SHIFTING GEARS

SHIFTING GEARS

The Story of a Small Town Simple Man

EDDIE THRAMER

iUniverse, Inc.
Bloomington

SHIFTING GEARS
THE STORY OF A SMALL TOWN SIMPLE MAN

iUniverse books may be ordered through booksellers or by contacting:

iUniverse
1663 Liberty Drive
Bloomington, IN 47403
www.iuniverse.com
1-800-Authors (1-800-288-4677)

ISBN: 978-1-4620-6843-2 (sc)
ISBN: 978-1-4620-6844-9 (ebk)

Printed in the United States of America

iUniverse rev. date: 11/30/2011

For my family, and anyone else who might care

CONTENTS

"I ain't nothin' but a simple man, they call me a redneck and I reckon that I am"
"Simple Man"
Charlie Daniels, Taz DiGregorio, Jack Gavin, and Charlie Hayward

INTRODUCTION

O CTOBER 15, 2008. It's just another day really. The air is crisp, thanks in part to the previous change from summer to fall, as well as the persistent afternoon breeze pushing gently through the Skagit Valley. What few clouds there are in the otherwise clear sky appear to rest peacefully on top of the Cascade Mountains, the aptly named mountain range that begins just outside of my front door and attracts thousands of tourists to the Pacific Northwest every year. Today's outside chores that consist of feeding the dogs and chickens and picking up limbs (thanks to last night's wind storm) are finished. The kids are at school and my wife is at work. The only significant thing about today is the fact that I finally sat down to begin a project that I have thought about doing for a couple of months—writing my autobiography.

It might be a little early in life for this, however. After all, I'm only five weeks removed from just my twenty-seventh birthday. I've never thrown a winning touchdown pass in a Super Bowl or pitched a perfect game in the World Series. I've never taken home an Academy Award or a Grammy. Hell, I haven't even won a lottery. I've never battled my way through drug and alcohol addiction or have repaid a debt to society. Outside of this valley, any mention of my name would leave people with a puzzled look on their faces. I'm just a plain, average guy. I work forty hours a week in order to earn enough money for a mortgage payment, put groceries on the table, insure my vehicles, turn the lights and the phone on, and see to it that nobody in the house goes without. I'm just an ordinary, tax-paying, American citizen who wouldn't have it any other way but that.

So just why am I doing this? I'm doing this because life doesn't last forever and there aren't any hints as to when one's birth certificate is going to expire. If I'm not around when my kids get older, how will they ever know anything about how their dad got to be the person that he was? Hopefully they would care enough to want to know all about me. Perhaps even fifty years from now, a future generation will need to do a report on family history, at which time this may become a valuable tool. Additionally, if my name is mentioned in a conversation or a story is being told about my past, I think that the truth and the reasons behind the situations should be factored in. Here you will have it. Besides, we live in a society that gets off on hearing and reading things about other people's lives.

Obviously, there are things that I'm going to forget to include, but I can assure you that it isn't going to be on purpose. In fact if that does happen, I'm going to be angry about it—enough probably to force me to sit down and write another book. But I will do my best.

This is all going to be written by hand at first, mainly because my typing skills leave something to be desired. The inspiration of doing it the old fashioned way came from a 1999 autobiography by Mick Foley, a professional wrestler whose book went to the top of the New York Times Bestseller List. He wrote his book by hand and on his own, without the help of a ghostwriter. I want to do the same thing. My goal is to eventually get this published into book form and have several copies printed up in case anyone cares to read it.

This isn't designed for me to take pot shots and to get people pissed off at me because their feelings might be hurt. It is, however, designed for me to explain my feelings and the reasoning for them following certain events in my life. Some feelings may have changed since then, others may have not, but I will explain that later on. Some readers may not care about certain things in this book and may or may not be offended by some of my opinions, but everything that I am going to talk about is because at some point in time they were important to me—why else would I remember them? Everything that happens in a person's life, albeit good or bad, makes them the person that they are on that given day.

I can't say how long this book is going to be or how long it will take to complete, but I would hope that it is pretty much going to write itself. I am a bit of a perfectionist, so it may not be all that easy. I don't know how it will turn out, either. I know the things that I want to talk about and the stories that I want to tell, but I have to tie that all in to avoid giving readers an extra doorstop or something to start a fire with. But I can promise you this—you will laugh, cry, and cringe with disgust.

As I look out at the mountains from the front porch of my own house, I begin to think of how I got here. Just two months ago, I was riding my Harley-Davidson through the fabled Big Sky Country of Montana. Off in the distance, I saw the symbol of our nation's freedom, a bald eagle, gliding across the terrain. I imagined what it would be like if I were in his place—flying over his past, his present, and his future. My mind began to wander and up in the sky I went.

As I flew over the mountains, valleys, streams, and prairies, I saw my life happening right below me. I saw Orth Way, Dad, Mom, and Jen. I saw Christmas with Grandpa, Grandma, and Grandma Murrow. I saw Disneyland, Donald Duck, Jonny Quest, Gilligan, and Jack Tripper. I saw the front door at kindergarten. I saw Mrs. Brooks and Mr. Prange. I saw Dr. Smith saying a prayer for me as I was strapped onto a stretcher. I saw Grandma T. I saw the Blazer and camp trailer in shambles on a frozen piece of interstate. I saw Uncle Robbie, Jake and Tristan shooting guns at beer cans. I saw Papa hand me a rifle that I would use to kill something twice my size with a single shot. I saw Joe Montana throw a touchdown pass to Jerry Rice. I saw Lawrence Taylor break Joe Thiesmann's leg. I saw Hulk Hogan bodyslamming Andre The Giant. I saw WrestleMania XIX. I saw Travis Tritt and Marty Stuart singing "The Whiskey Ain't Workin'". I saw Axl Rose belt out "Welcome To The Jungle" over Slash's electric guitar. I saw John Wayne, Clint Eastwood, Lee Van Cleef, and Eli Wallach. I saw Dad's log truck and my milk truck. I saw McDonald's and Dorothy and Aunt B.'s lawns. I saw Ron Russell and Dale Wicker yelling at us to keep going, as we put up eighty-two points during a single football game. I saw a personal foul and a disqualification. I saw Jay Breckenridge pounding the mat as the capacity crowd chanted my name in unison at Squalicum High School. I saw Mom on one side of the gym in Sedro-Woolley sitting with another man, Dad sitting alone on the other side, and me in the middle, staring a hole into the person I was finally going to take out all of my frustration and aggression on. I saw the stretcher taking me off the mat and to the hospital while Dad sobered up after a night of drinking and driving. I saw hunting camp and Slide Lake. I saw Yellowstone, the Grand Ole Opry, Little Bighorn Battlefield, the Grand Canyon, the Rocky Mountains, the Las Vegas Strip, Texas, and Graceland. I saw Sturgis, South Dakota. I saw my first dirt bike, the Kawasaki, the Magna, and my Harley. I saw Tuco following me home from school, saving me from a vicious attack, and dying in my arms in the bed of my truck. I saw Mike and Debbie. I saw Holly and Sharon. I saw Joey, Dustin, Greg, and Archy. I saw Pinelli Road, Burrese Road, and Willard Lane. I saw Katelynn riding her bicycle. I saw Elizabeth take her first breath of life. I saw tears falling in Nevada. And I saw me, riding motorcycles with Dad and Uncle Robbie into the sunset.

I shut my eyes for a moment in order for it to all sink in. When I opened them back up again, I was damn near in a ditch. Realizing that I better start paying attention, I looked up again at the eagle and gave him a waive of thanks before he disappeared behind a cloud. I couldn't believe that I had just seen my whole life replay in front of me. To help you understand, let me explain it all.

PART I

GROWING UP

CHAPTER I

Family Tree

Every child has asked it. If they haven't yet, they will. The only question is, when will it happen? It could be while driving in a car. It could be while dining at a restaurant in the presence of a waitress. It could be while standing in line at the ticket booth in Disneyland. With any luck, it could happen in the privacy of your own home. Out of the blue, your inquiring child will tug on the bottom of your shirt in order to get your attention so they can ask, "Where do babies come from?"

Even though you knew that it was going to happen eventually, it still catches you off guard. But how do you answer the question? You know what you want to say, but surely you can't tell them that. How can you put it in a way that a child can comprehend? That is up to you to decide. While technology gets more and more advanced every second of every day, it still takes a male and a female to reproduce. That is why we are all here, although none of us wants to think about our parents engaging in that sort of act. Well, it happened.

My father was born Ronald J. Thramer on June 20, 1959 at Saint Joseph's Hospital in Bellingham, Washington. The "J" is actually his entire middle name because had he been born a girl, his name would have been Jennifer. Naturally, that couldn't be on his birth certificate or he would have probably gotten beat up at school on a daily basis. The funny part is that people actually argue with him about it, saying how it isn't grammatically correct to have just an initial for a middle name. He was the second of two sons born to Robert Raymond Thramer and Doris Jean Thramer (Schenk). He came just two days short of one year after the birth of his older brother, Robert Kenneth Thramer, whom I know as Uncle Robbie, on June 22, 1958.

The Thramer name itself is of Austrian descent and can be traced back to the early 1800's. I have recently received a book that states that the first known Thramer was a man named Joseph. He and his wife, who nobody is certain of her name, had two daughters and a son in Hangendensten, Austria around 1838. In 1877, Joseph A., the son of the elder Joseph, left Austria with his wife and three children for New York. Once there, they boarded a train to

Platte County, Nebraska, where the family settled and grew. It wasn't until the early 1900's that the family began to learn the English language.

My grandfather, Robert, known more as Bob and referred to by me as Papa, was the seventh and final child born to William John Thramer and Catherine Opha Thramer (Lydon). Grandpa Thramer and Grandma T., as everyone referred to her, had five girls—Delores, Yuteva, Patricia, Madonna, and Catherine. They have always been known in the family as Jean, Teak, Pat, Donna, and Bonnie respectively. The youngest daughter, Bonnie, whom I know as Aunt B., was born alongside a twin brother, William, known as Bill Jr. The family was originally from Ewing, Nebraska alongside the rest of the Thramer Family, before leaving everyone else behind in order to move out to the Pacific Northwest.

The Schenk name is also of Austrian descent. My grandmother, Doris, was the fifth of as many children born to Robert Schenk and Edna Schenk (Rollins). The Schenks had one son, Robert Jr., and four girls—Elsie, Hazel, Lois, and Doris. The collectively resided in Bellingham.

Papa and Grandma separated and soon divorced only a few years after Dad was born. Both eventually remarried. Papa married Judy England and together they had a daughter, Rebecca. Judy had a daughter from a previous relationship, Jackie, who Papa legally adopted. Grandma went on to marry Gary Nutter and they too had a daughter, Lorie.

Dad and Uncle Robbie lived with their mom and Gary. In the mid to late 1960's, they moved every three to six months to places where Gary could find work. They moved around from state to state with stops in California, Arizona, Colorado, and even Hawaii. While living in Montrose, Colorado, Dad, whose early grade school pictures bear a striking resemblance to Theodore "Beaver" Cleaver from the *Leave it to Beaver* series that ran around the same time, would often ride horses and go on cattle drives.

In 1972, Dad and Uncle Robbie left their mom for good to move in with their dad in Sedro-Woolley, Washington. Papa was glad to have his boys back but with two girls and a wife already, money was in short supply. The boys picked berries, cut shakes from cedar blocks for roofs, and scrapped out old wrecked cars to help buy their school clothes and have a little spending money.

In their spare time, the boys put a lot of miles on their bicycles, which was their primary form of transportation, riding to local creeks and streams that they fished all year long. After years of pedaling his way to wherever he went, Dad eventually saved enough money to buy his first car, a 1966 Oldsmobile, for $200. The trouble was, it didn't come with a motor. That was purchased separately for an additional $100 out of a wrecked car. Dad and Papa worked on it during the evenings until it was ready to roll.

Dad was also into motorcycles, as was Uncle Robbie. When he was twelve, he had a Honda 55cc before moving up to a Yamaha 80cc at fifteen. His first new bike was a 1975 Yamaha 250 that he could ride on both the dirt and the highway. The new bike, which cost around a thousand dollars, was what he rode to school and his part-time jobs.

In his teenage years, Dad worked at the Exxon station in downtown Sedro-Woolley—pumping gas, washing windshields, and trying to score dates with girls. He would even put up an "out of order" sign on the pop machine so he could use it to chill down beer for weekend parties. Times have not changed in the past forty years, as high school kids still find ways to mislead their parents for a night of underage drinking and who knows what else.

My mother was born Brenda Lois Oliver on August 22, 1959 at United General Hospital in Sedro-Woolley. She was the second of two daughters born to Edwin Earl Oliver and Lois Elaine Oliver (Murrow). The eldest child was Sheila Jane.

My grandfather, Edwin, known more as Ed, and who is known to me as Papa but will be referred to in this book as Grandpa to avoid confusion, was the middle child of five born to William Oliver and Hazel Oliver (McCoy). The oldest child, Dorothy, was the only daughter. She was followed by Bill Jr., Grandpa, George, and Ken.

My grandmother, Lois, was also the third of five children. Gerald Murrow and Leta Murrow (Vanmeter) had the exact opposite of the Olivers—four girls and one son. First was Lenora Lee, followed by Garnet, Grandma, Ronnie, and Carol.

Mom lived in Sedro-Woolley throughout her childhood, teenage, and early adult years. Her and her sister lived on a farm with their parents just east of town towards Lyman. They too rode their bicycles to pick cucumbers and raspberries to earn enough money to be able to buy their school clothes.

My parents first met each other in junior high school. Several years later, Dad asked Mom to the junior prom while standing in the library at Sedro-Woolley High School. Mom thought it was a joke because, after all, Dad had already asked three other girls and was accepted by them all—and Mom knew it! They did end up going together, however, and would date steadily for the rest of the year. After graduation in June of 1977, they moved in together along with another girl, Kris. Oddly enough, a new sitcom came to television around the same time that chronicled one man living with two girls. More on *Three's Company* later.

On October 3, 1977, they two drove a 1966 Thunderbird to Coeur d'Alene, Idaho and were married at The Hitching Post. For the next couple of years, both worked and saved their money in order to buy their first house. Dad worked construction, as did Uncle Robbie and Papa, for his uncle, Bill. Mom, in the meantime, worked at a cafe with Uncle Robbie's wife, Sue. On weekends, Dad and his brother would often fish in the boat that Mom bought him for his birthday, or shoot guns at a local gravel pit. After the Thunderbird, they moved on to a Pontiac Trans-Am, just like the one that Burt Reynolds and Sally Field drove while trying to foil the pursuit of Jackie Gleason in 1977's *Smokey and the Bandit*. After a little more than three years of marriage, they then decided to start a family.

CHAPTER 2

1981

O N JANUARY 20,1981, Ronald Reagan, a republican who was preaching "Reaganomics," succeeded democrat Jimmy Carter, to become the fortieth president of the United States of America. Reagan was a former television actor before turning to politics, opening the door for Jesse Ventura, a former professional wrestler and actor who became Governor of Minnesota in 1998, and Arnold Schwarzenegger, who became Governor of California in 2003. (The two would ironically co-star prior to their political days in 1987's *Predator*.) Just minutes after the president-elect's inauguration, Iran released 52 American hostages that they had held captive for 444 days. It would be just the start of foreign affairs that would also see the ending of the Cold War during the two terms that Reagan would serve as president.

1981 was also an innovative year for the future. The Osbourne 1, the world's first personal computer, was introduced. The term "internet" was also first mentioned. But it was the identification of AIDS, the disease ultimately caused by exchanging contaminated bodily fluids, that proved to be the most important.

On June 12, *Raiders of the Lost Ark* was released in theaters. The film starring Harrison Ford as Indiana Jones, would go on to be the top grossing movie of the year, earning a then record $209,562,121, as well as spawn several sequels. Earning roughly $90,000,000 less was *On Golden Pond*, which starred Henry Fonda and Katherine Hepburn. The two would win Academy Awards for Best Actor and Best Actress for their roles in the film. Neither film, in spite of their popularity, would win Best Picture, however. That honor went to *Chariots of Fire*.

On the small screen, it was *Dallas*, starring Larry Hagman as J.R. Ewing in the prime time soap opera focusing on a Texas family involved in the oil and cattle industries. The fifth season of an eventual fourteen, topped the ranks of popularity while answering the question, "Who shot J.R.?"

On July 7, following a nomination from President Reagan, Sandra Day O'Conner began serving as Associate Justice of the Supreme Court. She was the first female to do so and would hold her bench until retirement in 2005.

With the popularity of music always on the rise, Music Television (MTV) was introduced on cable television on August 1. The all-music channel was designed to play continuous music videos, much like a radio station. Instead of being hosted by a DJ, they were hosted by a "VJ." While the channel would reignite the career of bands like ZZ Top, it would make casualties out of other artists. The first video to air on MTV was appropriately titled "Video Killed the Radio Star" by The Buggles.

For those who still listened to the radio, on September 5, "Start Me Up" by The Rolling Stones was the number one song in America. It would hold it's mark for a total of thirteen weeks. That weeks number one album was *Bella Donna,* the first solo album from Stevie Nicks, who had previously fronted Fleetwood Mac. Country radio was topped by Ronnie Milsap, a blind piano player and singer who once played alongside Elvis Presley for a series of recordings. Milsap's single "(There's) No Gettin' Over Me" would rule for two weeks.

On September 6, the National Football League began its regular season. The San Francisco 49ers lost to the Detroit Lions 24-17 in front of 62,123 fans at the Pontiac Silverdome in Pontiac, Michigan. The next time the Niners would play in that same venue would be seven months later for Super Bowl XVI, where they beat the Cincinatti Bengals 26-21 before 81,270. (I only mention the attendance because the Silverdome's record, as well as the world record for indoor attendance, belongs to WrestleMania III. That event drew 93,173 fans to witness Hulk Hogan wrestle Andre The Giant on March 29 1987. I'll have a bit more on professional wrestling later.) Also on the sports scene, Muhammad Ali would retire later during the year from professional boxing with a career record of 55-5 and seven World Heavyweight Titles.

1981—the year that a gallon of gas was $1.25. A single postage stamp was $.18. A new home went for an average of $78,200. This may seem like a dream but on the flip side, annual household income was a mere $21,000. And with the world population at roughly 4.529 billion, Ron and Brenda Thramer were preparing to welcome their first child into the world.

CHAPTER 3

In the Beginning

I WAS BORN EDMUND Dean Thramer at United General Hospital in Sedro-Woolley, Washington on Friday, September 11, 1981 . . . . Let me just stop right there. If you are truly taking the time to read and comprehend what I have written, I am positive that my birth date gave you an uneasy feeling. Don't feel bad, I hear it every time I give it out when I'm asked for it—whether it is over the phone or face to face. People always remind me about how it is a bad day in history. I just smile and kind of shrug my shoulders, never verbally acknowledging them. Why get into it? They won't understand anyway and I'm not going to waste my time explaining something that isn't any of there business to begin with. I often wonder just what they would think if I told them that I couldn't care less about the thousands of people that died in the infamous terror attacks of 2001. Of course I don't really mean that, it's just that September 11 has had a few more things hit me on more of a personal level than that.

Everybody always thinks of what happened in 2001, or 9/11 as they refer to it now, when they see that day on the calendar. While nothing can really compare to the tragedy in 2001, September 11 has been the date for other unfortunate events in history. In 1777, the British Army were victorious in Chester County, Virginia at the Battle of Brandywine over the Continental Army as part of the Revolutionary War. In 1992, Hurricane Iniki devastated the Hawaiian islands of Kauai and Oahu. In 2002, Johnny Unitas, Pro Football Hall of Fame quarterback for the Baltimore Colts, died at the age of 69. Just one year later in 2003, John Ritter, the star of *Three's Company* and my personal favorite comedic actor, died at the age of 54. There was also one other major one that nobody knows anything about, of which I will discuss later. But wait—this is supposed to be a positive book, not a sad and depressing one. Let me try it again . . . .

CHAPTER 3

In the Beginning

I was born Edmund Dean Thramer at Untied General Hospital in Sedro-Woolley, Washington on Friday, September 11, 1981. My first name was what Mom was to be named if she was a boy. All of my life I have been called Eddie, except when I was in trouble. If I did something small, it was usually Eddie Dean. If it was something big, it was Edmund. Otherwise, it has always been Eddie. I never even wrote my full name on a piece of paper until I bought my first house in 2003, at which time I had to use it in a signature. The lady just stood over me like a school teacher who was helping a student learn to write. Right now is only the second time in my life that I have written my full, legal name.

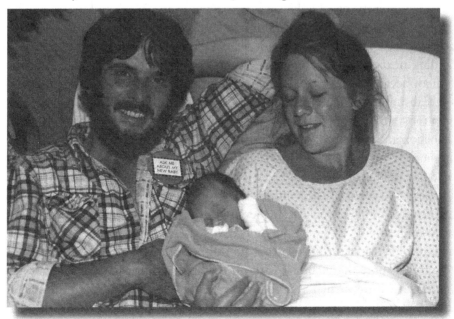

Dad, Mom, and me on the day I was born, September 11, 1981

Mom got her wish when I was born. She wanted to have two kids, a boy and a girl, with the boy coming first. It would be a couple of years until my parents would try their luck again in order to follow up on the second half of the wish, as Mom wanted me and my eventual sibling to be two-and-a-half years apart.

We lived on a dead end residential development on Calkins Place, a few hundred yards from the elementary school that I would be enrolled in when it was time for kindergarten. The house itself was small, standard for the time. It had an attached garage and three bedrooms, all crammed together into rectangular shape that made it look more like an oversized, brown shoebox.

Dad continued to work construction after I was born. Mom would get up early each morning and make his lunch and coffee for him. Dad soon convinced her to stay in bed rather than help him before dawn each day. Perhaps it was because she accidentally packed him a Budweiser instead of a Coke one day. Or it may have been the occasional wrapped slice of cheese that would mysteriously appear in his sandwich.

During the day, Mom stayed home and took care of me. She tried a few odd jobs, but they never lasted. She worked at a retail store in Sedro-Woolley for a little while and at a Texaco station for less than one full shift because she was afraid to work nights. It would be a long time before Mom got a full-time job. In those days, families could make it on a single income. Nowadays, it is a bit harder.

I went everywhere with my parents. They say that I was good and rarely ever cried, except for one time at a local Italian restaurant called Cascade Pizza, where word has it that I threw a fit for no reason for so long that we had to leave in the middle of dinner. We went to Disneyland when I was a few months old. Dad even drove down to the Mexican border and crossed, only to turn right around and get back into our own country after being bombarded by peddlers.

We had two black labs that Papa had given Dad for Christmas one year. I looked like a terrier standing next to those two giants. While I don't remember, I must have gotten along well with them because ever since I can remember, I have just loved being around dogs. They were typical labs, always roughhousing and digging bomb craters in the backyard. Allegedly one of them took a dump in the neighbor's yard, causing the angry man to threaten to put the pile in a shoebox and leave it on our front step. Mom told him that if he did that, she would return the shoebox to his step with his dead dog in it.

We would go camping on weekends when it was warmer out. Dad had a small green tent that was supposed to sleep two people. In order for that to happen, the two people would have to be midgets because that tent wasn't big enough to sleep even one normal-sized person. Mom hated sleeping on the ground so our camping days were put on hold for several years until they bought a camp trailer.

Dad had an old Chevrolet pickup that he dubbed the "Dyin' Pig" due to the fact that it wouldn't go much more than a block without the engine quitting. Not long after I was born, he laid me down on the bench seat to change my diaper, which was nothing more than a cloth—the cheaper alternative to disposable diapers. As soon as he removed the soiled piece of material, I sent a continuous arc of piss up into the air and back down into my face. I just kept moving my head from side to side and wiping my eyes with my hands, never realizing that I could turn off the faucet at any time.

In addition to his pickup, Dad also had a Honda 350 motorcycle that, oddly enough, had the same temperament as the Dyin' Pig. Grandpa and Grandma also had a motorcycle, a Honda Gold Wing, that they would take me for rides on. Sitting right in between them like a piece of bologna on a sandwich, I would ride with them periodically to places as far as north as Bellingham—a fifty mile round trip. Of course now, that would probably wind them up in jail and my parents would be forced to give me up for adoption for reckless endangerment of a child. It did, however, plant a seed in me for a lifetime desire to ride motorcycles.

Mom and Dad had a party for me on my first birthday. I had been on the verge of walking on my own for a few weeks leading up to that day. They tried all afternoon to get me to take a few steps while the company was there, but I didn't cooperate. Instead, I waited until everyone gave up and went home before I took off walking across the living room.

My first actual memory is something that I am reminded of each time I look into the mirror. If I partially close my right eye, I can see a thin scar that angles down my eyelid from my eyebrow to my cheekbone, reminding me just what happens when a child runs around in places that he shouldn't. I was probably three years old when I went with my parents to a furniture store. I was running around, goofing off, and pretty much ignoring everyone, when I smacked into the corner of a waterbed and put a gash right through my eyelid. While I don't remember how it felt (I'm sure it was painful), I do remember going to the hospital and getting stitched up. The best thing about that was getting a grape Popsicle for not crying while the doctor sewed me up. The battle scar comes in handy these days, providing a visual aid for children to help them understand just what happens when they make poor choices in public.

I don't really have too many other clear memories of living at the house on Calkins Place. The only other one that I have is of a clever way that Mom and Dad tried to break me of a habit. It is common for children to suck their thumbs when they get tired or bored, but usually it is for them to have a sense of security at bedtime. Always trying to outdo the rest, I would instead stuff two fingers in my mouth as opposed to just one. In addition to being just plain dirty, having your fingers in your mouth can also lead to dental problems in the future because your jaw doesn't close right if you have something wedged in it at all times. I don't know if that was the reason or if my parents were just embarrassed by it, but they had to put a stop to it.

After other attempts at it failed, they taped up my fingers so I couldn't so much as move them. Right before I could figure out what was happening, they put me in my room for the night. Once I realized that I couldn't shove anything in my mouth, I did what any toddler would do—screamed my head off. When I came to the conclusion that it was going to be to no avail, or I just became too tired, I gave up and went to sleep. After a few nights of that treatment, I was cured.

On March 2,1984, Mom got the second half of her wish fulfilled when she gave birth to a baby girl. Just a week shy of a full two-and-a-half years after I came, just as she wanted, Jennifer Renee

Thramer was born at the very same hospital. She would be the last child that my parents would have.

Later that year, we moved into the house that we would remain in for the next fourteen years. Mom and Dad had it built on a half-acre lot about a mile or so from the house on Calkins Place. It was on a small, dead end street that was about a quarter-mile long. While eventually roughly thirty houses would be erected upon the completion of Orth Way, only about a dozen lots had houses on them at the time. They were all spread out throughout the development so that (for a while) nobody lived directly next door to anyone else. Our lot, which was marked 709, would be the second to the last house on the left when it was all said and done, right at the start of the cul-de-sac.

Our house on Orth Way

The house was a three bedroom, two bathroom, basic rambler. It had vaulted ceilings and a wood stove surrounded by brick just inside the entry way. The living room was long and well-lit by the windows that bordered two sides of it. At the end of the living room, sat the connecting dining room that was just off to the left in front of the wall of windows. Next to that and just on the other side of the living room wall, was the kitchen. Outside the kitchen window sat the patio area, which then gave way to the backyard.

After exiting the kitchen through the swinging doors that were straight out of a western movie, the L-shaped hallway led to the bedrooms. Just before the turn in the hall was a tiny alcove for the washer and dryer. After the turn, sat Jennifer's room, which was painted pink. Next to her room was my room, which was (what a coincidence) painted blue. Across the hall from my bedroom door was the bathroom, which had a skylight directly over the toilet. Some people refused to use it, for fear that an airplane might fly over the house and catch a glimpse of their naked butts.

At the end of the hallway was Mom and Dad's room. Like my room, it had a large walk-in closet in it, while Jennifer, whom we all call Jen, had a much smaller, folding door closet. On the other side of the master bedroom was the master bathroom, which did not have a skylight in it, allowing insecure guests an alternative.

The outside of the house was originally painted a rust red color with dark brown trim. Outside of the attached garage was the driveway. What was unique about this, and to this day I haven't seen another like it, was the rock-marbled "T" that was embedded in the cement.

In the front yard bordering the street was a row of shrubs, which then gave way to a flower bed that led up the driveway. The portion of the yard on the side of the house resembled a small football field—twice as long as it was wide. Bordering the edge of the yard were evergreen trees that ran the full length of the property at ten foot intervals. Separating our backyard from a church and its accompanying two acre field, was a row of alder trees that provided shade in the summer and constant work in the fall.

Next to the alders sat our year's supply of firewood that would heat the house in the winter or any other time that Mom was cold, which was quite often. Behind the woodpile and off to one side of the church field, was a small pasture that corralled two cows. The cows would hang out at the end of the fence next to our property more often than not, as Dad used them to dispose of the grass clippings from our lawn. I would pick up clumps of grass and have them eat it out of my hands. If I didn't have any grass, I would feed them my raisin boxes boxes instead—they didn't seem to mind.

In front of the woodpile and alongside the other side of our house, was the spot where Dad parked the Dyin' Pig. He managed to get it running long enough to get it to one of his friend's houses one day, where he was going to prepare it for a paint job by sanding the body down. I went with him to help out, but was taken back home when I began sanding the windows instead of the body.

With only about a third of the lots sold combined with sparsely wooded, yet-to-be developed areas, there were always places to play. Most of the playing was done by me alone or with Dad after he got home from work, because Mom always had to take care of newborn Jen. Every time a new house was being built nearby, I would always find my way over there after the builders had gone home to make believe that I was building the house instead of them. I wonder what the workers thought when they came to work the next day and found nails half-driven into the framework? I never did thank them for the use of their hammers and the endless supply of nails.

CHAPTER 4

Life As I Knew It

L OGGING IS THE foundation of which the greater part of Washington State was built on. With a near endless timber supply in the Pacific Northwest and a vast demand for lumber, at the time it provided steady employment for men that were willing to brave the elements and risks in order to provide for their families. Once trees reach a certain apex, the owners of the land hire out logging companies to thin or clearcut sections of the land. A crew will come in and fall the appropriate trees and cut off the branches and limbs. Once that area has been cut (with the exception of a few remaining trees that are purposely left standing to keep environmentalists, local habitat, and the hippies happy), guys will come in with thick, heavy cable to attach to each log so that they can be winched up the hill by giant machine operating on a basic pulley system called a yarder. From there, another large machine with grapples called a log loader, picks through and sorts the logs by species. A second loader will then load specific sorts on certain log trucks, depending on which mill they are hauling to.

At the helm of one of these eighteen-wheeled rigs was Dad, who went to work for Hamilton Brother's Logging in 1985. Next to him in the passenger seat on some Fridays was me, starting a countdown to the day when I too could drive a vehicle that large. Every boy loves cars and trucks—especially big trucks. In those days I was just a mark, but a seed was being planted for something that I wanted to do someday.

The log yard that I remember hauling to the most was in La Conner, a small town on the edge of the inlet to the San Juan Islands. The coolest thing about that trip was crossing the big orange bridge that was built over the river that we had to cross. It was rainbow-shaped and could be seen from several miles away, thanks to its fluorescent color.

Once at the log yard, a huge loader that had grapples on it big enough to take the entire load of logs off the truck at once, would do just that. The tires on this machine were as big as the truck that Dad was driving! Carrying over 40,000 pounds of logs in front of it, the machine would take them and stack them into giant log piles that would eventually be shipped overseas.

After the truck was unloaded, Dad drove us over to a device that would pick up the empty trailer and set it on the back end of the truck, with the tongue sticking out front and resting on a bracket on top of the cab. If nobody was looking and only if I had my hardhat on, Dad would let me push the button that would activate the lift.

On the way out of the yard, we would stop at the building where Dad would have to turn in his paperwork. Inside, they usually had a box of donuts where I could snag lunch for our ride back to the mountain. I don't know why, but Dad always bought me a can of Squirt to wash it down with. Ironically on the way back to get another load, I would have to take a squirt in the empty pop can while driving down the road because Dad refused to stop. He was always pissed about how I never had to go when we were stopped—it was always as soon as we got on the road instead. I always told him it was because I didn't have to go then. He didn't buy it.

Dad and me hauling logs over Washington Pass

On the way back up the mountain, drivers used CB radios to communicate their position, or their "20" as they called it. With the roads so narrow and at frequent places very steep, drivers would tell others what mile marker they were at (which were nothing more than spray painted numbers on a tree or a stump) and whether they were going up or down the hill and if they were loaded or empty. If approaching too close to each other, the empty truck would pull off at a widened turnout, sometimes a mile or so sooner, so that the loaded truck had as much possible space to pass. I was usually the one to broadcast our 20 over the radio.

CBs could also be used for a little humor during the work day. Dad would sometimes disguise his voice to fool another driver or loader into doing something unnecessary—like taking a detour through town just so he could cut in front of them and be loaded first. We would also listen in to other driver's conversations, where Dad would again use a different voice and interrupt them—calling one of them a dick. It would usually get them laughing if they had a sense of humor. Some didn't, but we would do their laughing for them.

We would get about three loads a day, depending on how far it was from the landing to the log yard. Dad would crank the tunes all day long, as we listened to some of the most popular songs of the day like "Keep Your Hands to Yourself" by The Georgia Satellites, "You Give Love a Bad Name" by Bon Jovi, and "Legs" by ZZ Top. I only went with him once a week at the most, but I wished it could have been everyday.

On the days that Dad went by himself, I stayed home and entered own world of make believe just like every other kid. I wasn't pretending to be a cop or a firefighter, a dragon slayer or a pilot, or anything else—I would pretend that I was Dad. I would hitch my Radio Flyer up to my tricycle and take my own loads of logs to log yards. After I was loaded, I would take the same path down the road going in the opposite direction. Halfway down the "mountain," I would get off, put my hardhat on, and tighten my imaginary binders with a plastic baseball bat that I used for a cheater pipe. I did things exactly like he did because he always told me to never do a job halfway.

"You might as well do it right the first time," he would say. "Then you don't have to go back and do it again."

Sometimes I hauled Jen around instead of logs—pretending I was driving garbage truck instead.

The sandbox out back was where I spent the rest of my time while I was outside. Before I could play, I had to remove the pieces of scrap plywood that covered the sand to discourage cats from crapping in it like a litter box. Each week Dad would build new mountains, complete with roads and bridges, for me to work with. My front end loaders were always busy loading up the dump truck with dirt that had to be hauled in order to complete jobs. If Dad was home he would play too, but usually it was just me and maybe Jen. It didn't matter because I could stay out there for hours putting in my day's work. I would spend so much time out there that I would poop in my pants just so I didn't have to come in the house. I didn't have time to go to the bathroom when there was work to be done!

Dad, Jen, and me playing in the sandbox

When Dad would get home, I was all over him like a bad smell (no pun intended). I would follow him around and try to do the chores just like he did. If he was getting a wheelbarrow load of firewood, I would help him stack it and even try to show how tough I was by carrying a few chunks in my hand at once. If he was splitting wood, he would occasionally let me swing the ax. He was a bit better at it than I was. While he would drive through a piece just like a knife goes through butter, I would be content if I even left a slight mark on the wood.

When it came time to mow the lawn, both me and Jen would follow him with our mowers during every pass that he made in the yard. There was only one plastic lawn mower so the other kid would have to use the plastic wheelbarrow in its place. If I only knew then how many lawns I was going to have to mow over the years, I might have done something different instead—like watch.

On one early spring weekend, Dad cut up a bunch of cedar 2x4s and several sheets of plywood in order to build a tree house out in the backyard. Four of our alder trees grew together in a cluster, just like the fingers on your hand, which provided perfect support for our small shelter. Inside were the benches and picnic table while the outside had a porch that led to the ladder. It seemed like it was thirty feet off the ground while it was being built. In reality, it was probably closer to ten.

During the construction of the floor, Dad had spread out the boards onto the cross-members that were already nailed to the trees to begin fastening them together. I was up top with him trying to help, when I stepped out onto a few pieces that were not yet nailed down and found out the hard way about the dangers of heights. The boards went down with me and landed right on top of me, covering me like a blanket. I'm pretty sure that I cried over that one, but I learned my lesson about getting too close to the edge of something.

Below the tree house was a tire swing that hung down from a rope that was hooked to one of the beams. This was fun to do because if you sat just right, you could bounce the tire off the trees while you were swinging and not get hurt. But if you leaned to far back, your butt would drag and you would fall off. I would push Jen around on it when she was a couple of years old, causing her to hit the trees. I don't really remember, but it may or may not have been an accident.

Every April, Dad would take me fishing in his boat at a nearby lake. On occasion, Uncle Robbie and my cousin Jacob, who was about a year younger than I was, would go along with us. The boat really wasn't all that big, so it was a good thing that Jake and I were small or else the four of us would have been packed in like sardines. In between getting all four of our lines tangled up, we even managed to catch a few fish from time to time. It wasn't really enough to eat so we cooked hot dogs on a small propane stove right inside the boat for lunch instead of dining on our catch. It always paid to have a backup food plan when fishing with Dad.

I always preferred fishing off of the bank as opposed to in fishing in the boat. It was warmer on land and there was dirt to play in to pass the time between bites. Dad and I would drive a few miles east of town along Highway 20 towards the tiny town of Lyman and fish along the banks of the Skagit River. Dad would once in a while catch a few salmon while I played in the dirt until it was time to watch him reel one in. If he was having pretty good luck and reeling in more than a few, I would often ask the other guys that were fishing a few yards away if they were having as good of luck as we were. If they weren't, they would get disgusted and leave. The people that stuck it out would usually snag onto my long forgotten about line in the water.

We would hang out a lot with Uncle Robbie and Jake, just being boys. If we didn't go fishing, we would most likely go shooting at a gravel pit a few miles from our house, near where Papa lived. They would each buy a brick of 500 rounds of .22 shells and we would assault beer cans and open-fire on paper plates and sheets of plywood or cardboard. When the smoke cleared and all that remained was a thousand empty brass cases littered on the ground, it was time to call it a day.

Most of the time Jake and I used our cap guns. We would always have our endless supply of caps, but we wanted the real deal. Dad and Uncle Robbie began teaching us when we were probably around four years old. They taught us to handle, carry, and shoot their pistols. Safety was always the name of the game. It's too bad that other fathers don't teach their children how to use guns properly—there might just be a few less tragedies in the news.

For the first couple of birthday parties that I remember, I always wanted to go to Chuck E. Cheese's, the overpriced pizza place that also had games and slides for kids to run wild at. Unfortunately at the time, we had to go clear down to Tacoma to visit one. It wasn't until around 2000 that one made its way to farther north to Burlington. It wasn't too late for me to enjoy it because my kids like to go there for their birthdays also.

When summer turned into fall and the days became colder and shorter, there wasn't much sandbox or tricycle time. I would then spend my time with my favorite stuffed animal, Donald Duck, watching TV. I had another stuffed animal named Radar that I took everywhere until I accidentally left him at a dentist office in Burlington. We were gone about five minutes when I realized that he was gone but by the time we turned around and went back, Radar was gone for good. If you're out there reading this and have Radar, I want him back!

Now that Donald and I were on our own, we would lay together on the living room floor and watch *Donald Duck Presents* on the Disney Channel. I just thought that it was so cool that I could watch Donald and sit with him at the same time. I would lay on my stomach and rest my chin on the side of his head while I draped my arm over him so I could hold his hand. I still have him up in the closet and he still has the dents in his head from propping me up for so long.

The other cartoon that I watched was *Jonny Quest,* the Hanna-Barbara production that aired for just one season back in 1964. It chronicled the adventures of Jonny, his father, Dr. Quest, his bodyguard, Race Bannon, his friend Hadji, and his dog, Bandit. Over twenty years after they were originally produced, they aired every Sunday on syndication. They became so popular again that in 1986, they made another thirteen episodes. Don Messick, who was the voice for Dr. Quest and whose voice has been used on hundreds of Hanna-Barbara cartoons, was the only original cast member to return.

Aside from animation, only two television series interested me. Every child's favorite, *Gilligan's Island,* was on every single day on syndication. The show only ran for three seasons from 1964-1968. I wonder if CBS would have pulled the plug on Gilligan in exchange for *Gunsmoke* if they knew that it would still air daily over forty years after its final episode?

The other show was *Three's Company.* The series ran for eight years from 1977-1984, with a comedic look at the life of a guy who pretends to be gay in order to live with two girls in an apartment. The show was loaded with sexual innuendos and references that went straight over my head. Instead I was entertained by watching Jack Tripper, who was played by John Ritter, stumble and fall over everything and continuously get in a mess with food and drinks. It was a riot, but Mom eventually took it away from me for good when I started acting like Jack. I wonder it was because I was tripping over things or if it was that I was acting gay?

Today, I have all of the previously mentioned shows on DVD and I get to enjoy them all over again with my kids. They love watching them, just like I did twenty years ago. Looking at their faces while they watch along gives me an idea of what I looked like when I viewed the shows for the first time. For me, it just takes me back in time to when the only responsibility that I had was brushing my teeth and wiping my own ass.

Winter meant two things to me—Christmas and snow. Unlike now, I loved the snow when I was young. We didn't get a lot of it and when it did, it wouldn't stick around for very long. In the Pacific Northwest, it can snow for a few days and make everyone's life slightly miserable before the temperature suddenly jumps twenty degrees, causes the rivers to flood, and really make things difficult. But as a kid, I could care less about that.

Building a snowman out in the front yard was a tradition at our house. After one above average snowfall when Jen was about two or three, we went outside with Dad and actually built an igloo. After putting some plywood down on the ground for the floor, we filled a plastic bucket with snow over and over again to make the blocks. The bucket was actually a large hospital bedpan that we all called the "Puke Bucket" because up until the time we made the igloo, the only time it saw the light of day was when somebody was sick and fixing to toss their supper all over the place. The igloo turned out pretty slick. It wasn't very big, but it sure was fun to play around in for the few days that it was still frozen outside. Once it warmed up even the slightest bit, the igloo was off limits because it was turning into mush.

Christmas was a busy time of year. A few weeks beforehand, we would all go and pick out our tree. It wasn't just one of those artificial things either, it was the real deal. Some years we would get one from a tree farm, but most of our trees came right from the woods. Dad had keys to all kinds of gates that blocked off logging roads to the general public, giving us access to any tree that we wanted. Once we got it home and decorated, we would all sit down and sing some of the poorest versions of Christmas carols known to man.

Shortly before Christmas Day, we would load up in our Oldsmobile Cutlass Supreme (you know, the kind that only Mexican's drive nowadays after they convert them into low riders) and drive all over Sedro-Woolley, Mount Vernon, and Burlington to look at outdoor Christmas light displays. Some houses went all-out. When I saw these houses that were so extravagantly decorated, I would yell out "Claus! Claus!" I don't have any idea why—I guess it was just one of those things that reminded me of Santa.

Christmas Eve would always be at Papa's log house a few miles away. Going to Papa's was fun anytime we went. His wife at the time, Brenda, had a cool Corvette that I just loved to ride in (yes, for a while there were two Brenda Thramers living in the same town). Papa also had the coolest toilet in one of the bathrooms. It was the kind that had its tank up in the air and you had to pull a handle that was attached to a chain in order to flush it. Sometimes I would find myself going into the bathroom just to flush the toilet, without even using it first.

Uncle Robbie was always there too. By this time he was remarried to a lady named Karen. Since his separation with Sue, Jake was only with him on a few weekends from time to time, otherwise he stayed with his mom in Mount Vernon. In spite of all of that, he was usually always around for family functions.

After that get-together was over it was time to switch gears and start thinking about the next day—Christmas. Jen and I would set out a plate of cookies and milk for Santa Claus, get into bed, and try to stay awake in hopes of catching a glimpse of the fat guy in the red suit. Try as I may, it wasn't very long before I found myself sound asleep.

As soon as my eyes opened up the next morning, BOOM—I shot out of bed like a cannonball and woke everyone else up so we could go out to the living room and see what Santa had left. The cookies and milk were gone and, oddly enough, the dishes were even washed and put away. We would all dump out our stockings and open our presents one at a time, rotating in a clockwise order. When it was all over and before we could even play with our new stuff, everyone pitched in to clean up the wrapping paper that was strung out all over the living room like a giant rat nest.

Not long after the mess was disposed of, Grandpa and Grandma came over and we trashed the living room all over again. Then it was off to Grandma Murrow's house for a Christmas brunch. Jen and I would generally ride with Grandpa, who was a long haul truck driver and always seemed to head out on a week long trip immediately after we ate. We rode in the truck for the twelve mile trip to a Mount Vernon truck stop, where Grandma would then pick us up and take us the few remaining blocks to Grandma Murrow's.

Mom and Dad would be there already and once everyone said their hellos and gave their insincere hugs, it was time to eat. We would all bow our heads as Grandma Murrow rattled off a ten minute prayer that left me wondering if she was just stalling so that the food had time to finish cooking. We always had ham and some sort of stuffing that would give everyone diarrhea. The only really good part about her food was the rolls that she made—hands down that best that I have ever eaten.

After brunch, it was time for another round of presents. This time it wasn't fun at all. I would always get something ridiculous like a coloring book or something. When I was fourteen, she got me a firetruck—you know, the kind that THREE YEAR OLDS PLAY WITH! But it wasn't my gifts that made it miserable. The worst part was that we all had to set through a two hour stretch of her opening close to a hundred gifts. She would get so many that Mom had to write down in a notebook who gave her what so she would be able to thank the people later.

Next it was off to Burlington, were the entire Thramer Family would book the community center for a buffet-type Christmas potluck. We wouldn't stay for very long before we went home and could finally play with our new stuff. But it didn't last long, however, because we always left in the morning to go to Salt Lake City, where Grandma lived with her new husband, Milt—and we always drove straight through.

I have yet to figure it out but as soon as the ball drops in Times Square to begin the next year, I am usually blessed with a cold. It's nothing severe, just a cough and a bit of a runny nose. I found out that if I actually listen to the old saying of drinking plenty of fluids, it doesn't get too bad and I wouldn't have to go to the doctor. I was a very healthy kid growing up, and I still am today. I could probably count on one hand how many bad flues that I have had in my life—and getting sick from tainted restaurant food doesn't count.

It's funny (as in ironic) that every time I get sick, I completely lose any desire whatsoever to eat last thing that I consumed before falling ill. For my fifth birthday party that was at a McDonald's, I ate one of those heavily-sugared decorative pieces on the cake and was sick shortly thereafter. I don't think they were what got me sick, but thinking about it now still gives me a gritty taste in my mouth and a queasy feeling in my stomach.

Around the same time, I saw an add on TV advertising a nacho supreme dish. Mom made it for dinner a few nights later and I was up all night giving it back to her. I haven't eaten anything with sour cream since—I don't even like looking at the cartons. The funny part is that I have to because my job requires me to sell them every day. One time I dropped a five pound tub of it on my shoe and of course it exploded everywhere. I had to finish up the day feeling sour cream squish between my toes with every step that I took. I bought a new pair of shoes on the way home and left the other ones in the parking lot.

When I got sick and was throwing up, Mom and Dad would always let me sleep in their bed. As a parent now, I realize that not only does it make the child feel better, but it also lets the parents get some rest without having to get up every few minutes because their child is throwing up again. I do draw the line with my kids, however, and have them sleep on the floor. That idea came after one too many forearms to the nose and sudden kicks to the balls—plus it is also uncomfortable sleeping on the floor and they practically beg to go back to their own beds after waking up sore the next morning. I always slept better, as my kids do now, knowing that I was in the same room with my parents. It always gave me a small sense of security when I felt completely helpless.

The only time that they said that I couldn't was when I had the brilliant idea of swallowing an entire can of sliced peaches whole without chewing them first. I ate the whole can for dessert one night and by ten o'clock, I was puking them up in the exact same form that I swallowed them in. It didn't feel anything like the gliding sensation that I felt when they slid down to say the least. From then on I chewed every bite, just like Mom and Dad said that I should do from the start.

The other thing that found me in my parent's were bad dreams. Sometimes it would be just to wake them up to let them know that I had just had a nightmare. Other times I was in there for the night. One night, a locomotive with about eighty freight cars of explosives raced down the hallway of our house rather than on the tracks where it belonged. I screamed as loud as I could, but no sound came out of my mouth. I closed my eyes tightly and thought to myself *If I can go to sleep in my dream, then I might just wake myself up.* It worked and in just the nick of time. I never forgot that and since then, it has always been my way out of a compromising situation in a dream. Even today if something isn't going right, I just close my eyes and I am awake in a flash. Unfortunately in real life, you can't just close your eyes to escape your problems because they will always be there waiting for you to face them.

CHAPTER 5

Hulkamania Runs Wild

I'M JUST GOING to throw out the disclaimer that this chapter probably won't interest most people. But it is important to me and beings this is my book, I am going to take the time to explain what an impact that professional wrestling has made in my life. It has influenced my attitude, personality, and overall character. Things that I have or have not done in my life can all be traced to this simple form of entertainment.

To begin with, wrestling is the oldest sport known to man. Some might argue that running is older, but it is hard for me to imagine cavemen settling a dispute with a hundred yard dash. Men wrestled to stay in shape, honor their gods and kings, and they did it for fun. Even Abraham Lincoln was a wrestler who was said to have competed in over five hundred matches.

Professional wrestling essentially began as a sideshow in carnivals, in the sense that promoters paid traveling acts for entertaining audiences, following the Civil War. In 1887, circus manager P.T. Barnum employed Ed Decker, a 5' 6", 150 pound man, to take on all comers. Barnum would pay anyone $100 if they could pin the "Little Wonder From Vermont," or give $50 to anyone that could last three minutes without being pinned. Circus owners would also enhance their employees with colorful costumes and create fictional biographies about them to attract attention.

In the early 1900's, wrestling moved from carnival stages to small parks and gymnasiums as the public interest began to grow. In practically my own backyard of Bellingham on January 27, 1904, Frank Gotch defeated Tom Jenkins in straight falls to win the American Heavyweight Championship. Gotch would go on to lay claim as the world's first Undisputed Heavyweight Champion, having defeated all contenders in North America and Europe, when he pinned George Hackenschmidt in Chicago on April 3, 1908.

In the 1920's, wrestling fans began to question the legitimacy of the sport. Audiences became bored with seeing a single match taking sometimes nearly two hours to complete. After Gotch retired in 1913, what few fans remained didn't have a wrestler to get behind and cheer for. In response, Ed "Strangler" Lewis, who was World Champion at the time, teamed with Billy

Sandow and Joseph "Toots" Mondt in an attempt to promote a modified wrestling product to entice fans. The three men, known as the "Gold Dust Trio" due to their financial success, were the first to introduce time limits for matches, flashy holds, tag team matches, and the dreaded "foreign object" as ways to create excitement. Lewis would lose his title willingly to an opponent, sparking interest from fans who would then pay to see him get his revenge in a rematch. Lewis didn't worry about losing because he was unbeatable in real life. If his opponent would ever dream of double-crossing him in a match and not do what was planned, nobody could legitimately beat him in a shoot fight.

The Trio also were the first to use the same performers on a regular basis, paying them in exchange for a contractual commitment of several months or even years worth of work. This would also prevent men from working for other promotions or territories that were starting to pop up all over the country. These territories were ran independently but were all governed by the National Wrestling Alliance. The NWA had one recognized World Champion that would travel through each territory during his reign to work with local talent.

Wrestling entered its "Golden Age" in the 1950's with the advent of television. TV companies loved it because it was cheap to produce and it was easy to understand the drama and the comedy. During this time in the Los Angeles area, "Gorgeous" George Wagner was becoming the first "character" in the sports-entertainment world with his appealing flamboyance and charisma, setting a standard that would be followed and elaborated upon from then on.

In the early 1960's, wrestling went back on the decline. Promoters withdrew from the NWA with hopes of making changes in the business that were not allowed in the governing body. The two most successful promoters to withdraw and actually establish their own brand were Verne Gagne, with the Minneapolis-based American Wrestling Association, and Vincent J. McMahon, with the New York-based World Wide Wrestling Federation. Gagne was a former two-time NCAA Wrestling Champion in the 1940's with the University of Minnesota and was even an alternate for the 1948 U.S. Olympic Team. McMahon meanwhile, was the son of boxing promoter, Jess McMahon, who was the first to bring professional wrestling to Madison Square Garden in New York City in the 1920's. Though lacking the athletic background, McMahon had the more important business background that Gagne did not.

Wrestling remained stagnant for the next two decades, with promotions staying localized to run shows due to the lack of interest in fans outside of the major markets. In 1982, McMahon sold his company to his son, Vince McMahon Jr., who shortened the companies name to the World Wrestling Federation. Within two years, McMahon purchased surrounding territories along with its talent with a huge dream of taking his company to a national level. In spite of all of his recent business acquisitions, McMahon still lacked a major star. Then in 1983, he found the man that had not only the look, but that all-important charisma that could captivate audiences of all ages—Hulk Hogan.

Born Terry Bollea, Hulk Hogan was already known nationally. He made an appearance in *Rocky III* in 1982, starring Sylvester Stallone. Stallone, who was also the writer and director, used Hogan in the film as part of a boxer vs. wrestler scene that was designed to make Rocky Balboa look like a modern day David going up against Goliath. Playing the part of Thunderlips, Hogan was nearly a foot taller and over a hundred pounds heavier than Stallone, who was in phenomenal shape himself.

With Hogan signed along with other athletes of all shapes and sizes, including a 7' 4", 525 pound marvel known as Andre The Giant, McMahon kicked off the second phase of his expansion by syndicating his programs to TV stations across the country. In addition to just the wrestling, McMahon reached out into other entertainment fields with the idea of enhancing his product with celebrities, such as pop singer Cyndi Lauper and TV's biggest bad ass, Mr. T. As hoped for, audiences were enthralled and newspapers and news broadcasts across the country were all over it, reporting how "a vicious pro wrestler named "Rowdy" Roddy Piper kicked a defenseless Cyndi Lauper in the face for no reason." Now that everyone in the country was curious, McMahon set up a make-it-or-break-it event called WrestleMania, in which he hoped fans would want to pay to see at closed-circuit theaters across the country on March 31,1985. Not only was there a sold out crowd to see it at Madison Square Garden, but 135 additional theaters, gymnasiums, and convention centers were also sold out to watch it air live. The event was so popular that it prompted NBC to put wrestling back on network television in prime-time. CBS also capitalized on its popularity and created an animated series called *Hulk Hogan's Rock 'n Wrestling*. McMahon then began marketing clothing, magazines, videotapes, and toys to bring in even more money and to literally have his product everywhere.

This was where I came in. I began watching wrestling in 1985 as part of my regular weekly television routine. I watched the cartoon show on Saturdays and *All-American Wrestling* on Sundays. Every few months, NBC would air *Saturday Night's Main Event* at ten or eleven at night. Dad would always set the recorder on the VCR and we would all watch it first thing Sunday morning after everyone was up.

Hulk Hogan was, in addition to being the World Heavyweight Champion, a giant of a man with a deep tan and a massively muscled frame. He wore a yellow and red T-shirt, carried the American Flag, and came to the ring to Survivor's "Eye of the Tiger" as his theme song. Once inside the ring, he would rip his shirt off and go into a muscle posing routine that would send the crowd into a frenzy. Following his match he would give an interview and talk about how he lived his life by training, eating his vitamins, and believing in himself. Coincidentally, my favorite color has always been yellow since as far back as I can remember. My wife once asked me if it was because of Hogan and I didn't really have an answer for her. But it is probably true. Too me, he was the ultimate hero. In watching him, I saw that right always prevailed over wrong and cheating and taking shortcuts got people nowhere in the end. I also saw just what could happen if you trained, took vitamins, and believed in yourself. It's funny how such a simple form of entertainment has taught me the confidence and self motivation that carried me through childhood and still sticks with me as an adult.

Jen and me with Grandma in Salt Lake City

People have given me a hard time about watching wrestling most of my life. They would say, "How can you watch that fake shit?" or "That stuff is so fake." To me, "fake" is a monster in a movie. These are real people, some of the best athletes in the world, and great entertainers that can literally hold the audience in the palms of their hands. It isn't any different then those so-called reality shows on TV today where writers carefully set up circumstances and situations that grasps the audience's imagination. The only difference is that wrestling hasn't pretended to be legitimate in decades, unlike reality TV. But both can be enjoyed easily if viewers suspend disbelief for a few hours each week—and there isn't anything wrong with that.

Wrestling can be such a beautiful showcase between two athletes. Guys like Ricky Steamboat, Randy Savage, and Bret Hart could put on a clinic of holds and counter-holds that, when done right, would be just like a dance or even a ballet in the sense that it would tell a story. If people didn't like technicians, they might appreciate the villains—without even knowing it. "Rowdy" Roddy Piper, "Ravishing" Rick Rude, and Jake "The Snake" Roberts would insult the crowd, attack opponents from behind, and constantly cheat. The crowd's boos and other disapproving gestures were proof in the pudding that they were being controlled like marionettes. Then came the giants. People would stare in awe at the sight of Andre The Giant, Big John Studd, and King Kong Bundy, who were more than twice the size of normal men.

In addition to watching wrestling on TV, I also began playing with the action figure toys that were replicas of my favorite guys. The first two I got I came across by accident at a department store with my parents during our march through the toy aisle. The Iron Sheik and Jimmy "Superfly" Snuka were just laying there, out of their package, and just waiting to be played with. I snatched them up and could hardly wait until I could get them home and put them into action! Meanwhile as we continued through the store, I had them wrestle each other on shelves any time my parents stopped to look at something. The Sheik and Snuka battled it out on toaster ovens, microwaves, particle boards shelves, and even on paint cans, but there was never a clear winner—the matches had to continue.

Once we got home, I picked up the only thing in the house that resembled a ring—the Puke Bucket. If there was any other choice, believe me, I would have used it. Uncle Robbie came to the rescue and made me an actual ring for my birthday. It had a white canvas, black turnbuckles, and red, white, and blue ropes—just like what the real guys fought in at Madison Square Garden! It was only a matter of time until I was able to sign more wrestlers to an exclusive contract that guaranteed me that only the best wrestlers would compete in my room and not anywhere else. If there were wrestlers that I didn't have, odds are that Jake had them so we could have a bit of a talent exchange to keep the matches different.

Me and Jake with our wrestling guys

I still have all of my wrestling guys, but they have long since been retired. The paint from their tights and mustaches have peeled away in spots and there are even a few cracks in their arms and legs. But they did their job. The wars waged inside the squared circle between them live on in the solitude of a fanatic child's mind.

If I wasn't playing with the guys, I wanted to wrestle for real. Some nights after dinner and after Dad was done watching *World News Tonight* (which he seemed to revolve his life around much like I did with wrestling), we would wrestle in my room. Jen would join in too and together we would take turns jumping off my bed onto Dad's prone body with elbow drops, leg drops, splashes, and the dreaded butt-bomb. Dad would eventually get the upper hand and me and Jen would always have to submit—or he would just pin us down and fart in our faces. If that wasn't bad enough, he wouldn't let us up until we at least got one little whiff of his potent potpourri.

When Dad wasn't home Jen really didn't have any desire to wrestle with me, so I had to turn to my huge, three foot stuffed bear in order to have a match. I literally knocked the stuffing out of him over the years with bodyslams, suplexes, and elbow drops. When he was forced into retirement, he was as flat as a pancake.

Around this time, my parents signed me up for a youth wrestling camp that was, and still is, held once a year at Sedro-Woolley High School. The local wrestlers and coaches would volunteer their time to spark the next generation's interest in freestyle and collegiate wrestling. Obviously these forms of competition differ greatly from the style seen on TV, but the object is still the same—beat your opponent.

Very few kids actually knew holds. The rest like me would roll around on the mat and try to put the other kids' shoulders down. I won a few and lost more than a few, never getting better than a third or fourth place ribbon. To me it just wasn't the same as what was on TV, and I remember telling Dad on the way home that I didn't want to do it anymore.

"It's your decision," he said. "If you don't want to, then you don't have to. Just remember that it is your choice."

I sat there content in the back seat of the car and was more than happy with my decision. I never thought that I would ever regret that but let's just say that ten years later, I wouldn't have minded getting a do-over.

CHAPTER 6
Time For School

I N AUGUST OF 1987 and with school less than one month away, it was time for orientation and a trip to the doctor's office for a series of shots. With my legs and arms full of holes and a certificate that officially declared me eligible for kindergarten, all I could do was wait until it began in early September. I had gone through preschool the year prior, but that was totally different. Those were two or three hour days a couple of times a week and while kindergarten was still three days a week, they were going to be full days.

Just like every young kid, I made my share of mistakes and wound up in trouble. I had long since been banned from watching *Three's Company* and would be banned from watching wrestling occasionally as well. That was my punishment for everything no matter what I did wrong and how big or little it was—no wrestling. It was that way my entire time growing up until I was eighteen. I hated it, but it pretty much always taught me a lesson to where I never was a repeat offender of a certain offense. As a parent now I understand that if you take away the most important thing in a child's life, odds are that they will behave the way that you want them to. Of course at the time, I thought that my parents did it just to make me suffer.

I was in trouble way more than Jen was and as far as I was concerned, my punishments were always a lot stiffer. We would argue about something pretty silly most likely and she would generally resort to pinching or scratching me like a typical girl. I would then retaliate by pushing her or hitting her in the arm. She would then sell it like I shot her with a gun and screech at the top of her lungs. Mom or Dad would then come to her rescue like the U.S. Cavalry and drop the hammer on me. Jen of course got off Scott-free. It was that way until she grew up and finally stopped crying over everything, which wasn't until she was in her late teens. Then she would just tell on me and somehow always manage to leave out certain parts—like the ones that would get her in trouble too! And for the longest time, Mom and Dad always took her word over mine.

I didn't always need Jen to get myself into trouble because I could do just fine bringing it on myself. (Jen will love this story because she brings it up every time we talk about our

29

childhood). There was a dairy plant in Mount Vernon that produced cheese and one day after going to lunch at Grandma Murrow's, Mom took Jen and I on a tour of the production area. At the end of the tour while we were in the gift section, I committed my first crime. While nobody was looking and for a reason that I can't explain, I swiped a pack of whole wheat sandwich crackers with cheese in the center. I stuffed them under my shirt, just above my ass crack, and followed everyone out the door.

While we were on our way home, I decided to take out my stolen snack and dig in to them. Mom looked in the rear view mirror and with fury in her eyes, quickly jerked the steering wheel and spun us around right in the center of the road to take us back to the cheese factory. I then had to endure the most humiliating thing in my whole five years of life by walking into the store, handing back the crackers, and telling them that I had taken them like a miserable thief. I didn't watch wrestling after that for a month.

A few weeks before my one man crime crusade, Dad brought home my first motorcycle in the back of the Dyin' Pig. It was a Honda MR50 that was well-used but still in good shape. It was orange with a black seat and it had a few stickers on it. It was only a three speed so it didn't go very fast. Why should it? It was just a beginner bike.

I had been on motorcycles before, but never on my own. The last time I was on one was earlier in the summer when all four of us (that's right, ALL FOUR OF US) piled onto Dad's 350 and rode up to Baker Lake. We had done this, believe it or not, several times before. Jen rode in front of Dad on top of the fuel tank. I was sandwiched behind Dad and in front of Mom, who brought up the rear with half of her butt on the seat and the other half on Dad's homemade luggage rack. This time around we got pulled over and were sent home by the sheriff. No ticket was issued, which was not only amazing considering the amount of people on the back, but Mom and Dad didn't even have helmets on either! Needless to say, we didn't do anymore of that.

Even when we did go for ride on Dad's bike, it seemed to take hours just to get it to start. Me and Jen would stand in the front of the bike and look at the headlight, which only came on after the engine fired, while Dad jumped up and down on the kickstand and screamed, "Come on you piece of shit!" with every kick. We would get excited when the light would flicker, but it would most always fade out quickly. Sometimes it would run for a few seconds, only to quit again. Plan B usually meant Dad putting it in gear, rolling it down a hill, and popping the clutch to get it running. The three of us would then have to run and catch up with him and mount up while he was still rolling because if he stopped, it would likely die again.

My very first ride on my new bike was in the church field behind our house. Dad gave me a crash course in operating the bike by pointing out the throttle, the brake lever, and how to shift using the clutch lever. The hard part was starting out. It took several times of killing the engine (I guess it runs in the family) until I finally let the clutch lever out slow enough, while easing on the accelerator at the right time, to get the bike in motion. Once going, I went several laps without shifting out of first gear. Dad was planning on riding his bike with me, but instead he spent my first few laps jumping up and down and swearing at his temperamental machine (what a surprise).

A few minutes later, I finally worked up the courage to shift into second gear. I was a little nervous at first but after a few laps, I was settling down and getting a little more comfortable. I kept glancing back at Dad, who was by this time digging into his tool kit to mess with the spark plugs, wondering if he was ever going to join me. I chuckled a little bit and turned my head back to where it should be just in time to see that I was heading for a four-foot wide and four-foot deep irrigation ditch that ran the length of the opposite side of the church field. *No problem,* I thought. Dad told me to pull in the brake lever to stop the bike if I ever got into trouble. I quickly pulled in the lever and was getting ready to put my feet on the ground when I suddenly realized that I was still moving. By the time I figured out that I had pulled in the clutch lever instead, it was already too late and into the muddy ditch I went—bike and all.

It was about sixty yards from the ditch to where Dad was, but it might as well have been sixty miles. After yelling for him a few times to no avail, I figured that I was on my own to get myself out. Luckily the bike didn't land on me so I wasn't hurt, but I was still a little shaken up. It wasn't until I crawled out of the ditch with a big glob of mud on my face and helmet that Dad finally noticed where I was at. He then raced over to me to see if I was alright. He must not have been all that concerned because he was laughing the whole way over to me. That would be my only crash that I had for the next few years. I got right back on the bike and rode the rest of the afternoon.

I had to pick my spots when riding in the church field. Obviously, Sundays were out of the question so I had to do the bulk of my riding on Saturdays and weekday afternoons after Dad got home from work. Once I could start the bike on my own, I didn't have to wait for him to get home before I could go for rides. Eventually, I became good enough to pack Jen around on the bike with me.

Me riding Jen on my motorcycle

Evergreen Elementary School was about a quarter-mile from the old house on Calkins Place. It was a small, kindergarten through fifth grade school for the kids that lived on the north side of town. The south side kids went to Mary Purcell, while the outline kids went to Big Lake, Lyman, or Samish before everyone combined to begin sixth grade at Cascade Middle School, which was across the field from Evergreen. Following eighth grade it would be on to the high school, but that was a long ways out.

I remember on the morning of my first day of school shooting my arms in the air and and yelling "First day of school!" as soon as Mom came in to wake me up. As years went on I would groan the same sentence as my alarm rang to end my summer vacation, but not on this day. On this morning I was fired up and ready to go. School didn't start until 9:30 which meant that in the three hours that I had to spare, the adrenaline that was flowing had plenty of time to turn into nervousness. As usual, my uneasy nerves led to a bout with diarrhea. Sometimes I would just get my pants buttoned up when I would have to undo them again and sit right back down on the toilet for another round.

At 9:10 when Mom pulled the car out of the garage, the diarrhea was gone but I still felt like a criminal walking towards the gallows as we made the mile-and-a-half car trip. We parked the car and Mom walked me to the classroom. She bent down, gave me a kiss, and said goodbye before she turned to go. After I turned and faced the class and saw about twenty kids that I had never seen before, I decided that school wasn't for me. I took off out the front door and chased down Mom before she even made it back to the car, begging her tearfully to take me home. She then loaded me up in the car and took me home, telling me that I would never have to go to school if I didn't want to. Yeah right! She marched me back into the classroom and tossed me in just like a policeman does to an inmate—starting my thirteen year educational/prison term.

Aside from the first day, school was just fine. It was over at 3:30 in the afternoon, at which time Mom would pick me up and take me home. I only went on Monday, Wednesday, and Thursday, so I still had four days a week to myself. The only thing we had to do in kindergarten was learn our colors, letters, and shapes and how to get along with others. Depending on the kid, some of those topics were harder to learn than the others. Kids today go five full days a week and are reading small sentences by the time they are finished with the course. I had nothing like that, but I didn't turn out too bad if I do say so myself.

September is traditionally a very nice month around here as far as the weather goes. It can still get up to the mid-70 degree range during the day, but the cooler nights indicate that fall is coming as well as shorter days. The clocks at that time had to be set back an hour during the month of October, which meant that any outdoor activity after school was likely out of the question. I would usually spend that time catching up on *Jonny Quest* episodes that Dad had taped over the weekend, or wrestling—if I wasn't in trouble.

With it getting dark around five o'clock in those days, it would mean that trick or treating on Halloween would have that spooky feel to it when going door to door at dusk. The youngsters all over the surrounding neighborhoods would go out for a couple of hours in search of sweets. The fun was generally over around 7:00 when the older kids, some probably in middle school or even high school, would come out and trample everything in their path to get their greedy hands on free candy. Nowadays daylight savings isn't until November and those same type of senseless teenagers, whose parents probably don't care what they are doing as long as they are not in their hair, run wild in the neighborhoods without any awareness of children like mine who are just out to have a good time and show off their costumes. I don't think that Congress took that into consideration when they passed the new daylight savings time and why should they? It's the parents responsibility to keep their hooligan offspring off of the streets.

Now where was I? Oh yeah—Halloween. Halloween was a big day in elementary school. Every kid would dress up in their costume and the whole day was always a big party. We would have different activities that were both educational and fun. At the end of the day, probably with about an hour left of school, all of the kindergarten, first, and second graders would line up and go on a parade through each classroom in the entire building. Even the big kids, who were only in fifth grade but seemed more like adults to us, would get smiles on their faces as we marched along.

That year I dressed up as a logger, just like Dad. I wore my jeans like I always did, a flannel shirt, a miniature pair of suspenders, and a hard hat. Mom even put eye shadow all over my face to make it look like I had a beard. To top it off, Dad made me a chainsaw out of a shoebox that I could pack around all day. If I'm not mistaken, I think that I even won the class award for the best costume.

After Halloween was over, it was time to decorate the classroom with Thanksgiving decorations. We would learn about the pilgrims and the Native Americans and all that, and finish off by making a pumpkin pie as a group. Obviously that was everybody's favorite part as we got to eat the finished product.

We celebrated every holiday in school, but Christmas was the big one. We would make Santas out of construction paper and string them up all over school. There were also decorated Christmas trees lined up throughout the building and most of the teachers wore Santa hats for the entire month of December. Right before we left for Christmas vacation, we would all gather in the cafeteria for an assembly filled with Christmas music and Christmas plays.

Everyone participated except for the Jehovah's Witness kids, who wouldn't even come to school on the assembly days. They also wouldn't participate in any of the decorating activities leading up to it as well. It was like that throughout my years of school. Sadly, certain religious activists have made it to where these kinds of things don't happen anymore—no Christmas decorations, no Halloween costumes, or anything cool like that which, God forbid, could let a kid have fun. There are even some people who want the Pledge of Allegiance taken out of school also—what a crock!

During the winter months I lost my first tooth, or should I say that I got it jerked out of my mouth. It had been loose for a few weeks until finally it was just hanging there sideways. I was too nervous to try and pull it out myself, so I let Dad give it a try. I wish I hadn't because his way still turns my stomach. He would tie a piece of dental floss around the tooth and give it a quick jerk. Generally it wouldn't even come out because the floss would slip off during the tug, or he wouldn't do it hard enough and just pull at the tooth instead. It actually would hurt pretty bad, not to mention bleed like a stuck hog.

My way of pulling teeth on my kids may sound a little vicious, but I feel that it works better. I put a small piece of paper over the tooth and grip the sides of it with a pair of pliers. I then squeeze them just enough to where the tooth won't break but most importantly, they won't slip off. Then I just pull straight up in one slow but continuous motion. No jerks, no slips, and believe it or not, no complaints.

I lost quite a few more teeth in kindergarten than the rest of the class because I was older than most by at least a couple of months. I looked like a jack-o-lantern more often than not, making talking a little difficult at times, but I still wasn't as bad as Gabby Hayes by any means. Eating felt funny too but I didn't let that slow me down. I had to because my appetite was starting to increase—as was my size.

I ate pretty much anything unless it had sour cream on it. The funny thing was that I didn't like potatoes for the longest time and wouldn't even want to look at them. But I could eat French fries just fine, especially the ones at McDonald's. Mom would take us there for lunch once a month when we would drive from place to place paying bills. Why she didn't pay by check through the mail is beyond me. Maybe she just liked me and Jen's company in the car.

Eventually I got over the potato thing and ate them at dinner along with everyone else. My favorite dinner, however, was spaghetti and I would always eat two full helpings every time it was served. One thing that I never did was tell anyone at school that I ate the Italian dish or else they would call me "Eddie Spaghetti." Years later, kids started getting more creative and one moron drug it out to "Eddie Spaghetti, your meatballs are ready." It got a few laughs, even from me, until it got old. Then it just irritated me.

We didn't eat a whole lot of sweets at home because Mom didn't want us to have our teeth rot out of our head. The same went for pop—she would always buy diet soda so, again, our teeth wouldn't rot. I actually prefer diet pop now, not because I am worried about my teeth, but because I don't like the ultra-sweet taste. We made up for it by having ice cream on a regular basis. Mom would buy the normal chocolate, strawberry, and vanilla, but my favorite was chocolate marble. Except for the times when there was only one miniature ribbon of chocolate syrup in the entire carton, it was great. She would also get the flavor of the month once in a while, including spumoni, that we ended up throwing out because it not only tasted like shit, it looked like it too.

After Dad would dish it up, Jen and I would always compare to make sure that we were given the same amount. Naturally there would be whining by either one of us if they weren't the same, so Dad had to scoop it just right. Once, the ice cream was so hard Dad had to really bear down on it in order to get the scoop through. While pulling up on the scoop, the ice cream popped loose and he sent a baseball-sized chunk straight over his shoulder and onto the living room carpet. Everyone laughed except Mom.

We would have cake or pie every once in a while along with our ice cream. Mom got her cooking lessons from the Swedish Chef on *The Muppet Show,* so some of her confections left something to be desired. She would improvise all the time, including substituting baking soda for baking powder on a loaf of banana bread. It may sound bad but believe me, tasting it was much worse. She would also leave out key ingredients or skip just enough steps that her pies would look more like soup with a crust for a bowl.

She always got birthday cakes right, though, especially Jen's teddy bear cake. You see, when Jen turned four in March of that year, she asked Mom to make a cake for her in the shape of a bear. I don't know where Jen got the idea, but she has had Mom make the same cake for her every single year since then—and she is now in her mid-twenties!

When spring rolled around and the weather warmed up and it became somewhat drier, I was able to get back on my motorcycle once in a while. It wasn't an everyday thing, however, as our springs usually bring persistent rain. It may be good for the plants and flowers, but it was bad for kids who wanted to play outside.

The warmer weather brought the sounds of birds chirping and sometimes even sweet sounding melodies in the back yard. The sliding glass door in the dining room was always cracked in order to let the fresh air in. The birds would set out on the picnic table or on the lattice fence and just sing away. They would also fly around and gather grass and small twigs that they would use to build nests in our birdhouses or even the eves of the roof.

A lot of times they would fly right into the windows during mating season, thinking that their own reflection is another male bird. If we heard it, everyone would always go out to see if it was okay. If it was laying there just stunned, Dad would bring it inside and gently massage it until it perked up. Jen and I would even take turns petting it while it was still gathering its senses. One bird decided not to wait until we got it outside before it came back to life. He shot out of Dad's hands and off he went through the house. It took a while but with every door and window in the house open and us chasing him around, he eventually found his way back outside where he belonged.

For a while unconscious birds were the closest thing that we had to a pet, unless you count the rabbits and the deer that strolled through the yard from time to time. One day, Mom and Dad brought home an actual family pet—a baby puppy. It was a black and tan, short-haired, miniature dachshund named Muffin. We called her Muff or Muffy for short.

Prior to Muff's arrival, the only dogs that we played with were the ones that belonged to the neighbors. The neighbor on the west side of our house, Yvonne, had a mutt named Tiger who was every bit of twenty years old, couldn't hear, and could barely walk. That dog was pretty much off limits so we played with the black lab named Shadow that lived kitty-corner to us. She was a great dog who would come over every day to play fetch. You could throw a slimy piece of wood or a tennis ball for her all day and she would just have a blast.

Everyone was so excited to have a dog of our own. Of course she had to be house trained, but that doesn't take very long. Muff really liked Dad and would wait on the window seat every afternoon until he would get home from work. As soon as he pulled up, or anyone else did too for that matter, we had to take her outside to greet them. Even though she was house trained, she still pissed everywhere when she greeted somebody because she got so excited.

In the evenings, she would lay in Dad's lap as he hogged the recliner. He would have to hold her bone for her while she chewed it or else she wouldn't want anything to do with it (talk about spoiled). She played with her squeaker toys on her own, however, because she didn't want anyone messing with them. Her goal was always to pull the squeaker out and more often than not, she was successful.

The other new addition around the house was our new camp trailer. Actually it wasn't new at all. It was a single-axle, 1967 Aloha that was a whole thirteen feet long. Dad got it for pretty cheap and it was really in good shape. It was fully self-contained with a stove, a refrigerator, and a furnace and it could sleep six people (four people comfortably). It had a kitchen table and two bench seats that folded down into one bed. Above that were brackets that held a roll-out hammock. I slept in the hammock a few times, until I rolled off and smacked my head on the corner of the stove—then I traded spots with Jen. We had to get it if we wanted to camp because Mom refused to sleep on the ground anymore. The green tent was then only used when Jen and I camped out back or when Dad took me on our yearly camping trip to Slide Lake, which I will talk about later.

We had a few camping trips on some weekends right after we got it. We mostly went to Baker Lake or Grandy Lake if we went anywhere. We would fish and ride bicycles during the day and play Uno during the evening. On the days when it would rain all day, we would just play cards all day. We didn't really complain about the weather, we just made the most out of quality family time. When the weather got better once summer came and school let out, we went almost every weekend.

Even though it was much nicer outside after I wrapped up kindergarten, Jen and I would still watch our fair share of TV. We could watch anything at anytime as long as it was family oriented and we spent an equal amount of time outdoors. There was one hour each weekday that the TV was off limits for us because Mom absolutely had to have it turned to ABC to watch *General Hospital.* Let's put it this way—her daily soap opera was the equivalent to me watching wrestling. I don't know how she could enjoy it because for the entire program, she would be on the phone with her friend, Lisa, jabbering about what they thought was going to happen next. When that was over, they both watched a postgame-type show that would actually have people analyzing what happened during the show.

Mom and Lisa would talk several times each day. It wouldn't always be about *General Hospital,* but it wouldn't be about anything important either. They had gone to school together and Lisa's husband, Skip Shiefelbein, was friends with Dad in school. Every couple of months, both families would take turns going to the other family's house for dinner on a weekend night. They had two kids—a daughter named Brandy and a whiny, bitchy son named Brent. I cannot count the times that I got into trouble because of that little bastard. It wasn't so bad around this time because he was just a toddler, but for the next ten years or so, he was something else. (Augghh!! I get pissed off just thinking about it! I'll get back to him later after I cool down.) There was also another couple, Dan and Cori Hyatt, that we hung out around also.

Mom did some babysitting over the summer months in between her phone calls and *General Hospital.* I don't think it was for any money, but rather as favors. She would watch Brent and Uncle Robbie and Aunt Karen's new baby boy, Tristan. Tristan's real name is actually Robert Tristan Thramer, but I can imagine it being very confusing around their house because Karen always called Rob, Robert—especially when she was mad at him, which was often. It wasn't ever anything serious, they just bickered back and forth all the time.

Every summer, right around Dad's birthday, a local network television channel out of Bellingham called KVOS would broadcast five different Clint Eastwood westerns over the course of the work week. (By the way, have you ever noticed that all TV and radio stations around here begin with the letter "K"? That is because every station west of the Mississippi River does as well. All stations east of the Mississippi begin with a "W" instead. See, this book can be educational!) Dad and I would make it a point to watch all five of these movies. On Monday, it was *A Fistful of Dollars,* Tuesday was *For a Few Dollars More,* and Thursday and Friday aired *High Plains Drifter* and *Hang 'em High* respectively. I realize that I forgot Wednesday, but that was because Wednesday was special. It was on that Wednesday in June when I was just six years old that I first watched what instantly became my favorite movie—*The Good, the Bad, and the Ugly.* For the record, it still is.

The Good, the Bad, and the Ugly is an Italian western (better known as a spaghetti western) that was released in 1966. It was directed by Sergio Leone and starred Clint Eastwood, Lee Van Cleef, and Eli Wallach. It was actually the third and final installment in Leone's trilogy of films that centered around a man with no name (Eastwood), the first two being the aforementioned *A Fistful of Dollars* and *For a Few Dollars More.* Unlike most sequels to their predecessors, these films didn't follow the same storyline. This one was about three men traveling separate roads in life whose paths cross amidst a search for a stash of Confederate gold buried in a cemetery. The three would team up and double-cross each other throughout the movie. Eastwood was *The Good,* Van Cleef was *the Bad,* and Wallach was *the Ugly*—known better in the film as Tuco.

To me, this movie had it all. The dialogue was laced with humor, anger, passion, guilt, and sorrow. The footage of brutal Civil War camps and of just what life in this country was like in that era—torn in two—showed me that my life was a fairytale by contrast. It was full of action, suspense, and plenty of violence—all surrounded by a one-of-a-kind musical score that guides your emotions through each scene.

Composed by Ennio Morricone and played by a powerful orchestra, the songs on the soundtrack are perhaps the best ever written for a movie. The vocals were in Italian but were so haunting and even at times beautiful, that it didn't matter what they were singing about. The instruments were just your basic guitars, trumpets, and violins, but it was how they were used that brought feelings of sadness, anger, and triumph. There are very few musicians or writers that have the ability to make music real enough to feel, and Morricone was at the top of the list.

I'm not by any means a spokesperson for this movie but if you haven't seen it, you will not be disappointed.

Dad recorded it on the VCR because it was on so late. I would watch and re-watch it so many times that the tape would literally wear out. Other than that, the only fear I had of losing the movie was if Mom taped over it with some of her stupid *General Hospital* shows, which she did more than once. Eventually I was given the whole unedited VHS for my birthday so it would never happen again.

Why did I waste so much paper on this movie? It inspired the name of my best friend in the whole world who I will talk much more about later.

In 1987, Dad went to work for another logging company, Janicki Logging, out of Sedro-Woolley. After changing employers, my days of riding in the log tuck with him were over. It wasn't because they didn't allow it, it was because Dad didn't even drive trucks anymore—he ran a log loader instead because it paid more money. I still got to go with him when he worked on Saturdays sometimes. I would sit in the cab with him while he sorted logs and I would even get to move the joystick-type controllers that operated the grapples.

Since Dad started with Janicki's, with whom he still works for to this day, he has always gotten Christmas week and the week of the Fourth of July off. Over the Fourth of that year, we took a family vacation to Disneyland. This was my second trip there, but it was the first one that I really have memories of.

We drove the Oldsmobile down and stayed at motels along the way. We didn't take the camp trailer because there was no way that the Dyin' Pig could pull it across the county line—let alone clear to Anaheim, California. Besides, Dad sold it to finance our trip and with the intention of buying something a little more reliable and dependable for future trips.

Muffin went along with us on the trip, riding in her normal spot like she always did in the car—underneath the driver's seat. She would stay there from the time the car was started until it was shut off every single time. When we left her at home, she would hide under Jen's bed until we returned. She was just a real nervous dog and with her being so quiet and clingy, we had no problems sneaking her into motels that didn't allow any pets. Even when we left her in the room when we were inside Disneyland, the maid never found her because she stayed quiet as a mouse under the bed—and we all know that maids don't clean under there to begin with.

Finding a motel on trips like these were humorous, but often exhausting. It seemed every building that we came to had its "no vacancy" signs lit up, so we would be off to the next town. I swear that there were times that the signs indicated that they had room and when Dad went to check in, the Arab that generally ran places like that would say that they were full, so it was on to the next town. It wasn't just our bad luck, we were traveling on the Fourth, which is one of the busiest traveling weeks of the year. After this trip, Dad vowed to speed up his search for something to pull the trailer with so we wouldn't have to fight it anymore.

Our first day out of the car was at Knott's Berry Farm. Billed as "America's First Theme Park" in Buena Park, California, Knott's Berry Farm featured a *Peanuts* theme. *Peanuts* was a comic strip that was created by Charles M. Schulz and its most popular character Snoopy, was the focal point in the advertisement of the park. *Peanuts* also had a character named Linus van Pelt who would carry a blue blanket around with him everywhere he went. Ironically, Jen was rarely seen without her blue "blankie" either. Even today, Jen has a blue blanket, although much larger than the original, that she always has by her side when she is in her pajamas.

Knott's Berry Farm had several roller coasters and water rides at the time but in the 1920's, Walter Knott ran the area as an actual farm where visitors could sample and buy his fruit. It was also here that he first introduced a new berry that was cultivated by Rudolph Boysen, the boysenberry. Boysenberries are a combination of red raspberry, blackberry, and locanberry that were first discovered on that very piece of land. Another Walt, Walt Disney, visited the park on several occasions and even personally invited Knott to the opening of Disneyland on July 15, 1955.

The following day we went to Disneyland, and we were there from the time they opened until the time they closed. Jen and I were still not big enough to get on some of the rides. Space Mountain was off limits, as was Thunder Mountain Railroad, but we could do everything in Critter Country and Fantasyland.

After walking through Sleeping Beauty's castle, our first stop was Pinocchio's Daring Journey. *Pinocchio* was by far my favorite animated movie and I just had to go on the ride, which was a roller cart ride that took you through several dark rooms. The only light came off of the computer-animatronic characters from the movie. Although it was dark with loud voices, it wasn't too scary—until a roaring Monstro, the giant whale, shot up directly in front of our cart along with thunder and lightning. That was it for me—I screamed and cried until the ride was over. Here I was at the "Happiest Place on Earth," crying like a baby and wanting to go home.

Maybe it was to make me feel better, but Mom and Dad bought me a Donald Duck hat after the ride was over. The bizarre hat was white with eyes on it and had a giant yellow bill that extended out more than twice the standard size of regular bills to make it look like a real duck. Jen got a Goofy hat (no pun intended) that also had a huge bill that resembled a dog's snout and had two droopy ears dangling down from the sides of it.

I had the hat for only a few minutes before I almost lost it for good. We strolled over to New Orleans Square and got onto the Pirates of the Caribbean ride, where we boarded a boat that floated us through coves and towns that were being ravaged by pirates. During the ride, we went sailing down a twenty foot waterfall where, sure enough, my two foot long bill got caught in the wind and went flying off of my head. I turned around fully expecting to see it in the water, but found instead that an old man sitting behind us had it surprisingly land right in his lap. I was lucky, as were Mom and Dad—how many parents have kids that cry twice in one day at Disneyland?

During our trip to Disneyland, we began a family a tradition of stopping and eating at Carl's Jr. Although a standard fast food restaurant, Carl's Jr. was at the time only located around the south part of the country. It seemed every bit as popular as McDonald's because every building was always full of people. For the longest time the only one around our area was in Spokane, which at one time had more restaurants per square mile than anywhere else in the country. It was only a couple of months ago that we got one somewhat close to us in Marysville. Needless to say, anytime I'm in the area I must stop there for lunch.

My last big event before the start of first grade was me and Dad's yearly weekend camping trip to Slide Lake, a tradition that continued for over a decade. It was a three hour drive from our house, two of which were spent driving up over twenty miles of gravel logging road, a little south of the ultra-small town of Rockport. From there it was a little over a mile of hiking to get to the lake itself. Slide Lake got its name from a massive rock slide that completely blocked the path of Otter Creek, which itself is the result of continuous snow melt off of Snowking Mountain. With the sun radiating off of the high mountain peaks, the lake reflects the surrounding landscape as pristine as any mirror.

The two of us would get up there on a Friday afternoon and stay until Sunday morning. We packed a loaf of bread, a dozen eggs, some bacon, and a few cans of soup. We had all the comforts of home—a small set of pots and pans for cooking, a grill that was made out of the bottom part of a broken stroller, a refrigerator and bathtub (by way of the chilly lake), plenty of downed trees for firewood, and of course the green tent. They even had an outdoor toilet not far from our camp.

The john was actually an old crate-shaped wooden box with a lid on it that covered a hole that was dug into the ground. There were no walls around it, so you were out there for everyone to see. Generally when Dad or I was out in the woods and had to take a dump, we would just crouch down and lean slightly forward to avoid a potential catastrophe if one were to lose his balance. However, for more calculating and time-consuming dumps, the box was the only way to go.

Over the course of the weekend, we each had to use it at least once. I would always walk up there with him when he had to go so that I didn't have to wait at camp on my own. Dad was wearing a bright red hat at the time and didn't want to attract attention while he was making his deposit, so he set it on the ground. As he was taking care of his business, I figured that I might as well take a leak while I waited.

I had just started doing my thing when Dad yelled, "Goddammit, Eddie!"

I looked down to see that I was giving his hat a golden shower. I swear to this day that it was an accident.

We fished all day on Saturday. We walked around the entire lake, stopping to drop a line every hundred feet or so. There was no bridge across Otter Creek so in order for us to cross, we had to strip down to our underwear and wade across. Not only did we have to worry about tripping and dropping our clothes, but we had to somehow avoid getting glacier water anywhere near our nut sacks.

Provided we caught any fish, which we always did, we would grill them up for dinner. He was always really good about ripping the bones from the fish with just a flick of a wrist, never leaving any behind. His only flaw was not cooking it through completely, giving us an idea of what sushi would taste like.

In the evening, we would sit by the fire and I would listen and laugh as he told me stories about when him and Uncle Robbie were little boys. Those stories would never get old, even after I heard them a hundred times. It's even better when both of them are together trying to recount what happened, likely starting an argument.

"Bullshit, Ronnie," Rob would say. "That didn't happen."

"It did to," Dad would say, trying to reassure him. "Don't try and deny it"

I and whoever else was listening would just laugh at them all night long. Nobody needed television when these two guys were together.

As we headed home, we talked about how much fun that we had and just when we could go back and do it again. A year was so far away, but I had first grade coming up to help pass the time. It was going to be much different than kindergarten was, having to go five full days instead of just three.

CHAPTER 7

"Are You Ready For Some Football?!"

I FIRST GOT INTO watching professional football in the fall of 1988. My favorite team was (and still is) the San Francisco 49ers. People have always asked me why that is, most of which just assume it is because they were good at the time. Well, that is not exactly true. Granted, they had won Super Bowls XVI and XIX by that time, but things weren't going good at that point. Through the middle of November in the 1988 NFL season, they were just 6-5. The Buffalo Bills, Cincinnati Bengals, Chicago Bears, and even the Seattle Seahawks had better records at that point, so that wasn't it. Maybe it was the gold and red color on their uniforms. Perhaps it was the fact that a few months earlier on our way to Disneyland, we went through San Francisco ("Franscy Frisco" is how Jen said it) and crossed the Golden Gate Bridge. It could have been that *Full House*, a show that I watched when it came on the air around that time, was based in San Francisco. I really don't have an answer for anyone, nor should it matter—they're my favorite team and that's the end of it.

Every Monday during the season, I would get to stay up way past my bedtime to watch *Monday Night Football* on ABC. It was always the biggest and most anticipated game of the week. Hank Williams, Jr. would ask everyone who was watching "Are you ready for some football?" before breaking into a musical opening that was a remix of "All My Rowdy Friends Are Coming Over Tonight," which would get fans fired up.

Dad and I would bet a quarter on each game. It would be several years before dollars were at stake. Having just turned seven, quarters were just about all that I had at the time. Dad would empty out his pockets at the end of the week and split his coins up between me and Jen, providing me with my only source of income. There were no allowances for doing chores—they were mandatory and not rewarded for upon completion.

We would take turns picking teams each week. I didn't know much about win and loss records or statistics at the time, so I pretty much chose the team whose name or colors that I liked better. I would pick the cool sounding teams like the Vikings, the Raiders, and the Broncos. I stayed away from silly sounding names like the Dolphins, the Saints, and the Oilers.

We would pretty much trade quarters back and forth throughout the season. It wasn't about getting rich, it was about a father and son competing against each other and cheering on his team to clobber the other the other guy's teams—and I got to stay up late to do it!

Life in first grade was much different than I had been accustomed to the year prior. School was five days a week and was much more than just coloring and sharing. We learned to read, write, and do math. I didn't have any trouble picking any of it up and was ahead of most, if not all, of the class.

It was during this year that I really started to develop my own personality, some of which I got into trouble for. When you got in trouble in class, the teacher would write your name on the board. This was a small (but good at the same time) form of humiliation that let the entire class know that you did something wrong. Having your name on the board was merely a warning, but any check marks behind it got you time off of recess. Five checks earned you a trip to the principal's office. While I never made it quite that far, I did get my fair share of check marks.

The worst part about getting my name on the board was having to come home and tell my parents. Technically I didn't have to because the teacher didn't call any parents to tell them that their child got a few check marks, but that would be keeping secrets—and I knew better than that. I figured that if I made a mistake, Mom and Dad should know about and I should be tough enough to admit to it.

I don't remember getting into too much trouble when I got home and told Mom. She would just say, "You're gonna have to tell your father when he gets home."

If it was really bad, she would say, "Wait 'til I tell your father when he gets home!"

Having her say that was a punishment in itself. There was no real reason to fear him or anything like that, but I just didn't want him to be disappointed in me.

I got my share of spankings from time to time and if it was really bad, I had to drop my pants and get it on the bare butt. As I got older Mom would give it to me with a wooden spoon, which for some reason she won't ever admit to having done. It often times turned out more funny than painful because the spoon would occasionally break after hitting my butt cheeks. That really pissed Mom off because now I was laughing and having a good time when I should be receiving a punishment.

In addition to spankings, I managed to get my mouth washed out with soap a few times. (It wasn't until I was about twenty that I realized that the purpose of which was to "clean up the mouth.") I never could understand why something that was supposedly good for your body tasted so bad. One time Jen and I sat outside on the patio taking turns saying bad words to each other. Mom heard us through the kitchen window and came unglued. She marched us into the bathroom where we took turns biting off chunks of soap and chewing it for thirty seconds before we were allowed to spit it out. If we did it too early, we were awarded with an extra bite.

I don't remember getting diarrhea or anything from it, but I'm sure that I did. As a parent now, I don't use soap on the kids—I use Tabasco Sauce. It doesn't take much, but it painfully gets the point across without giving them the shits. If that were to happen the punishment would be on me because I would have to clean it up.

On October 15,1988, one of my biggest dreams came true. That Saturday afternoon, all four of us went down to the Tacoma Dome to watch our first live World Wrestling Federation event. Us and approximately 10,000 other fans watched two hours of wrestling action in person.

Pro wrestling peaked again in terms of popularity in 1988. Just one year earlier, 93,173 fans packed the Pontiac Silverdome in Michigan, setting a world record for indoor attendance that still stands today. The match that they came to see was Hulk Hogan vs. Andre The Giant as part of WrestleMania III. A few weeks later 11 million people tuned into *Saturday Night's Main Event*, eagerly anticipating what was going to happen in the aftermath. The television rating for that episode still holds the record for any program in the history of television shown in that time slot. Nine months later on February 5, over 33 million viewers watched a live, prime-time edition of *The Main Event* on NBC, setting a mark that still stands as the highest rated wrestling event ever on TV, to see the long awaited rematch between Hogan and Andre.

Casual fans then began turning away from wrestling, as they grew tired of Hogan/Andre matches, and it would be nearly a decade before mainstream attention returned. After all, like a soap opera, they all just led up to the next event anyhow. Hardcore fans, on the other hand, never tired of the same old song and dance.

Eight big matches went down that day in Tacoma. Jake "The Snake" Roberts wrestled "Ravishing" Rick Rude, Ultimate Warrior wrestled the Honky Tonk Man, and there were also some tag team matches—all of which led up to the main event between Hulk Hogan and the Big Bossman.

The Bossman, whose real name was Ray Traylor, came to the ring first for the big finale. Traylor's character was an evil prison guard who beat up everybody in sight while claiming to stand for law, order, and justice. After he made his way to the ring, the crowd stood in unison and turned to the entryway as his opponent entered the arena, just as a gladiator would have in ancient Rome. Hulk Hogan then hit the ring and tore into the evil prison guard. After about twenty minutes, Hogan came out with the win to the delightful cheers of the crowd.

Jen and I each got souvenirs from the show. She got a giant foam Hulk Hogan finger and I got my first of several hundred wrestling magazines. I would spend the next several years trying to convince her (or con her) into giving it to me. Just as we would have a deal, Mom would would usually step in and put an end to my devious scheme. I guess that at some point I was finally able to persuade her, because I have it right here at my house today.

There were just two drawbacks about my first live event. Randy Savage, the current World Champion, wasn't there. He was wrestling across the country at the Capital Centre in Landover, Maryland before a dismal crowd of under 3,000. He was really the ultimate loser because as champion he receives a small percentage of the gate, so his bigger payday would have been in

Tacoma with us. It also proved that Hogan was the better draw and the northwest region of the country could be a decent market.

Also conspicuous by his absence was Andre The Giant. I remember Dad wishing that Andre would have been there, and I felt the exact same. Just to see a man of that size up close would have been something that I would have never forgotten. Unfortunately, Andre was feeling the effects from Acromegaly, a disease that he was born with that would not let his body stop growing. In late 1988, he was taken off the tour schedule for good and thus only worked the big events and pay-per-views. Less than two years later, he was completely retired.

Despite the two disappointments, I felt like the luckiest kid in the world as I walked out of the Tacoma Dome. I had just been a few yards away from my hero, Hulk Hogan. For me, it was like seeing God in person. That may sound ridiculous but for a seven year old, it was a dream come true.

When I went back to school and reported in for show-and-tell what I had seen over the weekend, nobody cared. Even at six or seven, the kids in class were under the impression that wrestling was fake. But yet their cartoon shows were real, right? I stopped defending my reasons for watching it from that point on. Who cares if nobody else liked it? I didn't have to be like anyone else just to fit in. I figured that people should like me for who I am if they were going to like me to begin with, not for portraying something else.

Fortunately, most kids liked me anyway. The boys and I would play football during recess, emulating our favorite pro stars. The girls would stand out on the sides of the field and watch us show off while competing for their attention and adoration. The one girl that I had my eyes on, I won over instantly.

Kristen Andrews was a skinny, brunette-haired beauty that captured my attention from the moment that I saw her. From that point on and for the next several years, we were best friends, or a grade school "couple." Every kid in the class teased us about it whenever we were even near each other, singing that stupid song about "sitting in a tree, K-I-S-S-I-N-G." They sang it on the playground, in the lunchroom, and even in class. It became so persistent that the teacher had to move our desks clear across the room from one another. I then had to sit by the ugliest and fattest girl in the class, which got me teased and laughed at too.

That was standard procedure though—you always laughed at the kid who had to sit next to a hideous member of the opposite sex. Maybe it was because I was a boy, but it seemed that the ugly girls far outnumbered the ugly boys. Still, there was always THE ugly one that stuck out like a sore thumb. I regret how people like me treated girls like that. She never got a card on Valentine's Day, always got the "ew, gross!" look, and nobody wanted to so much as stand in line by her. If I had to sit by her in class, I would scoot my chair over as far as I possibly could away from her. When we lined up at the door after recess, I would wait until somebody else got behind her before I took my place in line. If she were to get in line behind me, I would actually get out of line and go to the end of it. And God forbid you touch her. Then you had to wipe off the part of your body that had been "soiled" onto something or someone else—starting a chain reaction

45

that would make its way around the class at least once and sometimes more. All the while, here is a lonely, fat, and ugly girl watching cool kids rubbing her germs off onto each other.

Looking back, we weren't the cool ones and we should be ashamed of ruining a girls' childhood but at that age, nobody cared about giving somebody a poor complex. You didn't realize the fact that the ugly girl might just grow up to be a gorgeous woman with a knockout body. Most likely though, she would grow up hating herself, her life, and everything else around her. She would probably get into drugs while looking for the slightest bit of acceptance and eventually die without anybody even knowing. That may seem a bit extreme but think about it—have you ever seen or heard about that one ugly person that was in every one of your classes growing up? Me neither.

Kids tease anyone that they can find even the slightest flaw in. Velcro shoes were an easy target because that meant that you couldn't tie shoelaces. If you wore a hand-knitted sweater that your grandmother put her heart and soul into making it for you, you could get your ass kicked. And if you brought one of your favorite toys to show-and-tell, it better be something that big kids used or else . . .

As much as first graders wanted to be big kids, nobody physically measured up. The playground at school was separated into two sides—one for kindergarten through third grade and the other for fourth and fifth graders. There was no way, no matter how cool you tried to be or how tough you though you were, that any younger kid would cross over to where the big kids played—you may not return! Nobody would admit their fear, however, because then you were a pussy. While no kid ever went over to that side, you had to act like you would go over in a heartbeat. If not, you were a baby and subject to constant ridicule.

Some kids had flaws that they couldn't do anything about, and I was one of them. For some reason, when I laughed really hard or was tickled to the point of laughing, I would pee my pants. Thank God nobody at school noticed or else I would have been screwed. To pull it off, I had to make it look like I fell in the water or spilled something on my pants—that includes "accidentally" falling crotch-first into a puddle and "accidentally" dumping a cup of water into my lap. Sometimes if water or mud wasn't an option, I had to improvise a little more and walk around holding something in front of my crotch—much like a teenager hiding a boner. I would even go so far as to pretend that I was sick so I didn't have to get up from my desk and go out to recess.

It's not like it would happen every day. In all honesty, it probably only happened around a dozen times throughout school. The last time that it ever happened was in ninth grade when some kid went to spit his Copenhagen out of an open window while sitting at his desk during English class. Instead, he missed and left a huge, tar-like spill on the glass. As always, I sent a squirt right into my shorts. The good news was, it hasn't happened since—no matter how funny anything has been.

My little handicap was cured over time to where the actual handicap kids at school didn't have the ability to outgrow their troubles. I don't know how many mentally or physically retarded kids that there are in every school district, but it sure seemed that we had more than usual at Evergreen. We had Downs syndrome kids, Cerebral Palsy kids, quadriplegic kids, as well as kids that spoke in such a way that it was is if their tongues were glued to the roof of their mouths. With the exception of a couple, they were all confined to a sanitarium in the building that reeked of piss and decay at all times. The teachers that had to deal with them and care for them should have been paid a fortune.

I signed up for and competed in my first team sport in 1988. Every kid starts somewhere, and for me it was soccer. I have no idea why I ever felt the urge to play, other than I enjoyed running around and the fact that I could trip people and make it look like an accident. I wasn't even very good. I would just run around and try to kick the ball towards the opponents goal. In the three years that I played, I didn't score a single goal—I even missed on penalty kicks. The best part about soccer was the after-the-game snacks that were passed out by the parents. We would always get a candy bar and a Squeeze-It, the popular fruit drink that was shaped like a beer bottle.

During the season, we had a fundraiser in which we were to sell candy bars for a buck apiece. If you could sell a whole box of fifty, you could get a prize of your choice. I went to every house on our street trying to get the box sold. The ones I didn't sell, which was the majority, Dad took to work and sold to overweight truck drivers who probably had diabetes also. Thanks to him, I was able to earn my prize—a 49ers pennant that I could display in my room.

The other sport that I began playing that year was baseball (actually it was T-ball, but you have to start somewhere). Like soccer, it was coed. Each team had thirteen or so players and with any luck, only a small amount of girls. The more females on the team, the more losses you would have. It was just a fact. Girls were slower and couldn't hit or throw the ball as far as the boys could. Things may be different now but at the time, boys ran around at recess building strength and endurance, while girls stood around and talked. If it were a talking contest, the boys would be the ones that were the detriment.

CHAPTER 8
Dealing With Reality

Until the spring of 1989, my seven-plus years of life was a continuous stretch of a well-lit road without stop lights, large speed bumps, or other traffic to get in the way. We were as close to a perfect family as a group could possibly be. Everything that we did, we did together. We went to town together, watched TV together, and ate dinner together every night. The only times that we didn't were on the sporadic days that Dad had to work late, but that only happened a couple of times a month.

On Saturdays when Dad didn't have to work, which at the time was most of them, we would all go down to the bakery in town for breakfast. (Dad and the other guys from work called it the "Suck Butt" for some reason.) By this time, I was done ordering from the kiddie menu. It wasn't that I was trying to be a "big kid" or anything, it was just that my appetite was growing rapidly. Mom would accuse me of ordering the biggest thing on the menu because I wasn't the one paying for it, when in reality all I wanted was enough to eat. She probably just didn't want to spend the extra money.

My appetite was growing right along with my body, as I was constantly getting taller. I would grow out of my clothes not long after just getting them, much to the dismay of my parents. With me being the oldest of any of the kids that my parents' friends had, I didn't have any hand-me-downs so everything that I wore was always new. Jen, on the other hand, got lots of them because she was the youngest.

I wasn't Andre The Giant-size by any means, but I was the tallest in my class. I remember wanting to be Andre's size when I grew up, but Mom and Dad quickly brought me back down to Earth by telling me that someone who is that big lives their life in misery. Clothes have to be special ordered, furniture has to be custom-built, and people would always stare at you. I certainly down-sized my wish after that.

With the constant need for clothes and food coupled with trying to save money to be able to buy a vehicle that would tow the camp trailer with, Dad began putting in an awful lot of hours. Any hour over forty was time-and-a-half on the paycheck, so he worked as much as he could. He even did some side jobs for the company to make a few extra dollars.

In the late 1980's the Northern Spotted Owl made headlines in the newspapers and television reports throughout the state because it was at a 7% decline in population in the Pacific Northwest and British Columbia, Canada. The problem was, this area was their only habitat and the old growth forest areas in which they lived, were becoming fewer and fewer. The land that was logged was thus considered uninhabitable for them. Although the legislature stepped in with new rules for logging, protesters would hold signs near logging company offices and shout their displeasure to passers by. To make matters worse, some would go up to the actual job sights at night and sabotage equipment, causing thousands of dollars in damage. Companies would fix the equipment, but often times it would happen again later. With the need to slow down and hopefully eliminate the problem completely, companies began to send out watchmen to the job sights to act as a security guard while the workers were home for the night.

With extra pay at stake, Dad took this position for a month long stretch towards the summer that year. He towed the camp trailer up to one of the sights with his work pickup and settled in for the month. He would got work during the day, which was literally just outside of his front door, and return in the afternoon with nothing but a light sleep to look forward to. Every couple of hours he would get up and check around the landing, making sure that nobody was out and about.

This was the first time in my life that I was in a single-parent situation. Dad came home at the end of the month, but most kids that were my age didn't have that day to look forward too—their parents were split up for real. They would have to go months without seeing the other parent, if they even saw them at all. Some kids that I knew had never even met their real father, yet they would act just like everyone else when inside they had to have their hearts full of sorrow and shame. And then there was me—a kid with a fairytale life who thinks that his world is ending because his dad is working out of town for a month. Now I knew how Jake felt every time his mom would come and pick him up from Uncle Robbie's house. I also realized how those kids might feel abandoned, because that was how I felt. I was too young to realize that it was all to benefit the family.

The toughest part about him being gone was at bedtime. It was only Mom around in the mornings and afternoons anyway, so I was used to that. Bedtime was different. Mom and Dad always took turns coming into my bedroom to say goodnight since the day I was born. Now it was just Mom. There weren't any cellular phones in those days, so there weren't any calls from him. I take that back, he did call once a week when he went into the nearest town to get a few groceries. By "nearest," I mean every bit of an hour away. He just couldn't leave the equipment up there unattended for that long on a nightly basis.

The three of us went up to see him on Fridays and stayed with him until Sunday. It was just like a weekend camping trip, only better. There was absolutely nobody around for miles and miles. There weren't any noisy campers around us, no fighting to get a camp spot, and Dad was getting paid to do it. On the weekends, it must have been like a paid vacation for him.

Dad had hauled my motorcycle up with him in his work pickup when he first drug the trailer up there. For the first time, I got to ride my bike all over muddy logging roads and gravel pits. This was way different from being confined to a church field and riding around in circles. Up in the mountains, there was a near-infinite amount of roads that went through thick timber and freshly logged hillsides. Twice each day when Dad had to drive the roads to check the equipment, I would follow right behind him. I would even have Jen on the back unless we had to go up a steep hill. I had to go up those on my own because the bike just couldn't handle Jen's weight!

While back at camp, we would shoot guns at pop and beer cans just about every day. While Jen was just learning to shoot, I was trying to improve my shooting and actually try and hit what I was aiming for. It was slow going at first but with four-straight weekends of practice, things were looking up. Even if my bullet hit the ground just under the can, it would fall over. It wasn't until we went over and looked at it that it was discovered that I had missed. *That's okay,* I thought to myself. *Even Clint Eastwood misses once in a while.*

All good things have to come to an end, and a weekend of motorcycles and guns were no exception. Sundays were the days that everyone hated. We had to go home and go back to school, while leaving Dad up there for another week by himself. The weekends went by just too fast. Looking at the bright side, there was only a five day wait until we would go back up and do it again.

After a few weeks of this and while just having caught a glimpse at the light at the end of the tunnel, things went sour again. While backing the car out of the garage to take me to school, Mom accidentally ran right over the top of Muffin. I remember feeling the bump followed by an ear-splitting yelp, before everyone jumped out of the car and screamed. Mom didn't want to look under the car, so I had to. When I did, Muff looked right into my eyes. She was holding herself up with her front legs like she would normally do while she was sitting, only now her back legs weren't under her butt—they were off to the side of her in opposite directions.

We took her to the vet as quickly as possible. It was a short ride because the vet was right across the field from Evergreen. After dropping her off, Mom took me to school. Before she dropped me off, I asked her, just like any kid would do, if the dog was going to be okay. Mom said that she would be fine and not to worry about it while I was at school. That's like telling the sun not to shine. I worry about everything, especially when something is up in the air like that. To this day I am the same way, I just can't help it.

I was down all day during school but I would brighten up with optimism when I would think about Mom assuring me that Muff would be fine. I didn't tell anyone in school about it because it was none of their business to begin with but more importantly, I didn't want to talk about it. I'm not one to bother people with my problems, no matter what they are.

Mom picked me up from school at 3:30 as always. This time though, she had tears in her eyes. I knew the answer before I could even ask the question. Muff had such severe damage to her back that the only logical thing to do was euthanize her. That was tough to take. I had never experienced a death in the family before. Yeah, it was just a dog, but it was still a member of the family. The only other death in the family up until that point was Dad's Grandma Schenk's, who died when I was only a year or two old—much too young to understand death. I didn't even know that she existed until I was much older and had to research my family's history for a report.

It was a tearful and blurry car ride home. I wasn't sure if it was just a bad dream or not. When I closed my eyes and opened them again, I was unfortunately still in the car. If it had been a dream, I would have woken up in my dark bedroom. This kind of darkness was different. Now, the only sound while opening the garage door into the house was made by the squeaky hinges. There wasn't any cheerful yelps or puddles of pee on the ground. I walked into the living room and saw well-worn steak bones and squeaker toys with the squeakers removed strung out by the wood stove that she used to lay under to get warm. Now, there was no warmth. The house and the hearts of those who were in it were cold and empty. And Dad wasn't there to help us feel better—we wouldn't see him for several more days yet.

Mom did alright handling it on her own. It must have been tough on her with everyone getting double-bulldozed during that month. Looking back, I wish that she wouldn't have told me that Muff was going to be okay after we left her at the vet. Maybe I shouldn't have asked. After seeing her underneath the car, I should have known. Then again, I was only seven and hadn't yet been introduced to the reality of life on Earth. I knew that everything that was alive would die. I even saw people die in movies. (I used to think that when somebody died in a movie, that they were really dead. I figured that they must have a terminal disease or something to justify killing them off in the show.) This wasn't Hollywood, this was reality. It would be a long time before I attached myself to a dog again.

Dad continued to put in long hours of work during the summer of 1989. He was gone later at night and worked most Saturdays in those days, continuously striving to provide as much as possible for the family and the house. We got a new Chevrolet Blazer from a local dealership in town that was more than capable of pulling the camp trailer. It was red and had four wheel drive but most importantly, it gave the family a second vehicle. If necessary, Mom and Dad could have the family in two places at once. Jen was now into gymnastics and it would coincide with my soccer turnouts. The biggest thing was that nobody was left home without a vehicle.

Throughout the summer, construction workers came each day to build a detached shop at the back corner of the property where the woodpile used to be. Dad and Papa poured the cement for the foundation first, wisely cutting down on the labor costs. After the shop was framed and sided by the workers, Dad finished the the roof himself. He spent several hours hand-splitting cedar blocks into roof shakes. He would bundle up a load and hoist them from the ground to the roof using a rope. I would go up on the roof with him and try and help out by nailing shingles into place. Dad would lay six or seven before I could even drive my first nail, but I was trying at least. Most of the time I missed the nail and split the shake in half.

After several weeks, it was all done. The only thing that was left was painting the outside, which meant that the house was going to be redone also to match. Mom, I assume, chose a pearl color with a pink trim that was not only hard on the eyes, it was also embarrassing to reside in. Luckily we lived on a dead end road and the only people that saw it were the neighbors. Surely if we lived in a heavily populated area, the repulsive sight of our house would attract teenage kids and their sophomoric pranks.

Even with all of the home improvement over the summer, we still found time to do a little camping. Mom and Dad also introduced Jen and I to car racing. Skagit Speedway was about twenty minutes from our house in the small community of Alger. It was an oval dirt track that attracted winged sprint car driver from neighboring counties. Fans would come from as far south as Seattle and as far north as Vancouver, Canada on a weekly basis between April and September to take in the action. After a couple of trips, we too became regular attending fans.

Just about every Saturday, we would pack a bunch of sandwiches and pops and head out to watch the cars go around in circles until around ten at night. It was so dusty and dirty there that we drove the Oldsmobile each week so that Dad wouldn't have to get so much as a speck of dirt on the Blazer. It was so dusty that when we got home, we would all line up in the garage and take turns vacuuming off ourselves with the shop-vac before we were allowed to set foot in the house.

We didn't go to every race, but we certainly took in our fair share. During our second or third trip there, I looked over at Dad and asked, "Have you ever heard of a car flying over the top of the fence during a race?"

As God as my witness, he no sooner than opened his mouth to answer me when a car flipped about fifteen feet into the air and went right over the top of the flagger's stand. Luckily the flaggers escaped with one broken leg apiece and the driver had only minor injuries, but it did end the night prematurely. I walked out of the stands that night feeling guilty that I was the one that caused the whole thing. But if I truly was Nostradamus, I should have given my parents a set of numbers for them to by Lotto tickets at the 7-Eleven. This was just a freak but tragic coincidence. Thankfully, that was the worst crash that we would ever see in nearly a full decade of watching live racing.

As the eighties were coming to an end and with a new decade on the horizon, the entire Thramer Family was going through changes from the top to the bottom. Grandma T., the matriarch of the family, was getting into her late eighties. She had lived on her own since her husband had died in 1975 but with declining health, it made sense that she have a little help.

Her youngest daughter, Bonnie, whom Dad affectionately named Aunt B. after a character on the *Andy Griffith Show*, had just lost her husband. One weekend, Dad and I went down to Maple Valley, which is just north of Seattle, and helped move her stuff up to her new place in Burlington, not far from Grandma T.'s apartment. The two then moved in together, both filling a separate void for the other.

Papa had divorced Brenda a while back, but the troubles with the name "Brenda Thramer" were felt in our house also. The soon-to-be former Brenda Thramer had ran up a bunch of credit cards and the Brenda Thramer that was my mother was getting the blame. This actually went on for several years before it became somewhat funny.

Papa got remarried once again, this time to a lady named Gladys Adams. In an odd twist of fate, the two shared the same birthday. After they were married, they continued living in the same log house.

Papa's marriage to Gladys was a packaged deal in the sense that she came with a young daughter named Carissa that was younger than I was. Gladys also had an adopted daughter named Renee who was about twenty years older, but she was already married and living with her husband, Larry. With Carissa technically my aunt, I told the other kids at school that I was older than one of my aunts. Nobody could ever figure it out, no matter how hard they tried.

We had a new addition to our house as well—a new dog. Bitsy was a black and tan dachshund, just like the one that we had to have put down a few months earlier. Her name came from her extremely small stature. It wasn't long until she was anything but small. It also wasn't very long until we had to have her put to sleep too.

She had been mildly aggressive for a while and one evening she bit Dad in the face while they were wrestling. A few weeks later, she bit one of his nostrils clean off his nose. He had to drive to the emergency room with it in his hand so the doctor could sew it back on his face. The doctor did a pretty lousy job on it, not lining it up correctly at all. (Dad says it feels like he always has a giant booger up there.)

The next day, Dad took her to the vet to have her euthanized. Before they could though, they had to first test her for rabies and give her an X-ray. The rabies test was negative, but the X-rays showed that she had bone spurs growing from her spine and jabbing into her nerves, causing excruciating pain. The vet said that this was a common result of people running puppy mills that had their animals interbreed and reproduce at unhealthy rates. After the tests, Dad went through with the euthanization. He would later admit that he would rather have taken her out back and shot her instead.

CHAPTER 9

Big Penises and F-Words

I N SEPTEMBER OF 1989, I started the second grade, about a week or so before my eighth birthday. Although I know it wasn't even close to being their idea, Grandpa and Grandma bought me an annual subscription to WWF Magazine for a birthday present, beginning a collection that I would build upon for the next twenty years. Now I could not only watch wrestling (when I wasn't in trouble), but I could read about it too! I got it sent right to my door at the beginning of each month, instead of otherwise only getting to look at them at the store while Mom shopped for groceries. Even after I started getting it at home, I would still look at the other wrestling magazines that they had at the store so I could stay up on the other wrestlers that performed in other promotions across the country. Only the WWF was shown in our market, so this was the only way to keep up with the business. Remember, there was no internet in those days.

My birthday was always the first in the class. Mom would send in cupcakes for the kids, which was a great way to get over with them right from the start. As years went on, it became less and less cool to have your parents do anything like that. If you kept doing things like that, people would start calling you a "mama's boy."

Kids, especially the boys, had to have a superior and chauvinistic attitude to even stand a chance with their peers. If you did something stupid and got yourself laughed at and made fun of, fine—just be sure that you find the weaknesses in others and the mistakes that other people make quickly, so you can put the heat onto them. Everyone only remembered the most recent event, everything else was buried in a hall of shame that only the victim had to deal with.

The most important thing for boys to have was a big penis—that's just the way it was. You always had to insinuate that yours was much bigger than anyone else had. If you got hit down there with a ball or something during recess, you had to be sure to sell your pain for a long time. The reason was because you had more mass down there, thus making it more pain per square inch. Some of the boys would flip out when they hit their thigh on the end of a table. Why? Because their dick was so long that they had to stuff it down their pant leg and have it resting on their kneecap. It wasn't a leg bruise that they had, it was a dick bruise. In all likelihood, everyone had a typical eight year old penis that was completely hairless. The only time that it had actual girth to it was when it would get hard, which nobody knew why that was. All we knew was that it was uncomfortable and it was free to go back to normal as soon as possible. Everyone was under the impression that an extra limp wiener was far better than a stiff one.

With a big pecker hanging down between a boys legs, the only other cool thing to do was to talk cool—as in, saying bad words. Kids were very smart when it came to swearing, only talking like that on the playground and never in front of an adult or teacher. Nobody wanted to get into trouble either, that was just as uncool.

I didn't say a lot of bad words at school. I said "hell," "ass," and "damn" mostly and only on occasion would I say "shit" just because I thought it sounded funny. (I still do, by the way.) These were all words that I heard at home. Mom and Dad would periodically say them, but not all the time. Papa said the most bad words, using the same ones that my parents did, only more frequently. I think that "son of a bitch" was his favorite with "bullshit" being a close second.

Up until I was eight, I had never even heard the F-word used. In fact, I thought that it was a brand new swear word the first time that I did hear it. I knew that it was bad because of how it was used. When I was at George Brookings' house, his step-dad called him a "fucking little asshole" because George had just called his mom a bitch. Aside from school, I didn't hear it out of Dad or even Papa's mouth until I was ten or twelve. I never used the word in elementary school at all. Even today I rarely use it unless I am really, really pissed off. I may also use it to jokingly say "fuck you!" to another guy at work. But other than that (and for an occasional climax aid in the bedroom), I don't say it.

Although swearing and penis size was generally the first order of business for the boys in the class, the next was competing to see who was the smartest and who got the best grades. All of the boys participated in it because it was a big deal to stand on top of the mountain and be able to look down at the mentally inferior. This, coupled with my own personal goal to make my parents proud of my academic accomplishments, was the beginning of my quest for perfection in school.

I wouldn't win the contest all of the time, sometimes I would totally bomb an assignment. If it was too bad, I would throw the paper in the garbage after it was graded so I wouldn't have to take it home and show my parents. I figured that they would be ashamed of me because after all, I was ashamed of myself. I wouldn't throw them away in my classroom because I thought that there might be a chance that teachers scour through the garbage cans at night. Instead I would take them down to the cafeteria, because nobody in their right mind would search through that shit. I even disposed of them nonchalantly, like I was Clint Eastwood dropping pieces of his cell wall out of his pants and onto the prison courtyard ground in *Escape From Alcatraz*.

The most hotly contested assignment was the daily multiplication tables that had a time limit in which to be completed. Each kid would have one minute to do thirty problems completely and correctly. There weren't too many better feelings than setting back and watching other kids try to beat the clock after I had already finished.

Sometimes it would be a one-on-one contest with flashcards instead. One kid would start and stand behind his or her opponent, the teacher would flash a problem, and the first to answer it correctly would advance on to the next kid. If the kid in the chair defeated the kid that was standing up, he would stand up and move on while the loser took his chair. I wasn't the only one to ever do it, but being able to march around and beat every single kid in the class one-on-one was just awesome. It truly set you apart from the others.

Not every subject was a competition. The final grades always were, but the gloves would come down when everyone was learning something completely new. Then nobody had a leg up on anyone. The planets of the solar system and the star constellations might as well have been written in Greek to all of us. With the exception or Uranus, which always got a chuckle from the kids who knew a thing or two about the human body, understanding different planets and temperatures took concentration and effort to understand.

On the playground, it was football as always. I had gotten a youth-sized football for a present one year and I brought it to school everyday. We would pick teams and play tackle football, even though it was against the rules. Naturally we only played that way when the teachers weren't looking but if they were, it was two-hand-touch. More often then not though, they were preoccupied with something else and we were able to get a few good licks in on one another. The same group of kids played together every day. Still, some of us had our quarrels that would generally be brought on by disputing whether or not somebody had been tagged down. Fists weren't ever thrown, but there were a few good, stiff shoves being tossed around.

Fighting on the playground was always an added attraction. Once one would start, it was like moths being attracted to a flame. Kids would catch a glimpse of it out of the corner of there eye, drop whatever they were doing, and rush over to get a front row seat. It wasn't very long until the playground attendants figured out what was going on and began shuffling their chubby asses over to break it up. If you got into trouble on the playground, you stood on the "Wall of Shame" for everyone to see while everyone else spent their time heckling you for getting caught. If it was real bad, it was off to the office for a visit with the principal. I limited my office visits to about one or two a year throughout my school years. Bringing home discipline notices were much different than coming home with the news of getting my name on the board. This meant big time punishments—no wrestling (as usual) and no Nintendo.

The Nintendo Entertainment System was the most popular thing out there in the late-80's. Originally designed by Masayuki Uemura and released in Japan in 1983 before finally coming to North America in 1985, the Nintendo was far superior in graphics and games than the Atari, which was the mainstay at the time. We got ours around the first part of 1990, complete with the original *Super Mario Brothers*.

We only had five or six games, but *Double Dragon II* was the best. Dad and I would play that together all the time, taking our guys from city to city to fight thugs and brawlers using knives, dynamite, chains, and our martial arts skills. There was even a mode where we could beat the hell out of each other if we wanted to. We would spend hours on rainy days and on weeknights playing, stopping only to go the bathroom.

Once the weather got better, I began turning out for technically my first year of baseball. This time there wasn't a tee or anything to fall back on. Players had to stand in there and take five pitches from their coach. If you got a hit, great—but if you came up empty after five swings, then you were out.

Just my luck, I had a girl coach who could only throw underhand rainbows that would always foul off the back side of your bat. Her son, Bjorn, who was on the team also, was the only kid in school who had gray hair. It was gray because it was full of dandruff and clearly he never washed it because it looked like a wire brush. He probably never even showered for that matter because he was always picking his butt or scratching his balls.

We lost just about every game. The team was so over-matched and under-coached, it was ridiculous. We had bright orange jerseys and hats that made us look like traffic cones that had been strung out in the field and to top it all off, our best hitter only had two fingers on his right hand. We were doomed from the start.

CHAPTER 10

The Instigator

EVERY COUPLE OF weeks throughout the year, we would go over to Aunt B.'s house and Mom and Dad would play pinochle with her and Grandma T. Jen and I would usually sit in the other room and watch movies while they played but after a while, they took the time to teach us to play as well. After Jen and I tired out in the later evening, they would keep right on playing until nearly dawn.

We still did our share of camping, although by this time we no longer went to Baker Lake because it was becoming more of a party hangout rather than a family relaxation environment. For an alternative, we spent time at a private campground alongside Grandy Creek, not twenty minutes from our house, that Papa and Gladys had recently bought a membership for. At the time, it was part of a campground chain called Leisure Time Resorts that were spread out all over the country. Using their pass, we could go up and camp or swim anytime we wanted, which was at least once a week in the summer months.

One weekend while we were there, they had a pie eating contest where you could win a T-shirt or a hat or something. There were three different races—one was for kids under thirteen, then it was fourteen through eighteen, and finally it was adults only. That meant that me and Jen were the first group to compete. There was probably a sixty second time limit, though I'm not completely sure. Regardless, I was victorious after downing two full pieces of peach pie.

With a heart full of pride and a stomach full of sugar, I stood behind Dad as he prepared to take on a table full of hungry men. I had seen Dad put down a whole chicken at buffet restaurants along with salads and desserts, so I knew that he could put away the groceries. (Not bad for a guy who weighs 150 pounds soaking wet.) He barely got one piece of pie down during his contest because he started laughing at one of his opponents. The guy that was in front of him stuffed one whole piece into his mouth and chewed it only twice before swallowing it practically whole. At the end of the time, he had put away ten pieces in a hilarious act of gluttony. I think that he won a bottle of antacids instead of a T-shirt.

From time to time in the summer we would also go up to Bellingham for a day of swimming on Lake Whatcom. At the north end of the lake was a nice beach, a long dock that surrounded a shallow play area, and another dock out in the deeper water that had two diving boards on it. One was a basic one meter springboard, while the other was every bit of fifteen feet off the water. The whole area has since been closed to the public but at the time, it was a happening place.

I had known how to swim for a few years by then but had never used a diving board before. I could dive from the edge of a pool easy enough, but this was different. It took a few tries to get the hang of taking that hard step that led into the spring jump. After a couple times of double-bouncing myself and jarring my entire body, I got the hang of it and figured that I was ready for the high-dive.

Following a few basic straight jumps and a daring head-first plunge, I decided to get a little more creative and try doing a front flip. I had never attempted a flip of any kind before and really had no idea how to do one correctly. It didn't take but one time for me to learn how to do one incorrectly.

I climbed up the ladder and walked along to the end, took a deep breath, and closed my eyes. I didn't tell Dad what I had planned to do, so I'm sure that he might have been just a little shocked at what he was about to see. While standing straight up, I just tucked my head and fell forward, landing on the water with the flat of my back. It hurt so bad that I didn't want to come out of the water right away because I had to have something touching my back to cool the burning feeling. I just wiggled around underneath the water like a fish for five or ten seconds with hopes that the pain would quickly ease—plus I was trying to fight off tears. When I did surface, everyone on the dock was waiting to see if I was okay. I just nodded my head, still trying to swallow the lump that was in my throat.

We swam back to shore to have lunch on the beach with Mom and Jen. Mom never would get into the water, so she always stayed behind. Jen wasn't yet big enough to make it out to the diving dock, so she played in the shallow end with anybody who would join in. During lunch, a pasty-white guy with light blue shorts laid his towel down ten or twelve feet behind us, next to a trio of blondes in bikinis. After laying in the sun for ten minutes (it would have taken ten hours to tan his skin), He got up and decided that he was going to show off for the girls by doing pushups. He did about ten of the sloppiest pushups in history before he got real gutsy and tried to do them with one hand. He didn't even finish the first one before he fell flat on his face. The funniest part was, the girls weren't even paying attention to this guy.

With us and just about everyone else on the beach eating lunch, the seagulls were out pretty thick trying to get a handout. People would throw bits of food at them and they would just about come up to your towel to eat it. "Blue Shorts," as we began calling him, went back to lying in the sun after his exhausting workout. A seagull then walked right over to his face and squawked, scaring the shit out of him. Ever the tough guy, Blue Shorts fired one of his sneakers at the bird and flipped it off before he went back to work on his tan.

After lunch, the three of us played around in the shallow end. Jen practiced jumping off the dock while I worked on my dives. (I wasn't about to try another flip that day.) While sitting on the dock and getting ready to call it a day, we were caught off guard when someone behind us let out a loud fart that excessively flapped his wet butt cheeks. As if we didn't already know who it was, we turned around to find a smiling Blue Shorts as the culprit.

On August 2, 1990, Saddam Hussein and Iraqi troops invaded their neighboring country of Kuwait, after accusing them of stealing their oil through slant drilling, with the intent of taking over the entire country. The United States, along with thirty-three other nations, began Operation Desert Shield as means of stabilizing the Middle East and with hopes that Iraq would withdraw without military force. For the next several months, the entire focus of the world was on the conflict in the Middle East. Every newspaper, every newscast, and everybody on the streets would talk about it on a daily basis.

In September, I began the third grade and was in Mrs. Brooks' class. During the year, we learned how to write in cursive, how to write short stories, and how to do reports. Whether it had to do with the Middle East conflicts or not I don't remember, but we all had to do a report on a foreign country. I chose Saudi Arabia as my country because they were in the news constantly and were one of our allies. I remember that George Brookings chose Niger just because he thought that it was pronounced "nigger." I also remember that nobody wanted to have anything to do with Iraq. It's funny how even at that age, kids understood what true evil was.

The kid that got stuck with Iraq, because he wasn't at school the day that we all picked our countries, was a somewhat handicapped boy named Josef. Born with autism, Josef got stuck with the evil country. Because he got stuck with Iraq, I started calling him "Josef Hussein," which damn near got me expelled. He was actually intelligent, but would purposely draw attention to himself by acting like a dumb ass.

Josef's main way of getting attention was by sneezing. Instead of doing two or three consecutive sneezes like normal people, we would do twenty or thirty. The first couple were legit but after kids noticed and started laughing, he would roll through a couple dozen just for show. It got to the point where Mrs. Brooks caught on to his game and started writing his name on the board for disrupting the class.

The other way for him to get attention was unfortunately at a girl's expense. Throughout the years that he was in school, he always selected one girl each year that was the love of his life and that he was going to marry when he got older. The girls were so embarrassed and were uncomfortable just being around him. The girl that year, Jennifer, eventually had to transfer to another class because he wouldn't leave her alone.

Josef had a few more "unique" traits, like the way that he held his pencil. He would lay it across all four of his fingers with the eraser underneath his thumb and the lead just resting against his pinky. To say that his writing was illegible would be the world's biggest understatement. He also had a cold lunch everyday that he would only eat two or three bites of. The rest he would put back in his lunch pale and bring it back the following day. It may not sound too bad until you factor in that it was a cheese sandwich and he had no way of keeping it cool—that rotten shit stunk up the entire class.

The other kid that I met for the first time was Joey Moore. To this day, Joey is the only person that I went to school with that I see on a regular basis, and not just because we work together. Before we even started working together, we would talk on a regular basis—probably because we shared the same passion for professional wrestling. If there is anyone out there who rivals my knowledge of wrestling, it is definitely Joey. He is without a doubt my closest friend but why he liked me in those days, I'll never know.

At the time, Joey was a white version of Steve Urkel, a nerdy kid from *Family Matters* which aired in the 90's. Both Joey and Urkel were tall and skinny with short hair and a pair of glasses with abnormally large lenses. Joey was, and still is, the easiest person to piss off—and I was the master at setting him off.

Mrs. Brooks had this discipline system in class that was color coded. Each kid started out with a green tag at the beginning of each day. If you had to pull the green card, you now had a yellow warning card in its place. Behind that was a red card that meant no recess. After that was a brown card which meant that you had to go to Principal Brown's office. My personal goal was to get Joey to his brown card as often as I could by being a devious little prick. I would put his pencil on another kids' desk, knowing that he would yell at them and accuse them of stealing his stuff. I would hide his lunch pale and blame it on someone else just to watch him try to get even by throwing their stuff in the garbage can. I would slyly point it out to Mrs. Brooks as he was dropping somebodies stuff into the trash. She would have him pull a card and he would start screaming and swearing that he didn't start it, which got him into even more trouble.

As if that wasn't bad enough, there were times that I would cheap shot him also. There was a wooden bridge on the playground that had wooden planks for a floor and was really unstable. If you timed it just right, you could catapult someone off of the bridge and onto the gravel. One day as Joey was running across the bridge, I jumped down just right and launched him right into the rocks, cutting him up pretty bad.

The worst thing I ever did to him (in third grade anyway) happened right inside the classroom. He was sitting across from me while we were in the middle of doing a group project and he leaned back in his chair and yawned. Normally I would just lift up the leg of his chair while he was tipping back in it so he would fall over, but this time I decided to take advantage of his yawning. While his mouth was open, I spit a huge snot ball right into his mouth. Yeah it's hard to believe, but all you need to do is ask him—he'll tell you that it's the truth.

Each week, one student was the V.I.P. of the entire class for the full five days. The V.I.P. was usually determined by who had a birthday around that particular week. They would get to bring in some of their favorite things to display for the week and on Friday's, they would stand in front of the class and explain those things were important to them. If you wanted, you could even have a parent come in.

With my birthday being in September, I was the first one out of the gate. I brought in a lot of my wrestling stuff that only Joey thought was cool. Kristen did too, but I know that the only reason was because it belonged to me. When Josef's turn came around, he brought in his father, Larry, who gave some presentation about trains and maps. While he was talking, I was up to no good and starting shit with somebody.

"Son, you know what you are?" he asked after walking up to me when he was finished talking.

"No," I said smiling. "What am I?"

"You are an instigator."

"What's an instigator?" I asked.

"Look it up in the dictionary," he said as he turned around and walked away.

I didn't even know how to spell it, so I didn't bother looking it up right away. When I finally took the time to sit down and sound it out, I grabbed my Webster's Dictionary and read the definition. Not only did it fit me to a T, but I also found a picture of myself next to it.

Boys think that farts are just about the funniest things on Earth. Girls will never admit to them, but they, as well as every other air breathing mammal, do it. (I just did it myself as wrote this sentence.) Fart, let drive, cut loose, rip one, cut the cheese—however you want to put it, it was the highlight of the day whenever someone did it. Everyone would then burst out laughing, no matter what was going on in class.

Following lunch recess, Mrs. Brooks read to us as a class out of a chapter book. During one of her reading sessions in which all of us were circled up on the floor around her chair, a girl named Sarah let one fly. It was her own fault that it was so loud because her knees were tucked up under her chin, causing it to echo off the floor. Her face instantly turned a dark shade of crimson as she bowed her head in shame. Everyone else started laughing and pulled their shirts up over their nose like it was a gas mask, which was the cool way of separating your nose from the bad smell.

Prior to that year, I had never seen anyone do that before. People would always pinch their nostrils with their fingers or cup their entire hand over their nose. While I'm sure it had been done long before I started burying my face in my shirt, I was the first to do it in the class—starting a trend that never died. Anytime someone smelled anything that resembled a fart, everyone would let out a groan and lift up their shirts. Sometimes nothing ever happened and you could just lift your shirt up and everyone would go into the same routine. Without really even smelling anything, they would groan like they were smelling a week old diaper.

After Sarah's fart and after everyone put on their makeshift masks, Mrs.Brooks, who had clearly had enough of this behavior by that time, tried to show us how dumb we looked by lifting her scarf over her nose.

"What does this do?" she asked. "Do you kids know how stupid this looks?"

We didn't care how stupid it looked, it was even funnier now that our teacher did it. She did it to try and get us to stop, but it just didn't work. Every fart was still met with immediate laughter.

To this day, every guy that I know, regardless of their age, will laugh anytime the sound of passing gas is heard. I think, however, that it is just as funny to fart without it making a sound. Of course it has to really stink to make it worth the effort. The real humor starts when the supplier vacates the area immediately after doing the damage, leaving those left in the crowd to point their fingers at each other in denial. That never gets old either.

At home, Mom wouldn't allow us to even say the word "fart" until we were at least ten. For some reason she treated it like a swear word, which meant that saying it would land a bar of soap in your mouth. After a while, she even began punishing me for farting. It wasn't a capitol crime so I didn't lose wrestling or anything, but she did charge me a dime every time that I did it out loud and laughed about it. I think that her idea was to get me to stop thinking it was so damn funny, but obviously that didn't work. Even though I was lighter in the pockets, I still did it. Once she figured out that it was a losing battle, she gave up. Oh yeah, by the way, she's one of those girls who claims to have never done it, but I'm here to tell you that just ain't true!

CHAPTER 11
The Home of the Brave

O N JANUARY 16, 1991, Congress narrowly passed the authorization for President George H.W. Bush to begin using military force to get the Iraqi soldiers out of Kuwait, which became known as Operation Desert Storm. With the war taking place overseas, nearly everyone in the country flew the American Flag in front of their house and tied yellow ribbons to their mailboxes in support of the fighting men and women. Regardless of whether people agreed with the Persian Gulf War or not, everyone showed their support for those who were in combat.

Although the war was tens of thousands of miles away, the United States was under heightened security everywhere, especially at major sporting events. Basketball and hockey were going on but both seasons were in their infancy. Football, on the other hand, was building towards Super Bowl XXV and fans' interest was at its peak for the year. The major difference between the three sports was that football was played outdoors with larger audiences, creating a golden opportunity for enemy forces to strike.

A week prior to Super Bowl XXV, the 49ers hosted the New York Giants at Candlestick Park in the NFC Championship on January 20. The 49ers had been victorious in the previous two Super Bowls, bringing their Super Bowl record to 4-0. Only the Pittsburgh Steelers (Dad's favorite team) had as good of a record in the big game as they had. The 49ers were favored to beat the Giants and advance to and win their third straight Super Bowl, which had never been done before. The victory would then hand them their fifth Vince Lombardi Trophy in as many tries, also a record.

The game was a defensive battle from start to finish. In the fourth quarter with San Francisco leading 13-9, Joe Montana dropped back to pass to try and put a dagger in New York's heart. Leonard Marshall, the defensive end for the Giants, came from seemingly out of nowhere and blindsided Montana with one of the most vicious tackles that I have ever seen. Although it was a totally legal hit, it was the end of the game for Montana. It would also keep him on the sidelines for the entire season the following year, theoretically ending the 49ers reign of supremacy. The Giants won 15-13.

One week late on January 27, Super Bowl XXV went down in Tampa, Florida. With the war less than two weeks old, both fans in attendance and watching at home weren't ruling out the possibility of an attack on American soil. I'm not condoning evil by any means, but there wasn't a better time to attack us with the entire country and most of the world watching. Thankfully, it never happened.

Before the game started, the country came together as one with THE most incredible music performance that I have ever seen in my life. Whitney Houston, at the height of her popularity, walked to the center of the field and delivered "The Star Spangled Banner" to a tearful United States audience. The tears that were shed that day were not those of sadness and sorrow, but rather of pride and honor. If you ever get the chance to watch it in its entirety, I assure you that you will cry the same tears all over again. That's the thing about music—if it sounds good, you'll here it, but if its real, you'll feel it. It's not my line, it's written on the sleeve of every Kid Rock album, but it's the truth.

The game itself was played between the Giants and the Buffalo Bills. Ironically in addition to both being from New York, both teams colors were red, white, and blue. Unlike most Super Bowls up to that point, it was evenly matched and came down to the last second. The Giants won 20-19, the narrowest margin in Super Bowl history. The Bills meanwhile, began a run of four straight Super Bowl appearances. While they may have went 0-4, the feat has yet to be matched.

Much like we did for *Monday Night Football*, Dad and I put some cash down on the game. This wasn't for just a quarter though, it was for big money—two dollars. This was our second year of betting on the Super Bowl. The year earlier, I had picked the 49ers and walked away with a crisp dollar bill. We decided that it should go up a dollar each year to keep it interesting. When I lost, I had to pay him in nickels and pennies because I had no paper bills.

We still bet on the Super Bowl today, with the bet still increasing each year by a dollar. The stakes are a little higher as the dollar amount now coincides with the number of the game itself. Dad accuses me of raising the stakes when it was my turn to pick the game, which just happened to be a mismatch. (He might be right.) I pick on the even numbers and Dad picks on the odd numbers. I have to be smart with my picks and choose with my head and not my heart or else I could go a few years without winning.

The war ended on about a month later on February 28. Although major fighting ended that day, problems still exist in Iraq as I write this. There was a second Gulf War in 2003 that lasted for over seven years—even though Saddam Hussein was captured and executed a few years into it. But at the time, things were getting back to normal in the country. As the troops came home, a satisfied country collectively took down their flags and yellow ribbons.

The war affected just about everything and, although not too many people know or even care, pro wrestling was one of them. On March 24, WrestleMania VII was to take place at the Los Angeles Memorial Coliseum in front of over 100,000 fans. The event was moved to the nearby L.A. Sports Arena due to, among other things, a threat made to one of its performers.

Robert Remus played a character by the name of Sgt. Slaughter. In the early 80's, he was so popular that he had a G.I. Joe doll replicated after him, and he even provided his voice for the same character on the G.I. Joe animated cartoon show. But now, Slaughter played the role of an Iraqi sympathizer. He would walk out to the ring with an Iraqi flag and wearing a pair of boots that he claimed were given to him by Saddam Hussein. This was done simply to get the audience to hate him and, in turn, getting them to cheer for the person wrestling him. With some people still in the dark about wrestling's legitimacy, they took Remus' character that he was portraying seriously. He had to have security stand guard at his home at all times for a three to four month period. His entire family, children included, had even received death threats.

With the event being held at an outdoor venue, promoters couldn't take the chance on something tragic happening at an entertainment show that was going to be seen all over the world. Thus, it was decided that it must be held indoors with a thorough security check given to all spectators. After Slaughter lost the main event match, he quickly changed his character back to and American soldier to get the heat off himself and his family.

Just before Easter came, it was time for yet another new dog to be welcomed into the family. Obviously black and tan dachshunds were not going to work, so Mom and Dad tried something different. This time they brought home a Pomeranian puppy named Shiloh. She was a purebred, unlike our previous dogs, so they paid a pretty penny for her.

She was a good dog. She was good in the car, behaved when we left her at home, and I don't think that she ever went to the bathroom in the house. Her only fault was her barking. Anytime there was even the slightest noise made, she would start in. She barked at everybody that walked by, drove by, and at the birds that flew by. She even barked when the phone rang. It drove Mom and Dad over the bank, but they stuck it out in hopes that it was just a phase.

Dad's mom came up from her new home in Las Vegas for Easter weekend. She didn't stay with us, or even come to our house for that matter. Instead she stayed with her sister, Hazel, who lived in Deming, just a few minutes east of Bellingham. We went up there for Easter dinner along with Uncle Robbie and his crew.

After dinner while playing with Jake, Jen, and Tristan in the living room, I started to feel a little sick. It wasn't a throw up kind of sick, but rather just a lethargic feeling. I got real warm all of a sudden, but yet felt like I was in a refrigerator. I still managed to go through the family picture routine and that, but I got even worse as we started for home. Thinking it was something that I ate, I just sat back and waited for that urge to puke it up. It never came. What showed up instead was a case of the chicken pox. I started breaking out in red sores that popped up like a pimple on prom night all over my body—and I do mean ALL OVER. And talk about itch! I thought bug bites were bad, but at least they were centralized to one spot. These showed no mercy.

With chicken pox being so highly contagious, I had to stay home from school for a few days. I hated doing that—I would much rather go to school sick so I didn't have to make up the work later. Plus I didn't want to miss out on anything cool. I didn't have a choice with this.

Mom went to the school and picked up my work and I sat on the top of my new bunk bed and did every bit of it in one day. I then got to watch rented wrestling tapes for the rest of the week, which certainly wasn't a bad thing. When it was all said and done, the chicken pox didn't leave a single scar. Mom had to put calamine lotion on them to ease the itching, so it wasn't done with just my will power. Within a few days, Jen came down with them too and Mom had to start the process all over again.

When I returned to school, our next assignment was writing a short story. The two best stories would earn the kids that wrote them a trip to Skagit Valley College for a young author's class. I didn't necessarily start writing with the intention on winning, but I did want to write a good story. With me being so into sports, it was an easy decision to write about something along those lines.

I chose to write about Super Bowl XXV that had taken place just a few months earlier. As a twist, I didn't write about what happened in the game that people saw on TV—that was already in the newspapers. Instead I wrote it as if it was from the perspective of Bill Parcells, the coach of the Giants. He was the main character and the story revolved around him coaching his team to victory over the Bills. Keep in mind I was only in third grade, so it's not like it was destined to be a New York Times Bestseller. It did, however, earn me a spot on the trip. Although I didn't really want to go, I was certainly proud that my story was good enough to be in the top two of the whole class.

Right around the time for the field trip, baseball season began. This time we actually learned something because we didn't have Janis Joplin for a coach. The cool thing was that every boy that was in Mrs. Brooks' class who played was on a different team. It was probably only four or five kids, but bragging rights were on the line nonetheless. With that kind of competition for about eight weeks, it was like the World Series was being contested each day.

I didn't contribute much to the team, considering that it was technically my first year with actual instruction from a knowledgeable coach. I was average at best when it came to hitting and defensively, I played third base and outfield. We won a few and lost a few, but had fun all season. In class, it was all evened up and nobodies team had anymore wins then the other guy's. It was a good thing too, because having an ultimate victor would feed a guy's ego all the way up to the next season.

School let out for the summer in June and with me being just a few months away from my tenth birthday, Dad felt that it was time that I start taking over some of the chores. During the summer was when we replenished our firewood supply for the upcoming winter. Dad would haul some home in his work pickup, split the pieces that were to big to fit in the stove, and leave it all in a pile in the yard for me to put away during the next day. It would take me a while because I wasn't quite strong enough to pack a full wheelbarrow load to the woodshed, making me have to make double or even triple the trips that an adult would make. He would bring home two to three loads a week until the shed, which ran the full width of the shop, was completely full. With me being the one who was doing the stacking, I thought that it would never get full.

When I wasn't stacking wood, I was doing my other new job—mowing the lawn. I actually got paid to do that, to the tune of a five dollar bill. That was pretty good money for a nine year old and with a lawn that needed mowed twice a week. Raking in about forty bucks a month, I soon had enough to open my own savings account at the bank in town. Since that time, that particular bank has gone through countless employees and about four different name changes, but I still have that same account that I opened that summer.

As far as I'm concerned, I earned every dollar that I made mowing our lawn. It was pretty good sized and I had to do it all with a push mower. It wasn't self-propelled, so the only way to get it to go was the gas in the tank and me doing the pushing. The reason that I had to mow it so often was because Dad fertilized and watered it all the time and if I let it go a day or two too long, it would be a real bitch to do.

Another thing that made mowing difficult at times were my allergies. For as long as I can remember, I have been allergic to grass and weed pollen. It generally starts around March and stays with me until it dries out a bit in July. Sneezing, itching, watery eyes, scratchy throat—you name it and I get it, sometimes so bad that my eyes swell shut and I lose my voice. At night while I'm sleeping, my eyes will ooze so that when I go to open them in the morning, I can't because they are literally glued shut. I then have to take my fingers and rub all of that shit off in order to open them which, in turn, causes them to get inflamed all over again.

There isn't a medicine out there that will stop it either. Some will ease it up a little, but most don't do anything. I've tried A.R.M., Seldane, Dimetapp, Allegra, and Claratin over the years, none of which works. The best thing that I can do when things get really bad is just go inside for a little while and get out of the air. After about an hour it will ease up and I can go back outside, but it won't be long before I'm right back in again and praying for the rain to come to settle that nasty junk.

I also got another lawn mowing job that summer, but for an entirely different reason. Aunt B. could no longer mow her own lawn because the last time that she had done it, she didn't let go of the starter rope when it retracted and it subsequently jerked her to the ground. Additionally, Grandma T. needed more attentive care by this time and a couple hours of leaving her unsupervised wasn't an option. The good part about her mower was that it was self-propelled, but the bad part was that it only paid two dollars. That was actually Dad's idea based on the costs of the continuous medical bills. I didn't complain about it, but I didn't like it either.

Aunt B. became a full-time caretaker in hurry after Grandma T. took a turn for the worse in the latter part of June. We just so happened to be over there visiting in the kitchen one day, while Grandma T. was sleeping in the recliner in the next room. While everyone was talking, we all heard a loud thud.

"What the hell was that?" Dad asked while looking around the table.

"That's Grandma!" Aunt B. yelled as she hurdled over the table as if she was Carl Lewis. Everyone dashed into the living room to find her laying on the floor ten feet away from her chair. She was okay, but unable to get herself up. Now Grandma T. was a big lady, and it took Dad, Aunt B., and myself to lift her up off the floor. Within a couple of minutes she was fine, but very sore. Everyone just chalked it up to sleepwalking, but it proved to be just the beginning of a rough couple of months.

Over the week of the Fourth of July, we packed up the camp trailer and took off on our first big trip in three years. Mom and Dad had put all of their extra money into the shop and the Blazer, so there just wasn't enough to go on one for the few years prior. This time around, we were going to check out a part of this great country that only Mom had been to before—Yellowstone, our nation's first national park.

We left after Dad got off from work on a Friday afternoon and drove to the other side of the state around Spokane before we stopped for the night. Rather than near a lake or creek like we were used to, our first campground was a rest area off of Interstate 90. After crawling into bed to go to sleep, we all collectively found out that the person who was in charge of packing the pillows had not held up there end of the deal. For the next week-and-a-half, we were subject to waking up with stiff necks after resting our heads on coats during the night. That was just a little bump in the road, but it wouldn't be the last.

A couple of days later while driving across Montana, one of the tires on the camp trailer disintegrated as we rolled down the highway. It wasn't really a big deal because we had a spare in the storage compartment, but it just seems like our trips always have to have some sort of malfunction go on during them. It really can all be traced back to this trip. No matter what we did to prevent them, something was just bound to happen. At least at this time, the minor little hiccups were comical and made for a few laughs throughout the trip.

To pass the time on the road, we started a little contest between all four of us and even Shiloh. When we passed a sign with one of our first or middle names on it, that person got a point and whoever had the most points at the end was the winner. The contest wasn't even close. Shiloh destroyed us all because every town that we came to had a Shiloh Inn, giving her an insurmountable lead from the onset.

Throughout the entire trip, temperatures were pushing a hundred degrees just about everyday. While at one stop in Jackson, Wyoming, Dad wanted to take a picture of me and Jen as we sat on a statue of a buffalo. I practically trampled Jen on my quest to be the first one to mount up. I straddled that thing without even thinking about how hot it was and after crisping my hot dog, I decided that we should just stand by it instead.

After a couple of days of travel, we finally made it to one of the entrances to Yellowstone. We spent the next two or three days seeing all of the hot springs, geysers, and wildlife that attracts people from across the world. I had seen deer and elk before, but never had I seen a buffalo. They were everywhere, and they could care less about all of the people around them.

Upon entering the park, everyone was given warnings about not approaching wildlife, but not many people took heed. People would foolishly walk up to them as if they were trained dogs in order to get a picture. While I haven't seen anything happen, I'm positive that something has over the years. We weren't as stupid as most people and the closest we got to one was about twenty or thirty feet away from it as it was sprawled out up against the Roosevelt Lodge.

After a few days, we left the park and headed towards home. The last stop was at the laser lights show at the Grand Coulee Dam. After spending the night in a post office parking lot in Electric City, we made our way down to the base of the dam where we would watch the laser show and the fireworks display at the end. Forgetting about the lasers, the sight of the dam itself was amazing. It is just a few feet shy of one mile long and it is twice as tall as Niagara Falls. It is the largest concrete structure and the largest electric power producing facility in the country and fifth largest in the world. The dam is also built with enough cement to build a four foot wide and four inch deep sidewalk that would wrap around the equator twice.

The next morning we headed for home following over a week on the road. This time we made it home in one piece, next time we wouldn't be as lucky.

CHAPTER 12
The Cost of Living is Dying

FOLLOWING THREE UNSUCCESSFUL and uneventful years of playing soccer, I had no desire to sign up for another season. I never even scored a single point and wasn't even a factor in the outcome of the games, so it was time for a change. It was time for me to do something that I had a passion for, something physical—it was time for me to play football. It wasn't going to be no chicken shit flag football either. It was going to be real, tackle football—just like I watched on TV.

In 1991, it cost fifty dollars to sign up and play and all of the gear, minus the nut cup, was provided. Turnouts were every night at the carnival field on Metcalf Street in downtown Sedro-Woolley. There were three age groups that each took up one section of the field. The giant-sized seniors, which were only eighth graders, played at one end, the juniors played in the middle, and the fourth and fifth grade midgets played at the opposite end.

I was in a bit of unfamiliar territory with my new sport. Instead of being one of the oldest like I always was, I was one of the youngest. Only two kids were in my grade, while the others were older and bigger, which was the first thing that our coach addressed.

"We have guys of all sizes," he said. "What we are going to do is make everyone just as tough as the next guy and weed out all of the pussies."

You couldn't talk like that in any other sport, but football was different. Not one of us standing there in our gear wanted to be called a pussy. It was the fear of being singled out and humiliated that motivated and inspired us to prove ourselves at all times. It lit a fire in us that burned constantly, and pushed us to do things that we didn't know that we could. Sadly, that's what is missing in today's society. It isn't politically correct to yell and scream at players. We have become soft, and soft doesn't win in football, regardless of the age of the players.

For the first few days we didn't even suit up. We just ran, ran, and ran some more as the coaches tried to get us into shape after a summer where most kids did nothing but watch TV and eat chips and cookies. Nobody quit, though, no matter how tired we got. The kids that turned out wanted to be there and wanted to put themselves through that. Once we did get the pads on, we ran, ran, and ran some more, carrying a much heavier load. Still, nobody quit.

After a week or so of nothing but conditioning, we finally got down to the hitting drills. One particular drill, "Rest in Peace," was designed to prove if you were man enough to be playing football to begin with. In this drill, which was damn near like committing suicide, a kid would kneel down on his knees and shut his eyes. From ten yards away, another kid would come at him at full speed and hit him just as hard as he could. The victim had until the count of two, after just about being decapitated, to get up and return the favor to his opponent.

Another drill that we did called "Blood Alley" was designed for a kid to go through three defenders without getting tackled. If tackled, the kid had to run a lap of nearly a quarter-mile. If he ran through the all three defenders without being tackled, the defenders would then have to run the lap for missing the tackle. A drill like this could teach offense and defense at the same time, making more time for learning how to execute plays.

When it came time to get down to playing football, the best tacklers from Blood Alley were designated as the starting defense. The bigger of which played on the line, while the smaller but quicker ones played linebackers and in the secondary. The offense was decided by tryouts. If a kid had an interest in a particular position, he was welcome to give it his best shot. Having never played before, I figured that I might as well try for quarterback, just like Joe Montana.

For the next week or two, I was the guy. I had our playbook down, which was real simple. I was the one back, and we had three running backs—a two back, a three back, and a four back. The right side of the line had even numbered holes between the center, guard, tackle, and tight end and the left sides holes were odd numbered. With all of our plays being running plays or bootleg options, it was a piece of cake. A 32 meant that I would hand the ball to the three back who would then run between the center and the right guard. A 17 was me running around the tight end on the left side.

As my shitty luck would have it, the quarterback who played the year before was late to sign up and when he did, he was given all of the reps while I just watched. He was better, more experienced, and stronger, so he took my job. Football is a team sport and if a guy is better than you and it is better for the team that he plays, then he should be the guy. While I was a little down about it, I understood it—he's better, so he should play. I then gave up on the whole quarterback thing and went to the offensive line, which suited me better to begin with.

During our second or third game, us rookies found out just how violent that the game truly was. The coaches son, who was our lead running back, broke his arm right in half about ten minutes into our game in Oak Harbor, which was always our toughest opponent each year. Every single kid was black, which wasn't a big deal but was still kind of a culture shock. At the time, the only people that weren't white in our school were Indians. We didn't have a single black kid and it would be several years before we started seeing a lot of Mexicans come into our area. These Oak Harbor kids were faster, stronger, and tougher than us, and the beat us until we were black—oh, and blue too.

We had to travel to play most of our games because youth football in our area was still in its infancy at the time. We had our team, as did Oak Harbor, Stanwood, Mount Vernon, and Friday Harbor, which was a little tourist town out in the San Juan Islands. It was a two hour ferry ride from Anacortes just to get there, after which we were loaded up in a truck like a herd of cattle and driven to the field.

That game against Friday Harbor was the first of just two games that we were victorious in all season. We felt so good that we sang excerpts of Queen's "Another One Bites The Dust" for the entire two hour boat ride home. It felt good to win, because losing sucked. Though we lost most of the time, we were not allowed to whine and complain about it—pussies did that, and pussies didn't belong on the football field.

At the awards banquet at the end of the season, I watched as some of the gigantic kids from the senior team walked up to the front of the room to receive really nice commemorative plaques that symbolized that they had completed five years in the youth football program. I decided that I was going to hang around the sport long enough to get one of those myself. Although I didn't get one that year, I got the next best thing—a trophy that was double the size of those that the rest of the team got, indicating that I was the most improved player on the team. I didn't really know what to think of it at first. *Was I just plain shitty at the start of the season and went on to become okay by the end?* It wasn't until many years later that I realized that getting better all the time is necessary in sports, and that year did that more than anyone else.

I began fourth grade in the fall of 1991, starting a school year that was full of downers. Just before the first day, we got rid of Shiloh because my parents just couldn't take her barking any longer. They put an add in the newspaper, listing her for the same price that they paid for her. When the time ran out on the add and nobody had called, they cut the price in half. Once that add ran its course and the same number of responses came in, they listed her in the free column. The next day she was gone. After her departure, there wasn't any plans on getting another dog—three strikes and we were out.

Back at school, some girls, as well as boys, thought that the members of the opposite sex were gross and that they surely had cooties (whatever they are), but others like me didn't think of silly stuff like that. I liked girls, but the only problem was that Kristen wasn't in my class anymore. To top it off, she started hanging out with a new boy and acted like I didn't exist.

After lunch recess one day, everyone was jogging back towards their classrooms after the bell rang and after seeing Kristen with her new pal, I stuck my foot out and tripped her onto the cement. Why I tripped her and not the other kid I don't know, but it seemed like the right thing to do at the time and it gave me a great feeling of satisfaction. But when I saw her rolling around on the pavement in obvious pain, I thought that I might have made a mistake. When everyone pointed at me when the playground attendant asked who did it, I KNEW that I made a mistake.

As I made my way to the principal's office, I could hear her bawling in the nurses office. I really started feeling shitty as I listened to her from across the hall while I sat and waited to see the principal, who was no doubt going to send me home with the dreaded pink slip for my parents to see. When he did come in, he didn't for a second believe my "it was an accident" story. I was sent home immediately and Kristen was sent to the hospital for X-rays.

When Judge Dad got home, he handed down my usual sentence of no wrestling for a month. If that wasn't bad enough, Dad then drove me to her house where I had to apologize to her and her parents. Man, was that humiliating, but it was certainly the right thing to do. Dad offered to pay for the medical bills, which they gladly accepted, causing me to have to repay a portion of that by mowing the lawn for the rest of the season for free.

Kristen ended up with a sprained wrist and a permanent dislike for me from then on. I couldn't blame her—who wants to hang around somebody that will happily inflict pain on you in a senseless act of rage and jealousy? She didn't and now neither did any other girl, ending my relationship opportunities with any girl for the next eight years. (And no, that doesn't mean that I became a switch-hitter!)

During the early fall, as well as much of the summer, our family time was spent over at Aunt B.'s. Grandma T.'s health was rapidly deteriorating and she was now confined to a wheelchair. Other than her occasional ventures to church, she rarely left the house. One of her last times that she was out and was still somewhat healthy enough to know what was going on was when she came over to our house for a family get-together. While I don't necessarily think that it was for my birthday, it was right around the time of it.

Shortly after that began the eleventh hour and she was soon bedridden in the den of Aunt B.'s house. Hospice had even began coming in to tend to her for the rest of her time. I remember going in there and watching her get worse and worse seemingly by the minute. You could literally smell death as soon as you stepped through the front door of the house. If anyone out there has experienced that, you'll know the smell I'm talking about.

It was really hard to watch because she would be in a normal frame of mind one minute, and be completely senile the next. At one point, she thought that Dad was a fireman and that Aunt B. was wanting her to hurry up and die. It was sad to see somebody get sick and become terminally ill right before your eyes in a matter of only a few months. Prior to this, the only deaths in our family that I was aware of were when the dachshunds had to be put to sleep.

We finally got the call on October 18, 1991, that Grandma T., the matriarch of the Thramer Family, had died at the age of 89. We went over to Aunt B.'s house later that night to give her some support. The house was packed full of people that were crying and trying in any way to cope with things. Everybody knew that the day was imminent but no matter how prepared they thought that they were, it still seemed like a bad dream.

When we got home and parked the Blazer in the garage, Mom and Jen went right into the house. I was a few seconds behind them and when I turned around to see if Dad was coming, I saw him crying with his head against the steering wheel. The engine was off but he still had the radio on and was listening to Chris Isaak's "Wicked Game." It's been almost twenty years since that night and my eyes still well up with tears when I hear that song—music just does that to me sometimes.

A few days later was the funeral, and not just a regular funeral, it was a Catholic funeral. Anyone who has ever been to one will know that they are almost endless because there is so much prayer involved. Both Dad and I were pallbearers. He was one of the casket bearers, while I was an honorary pallbearer who carried around a bowl of some type of hardened substance that signified the holy food. I felt extremely honored to be a part of it beings I was just ten years old.

CHAPTER 13

Was it Something I Ate?

WITH THE DEATH of Grandma T. a few months earlier, the Thramer Christmas gathering at the community center in Burlington became a thing of the past. Everything else as it pertained to Christmas was the same—Christmas Eve at Papa's, Christmas morning with Grandpa and Grandma, and Christmas dinner at Grandma Murrow's. Even with one less event over two days, it was still go-go-go as usual.

On the Saturday after Christmas, we went to Skip and Lisa's for their pre-New Year's Eve party. She fixed enchiladas for dinner and other than them being a tad on the greasy side, everything tasted fine. A few hours after dinner, though, I started to get a bit of a stomach ache. It was nothing serious, I just figured that the extra grease wasn't agreeing with me. When we got home, I went right to bed knowing that I would feel just fine in the morning.

Around three o' clock in the morning, I woke up from tossing and turning in my bed. I rolled off the top bunk and painfully walked into Mom and Dad's room. It hurt to breath, to walk, and even to hold still—it was like someone had stabbed me with a knife in my right side and was twisting it around and around.

"Dad," I said, trying to wake him up as calmly as I could. "My stomach hurts really bad."

Probably figuring that it was just gas or something from dinner, he replied, "Go back to bed and try laying on your side with your legs tucked up by your chest."

I figured that he knew better than I did so I went back into my room. It took two or three tries to get back into my bed because it hurt so bad. Once I finally made it, I had to reach down with my arms and pull my legs up because my abdominal muscles were off limits. I gave it about twenty minutes, but it just wasn't working—there was no way that this was just a belly ache.

"Dad," I said quietly, knowing that he was probably getting tired of being disturbed. "My stomach is killing me!"

"Okay," he said. "Try going into the bathroom and going poop."

"I did already."

"You went?"

"No, it hurt too bad to try and push it out."

"Oh," he said as if a light bulb just lit up in his head. "Come over here and take off your shirt."

I slowly took off my Hulk Hogan pajama shirt and stood there as Dad pressed down on my side. I almost cried right there on the spot.

"I think it's his appendix," he said, looking over at Mom.

Once it got light out, we loaded up in the Blazer and went down to the emergency room at United General Hospital. Believe it or not, this was my first trip there since the day I was born. I had gone to the doctor before, mostly for ear infections, but never to the hospital. Just like your typical emergency room, I just sat and waited until the nurses decided that they had a few minutes to listen to my problem. Billing always comes first you know, and if you're lucky enough to not die in agony, you just might get in once you have suffered in the waiting room for at least an hour. Once the doctor finally came in, the prick actually sent me home to see if it would go away.

So back home we went. I felt every single bump in the road and even if I tried bracing myself first, it would hurt just as bad. When we got home, I sprawled out on the couch and watched *All-American Wrestling* at noon, just like I did every Sunday (when I wasn't in trouble). For the first time in my life, I didn't even enjoy watching it. I either wanted to go back to the hospital or just shoot myself. I tried eating a little Jell-o, but it was too painful to even open my mouth at this point. Later in the afternoon, we went back to the hospital again. Dad, of course, hit the exact same bumps in the road on the way there. You would think that after two times down the same road he would know which ones to avoid, but I had no such luck.

Once back at the hospital, they started preparing me for surgery. I took off my clothes and put on the ever-fashionable hospital gown that always seems to open up so the world can see the patient's ass. After they took my temperature and blood pressure and hooked me up to an IV, the doctor put on a rubber glove and lubed up his finger. I looked over at Dad, who purposely had his head turned to hide the grin on his face, for some sort of an answer. The doctor then told me to lay on my stomach with my legs apart. Still not knowing what was going to happen, I did what I was told. He then viciously shoved his finger seemingly a mile up my ass, while my eyes rolled up in my head from the pain.

"Why didn't you tell me that was going to happen?" I asked Dad after the doctor/rapist left the room.

"I didn't know," he replied with that same grin that he wore just a few minutes earlier.

After a while, I was loaded up on a gurney and taken down a hallway and through several swinging doors. My parents had assured me all day that after surgery, everything would be fine. They told me about being under anesthesia and that I wouldn't feel a thing. I was okay with all of that and prepared for what was going to happen—or so I thought.

After Mom and Dad left the area, Dr. Smith, who was going to perform the procedure, introduced himself to me and said that he would like to say a prayer before he began. I agreed to let him do his thing but after he was finished, I asked him why he did it.

"Because I want God's assurance that you won't die in the operating room," he answered, as he turned and disappeared into a dark room.

I just laid there speechless and closed my eyes real tight, hoping that I would awaken from a horrible dream. *Why did he have to mention the word "die?"* I would have been fine if he hadn't have opened his mouth—now I was scared to death.

Once in the operating room, I saw four or five people wearing masks and hairnets. *How many people were going to do this anyway?* One of them put what looked like a gas mask over my face and started talking about next week's Rose Bowl that the Washington Huskies were playing in. As I told her that I wasn't going to watch it, I began to smell a scent that combined cherries and burnt plastic. The lady then told me to count backwards from one hundred.

"One hundred . . . Ninety-nine . . .Ninety-eight . . . . Ninety—seven . . . . Ninety . . . . Six."

I have no idea how long I was out, but I woke up with a gag in a different room than I was in before. A nurse quickly came over and stuck a bedpan by my face and walked away. Nothing came out, but boy did that gag hurt my stomach. I reached down and felt my side, which had a mound of gauze and tape on it. It hurt just to touch it.

"I thought I wasn't supposed to hurt anymore," I said to the nurse.

"The pain is from the incision and from the cutting of your abdominal area," she said as she left the room.

"Where's Mom and Dad?" I called out.

Nobody answered. *They said that they would be there when I woke up. What happened?* I thought about it for a few seconds before I fell back asleep.

When I woke up the next time, I was in a hospital room. Dad, Mom, and Jen were all there finally, asking me how I felt. I kept drifting in and out, trying as hard as I could to stay awake. Dad stayed with me in the room on a cot, just like he said he would, after Mom and Jen went home. I don't remember much about that night other than about every hour somebody would come in and check my vital signs and give me shots through my IV.

The next morning, I woke up well rested, but still very sore. With the core muscle responsible to aid nearly every movement by the human body, I was in pain with everything except blinking my eyes. The doctors wanted me to fart before I could eat solid food. This normally wasn't a problem, as I could strain out a fart anytime. But I was afraid to now, knowing it was going to hurt my stomach. On the other hand, I had to do it soon because I couldn't leave the hospital without taking a dump, which required me to eat solid food first.

People came in to see me throughout the day, bringing with them cards, books, and all kinds of cool stuff. I was finally able to squeak out a tiny fart so I could get something to eat. Now I just had to digest it and pass the waste so I could get on my way. To pass the time, I looked at my new stuff and got up every little while to take walks. I'm telling you, it was hard to move! A twenty foot walk would take ten minutes, after which I would have to take a nap.

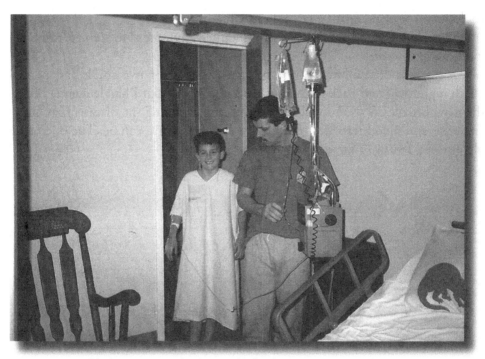

Dad helping me in the hospital after having my appendix out

After I woke up from one of my naps, I looked up and saw that the TV was on, so I started watching what was airing. It was *I Love Lucy* and and all that I remember was a pie-throwing spot that brought on literally side-splitting laughter. It hurt even worse to laugh than it did to walk. I had to have the TV shut off and I have never watched that show since out of protest.

Following one more lousy night, I was able to drop that elusive shit and earn my release. I was thrilled to get out of that stupid gown, but I had to wear sweat pants, which I hated. I wasn't allowed to wear my jeans because they would rub on my staples. I was able to walk better each day, but even after a week, I couldn't bear to laugh—or sneeze—or fart. It was too bad because farting and laughing about it was one of my favorite things to do.

Two weeks after my surgery I was able to get my staples out. It couldn't have come at a better time because I had long since grown tired of showing everyone in school that I had a stomach full of staples. For the longest time, my scar was like a thermometer, turning blue when I was cold and red when I was warm. My appetite didn't come back for a while, either. I was usually nauseous in the morning and wouldn't get hungry until later in the day.

"Maybe you have morning sickness?" Dad suggested.

"Do you think I do?" I asked, hoping that knowing what was wrong with me would make me feel better.

"I would if you were pregnant," he said, bursting into laughter.

I'm not sure that I found the humor in my father anymore. He seemed to be taking too much pleasure in my pain.

After a few weeks of drinking instant breakfast shakes for two meals and picking at my dinner each night, we went back to the doctor. Mom swore that I had leukemia because at the time, the news broadcasts were spending a lot of time covering the disease. Of course I didn't have leukemia, and blood tests showed that I was as healthy as can be. The doctor said that I probably just had I virus. *Thanks, Doc.*

CHAPTER 14

Not the Hospital Again!

My APPETITE AND ambition came back around early spring, about the time that baseball started. Going into my third year, I played a little more often in the infield. I'm sure that the reason was because the outfield was reserved for the two older kids who failed to qualify for the upper-level league, as well as a kid named Calob, who had Down's syndrome.

Calob was an always entertaining and often embarrassing member of the community. He never once hit the ball all season long but would run the bases anyhow, culminating in a head-first slide into home plate as if he had just scored the go-ahead run in Game Seven of the World Series. As a team, we had to be the laughing stock of the whole division. It didn't help that our coach didn't know jack about baseball. He didn't know the difference between a stolen base and a stolen car.

With our baseball team being the polar opposite of competitive, I set my sights on a school competition instead. This wasn't just about who got the best grades in the class or about how quick the work was completed, this was a contest involving the entire fourth grade to determine who could read the most amount of minutes in a single month. This was something that I decided right from the start that I was going to win.

First of all, I love to read, especially if it is a compelling story that I can visualize actually happening in my head. These days, I usually read biographies on wrestlers or musicians who I am interested in. In the winter months, I can knock out a four hundred-pager in two or three days. Once I get into a book, I can't put it down. I'll read in the shade outside, on the front porch while it's raining, in the recliner while the kids watch TV, and, of course, while sitting on the toilet as I make a deposit.

During the contest, as is such with most competitions, there is always a way to cheat. Minutes were logged by the person who did the reading. They didn't have to be monitored by a parent or teacher, it was on the honor system. Each day, students would highlight a graph with each block representing twenty minutes of reading. I personally witnessed several kids casually filling in extra blocks as if nobody was watching them. I, however, never once added extra blocks and am not exaggerating when I tell you that I read an average of 400 and 420 minutes a day—the equivalent of seven hours. The parent of the runner-up kid said that I would have to go with out sleep to accomplish that.

Here's the deal—each school day, I got up at 6:15 and jumped into the shower. By 6:30, I was reading in the living room. When Mom fixed breakfast at 8:00 or 8:30, I read while eating. School started at 9:30 and we lived just minutes away, so Mom took us at 9:00 so we could play at morning recess. So before the school day even started, I had two-and-a-half hours under my belt. During school, I would get at least ninety minutes of reading in because I always had extra time from finishing my work early. When school was out at 3:30, I had a total of four hours in. By the time I got home and had things put away, I was able to start reading around 4:00 and would read until dinner was served at 6:00. After dinner, I would read from 6:30 to 7:30 when it was time for bed. Add it all up, and you get seven hours of reading and plenty of time for sleep, school, and eating. So fuck off, Eleanor Nakis!

When it was all said and done, I more than tripled the amount of minutes that the second place finisher logged. I won a gold medal, which I still have but now resembles a worn-out 1972 penny, as well as the choice of any book in the library. I was very proud of myself for what I had accomplished and it meant a lot to me that I was better than everyone else in the fourth grade—and I did it all by doing something that I enjoyed.

Shortly after that, I won another contest—a second-straight young author's award for my newest short story. Instead of being about football, this time it was about a storyline in wrestling that I really wanted to see play out on television. Unfortunately, promoters nixed the idea and the only place that the match happened was in my story.

WrestleMania VIII was held on April 5, 1992 at the Hoosier Dome in Indianapolis, Indiana. Ric Flair, who has held more world titles than anyone in history, was finally in the WWF after a twenty year run in the NWA. Hulk Hogan was still the main draw in the WWF and a match between the two would fulfill every wrestling fan's dreams. The match was teased, but decided against at the last minute in favor splitting the two up to wrestle in separate matches. Flair wrestled Randy Savage in a classic and Hogan wrestled Sid Justice in a snooze-fest.

My story began, as it did on television, with a sneak attack on Hogan that was perpetrated by Flair. For the next couple of weeks, the two trained and cut promos on each other and all roads led to the final showdown at WrestleMania for the World Heavyweight Championship. The two then put on one of the greatest matches in history, but that was on paper. In reality it would be nearly three years until the two finally met in a match but by then, they were in a smaller organization and their performances were sub-par at best.

As I did every spring, I began to spend more and more time riding my motorcycle. By this time, I was outgrowing that little 50 so bad that I looked like an elephant getting a piggyback ride from a turtle. My knees rested above the gas tank and were interfering with my hand controls, while my feet hung very low to the ground over the foot pegs. As funny as it looked, seeing Uncle Robbie riding Jake's motorcycle, which was even smaller than mine, was hysterical.

Uncle Robbie riding a motorcycle much smaller than he is

At his house out behind the chicken coop, which housed his fighting cocks, was a little set of trails that he made for motorcycles and ATVs. Right after he first built them, we went over there for a few hours on a Saturday afternoon to test them out. Dad and Uncle Robbie would switch off with me and Jake on our bikes so they could get some riding in too. Papa was there also and brought with him his new four wheeler to ride along with us. He even taught me how to drive it, which went much smoother than my trials on motorcycles. There wasn't a clutch lever that led me into a ditch and a had two more wheels that did all of the balancing for me.

About halfway through the day, I was following Papa out in the field when a gust of wind came by and lifted his leather cowboy hat off of his bald head. Me being the gentlemen that I am, I did the only logical thing that I could think of—I ran right over the top of it! I had to stop about ten feet away from his freshly flattened hat because I was laughing so hard. Papa circled around and pulled up alongside it, got off the four wheeler, and began to survey the damage. The otherwise new hat now had a tread mark that ran its full length, giving it somewhat of a leopard print.

With an evil grin and a stern voice, Papa looked at me and said, "Payback's are a bitch, kid."

More than thirteen years went by before he found his opportunity to get even—thirteen years! Dad and I were at his place for some reason and we were all out in his pasture shooting guns. We had everything from shotguns to rifles to .44 Magnums as we peppered targets with lead. While I was loading up to take my next turn, Papa ripped my 49ers hat off my head and emptied his fifteen round clip in it.

With the barrel still smoking, he looked over and said, "Now we are even."

I knew exactly what he was talking about and just to prove that I was a good sport, I shot my own hat with a twelve gauge shotgun from ten feet away.

Probably after seeing how much fun could be had on dirt bikes, Dad decided to attempt to get his 350 running again. I know it may be hard to believe, but whatever he did to get it going this time worked and it stayed running until the day that he sold it. Finally the days of him kicking and kicking in order to get it to fire were over and all of the swearing and hollering over it was now a thing of the past. Now we could finally spend our time riding, rather than just trying to catch a glimpse of brightness from his headlight.

Our neighborhood was growing nearly every day. All of the lots on Orth Way were now sold and had houses on them and all of the fields and woods of the surrounding areas were cleared and subdivided into several other streets just like ours. Soon, there would be over a hundred new homes right in our laps. These houses were being put up faster than a child building one out of Lincoln logs, and probably with about the same quality of craftsmanship. As more and more people moved in, everything just got more complicated—more traffic, more kids in classes, and more headaches.

On the positive side, the development and construction stages of these areas made for some pretty good motorcycle tracks. Bulldozers cleared areas for foundations and just piled all of the dirt up out of their way, which we rode over just like motocross guys—minus the tricks. They also dug huge irrigation ditches that we could ride all over inside of. Dad would ride down into one and send gigantic rooster tails of mud into the air as he held his breaks and poured on the throttle. I, on the other hand, would just splash through the mud and get as filthy as possible. We just had a blast, except for one time.

The story of what happened is the same on my part as it is on Dad's, except for the matter of whose fault it was. In my book (which this is, by the way), the blame rests on his shoulders. We were riding along the top of one of the ditches, Dad on the inside closest to the ditch, and me on outside. While cruising at a steady pace, I looked over my left shoulder and motioned with my head to go down into the mud again. As I turned to go down into the ditch, Dad twists on his throttle, thinking that I wanted to race, and plowed right into me. His front fork slammed right into my foot peg—at least it would have if it hadn't hit my foot that was hanging over it. Not even caring about my bike, I just tipped it over on its side and began yelling in pain. Dad, thinking it had bumped my infected big toe that I had at the time (which hurt like hell if I so much as grazed it), just assumed that I was hollering about that. When he took off my shoe and sock, he changed his tune.

"Oh," he said. "I think we need to take you to the hospital."

"Not the hospital again!" I cried.

Not wanting to look for myself because I was too afraid of what I would see, I asked him how bad it was.

"Bad enough that we need to take you to the hospital. And by the way, you better stop crying by the time we get home or Mom won't let you ride your bike no more."

With that, I shut the faucet off and loaded up on Dad's bike. It was my only way of getting home, as I couldn't ride my bike because I couldn't shift and I couldn't put any weight on my foot to walk. Dad pushed the bike home with me stretching my leg out on the seat so it wouldn't bleed so much. It was then that I got my first look at the injury. Yeah, I needed to go to the hospital. *Swell.*

The idea to not cry around Mom worked because I don't remember her being all that mad, or maybe she just waited to yell at Dad when I wasn't around. She helped me into the Blazer as Dad ran back to get my bike. Once he was back, the two of us drove the all-too-familiar route to the emergency room.

"At least you won't get the finger check this time," Dad said with a smile.

"Yeah, but am I gonna have to wear a cast?" I asked.

"I don't know—maybe."

We pulled into the parking lot and Dad gave me a piggyback ride into the building. After the standard two hour wait, the doctor came in to look at my foot. After an X-ray, I found out that my second toe was broken. Luckily it was a clean break right at the joint, rather than a shattered bone. I then had to get a few stitches to close the gap between my second and middle toes. Once that was done, I was fitted for a plastic splint that covered the bottom part of my foot and went up the back of my leg. The doctor finished my new ensemble with a set of crutches.

"It will take three or four weeks to heal the break, so you must not put any weight on it until then," the doctor said. "And you must use the crutches at all time also."

I felt just like a man getting sentenced for committing a crime when he told me how long that I was going to be laid up. I had to deal with people pointing and laughing at me for a whole month. *This was all Dad's fault.*

Before I could get laughed at during school, I beat everyone to the punch by unzipping my pants and putting the rubber arm pit pad in my fly to make it look like I had a giant penis. That trick never got old, but I had to stop after a trip to the principal's office. He didn't find the humor it for some reason. After about two or three weeks, I began trying to walk, or at least stand up on my own feet, so I could ditch the crutches. By the time I was to go back and see the doctor, I was able to walk into the exam room on my own. The doctor said that my bone was back to normal and probably stronger than it was before. While this was my last trip to the hospital due to a personal injury for nearly a decade, it would be only about six months before I was back in the ER yet again. This time, the whole family came too.

CHAPTER 15
The Good Outweighs the Bad

WHEN SCHOOL LET out for the summer, Mom entered me and Jen into a reading contest at the Sedro-Woolley Library. There were three different age groups and the winner would be determined simply by who read the most books in sixty days. Participants could check out up to ten books at once and once they were read, they could be returned for another ten. Needless to say, I was back at the library to check out another ten about every three days.

At first the librarians questioned me about the validity of my reading log, but they backed off when Mom stuck up for me and said that I spent hours upon hours with my face buried in various books. I just couldn't understand why people weren't buying what I was selling. To be fair, I was reading intermediate chapter books as opposed to eight hundred page Steven King novels. These books were about eighty to one hundred pages with larger text, pictures, and aimed towards nine to twelve year old kids. Since I was ten, I was right within my age level. As I said before, I'm a quick reader and books don't get put down when I am really into them. It's a pretty simple concept to understand to me.

When it was all said and done, I read 206 books—cover to cover—in sixty days. For you Rhodes Scholars, that is just short of three-and-a-half books per day. Naturally, I won the contest—and it wasn't even close. My margin of victory was about 150 books more than the kid in second place. Not only did I beat everyone in Sedro-Woolley, I beat everyone in all of Skagit County. I received another gold medal for my achievements and a lifetime library card if I'm not mistaken. I even had an article written about me in the paper.

The library itself was in a contest with the other libraries in the county. At the end, each library added up the total amount of books that each kid read and the town that had the most would be the winner and get to display a two foot tall trophy for a full year. I think that I should have gotten the trophy because Sedro-Woolley won because of me—two hundred books over Mount Vernon's total. If I hadn't entered the contest, they wouldn't have gotten shit unless they scooped it themselves from the horse stalls of the Skagit County Fairgrounds, where the awards ceremony was held.

If you assumed that I did nothing but read all summer, you're wrong. In addition to the reading olympics that I was in, I was also introduced to the real Olympics for the first time in the summer of 1992. The two-and-a-half week long event that comes just once every four years was held in Barcelona, Spain from July 25 to August 9. For the two hours that it was on each morning and the three hours that it was on each night, I was glued to the TV watching diving, swimming, weightlifting, and gymnastics.

Recently, Jen had taken up gymnastics and I absolutely hated going to her meets. I actually liked watching gymnastics, it was just the fact that her meets were almost endless. She would compete in four events—floor exercise, uneven bars, vault, and the balance beam—but it would take all damn day. To top it all off, they were happening just about every weekend. So with gymnastics popular in our house at the time, we all tuned in to the hotly contested women's individual all-around final. The rest of the world did as well, as gymnastics is traditionally the highest rated event in each Summer Games.

In 1992, the team medal battle was a two horse race between the United States and the Unified Team. Since the dismantling of the Soviet Union a year earlier, Estonia, Latvia, and Lithuania sent their own teams for the first time since 1936, as the other Soviet counterparts competed as the Unified Team. At the end of the Olympics, the Unified Team finished with 112 medals and the United States finished with 108. That being said, it was no surprise that each team was well represented in the women's all-around. But it was the showdown between the Unified Team's Tatiana Gutsu and the U.S.'s Shannon Miller that earned the ratings that the Olympics drew that year. In the end, Gutsu won the all-around by 0.012 points—the closest margin of victory in Olympic history.

I also added another lawn to my job list over the summer. This one I would go on to mow for a total of seven years, longer than any other one. Dorothy Cinnamon (yes, that was really her name. I wonder if her cousin was Burt Sugar?) was a widow that lived about three houses down from us on the opposite side of the street. This lawn payed me eight dollars but by the time I was finishing up when I was seventeen, I was getting twenty bucks for it. Now with three lawns a week, I was bringing in pretty good money for a ten year old.

With the money that I was making, I wasn't afraid to spend some of it if I wanted something. To avoid pissing money away, Mom and Dad always taught me not to buy the first thing that I saw just because I had some money. If the next day comes and I still wanted it, then I should get it. Believe it or not, I still follow that rule pretty closely today. There are exceptions to every rule, however, as sometimes there are things that I just got to have—like my first WWF home video tape. It was *Hulk Hogan's Greatest Matches*. At just over sixty minutes long, I could watch it every day if I wanted to—and I did just that, unless of course if I was in trouble. This tape started my collection that still grows to this day. Later on, I will tell you just how big my collection is.

It was also with my lawn mowing money that I bought my very first music album. I had really been into hard, southern, and classic rock music ever since the days of riding in the log truck with Dad. In spite of the arrival of grunge rock, which came from Seattle, I was still very much into the the hair bands of the fading Los Angeles glam metal scene. My favorite was, and still is to this day, Guns n' Roses.

In 1992, Guns n' Roses was the hottest band in the world (sorry, KISS). Led by the volatile Axl Rose, whose voice range is from another world, Gn'R was on top of the music ladder after only five years on the scene. Lead guitarist Slash, whose real name is Saul Hudson, played bluesy solos underneath his trademark top hat while smoking a cigarette. Bassist Duff McKagen, who was born in Seattle, kept the beat going along with rhythm guitarist Izzy Stradlin and drummer Matt Sorum, who had recently taken over for Steven Adler, after he had been fired for excessive drug use. If you know anything about the "World's Most Dangerous Band," you can bet that he must have been a mess, considering the band's nature to begin with.

Just under a year earlier, in September of 1991, they released two albums on the same day. *Use Your Illusion I* debuted on the Billboard charts at #2, while *Use Your Illusion II* took the top spot. The first of which contained my favorite ballad, "November Rain." More than just a hard rock song, "November Rain" was complete with an orchestra arrangement that upset many rock fans. But not me—I don't care what goes into a song, just as long as it sounds good. It could be rock, country, jazz, blues, and even a little hip hop, and I can dig it.

So there I was, at the Sam Goody store in the mall with twenty dollars burning a hole in my pocket. As I would come to learn, record stores were not the place to buy music. They wanted $19.99 plus tax for a compact disc and remember, that was in 1992. Knowing that I didn't have the money for a CD at that place, I opted to buy a Guns n' Roses hat for ten bucks and have Mom and Dad take me to Target to buy a cheaper album. With only ten dollars left though, I had to settle for a $7.99 cassette tape instead of a CD. The only problem I had now was choosing which one to buy. After a half-hour debate between *Use Your Illusion I* and *II*, *Gn'R Lies,* and *Appetite for Destruction,* I decided on *Appetite*.

Released on July 21, 1987, *Appetite for Destruction* became the fastest selling debut album in history (it still is, by the way). It has been ranked #1 on the Billboard album charts on three separate occasions and has sold 28 million copies worldwide since its release. (I can vouch for three of them because after I wore out the tape, I bought the CD, wore it out, and bought a second one.) The album itself has been ranked #32 out of 200 by the Rock and Roll Hall of Fame, #61 out of 500 by *Rolling Stone*, #42 of all-time by VH1, and #1 in history according to *Kerrang!*. But most importantly, it is ranked #1 in the opinion of one Eddie D. Thramer.

Appetite kicks off with "Welcome To The Jungle," arguably the greatest hard rock song ever recorded. It is played at every pro football game, hockey game, baseball game—you name it—commercials, movies—everything. The reason is simple, the intro instantly grabs your attention and gets your adrenaline flowing, even twenty-five years after it was written by Axl Rose in Seattle in just under three hours. With "Sweet Child O' Mine," "Paradise City," and nine other rocking tunes, it's hard to question the greatness of the album.

As far as Mom was concerned, it didn't matter my reasoning for buying anything just as long as I hurried up and got it done so we could leave. The good part about getting the cassette was that I could listen to it in the Blazer on the way home. Beings it wasn't Michael Bolton, Mom wasn't to thrilled about listening to it, but she was going to let me play it anyway so I would shut up.

I tore open the cellophane as quickly as I could, ignoring the parental advisory sticker on the outside that I honestly didn't notice while I was shopping. When I opened up the case and saw Robert Williams' painted picture of a robotic rapist and a ravaged woman with her underwear down around her ankles and one of her boobs exposed, I figured that illustration was what the sticker was for. I figured that if I didn't show it to Mom, everything would be fine and I could keep my tape. But it wasn't the painting that I had to worry about, it was the lyrics. The songs that I heard on the radio, although suggestive, were free of bad words. The same cannot be said for some of the deeper album cuts.

Unaware of what was to come, Dad put in the tape as we pulled out of the parking lot. "Welcome to the Jungle" was up first and sounded as good as ever, much to the chagrin of Mom. Next came "It's So Easy" and somehow three or four F-words went unnoticed by everyone, including me. "Nightrain" was third and was clean, but then came "Out Ta Get Me," and my tape was taken away. Unlike the F-words from two songs earlier that were covered by background vocals and guitars, this time the lyrics were clearly heard over the band, which was the intention of the song.

Leading up to the first chorus, Axl yelled, "'cause I've got somethin' that's been buildin' up inside for so fuckin' long . . ."

"What was that, Ronald?" Mom yelled. (Like Edmund for me, it was Ronald when Dad was getting hollered at by Mom.)

"What? I didn't hear anything," Dad untruthfully replied.

Two lines into the chorus and right after Dad finished his sentence, Axl put the nail in my coffin when he yelled, "I'm fuckin' innocent!"

"That right there!" Mom furiously exclaimed. "Shut that shit off!"

With that, my brand new tape was taken away and put in the garage with Dad's stuff. It wasn't an entire loss because when Mom left me home alone, as she and Dad began to do for short times, I would listen to it anyway!

These days with my music collection checking in at nearly six hundred albums, a fair amount of them has some bad language included. Of those, only a few of them I won't let my kids listen to—like the ones with songs that blatantly talk about sex, rather than in a creative fashion. The rest are okay. They know what words not to say, or maybe they just don't say them around me.

The school scene was fixing to change for me going into the fifth grade. With elementary classes getting larger, the district elected to renovate Central Elementary School on the south side of town, which was built back in the 1920's and had been vacant since the 1960's. Once redone, all of the fifth and sixth grade students from both sides of town would go there, thus making the junior high school only a seventh and eighth grade establishment.

With Central on the other side of town and with Mom starting a job with the district in food service, I had to start riding the bus home from school everyday. It was different, but it wasn't bad and could actually be very entertaining. I liked goofing off as much as anybody, but I knew when to keep my mouth shut. Other kids didn't, and of course my instigating didn't help matters.

That gray-haired Bjorn rode the bus everyday, unless he was kicked off. He was usually kicked off for calling the bus driver a "dumb bitch" because she just couldn't seem to pronounce his name right. She pronounced it "Buh-rorn," which I thought was just great. So me and a couple of other kids would do anything to draw attention to him.

"Sit down in your seat, Buh-rorn," she would say.

"My name's Bee-yorn, you dumb bitch!" he would yell back.

She would literally stop the bus, get right into his face, and shout, "You're off this bus for two weeks, Buh-rorn!"

He finally shut up and would then start bawling until she dropped him off at his house. Sadly, I would have to wait two weeks until the process started over again—which it always did. In the meantime, we could get her to yell at another hot-headed kid with red hair that she always called, "Red."

"Shut your mouth, Red, or you'll be settin' home with Buh-rorn for two weeks!"

It was classic.

Of course with the beginning of school, meant the beginning of football season. This year instead of being one of the youngest, I was now one of the oldest. It was this year that I starting playing a position that I hated at first, but would go on to play it for the rest of my years.

Coach Dale Wicker needed a center (the guy who hikes the ball for all of you who don't know about the sport) and nobody wanted to do it. Maybe it was because the quarterback's hands pressed not-so-gently on the back side of your ball bag before each play. Nonetheless, with me being much taller than everyone else, I was designated as the guy who liked to get his nuts felt. On the bright side, I played every single offensive play of the season. Not very many others could say that.

My second year of football

We were surprisingly very good that year, losing just one game all season. Our running attack was designed around two quick and illusive backs, J.J. Lopez and Casey Olson. J.J. would play the first half and a fresh Casey would come in and play the second half, when the defense was getting tired. The system works, just ask Mike Shanahan. He led the Denver Broncos to back-to-back Super Bowl titles in 1997 and 1998 doing the same thing.

The only downside of our season was our assistant coach, Eddie Pole. After meeting this dude, I truly wished that I had been given a different name. This guy was an ex-Army reject who treated our turnouts like boot camp. We would jog in a single file line and recite a ridiculous cadence that made us look like we were filming a low-budget slapstick comedy. Usually Dale would knock G.I. Joe off of his high horse just before he would line us up for military haircuts and a serving of hardtack. He is one of those guys that when you see him in public, you must do everything you can to make sure that he doesn't see you. This guy was so clueless, when *Monday Night Football* was on, he would stare at the radio and wonder what was wrong with his picture.

Back in the classroom, school was as easy as ever. So easy in fact, that I would spend most of my time goofing off and disrupting the class after my assignments were done. Soon, I became all about being a cut-up and my grades started slipping. Just like a junkie that's hooked on dope, I finally hit rock bottom when I received what was to be my lowest grade on a report card ever—an 80% in science.

Some people would do anything for a B-, but not me. I felt that a grade like that was beneath me, and it was. To me, a C was a failing grade, and I damn near failed by being a screw-off. After that, I concentrated much more on my school work. As long as I kept my grades up, I could still screw off, right? Not hardly. It got to the point where the teacher sent home a note to Mom, that I knew nothing about, saying that I was out of control. That went over like a lead balloon at home. Not only did I lose wrestling until the end of the calendar year, but Mom had to come in during school every couple of days to talk to the teacher to make sure that I was behaving better. After a few humiliating visits, I finally got the picture. I would still have my fun, but I had to think of other ways to have it without disrupting others. Several weeks later, she sent home another letter that said I was a pleasure to have in class again. I still didn't get wrestling back, though. Mom and Dad continued to dangle that carrot in front of me just so I wouldn't relapse.

As winter rolled around, we began to focus on our family vacation. This would be our first big trip since our trip to Yellowstone eighteen months earlier. For this one, we were going to be gone for two full weeks. Our plan was to load up the camp trailer and head south on Interstate 5 into California. We would stop in San Francisco, Six Flags Magic Mountain, Disneyland, and in Las Vegas, to spend Christmas at Dad's mom's.

With several thousands of miles to be covered, Mom and Dad said that as long as Jen and I didn't bicker back and forth, we could have the back seat of the Blazer folded down for the entire trip. It was like traveling on a full size bed at all times. We never sat in our seats once—no seat belts, no restraints. We could move around at will and not ever have to worry about getting uncomfortable. When we were tired, we could just stretch out and go to sleep as if we were in a regular bed.

For the last few months of lawn mowing season, I had saved a fair amount of cash for the trip. Knowing that we were going to visit San Francisco, I made it clear to my parents that I wanted to buy a 49ers hat with some of my money while we were in town. You wouldn't believe how proud I was to pay for my own 49ers hat in downtown San Francisco. To top it all off, I even took a picture with Joe Montana as we walked along Fisherman's Wharf! Well, not exactly. It was a wax replica of the future Hall of Famer, but it was good enough for me.

It was already dark when we were touring the city, but we had to get out of town a ways to a rest area or truck stop or something so we could spend the night. After we left town, it just started dumping down rain. People sometimes say "raining cats and dogs," but this was more like horses and cows. When we pulled over to camp for the night, there was no less than six inches of standing water in the parking lot. Johnny Cash must have been standing in that spot when he wrote "Five Feet High and Rising."

Dad took his shoes off and carried Mom into the trailer, where they could light the furnace, get the place warmed up, and get the beds ready. Dad came back and got Jen next but when it was my turn, Dad managed to trip and send me directly into the furnace vent on the outside wall of the trailer, which was by this time a bright shade of orange from the radiating heat. It instantly singed an unwanted brand mark forcefully onto my right arm, leaving me with a scar that I can see plain as day as I write this sentence. Mom thought that it would be a good idea to rub butter on it to relieve the burning—it didn't work.

A day or two later, we stopped in Valencia, California to spend the full day at Magic Mountain. Known for its Warner Brothers theme, Magic Mountain was much more than Bugs Bunny, Daffy Duck, and Elmer Fudd (Uh-huh-huh-huh-huh-huh), it was also home to some of the largest roller coasters in the world. In addition to Colossus and Cyclone, it also featured a new ride called The Viper that raced you through seven vertical loops at over seventy miles per hour. One of the loops was fourteen stories high, the tallest for any roller coaster in the world. Only Dad and I got to ride it, however, as Jen was turned away at the final height checkpoint. Finally, somebody caught on to the old "stand on Dad's toes" routine. She didn't stop whining about that for the rest of the trip.

Never one for roller coasters, Mom found her delight in watching us race around on carts until our stomachs couldn't take it anymore. The three of us nearly soiled ourselves when she requested that all of us ride the giant Freefall that stood ominously at the other side of the park. As we got closer and closer, however, Mom started to freak out. Unfortunately for her, there was absolutely no line so she didn't have a chance to change her mind. As we were strapped in and elevated ten stories into the air, you could tell that Mom was wishing that she had kept her words soft and sweet because now she was having to eat them. As we moved closer to the ledge, Mom was practically in tears. But just before she could squeeze out a single drop, down we went to the ground below in about two seconds. Once we all swallowed our stomachs, putting them back where they belonged, we bailed out of the car and set foot back on the pavement. To this day, I have not seen Mom back on a roller coaster ride of any sort.

After the park closed, we headed south to the "Entertainment Capitol of the World," Las Vegas, Nevada. It was pretty late at night when we got there, but you wouldn't know it. Both sides of The Strip were lined up with people and the traffic congestion resembled that of a Friday afternoon commute in Seattle. The neon lights of the magnificent casinos pierced through the night sky. Even the McDonald's was illuminated with flashing lights.

Grandma lived a few miles off of the main drag. When we got there, I noticed something that I had never seen before where we lived—metal bars on the outside of the windows on every house in the neighborhood. Whether they were there because of frequent burglaries or to deter burglars, I don't know, but it was a much different scene than on Orth Way.

The next day was Christmas Eve but if you walked outside, you would think that it was the Fourth of July with the heat and humidity. We were all in T-shirts enjoying the "summer" weather, while Grandma was bundled up in no less than four layers of clothing. Granted, she only weighed about a hundred pounds, but I just can't remember ever seeing her without warm clothing—ever.

We celebrated Christmas on Christmas Eve, which was also much different from the norm. Mom and Dad had hauled all of me and Jen's presents down in the camp trailer, thus solving one of life's greatest mysteries. Unless Santa Claus made his deliveries a week in advance, he was a figment of a child's imagination. In all fairness to the jolly old fat man, I would start believing in his magic once again when I saw it through the eyes of my kids.

We stayed a couple of days more before we headed back north. It wasn't a Christmas present but the day that we were leaving, Grandma gave me an acoustic guitar. It was smaller than the standard size, but it did come complete with its own case. I never asked for it or anything, she just gave it to me. I still have it today, as it is displayed with some of my collector's stuff. I've had it re-stringed, but have yet to play a note on it. I've been saying it since 1992, but someday I'm going to learn to play it.

After we said our goodbyes, we drove back into California to a campground that was part of the same Leisure Time chain that Papa and Gladys belonged to. Mom and Dad committed identity theft as they used their names so they could camp for free. (It's not cheating, it's just being smart if you ask me.) We went to bed early that night because we were going to need every once of energy we had for our visit to Disneyland the following day.

We got up the next morning, leaving the trailer at camp so we had a guaranteed spot to sleep after the park closed at midnight. It was about an hour drive into Anaheim and with any luck, we would be there right when Mickey Mouse opened the gates. Well Dad, being the Rhodes Scholar that he is, parked the car and stepped onto the parking lot of the "Happiest Place on Earth" before he realized that he was still wearing his slippers. So back we went to get his shoes. Two hours later, we finally walked past the statue of Walt Disney—too bad we had to miss out on some action because of Dad's stupidity.

Finally, now that I was making my third trip to the park, I was able to get on all of the rides—Space Mountain, Thunder Mountain Railroad, and the fairly new Splash Mountain. The park wasn't that busy at all, which meant that there were hardly any lines to have to wait in. We met all of the best characters and got to take pictures with some of them without anyone else getting in the way.

A few months earlier, Disneyland opened their newest section of the park called Toon Town. Although light on the rides, Toon Town was like walking through an actual cartoon. Mickey and Minnie Mouse each had a house (hey, a rhyme) that you could walk through. You could set on their furniture, watch their TV, and pretend like you were in your own sketch. With Toon Town being new, this was the most populated section of the park, so we didn't spend a whole lot of time there. As we were heading back to Tomorrowland, a plane flew over with a banner behind it. Dad pointed up to it and commented on what the sign read.

"What does it say?" I asked.

"Can't you read it?" Dad asked.

"No."

"What do you mean?" Mom butted in.

"I mean, I can't read it," I humbly answered.

"Well, we will have to get your eyes checked when we get home," she said.

Great—I just knew that I was going to have to get glasses. I was going to be called "four eyes" and "window face" and shit like that. People were going to laugh at me and think that I was a nerd—just what I always wanted.

The truth was, I did have trouble seeing. Mom must have passed me that gene because she didn't have very good vision either and had been wearing contact lenses for the past couple of years. I, on the other hand, seemed to be getting worse as time went by. But it was the fear of getting glasses that kept me from telling anyone about it. I could see fine if I was reading a book and I could see people, but if there was a spider crawling on their forehead, I couldn't see it. I had a hard time seeing words on the chalkboard but luckily, because of my behavior in class, I was put up front where the teacher could keep an eye on me, which meant that I could be closer to the words. Regardless, it was just one of those things that I was going to have to accept—I needed vision correction.

Despite the whole vision issue, we had a great time at the park. After the parade concluded, the crowd shuffled out of the park and began hunting for their cars. Dad always knew right where ours was at, while others crisscrossed the lot, trying to remember where their vehicles were. Now if Dad hadn't have been there and me and Jen were just with Mom, we would probably still be looking for the Blazer right now.

The next night was spent at yet another campground. That night, we all went into the clubhouse to watch *Monday Night Football*. This wasn't just any regular game, however, this was the end of an era. It was on that night, December 28,1992, that Joe Montana played his last game as a San Francisco 49er. After being out with that same back injury since the NFC Championship against the Giants, Montana's contract was up and a trade was looming. Leading the Detroit Lions just 7-6 in the third quarter, he came off the bench for his final encore. His performance that night captivated audiences once again. Completing 15 of 21 passes for 126 yards and two touchdowns, Joe Cool rode off into the sunset with a 24-6 win at Candlestick Park. Two months later, as expected, he was traded to the Kansas City Chiefs. I will truly never forget watching the team that turned me on to football and probably the greatest quarterback in history compete as a unit for one last time on that given night.

In the morning, we continued north on our way back home. As we got into the higher elevations of the Sierra-Nevadas, we began to see snow and would not see the bare ground again for the rest of the way home. We drove through the Redwood Forest to see the awe inspiring sequoia and redwood trees, which is one of the most magnificent sights on this Earth. To say that they were big would be like saying that Babe Ruth was just an average hitter. Being able to stand there and be captivated at what nature was able to create over time was nothing short of extraordinary and I would highly recommend a trip there for anyone who hasn't seen them.

As we dropped down in elevation and came into Oregon, there was no let up in the weather. The whole west coast was socked in with a heavy snow storm and forecasters said that it would be a few more days until temperatures would raise enough to turn the snow into rain. Until then, it was a blizzard. On top of all of that, the freezing temperatures made for icy and very slippery road conditions. We spent the next night in the central part of Oregon. In the morning, Dad decided that it was time to go home. He was going to drive straight through, which was only about six hundred miles away. On a normal day, we could have made the trip in about ten hours towing the camp trailer. But with the adverse road conditions, it was going to take substantially longer. Our caravan traveled down the interstate not much faster than the settlers from the east did as they made their way along the Oregon Trail a hundred years earlier.

To pass the time, we sang along to the country music tunes on the radio dial, which I had really just been exposed to during that particular trip. At the time, country music was transitioning from western themes into a more up-tempo dance style. The radio played a mixture of each to appease both audiences. They also played a more southern rock-type, much like that of Lynyrd Skynyrd from fifteen years earlier. Travis Tritt and Marty Stuart played and toured together, wearing biker gear as opposed to the traditional cowboy hats and Porter Waggoner suits. Their song, "The Whiskey Ain't Workin'," was played every couple of hours, eventually garnering enough accolades to earn the two a Grammy. It was their style that turned me on to country music. I liked the more outlaw-type style of them, Hank Williams, Jr., Dwight Yoakam, and Lee Roy Parnell, but I could still dig traditional stuff from George Strait and Alan Jackson as well.

As night fell, the storm didn't let up. Temperatures were still in the 20's and home was still over three hundred miles away. Traffic was actually light, which was odd because it was New Year's Eve. Apparently, people had more sense than we did and stayed home and off of the roads. Jen and I went to sleep in the back of the Blazer with the seats still folded down. Before I fell asleep, Dad promised that he would wake me up as we got closer to Seattle so we could listen to the last ten songs of the KISW Top 1000 Rock Song's of All-Time. I was all for it—anything for a chance to hear "Welcome to the Jungle" without having to sneak around about it.

I have never been able to sleep very well in the car. If it makes any sense, I am able to rest enough to where I begin to dream and still be coherent enough to know what is going on around me. Any time that the car goes over a bump, my eyes open right up. Once everything is safe and sound, I drift back off.

What happened next was much different and in a matter of a mere fifteen seconds, really changed our lives. I quickly awoke to a sound of spinning tires as Dad had driven over a lengthy patch of black ice. I was lying on my stomach and within a split second, the car kicked to the side. Up front, Dad began trying to correct the steering while I laid in the back thinking that the car was out of control, violently jerking from one side to the other. I held on to the back of the horizontal seat as tight as I could, unsure of what was going to happen. Outside, the camp trailer whipped around and hit the side of the Blazer, causing it to bounce from side to side before rolling over onto its top. Now upside down, I held my death grip until we stopped sliding. The smell of burnt metal freshly ground into the wet pavement was a scent that I have never forgotten and I can practically smell as I write this.

After the car stopped sliding, I let go and fell to the roof. The only way out was to crawl through the broken glass that used to be the rear window. As I carefully crept over pieces of glass, I looked up and saw Mom sprinting south on the freeway where we started losing control. Off to my right, the camp trailer was unhooked and laying on its side about thirty feet from me. Dad was in the process of launching the propane tank over the bank so we wouldn't blow up. I stood up on the wet and cold pavement totally barefoot, trying to absorb what had just happened. Mom and Dad frantically looked around the road, the ditches, and on both sides of the debris. *What were they looking for?*

I don't remember any words said during or after the crash until they came to me and yelled, "Where's your sister?!"

I don't remember even answering them.

As a father now, I can only imagine what Dad must have felt like as he began crawling through the wreckage to find his daughter. But it had to be done. She was lying there in her sleeping bag, motionless, on what was left of the interior ceiling. Dad picked her up and hauled her out of the car. Then her eyes opened up, or should I say, then she woke up! How anyone could have slept through what had just happened, I'll never know—but she did.

Dad brought out my sleeping bag and told us to bundle together on the shoulder of the freeway. I just sat there and looked at the carnage, as Jen stared off in the distance. Here were four people stranded on the freeway about a half-hour north of the Washington state line. There were no lights other than the headlights that were still shining on the Blazer. There were no cell phones either. It felt like a month, but in actuality it was probably only about two minutes, before another car came up on us. It was two Asian guys, one of which thankfully had a cell phone, and they called 911. They even gave me and Jen food before they left, but who wants to eat after something like that?

It wasn't long until the flashing lights signifying help faintly began to appear in the distance. The state patrol and the ambulance pulled up to the crash site seconds later. They asked if everyone was okay and loaded us into the ambulance to get us off of the road and thankfully out of the dreadful cold. Mom was placed on a stretcher because her leg was bleeding but other than that, there wasn't a mark on any of us. After the cop won the "Asshole of the Year" and "Most Insensitive Prick Alive" awards for issuing Dad a citation, we sped off to the hospital, leaving everything else behind. As I sat in the front seat with the driver, I looked out the window and smiled because it was New Year's Eve, which traditionally has the highest crash rate of the year, and we were helping pad those stats. Not only that, but we were all going to live to tell about it.

The Blazer after rolling over on I-5

Exhausted, we all fell asleep in the hospital room and waited for Grandpa and Grandma to come down and get us. A few hours later, they arrived in their van, loaded us up, and took us to the wrecking yard so Dad could try to salvage what was left of our stuff. Everything was in pretty good shape. Our things that were in the car were wet, but otherwise okay. Aside from looking like a bomb had exploded inside the trailer, everything in there was also fine—even my guitar was in one piece!

Dad and Grandpa loaded everything up and we started for home. The roads were still shitty and it was beginning to snow again. We had been on the road for maybe an hour when all of a sudden the van began slipping and sliding. I thought for sure that we were going over again and would have to go through the whole routine again, but Grandpa was able to straighten it out. We made it home a few hours later.

Following this trip, our family began practicing a new set of rules. First of all, there were going to be no more winter trips. Secondly, and most importantly, there was going to be no more riding in any car without a seat belt. The stars were aligned just right that night. We used our "get out of jail free" card. We dodged a bullet. No matter which cliche you use, the bottom line was, we were lucky.

CHAPTER 16

Changes

Following the wreck, we were back to using the Oldsmobile as our primary means of transportation. Dad fought with the insurance company for weeks until they finally gave in and went well above what the car was worth based on its condition. Today with my cars, I take an updated picture of each one a couple of times a year after I detail them, from top to bottom and from inside and out, to avoid any prolonged corporate battles should one arise.

When the check came, Dad and Mom put the money down on a brand new Ford Explorer. With any new car comes the recalls and defects that are usually covered under warranty. This car, however, seemed to just have a little more. It seemed that Dad was always taking it back to the dealer for one thing or another, but most of the time it was for the transmission. It got to the point where Dad, the mechanic, and the owner of the dealership got into a shouting and swearing match that I sat ringside for. I don't remember the outcome, other than he was no longer welcome at that particular dealership.

When the Explorer wasn't in the shop and we were actually able to drive it, everyone who was in the car had their seat belts latched. Jen the tattle-tail would always point out that I was the last one to buckle up which, according to the new rule, meant that I owed everyone a quarter. I thought that the whole thing was stupid because, even if we hadn't left the driveway and I was still getting situated, I would have to pay because I was the last one buckled. Mom and Dad must have been giving her their money—why else would she be such a snitch?

As promised, after the whole car buying ordeal, I went to the eye doctor for a test of my eyes. Sure enough, I needed vision correction. Ever since Disneyland, I had tried to persuade my parents into letting me get contacts. I pushed and pushed until they agreed to let me give it a try. Mom was now working steady for the school district and her medical, dental, and vision benefits were pretty good to say the least. The insurance company would cover a pair of glasses or a six pack of contacts.

Learning to put the lenses in my eyes was a real treat. If you're not used to doing so, try sticking your index finger right onto the pupil of your eyeball. Your natural instinct is to flicker your eyelids but when your trying to stick a lens in your eye, you have to force yourself not to do it. When my lids did flicker, the lens flew right off of my finger and could land virtually anywhere. I think that finding a needle in a haystack may at times be easier than finding a clear plastic lens that is smaller than a dime. The worst part about losing one is the fact that you only have a matter of minutes until that thing dries out and begins to solidify.

Over the years, I have found them on the floor, the sink, the faucet, and my shirt. I have found them on the toothpaste container, my toothbrush, and on the toilet handle. I have found them on the bathroom door and on the hand towel—and that is just in the bathroom. I've had to search for those bastards anywhere that you could possibly imagine. More often than not, I have found them. Unfortunately, sometimes it wasn't until days or even weeks later.

When I first started learning to put them in, it would take about twenty minutes per eye. Within a week or so, I cut it down to around five. After a month, it was second nature and I could go days before I missed putting one in on the first try.

From then on, I had to be careful about rubbing or even wiping my eyes. If I didn't do it just right or if I did it once to often, one of them would spring free. If I had a bottle of saline solution with me, which was rare, I was fine. If not, I had to improvise. I would use water if it was available, but a lot of times it was my own saliva that I would use to moisten them up enough to put back in. If they fell out because my eyes were irritated from allergies or from just rubbing them too much, I would have to go without one for about twenty minutes until the redness went away before I could put it back in. Hopefully I had a place to store it in, but usually I would have to improvise again and use a cup, a pill bottle, or even a bottle cap to store it in. It is safe to say that over the years, I have mastered the art of contact lens usage.

Now that I had them though, I could see perfectly—no more squinting or just acting like I saw something. Everything was clear as a crystal and as sharp as a knife. I didn't have to worry about being a nerd with glasses, either. Actually, it would be another ten years before I was to get my first pair of glasses. Initially, I would wear them at the end of the day to give my eyes a rest. Five years after that, I started wearing them all of the time. It's been several years since I have had a contact in my eye and people might think that I am a dork, but I'm long past the point of giving a shit.

On the morning of January 27, 1993, Dad woke me up with the news that Andre The Giant had died of a heart attack at the age of 46. I had been around death before, but this was different. For the first time, I realized that the wrestlers that I idolized were not super-human. They breathed air just like you and me and they too will eventually die. Worse yet, it only just began a string of early deaths that still haunts the business.

In school, things were drastically changing. For the young author contest this year, I decided to write a short biography for whom I felt were the ten greatest quarterbacks in NFL history. I put a lot of research and effort into writing it but since it wasn't an actual story, I wasn't selected. The teacher said that if it had been an essay contest then I would have won, but it didn't change the fact that I got picked over for stories that were as interesting as a two year old reading excerpts from the bible.

The main change was in everyone's appearance. Some of the girls began to stretch the limits of their T-shirts with their developing chests. One girl even carried around a set of DD's—double delights! For the boys, it was arm pit and nipple hair, but most importantly, that all-important pubic hair. It may have only looked like a caterpillar lying perpendicular over my penis, but dammit it was hair!

With puberty running wild all over school and hormones beginning to rage like a forest fire, it was time for the entire fifth grade to be educated about sex. They weren't teaching us about the purpose and the pleasure, but rather the dangers and repercussions. The boys and girls were split up into opposite groups for the duration of the classes. We watched videos of people with HIV and AIDS and saw close-up still photos of people with visible signs of other venereal diseases covering their private parts. During some of the videos, to take our minds off of the disturbing images that we were seeing on screen, we would pass around drawings of stick-figured chicks with huge tits. Never being one of true artistic ability, my drawings merely looked like girls with an upside-down McDonald's Golden Arch hanging from their chests.

I'll never forget that when we all converged back into the same classroom, one of the girls asked me if I got a boner during the video. I simply replied "no," all the while wondering if she had watched the same tape I had or if she was just some sort of a twisted freak.

October 15, 2009. It has been one year to the day since I began writing this. Clearly I haven't gotten very far, but it hasn't been for a lack of trying. I was able to do quite a bit of writing over the winter months, thanks to our lousy winter. The spring and summer brought a lot of changes in their own rights, thus making it difficult to find the time to sit down and write. Hopefully I will be able to pick up the pace because at this point in the book, I'm just eleven years old—I've got another seventeen years to go to bring it up to date! So where was I? Oh yeah—changes.

Ironically, the biggest change that affected the family didn't occur at 709 Orth Way. A couple of mile up Highway 9, Uncle Robbie and his crew, which had now grown to four with the birth of their daughter, Torrie, packed up and moved over three hundred miles away to the Eastern Washington town of Springdale. Technically it is a town because it has a post office, but the reality is that, in addition to it, there is only a small convenience store, a K-12 school, and three taverns in it. Stranger still, it is every bit of a thirty minute drive to a town with a few more options in it. Any of the major stuff is over an hour away in Spokane.

There were several factors into their decision to move away, most of which revolved around Karen. There she would be closer to her parents, who lived just about five minutes away. Also the drier climate was much easier on her allergies. Having allergies pretty bad myself, I can certainly appreciate that as I can vouch for the difference based on personal experience.

The change hit Dad pretty hard. It was the first time that he and his brother lived that far apart from each other. They had lived together in numerous states growing up and within minutes of each other after leaving home, now things were going to be different. Instead of possibly seeing each other any day of the year, you could now count the number of annual visits on a single hand—and that would require a six to seven hour drive one way alone.

At first, right at once a month, either we would go over there or they would travel over our way. At the time, Uncle Robbie was seeing a surgeon at the University of Washington as the result of a shoulder injury. Several times a year he had to come back for checkups on the progress of his rebuilt ball and socket. Once the healing process was over, so too were their trips to this side of the mountains. These days, it may be just once a year that he comes over the pass.

We helped them load the moving truck with all of their stuff but didn't make the trip over to help them unload for reasons that I can't remember. Instead, we waited a couple of weeks to come over and check out their new place until we figured that they would be settled in. Up until then, all we had seen were pictures of a cute, secluded little log cabin-style house on nearly thirty acres of land. Their plan was to select log the property in order to finish the previously unfinished upstairs level of the house. Once completed, Tristan and Torrie would have their own bedrooms and there would also be a guest room. While the logging was done right away, it would be many years before the second level was done, meaning the kids resided in the living room—so too did their guests.

Our first trip over to their new house was our first long car trip since the big wreck eight months earlier. Albeit in the middle of summer and the chance of snow about as likely as the Seattle Seahawks winning a Super Bowl, the dramatic experience was still fresh in our minds and everyone was a bit nervous. It was just a natural feeling of insecurity, no different than anyone else in the world would feel if they too had gotten in a wreck. But if Dad, Jen, and myself were nervous, then Mom was hysterical. With the latter half of the trip being in the dark combined with the fact that towns on that side of the state are at least twenty minutes apart, street lights were virtually nonexistent. The only lights out there were those of oncoming cars. Mom would doze off a little bit and then jerk herself awake just in time to see the headlights of another car.

"Jesus Christ, Ronald—I see headlights!" she would cry out while trying to grab for the steering wheel.

"Relax Brenda," Dad would say. "Other cars are allowed to drive on the highway.

Not appreciating the humor of Dad's sarcasm, Mom would try to get him to understand that she was genuinely scared. Things did not change for the rest of our trips growing up. Although I haven't taken a car trip with Mom for ten or twelve years, I can safely say that she is probably still uncomfortable on long drives at night.

Our first trip over there seemed to take days. Not because of Mom's panic attacks, which were able to be controlled while traveling down the highway, but rather by having to stop practically every ten minutes for Jen to get out of the car and puke. It wasn't anything that she ate, it was just that she too was nervous on a car ride of that length with the aftermath of our accident still fresh in her mind. After a few trips back and forth, hers went away. For that initial trip, however, she spent more time gagging and heaving on the shoulder of the road than she did sitting in her seat.

We finally got there in one piece, which is really saying something because Uncle Robbie's quarter-mile driveway was so uneven and bumpy, I couldn't believe that the bolts on the

Explorer's frame didn't rattle loose. Believe me, I'm not exaggerating too much when I say that his driveway would present a problem for motocross riders. Once we stopped the car after our wild ride, their dogs ran out and greeted us as they would always do—by pissing on the tires.

Saturdays were always the funnest on our trips over there. After all, Fridays and Sundays were traveling days so the bulk of our activity was sandwiched in between the two. Now, what I'm going to talk about didn't all happen on our first trip. Although some of it did, most of it took place over the course of several trips.

With their upstairs section undeveloped, we had to sleep out in the living room, along with the Tristan and Torrie, on air mattresses and sleeping bags. Mom and Dad's mattress would go flat half-way through the night every single time. But it wasn't their grumbling about the sleeping arrangements that kept us awake, it was Uncle Robbie's snoring. People often joke about "sawing logs" when they snore, but this was ridiculous. Honestly, I have heard quieter engine breaks on semi trucks compared to the racket that he made. I had to go to bed before he did if I wanted to get any sleep.

In the mornings, if it wasn't the dogs barking at absolutely nothing that woke us up, it was Tristan. Always full of energy, he would be up and playing his Sega Genesis, the upgrade of the Nintendo, with the volume cranked to the max. He would then do his own commentary on his games and belt out his silly laugh that sounded just like Tigger from *Winnie The Pooh*—"Hoo-hoo-hoo-hoo!" The energy that he had built up inside him was so perplexed, it was often difficult to understand him. He would get so excited about something that he would stutter his words. Unlike most people who stutter slowly and drag out their sentences, he would stutter so fast that you would lose track quickly of what he was trying to say.

In addition to his stuttering problem, Tristan also had a swearing problem. While he held off on the F-word until he was ten or so, he was always saying "shit" and "dammit." His parents didn't encourage this, but they didn't discourage it either. They mainly ignored it, pretending that it didn't happen. One time, Karen was talking to Mom and Dad about his swearing and the fact that he was going to be starting school.

Listening in from the other room, Tristan hurried over to his mom and said, "You-you-you-you-you-you-you don't need to worry, Mama. I won't say goddammit, I'll say Jesus Christ instead!"

"That would be fine, sweetie," she replied.

He then headed back to his video game, shouting "Jesus Christ!" every time his player died.

After a breakfast that cardiologists would not believe, consisting of bacon and sausage and eggs that were fried in the pork grease, all four of us would instantly test the limits of their septic system. It's not that Karen was a bad cook—she wasn't. In fact, her food was really good. It just wasn't what we were used to, like any restaurant food would be for that matter. Haven't you ever noticed that when you eat at a place away from home, it isn't long before you have to go rest in the restroom?

Following our colon cleansing, the boys would head outside and usually shoot guns. Uncle Robbie had recently gotten into the rather expensive hobby of collecting guns. He had all kinds—pistols, rifles, shotguns, handguns, and machine guns. We shot at targets behind his house, or towards the highway in front of his house. I know that sound bad, but remember how long his driveway was? He was a long way from the highway. We didn't shoot to the left or right of his house because there were people living on each side. The left side in particular housed three male slobs that he called "The Bachelors." (Three guys living together—no girls—Hmmmm . . . .)

We would shoot for hours and hours, burning up tons of powder and never having a problem with the neighbors. We even got into what we thought was a contest with the people who lived to his right. After going through hundreds of rounds already, they started shooting louder guns. Never one to be outdone, Uncle Robbie would get out a louder gun and shoot back. Again, they would trump him.

"Fuck those guys," he would say. "I would like to see them beat my fuckin' AK-47!"

With that, he went into his house, brought out the gun, and sent twenty-five rounds into the dirt in less than two seconds.

"Beat that, cocksuckers!" he yelled as he went back into the house to put his assault weapon away.

As it turned out, they were shooting distress shots—at least that is what the sheriff said after he showed up in Uncle Robbie's driveway a short time later. Luckily the cop never saw the illegal guns. Although he never told us to stop, we figured that we had enough empty brass on the ground to satisfy any male ego.

The girls would go into Spokane shopping most of the time while we were shooting. They would come back and put the grocery bags inside on the kitchen floor because there wasn't any room on the counters. The bad part about that was, the kitchen floor was also where they kept their grocery bags full of garbage. I don't know how many times that I tossed garbage into a bag of fresh food. Most people who know me would say that something like that is not an accident, but it really was.

In the evenings, we would all go for a drive in Karen's Jeep Cherokee. And when I say all of us, I mean BOTH families. There were nine people in all, because Jake would come over with us for the first several trips, piling into a Jeep that was meant for six. Uncle Robbie and Karen sat in the front because they were the biggest (and I'm not talking about height), Mom, Dad, Jake, and me sat in the back seat, while Jen, Tristan, and Torrie sat in the cargo area. We looked like we belonged in a circus. But then again, we were in Springdale.

On Saturday nights, we always had tacos for dinner and man, were they good—and greasy. Between everyone, there were probably fifty to sixty tacos consumed in one sitting. All of the toppings were piled up on serving platters and they even would go through an entire five-pound tub of sour cream, most of which was used by Tristan. He would sit at the table, wearing only his underwear because he was such a sloppy eater, and stuff a taco shell filled with one bite of meat and about three tablespoons of sour cream into his face. Before he was done, his entire face was covered with sauce, his chest was splattered with sauce, and that one bite of meat that was in his taco was stuck in his bellybutton. He would then go straight to the tub to take a bath. When he got out, he would put on his trademark tighty-whities and not a stitch of anything else. I swear he would only put on regular clothes when he went outside, otherwise he paraded around in his shorts—and he did it for years.

After dinner, we would all gather around the TV and play video games. The most popular game for us was one called *Road Rash*, where street bikes raced each other around town trying to avoid cops and oncoming cars. You could pull up alongside another bike and punch him, kick him, or hit him with a chain in order to get him out of your way. We would have the greatest of times taking turns racing. It was just as much fun to watch someone else play as it was to play yourself.

As with everything, all good things must come to and end. Sunday was always a sad day. Nobody wanted to leave but once we were on the road, we had eight hours of talking and laughing about the weekend that was. Besides, it wouldn't be long before we went back again or before they would come over our way.

On Saturday, August 14, 1993, we went to the races at Skagit Speedway, like we did most of the summer weekends. As always, we got home around eleven or so. Mom always checked the answering machine when she came into the house (even if she just went out to check the mail), probably just to make sure that she didn't miss a call from Lisa. The message this time wasn't from Lisa, it was from Gladys. She was calling to tell us that Papa's only biological daughter, Becky, was killed in a car accident in California earlier in the day.

We quickly got back into the car and went up to Papa's. When we got there, Papa was at the kitchen table with his face buried in his hands, crying his eyes out. While it's not unusual to see a grown man cry over something catastrophic like that, it was the first time that I had ever seen him shed a tear. He didn't even cry when his mom died, so I didn't think that this big, honorary man even had tear ducts. I was proved wrong that night as I saw a father try to cope with something that no father should ever have to live through—the loss of a child. With me being a father now, I can't imagine the pain that he was feeling.

Right before school started, I took my last trip to Slide Lake. What was different about this trip was that Jen came along with Dad and I. The reason was, she was getting deep into gymnastics and most of her weekends were spent at competitions. That combined with football starting for me in the fall and Dad still working those occasional Saturdays, meant that any camping that was going to be done would have to be with both of us instead of one at a time.

Dad and me at Slide Lake

Going into my sixth grade year would be a positive change from my previous years in school. For the first time, I was going to have a male teacher overseeing the class. Mom had requested me to be put in a class like that specifically, knowing that it would be better for both my education and my behavior. So too did the other mothers of boys in my grade because there were going to be just five girls in a class full of boys. This set the stage for my final and most favorite year of elementary school.

PART II

THE TEENAGE YEARS

CHAPTER 17
Boys Will Be Boys

C AN YOU IMAGINE being a teacher that has to teach (and control) a classroom of over twenty boys and just five girls? Who would want to be in charge of that many boys who were eleven and twelve years years old, developing attitudes, becoming aggressive and confrontational, and each of them having an ego that was off the charts? Not to be sexist, but a woman, in my opinion, not only probably would not, but could not do it. You don't see female coaches with a team full of males do you? It would never work. Males relate better to male leaders, it is just nature. Men can relate to boys in way that women can't. To be fair, the same can be said for females teaching or coaching girls.

My teacher that year, Mr. Prange, had to take control right from the beginning and maintain it throughout the year and he did so in a rather unique way. At the beginning of each day, he would write a sentence on the white board. His sentences weren't your basic ten to twelve word sentences either, they were more like full paragraphs. For example:

I started today of on the wrong foot. Instead of behaving properly,
I took the low road and misbehaved. Obviously, I need a reminder
on how to behave in class. That is why I am writing this.

If he felt that you weren't behaving right, without even a warning, he would just look at you and give you a number. That meant that you packed up your stuff and went out into the hall and wrote the day's sentence until you reached the number that he said to you. You couldn't come back in the classroom, go to lunch, go to recess, or anything until you were finished. I should know, because I had to do it a lot.

As long as Mr. Prange was the one in charge, students didn't have to worry about notes or phone calls to their parents. It didn't matter if a fistfight broke out in the middle of class (which happened more than once), he would just remove the problem from the room. If a situation required a stiffer punishment, you would be confined to doing your assignments in the principal's office for a week at a time. But again, no parents would know, unless the principal got tired of seeing you in her office—or your mom worked at the school.

Mom's latest gig as part of the lunch program brought her right to my school once in a while. Of course every time that I was sent out to the hall for goofing off, Mom would see me sitting there writing sentences on her way to the office to turn in the meal money.

"Out here again, son?" she would sarcastically ask. "Why don't you just move your desk out here?"

I never had much of a response. What could I say? It never failed, I was always caught red-handed by my mother. She always knew that I had gotten in to trouble no matter what. On the rare times that she didn't catch me out in the hall, some dickhead would tell her at lunch that I had gotten into trouble. I would have had a much easier time sneaking an elephant into the building than I had of trying to keep things from Mom.

My trips to the hall probably occurred once a week but when Mr. Prange read *The Adventures of Huckleberry Finn* aloud to the class, I was sent out there every single day. Eventually, it got to the point where I would be sent out before he even opened up the book to begin reading it. Until that book was finished, I spent thirty minutes out in the hall each day after lunch, and all because of a single word. Written in 1884 by Mark Twain, the book freely spoke of black slaves as niggers. It wasn't a derogatory term then, it was just a word that was socially accepted. Slaves were called niggers, and thus just about every other paragraph had that word in it. What made it so funny was one particular kid's reaction to it.

Josh Williams was a kid who was renowned by people that I went to school with for his embellishing, to put it politely, of just about every event to ever occur in his life. Through the years, he would say things like how he was being recruited by major college football and basketball teams, his family was worth millions of dollars, he knew famous musicians personally—any preposterous shit that you can think of. Among them was his claim that his African-American father was the head coach of the Miami Hurricanes. Honestly, I don't think that he had ever met his father and it was just some sort of fantasy, but he rolled with that story until graduation. As far as the man being black, I have no proof that he was or wasn't, nor do I really care.

So me being the instigator that I was labeled as back in the third grade, naturally I had to stir the pot. Every time that Mr. Prange said the word "nigger," I would look over at Josh and give him a grin. You could practically see the steam shooting out of his ears as he would flip me off in retaliation. Another kid, Greg Mahle, who was ironically half-black himself as well as half-Indian, would help me out in the cause. For the first couple of days, Mr. Prange would catch Josh with his middle finger in the air and send him out in the hall. After about the third day, he would start taking him to the principal's office. With Mr. Prange standing by the door waiting for him, Josh flew out of his chair and actually challenged him to a fistfight right there in the middle of class. The whole class was laughing hysterically as the two marched to the office. It wasn't long, though, until Mr. Prange caught on to the fact that it was me and Greg starting the problem, which bought our tickets to the hallway and fifty sentences per day for the remainder of the story.

Once that book was finished, he read others like *The Outsiders,* by S.E. Hinton and *Hatchet,* by Gary Paulson. He also read some sleepers as well and although I wouldn't literally fall asleep during them, I would lounge back in my chair and space out a little bit. Others actually did fall asleep. Never missing a beat from his reading, Mr. Prange would slam his yardstick, that he carried around like a prison guard all day long, onto the snoozing kid's desk. The kid would shoot up like he had just been poked with a sharp stick and pay immediate attention.

My way of fighting off the grogginess that was brought on by some of his books was to lean my chair back on its back legs and put my feet up on the inside bars of my desk. If I was caught, and I usually was, I lost my chair for the rest of the day. If I wasn't caught and I leaned it too far back until I fell over backwards, I lost it for a week. I would then have to kneel on my knees to use my desk or sit on the floor and use a book to write on. As uncomfortable as it was, I guess that it didn't bother me enough to stop leaning in my chair.

It did make for a pretty fun game, however. Everyone thought that it was funny when someone lost their chair so to ensure that it would happen more often, kids that sat across from a chair tipper would lift the already elevated legs past the balance threshold and dump that person on their back. Or if another kid saw a chair tipper behind them, they would grab a hold of the back of their shirt and jerk them to the ground. Regardless of how it happened, the one on the ground was in trouble and was going to be without a chair for a while.

The best one ever was when Josh fell out of his chair and his desk followed him to the floor as well. Somehow he had gotten his coat that was draped over the back of his chair caught on a desk bolt. When he fell over, so too did his desk, which emptied itself of all of his books and pencils. Supplies were everywhere and here he was stuck on the ground because his coat was still hooked on the bolt. Mr. Prange helped him to his feet and then helped him move his entire desk out into the hall for the next week.

Once Mr. Prange identified the four or five of us that were causing all of these mysterious accidents, he isolated each of us to one side of the classroom. There we would sit, with nobody within ten feet of us, just so we couldn't cause as much trouble. Josh faced the closet by the front door, Greg faced the back wall, George Brookings faced the wall opposite of Josh, and my desk was directly in front of and facing Mr. Prange's. We would have those seating arrangements for the duration of the year.

Since moving to Central School a year earlier, football at recess wasn't really an option. There was only one field and it was never really able to grow grass because of all of the baseball games that were played during the year. So it was either go out and get muddy every day and have your mom yell at you for getting filthy, or play something else on the asphalt.

One game that we developed, improvised, adapted, or whatever you want to call it, was wall ball. Using just a tennis ball, players would scatter around about ten to fifteen feet away from the brick wall of the gym and throw the ball at it. The object of the game was to catch the ball off the bounce but if you didn't, you had to run and touch the wall before somebody could grab the ball and throw it back against the wall. If you beat the ball, you were fine, and the game continued. If not, the person whose throw beat you to the wall got a free throw at you while you stood face-first against the wall. The best you could do was just hope that somebody had bad aim and would miss you entirely, or at worst hit you in the butt. The game came to a permanent end when one kid got drilled in the back of the head and was knocked out cold.

After wall ball was terminated, we moved on to basketball. Now I hate basketball and to this day I have never watched one on television, but this was fun—at least every other day when Mr. Prange would come out and play too. The cool thing was, he was just as competitive as we were. If he was hot and was hitting every shot, he would rub it into the opposing team just like the rest of us.

"I'm thirty years older than you babies," he began. "Do you think that I should and play against the girls so I can get some real competition?"

Of course when he was off, we would fire it back in his face.

"Come on, old man. Can't you hang with a bunch of kids?"

In addition to our normal recess everyday, Mr. Prange would let us spend the last half-hour of school at least twice a week in the gym playing kickball or dodge ball. He would always play too, proving that boys will always be boys.

CHAPTER 18
Reasons to Kill

O N THE WEEKEND after my twelfth birthday, we went up to Papa and Gladys' house for a barbecue. They didn't live in the log house anymore, instead they lived in a large double wide mobile home on a two acre lot. The funny thing was, it was right next door to the log house. They literally moved three hundred feet from their old house.

On their new lot, Papa built a huge four wheeler track that went around the perimeter of the property. There were lots of trees and brush, making it look like taking a ride out in the woods. I put a lot of miles on his four wheeler over the years racing around his track. This weekend was no different, but my ride came to an end when Dad came out and told me to park the four wheeler because Papa wanted to talk to me.

"About what?" I asked, wondering what the hell I did wrong.

"I don't know," he said. "But you better go find out."

Great, I thought. Papa wasn't the kind of person that you wanted to piss off. If I did something wrong under his watch, he would angrily let me know. His bark was warning enough not to fuck with his bite.

I parked the four wheeler in the shop and made my way over to the house. It was like walking to the gallows as I made my way across the driveway. The only thing that I could think of that I had done was putting dog food in his boots one time too many. *There was no way that was it. He wouldn't be mad at that, would he? Wouldn't he have just gotten even instead? Besides, Dad did it too.* He would even add bark and gravel to the mix. As I stepped up onto the porch, I saw him standing with his hands behind his back and a scowl on his face. *Oh shit, here it comes.* But when I got right up to his face, his scowl turned to a smile.

"Happy birthday, Ed," he said, taking a rifle and a box of shells out from behind his back.

Papa giving me my first rifle

If anything came out of my mouth, it probably would have been "holy shit!" He was giving me a 30-30 lever action rifle. Now Dad had given me a pistol a few years earlier as well as a 20 gauge shotgun, but this was my first rifle. This was the big time. This was like the passing of the torch so to speak—the gates were now open to manhood.

The next weekend, Dad and I went up to the same gravel pit where we used to shoot pistols to try out my new gun. As cool as it was to have a rifle and even as grown up as I thought I was for having it, I was still concerned with how hard the recoil would be after I fired off my first round.

"If Papa heard that you were being a weenie about this, he'd probably want the gun back," Dad said. "It ain't going to hurt—now shoot."

I took aim at an empty beer box with a bright orange circle on it that Dad had spray painted upon it. I pulled the hammer back with my thumb and held the stock tight against my shoulder. Just before I pulled the trigger, I shut my eyes in preparation for the kick.

"Hey!" Dad yelled. "How in the hell are you supposed to see what you're shooting at if your eyes are closed? Keep 'em open, or don't shoot!"

So I tried it again. This time I kept my eyes open and fired. The recoil didn't hurt all that bad and I even came within a hair of the target. I shot four more times was all, but I hit the circle on three out of the five shots. I was comfortable shooting it and it was sighted in correctly, so there wasn't a whole lot of need to keep shooting. Besides, at about seventy cents per round, it could get costly in a hurry.

Less than a month later, deer hunting season opened up for its usual sixteen days in mid-October. I'd gone along for the ride on logging roads with Dad in the past few seasons, but that wasn't really hunting. It was more like driving in a car with a gun in the backseat, hoping by chance that a deer would walk out and just stand there and wait to be shot. It's not all that likely, but road hunting isn't necessarily a bad thing either. It gives you a chance to warm up after walking out in the cold and gives you a chance to have a snack as well. Most importantly, you can see which areas are most populated with game. The more tracks, shit, and broken branches seen in an area leading into a patch of timber indicate well-traveled game trails. While they may not be traveling at that moment, the fact remains that they are in the area.

On Sunday, October 25, 1993, Dad and I loaded up our guns in the Oldsmobile and headed out to some logging roads around Lake Cavanaugh, where Dad had job watched before. We drove for a while and got out and tromped through the brush for a while as well. I didn't have a strap to carry my gun over my shoulder like Dad did, so I just carried it in my right hand just like you would carry a large stick. I found myself always looking at the ground while I was walking, avoiding sticks and twigs and things like that that would make noise if I stepped on them. At first, I walked right next to Dad but after he got tired of me stepping on too many branches, he told me to follow him and step in the exact same places that he did. Looking back, that may not have been all that bright of an idea. Although the chances are rare, if I tripped and fell just right, Dad would have been turned into Swiss cheese.

Throughout the day, we would drive a half-hour, walk a half-hour, and so on. It was getting to be early afternoon so we started driving back down the gravel road towards the highway. About a mile or two from the pavement, somebody that Dad worked with passed us on his way up the hill. He said that he had just seen a couple of doe walking into the brush just back around the corner, causing Dad to want to hit the brush one more time before we left. *Damn!* I was so close to being able to go home. Now I had to put my orange vest back on, load my gun, and go out and get soaked some more. *Great.*

We weren't in the brush but maybe about five minutes, when Dad just happened to glance behind him to see how I was coming along and instead saw a deer.

"Eddie," he whispered. "There's a deer behind you. Turn around slowly."

I turned ever so slowly and sure enough, there he was. Believe it or not, he was following us. It just shows you how good of hunters that we were—the deer was stalking us!

"It's got horns," he continued. "It's a spike."

"Cool," I said. "Now what?"

"Shoot it."

"Shoot it?" I questioned.

"Yes. Shoot it."

"Where?"

"Right between his eyes."

I couldn't believe that this was happening. Even with us talking, this deer was continuing to walk right up to us. It was almost as if we were at a petting zoo or Yellowstone—this animal just didn't care. I slowly pulled my gun up and gently pulled back the hammer. Dad was doing the same thing behind me, but he was going to let me fire first. I lined up my sights and placed the bead of my rifle right between his eyes, which were now no further than twenty feet away. My heart was pounding and I was literally shaking in my shoes as I kept my eyes opened and focused. I took a deep breath and slowly squeezed the trigger—BOOM! Down it went. It didn't make a movement whatsoever, its knees just buckled and he hit the ground.

"Holy shit, you got him!" Dad yelled. "Jesus Christ, you killed him!"

I wish that I could tell you that I was just excited as he was. I wish that I could tell you that we both did back flips and popped open bottles of champagne to celebrate. I wish that I could tell you that. Instead as Dad drew his knife and hurdled over stumps in order to cut its throat, looking like Sylvester Stallone in *Rambo*, I just stood there and began to cry. Let's face it, I was still just a twelve year old boy and I had just killed a large, living animal. This wasn't a fly, a fish, a cat, or a bird, it was a 150 pound animal and I had just taken away the only thing that it had in this world to itself—its life.

After Dad cut its throat, he rolled it onto its back and sliced him open from the middle of its chest all the way down to its asshole. He then reached into the ribcage and began pulling all of its internal organs out. As the steam arose from the gut pile, I caught a whiff of the odor, so now I was upset and nauseous at the same time.

Knowing that I wasn't sharing in his jubilation, Dad looked up while he was field dressing and said, "Son, you didn't do anything wrong you know. It's okay for you to kill something for food or for survival. This animal is for us to eat. It is no different than a cow being killed—it's for food."

"Yeah, well I didn't kill the cow. But I killed this."

"And we will use it, just like a cow."

I knew what he was saying and my emotions were starting to change. I thought to myself that there probably weren't too many people who killed a deer on their first shot, on their first day of packing a gun, all the while only being twelve years old. Yeah, I did have something to be proud of!

The nausea came back a little bit as we drug the deer through the brush and back to the car. When Dad cut its throat, he cut all the way back to his spinal cord so, in turn, every bump that we went over, the head bounced in all different directions like one of those bobblehead dolls.

Most hunters drove pickups so they could just pitch their animals into the bed and not have to worry about blood or mud. Well, we were in the Oldsmobile, giving us a trunk as our way of transporting it home. Try to picture this—two people driving a car with the back end dropped like a Mexican low-rider and bloody hand prints on the trunk and bumper. We had to stop at stop signs and stop lights on the hour drive home and you know how people that pull up behind you always look at the back end of your car? What the hell was going through their minds?

When we pulled into the driveway, Mom came over from picking up leaves in the flower beds to see how things went. We were all smiles and asked her if she could open up the trunk for us so we could start unpacking. Knowing that something was up, she declined.

"I don't want to see it! I don't want to smell it! I don't want to eat it! I don't want to clean up the mess!" was all that she said before she turned around and walked into the house.

She didn't even wait around to find out which one of us that it was that did the shooting. To tell you the truth, I don't remember when she finally found out that it was me.

Me with my first kill hanging in the shop

I helped Dad skin it, saw it in half, and hang it up in the shop. A few days later, we butchered it. I helped him cut and wrap the portions to be put into the freezer. Because of the circumstances surrounding it all, only the two of us ate it so we usually had it on Tuesday nights as we watched John Wayne movies while Mom and Jen were at gymnastics. The meat lasted us almost a full year before we ran out.

I still have its horns, which aren't much bigger than my two middle fingers. I also still have the empty shell casing, as well as the bloody deer tag that I decided to keep for a souvenir instead of mailing to the Department of Fish and Wildlife. So whoever is in charge of the records, the 1993 census should have one more recorded deer kill on it—mine.

CHAPTER 19

Getting Color

J UST AFTER SPRING break, the entire sixth grade class went to spend five days and four nights at Camp Orkila in the San Juan Islands. There, we could study marine life, forest life, and plant life all in one spot. The boys and girls were split up and stayed a couple of hundred yards apart in several different cabins. Now being twelve and full of hormones, one could only imagine what it would be like if boys mixed with girls.

To prevent anything from happening, each cabin had a chaperone. That person had to control ten boys day and night—not easy. Even the chaperones had to sleep so to prevent anything from happening at night, teachers were on night watch at various places around the camp. Even a trip to the bathroom at midnight to have a bout of diarrhea, thanks to the wonderful camp food, would earn a few seconds of interrogation from a dark silhouette wielding a flashlight.

With it still being technically winter, the nights in the three-sided cabin were flat cold. Hoping to warm up with a hot shower was out of the question because there was zero hot water, so I refused to shower. So did everyone else, so you can only imagine the stench that came from the school buses on our way home. Mom nearly puked when she picked me up on Friday. Let me tell you, it felt great to take a nice, warm shower as soon as I got home.

When baseball season began a few weeks later, I went into it with the intention of it being my last year. The first three years were okay, but the previous year found me in the outfield exclusively. There were a lot of older kids on the team that were better than me at both hitting and fielding. I just wanted to have one more year with me being the older kid and getting a bit more playing time. I'm glad that I did because it turned out to be my best season ever, and it all just happened by a stroke of luck.

Height wise, I was literally head and shoulders above the other players. Just because of my height, our assistant coach, Landy Morgan suggested to our head coach, Larry Kilcup, that I should play first base. After my performance last year under Larry's guidance, I bet that if I had heard his response, it would have been, "Are you crazy? This kid's awful."

So here I stood at first base and I just began operating like a fine-oiled machine. I could stretch out just short of doing the full splits and snag a throw from the third baseman while my left foot remained on the bag to force out a batter. I could also reach up and pull down a would-be over throw from the second baseman. I never played another position again, unless you count the one inning at the end of the season when Landy let me pitch.

I only faced three batters. The first one hit my second pitch but was thankfully thrown out at first base. I went on to strike out the second batter, which surprised me more than the batter. The third, I hit square in the head with a wild pitch. I went back to first base permanently after the batter took his free base, ending my pitching career. I was satisfied, one strike out and no hits—not bad for 2/3 of an inning of work.

Not only was I excelling on defense, but I finished the season with over a .400 batting average that not only led the team, but was near the top of the entire league. I never hit a home run, but I had countless triples and doubles and minimal strikeouts. I had such a good year on paper that I was elected to the all-star team. I declined the invitation because the all-star tournament against surrounding towns began on Fourth of July weekend, and our family was already planning on being out of town in Lake Chelan for that week. That fat slob Buh-rorn took my spot, and the team finished one game shy of earning a trip to the West Coast tournament in California. I think that I'd like to have that one back but at the time, I didn't want to miss out on the trip.

Lake Chelan is a very large lake in the central part of the state that stretches some fifty miles from one end to the other. As large as it is, it barely registers on the North American atlas. Compared to the Great Lakes, it is a small puddle. Located in Chelan County, it is one of the most popular summer vacation destinations in the state.

We were going to stay in a rental house at the south end of the lake, about an hour north of Wenatchee. We weren't going to be staying in the house alone, as Skip and Lisa and their kids, Dan and Cori and their kids, as well as Dan's sister, Pam, and her son, Matthew, would all be staying there too. There was plenty of room because the house was two stories with about six bedrooms in it. There was little yard, but we weren't there to hang out in the grass anyway, we were there to do everything else. There were bicycle trails, fitness trails, tennis courts, miniature golf, and large open grass area for throwing a Frisbee or a football—and that was just on land. The water was the main attraction where we could swim on the beach, cruise on paddle boats, and water ski.

Dan and Cori and their crew towed their boat over and got there a day ahead of the rest of us. We left along with Skip and Lisa the following day. We had to tow Skip's boat over for him because he didn't have a vehicle to tow it with. (Good thing he had a boat, huh?) We stopped for breakfast in Wenatchee at, in my opinion, the absolute shittiest place to eat ever—Denny's. Their food is just so plain, with no flavor, and far from satisfying.

I don't even remember what I ordered but when the waitress asked everyone how they wanted their eggs, Skip and Lisa's son, Brent, looked her dead in the eye and answered in his low and dilatory voice, "Hard boiled."

The waitress glanced over at Lisa as if she was going to ask, "Is this kid really that stupid?"

"He means over-hard," she corrected.

Everyone laughed at the blunder, sending him into one of his trademark temper tantrums. He was one of those jerks that could laugh at anyone else, but nobody could laugh at him. It didn't help that his mom always, and I do mean ALWAYS, stuck up for him, no matter what he did. He would get so mad at the smallest things, usually brought on by himself, and he would take out his anger by pushing, scratching, or kicking the first person that he saw, which was generally me because I was always standing there laughing in his face. Then I would get mad and put him in a full nelson or something and tell him never to touch me again unless he wanted to die. After I let him go, he would turn on the tears and go whine to his mom. She would then storm in and start scolding me. Even my own mother never stuck up for me, I was always the bad guy.

To be fair, I can't say that I was always innocent. You may not believe this, but I occasionally did things to stir the pot. One time, I stuck a big wad of gum in his hair for really no reason other than to laugh at him until he cried. The laughter was elevated even more when Lisa thought that of all things, peanut butter would take it out so she wouldn't have to cut off some of his hair. So there he sat in a chair with his fists clenched and his lips pursed so hard that they were purple, while his mom massaged an entire jar of peanut butter into his hair. It didn't work and she had to cut his hair anyway. I earned my punishment for that one, but damn, it was worth it.

Anyway, after we left Denny's we drove the last hour to the lake. When we got there, we spent most of the early afternoon unpacking and settling in. We didn't go out on the boats until the next day. The rest of that day was spent checking out what all the resort offered.

The next day, everyone took turns water skiing. For those who couldn't, meaning us kids, we took turns taking lessons. I don't know if he volunteered or if he was volunteered, but Dad was the designated teacher. He ended up getting a bit of hypothermia from spending a couple of hours straight in the glacial lake. To this day when his hands or feet get cold, they turn a shade of yellow like a stick of butter. It took several attempts, but I was eventually able to get up on the skis. I couldn't do anything fancy like any of the adults could do, like dropping a ski and continuing on using only one, but I did alright. The hard part was leaning back just enough on the tow rope and keeping my legs shoulder length apart.

I had my share of crashes too, most of which would be caused by the wakes of passing boats. At first, I struggled with entering the wakes properly and one of my skis would always snag and I would crash on my face into the water. Brent did that on one of his turns and actually broke off one of his front teeth after his ski flew up and hit him in the face. (What a shame.) My worst crash was caused from me leaning too far back on the rope. I tried to correct it, but I ended up scooting on top of the lake, spreadeagled, and literally giving myself an enema.

Water skiing was alright, but inner tubing was by far the best part of the trip. These tubes weren't your basic tire inner tubes, these were made with handles and materials designed to skiff around on the water. Somewhere along the way, somebody got the idea to lay down on their belly and try to do a barrel roll while riding over a wake and manage to stay on the tube without falling off. I wasn't the first to do it, but I was the second. It got more extravagant as the days went on. First, it was one roll, then it was two consecutive rolls, then it was rolls with two people riding on the same tube, and finally it was synchronized rolls with guys on separate tubes being towed by the same boat. Real safe, huh?

Of course, the crashes were the highlights of the whole experience. Sometimes the rider would catch so much air that they would get thrown from the tube and fly over the water like an eagle in search of a fish. Bloody noses, split lips—it was all worth it. Dad's crash went down in history and somewhere there is authentic video evidence of just what happened.

Let me back up just a little bit to set the stage a little better. Before we left for the trip, Mom bought everyone new swimsuits. For some reason, Mom bought Dad and I matching trunks. She always bought us matching shirts or shorts if we both needed them at the same time. I thought that it was cool to look like Dad at first but the older I got, I found it embarrassing. I didn't want to look like his twin. Anyway, his trunks didn't have a drawstring. Either somebody pulled it out while they were on the sales rack or they just didn't have one put in them originally. Simply put, he couldn't tighten up his drawers.

During one of Dad's turns on the tube, which just happened to be being filmed on a video camera, he attempted to do his barrel roll. He didn't make it. What happened instead was, while he was in the middle of his roll and scooting along on his back, he shorts came completely off. Now the boat is probably going at least thirty miles per hour and by the time that he realized what had happened and he let go of the tube, he was quite a ways ahead of his trunks. Dan, who was driving the boat, saw that he fell off and circled around to pick him up. Once we pulled up to him, we noticed that he was swimming frantically away from the boat towards a floating object several yards away. Dad was wearing a life jacket which kept him above water, showcasing his doughy, white ass for everyone to see. After this incident, he named his shorts "The Automatics" for obvious reasons. The highlight of that evening was watching the film footage over and over at least ten times straight.

A couple of days later, everyone who wanted to was given the opportunity to parasail over the lake by a boat that was operated by the resort. The ride lasted maybe five or ten minutes, but it was cool being up really high in the air and checking out all of the views of the lake from above. I would say that each sailor was every bit of a hundred to two hundred feet in the air. It was certainly a lot easier doing that then it was skiing. The only bad part was that you didn't even touch the water. They just sent you out and reeled you in from the back end of the boat.

After nearly a week of constant sun exposure, everyone became much darker. Dad didn't wear any sunscreen throughout the week because he wanted to "get some color." That idea sounded good to me, so I followed suit. Boy, was that a bad choice.

Apparently neither one of us learned our lesson about a month or so prior to the trip when the four of us went to the water slides in Birch Bay, about five minutes down Interstate 5 from the Canadian border. It was there that we got seared from the sun so bad that I personally couldn't wear shoes for a week due to the blisters that I developed on the tops of my feet. After that, I always put sunscreen on my feet—just not anywhere else.

By the end of our week in Chelan, I was burnt so bad that I felt like I was in an oven at all times. Cori told me that aloe would cool and soothe my skin in seconds. This sounded great, so I lathered myself up from head-to-toe and waited for that much needed sense of relief. It never came, instead I broke out in hives and started itching like crazy.

"You can't be allergic to aloe," Cori said. "Nobody is"

"I don't know, but I gotta get this stuff off!" I shot back as I ran to the closest shower.

God, did that ever hurt, standing there under hot water and scrubbing that shit off. The itching went away as soon as I got out of the shower, but the burning sensation was still there. She brought over another bottle of some sort of moisturizer for sensitive skin.

"Try this," she said, handing me the bottle. "Don't worry, this stuff has no aloe in it."

So I lubed myself up with this new stuff and within seconds, I'll be damned if I wasn't wanting to tear my skin off again. Back into the shower I went to scrub it off again. When I got out, I walked right back into the living room and grabbed the bottle. Aloe wasn't listed in the official ingredients but just under that in real small letters, it stated that "this product may contain traces of aloe." It was a very uncomfortable way of finding out that I was allergic to an African flower that was supposed to soothe skin. From then on, just like anyone with an allergy, I have to look at any lotion or soap that I put on to make sure that I don't go through that hell again.

By the end of the week, everyone was ready to go home. You learn a lot about people after spending night and day with them for a week straight. While I didn't really get into the differences from an adult perspective, I knew that I really couldn't stand the other kids there. Brent and his sister, Brandy, were both whiny brats. Dan and Cori's son, Galen, was fun to be around, but he was only about five fears old. Their daughter, Sarah, was alright too, but she only hung out with the girls. Their cousin, Matthew, was a loner, so I didn't hang around him at all.

Several years later, he wound up hanging himself. I remember that Mom and Dad tried to force me to go to the funeral, but I refused. I felt that if he didn't have enough respect for himself and his family by committing suicide, why should I show him any respect and go to his funeral? I felt the same way about the three or four other kids that I went to school with that did the same thing over the years. I feel the same way about celebrities and sports stars that do it—pro wrestlers included. I understand that tragedies or a lack of acceptance can cause people to lose their willpower and hope and therefore resort to desperate measures and maybe I haven't experienced it myself on a high enough level, but I just can't see myself doing that to solve a problem. I couldn't put my family through the pain just to ease mine.

Okay, back to the trip. All in all, it was a pretty good time—good enough that we would all go together again the next two summers. Although I may use this analogy again later on, it was kind of like a movie that has one or two sequels—they usually don't live up to the quality and expectations after the success of the original.

I personally began spending less and less time with the group, mainly because I was sick of getting into trouble for shit that I didn't start. During the summer, Mom and Jen would go to Skip and Lisa's to swim in their pool. Occasionally I would go, but more often than not I would just stay home and mow lawns, watch wrestling, or listen to some tunes.

A couple of weeks after we got home from Lake Chelan, the blisters from my sunburn finally went away. It was slow healing because I would scratch the sores until they bled. At first it felt good, and then it became painful, but I couldn't stop because it constantly itched. I had to be outside constantly because by now I was mowing six to seven yards, so it prolonged the process.

My hard work paid off in early August when, just a month short of my thirteenth birthday, I bought my very first motorcycle with my own money. It had been some time since I last rode the 50 due to my size, which was getting me close to passing Dad's height. With this bike, I no longer looked like a circus stuntman. It was a red Kawasaki 100 that was both street and trail legal. It was a 1974 model that came with a load of extra parts, including an extra fuel tank, motor parts, and maybe even an extra seat if I remember right. I paid three hundred dollars for it from a guy that lived two houses over from us. Dad and I had been scanning the classifieds for months looking for something that would be good for me. Just by luck, the neighbor was having a garage sale one day and he had it out in his yard with a for sale sign on it. It couldn't have worked out better. I hopped on that thing and hit the church field until I ran out of gas. It felt good to be riding again and at the same time, it felt just a little extra special because it was purchased entirely by me with my own money.

Me on my second motorcycle

A few weeks later, Dad had a great idea to ride it together up in the woods to go camping overnight. The bike was okay with just me but with two of us and gear, it was back to a circus act. We made it about eight miles up the highway before the spark plugs got so caked-up from running so hard that the bike died. We took turns pushing it to the nearest gas station so Dad could call a friend of his to load us up and take us home.

After that experiment, I had to clean the spark plugs every few weeks to keep it running well. Sometimes it was hard to start, so I relied a lot on starting fluid—that is until it caught fire with me straddling it. The blaze only lasted about two seconds and did zero damage, but anybody watching would have laughed hysterically after seeing me jump off the bike and try blowing it out as if it were just a match.

That wasn't the only mishap that happened during my first month of ownership. Grandma and Milt were staying with us for a few days after coming out from Las Vegas. I was showing off (as usual) out in the church field when I got the idea to ride underneath their volleyball net. I figured that if I got low enough, the net would just brush along my back. Instead, my handle bars got caught in the net. The worst part was, both of my hands were pinched between the grips and the clutch and brake levers. The engine died and I just sat there like a huge fish, unable to move. Dad took his sweet-ass time coming over to untangle me just so he and everyone else could get a good laugh. That was the end of my motorcycle stunts.

In late August, we made our last regular visit to Skagit Speedway as a family. We would go very sporadic over the course of the next couple of years, but this ended our weekly run. It was the biggest event to ever come to the area, featuring the best sprint car drivers from around the world who traveled around the country and raced local talent. Known as the World of Outlaws, they were the sprint car equivalent to NASCAR coming to Alger. For you non-racing fans out there, it would be like the NFL's Pro Bowl or Major League Baseball's All-Star Game, each on a traveling tour of the country.

The World of Outlaws became a traveling series in 1978, stopping annually at Skagit Speedway. But as the sport got bigger, the Pacific Northwest got the snub for over twenty years. Their schedule featured over sixty races each year, covering nearly all of the other states in the country. They finally returned to our area on August 26 and 27, 1994. Only a few of the local guys could keep up with them. They shattered track records by nearly a full second. They drove flawlessly against each other at over 120 miles per hour. Over ten thousand people attended the show each night, not one leaving unsatisfied.

CHAPTER 20

Champions of Our World

H AVE YOU EVER felt like you could literally take on the entire world or accomplish the most physically demanding task ever devised? If you answered "yes," then ask yourself the question again, and be sure that you don't include the times when you were under the spell of the false courage of drugs or alcohol. If you're telling yourself the honest truth, then you can probably count those instances on a single hand. I personally have legitimately felt that way just twice in my life. The second came several years later, but the first happened every Saturday for about eight weeks.

In the late summer of 1994, I began my fourth and, as a team, my most successful season of football. Every week was full of controversy due to my nearly six foot, 150 pound body. Before every game, I had to strip down to my underwear to make the 150 pound weight limit. I also had to carry my birth certificate with me each week to prove that I was thirteen or younger. I swear to God, most referees and coaches thought that I was in high school but little did they know, I had only just begun junior high. Dad even had to come into the locker room with me to say that I was legal. I'm not sure what good that did because by now, I was as taller than he was.

Grandma, me, and Grandpa before a football game in Mount Vernon

The team was pretty much the same as it was two years earlier, guided once again by Dale Wicker. The year before, he had stayed with the midget group while half of us went up to the junior division. Now we were all back together again and joining him was the president of the whole Sedro-Woolley organization, Ron Russell.

Ron was one of the greatest human beings that I have ever had the privilege of meeting. While I respected all adults to a certain extent, very few did I have unlimited respect for. Today, not many people get that from me as I can see right through people. As an athlete, Ron made you feel good about yourself while at the same time pushing you to do better. He had a unique passion, not just for the game, but for the performances of the participants. He was such a great motivator that he could push you to what you thought was the limit of your soul, find a little something extra, and then crest the highest peak. It wasn't something that was just saved for game day, it began at turnout.

The biggest and most important thing that we learned was discipline—as in self-control. Both coaches demanded perfection, not in performance, but in execution. Obviously every play wasn't designed to score points, but rather to just keep advancing the ball down the field. If we ran every play as it was designed and everyone did their job correctly, we would be successful—and it all started with the snap count.

The snap count is the only true advantage that the offensive line has over the defensive line. While the defense must watch the ball until it is snapped before they attack, the offense knows exactly when the ball is to be snapped and thus has just a split-second advantage. It took a lot of work to get it right, believe me. Night after night during turnout, we would line up to run a play and somebody would jump early, which is called a false start. Then everybody on offense would have to run a lap while the defense just sat back and watched. While we were running our lap, we would cuss out the perpetrator, not necessarily belittling him, but rather humbling him just enough to light a fire inside him to get it right. If he did it twice in a row, forget about it—he was in deep shit.

With me being the center, if I snapped the ball too early, the offensive line would take off but the quarterback would likely drop the ball and really foul things up. To add insult to injury, his hands may not be ready and in position, causing me to slam the ball directly into my nuts. To make it worse yet, I would have to run a play in complete agony. So it was ultra important for me to get the count right.

Forgetting the snap count is easy to do. In the huddle, the quarterback says a series of numbers, colors, and letters that each indicate a scheme for the line, the backs, and the receivers. At the very end, he will say the count and break the huddle. As the line jogs to the line of scrimmage, each person reminds themselves of their responsibilities based on the numbers, letters, and colors, thus making it very easy to forget about the last but not least part. The whole thing can only take thirty seconds from the end of the last play, to the huddle, to the call, then to the line and finishing with the snap of the ball. Usually if anyone forgot, they would quickly ask before we lined up on the ball to avoid a lap during turnout, or an ass-chewing during the game. When I forgot, the quarterback would not-so-gently press his knuckles against my nuts to give me a reminder that he wanted the ball right then. Sometimes he even did that because we wouldn't have a snap count and we would just set and go, totally catching the defense off guard.

I better explain the testicle issues real quick. You're advised to, but not required to, wear a cup over your goods. I never did and most players don't either, even in the NFL, because it is so darn uncomfortable. It leaves rashes on each side of your package from its edges rubbing against your crotch while you are running. Combine that with the salty sweat and the eventual open sores, you're going to walk around like you have something stuck between your butt cheeks. I decided to take my chances. The damage must not have been too severe because they still work.

In addition to our plays during practice, we would collectively practice snap counts as a team during our wind sprints at the end of each turnout. We would all line up and Ron would go through a cadence as if he was a quarterback and we were all down linemen. He would say that the count was on "B" for instance, and we would all wait for his big, booming voice to get us going.

"GO!!"

Hopefully nobody moved, but you couldn't blame them if they did.

"Forty-five. Set. Blue. HIKE!!"

By now, somebody was sure to move and we would have to run a lap before starting over.

"GO!! Thirteen. Red, sixty-one, HUT! Blue, hut, HUT! Seven, twelve, black-eighteen, GO! Set, red—B!"

We would do this to begin our forty yard sprints and turnout would not be over until ten snaps were completed flawlessly. Sometimes it took an hour but by season's end, it only took ten times.

We would always end turnout with Ron giving us a motivating speech about our upcoming game. Some coaches you can look right through and see that they are only saying things because they have to, but not Ron—it came from his heart. He believed in us and he wanted us to believe in ourselves even more. We, in turn, would want to do nothing short of making him proud. He must have known what he was doing because we didn't lose a single game that season and won the league championship. Four years later with a different coach but the same players playing the same opponents, we rarely won. It's no coincidence, folks.

Our biggest and most dominating victory came mid-season against Stanwood. The opposing coaches just plain didn't like each other and we were told to beat the living shit out of them, but legally. By halftime, we were up 40-0. We didn't let up and in the second half, we actually outscored ourselves. The final score was 82-0.

Not all of our games were shutouts, some were actually pretty close. Some we even trailed in the fourth quarter but with one of Ron's speeches during a timeout that pierced into our veins like an adrenaline needle, we battled back and took the lead no matter what. If we needed two touchdowns in two minutes—so what—our offense scored, the defense would get a takeaway on their next possession, and our offense would march right back down and score again. There wasn't anything that could stop us.

Both coaches never let a single player take credit for anything. Without the other ten teammates involved in the play, he wasn't shit. If one of the linemen missed a block, the running back wouldn't have gotten those sixty yards. Yeah, the quarterbacks, receivers, and running backs get all of the statistics, but they couldn't do it without a good offensive line. Casual football fans know Peyton Manning, Jerry Rice, LaDanian Tomlinson, and Boomer Esiason, but how good would they be if it wasn't for Jeff Saturday, Harris Barton, Alan Faneca, or Anthony Munoz? Only people that know the game know the answer.

After each victory, which was each game, Ron bought us either pizzas or full hamburger and French fry meals. Now the tab on that has got to be pretty high and Ron wasn't a rich man. Though it eventually got him banned from the league, the money came from bets that he made with opposing coaches. Most people might think that it is wrong to bet on kids' games but if the money was spent on us who were doing the winning, what's the big deal? So what if he bet a hundred bucks a week on us, just how much do you think that it costs to fill up 30, thirteen year old kids? I didn't have a problem with it then and I don't now. If he stuffed the money in his pocket for a bottle of booze for himself, then it's a different story. None of that ever happened and as far as I'm concerned, his banishment from the sport only ruined the opportunity for future players to be coached by a great leader.

CHAPTER 21
Brace Yourself

As I BEGAN the seventh grade in the fall of 1994, I was moved to another school—the middle school. In middle school, you have thirteen to fifteen year old kids who want nothing more than to be accepted by their peers. Everybody has to be cool, do the coolest things, wear the coolest clothes, and have the coolest hair. But who is the one that decides what is cool and what is not? I don't know but if you do, don't bother telling me—because I don't care. I suppose I went through middle school not being cool because none of that shit appealed to me.

Starting at the top, it was the hair. All of the alleged cool guys bleached their hair yellow. They looked more like a Q-Tip that had just been pulled from someone's wax-encrusted ear. When that phase ran its course, it was shaving your head completely bald. And every "cool" kid did it within a week of each other. I just stuck with a plain old haircut, I didn't have a style.

Next came the clothes. Guys would were anything from sports-themed T-shirts and jeans to stupid looking khaki dress pants and a sweatshirt. Other guys would wear grungy clothes that came from the store with holes and bleach stains in them. The "cool" thing was to have saggy pants that were kept up by a belt that was placed purposely below your ass, exposing a pair of scroungy boxer shorts. I stuck with my T-shirts and Levi's.

Finally it was the shoes. All of the "cool" kids had to have a hundred or even two hundred dollar pair of shoes. What the fuck for? Do they really make you run faster, jump higher, and look cooler? Whatever. I had twenty or thirty dollar Spalding or Riddell shoes that lasted for the whole year, kept my feet dry, and didn't give me blisters. I was comfortable. Maybe I wasn't cool to everyone else, but I had something that they didn't have—a personality. We might as well have been going to school in a barnyard because most of the kids were nothing but sheep.

I almost forgot about the girls. By now most of them were shaping up quite nicely, if you know what I mean. Now granted, rules were established for preventing too risque styles of clothing from being on display and while some girls pushed it to the limit, other girls covered everything and wore all black. When it came to make-up, girls wore none at all or caked it on so thick that they must have had to remove it at night with sandpaper. The eyeshadow they piled on looked like their parents took turns punching them in the face before they left home. As for the blush and lipstick, it looked like someone shot them with paint balls. While I enjoyed looking at pretty girls just as much as the next person, there wasn't too many choices. I would like to have met someone in the middle, but there wasn't any yet.

It was interesting to sit back and watch people trim themselves to fit the world while whittling themselves away. I found out who my true friends were and which people to stay away from as they strayed off. Hopefully, people headed down the wrong path would find their way back. It took a while, but most did. Others were never seen or heard from again. I feel that between seventh and tenth grade, you better get all of that shit figured out or else it's going to be a long trip home. By now, most kids had tried smoking cigarettes or marijuana. I didn't (and still haven't) for the simple fact that I absolutely hate the smell—never mind the fact that continuous use makes you rely on it just to function during each day. Then in the end, you get rewarded with cancer. I'll pass. And while drinking alcohol and having sex hadn't begun just yet for everyone, it wasn't very far off.

On September 11, 1994, my thirteenth birthday, I watched and rooted against the 49ers for the first and last time ever. They traveled to Arrowhead Stadium to play the man that led them to four Super Bowl titles, Joe Montana, and the Kansas City Chiefs. It was the first and only time that Montana would face the team that traded him almost two years earlier. Like most fans, I was still bitter over the trade but at the same time, I understood that pro football was just as much a business as it was a sport. It makes perfect sense to get money or draft picks out of a star player while he still has some gas in the tank. That said, I cheered the Chiefs on to a 24-17 victory.

The 49ers bounced back though, as I knew that they would. Four months later, they beat the San Diego Chargers 49-26 on January 29, 1994 at Super Bowl XXIX in Miami. The victory not only was their fifth in as many tries over the course of fourteen years on football's grandest stage, but it also earned me well over fifty dollars off of various bets that I made with some of the guys in school. They haven't been back since but, even though I've told myself this for over fifteen years now, there's always next year.

The day after my birthday, I got to get out of school early and miss a few hours of work. For most, it would be something to be excited about. For me, however, it was nowhere near exciting—I was going to be having braces affixed to my teeth. My teeth weren't really all that bad but Mom had such good insurance working with the schools, it wouldn't cost an astronomical amount of money for me to have perfect teeth. Although I was against it, deep down I knew that they would be fools as parents not to take advantage of it. Still, they weren't the ones that had to have a bunch of metal in their mouth and have to go and get them adjusted every few weeks. All I wanted to know, was just how long they had to be in my mouth.

"Less than two years," the orthodontist said. "Probably 20 to 22 months."

Just fuckin' great, I thought. I almost said it, but Mom was in the room so I opted for, "How often are you right with your predictions?"

"Ninety percent," he guessed.

That was good enough for me. While I wasn't happy about the nearly two year sentence, I could live with the fact that it wouldn't be any longer than that. I mean, nine in ten is great odds—I would take a bet like that any day of the week. As my luck would have it (probably because it was around my birthday), I ended up being in the tenth percentile. When it was all said and done, I would have them on for two weeks shy of three years. Thanks Dr. Engst, you jerk!

In order to be able to cement a bracket to each of my teeth, my mouth had to be totally dry, which isn't possible because of the mouth's natural salivation. To counteract this, they stretched out my lips as far as possible—and a little more. (Try to imagine four hands stretching your mouth in all four directions and holding it for thirty minutes.) Then they blew forced air into my mouth to immediately dry any saliva. After a couple of minutes, they cemented one bracket to each of my teeth and then took a tiny wire and used rubber bands to attach them together. When they were finally finished and able to release my lips back to their normal position, they were totally numb and looked like a worn out piece of elastic. I looked like one of those Ethiopians that pierce a hole in their lip or ear and stick a disc in it in order to stretch it out.

My mouth did nothing but bleed for two months straight. The cuts would turn into sores and would rub on the brackets every time my jaw moved. Just when one would heal, another one would turn up and start the process all over again. It did get better after a while when the inside of my mouth toughened up. Once that happened, I would almost have to be punched in the mouth for it to bleed. When it came to eating, certain foods were off limits. I couldn't have hard candy (which I never cared for anyway), corn-on-the-cob, or certain meats—unless they were cut into pieces that wouldn't even make a toddler choke. I also was advised not to drink pop unless it was through a straw.

I followed their guidelines for the most part because I found that it was easier if I took their advice. I must have done alright because I only broke one bracket in the time that I had them on. If I ate a steak, it would take probably five minutes to floss what was left of it out of my teeth. The corn I would cut off the cob to eat, still leaving it with that distinctive taste that isn't found in the can. But when it came to pop, I refused to drink it through a straw.

Mom packed me a Diet Pepsi (which I hate) every day in my lunch. Right next to the can though, was a straw—she couldn't forget that. At first I threw the straw away and drank it like a normal person, refusing to look like a three year old in the cafeteria. A couple of weeks later, out of the blue, Josh Williams asked if he could buy my pop from me. I wasn't really interested until he flashed his entire two dollars worth of lunch money, then I couldn't resist. From then on until the end of the year, I ran my own pop distribution business, selling my can to the first kid who threw his two bucks my way. I bet I pulled in three hundred dollars over the course of the year.

At the middle of each month, I would get out of school maybe an hour or two early and Mom would take me to Mount Vernon to get my hardware adjusted. For this, they would cut off the bands, put on a thicker wire, and and them back up. Every month, I would ask them to put on even thicker wires.

"Your teeth would hurt too much," they would say.

"If it knocks off a few weeks, let 'em hurt," I replied.

They said that they could up it a little bit, but they must have lied and never did it—why else did I have them on for so long?

When it came time to band them up, I was able to pick the colors. It may sound silly, but I would do orange and black for Halloween, red and green for Christmas, and red, white, and blue for the Fourth of July. I even did red and gold for the NFL Playoffs, showing my 49er pride. Surprisingly, nobody made fun of my corny little game, nor did they call me "brace-face" or "railroad mouth"—at least as far as I knew.

Now that elementary school was over, I no longer had just one teacher all day long. The day was separated into six periods, seven if you count homeroom, all of which had different teachers. I take that back—my first and fourth period classes had the same teacher. This was called core class, which was language arts, history, and reading all rolled into one. There was also a period of each of science, health or P.E. that alternated quarterly, math, and an elective, which was a quarter of each of, computers, reading comprehension, art, and wood shop.

I was straight A's all year, except for a couple of B's in math. This was the first year that I somewhat struggled enough to where I had to do constant homework and studying to maintain my grades. I was one of maybe two or three seventh grade kids amongst a class full of eighth graders in a course called pre-algebra. While I was doing better than most of them, I still had to work hard. I would bring home worksheets and do them every afternoon. Mom would grade them with the answer key because she didn't have the slightest idea how to do it. Dad tried to help, even bringing out his log scaling book for some reason, but he was not much use. I was pretty much on my own with this stuff.

When it came time for tests, I was a wreck—and that wasn't like me. I rarely studied for any tests in other subjects and couldn't care less that I had to take them. I dreaded these. When I found out on Monday that there was going to be a test on Friday, I would have diarrhea until test day and then continue to have it until it was graded. On some of these tests, I saw letters that I had never seen on the tops of my papers before—C and D. If I got a D, my only hope was that every other kid in the class did about the same, which would mean a redo. More often than not, that was the case and I would get at least five or ten percent higher on the second time around.

Seventh grade was the first and only year that I took a keyboarding class. The teacher taught the importance of posture as well as the proper way of typing. I passed all of my skills tests correctly because I had to. Once that class was over for me, it was back to "hunting and pecking," which is just plain old, two-fingered typing. The only reason that I took computers in the first place was that I had to in order to take the class that I really was looking forward to—wood shop.

Wood shop was the class that I tried the hardest to perfect. I would only pick wood that had no knots in it at all, which was difficult to do because the school only received rejected maple planks from saw mills. I would sand every piece more than perhaps I needed to so that it would be as smooth as silk. It would take several weeks for me to make a single project, but the proof was in the pudding.

Over the course of the two month class, I made a sign board with my name on it, which Mom thought was an insult because she was wanting one to put on the front door. I figured that I would make one like that later but in the meantime, I wanted to make one for the foot of my bed. With the sign reading "Eddie Thramer," other kids got quite the laugh writing notes on the drying paper that it laid on over night each time it was either, painted, stained, or varnished. Next to it, some clown would write "is gay," "likes boys," or "sucks dick." At least they didn't write it on my board, I guess. While I can't confirm it, I'm pretty sure that it was Greg Mahle, who was in shop later in the day. I can't blame him, I would have done the same thing to him if I knew what he was making. I also made a CD rack for my increasing number of albums, a hand mirror for Mom, a napkin holder for the dining room table, and a gun rack for Dad. They weren't perfect because I was still learning to operate a jigsaw, band saw, and a router, but it was a foundation for what was to come later.

Although it was only every other quarter, it was great having P.E. everyday. We would change into our workout clothes, that we kept in the lockers that we had for the duration of the quarter, before we would hit the gym. The idea was to take them home at the end of the week and wash them, but some kids never did. About a month into the course, the locker room would smell like a dead fish. I got fed up with one particular kid and threw all of his shit in the garbage when he accidentally left his locker open one afternoon. I pleaded my case, but received a discipline notice for it anyway.

I was awarded another discipline notice in P.E. for making one of the most amazing shots ever, the problem was it wasn't on the basketball court. There were always small jokes being pulled in the locker room like switching locks, tying shoelaces together, and crap like that. I forget who it was but somebody (probably Greg) tied my laces together in no less than thirty knots. When I saw this, I just picked up the nearest shoe and threw it into the shower area, which nobody ever used because nobody wanted another guy to see their pecker. The shoe hit the handle and knocked it to the floor, which somehow caused the water to turn on. The shoe then landed right in the middle of the stream of water, thoroughly soaking it. The owner of the shoe wasn't too happy because he had only one shoe for the rest of the day. I was completely amazed because I couldn't have made that shot again in a million tries, but I was written up for destruction of property.

During P.E. itself, we would play seasonal sports like baseball, basketball, soccer, and even wrestling. I hadn't wrestled since the afternoon that I told Dad that I didn't want to do it anymore. After a couple of weeks of wrestling in P.E., I pinned the school's varsity 175 pounder. I told Mom and Dad about it and they suggested that maybe I should turn out for wrestling. That year was out of the question because at the time, the season only had a few weeks left in it. I would have to wait until next year, which would also give me time to decide if it was something that I really wanted to do.

The most time during the school day each day was spent in core class, which remained constant all year. Our teacher, Mrs. Granberg, was an older, bitchy lady that was gone frequently for medical reasons. Nobody ever believes me when I say this, and you surely won't either, but the two most often used substitutes were Mr. Queen and Mr. Whacker. I was one of only a few kids that knew the slang term for "queen." That was because it was a regular name that Uncle Robbie would call people, along with "hump" (short for butt-hump) and "spade." I let everyone in on the joke so the entire class could join in on the amusement. As for Mr. Whacker, no explanation was needed for a laugh. If you're already doubting the validity of these names, than you're really not going to believe this—Mr. Whacker's first name was Richard. It's true, I swear to you on my kids' lives. He announced it every time he was there to fill in, even if he had just been there the previous day.

"My name is Mr. Whacker," he said. "I'm telling you now, my first name is Richard. You will call me Mr. Whacker. If anyone calls me 'Dick Whacker' or anything else, you WILL be expelled for twenty days. If you don't believe me, try me."

"How about 'Pud Whacker'?" a kid named Curtis asked.

Mr. Whacker quietly walked over to the phone and called the principal, Mr. Callero. Within minutes, Mr. Callero came in and hauled the kid off. We didn't see him again for exactly twenty school days.

"Anyone else?" Mr. Whacker challenged.

Everyone remained silent, as we did our best to hold in the laughter until after class.

One of the times that Mr. Whacker was our substitute, I was standing up at my desk while I was cutting something out for a project. Unbeknownst to me, Greg set up ten or twelve thumbtacks on my chair. Since my desk was in the front row, everyone but me and the teacher knew what was going to happen next.

"MOTHERFUCKER!!" I yelled as I sat down on the bed of nails, which turned my butt cheeks into Swiss cheese.

"You're outta here, fella!" Mr. Whacker exclaimed after he heard my outburst.

"No way!" I argued. "What would you say if you sat down on a bunch of tacks?!"

I turned around to show him the evidence.

"Oh dear," he said, walking towards me. "Let me help you."

"Don't touch me!" I yelled at him, slapping his hand away. "I'll take care of it myself."

"Who did this?" I asked.

I knew exactly who it was, but I didn't turn Greg in. I figured that I would get him back later. Our friendly feud went back and forth until the day that we graduated.

Despite my profanity, I wasn't in trouble. I did, however, earn my first suspension a short time later. Josh Williams decided to make a comment about my mom, who was now tormenting me by working at the middle school. (I swear that she only transferred jobs to make my life miserable.) With Mom being an attractive lady, combined with a bunch of horny teenagers, it was a recipe for disaster. I usually got even by doing something that involved a little thought, but not this time.

I don't remember exactly what he said, something sexual for sure, and I quickly shot back with, "At least my dad ain't a nigger like you say that yours is."

He flew out of his chair and we started scuffling right in the middle of class. It was broken up before any punches were thrown and he stormed out of the room crying like a pussy. Mrs. Granberg went out after him and I just sat back down to my assignments. She came back in a minute or so later and told me to go to Mr. Callero's office. I did what I was told and after he heard both of our stories, which were the same, he sent Josh back to class.

"As for you," he said, "I am giving you an in-school suspension for three days."

An in-school suspension, or I.S.S., consisted of me doing all of my school work in a small room with five cubbyholes in it. There was a twenty minute break for lunch and two, five minute breaks to use the restroom—and no talking.

"So it's okay for him to talk about my mom like that?" I asked.

"No," he said. "But it is completely unacceptable to use the racist term that you used."

So then, I was labeled as a racist for a while.

Let me tell you about my views on racism and how it relates to me personally. I do not dislike African-Americans, although I must be fair and say that I don't know too many. Where I live, there just isn't very many. As for the word "nigger," I don't have a problem with it. To me, a nigger isn't a slave from the 1800's, but rather as person who uses their ethnicity to their advantage. There are laws in place that require establishments to interview or hire black people, but the niggers pull the race card to prevent them from doing what they don't want to do on the job. White people are just as guilty too so anytime that a black person wants to use derogatory terms towards whites who behave the same way, I'm all for it. Around this part of the country, there are Mexicans that do the same thing, along with East Indians and Asians. They come to this country because they are given convenience stores to run by the government. They only work their family, instead of hiring employees, so they don't have to pay out any wages. And in a country where English is the spoken language, they will stand right in front of you and talk amongst themselves in their native tongue. For all I know, they could be belittling me right in front of me and I wouldn't have a clue about it. If I am a racist, then so are they—you can't expect to be treated equal if you don't do the same to others. White, black, Indian, Mexican—I don't care—it's all of us that do it. Or perhaps everyone has just become white. Think about it.

Anyway, I was sent to I.S.S. For three days. Obviously I couldn't take my shop projects in there with me, so the teacher gave me sentences to write. They were nothing compared to Mr. Prange's sentences, so it was a breeze. The good thing about the suspension was that I got lots of time to study my pre-algebra.

On November 26, 1994, I went to my very first concert at the Tacoma Dome. With country music being what everyone could collectively listen to enjoyably as a family, it was an easy sell for us to go to see Reba McEntire. While Reba is an amazing vocalist, she isn't much of an entertainer. She would stand up there on stage and belt out the songs with her unique voice range, but it didn't seem that she was all that into it. Singers that I had seen on TV would dance and get into their music, but she didn't. While I'm sure it was just because it wasn't her style, to me it just made it look like she was only out there because it was her job. I mean let's face it, it is a job. You put on concerts to attract an audience so that they will buy your merchandise and records and vice versa. Her style clearly works for her, as she has had a thirty-plus year career with dozens of platinum records.

Her supporting acts were much better. A newcomer named John Berry opened the show. With only having one album out on shelves, he played every song on it at least once, if not twice. He went on to put out a few more albums, have a few hits, and the faded away within just a few years. That being said, he achieved more than most people who are in that line of work. The guy that I really dug was John Michael Montgomery. He was put on a pretty high pedestal after he came out of the chute with three or four straight #1 hits—many thought that he was the next Garth Brooks. He played his hits and a few album cuts but it was his version of a popular classic rock song that really turned me on.

"Sweet Home Alabama" was a song that was released by Lynyrd Skynyrd on their *Second Helping* album in 1974. It is one of the most recognizable songs ever, as people instantly know it after just four chords. While it is nearly impossible to sing a song like Ronnie Van Zant did, or have the triple-guitar attack of Gary Rossington, Allen Collins, and Steve Gaines, Montgomery did an excellent job. He played a ten minute version of it, seven minutes of which was just him doing an electric guitar solo.

Although he was around a lot longer than John Berry and had a slew of hits, he didn't make it to the Garth Brooks-level of success. It wasn't for a lack of trying, though. Music is a popularity contest in which good looks often over shadow musical talent. There are lots of pretty boys that sing songs that somebody else wrote. The good ones do it all—write the lyrics, write the music, and piece it all together. Most of the time, that only plays second fiddle (as it were) to a guy in a tank top with a spray-on tan.

With the shorter days and cold nights, we spent about three to five evenings each week sitting in our new hot tub that we got a few months earlier. It was rarely used over the summer, unless it was on a cooler than average night, so the winter months were the times that we got the use out of it. With the temperature of the tub set at 105 degrees, it mattered not what the temperature was in the air. During rainy nights, we would sit out there and enjoy it just as much as if it was dry. You're already wet anyway, so what does it matter if it is pouring down rain? If anything, it cools you off a little so you can maybe stay in there longer than thirty minutes.

We would drag the time out quite a bit longer if there was snow on the ground. I don't really know how it started, but we got to where we would take turns daring each other to do something in the snow. It could be anything to running laps around the yard, to making snow angels, to turning somersaults. The most common dare was to see who could lie in the snow the longest. Mom wouldn't even try any of them, the only thing she did was set her butt in the snow for 1/10 of a second before she shuffled back into the tub to warm up. I don't think that anyone ever made it for a full minute, but the three of us tried.

The true record holder for anything meaningful belonged to Jen for doing somersaults. She did fifty in a row before she staggered her frozen body back to the spa. She looked just like a bowling ball rolling down the alley, as it took her just over a minute to get it done. I thought for sure that I could beat her but after trying several times over the course of that winter and for many years to come, the closest I could come was thirty. I must give credit where its due, she beat me like a drum.

Seventh grade marked the last time that the boys played football nearly everyday at lunch. Most kids were now loitering around the cafeteria and hallways talking about who was French-kissing who this week and who was hot and who was not. I guess that some of us weren't quite ready for the tabloid world.

We played out back behind the gym, out of the way of everyone else. Once in a while a teacher would check in on us, but not very often. There wasn't ever a whole lot of trouble going on except for the usual disagreements between players. It was the normal stuff—if it was it a catch or not, if it was it a first down, or if it was out of bounds. Most of the time it was argued with raised voices and swearing, but would get resolved without incident. About once a week though, it could get physical.

It was just an added bonus if two guys got into it with each other. Usually two or three pushes back and forth would get out the frustration, everyone would step in, and we could get back to the game. Once during one of my shoving matches, I pushed a kid and just after he reared back and was set to return the favor, I sidestepped him and he flew flat on his face. He called me a "pussy" for moving, but I, along with everyone else, was laughing too hard to care.

Sometimes, pushing just wasn't enough. There were times that there had to be a knock-down, drag-out fight. Fights were generally brought on after a couple of weeks of two guys not seeing eye to eye. It was almost impossible for guys to reconcile because there were always ten or twelve kids like me who stirred the pot. It could have all stemmed from the classroom and just continued to build with the smallest, stupidest shit. When a fight was fixing to go down, it wasn't a spur-of-the-moment thing, it was mostly planned.

Lunch was a great time for it. One person would stand watch by the edge of the building to make sure that a teacher wasn't coming. The rest would circle up in a large circle, with the two participants slugging it out in the center. As soon as blood was drawn, that was it—or if a tear was shed. There weren't any all-out assaults that ended in knockouts or broken bones. Each person got a few good shots in but if they didn't keep on their opponent, they would lose. Not one fight lasted more than a minute, then it was settled, and then we could play again. Against the rules? Yes. A major concern? No. The issue was solved without teacher intervention and doubled as great entertainment.

During the spring, I played my last enjoyable season of baseball. While I would still play one more season afterward, this should have been the way that I finished. While my hitting dropped considerably, my fielding was even better than the previous year.

Dad was the assistant coach and designated taxi driver for the guys that lived in town. The head coach, Dennis Russell, was the other taxi driver for the kids that lived in the Hamilton area near him. We had to take turns with the other teams that used the high school field in town. The reason for that was, at the time, it was the only field with a ninety-foot baseline. The rest in town were sixty-footers. When it wasn't our night for the field, Dad loaded up a carload in the Oldsmobile and hauled us up to Dennis' house for batting practice in the cage that he had built out of logs that Dad had hauled home for him. (Dad had by this time returned to driving log truck and moving the machinery from job to job.)

Dennis had the same type of pitching machine that high schools, colleges, and even the pros use. Its speeds varied, as did the position of the pitches, so no batter got the same pitch twice. The machine saved our pitchers from wearing out their arms, and it did the same for Dennis. He would just stand behind the fence, feed the machine, and not have to worry about the batter ripping one back to him.

He did get clobbered in the worst possible way while he was pitching for one of our seven-on-seven scrimmages. He fired a pitch over the plate and Donny Hoffecker swung on it, sending a line drive directly into Dennis' nuts. Ever the competitor, he picked it up and threw it to me to try and make the play at first base. I would have had to have been Andre The Giant standing on a ladder to pull down the throw, as it was every bit of twenty feet over my head. As it turned out, one of his nads swelled up to the size of a grapefruit.

Turnouts at his house were more than just baseball. He had a trampoline that we all took turns wrestling and doing flips on. His son, Micheal, could do a front flip, land on his feet, and bounce immediately into a back flip, like a pendulum, and do it for a minute at a time. Our trampoline privileges were removed after Evan Lemley ungracefully tried a back flip and landed on the back of his head with the rest of his body lying on his face. It was a good thing that his dad was the local mortician, because it seemed to be exactly what he needed from where we sat.

We played teams from as far south as Everett to as far north as Mount Baker, compiling a pretty good record. We made the playoffs but were defeated in the second round and sent to the consolation bracket. We lost again, ending our season, but it took twelve innings for the other team to beat us.

I played just one more season after that, as I had absolutely no interest in playing in high school, but I wish that I would have never even done it. Since quitting at mid-season wasn't an option for me, I had to stick out a season in which "fun" wasn't the proper F-word that would accurately describe it. This time around, Denny Steinman was the coach and his son, Matt, just happened to play first base as well. Matt was over six feet tall and built just like a beanpole, with about the same amount athletic ability as one. He couldn't, and wouldn't, play another position.

To Denny's credit, I started every single game. I would play six of the nine innings before being pulled if it was close game, but only five if it was a runaway. I would sit on the bench and watch as Matt embarrassed himself, the team, and the entire game, all the while assuring myself that if I ever coached one of my kids in any sport, they would be treated just as hard or harder as everyone else on the team.

CHAPTER 22
Wing Nuts

IN ADDITION TO mowing lawns as usual over the summer, I found another way to rake in a few extra dollars. Actually it was a lot of extra dollars, as it was an hourly wage of five or six dollars an hour working a couple of nights a week in the hay fields in Lyman. Strangely, with as bad as I was known to suffer from allergies, working in the hay didn't bother me. I got the job thanks to Dustin Hard, my best friend in those days, who lived across the street from an old man named Alf Albertine, who had a huge farm where he raised beef. He was too old to do any of the work, so his girlfriend, who's name was Patsy and was thirty years his junior, cared for his house and land. Her kids, who were grown up, did all of the farm work and she hired out young guys like us to buck hay.

Bucking hay is a great way to stay in shape with all of the lifting that is involved. After the tall grass is cut, raked, and bailed, a farm tractor and a trailer would drive along in the field as guys would load it with the hay. After the trailer is loaded, it is taken to the barn to be unloaded, stacked, and stored away until the winter. It is much easier with four or five other guys, but it can be done with just me and Dustin also—and we ought to know.

As for our coworkers, sometimes they would work and sometimes they wouldn't show up. Other kids would only work long enough until they had enough money to buy a quarter-ounce of pot from one of the neighborhood suppliers, and they wouldn't be back either. There were many times when it was just the two of us loading and unloading acres of hay in a single night. Often times we wouldn't be done until two or three in the morning. We didn't start until five or six in the evening anyway, after it was cooler outside. Sometimes we would be so exhausted that we would take a quick nap on top of the load as the tractor eased along the mile trek back to the barn.

When I first started, Alf sat in his car in the middle of the field and watched everyone work. His car was always in the way and we would have to walk farther to get some of the bails because his car blocked the road. Tired of this, Dustin asked me to come along with him as he asked him to move.

We walked up to his window and Dustin said, "Hey, you fuckin' cocksucker. Move this piece of shit before I throw your worthless ass out of the seat and do it my fuckin' self. And I need a raise, you cheap, slave-drivin' fuck."

My eyes were the size of dinner plates and I instantly became sick to my stomach as I stood there and waited to be fired on the spot, thanks to my soon-to-be ex-friend. Alf then looked over and handed Dustin a notepad and a pencil, on which Dustin wrote, "Sir, could you please move your car." Alf looked at it, nodded, started his car, and drove off.

"By the way," Dustin said with a grin. "Alf is totally def."

"What a relief," I replied. "I thought I was going to have to pound you for getting us canned."

We did hay for another guy one time who was nearly as bad as Alf. He pulled us on a huge flatbed trailer with his tractor out to his field to get a load of some of the heaviest hay that I have ever lifted. He was flying down this gravel road that was riddled with chuckholes and we had to hold a death grip on the rails in order to keep our balance. After one too many bumps, the trailer came unhooked and we had no choice but to ride it out until it stopped. Meanwhile, the tractor just kept chugging along, entering the field and making its rounds like always. The old man made about two laps before he realized that the hay was still on the ground. I wonder what he was thinking as he turned around to see what the hell was going on and discovered instead that he was flying solo?

The best thing about working for that guy, whose name was Virgil, was not only the seven dollar an hour wage, but his wife fed us at the end of the day. It wasn't sandwiches and a pop either—she fixed pot roast or chicken with all the fixings, including dessert. We only got a lousy candy bar when we worked for "Fatsy."

As with any job that must be done, there can always be an element of fun—just ask Mary Poppins. While it doesn't exactly take your mind off of work, it just makes doing the work more enjoyable. We wrestled around in the barn, throwing each other from the much higher stacks to the lower stacks below. It was a wonder how nobody got hurt, especially when we would drop bails on top of each other. Granted these were light bails, but it still was pretty dangerous—just not dangerous enough to deter us.

Working until that late at night made it impossible for me to get home, so I ended up staying overnight at Dustin's just about every time that we worked in the hay. We also took turns staying over at each guy's houses for fun as well. Most of the afternoons and nights, we would have marathon Nintendo tournaments that went on for hours. Other times we would play football out in the yard, concocting strange plays that we felt could work in actual games.

Dustin was home alone most of the time, as his mom worked nights and her boyfriend, Bill, worked out of town frequently. He was always in charge of heating up his own dinner, doing the dishes, and washing and folding the clothes. On days that I was over there, I would help him get finished so we would have more time to goof around.

For some reason, I always got diarrhea when I went over there. I don't know if it was the food or if it was Dustin's half-ass way of washing dishes, but it happened. It wasn't a bad case of the runs, but it did require two to three trips to the can during each visit.

Bill just happened to be home and using the bathroom one of the many times that I felt the urge to explode, and I accidentally walked right in on him. In the split second that I was in there before I turned around to leave, I noticed that he was reading a magazine. Actually he wasn't reading anything, he was just looking at the pictures. These weren't regular magazines that I looked at, these had naked women in them—and I don't mean *Playboy*, that had just naked women posing for a camera, these pictures were of guys and girls having sex, girls having sex with girls, and full-on orgies. I quickly lost the urge to shit and ran back into Dustin's room.

"Hey man," I said. "I just walked in on Bill taking a dump."

He started laughing and asked, "Why didn't you knock first?"

"I don't know, but he was looking at magazines with naked chicks!"

"That's nothing," he said. "Wait until he leaves and I'll show you some other stuff."

A few minutes later, his mom came home, picked Bill up, and left for town to get groceries. As soon as they left, Dustin pointed out a stack of *Hustler* magazines that that were tucked behind some towels in the bathroom closet.

"How did you find these?" I asked.

"I do the laundry, remember?" he replied sarcastically. "And that's not all—he's got other stuff—come here and check these out."

With that, he led me into their bedroom and showed me a whole shelf that was full of X-rated videos that he had covered up with a blanket.

"Jesus," I said. "If they know that you do the laundry, why don't they hide this stuff somewhere else?"

"I don't know," he said. "Maybe they think that I won't notice."

"Well, let's put one in and check it out," I said anxiously.

"No, we better not."

"Come on, don't be a pussy."

"Fine, just remember that we have to put it back exactly where we found it."

We pulled out a tape called *Pastor Fuzz's Confessionals*, went into the living room, and put it in the VCR. Too caught up in the thought that we were actually going to see people having sex right on the TV, we didn't even notice that we walked right over his mom's purse that she had accidentally left behind. He pushed the play button, turned on the TV, and there it was—sex right before my very eyes. I saw a blonde chick with gigantic boobs shove a guys dick right into her mouth, practically swallowing it. She then took it out, bent over, and had him ram it into the promised land as she stuck her own finger deep into her asshole. We sat there in amazement as the two moaned with pleasure and just out of the corner of our eyes, we caught a glimpse of his mom and Bill pulling back into the driveway.

"Holy shit!" I yelled. "I thought they were at the store!"

"So did I! Quick, take the tape out and go put it in my room while I go and cover his shelf."

He took off into their room while I fiddled with the VCR remote. The batteries must have been dead because the damn thing wasn't working at all. Running out of time, I just hit the power button on the VCR, switched off the TV, and sprinted into Dustin's room. Talk about having a heart attack—if our heart rates were up already from watching porn, they must have been at stroke level when we were dropped in on without warning.

We sat in the room and waited, trying to catch our breath. Just then, Bill opened the door and glared at Justin and motioned for Dustin to follow him. I just knew that we were in deep shit and that my parents were going to flip out when they found out about it. They probably wouldn't let me come over there anymore, which would likely end my job working in the hay as well. Justin came back a minute or two later, looking like he could cry at any moment.

"What happened?" I asked, not really wanting the answer.

"He knows."

My heart just sank. I felt like I had just been kicked in the guts by a mule.

"What's going to happen now?" I asked.

"I don't know, but I told him that you didn't do anything and that you were still playing Nintendo."

I felt even worse now. I couldn't let him take the blame for an idea that was mine to begin with.

"Well, I guess I better go tell him the truth," I said, turning to leave.

Dustin then burst out laughing.

"What could possibly be funny?"

"If you go confess, you will give us both up," he roared. "He was mad about the glass that I left in the living room that he tripped over and broke."

"Thank God!" I exclaimed with relief. "And that wasn't funny!"

He got me that time, but I made up for it another time that I was over there. As usual, I had a stomachache while I was there from whatever it was that was causing it. I let out one of the raunchiest farts that one could cook up that made him choke and gag. I'm the kind of person that follows suit if I see anyone starting to puke, so I rushed to the kitchen and emptied the entire contents of my stomach into the sink. It wasn't until the next morning when he went in to do the dishes that he discovered that the sink was still full of my vomit, just sitting there marinating. Apparently, someone had left the drain plug in the night before.

Dustin and I were pretty good friends through our senior year of high school football. He wasn't in any of my classes in those days and I was hanging out with other guys, so we didn't see each other much after that. After graduation, I saw him a few times in town and we exchanged phone numbers. He called once, but I was in California on a trip and I told him that I would call him when I got home. I never did—some friend I am.

A new era in my life began over the summer when Dad bought a motorcycle that was strictly for the highway. It was a 1976 Honda Gold Wing GL1000 Limited Edition—one of only two thousand made. This bike was in excellent to near-mint condition, despite being almost twenty years old and having over 40,000 miles on it. This bike was designed for cross-country trips and over the course of the next four years, it was used for just that.

Dad stole it for around $1,500 from a guy that used to work with him at Janicki's named Dick Snell. Dick babied and pampered that bike since the day he bought it. He would go on bike trips with his brother, Russ, and some other guys to as far away as Florida and never go over seventy miles per hour the whole time—the polar opposite of Russ, who never rode LESS than seventy. He would park it inside the motel rooms that they stayed in at night and clean it up. There is an old expression about "going over it with a fine-toothed comb," well Dick did them one better by cleaning every nook and cranny with a Q-Tip.

Dick was getting rid of it because he not only didn't ride it anymore, but his health was slipping and it wasn't safe for him to do so. Along with the bike, Dad also received a full set of leathers. With Dick standing over six feet tall and weighing well over two hundred pounds combined with the fact that Dad would never reach those marks, I got the leathers instead! Dad already had a set anyway, as he had gotten his from one of the guys that his mom was married to when he was younger. Speaking of his mom, she was in town around the time that Dad bought the bike and when Russ came over for some reason while she was there, she recognized him—the two had dated each other some forty years earlier.

I went with Dad over to Russ' house to pick up the bike, which had been stored there for several years. When we got there, they were just finishing up wiping the dust off of the paint that had accumulated under the bike cover. The bike had an after-market ferring on it and its paint didn't quite match up to the rest of the bike. With the bike having been built in 1976 and with the Gold Wing in only its second year of production, they didn't come with one like they do now. In order to pack enough gear for such long trips, Dick had to improvise. The ferring and a hand-built luggage rack on the rear fender filled the void. The bike also had two unique features as well. The rims were gold (not solid gold, obviously) and the companion tool kit that was stored on the bike had chrome tools. These may not seem all that cool nowadays, but this was in 1976—the year our nation celebrated its bicentennial.

I rode home with Dad on the back of the bike, which had a passenger seat but no backrest. Longer rides might lead to a little issue, but for now it wasn't bad. We rode an hour or two at a time, cruising Skagit and Whatcom County, nearly every night after Dad was off work.

This next part might sound repetitive as you continue to read along. There were four occasions in which the Gold Wing was tipped over, while Dad was the rider, during the next three years. When it's time, I will explain each one. The first incident, contrary to what some may think, was the only spill that I am willing to share some of the blame.

Riding solo and riding with a passenger are entirely different. When you ride alone, you only need to be concerned about yourself as you lean into corners and make turns while you are moving. You know which speeds are safe for which corners. When you have a second person along with you, riders have to account for them as well. A good passenger just sits still, relaxes, and goes with the flow. An inexperienced passenger, on the other hand, will often tense up going into the corners and cause the bike to straighten prematurely. They may also shift their weight around without warning the guy in charge, again throwing the motorcycle off balance. It takes time to get comfortable for both.

Within a week after Dad brought the bike home, we rode by Skip and Lisa's house so Dad could show Skip his bike. Dad had originally wanted to buy Skip's bike that had belonged to his late father, but he wasn't ready to part with it yet. Lisa's twin sister and her family were there, as well as a few others, so we didn't stay but for a minute. When it was time to go, Dad loaded up first and held the bike still so I could board. I hopped on and Dad walked the bike backwards, turning us around so we could go. I wasn't quite comfortable so I shifted over to the right so I could lift my left leg up to pull my pant leg down a little so my balls were not squished. As I was doing that, Dad was leaning to his right as well in order to flip up the kickstand (that he kept forgetting to raise) with his left foot. With both of us leaning to the right, the bike passed that all-important stability threshold and over we went. Naturally, everyone burst out laughing.

"What the hell's wrong with you?" Dad yelled toward me, obviously embarrassed.

"What do you mean? I didn't do anything!" I yelled back in defense.

"Just get on and don't move."

We tucked our tails between our legs and rode home. The truth was, it was my fault for moving without telling him. In Dad's defense also, it can't be easy having a passenger that is taller and heavier than you are. Something that wasn't my fault was the fact that his bike sat higher off the ground than most, making it rather top-heavy. Couple that with Dad having short legs, and accidents like that could be a little more likely to happen. So for the next couple of weeks, we took our time loading and unloading and I made sure that I warned him before I was going to adjust the way I was sitting. Things went pretty smooth as we cruised the county roads at forty, just like a Sunday drive. We each got accustomed to riding with each other—then we went on the Lawman 1000 with Russ.

Dad and me on his Gold Wing

The Lawman 1000 was a charity ride in which all entry fees went to the Fred Hutchinson Cancer Research Center in Seattle. Riders pay the fee and go for a day long ride, covering Washington and even the north end of Oregon. There are two checkpoints along the way that riders must get a receipt from a purchase that they made in there, proving that they made the stops. We could take any road that we wanted to get to any of these towns. At the end of the day, everyone gathered at the final checkpoint, which was a county park. When the participants showed their receipts, they were awarded with a salmon dinner. In 1995, the ride began at the Sea-Tac Mall, just south of Seattle. The two checkpoints were in Naches, Washington, and Heppner, Oregon. The final stop was in Richland, Washington. With the ride not ending until late in the evening, we would have to spend the night and ride home the next day.

We met Russ and some other guys at his house just after daylight. With Seattle being over an hour away and with a slight schedule that had to be followed, we had to get moving. We flew down the freeway at around eighty miles per hour, getting to Sea-Tac in less than an hour.

I wasn't too nervous going that fast because it was the freeway after all and at that time of the day, there wasn't much traffic.

After we signed in and hit the road, we didn't go any slower. To make matters worse, we were done with the freeway for a bit and riding those speeds through Mount Rainier National Park!

If Dad was going to keep up with Russ and the others, he had to go just as fast. We took thirty miles per hour corners at sixty and I thought for sure that we were going to crash. I even went so far as to put my foot down while we were in the middle of a corner. As a result, we shot straight into oncoming traffic. Luckily nobody was coming and we miraculously didn't crash and die.

The Gold Wings that we were riding weren't the same as the street legal racing bikes that most people refer to as "crotch rockets." I prefer to call then "knee-draggers" because riders come within centimeters of doing just that when flying through a corner. Even on a much bigger and less aerodynamic bike, we were leaning so far over that the lower ferring rubbed on the pavement.

Riding that fast was just Russ' style. Even though he was riding a 1500 Gold Wing, that even came equipped with a reverse gear, he took corners just like a professional motorcycle racer. This crazy cat even set his cruise control to eighty-five while shooting down the freeway, stood straight up on his pegs with his arms folded on his chest, and rode that way for over a mile. This was something that you could only see at a circus—or while riding with Russ Snell.

With Dad's bike not having a backrest and us riding so erratically, I was to the point where I couldn't ride with him anymore. I jumped out of the frying pan and went straight into the fire when I saddled up with Russ, who was the only one in the group that I knew for more than a few hours who had a backrest. He didn't slow down any, but at least I could brace myself and hold on for dear life without causing him to wreck. His passenger seat was even equipped with armrests. It was like sitting on a high-speed roller coaster—minus the seat belt that I sometimes wish that I had. We had the opportunity to see a ton of pretty country but when you go so damn fast, you don't catch all of it. You often miss the little stuff, like wildlife. In the areas that we traveled that day, we were certain to see deer at least, but not us—it was eyes on the road at all times or else . . . .

Late in the evening, we made it to Richland in one piece. Russ was just a tad shorter than he was at the beginning because somewhere along the way, he stepped in some gum and his remedy was to just grind down the soles of his boot on the pavement while riding. Dad had cramps in his fingers from gripping his handlebars so tight. I, on the other hand, was in great shape—except for the load that was in my britches.

During dinner, I got a first-hand look at how bikers look. Most are covered in leather. If they have any skin exposed, it is likely covered by a tattoo. Some guys have long hair with shaggy beards and look like they are allergic to soap. Others are even worse but they all have one thing in common, they are just as friendly as can be. The women look just like them, and some didn't even have beards! There wasn't any flesh on display like there is at other bike rallies. The only nipples that were out belonged to some of the guys that were shirtless. The women stayed covered, which was a shame because one lady had boobs that were so big that if she lied down and you got on top of her, your ears would pop.

"You want to stay away from ones that are that big," one guy said to me, noticing that I couldn't take my eyes off of them.

"Why?" I asked, wiping the drool away from my mouth.

"Because they just get in the way," he said as he spread his arms away from each other, like Moses parting the Red Sea. "You have to work to hard to get to the woman—you always want to remember that."

I have never forgotten what he said, though I may not have always taken his advise.

We spent the night at a motel in Yakima called the All-Star Motel. If it were to be rated with stars, it wouldn't even register. This shithole had stone walls the beds being just as soft. For what we got for the money, we could have saved the cash and slept out in the parking lot. Although it was partially because of who we rode with, this was the only night that we have ever, or probably will ever, spend in a motel.

All told, we logged on just about sixty miles short of a thousand miles in less than thirty-six hours. Dad and I had briefly entertained the idea of a trip up to Bellingham and back just to hit the quadruple-digits, but we just couldn't bring ourselves to it. Our bodies just were not used to that kind of travel—yet!

With both working in the hay and mowing lawns, I was raking in the cash pretty steadily. I put everything in the bank, except for the money that I spent on wrestling tapes that I found for sale at video stores. They weren't new but after I took the rental stickers off of the cassettes, nobody knew the difference. Buying them used for around ten bucks was the only way to afford them because new ones from the producer in New Jersey cost around forty. I would, however, buy one or two of those every couple of months when they had a 50% off sale and could get them for twenty.

I was saving the rest of my money for a street bike of my own. Yeah the Kawasaki was legal, but after the camping debacle the year before, it wasn't ever going to see the pavement again. I needed something bigger, something that I could take on Lawman's. Although I was just over two years away from getting my driver's license, it wasn't too soon to see what was out there for the money that I had to spend. Dad and I checked the classified adds in the newspaper almost every night and looked at the all-motorcycle *Cycle Trader* magazine each time that we went to the store. Some of the bikes that were listed for around a thousand dollars, we would actually go and check out. Most were shit-heaps—bikes that hadn't seen the light of day for years. It's a good thing that I still had two years left because at that rate, it was going to take a while to find something good.

Meanwhile, we rode the Gold Wing several times a week. Mom and Jen were at gymnastics as usual, so we had a couple of hours for riding almost ever night. We rode to every motorcycle shop that was within fifty miles of our house to check out bikes. After looking at what they had to offer, we would eat their free hot dogs and popcorn, that they had for their "customers," for our dinner. It got to the point where the two of us were worse than the homeless people who lined up at the soup kitchens—at least they needed it.

On Saturday, we rode down to Lynnwood, which is just north of Seattle, for one of Jen's gymnastic meets. It was a little cooler, so we dressed in our leathers in case it happened to rain. Jen's session was later in the day so we had a choice of watching other kids who weren't even on the team perform, or we could ride around for a while. It was a difficult choice, but we chose the ride. We rode to the motorcycle shops that were in the area to check out their inventory. For the money that I had, I was looking for bikes like an early 1980's Gold Wing or the Kawasaki equivalent, a Honda Shadow, or a Suzuki Intruder, all of which that had been pretty well used. These places didn't have any grub, so we went looking for a place that did when it came time for lunch.

With it being the weekend, Costco, the members-only food wholesaler, always had food samples. Thanks to Mom working at the schools, we had a membership that allowed us in—even if we were dressed from head to toe in leather. For the next half-hour, we pushed around shopping carts and dined on the free samples. To try to make it look like we were on the level, we went so far as to put groceries in our carts as we made our way down the aisles. After hitting each station two or three times, we decided that it was time to go.

"Too bad we didn't have dessert," Dad said, as we pushed our loaded carts down the candy aisle.

"I'll fix that," I said as I opened up a box of Carmelo bars, took two out, and put them in my pocket for the ride back to the gym.

We just left our loaded carts right there in the middle of the aisle and walked back to the bike. I haven't been back to the Lynnwood Costco since.

Believe it or not, there were times when we actually paid for our food. We would get a bag of chips and a couple of bottles of pop at a store and stop at a shady spot on the side of the road for our meal. We would have our snack and then saddle up and go. It was a cheap way to have fun. With gas just over a dollar a gallon, you could ride all afternoon and have snacks for two for under ten bucks.

One of our treks took us up to the ski resort at the end of the Mount Baker Highway. With it being the middle of summer, you wouldn't even know it based on all of the snow that was covering the ground. There were people up there riding inner tubes, building snowmen, and having snowball fights. There were even girls in bikinis who took their tops off for their friends to take pictures. As luck would have it, I couldn't see anything because I had to take my contacts out after an earlier allergy attack.

I don't remember how the idea came about, but Dad took out the plastic trash bags that he had in the ferring, tore three holes in each of them, and made instant ponchos that we could slide head-first down the snowbanks with. It garnered a lot of laughs from other people, but it sure was fun. We would even make that a yearly event for the next couple of years.

In late August, Papa and Gladys bought a house in Newport, Washington, which is a stone's throw from the Idaho border. They had talked about it for years, but now it was going to happen. He didn't show it much, but Dad had to be sad with his mom, his brother, and now his father living far away. (Maybe nobody liked him?) Now, in order to see both Papa and Uncle Robbie, we would have to take even more trips over to Eastern Washington.

Papa's house actually sold a couple of weeks before they were to move. In the meantime, they rented a house about a quarter-mile from where we lived. With me being on summer vacation, I helped him load all of his stuff into a Ryder truck all day on a Friday so they could take off the next morning. Dad was at work, so it was just me and him loading all of the heavy stuff as Mom and Gladys took care of the little stuff. When Dad got off work, he came up to help finish things off. By the time the door was shut, there was enough room for maybe an ant. There wasn't any wasted space, as every nook and cranny was filled with anything from a pair of shoes to a blanket. It was so full that when we pulled up to the truck scales between Sedro-Woolley and Lyman, the scale read, "One at a time please."

Actually, going to the scales wasn't on the list of things to do. Papa wanted Dad to drive the truck down to put as much diesel in it as possible for the long trip. Since he was paying by the mile and the weigh station was out of the way, it cost him extra to find out what he already knew—the truck was way overweight. It may have cost an extra quarter to find out the weight, but it might as well have been a quarter-million the way that Papa reacted. In his defense, moving is one of the most stressful things that a person goes through in their life, but this was just the beginning. We still had to take the near-four hundred mile trip over and unload him.

The next morning, Papa loaded Gladys, Carissa, and their new dog, Claire, that they had just bought the night before, into their Bronco and led the way to their new house. Behind them was Renee in her van with her kids, Mom, and Jen. Next was Dad and I on the Gold Wing and about eighty miles behind us, was Larry, inching along in the Ryder truck.

Believe it or not, it wasn't the truck that was slowing us down. Every twenty minutes, Papa would have to pull over to let Claire out to take a shit. When it first started, he would turn his blinker on, gradually change lanes, and pull over like a normal person. After about five times, he just jerked the car across all lanes of traffic, regardless of how busy the road was, and skidded to a stop. At the top of Steven's Pass, we all pulled over for her to take another dump, as well as to wait for Larry to catch up. Papa flew out of the Bronco, opened up the back end, and dumped an entire fifty pound bag of dog food onto the ground.

"I'm done feeding this fuckin' dog," he barked. "All it does is shit—it's got to be the food." (Or it could have been the fact that they had just got her a day earlier and now they were driving across the state.)

A few minutes later, Larry crept up to the summit and we were able to hit the road again. Dad and I began stopping every little bit to let a bunch of cars pass us, only for us to race up behind them and pass them back. Papa got pissed off about that too and he let Dad know about it the next time that we had to make a shit-stop for Claire.

"Can't you just ride along with us without dicking off?" he asked

Dad didn't say anything but as Papa headed back to his car, he said, "Man, the old bastard's being a real prick today."

"Yeah he is," I agreed.

"I WANT TO RIDE!!" Dad yelled.

Just then, Papa jumped out of the Bronco and ran back to us.

"What's the matter?" he asked. "Didn't you just holler?"

"No," Dad replied sheepishly.

Papa then turned and stormed back over to his car, shaking his head the whole time. I couldn't hear what he said, but most of the words likely started with and "F".

At the next poop spot after that, Dad told Papa that we were going to ride ahead of them, stop at Uncle Robbie's house to pick them up, and we would all be there to help him unload the truck when he got to his house.

"Okay," he said, in a little calmer of a voice than earlier. "I don't want to stop when we drive by because I still have another hour of driving after that and I'm so goddamn tired of stopping as it is. I'm just going to honk, so listen for it and be ready."

After the general let us go, we sped off ahead towards Rob's. We figured that by the time that we got there, Papa and the caravan would be a good half-hour behind us. We would have plenty of time to sit out on the porch and bullshit while we listened for the signal.

When we got to Rob's, Dad showed off his Gold Wing to his brother. Rob did have a street bike of his own, a late-60's Harley-Davidson Duo Glide, that he was in the process of restoring. Seeing Dad's bike and hearing the stories about how much fun that we had been having on it over the past couple of months, got him thinking that he wanted one as well. Before we knew it, we had been there close to three hours!

Once we came to our senses and had Rob lead us to Papa's, we knew that we were in for it. Surprisingly, Papa never said a word about it. His face, on the other hand, was beet red and the steam was shooting out of his ears as he packed in the last item from an otherwise empty Ryder truck. To this day when the story is brought up again, he reverts to the same look that he had on that day, biting his tongue, and holding in fury the likes of which this world has never seen.

CHAPTER 23
Same Day, Different Way

I N THE LATE part of the summer of 1995, I began a near-obsession of building my own pro wrestling video library. Previously, I had just been buying old tapes from the previous ten years when they were on sale at video stores. One day, I just decided to start recording the current televised programming with the idea of maybe watching it five years later. At first, I could get six, one hour editions of *Monday Night Raw* on a blank VHS tape. In order to get even more wrestling per tape, I then started editing out the commercials. I could then pack a single tape with eight episodes.

Raw was now the main program for the WWF. *Saturday Night's Main Event* stopped airing in 1992 and in 1993, the USA Network began airing the new weekly show on Monday nights. The ratings weren't staggering by any means over the first couple of years, but that all changed in September of 1995 when a different company left local syndication for national exposure—with the help of some familiar names.

In the late-80's Jim Crockett Promotions, a North Carolina territory of the National Wrestling Alliance, was purchased by Ted Turner and renamed World Championship Wrestling. Perhaps you might have heard of Turner—he is the media mogul out of Atlanta, Georgia that is responsible for national television networks such as Turner Network Television and Turner Broadcasting Network, to name a couple. You know them as TNT and TBS, which can be found on any cable or satellite channel guide.

Although the owner, Turner had far too much on his plate to do anything other than to pay the talent with his loaded pockets. He hired a successful salesman by the name of Eric Bischoff to run the company and acquire talent. Wrestlers were offered large contracts with guaranteed money to work for the company. He brought in guys like Hulk Hogan and Randy Savage, guys that fans still wanted to see despite their advancement in age. Together, they gave Vince McMahon and the WWF something that nobody had ever given them—competition. They began airing a one hour show opposite of *Monday Night Raw*, called *Monday Nitro*. It aired at the same time on opposite channels so fans could choose which show to watch. With us

153

living on the west coast, I could watch *Nitro* at five and *Raw* at eight because USA at the time, delayed their prime time programming three hours out here. I could not only keep up on my old favorites, but I could check out the new guys also. Plus, I could watch and record two hours of the finest wrestling each and every Monday night.

With the head-to-head competition, it forced each company to elevate their production. It would be like *American Idol* and *Dancing With The Stars* in the same time slot on separate networks, the World Series against the Super Bowl, or *Seinfeld* against *Friends*. Wrestling began a resurgence in popularity that over the next three years would dominate all televised programming on Monday nights. Suddenly, watching wrestling was cool for the hardest to reach audience in all of television—males, age 13 to 35. Wrestling was now viewed as interesting, intriguing, and exciting. Hmmm, how long had I already known that?

Eighth grade was just about the exact same as seventh grade, just a step higher. I was able to take algebra, which meant that upon completion for the year, I would receive a full year's worth of high school math credits. Most importantly, with the district only requiring two years of math credits to graduate, I would need just one more year to meet it. I had to work hard again to be sure that I was maintaining a grade to my satisfaction. I studied at home like the year before and seemed to understand it a little better. According to teachers, everyone would use it someday so it was important to complete. They were right, I have used it in my adult life—to help others learn how to do it!

The only real purpose of taking algebra is to strain your brain in a positive way, opening up the doors to deeper thinking. Everything else I just store in a cellar, collecting dust because it can't even be given away at garage sales. Pie=3.14. The quadratic formula is X equals negative B plus or minus the square root of B squared minus 4AC over 2A. Solve a problem in the order of exponents, parenthesis, multiplication, division, addition, and subtraction. Fifteen years after I have learned it, I have only used it to help other confused people.

The only class in the eighth grade that I have utilized in life recently was wood shop, which was now a full semester course! With being a year older, we were now allowed to use the table saw and the planer without a teacher's supervision. I made a bunch more projects than I did the previous year, all of which scored in the upper-ninety percents. The teacher never gave out a perfect score because there was no such thing as a flawless project, so the 97% that I got on my media shelf was as good as it got.

Shortly after I left middle school, I learned that the shop had been closed down and renovated into a technology lab. I may not like it, but I am fully aware that we live in the computer age. Still, I think that there is room for both. God knows I pay enough in taxes to make it possible. Maybe it just doesn't matter to anyone anymore, maybe nobody cares. Oh well—let the next generation hire out a small building job like building a fence, making a cabinet, or constructing a porch swing. I mean after all, at least they know what to if they aren't receiving E-mails. Good for them.

A positive change that occurred when I was there was a lunchtime sports activity that was designed to cut out loitering around in the hallways and around buildings. Throughout the year, kids could sign up to play various sports during lunch. There was football in the fall, basketball and hockey in the winter, and soccer and softball in the spring. The teacher would choose a captain to pick the players on his or her own team. For each sport, there were eight teams and we would play each other once. After that, we would be seeded in an elimination tournament based on our win and loss records. The winner of the single-elimination tournament would get their team picture in the yearbook and a ticket for a field trip to Enchanted Village in Federal Way in May.

I was selected as a captain for one of the football teams the first time out. I couldn't pick the team name because the teacher assigned them to prevent arguments. My team was the Lions, which wasn't exactly a team that was known for championships—just ask the city of Detroit. I was going to play quarterback because I was the captain and I could use my other picks to select the best of the other position players. I picked the best receiver that I knew, Greg Mahle, first. Second, I picked the fastest runner that I knew, George Brookings. I picked a few others that I don't recall off hand, but they were quick on their feet and could play defense. We went undefeated in the round robin and cruised through the tournament to win the championship.

I couldn't captain anymore sports that year, but I could still be picked for a team. I played every single sport that was offered, but never made it past the semi-finals of the tournaments. No big deal—I was already going on the field trip and was the champion of the sport that I was into the most.

Back in the classroom, another new course that was offered was peer helping. In this period, students would walk across the field to Evergreen, the same school that I went to until midway through the fifth grade, to work as a teacher's aid to second and third grade classes. Ironically, I was put in Mrs. Brooks' third grade class, five years after I was in there myself. While I didn't tell on them, I watched watched a few of the kids pull the same kind of stunts that I pulled at their age. They didn't know that I was watching and therefore I'm sure that some of them thought that I was strange for chuckling to myself nearly everyday.

It was also a throwback to the third grade in English class with the presence of one of my classmates. After five years of not having the "pleasure" of his company in class, Josef returned out of exile. He grew out of his sneezing routine but still set his sights on a girl that was going to be his wife. This time, however, it was the teacher.

Mrs. Malcom had to be every bit of fifty, but attractive to other people her age. She wasn't even close to the teacher that David Lee Roth and the other boys in Van Halen were "hot for" in 1984. Undeterred, Josef would do everything that he could do to profess his affection to her. He called her "Dr. Malcom," because she "had the intelligence level of educators of the highest level." He would write her notes and bring her flowers and chocolates once a week. When Valentine's Day rolled around, he actually bought her a pair of earrings.

About six months too late, Mrs. Malcom finally had enough when Josef gave her an extra steamy love note. He was taken out of the class and may have even been removed from the school for a while because it was a couple of years before I saw him again.

I myself got a love note during health class one day. (I guess that lessons of human reproduction can stimulate more than just the brain.) I knew who it was who had addressed the note to me from "Anonymous." I was the second one in class when I went up to my desk and found the note. The only other person in the room was a girl named Sara, who sat about two rows behind me. Without even reading it, I threw it in the garbage and sat down. When I turned around, she was gone. I figured that if nobody had enough guts to sign their name, then I wasn't going to give them the time of day.

I wish that I would have handled that a little differently, not because I liked her, because I didn't, at least not that way. I would have instead just put it in my notebook and threw it away later, where she didn't have to see it. Writing that was probably a big risk for her and something that she had worked up the courage to do for weeks, then here comes some arrogant asshole that crushes her spirit with one heartless act. Hopefully, she found someone more respectful than that inconsiderate prick in eighth grade.

In late October, I took a full week off of school to go hunting with Dad over to Papa's and Uncle Robbie's. We were going to spend the first couple of days at Papa's and the second half at Rob's. I was drawn for a special tag that allowed me to hunt either sex of whitetail deer. Dad put in for the same, but wasn't drawn. We left home early on a Saturday morning with a week's worth of healthy hunting food—chips, pop, cookies, and candy bars. We had our unloaded guns lying on the backseat of the Explorer, which we took because it had four wheel drive and we were going to be in the mountains, and in plain sight in case we were stopped by a cop.

Sure enough, Dad got pulled over for speeding about halfway there. He didn't get a ticket, but it began a record-setting streak that had us getting pulled over either on the way over or on the way back, and once even both ways, for close to a year straight. Never once did he get a ticket but if the officers took the time to check their recent records, they would likely have suspended his license because they were all for speeding—unless you count the time that we got stopped while I had my feet out the window. Just for the record though, the cop said that Dad was speeding also.

We got to Papa's in the early afternoon, too late to do anything other than drive around a few backroads near his house and look for deer sign. We found areas that were more populated with wildlife than others, so we pretty much figured on spending the next couple of days in these spots. It's funny because over there it seems that deer outnumber the people by about a hundred to one, but you have a hard time tracking them down while hunting. Finding them while driving is a bit easier.

When driving around there in the early evening around sundown, drivers must keep a sharp eye out for them. They can, and will, appear out of nowhere and try to cross the road. You can go around a blind corner and have one staring you down right there on the center line, giving you almost no reaction time. Thousands of deer are killed by cars over there each year. One such incident occurred on the first night that we were at Papa's.

We were all out in the shop that sat kitty-corner to Papa's house, when some lady walked right in unannounced and scared the shit out of us. Papa's house sat about fifty feet off of U.S. Highway 2 and the lady had just hit a deer right in front of his mailbox. With only two houses to choose from for the next several miles, she picked his place as the one to seek a telephone for a call for help. When she went inside to use the phone, Papa and Dad jumped into Papa's pickup and went down to load up the dead deer to bring back up to see if any meat could be salvaged. Papa started cutting it up, but everything was so badly bruised and bloody that we could only salvage a chunk off the right shoulder. Papa took the rest of it up into the woods and threw it out for the coyotes to eat.

The next morning, we got up early and got dressed to go out and sit on a hill behind Papa's house that overlooked the rest of his property. With any luck, we could just sit out there, freeze our balls completely off, and maybe see a monster buck walking around out in the clearing looking for breakfast.

Before we went out there, Gladys called from the kitchen and said that there was a deer right in the backyard under the porch light. While it was certainly possible, I wasn't sure if she was joking or not because I never got to see it. As soon as she made the announcement, I jumped out of a chair and took off for the backroom to get my gun. I leaped off of the two steps that separated the dining room from the living room and planted my foot to make a quick left turn down the hall. When I landed, though, I hit a small patch of linoleum with my insulated socks and my feet went right out from underneath me, sending me shins-first into the corner of the wall. It put identical holes in each leg of both my jeans and long underwear. I also had two huge chunks of meat taken out of my legs, exposing both bones. If there was a deer out there, he probably joined in with everyone's laughter before he strolled out of sight.

It might have been a blessing in disguise because now I could hardly walk. That, in turn, meant that I didn't have to go tromping through the brush in the freezing cold. Instead I could ride around in the Explorer with Papa and stay nice and toasty. We cruised around some logging roads for a few hours on Sunday while Dad pounded the brush.

That afternoon, we all loaded up into Papa's Bronco and went over to Rob's house for Tristan's birthday party. Karen fixed a huge pot of chili that was unbelievably good. I ate about four bowls because I was starving after skipping breakfast following my acrobatic act. We stayed until the early evening and then headed back to Papa's house.

When we left for the nearly hour ride home, my stomach started rumbling like a volcano. I didn't feel like puking by any means but my intestines were cramping so bad, I though I was going to die. I let a huge fart that didn't make any noise, but did relieve some pain—then it started to stink. Nobody said anything, but they had to have smelt it. I didn't laugh or anything, so I kept my cover—then I did it again.

"Jesus Christ!" Papa yelled. "Who shit?"

"I'm sorry," I said, bursting out into laughter. "I couldn't help it. It was Karen's chili."

"Goddamn!" was all Papa could say.

I few minutes later, I did it again. Papa started hollering again and rolled down my window from the front seat and locked it. Temperatures had to be in the teens outside but he didn't care, he was trying to air out his car. The same routine went on about every five miles all of the way back to his house. Once we got out of the car, I could be a little more creative. When we got back, we all sat down to play cards at the dining room table. After a couple of hands, I got up to get a drink of water—after I left a gift at the table. Before anyone even noticed, Papa had me figured out.

"Get back in here, Ed" he said calmly, without even taking his eyes off of the cards.

"Why?" Gladys asked.

"Because," he said, still looking at his cards. "He just shit his pants and went over there to shake his leg and leave us with the smell. If I have to breathe it, then so does he."

Thankfully it went away before bed. Since Dad and I had to share a bed, he said that I was going to have to sleep on the floor if I was going to soil the sheets all night. Up to that point and since, I have never had such foul smells emerge from my body. It wasn't all fun and games, either. Each fart came with a fiery burn along my colon, so I too was happy when it was over.

A few days later, we went to Rob's for the rest of the week. It was rainy and nasty the whole time so I didn't feel like hitting the brush. Instead I sat in the Explorer with Rob, ate junk food, and took naps while we waited for Dad to possibly flush something into the clearing. He would be gone for hours at a time, only to come back and find his car full of crumbs and us both sound asleep.

"You fuckers," he began as he got in the backseat and slammed the door. "I can't believe you guys. I ask you two to watch the clearing and you fuckin' sleep—and eat all of the food."

We headed back for Rob's because Tristan was going to be home from school soon.

"Hold it, Rob!" Dad yelled as we bounced down his driveway.

Rob stopped the car and Dad pointed out two doe that stood parallel with the passenger side of the Explorer, less than a hundred feet off the driveway. Dad handed me his rifle and told me to shoot the one in the back because it was bigger. I stared to open the door, but Dad stopped me.

"You'll scare it," he said. "Just roll down the window and shoot her in the lungs."

So here I am with a gun that I had never shot, sitting in the front seat of a car, and twisting my body to the side to be able to shoot out of the window. The irony of this was, it was October 25—two years to the day after I killed my first deer. Even though I was in such a shitty position, I fully expected to have the animal drop like the spike did at Lake Cavanaugh.

"Watch out for the Bachelors," Rob warned as I pulled the trigger.

Nothing—the safety was still on. The two deer started walking as I switched the safety off.

"Hurry up!" Dad yelled.

I pulled the trigger again. BANG!! The deer took off running with its left rear leg flapping in the wind.

"Goddammit, Eddie! You blew its back leg off!" Dad scolded, as if I didn't already know it.

"Calm down, Ronnie," Rob said. "These things happen. It won't get far, so let's go find it."

We all got out with our guns and headed down over the bank behind Rob's house. Dad bitched me out the whole way down there. I don't remember what all he said, but I just stood there and took it because I was too afraid to stand up for myself. I didn't need him coming down on me anyway because I was already angry at myself for making the animal suffer.

The other deer was long gone but between the three of us walking about ten feet apart from each other, we were able to track the wounded one. Dad and Rob followed a trail of broken and bloody branches while trailed behind them a few feet. I bent over to pick up a bloody chunk of bone and as I went to step forward to catch up to them, the deer's head popped up from a large patch of grass and sees us.

"Here she is!" I called out, as she took off into a giant patch of cattails that stood no less than eight feet high.

Dad and Rob each pulled up and shot simultaneously. Rob hit its front shoulder, really crippling it, while Dad missed completely. Of course, he didn't yell at his brother for wounding her like he did me.

With it now in the marsh and in the thick cattails, the only option was to go in after it and try to flush it back out in the open. Rob and I stood up on a level spot while Dad went into the swampy mess. We heard the rustling just fifteen feet away from us and saw the cattails moving, but we couldn't see who was who. Dad identified himself by sticking his bright orange hunting hat on the barrel of his gun and lifting it up in the air. He was still about ten feet away from it, but he was moving faster than she was. We directed him in the right direction until he was right up to her. He still couldn't see her until she mule-kicked him right in the knee. Dad feel down but got up with his knife, jumped on it from behind, and cut its throat as if he was a Viet Cong soldier in 1968 Vietnam during the Second Indochina War.

While I would go on just one more hunting trip (mainly for the trip itself), my desire for hunting was gone. It wasn't entirely because of injuring the deer before killing it because that was bound to happen, but it was because of the way that Dad degraded me for doing it. It was like pouring salt in the wound—I felt bad enough already. I should have just not pulled the trigger. I should have just taken the chance and gotten out of the car to try and get a clean shot. I didn't. The deer became a victim of my own greed—wallowing in the muck of my mind forevermore.

CHAPTER 24

Pins and Needles

"WHAT ARE YOU doing here, Ed?" David Kilcup asked me as I came into the locker room after school had let out on a cold January day.

"I'm gonna turnout for wrestling," I answered, setting my gym bag down.

"Have you ever wrestled before?" another kid asked.

"No, not really, but I did beat your varsity 175 pounder last year during P.E." I said, pointing over to him. "Maybe I can do it again and you guys won't have an automatic loss at that weight. Or maybe not, but I want to give it a go."

"He won't be varsity this year anyway," Troy Hanson said of last year's loser. "Nobody's going to beat Travis Geiger anyhow."

"Who's that?" I asked. "I've never heard of him."

"He's going to start school here," Troy replied. "In a few weeks, he will be eligible to compete after all of his transfer papers are done. He's a big fucker that is strong as hell."

I turned back and started changing my clothes. I didn't know how the varsity lineup was decided. Hell, I didn't even have a pair of wrestling shoes yet. I felt a tad out of place because everyone in there had wrestled before. All I knew was, I wanted to give it a try.

We all walked into the cafeteria where the floor was now covered with roll-out wrestling mats. The janitors rolled them out and cleaned them right before the final bell rang to end school so they would be ready for us at 2:30. After turnout, it would be our job to roll them back up and stack them over by the wall next to the stage so kids wouldn't mess with them during lunch.

There were probably forty kids or so gathered around the mats, talking wrestling, and practicing a few moves and holds. Out of the small weight room walked a long haired, lean, and muscular guy with a Hulk Hogan mustache. He introduced himself as Greg Bisbey and then introduced us to his assistant coach, whom I already knew, Ron Russell.

"The most important thing about wrestling is being in shape," he said. "It is impossible to compete in a match with a talented wrestler unless you are in shape."

Having said that, he told us to start running laps around the cafeteria. We would stop just long enough to do twenty push-ups, twenty sit-ups, or twenty jumping jacks, then it was back to the running. One hour later, we finally stopped. He let us catch our breath and get a small drink of water before having us start the process over again.

"Tomorrow, those of you who stick with it and not quit after the first day will be rewarded—" he said, beginning an evil grin. "With HARDER work."

When I got home that night, Dad asked me how wrestling went.

"I don't know," I said. "But the track meet was hard."

He looked at me funny until I explained to him the story. That night, we went to the sporting goods store to get me a pair of wrestling shoes. After running all afternoon barefoot, I wasn't about to do that again. The bottoms of my feet were black from the dirt of the mats and cracked from one side to the other from drying out during our marathon. As bad as that felt, it didn't hurt near as bad as my calf and quadriceps muscles. It even hurt to lay down when it was time to go to sleep.

The next day, we ran for only about a half-hour before we started drilling actual wrestling moves. We practiced collar and elbow tie-ups, crossfaces, and arm bars. These weren't the most technical moves by any means, but they are essential for basic wrestling.

After about a week, Greg and Ron weighed everybody in and grouped us together by weight in fifteen different classes, beginning at just 80 pounds and going up by five to ten pounds until 175. From there it went to heavyweight, with a maximum weight of 250 pounds. Guys were then put into a tournament bracket to determine the varsity and first string junior varsity wrestlers in a series of one fall matches called "challenges," which would be held once a week for the first month of the season. Just because a guy was named varsity one week, didn't mean that he was going to be the week after. He would, however, have to be beaten twice by the same guy in the same day to lose his spot. After the fourth week, there would be no more challenges and we would have a set lineup.

In the 175 pound class that I was in, I had just one match to win against a kid named Jordan Brown to be named to the varsity squad. I muscled him to the ground and rolled him over for the pin, without using a real hold, in a match that lasted maybe twenty seconds. I didn't care how I did it, I just knew that I had to put the guy on his back to win. I was varsity for the week my first time out, which culminated with a takedown tournament at the high school against three other schools.

I was more than a little nervous as I put on my spandex singlet for the first time. Although this tournament didn't count towards the season statistics, it was still my first actual one-on-one competition in front of an audience. I didn't want to be humiliated in front of people by being out-wrestled by a better kid. If I was going to have any sort of success, I was going to have to explode on my opponents and out-muscle them before they had a chance to out-wrestle me.

Things weren't starting off on the right foot, however. As I continued to slip on my tights, something wasn't right. I always wore boxer shorts for underwear and they bunched up and looked silly underneath my singlet. Everyone else had worn a pair of briefs. I didn't even own a pair and hadn't for years, so I just decided not to wear any underwear at all and pray that my tights wouldn't get torn. If that happened, my wrestling would be the last thing that everyone laughed at. Everything turned out fine and from then on, I would wrestle every match that I ever had without underwear.

Unlike regular matches, these jamboree matches would be just one, one minute period. After each takedown, the whistle would blow and both guys would start back up on their feet. If a kid got taken directly to his back, however, you could record a pin before starting back neutral (both guys up on their feet) again. The match was over at the end of one minute, meaning you could pin or get pinned a few times during the contest.

When it was my turn to wrestle, I walked out onto the mat and stared a hole into my red-head opponent. When the whistle blew, I hooked the guy's head and arm and jerked him over my right hip to his back. The referee slapped the mat, indicating a pin, and we started neutral again. The whistle blew again—same thing. I pinned the guy five times in the sixty second match without giving up a single point. The next two matches went the exact same way. It wasn't until my fourth match, when I began to get a little cocky, that I got a point scored on me. It didn't matter to me, I got first place in my weight class with a 3-1 finish. Not bad for a rookie.

The following week, Travis Geiger came into turnouts for the first time. Honestly, I have never met such a pain in the ass in my life. He wasn't a bad person, he was just a screw-off. He would flick somebody's ear from behind or trip them when they walked in front of him or some stupid, childish shit like that. He was the kind of person that you just wanted to punch in the mouth, which was what one kid did a few years later after Travis stuck his muddy finger into the kid's earhole.

When challenge day came around, it took me all of four seconds to head and arm Geiger to his back for the pin, earning me the top spot for another week. So much for him being unbeatable. Matches aren't won by size and strength alone and being bigger doesn't make you better. Most importantly, it solidified my spot with the other wrestlers on the team. I may have been new, but I could pull my weight. Now, I was accepted as a wrestler by my peers.

The first actual duel meet match was at Burlington. I was the last match of the night because our heavyweight, Matt Denmark, was overweight and couldn't wrestle. Only two kids on our team lost that night before I stepped onto the mat, so I couldn't be one of them. It wasn't a dominating performance, but it was a win. Thirty seconds into the second round, I turned the guy to his back for the pin.

The next week during challenges, I learned my first of many wrestling lessons—never look past an opponent. Just because I beat him once, didn't mean that I was a shoe-in to beat Geiger again. He beat me by fall in two rounds. *No big deal*, I thought, *he has to beat me twice*. That was lesson number two—don't go into a match with the idea that you don't have to win. He pinned me again and just like that, I was JV.

Beings I didn't have a match during those nights when he wrestled varsity, I sat up in the stands for the matches and quietly cheered the opposing team when Geiger was on the mat. That may not be a good thing from a team standpoint but with my only focus being on him, his loss could be an opening for my win. Sure enough, he was pinned inside of two rounds. I couldn't wait until Monday when I would have the opportunity to get my spot back.

When it was our turn to wrestle during challenges, I beat him. My confidence was back, but not exactly in a positive way. I had to find the difference between confidence and arrogance. After he beat me during the second match to retain his spot for another week, I found it. This time around, I had to sit in the stands for two matches. Although he was victorious in both, I used this opportunity to watch him wrestle instead of just rooting for him to lose. He always kept most of his weight halfway down his opponent's body when he had them down instead of being directly on top of them like he was supposed to. That meant that, with a little effort, the guy on the bottom could get out.

The next challenge would be the last one of the season and the winners would lock in their spots for the final six matches. It was all or nothing. My last chance. Do or die—and I had to beat him twice in a row. To sweeten the pot, Mom said that she would buy me any wrestling tape that I wanted if I could beat him. I picked WrestleMania III, which had to be special ordered from Coliseum Video's warehouse in New Jersey—price tag $39.95 plus shipping and handling. No sweat, Mom said that she would order it over the phone the next day if I delivered.

Me and Mom before a wrestling match in Sedro-Woolley

I won the first match easily, but the second one was more of a struggle. I was down by a few points towards the end of the match and would pretty much have to pin him in order to win. All that I could think about was getting that tape, the one that contained two of the greatest matches ever on the same video. In the closing seconds, Geiger wore down just enough and I was able to turn his tired carcass for the pin. Greg and Ron were right—you have to be in shape. While Geiger tripped kids and pulled down their shorts from behind, other guys were training hard.

True to her word, Mom ordered my tape the next morning. Two days later, I wrestled for a total of fourteen seconds against a black kid from Oak Harbor. I was named wrestler of the day and had my name and picture displayed in the gym for a whole week. My match was the quickest fall of the year to that point, with the next closest being thirty seconds longer.

I rolled through my next four matches, pinning all of my opponents without much of a struggle. The final match was at Arlington and I was going to face the kid that pinned Geiger a few weeks earlier. Team wise, the duel meet meant nothing. Even if our team lost, we would still be the league champions. That match was the only match of the year that I trailed in. He led all of the way through, but I kept within a few points of him throughout. I needed a two point reversal to tie it, or an escape and a takedown to win the match by one. I was able to reverse him and even managed to put his shoulders to the mat for the fall with only seconds to spare, ending my season with a perfect 7-0 record.

I was so exhausted after the match that I went into the locker room to get a drink of water and to rinse the sweat out of my burning eyes, blowing off the last bout of the night. I no sooner than got in there when I heard the crowd roar. I shrugged it off and went about rinsing my eyes.

"Holy shit, you missed it!" Michael Russell said as he flew through the doors.

"Missed what?" I asked.

"Matt just flopped his guy and stuck him in four seconds!"

Great. Not only did I miss the whole match like a bad teammate, but my season record for the fastest pin was beaten on the very last match of the season. *Damn!*

A week or two later, we had our team banquet at a local restaurant. Awards were given out for various things to various wrestlers. There was the Fish Award, which is wrestling jargon for "pussy," that went to the biggest fish. Matt got the "It's Over" Award, which was a piece of pie that signified the end of his diet. I was given an award for being "The Pinner," which was a giant brass safety pin that measured nearly a foot long. It kind of pissed me off when Greg introduced me as the recipient saying, "This guy just started wrestling and he doesn't even know how to wrestle, but he knows how to pin." The more I thought about it though, the more I found it to be the compliment that it was intended to be. A guy named Kevin Kesti was awarded the MVP. He too was undefeated, but he only pinned six guys. I pinned seven and although I didn't wrestle a full schedule, I did more in seven matches than anyone else. I honestly felt that I should have won that award.

All told, of the forty kids that began that season, only twenty finished. Of the twenty, only myself, Monte Peterson, Troy Hanson, David Kilcup, Matt Denmark, and Travis Geiger ever wrestled a match in high school. Of the six of us, only Troy and I competed for the entire four years and were the only ones that survived the reality of high school wrestling—it was a totally different world up there than what we had known for the previous two months.

CHAPTER 25
Tuco

PERHAPS IT HAS become a cliche that is too often used. When people use the term "man's best friend," do they say it so fast as part of their everyday language that they take for granted what it actually means? Most likely, few if any, don't take the time to analyze what they are going to say about any subject, let alone this one, but how true are these words? You could've had the shittiest day ever at work or in your personal life and yet when you get home, your four-legged pal is there wagging his tail as happy as can be to see you. Not that I advocate this, but you could beat the hell out of him for no reason and he would be pleased as punch to see you when you came back around. Some would argue that these examples only prove how stupid dogs are, but sensible people acknowledge this as loyalty.

As people, we don't always get along. Everybody has their differences, some of which are simple, others escalate into feuds. Husbands and wives argue. Fathers and sons battle back and forth. Bosses and their employees collide. Most are temporary, while others could lead to divorce, estrangement, or termination, but a good dog is your friend until the end—your best friend.

I met my best friend on a Thursday afternoon, April 25,1996, while I was walking home from school. I had actually seen him two weeks earlier, walking with who I presumed to be his owner, in approximately the same area. That day when I saw the yellow-colored Labrador with a slight curl to his tail, I thought to myself, *Gee, I'd like to have a dog like that someday*. As fate would have it, he strolled right up to me that day during my walk home from school. He could have just as easily have picked any one of the eight or nine kids in front of me, or the couple dozen that were behind or to the right or left of me. If dogs weren't color-blind, I would've thought that it was because of my red 49ers shirt and hat that stuck out from everyone's Gothic-black outfits.

As I was petting him, I noticed right away that he wasn't wearing a collar. Come to think of it, I don't recall him having one the last time that I saw him either. *This had to be the same dog—he had the same curly tail*. Without a tag, I had no idea what his name was, so I just called him "Boy" as I patted his head.

When I began walking towards home, he started to follow me. I continued along but stopped every few feet to turn around to see if anyone was out looking for him. Surely if somebody had their dog take off, they would know almost immediately. These were small neighborhoods with small lots, no more than a quarter-acre, and there weren't many places to hide. With each step I took, I figured that before I turned off the highway down Orth Way, somebody would retrieve their dog. Deep down, though, I hoped that I could take him home.

As we kept walking along, I started thinking more and more that he was a stray. I had walked this same road home from the middle school for almost three full years now and although this dog looked to be about a year old, I never once saw him before. Every other yipper and lazy mutt along my route I had seen hundreds of times—this one was different.

Sure enough, he trailed me all the way home. I walked into the garage and opened up the door to the house.

"Mom, come here for a minute," I said, looking down at the dog as he sniffed around the garage.

"What is it, son?" she asked as she came to the door.

"I think we have a new dog," I said, pointing over to him.

The truth was, the entire family wanted another dog. It had been four years since we had Shiloh and for the past couple of years, we had been talking about getting a big dog—one that didn't bark all the time or that Mom couldn't back over with a car. The only problem was, our neighborhood wasn't really set up for big dogs. We had no fence, no doghouse, no chains—nothing. It was like the old "someday" thing, you know, the idea that sounds okay but isn't too likely to occur.

Well, like it or not, the big dog was now here and it was late enough in the afternoon where he was going to have to at least spend the night. If we were going to be able to have a big dog, then this was going to be the test. If it worked, maybe "someday" might come after all. The only trouble was, I wanted this dog. After Dad and Jen met him, it was unanimous. The only thing that stood in our way of keeping him was Jiminy Cricket telling us that the right thing to do would be to run an advertisement in the newspaper about a found dog. The add would run for one week. If nobody answered, the dog would be ours.

In the meantime, he needed food. He ate a whole loaf of bread in the first couple of hours that he was there, but he needed dog food. Mom went to the store and bought a collar and a leash as well as a twenty pound bag of Western Family dog food, which she only selected because the dog on the front of the package looked the same as our visitor. While she was at the store, I gave him a bath with the garden hose and Suave peach-scented shampoo. If he was coming in the house, he had to be clean first. It took the biggest towel that we had to dry him off, which just happened to be one of my beach towels.

After his bath, I threw a tennis ball with him for a while. He would go get the ball after it was thrown, but he had no desire to bring it back to me. It wasn't until I got a second ball that he would bring it back, in hopes of getting both of them. It would become a game between the two of us to see if he could retrieve the first ball and capture the second before I could. After he had them both, I had to get a third ball. He eventually got that one too—carrying all three around in his mouth at once.

We brought him in the house in the late evening around bedtime. I wanted to be the one to take care of him, so I wanted him to stay in my room. This wasn't going to be a phase, I really wanted to make this work. I went so far as to shut my door and sleep on the floor with him. Anytime he stirred, I got up and took him outside to see if he had to go to the bathroom. Usually it was a false alarm and all he would do was just walk around and sniff. Other times he would lean into a sprinter-like stance to take a piss—he rarely lifted his leg like normal male dogs.

The next morning, it was time to leave him on his own while Jen and I went to school and Mom went to work. The only logical place to leave him in was the garage. There he would be locked up, but with plenty of room to move around and he couldn't do a whole lot of damage. As we pulled out of the driveway, he stood up on his back legs and looked out the glass window of the roll-up door at us leaving. All you could see was his wet nose and beady eyes as he tried to catch one last glimpse of us.

It all became routine in the week that the newspaper add ran. Only one person came to the house with the hopes that we had his dog, but it wasn't even a close match. By the following Friday, eight days after he followed me home, he was part of the family. All he needed now was a name. "Boy" and "Pup" weren't going to cut it.

I felt that I should be the one to name him. While I wasn't financially supporting him (yet), I was the one that found him, bathed him, fed him, walked him, took him out throughout the night, and played with him the most. I won the argument and selected a simple name, after my favorite character in my favorite movie—Tuco.

Without a doubt, Tuco had a name that he went by previously, but with constant repetition, he began answering to his new name in no time. He may not have came when he was called yet, but he would at least turn his head and look at you in the eye. Strangely enough, when you said, "Tuco, outside," "Tuco want a treat?" or "Tuco go bye-bye," he would always come running.

It took several weeks before I started sleeping in my bed again. Tuco didn't wait. He was at least smart enough to sleep on the never-used bottom half of my bunk bed. After he found out that it was okay to get on there, he slept there every night and for naps as well for the remaining two years that I had that particular setup. Another spot in the house that you could find him was in Dad's recliner. He would lay there until until somebody came along and wanted to set down. As soon as it was no longer occupied, he would crawl back up there. There were also times when he didn't wait and would just crawl up in your lap and flop down. When this happened, you had no choice but to get up and let him sit there by himself.

Tuco in his recliner

Now that he was completely house trained, the only time that he would get up at night was when he was sick. I would always wake up to his stomach rumbling, which sounded like a sluggish car trying to turn over. I would fly out of bed and lift his eighty pound frame and carry him across the hall as quickly as I could so he could puke on the linoleum floor. At least then it would be easy to clean up, as opposed to the mess that he would leave on the carpet.

It's hard to believe, but it was probably close to two weeks before he barked. We actually got to the point where we thought that he couldn't, much like a mute person. Once he finally did, it was a deep and intimidating bark that would definitely get some attention. He rarely barked but when he did, there was a good reason. Most of his vocal communication came by way of his unique howl. He would greet you with a howl that would sometimes go continuously for several seconds. Often times he would continue howling as long as you kept talking to him, sometimes carrying the conversation on for several minutes.

Within a few weeks, we took him to the vet to get neutered. Since we had no idea of his age, the vet guessed him at being right around a year old. The other puzzling thing was his slightly curled tail. The vet said that was a sign of being a mixed breed. He said that he could be part golden retriever, chow, or both, mixed with lab. Basically we left not only without Tuco's nuts, but without any definitive answers about his past as well.

He was down for a day or so, but it wasn't long before he was ready to play again. In addition to playing fetch, Tuco loved to wrestle. I could beat on him and give him bear hugs and try to hold him down, but he just kept coming. He would gently latch onto my forearm and take me down that way. While he did leave scratches and welts up and down my arms, he rarely drew blood. Luckily we were only playing because as strong as he was, he could have bitten clean through if he wanted to.

I would be lying to you if I said that having Tuco was all fun and games. Believe me, he wasn't Lassie or any other canine hero that you see on television by any means. He was mischievous, easily distracted, and often times wouldn't come when he was called. He would turn around and look you directly in the eyes when you called his name and then bolt. It was almost like he was challenging you to come and get him or he was giving you the old "F-you" in dog terms.

When he was left alone in the garage, he had plenty of room to himself, unlike most dogs that get locked in crates. Because the cement floor was always so cold, we would lay down a blanket for him to stretch out on. On it, we would spread out bones, chew toys, and a few dog biscuits. At first, he didn't touch anything, including his biscuits, which he would eat as soon as we got home. Then it got progressively worse.

It started with him dragging his blanket all around the garage. Once that went over without repercussions, he moved on to knocking down brooms and tipping over stacks of firewood. Next came chewing on the pieces of wood and stringing bark from one side of the room to the other. While it did make a small mess that had to be picked up, he really wasn't hurting anything. He finally crossed the line when he started messing with the shoes that were kept under a bench near the entry door to the house. Initially, he brought out one shoe (mine) and left it laying in the middle of the floor. Then he chewed on them a little. Finally, he ate over half of one of them.

Unfortunately, this was the beginning of my inevitable clashes that I was going to have with my father. Rightfully so, he beat Tuco with the same shoe that he had for lunch. On the other hand, I felt that he kept going a little too long with it. A couple of smacks was fine, but not more than that. I thought that was a bit too much and I told him so.

"You're not in charge," he said. "I am. I pay for the shoes—not you!"

In order to prevent future shoe store visits, we started putting them all up on the workbench out of the way. Tuco didn't care, he just climbed up there and pulled them down anyway. What began as a joke about the funny things that we would find upon our returning home, became a leery feeling throughout the day. Knowing that Dad was going to beat the shit out of my dog, I would just be a weenie and sit in the car and let it happen to avoid any confrontations.

The end of his garage days came one day when he skipped dinner and went straight for dessert. He ate, wrappers and all, over twenty chocolate candy bars that Jen was supposed to sell for gymnastics. I've heard it said that chocolate is poison to dogs, so how he got away with nothing more than diarrhea and a bellyache is beyond me. After this, he was banned from the garage and we began tying him up outside. That went fine for a few days until he found out that he could chew through the rope and run wild all over the neighborhood. After we started hooking him up with a chain, he would just slip out of his collar and take off. Now instead of worrying about what he was going to chew up, we just wondered if he would still be home when we got back.

Tuco would run off at least once a week in search of adventure. He wouldn't just do it when he was left alone, he would run off if you so much as turned your back on him for even a few seconds. He would chase birds, cats, and people who were walking as far as a hundred yards away. Once he would take off, he would get distracted by something else and, in turn, go after it. You could call him until your voice was gone and I swear that he would smile and just keep on going. Sometimes he could be caught in a few minutes but other times, it was a few hours. He wasn't stupid of deaf, he just wasn't trained properly.

There were two ways to fix this issue—get rid of him or put him through an obedience course. The latter was chosen and once a week for the next two months, all four of us went with him to train. Not only did the class train him, but it also trained us to be able to handle him. While everyone else in the class used dog biscuits, we used hot dogs as rewards to teach Tuco to sit, lay down, stay, come, and even crawl.

I would make it a point to work with him each day, aside from his once a week class. Before long, he could hold a "stay" command even if a tennis ball was thrown right in front of him. He didn't want to and his back legs would be shaking like crazy, but he didn't move. For the last day of the class, there was a stay contest between all of the enrolled dogs and the demonstration dog. People used treats and sudden movements to break their concentration and eliminate the participants rather quickly. It all came down to Tuco and the show dog and after a twenty minute standoff, the contest was ruled a draw.

Come to find out, Tuco was tearing up all of that stuff because he was acting out for not being left in the house while we were gone. Once we started leaving him inside, he never messed with anything. He might throw up if he was sick and once even shit from the garage door clear across the living room after eating a full bottle of my allergy pills, but that was it. From then on, he was left in the house if we went out.

Although it wasn't always possible, Tuco loved to go for rides in the Explorer. He got to ride in the cargo area behind the passenger seat and would just love to stick his whole head out the window, regardless of the weather. Either Jen or I might be cold, but one of the windows had to be down. If not, he would whine until it was.

Of course, he didn't like being left in the car alone. If that happened, he would get even by chewing up the vinyl retractable cover behind the backseat or by chewing seat belts in half so they would rewind into their casings and disappear. Not only that, but the dog hair and nose prints that he left behind were murder to clean up. He was then restricted to only going on short trips, with only one or two quick stops, or real long trips to Papa's house.

After the few years of going to Lake Chelan over the Fourth of July had run its course, everybody but Jen wanted to do something different. While she wanted to hang out with the girls on the water and bleach her hair like the following sheep that she was, and then try to lie about it to Mom, everyone wanted to go back to Yellowstone. A few months earlier, Mom and Dad bought another camp trailer, finally replacing the destroyed Aloha. This one was quite a bit larger but even with the couple extra feet of length, it was still cramped because Jen and I were now bigger and we now had an eighty pound dog that was like having a fifth person in the family.

Our first stop was a horseback ride at a ranch near Columbia Falls, Montana, about a half-hour from Glacier National Park. We left Tuco chained up to the camp trailer and took off on an eight hour ride through the wilderness. It was new and fun but unless your body is used to being in the saddle, it can be painful. While I enjoyed the experience and the scenery, I've had no desire to get on very many more horses—it just ain't my thing. I tried riding Papa's horse a couple of times after he first moved over there, but the bitch kept bucking me off onto the cement-like ground of Eastern Washington.

After waking up saddle-sore the next morning, we made our way towards Yellowstone. We no sooner than got on the highway when we passed a giant go-kart track in the next town. This track ran close to a half-mile and was shaped like an inflated letter "C." Dad pulled over and went into the entrance to check it out, quickly running back to order us out of the car so we could try it. Although Mom didn't ride, the three of us had a great race. It was so fun, we ran it again for a second time. The cars went pretty fast and with both up and down inclines, it could make for some pretty interesting passing attempts. In the future, we would actually ride motorcycles all the way over there, nearly six hundred miles one way, just to race. I went by there a while back during a motorcycle trip and was saddened to see that it was out of business and the track had grown over with grass and weeds. We sure made the most of it while it was going, though.

We took our time getting to Yellowstone. With it being so hot outside, we would pull over and stop and swim for a while in a river or a creek. Tuco would swim too. He was right at home in the water. He would jump in and swim around and duck his entire head underwater to try and see if he could scrounge something up. He would even play fetch with large pieces of wood that we would throw into the water.

Once we got to Yellowstone, we parked the camp trailer in a campground and drove around the entire park for three-straight days. We saw the usual elk and buffalo, roaming wherever they pleased. One such buffalo was standing right next to a stop sign as we pulled up to it. He was so close to the car that you could've reached out the window and plucked a hair from his back. Tuco nearly went through the window, barking and snarling like a rabid dog to scare him off. The buffalo thankfully just went on eating his grass.

I don't remember how it started, but somewhere along the line somebody came up with the idea to trick other park visitors into stopping and looking at something that wasn't there by pulling over and pointing into the woods. Without fail, the very next car that came by would pull over to see what was going on. Every other car behind them would also do the same thing and before you knew it, there were ten cars lined up to take a peak. We would then take off and leave them trying to find a figment of our imagination. Once, this Chinese guy asked Dad what we had seen. Dad told him that it was Sasquatch before we drove off.

Once we left the park, we stopped by Papa's for a couple of days before going home. Uncle Robbie and Karen and the kids even came over for a barbeque while we were there. Tristan brought along a bag of plastic army men and Papa, Rob, Dad, and myself sat out in lawn chairs for hours throwing rocks and golf balls at them, trying to knock them off a dirt pile. Whether a boy is eight or fifty-eight, it's the simple things in life that can be the most fun.

A few weeks after we got home from Yellowstone, Dad heard an add on the radio that the WWF was coming to the Key Arena in Seattle for a *Monday Night Raw* broadcast. He said that if I bought my own ticket, we could go to the July 22 event. Without hesitation, I agreed to the stipulation because tickets were only twenty bucks. We even brought Dustin along with us, as he had never gone to anything like that before. It was only fair because his mom had already taken us to a few Seattle Mariners games in recent years.

As soon as Dad got home from work, we loaded up and headed down to Seattle. We got to the arena just after the doors opened and found our way to our seats. We were probably twenty rows from ringside in club seats just above the entrance way were the wrestlers came out from behind the curtain. After a couple of preliminary matches, the show went live on the USA Network.

An hour into the show, the matches and interviews just kept on coming. The red lights on the television cameras indicated that they were still filming. I couldn't figure out why, because I knew that *Raw* was just a one hour show. The only thing that I could think of was that they were possibly filming matches for an upcoming home video release. Once it was all said and done, we sat through a total of four hours of wrestling!

The next day, I watched the telecast that I had recorded on the VCR. Although you couldn't make us out, I could see right where we were sitting during certain shots. At the end of the show, they advertised next week's *Raw* in order to begin building interest. I was shocked to find out that next week's matches actually already had happened the night before while we were there.

Little did I know, that using videotape to record events was precisely what helped make the wrestling business the money that it did. Recorded wrestling matches could be seen around the country, while live events with the same wrestlers could draw money at different arenas around the country or even the world. Although the matches were identical, nobody cared. The reality of it was, each month the WWF would broadcast worldwide on pay-per-view, culminating a month's worth of feuds. The next night, they would broadcast *Raw* and tape an additional three episodes at the same building to air in the weeks leading to the next pay-per-view. Only having to put out a live feed twice a month was a great way to save money.

On the downside, their competition had the extra money with Ted Turner's checkbook to go live every week. Thus, WCW would win the television ratings battle because they would adapt to what the WWF was going to air on their taped weeks. Within two months of the event in Seattle, the WWF had to start kicking out the extra cash and go live more often in order to compete. The four hour events were now over and the ticket prices went up to offset the television costs. Now for 50% more money, you could get 50% less wrestling.

As the summer winded down, Dad and I took a rafting trip down the Skagit River. We each had our own raft, fishing pole, and sleeping bag and with the exception of a few cans of pop and beer and a frying pan, that was it. The whole idea was to launch the rafts and let the rivers' current carry us along. The oars were only used for paddling away from debris, or for rowing ashore for the night.

It was fun and relaxing. We caught a few fish for dinner and just threw our sleeping bags on the sandbar and slept under the stars, listening to the river roll. I'm not much for boating or rafting, but it was something new. The comparison between doing this and riding motorcycles wasn't even close—I would much rather ride any day of the week.

A few weeks before my fifteenth birthday, I bought my first street bike. After a couple of years of casually looking at bikes, I found the bike that I wanted. It wasn't in a magazine or a newspaper and it wasn't quite as close as where I found the Kawasaki, but it was just behind the garage door in the driveway where Dad had tipped the Gold Wing over a year earlier—Skip was finally ready to part with his dad's bike.

The bike was a 1982, metallic purple, Honda V45 Magna. It was 750cc's and had a six speed transmission. When it was initially produced, it was one of the fastest accelerating bikes on the market. Unfortunately, Skip wasn't much of a rider and let it set for years between the rare instances when he would ride it a whopping one mile to work and back. Still, it was in phenomenal shape and it only had just over 7,000 miles on it.

I think the only reason that Skip sold it was because he needed the money. Dad had tried to get him to sell it to him before, but he wouldn't let go of it. It took just about every cent that I had when I laid out twelve, brand new hundred dollar bills on his kitchen table. With the money and a verbal commitment to Skip that I would give him the first shot if I ever wanted to sell it, I had my very own means of transportation. The trouble was, I would have to wait another year until I rode it—or would I?

CHAPTER 26

"Oh Look—A Freshman."

Inside most teenage minds in the weeks leading up to their entrance into high school can be a storm of mixed emotions. Soon they will be driving, going on dates, perhaps getting a job, and they begin counting the days until graduation. Then there is that other voice that tells them to do whatever it takes to fit in, show people how cool you are, and build a reputation. Some never quite grasp that a reputation is who people "think" you are, while a person's character is in fact "who" they are.

There may only be three years difference between a senior and a freshman, but it is easy to spot the difference. You name it—height, facial hair, body shape, voice—everything is different. Kids coming out of the eighth grade might think that their shit don't stink and that they are just as cool as high school kids. Oh man, is that a recipe for disaster. Upperclassmen were going to test everyone that came in riding on a white stallion. It's no different than two packs of wolves out in the woods—they will establish dominance. It's life. People do it to new employees at work. There is a food chain, and it's been around since the dawn of time.

There was no older brother or sister to give me advice upon entering high school, so I had to learn it on my own. I was going to be myself and not pretend to be somebody that I wasn't. I would be firm, but humble. Height wise, I was as tall as I would ever get by the time that I left eighth grade. I was 6'1" and weighed less than 180 pounds. If I thought that I was a bad-ass, I would have been I primary target to get my ass kicked because I stood out a little more, as the other kids my age weren't as big as me. I figured that if I just played it cool and didn't look for trouble, I would likely be fine—then came my first day.

Three periods of six into my first day, I had to take a piss. Classes for all ages were strung out across the campus but each grade, however, had their designated ares and hallways where they hung out between classes. This included lockers and bathrooms. It wasn't that you couldn't use any bathroom that you wanted to, you might just not have too many friendly faces in there waiting for you. I asked the teacher if I could use the bathroom and went out into the hall. I had really no idea where the closest one was, so I just walked around until I saw the first sign that read "boys."

I walked inside the first one I found and right away found two older guys each putting in a dip of chewing tobacco, while another guy was counting what was left of his cigarettes. There was no way that I could turn around and leave without getting destroyed, so I just walked up to the urinal.

"Oh look," the biggest guy said. "A freshman."

"Yeah," said his buddy. "I wonder if we can get him to push a penny?"

Pushing a penny is a crawl of shame where a person crawls on their hands and knees and pushes a penny across the floor with their nose. There was no way that I was going to do that, so I had two choices—I could either just start swinging and land only one or two punches before I got double-teamed into the ground, or I could begin to get on my knees and then hit one guy in the nuts in order to get the other guy one-on-one. Either way it wasn't going to end good because at the time, I still had my dick in my hand.

Thankfully before anything could happen, the cigarette counter said, "I don't think you guys can make him push a penny."

He lit one of his smokes before he added, "Especially with me around."

After the two guys left, he offered me one of his cigarettes.

"No thanks," I said. "I don't smoke."

"I didn't used to either," he said as he took another drag. "Now I'm having trouble stopping."

I don't know why that guy stepped in. Maybe he didn't think that two against one was fair, or maybe it was because he was older than the other two guys and wanted to put them in their place. Whatever the reason, nothing went down that day. As fate would have it, I was never in another position like that again. I didn't press my luck and use the wrong bathrooms anymore either, by the way. Avoiding trouble doesn't make you a pussy, it just shows that you are smarter.

Even if I wanted to, I couldn't avoid being around upperclassmen. I was the only freshman in both my biology and algebra/trigonometry classes. The two elective classes that I chose, wood shop and farm shop, were also filled with older students. The only two classes that I had with entirely one age group were P.E. and English.

I think that P.E. was segregated for two reasons. In addition to avoiding the inevitable locker room mischief, the biggest share of it was the difference in athletic ability. Unless you were fortunate enough to have God-given talent, a freshman couldn't keep up with an older athlete. High school football was the same way—freshman had their own squad that played freshman from other schools, while everyone else was on the actual high school team.

English was a two-level course that had to be passed in order to graduate. It was supposed to be for ninth and tenth grade students, but they had more than a few older kids in them who failed the previous year and needed to make it up. It wasn't uncommon, and in fact was very likely, to have a senior in ninth grade English.

Each student had to earn a certain amount of credits in each subject in order to graduate. As I said earlier, some of them could be earned in middle school. With me taking algebra the year before, I only had one year of math left to go. I also had to complete two years of science and two years of English. I figured on getting them done within my first two years so I could take more electives (which I had to do also) later on. The only other requirement was two years of history, but those courses couldn't be taken until eleventh and twelfth grade. It was just as well, because my plate was full with algebra and biology. The science wasn't bad, but the math was work. As usual, I did A's and B's, but it took a strong effort. The only saving grace was the fact that come June, I was done with math—period.

Biology was actually pretty cool. We did lab experiments all the time like dissecting pigs, growing ecosystems in a jar, and studied organisms under microscopes. Whether it was plants, mammals, or sea life, we studied it all from feeding to reproduction.

I'll never forget when the teacher introduced the human reproduction unit.

"We will use proper terminology," she said. "We don't say 'tits,' we don't say 'fucking,' we don't say 'cocks,' and we don't say 'screwing.' Any questions?"

We all just sat there, not really believing what we had just heard come out of our teacher's mouth. The only other time that I heard a teacher swear was during a class on drugs when they said that hallucinogenic mushrooms grew in "cow shit." Unless it was a coach, district employees kept it clean on school grounds. I often wondered what some of them were like when they weren't on the job.

The most important thing about high school academics is to prepare students for the future. There are courses to prepare you for college and basic labor jobs. Even military recruits are around to sign up those that aren't sure what they wanted. While I wasn't sure about what I was going to do, I knew that I was done with school after the twelfth grade. I didn't want to go to college—I didn't want to spend another four to eight years taking classes.

Now fifteen, still the only thing that I wanted to do in my adult life was drive a truck. Since Dad had started driving again, he was now bringing his truck home at night. I looked out the window at it everyday and wanted nothing more than to drive something like that. It didn't have to be a log truck, maybe I could drive long-haul like Grandpa did and be on the road all of the time and see the country. Whatever the type of driving, I just wanted to do it.

I wasn't going to be the type of person that worked a nine-to-five desk job. I didn't want to be lawyer. I didn't want to be a teacher. I surely didn't want to be a doctor because I just knew that I would puke the first time that I saw some fat, sweaty lady with no clothes on. After seeing a sign at school that read, "If you do a job that you like, you won't have to work a day in your life," I knew exactly what my future plans were.

During career week in English class, my teacher, Mrs. McCann, said that it was a ridiculous choice.

"Why would you waste your time with that?" she asked. "You could do any other job and make more money doing it."

"I know," I said. "I know for a fact that I could do any job that I want to. The fact is, this is the only thing that I want to do. Right now, I don't care about the money. I'm not going to do a job that I hate just for the money."

"You're wasting your brain."

"And you're wasting my time."

For the next couple of months, we butted heads about everything. She once even tried to have me suspended for assault when I was merely roughhousing in the hall one day. The principal even thought that it was ridiculous, but gave me a weeks worth of detention so she would drop it and leave him alone. Slowly but surely, once she got to know and understand me better, we started to get along. Who she thought was an arrogant jerk, was nothing more than a confident kid. Although they are often misconstrued, there is a big difference between conceit and confidence. In fairness to her, she wasn't the first to get the wrong impression of me—and she won't be the last. I can't apologize for having a personality.

After five seasons of playing little league football, it was time to begin playing ball at the high school level—well, sort of. There was a relatively new rule that restricted ninth graders from playing football at the varsity level, which was a benefit in the sense that we got more playing time—like a full season compared to maybe only a play or two. We were basically third string on the varsity depth charts, or C-Team. The varsity, of course, played their games on Friday nights, the junior varsity played on Thursday nights, and we played on Monday afternoons. We practiced in our own group, while the three older classes practiced together. We had our own coaches that were not part of the varsity squad. Our only interaction with the varsity team was when the head coach punished the entire organization for a food fight that took place during lunch one day.

The food fight had actually been brewing for a few weeks before it erupted. During lunch, kids could get sandwiches, salads, burgers, or whatever the daily entree was. You could also get as much fruit as you wanted like grapes, oranges, and apples. I really don't remember how it started, but a few grapes would sail across the cafeteria everyday during lunch not long after school began for the year. I thought it was funny, so I would grab extra grapes at lunch and launch them with a plastic spoon that I used for a catapult.

This went on for several days. Soon, there were a few more members of the staff watching for flying objects. That was no big deal because you would just wait until they weren't looking before you sent the objects airborne. The supervisor would hear them hit the window and then head over to the other side of the cafeteria to investigate. Then, someone would zip one past his ear and he would turn around and go back the way he came. He would have made a better ping pong ball than a supervisor.

Finally on one day, someone upped the ante and sent the entire half of their sandwich across the room. The person whose ear was then covered with mayonnaise then picked up their open carton of milk and flung it over their shoulder. Then all at once, everyone in the room stood up and threw their entire plate of food towards the center as they backpedaled to the surrounding walls. Only one kid didn't throw his food—B.J. Faye. He didn't even know what was happening until until it was too late and he was wearing fifty pounds of school lunches. He didn't hear the eruption because he was listening to music in his headphones.

It took about three-and-a-half seconds to make the biggest mess that I had ever seen in my life. There was ham and turkey stuck to the walls, milk dripping down from the windows, and pools of ketchup and mustard on the floor. There was going to be hours worth of cleanup for the lunch workers and nobody for them to punish. This incident may have led to our school installing video cameras because they were put up within a few weeks afterward.

The whole school was abuzz over what had happened and that nobody was able to be punished for it. The varsity coach, whose name I don't remember because I didn't play for him and this was to be his last season coaching, made the entire football team runs sprints for two hours straight as a punishment. It was funny because about two-thirds of the team wasn't on that lunch schedule to begin with, which meant that they obviously had nothing to do with it and had to run anyway. Better yet, B.J. was on the team and he did nothing but wear everyone's food. The coach punished us all because he said, "Football players don't behave like that." Yes they do, Coach.

As far as our C-Team record went, I'll just say around .500 because I really don't remember. The fact is after our undefeated season in 1994, we would never be anything but just an average team again. We didn't have good coaching, which caused us to give a shit less if we won or lost. I even skipped the last game of the season that year to go on a hunting trip instead.

Thanks to Dad's tirade last year following my indirect shot at the doe in Uncle Robbie's driveway, I had pretty much sworn off hunting with Dad. Apparently he was too good of a shot and never made mistakes, so I clearly wasn't in his league. Plus, I didn't like the idea of wounding an animal the way that I did and I was afraid that I might do it again. I decided to go on the trip anyway. It wasn't for the hunting, it was for the trip itself.

The trip was pretty much like a camping trip, with a little hunting mixed in with it. Myself, Dad, Papa, and Rob all were going to spend a week in early November camping in the Colville National Forest off of US-395, near the Canadian border. The four of us, along with Papa's chiropractor, Dan, set up two large, canvas tents, complete with wood stoves in them for heat, and connected them with a canvas tarp, making a third room that we used for the kitchen. We folded out benches and tables for eating and even built a do-it-yourself outhouse for us to shit in—several feet away from camp of course.

Hunting camp, not far from the Canadian border

After we had set up camp, Papa went into his truck and brought back a few bottles of whiskey and some peach flavored brandy. He took a few pulls off of the brandy and passed it to Rob, who took a big swig himself. Rob then held the bottle out as if he was going to hand it to me. I just looked at him instead of reaching for it.

"It's okay, Ed," he said. "You're at huntin' camp."

"Yeah," Papa added. "You better get it while there's still some left."

So I took the bottle and took a big drink of it, just as if it was a bottle of water. For a split second, it was like drinking peach juice—then I felt the burn and the instant buzz of the alcohol.

"Whoa," was the only thing that I could say as I blinked my eyes several times, trying to focus on what was happening.

"You're supposed to sip it," Papa said as everyone laughed.

"Thanks for telling me now."

"Care for some more?"

"Not just yet, thanks."

I was still trying to gather my senses. I did have a few swigs (not guzzles) throughout the week, but not enough to get drunk. That wouldn't come for over a year yet, which I will definitely get into later.

The rest of the day, we gathered enough firewood to get us through the week. We needed some for the campfire and enough to keep both of the tents warm at night, thanks to the twenty degree temperatures. Once we had enough wood, we got everyone's sleeping arrangements figured out, Dad and Dan were going to sleep in the small tent, while me, Papa, and Rob would get the big tent. Papa and Rob each brought fold-out metal cots that were so rusty, all you had to do was look at them and they would squeak. You can imagine the noise that they made when their fat asses were on them tossing and turning all night. Between that and their snoring, I barely slept. The amount of noise that those two made snoring, I'm not kidding you, sounded like two grizzly bears fighting in the wild.

Dad did the cooking for breakfast and dinner. We had steaks and potatoes, hamburgers, and roasts for dinners and eggs, potatoes, bacon, sausage, and toast for breakfast. There was always plenty of food to go around and it was even good on top of that.

Unfortunately, that was about all Dan was good for. He had no sense of humor, no common sense, and a shitty attitude. He didn't do any hunting—period. I was a little better in the sense that I at least road hunted with Papa and Rob in the pickup. Instead, Dan sawed firewood all day where we were hunting, making a ton of noise with his chainsaw and scaring away every living thing within a ten mile radius. At night, he would take his pickup load of stolen firewood home and drop it off. He would then stop at the bars on his way back to camp and have enough drinks to get himself good and lit up.

One night, he got so drunk that he crashed his pickup in the ditch instead of turning into our camp's driveway. He then stumbled his way into camp, knocking over the chairs and even the table before passing out in bed. The next morning after we all spent a few hours digging his truck out, he promised not to go back into town at night. What a relief—now we got to spend even more time with this fool.

As I said, he had no sense of humor. When I was setting the table for one of our meals, I inadvertently gave him a child fork instead of a regular one. After he put up a big stink over it, he went over and got himself a regular one. For the next two or three meals, I set it that way on purpose just to piss him off. It worked—he screamed and hollered each time, not finding the humor in at all. Rob then gave him a giant meat fork for another meal and said, "Is that fork big enough for ya, you fuckin' asshole?"

Once he started acting like a whiner, I really started laying it in on him. I loosened his salt shaker lids, put dirt in his sleeping bag, a cat skull in his pillow case, and grease on the door handle of his pickup. The best part was, he thought that it was Dad the whole time and tied all of his clothes in knots in order to get even with him. Papa then politely asked me to stop, just because he was sick of his attitude and wasn't far from kicking his ass.

The jokes may have stopped, but he kept his attitude. He was bragging one day about all of the deer that he had killed and that his .300 Weatherby could shoot a fly off a horses ass at three hundred yards with open sights.

"How far?" Papa challenged.

"Three hundred yards," Dan said, pointing away from camp. "From here to that big stump."

"That stump ain't three hundred yards away," Papa said. "Ed, you play football—how many football fields is that?"

"One, exactly," I judged.

"Bullshit," Dan said. "He don't know what he is talking about."

Papa then instantly got pissed off, got right up in his face, and said, "Do you want to step it off?"

Dan didn't answer. Papa then turned and headed directly for the stump, taking even, three-foot steps the entire way.

"Ninety-seven yards!" Papa hollered back, after he reached the stump.

Dan looked over at me and I gave him a huge, cheesy smile and a towel to wipe the egg from his face. When Papa came back, he told Dan to shove his Weatherby up his ass. Getting madder by the second, Dan stormed into his tent and came out with a pistol.

"Fine," he said. "There are six shots in here. Watch how many times I hit this beer can."

He stood back about fifty feet or so and hit the can four times out of six.

"Not bad," Rob said. "Mind if I try?"

Rob loaded the gun and just like a scene in a Clint Eastwood movie, he chased the can across the road, hitting it all six times. Dan then went in and took a nap, but probably cried himself to sleep.

Later in the evening after the guns were put away, we all played poker in the big tent. We used match sticks for poker chips and everyone was worth a dime of real money. Dan was doing well until he called for a game that put an ace and a two face-up on the table and flipped over a third card, which people could bet against him if the fourth card would be higher or lower than the third. When it was my turn, he dealt me a king of spades, so I bet my whole pile of matches that the next card was going to be lower. Sure enough, I was right and won every single one of his match sticks. Of course that was the end of the game, as he stormed off to bed.

After we started cashing in our match sticks, I wound up twenty dollars richer. Somehow, there was more money than match sticks on the table at the end, so Papa took it upon himself to shove the money into his pockets. Rob, Dad, and I just looked at him confused.

"What?" he said. "That's about how much I lost. Beings he quit, I'll take this, and we'll all have some of his money."

As for the actual hunting part, Dad was the only serious hunter who would try to hunt all day. He would pound the brush while I would ride around with Dad and Rob. We would just keep picking him up and dropping him off again as he searched for deer that were probably long gone due to all of the commotion.

All in all, it was a great time. There were no phones, TVs, radios, city lights, people, or cars. As a matter of fact, the presidential election was on that Tuesday and we didn't know that Bill Clinton was reelected until we got home on Saturday, likely making us the last five people in the country to find out. Although we talked about doing it again, this time without Dan, it never happened. It was a one time deal, but I will certainly never forget it.

CHAPTER 27

Two and Too Many

WINTER CAME EARLY towards the end of 1996, with snow piling up in town in November. It would stack up to be a few inches high and then be totally melted the next day when the temperatures would jump to fifty degrees, making it seem more like spring outside. This kind of stuff caused streams, creeks, and rivers to flood, giving this area of Washington national news coverage. The snow didn't affect us directly, other than it gave Dad some time off because he couldn't get to the job sights with all of the snow anyway, and it gave us a chance to ride dirt bikes in the snow and drag each other on sleds.

I was now legal to be on the road and operating a motor vehicle—sort of. I got my learner's permit around Christmas after I completed a two month long driver's education course prior to the beginning of the school day. This meant that I could begin to drive a vehicle anywhere with a licensed driver, so I was most likely the one driving anytime I was in the car with Mom or Dad.

I started out driving the Explorer and other than accidentally shutting off the headlights on an extremely dark road instead of turning on the wipers, I thought I did pretty good. Learning to drive Dad's bright orange GMC Jimmy, that he picked up after selling the Oldsmobile, was a little tougher. With it being a manual transmission, I had to push in the clutch pedal and shift at the right engine speed so I wouldn't lug or over-rev the engine. Yes I killed it at almost every intersection, but who doesn't? Both Jen and I would learn to drive it and nearly 200,000 miles were on it before Dad had to put in a clutch, so I didn't do that bad.

At the time, permits didn't apply to motorcycles and people couldn't get licensed until they were eighteen. I could, however, get my license at sixteen if I took a rider training course. The only requirement for the training course was a driver's license, so I was less than a year away from being able to do that. This didn't mean that I didn't ride my new Magna on the highway illegally, because I did.

The Jimmy was in the shop getting the four wheel drive fixed after Dad bent the shifting forks on our hunting trip. At the same time, the Explorer was in Mount Vernon having a recall procedure done on it and had to be picked up. Mom and Jen were at some gymnastics seminar, so the only option was for me and Dad to ride my bike to Mount Vernon, pick up the car, and take separate vehicles home. I would just follow Dad home on my bike and everything would be fine. It was only about ten miles from the shop to our house, so what could go wrong?

Dad rode bitch as the two of us rode to Mount Vernon to drop him off. He got in the Explorer and I followed him onto the freeway, which we only had to be on for two miles. As soon as I got the bike up to sixty, it sputtered and died. (I had to look down to see if I wasn't on Dad's 350.) Dad had no choice but to get off at the next exit, go southbound on the freeway back to the car lot exit, exit again, and get back on the northbound lane to get back to me. With all of the stoplights, it would be at least five or ten minutes before he got there.

I didn't know what the hell was wrong with my bike. I started right at the start by checking the gas tank—bone fucking dry. To begin with, I didn't have a fuel gauge on the bike to tell me how much gas I had left. Instead I had a sensor that would light up on my speedometer when I had a little less than a gallon remaining. The sensor sure picked a great time to stop working, leaving me on the side of the freeway with no license or permit. With nothing going to happen until I got gas, I just started pushing my bike towards the exit while I waited for Dad. I made it about fifty feet before, of all people, a state patrol pulled up alongside of me.

"Everything alright?" he asked.

"Yeah, I'm just out of gas," I said.

"Need any help?"

"No, I think I got it"

With that he drove off and I went back to pushing, although I was shaking so bad that I was lucky that I didn't tip my bike over. I made it to the off ramp, which thankfully had a downgrade, so I hopped on and coasted into the gas station at the bottom of the hill. Dad got there just in time to pay for the fuel. I learned a pretty good lesson that I follow to this day, and that is that you can't trust a fuel gauge. Since then, I reset my trip meter each time I fill up any of my vehicles and beings I know approximately how many miles that I get on each of them per tank, I will never run out of gas in any car again.

Wrestling season began just before Thanksgiving, around the middle of November. As I said earlier, only five of us from last year's middle school team even turned out. It was way, way different to say the least. The older wrestlers were much bigger, much faster, and much stronger. While some people may not be able to tell a sophomore, junior, or senior apart, if you add a freshman into the mix, he will stick out like a boy at an all-girl school.

Our coach, Sherm Iverson, led a varsity squad that finished second in the state the previous year and was favored to make a run for the team title again in the '96/'97 season. His goal was for the whole team to be in superior shape first, then work on the wrestling second. For the first few weeks, we did nothing but run. We ran in the one hundred degree mat room, mixing it up with wind sprints, push-ups, and sit-ups. For a break from the heat, we would get to run up and down the hallways in the school, upstairs and downstairs, or even outside on a five mile stretch that covered both the main parts and the outskirts of town. Those that were able to withstand the conditioning, were able to compete for a varsity spot. A few older guys quit, but everyone stuck around for the most part.

With an undefeated record a year earlier, I was expecting to do alright. I knew that I was going to have some hard times, but I wasn't expecting the very little amount of success that I was about to have. After getting squashed by Tyler Bridgman during challenges in under thirty seconds, I was the designated junior varsity wrestler for our team at 190 pounds. The problem with that was, the guys that I would be facing were a developed 190 pounds. I wasn't quite so defined and was closer to 170 pounds than I was 190. I'm not trying to make any excuses, but the three year difference between fifteen and eighteen is much different than say thirty and thirty-three. The three year difference that I was on the low end of might just as well have been ten.

My first high school match was actually at the varsity level as part of the Stanwood Wrestle-Rama. It was a four man tournament between four schools and I somehow got one of the spots after one of the guys from another school missed the weigh-ins and couldn't compete. How I got his spot instead of another kid from another school was beyond me.

Nonetheless, there I stood looking across the mat at a rock-solid dude from Mount Vernon. I was giving up at least ten pounds right at the start. I could have easily made the weight lower of 178, but I would have been third or fourth string on our team's depth chart. At least at 190, I could get some mat time. I didn't know how long this guy had wrestled for, but I'm pretty sure it wasn't his first varsity match. When the whistle blew, I sunk in a head and arm and took him directly to his back. I scored two points for the takedown and three points for the near-fall before he escaped from my pin attempt, scoring a point. I was up 5-1 just like that when we went to lock up again. I figured that I would go ahead and try the head and arm again beings it worked the first time. The thing about the head and arm, though, is that it is easily reversed if the guy throwing it isn't prepared for it. This time after I hooked it up and threw him, he rolled me right through it and took me to my back. Within five seconds, I was pinned for the first time in school vs. school competition. It certainly wouldn't be the last time that I was stuck that year.

The rest of the season for me was spent exclusively at the junior varsity level. It took four or five consecutive pinfall losses before I realized that the head and arm simply doesn't work against a legitimate wrestler. I was going to have to learn to wrestle and not just brawl or else I was going to have a long four years.

Nearly every Saturday during the season was tournament day. The varsity would go all over the state to wrestle in varsity tournaments, while the junior varsity would travel to a more local JV tournament. As for the twice a week team matches, we would go on first and the varsity would compete later on under the spotlight in an otherwise dark gymnasium.

We would all line up and weigh-in together as a group according to weight class. We all had to be completely naked throughout the whole process so we could be checked for rashes and and other skin diseases that were prevalent amongst wrestlers. Everyone's favorite running gag was to lightly push the guy in front of you so his dick would go between the butt cheeks of the unsuspecting guy in front of him. It was shit like this, combined with the group showers that had to be taken before and after turnouts, that gave us wrestlers a reputation of being slightly homosexual. Remember, a reputation is merely who people "think" you are, but it didn't help our cause when we would go up to the basketball players in the locker room, stand on the benches while they were sitting down tying their shoes, and act like we were going to stuff our peckers in their ears.

After we weighed in, everyone would eat a little something before their match. Most guys would drink a glass of Gatorade and eat some fruit or a sandwich. Other guys would eat cheeseburgers and French fries. I even saw one dude drink and entire half-gallon of egg nog less than thirty minutes before his match. Guess what he did on the mat thirty seconds into his bout?

Some guys hadn't ate or drank anything in a few days in order to make weight. It was nothing for them to gain ten or fifteen pounds in a day and then turn around and lose it all two days later. Most lost weight just by putting on heavy clothes and running in the hundred degree mat room, profusely sweating it all off. Other would go so far as to put on trash bags underneath their heavy clothes to further aid the sweating. Obviously that is illegal, not to mention seriously dangerous. The coaches knew it but if they didn't see it, then it didn't happen—whatever it takes to make weight. It has been that way for years, and will be for many more. That is why you hear about athletes dying way to early from heart attacks and heart disease. It's the nasty, but very real, side of sports.

For this season, I didn't have to watch my weight. I could eat whatever I wanted, whenever I wanted. Usually my prematch meal would be a can of fruit cocktail in light syrup. I would drain the syrup out to avoid ingesting unnecessary sugars. When it came to tournaments, we would weigh-in around eight in the morning and have a full two hours before the matches began. That, combined with me wrestling in the twelfth of the fourteen weight brackets which added an extra hour on top of that, meant that I had enough time to eat a normal breakfast of an omelet and toast at a nearby restaurant.

Every single tournament was long and drawn out. All weight classes had sixteen guys in each tournament bracket and were a double-elimination format. In order to win, a guy would have to wrestle and win four different times. One loss meant that the best that he could do was place third. My tournament days in those days ended after two straight losses, or "two and through," as it is known in the sport. For my first series of matches at tournaments, I was usually pinned inside of the first, two minute round. It wasn't until two months into the season that I lasted into the second round. Even then, I was typically pinned within the first few seconds of the round because I couldn't wrestle from the bottom.

At the end of the first round, the referee would flip a coin and award position choice to the coinciding wrestler. A rule of thumb is for the winner of the toss to defer his choice to the third round. The other wrestler would then get the choice of top, bottom, or starting neutral with both men on their feet. If I won the choice, I would defer to the other guy as I was supposed to. He then, knowing he was wrestling a fish, would choose top so he could quickly put me out of my misery without wasting anymore of his time. If the decision was deferred to me, I would choose top and try to turn the guy over. Instead, all I managed to do was let him reverse me and turn me over for the pin.

On the bright side, I only had to get beat one time during duel matches rather than having to be humiliated twice a day in tournaments. Match after match, I was beaten and battered and left lying on my back and staring up at the lights. My confidence was nowhere to be found and I just couldn't wait until the end of the season so I didn't have to suffer anymore.

Finally, on the second-to-last tournament of the year in Concrete, I managed to pick up my first win. It felt so good to get that monkey off of my back that, just for a moment, I felt as if it was the previous year during my undefeated run. As fate would have it, I even chalked up another win during the same day. Of course I lost my two matches and was eliminated, but I finally had something in the win column—and that was like winning the whole tournament as far as I was concerned.

I fully expected that to be my last match of the season. The following week was the league tournament in Sedro-Woolley, the first of two tournament steps to qualify wrestlers for the state tournament at the Tacoma Dome. Wrestlers that placed in the top two at league would qualify for the regional tournament the following week down south. From there, the top two again would advance to represent the area at state. I don't know if it was because we were the host team or if it was because the bracket needed filled up (it sure as well wasn't because of my record), but I somehow got a spot in the tournament, which was unheard of at the time.

Unfortunately with my record being two and too many losses, I was paired with the top seeded guy at 190 pounds in the first round. A mere twenty-one seconds into the match, I was tied up and pinned by the guy who would go on to win both the league and regional tournaments and finish second in state. With that particular tournament being a two-day event, I was done for the night but still had another day to go.

The next morning after weigh-ins, Sherm called a team meeting in the mat room. He talked about every match counting as points for the team and that any points would help us win the team title.

"Let me give you guys an example," he said. "After losing all season, here is Eddie Thramer—his consolation round opponent is out with an injury and he advances to the next round, giving us two team points."

Everyone clapped. I just sat there in awe because this was the first that I had heard about it. A win at league meant that you were guaranteed a sixth place finish. Although I would've had to have the rest of my bracket withdraw to make regionals, I was satisfied with the outcome.

It took two more pinfall losses for me to officially place sixth in league without technically winning a single match. Nowadays that would qualify a guy for regionals but back then, only two guys made it out in each bracket—every other guy was done for the year. For the seniors who didn't make it, their entire career was over. Not one of the seniors whose career ended that day didn't cry. Wrestlers are supposed to be tough and vicious, but we are still human.

Back then in order for a guy to letter in wrestling, he had to either wrestle half of the season at the varsity level or place at a postseason tournament. Although by sheer luck, I accomplished the latter and thus earned a letter. My fellow classmates, Monte, David, Matt, and Troy, all received one as well for wrestling varsity. Monte, Matt, and David had earned their spots, while Troy inherited his due to a starter's injury. Like me, he caught a lucky break to earn his letter but at the same time, he had also suffered the same amount of abuse throughout the year to deserve it—maybe even more. At the close of the awards ceremony where the letters were handed out, Sherm advised all of us to hit the gym and get stronger and go to a week long wrestling camp at North Idaho College in Coeur d'Alene in the upcoming summer.

With summer vacation's wrestling camp still a ways off and with weight training only offered as a class for tenth grade students and higher, the only way of taking his advice immediately was to join the local fitness gym in town. For the next eighteen months, Dad and I went down to Joe's Gym in town to pump iron five days a week.

We couldn't have been more out of place when we initially walked up the flight of stairs into the facility. There were slim, tanned, and toned men and women doing everything from treadmills to free squats to the bench press. Next, there were bigger and more muscular men doing dead lifts and dumbbell curls. Then we saw the owner, James, who had THE biggest arms that I had ever seen in person. His biceps must have measured some twenty-six inches around as he standing-curled over two hundred pounds for reps of ten.

The guys down there got us on a routine that worked our chest, shoulders, and triceps the first day. The second and fourth day was all lower body, while the third and fifth day was backs and biceps and a total body workout respectively. At first we couldn't lift a lot of weight but after we each got the proper form down, we were able to steadily increase our lifts.

We also got on this high-protein diet that was designed to build muscle. The idea was to eat one-and-a-half times your body weight in grams of protein daily. Within weeks, we would gain ten pounds of muscle and begin looking huge like them. They forgot to tell us that in order to get that look, we had to also take fat burners and metabolism boosters as well as illegal anabolic steroids. For two months, Dad and I consumed over two hundred grams of protein each day by drinking pasty shakes and eating egg whites, tuna fish, and pretty much anything with a fair amount of the nitrogenous substance that we could find. As promised, we put on quite a bit of weight. Without the other "supplements," however, it was almost all fat.

The worst part about it (or best part, depending on how you look at it) was the gas that it caused. The human body can only use so much protein and the rest is digested and expelled in the worst way possible. This made the time in Papa's Bronco seem like a walk through the flower garden. This didn't happen just sometimes either, it was on a daily basis. Even an otherwise routine trip to the toilet was now an epic event. Soon, we ditched the diets all together and focused on just the lifting.

The workouts continued to get better, despite the lack of a "necessary" diet. We even jogged at home every night to stay in good cardiovascular shape. Dad and I would run a mile or so, regardless of the weather, almost every night. There were times that it would pour and we would get back all muddy from splashing in the puddles that were on the street. When that happened, we had to strip down outside of the garage so that nothing would get tracked in.

Once after an extended rainy session, I stripped down and walked in first with an arm load of clothes. Thankfully, Dad warned me about the chainsaw that he had left in the middle of the path so that I wouldn't trip over it barefoot. After the warning, I stepped over it on my way inside the house. Dad, on the other hand, made a fillet out of his foot on the same saw that he had just got done warning me about.

Once school ended for the summer, the five day wrestling camp in Idaho began at the start of the subsequent week. Ten to fifteen of us returning wrestlers made the trip over in a couple of carpools. Dad actually drove me over two days earlier so we could spend a weekend at Papa's first. On Sunday afternoon, he took me a half-hour up the road to the college and dumped me off, just as the rest of the team was getting there, before going back home.

Four guys were assigned to each room. Troy, David, Monte, and myself all decided to share a room together. When we opened the door to the room, all we saw was one bunk bed, a small closet, and a desk with no chair. There was no possible way that two guys could sleep on each twin bed, so something had to be wrong. As we unpacked, a supervisor came around and pulled out two, paper-thin mats from under the bed.

"It ain't so bad, guys." the guy said with a grin as he left the room.

"I'm glad my parents paid for this shit," Monte said, pressing on the mats.

We agreed.

As for the camp, three times a day for two hour stretches apiece, we all went into the pavilion for turnouts. There were college coaches and freestyle wrestlers from all over the country giving instruction. Even an Olympic gold medalist from the previous summer's Olympics in Atlanta, Kenny Monday, was there to teach a couple of sessions. We were fed cafeteria meals three times a day that were served buffet-style and we could eat as much of anything as we wanted. The food was okay, not great, but after a tough session, you were so hungry that sometimes taste didn't seem to really matter. There was also a fair amount of free time each day for swimming in Lake Coeur d'Alene, on which the campus sat on the banks of. Generally right after the midday session, everyone would head directly for the water.

On the day before camp ended, many of the guys in camp started getting ill. Many of them were sprawled out in the lobby of the dorm, moaning in pain. It almost looked like a mission that housed the wounded soldiers during the Civil War, only without the blood—that is unless you count the unflushable football-sized turd that somebody painfully deposited in one of the bathroom's two toilets. There was blood all over the sides of the bowl as well as the seat and floor as a result. The poor person who had to go through such an ordeal was never identified.

By Friday, everyone was sick. I woke up with a terrible case of diarrhea. I couldn't get more than three feet from the bathroom before I was back on the pot again. Monte was taking a shower, hoping that it would help him feel better, while I was limping over to the sink to wash my hands. He let out a loud yell like he had just been stabbed, causing me to look over just in time to see him shoot vomit onto the wall while at the very same time, sending a waterfall of liquid shit out of his ass and onto the floor. Of course I immediately puked after seeing that.

Four days later, and ten pounds lighter, I was finally able to eat again. I don't know if it was food poisoning or a quick-spreading virus, but it was a terrible experience. I may have been almost as sick since then, but never worse. I get nauseous just writing about it.

CHAPTER 28
Planning Ahead

FOR SEVERAL OF the previous months of 1997, Mom had been suffering from severe lower abdominal pain. Eventually doctors found a large cyst growing on one of her ovaries and determined that it had to be removed. The surgery was scheduled for late June, the day that we were supposed to leave for our family trip. This year, we were going down to Las Vegas to see Dad's mom, who was supposedly real sick in her own right. Apparently, doctor's didn't know what was wrong with her or why she weighed less than a hundred pounds. (It couldn't have been from her steady diet of two packs of cigarettes, a half-case of Budweiser, and three crackers that she consumed on a daily basis could it?) The trip should have been postponed a couple of weeks but I had three tickets for *Monday Nitro* at the MGM Grand on June 30 and would have been out over a hundred dollars of my lawn mowing money if we didn't go, so Mom sucked it up and unselfishly made the choice for the trip to go on as scheduled.

On the day before the surgery, we left Tuco at the same place that he did his obedience training, which had now been expanded to include a row of kennels to house pets while their owners were away. I was so worried about leaving him there for a week because I thought that he might think that we abandoned him and would forget about us. He had never had to be without the entire family collectively yet. The lady assured me that he would be just fine. Some people left their dogs for months at a time and once they reunited, it was like nothing had ever happened.

Once Mom was out of surgery, and completely against doctor's orders, we loaded her up in the front seat of the Explorer and headed south. Other than to ask for a few pain pills and and to pull over from time to time so she could get out and move, Mom never bitched once about the ride. Although the trip down there can be done in one full day, we split it into two to make it easier on her. We made it to town on Sunday and unpacked the car for our four or five day stay. Mom got into Grandma's house and just stretched out in bed. She had a couple of days to relax before we loaded up and did it all over again. Each day she was up and moving easier and easier and by the time that we did leave for home, she was back to normal.

The next day was *Monday Nitro*, which was to be televised live on TNT. The MGM Grand was still buzzing because just two days earlier on June 28, Mike Tyson literally bit off Evander Holyfield's ear in their rematch for the World Heavyweight Championship. There were still news trucks and reporters surrounding the building and Tyson's nearby home that we drove by on the way to the show.

As I said, I had purchased three tickets for *Nitro*, one each for me, Dad, and Milt, which was the only way that Mom would let me go for some reason. At the time, it was worth it to me so I didn't put up a fuss. I scored fifth row seats for the night and if you check the tape from that event, you could even see us on the nationally televised event. To top it all off, I even got to shake hands with an up and coming Chris Jericho.

Getting to the arena was a piece of cake. Milt took us the ten minute drive from the house to Las Vegas Boulevard. He took side streets and allies to get us to the building the quickest. In Las Vegas, you have to be an aggressive driver or you won't make it anywhere. They might as well take down all of the speed limit signs and stoplights because nobody follows them. A couple of days later, we actually sat in an intersection at a green light while the cross traffic cruised through their red light without a care in the world. Once inside the building, it took us forever to get down to the arena level. Milt had a pacemaker and couldn't overdo it, so we had to stop and take breaks every few feet so he could catch his breath. After the show, it took us even longer to get to the pickup because the evening gambling crowd had recently filed into the casino.

For the next several days, we went to town during the day to see all of the big time casinos on The Strip. Grandma and Milt each worked during the day, so it was either do that or sit around the house. We went to most of the casinos on the south end—New York, New York, Excalibur, Luxor, Caesar's Palace, and Treasure Island. I even illegally dropped in a few quarters at various machines just for the heck of it. I didn't win, but I was asked to stop by security guards.

When the trip was over and we picked up Tuco and went home, Mom's doctor had left a message for her to come back in for a follow-up. It was during that follow-up that the doctor suggested that Mom have a total hysterectomy as soon as possible to prevent any further problems with her reproductive organs. Within a week, she was taken into surgery and gutted like a fish. I was designated to do all of her chores while she recovered, Jen was her personal nurse, and Dad went to work all day before he came home to spell us.

As August approached, Mom was back on her feet like nothing had ever happened. With that in mind, Dad and I took off on a weekend motorcycle trip. This time, instead of me riding on the back of his bike like before, I was going to ride my bike—by myself. Yeah, I was still a month away from getting my driver's license, but I did it anyway. I even rode it all the way to Montana.

It wasn't without excitement though. On our way back to Uncle Robbie's on Saturday afternoon, we were traveling along a stretch of highway about fifteen minutes from his house, without another car on the road for miles. It had been five minutes since we had seen a car when all of a sudden, I noticed a cop flying up from behind us with his lights flashing and his siren blaring. *Shit.* I knew that this was it. I had chanced it one too many times and now that I was a month away from being legal, I was finished. *Fuck*. I pulled over to the shoulder, as did Dad, and the cop just flew right on by. What he was after and where he was heading, we never found out.

When we got back to Rob's house that night, we told him again about all of the fun that we had been having recently on motorcycles. He still was in the process of restoring his old Harley that was a lot like Dad's 350 in the sense that was so temperamental. Rob would crank on it forever until it would cough and sputter just enough to make him think that it would turn over any second—it rarely did. If he was ever going to leave the driveway on a motorcycle, he would have to do something different.

"I know!" he said. "I'll buy a Gold Wing like yours, Ronnie, and all three of us will take a motorcycle trip next year. Yeah! We can even go to Sturgis!"

Sturgis is a small town that covers a mere two exits of I-90 about a half-hour into the western side of South Dakota. It is known exclusively for its Black Hills Motorcycle Rally that takes place for nine days each year beginning the first full weekend in August. It began in 1940 with about ten or twelve guys just hanging out at a local park, but has since grown to the largest and most popular biker rally in the world with nearly a half-million bikers riding into town over the course of the week. It isn't just for Harley riders, either. You can come on a Honda, Yamaha, or whatever. There's everything from knee-draggers, bikes with car engines, and bikes that look like animals—with fur and everything. You can even come in a car, but getting around town in one of those is next to impossible.

As soon as Rob finished his sentence, we all began looking at maps and picking out places that we wanted to see.

"We have to go to Little Bighorn Battlefield to see Custer's Last Stand!" Dad said.

"And I want to see the Devil's Tower!" I yelled. "And Mount Rushmore!"

"And the Badlands!" Rob added. "We can even go through Yellowstone!"

"Yeah, and I want to stop at every historical sign that we drive by because Brenda never lets me do it," Dad continued.

"We're going to," Rob interrupted. "We will have no women nagging in our ear. We can do what we want, fart as loud as we want, and shower IF we want."

Now we just had to wait one full year until it was time to take off.

A few weeks later, both families met in Walla Walla for a Schenk Family reunion. We spent the whole day on Saturday talking about plans for the trip—where we could potentially end up at the end of each day and what we would do for food.

"I figured that we could sometimes cook our own food on these," Rob said, taking out a small fold-out stove from his car that he said would fit in his saddle bags. "We can even make coffee in the morning too!"

It was difficult, but we managed to stop talking about the trip long enough to check out an old museum in town. Even then though, something would trigger thoughts about the bike trip and we would be all right back into it. Mom and Karen had to be just rolling their eyes and praying that the twelve months would go fast.

The day of the reunion, Rob took his crew home without even going. He had seen his mom, who had flown in from Las Vegas, on Saturday night and figured that was good enough. The rest of us went and sat through an endless afternoon, staring at a collection of some of the strangest looking and strangest acting people known to man.

Not two weeks later, Rob and Karen came to our house for the weekend for another one of his doctor check-ups. After he seen the doctor, he would put his shoulder through his own unique form of physical therapy—wrestling on the trampoline. Everyone would all pile on the there and have a huge brawl, trying to throw each other off. Real safe, huh?

For a while, all the trampoline was used for was wrestling. Dad and I would wrestle on there constantly and sometimes things would even get a little dirty. Once, Dad raked my sunburned back so bad that I thought I was going to stop breathing. In turn, I reached over and dug my finger nails into his sunburn that was on his thigh. We spent the next several minutes laying there and yelling in pain.

The trampoline wrestling ended for good when I gave Dad a flying dropkick that sent him airborne off of it and onto the grass. Remember that kid named Evan that I told you about earlier? That is exactly what happened to Dad—except Dad landed on the unforgiving ground from a much higher point of descent. The only reason that I laughed when it happened was because Dad got up and ran around in circles like a dog chasing its tail. He was convinced that I was laughing at the fact that I had hurt him. To me, that wasn't funny because it prematurely ended the playful wrestling between us forever.

Anyway, the Sturgis planning continued to go on. Dad and Rob would call each other weekly, or if at anytime they they had something new and important to share. For every accessory that was bought, whether it be a tent, a sleeping bag, or a bed roll, it had to be shared with the group. Rob sold me a nice set of leather saddle bags that looked and fit perfectly on my bike. My bike had came with its own bags that were big, green, and ugly. I didn't put them on because I thought that they looked gay. I decided to give them to Dad so they could look gay on his bike instead.

On our last trip over there before school started, we actually packed both Dad's and my bike with what we were going to bring on the trip, which was now one month closer than it was when we first started talking about it. My bike looked pretty normal, with full saddle bags and my sleeping bag and bed roll strapped to my sissy bar. Dad's bike on the other hand, looked more like a pack mule straight out of a John Wayne movie. Remember, his bike didn't have a sissy bar on it, it only had a small luggage rack. The only way to put saddle bags on his bike without altering it from its limited edition look, was to put a plywood box that surrounded a Styrofoam ice chest on the luggage rack and then put the saddle bags across that—making it even more top-heavy than it already was. It may have looked silly, but it was going to do the job. Again, all we had to do now was wait.

CHAPTER 29
Street Legal

M Y FIRST SEASON of full-on Friday night high school football began a few months earlier in June, just before the Fourth of July. The new head coach, Dave Williams, led the soon-to-be sophomore, junior, and senior classes into a week long pre-preseason set of turnouts to introduce his playbook and plans for the upcoming season. At the conclusion of the five day stretch, every player was asked to go to Eastern Washington University in Cheney for a week long camp, just like the one I went to not even a month earlier for wrestling, which just happened to be during the same week as our trip to Las Vegas.

During the very first practice, Coach Williams sat us all down and preached the importance of camp.

"Fellas, you gotta go to camp," he kept saying as he patted his clipboard in rhythm with each word that he spoke. "If you can't afford it, you can borrow the money and work it off during the summer. You must go—everybody goes. No excuses."

Great, I'm going to introduce myself as the only guy who can't go to camp. My first one-on-one conversation with the new coach was going be me telling him that I wouldn't be going.

It wasn't that I didn't want to go, but the family had already made plans for the Las Vegas trip—not to mention the wrestling tickets and the fact that Mom's surgery wasn't even going to stop us. Plus, family trips are something that don't last forever and I always looked forward to them.

As we all got in line to formally introduce ourselves, I just knew that this wasn't going to go well.

"Hi, Coach. My name's Eddie Thramer and I play center," I said.

"Welcome aboard, Ed," he replied while shaking my hand.

"I've got a little issue with camp, I—"

"Don't worry, we'll pay for it and you can pay me back with work," he said before I even finished my sentence.

"No, that's not it. See, my family has had this trip planned for months—"

"Football or family, Ed" he interrupted again. "You choose."

"Just forget I even brought it up," I said as I turned to go.

This was just swell. I had played football for six years and I had just three more seasons to play in my life, and this fucker was the guy that was going to be the coach. This guy, who wouldn't even let me explain a situation to him, was the guy that I was to call "Coach." He had been hired for not even two weeks and we had to rearrange our whole summer to fit his stupid camp schedule? If it had been something that had been planned every year then fine, I would have been prepared and not gone on the trip. First impressions mean a lot to me, and probably to him, so needless to say, we never did get along for the rest of my playing days. Just for the record, you'll notice that I was on a first name basis with all of the coaches that received and returned my respect—this guy wasn't one of them.

While the all-important camp was going on in Cheney, I was in Las Vegas as scheduled. I did, however, show up at every optional weight lifting session that went down in August. Only four or five other players made it as often as I did. When two-a-day turnouts started, I was running faster sprint times than every other offensive lineman, which ought to tell you how slow our team was because I was no speed demon. In my mind, I was more than making up for what I had missed.

"One thing I forgot to mention, fellas," Coach Williams began to say, conveniently after the last two-a-day. "Only juniors and seniors will start on this team. For some of you select sophomores, you will get to play on special teams and special teams only, unless a starter is injured. In order to earn a letter, you must play in half of the total quarters played in the regular season."

Some good camp would have done, huh? Special teams was kickoff, kickoff return, punt, punt return, and field goal units. You were guaranteed one kickoff and one kickoff return per game, and the rest depended on how good both our team's offense and defense performed. On the bright side, only sophomores and some less talented juniors played Thursday afternoon junior varsity games. That at least meant that all of us underclassmen got a full game in each week. We had an extra opportunity to get better for the future against the same guys that we would be facing in the coming years, so it wasn't all bad.

In high school, the number that you got in tenth grade was the number that you wore until the end of your senior season—no exceptions. You could choose any number that was available as long as it coincided with the position that you played. Offensive and defensive linemen got to pick from numbers from the fifties through the seventies as well as the nineties and the backs and receivers got the rest.

Me during my high school football days

I chose number 56. The most famous player to ever wear that number was Lawrence Taylor, who redefined the outside linebacker position throughout his Hall of Fame career during the eighties and early nineties for the New York Giants. Taylor was a vicious player who was responsible for ending Joe Thiesmann's career by breaking his leg during *Monday Night Football* on November 18,1985. While it was accidental, it was still the most stomach-churning play that I have ever witnessed in football. Once his playing career was over, Taylor even wrestled at WrestleMania XI against Bam Bam Bigelow in 1995. Plus, with the Giant's colors being red, white, and blue like ours, it was a no-brainer for me.

Some of the other guys got the numbers that they wanted too. Greg Mahle chose number 80, the same number worn by the greatest receiver of all-time, Jerry Rice. While nobody on this planet could ever or will ever be on Rice's level, Greg was as close as they came in small town Sedro-Woolley. He could pull a ball in from out of nowhere, even with one hand. David Kilcup chose number 22 after Emmitt Smith, who would eventually become the NFL's all-time leading rusher. Other guys didn't get so lucky, either the number that they wanted was taken or it wasn't available. Michael Russell was pissed because he wanted number 16 like Joe Montana. He had to settle with number 15 instead. All of us didn't wear these numbers because we thought that we were like these greats, but rather out of respect for what these guys had done.

I've got to say, suiting up and playing on Friday nights under the lights, even if it was for only a few plays each game, was amazing. The crowd was always buzzing, regardless of the win and loss record. The band played loud and proud and it was impossible not be excited when you stepped onto the field. It was as high as it would ever get on a football level for any of us that played that year because not one of us would go onto the college level. On Friday's, however, we all felt like pros.

For my sophomore year, I played kickoff return, punt team, and on the field goal unit. That meant that I played at the start of one of the halves, when we had to punt on fourth down (which was a lot), and every time we attempted a field goal or PAT (point after touchdown). Because these were my only chances to play, I stood on the sidelines and hoped for situations that would get me in the game. I wanted the other team to score so they could kickoff to us and I wanted our offense to sputter so we would have to punt. It may be selfish from a team standpoint, but I wanted to play—simple as that.

For kickoff return, I was the center guy on the front line. When the ball was kicked by the opposing team, I would turn around and run back twenty of thirty yards and form a wedge with the other front guys. They would all fall in behind each side of me and we would start running forward to block for the returner. Meanwhile, the opposing team would be coming full-bore at us to try and break the wedge and tackle the runner. Do you see where I'm going with this? I was the unprotected pawn designated to get destroyed in order to slowdown the oncoming tacklers—sounds to me like punishment for skipping camp.

I made the most of it, man. I didn't care if I was going to get clobbered or about how dangerous it was. I got myself so jacked for that one play a couple of times each game that it didn't matter what else was going on around me. I would take their kamikaze's best shot and just keep fighting with him. We'd scuffle back and forth, practically throwing punches while still making it look like we were just battling for position.

About midway through the season, I actually got to start at center in a game against top-ranked Ferndale. The starter, an uncoordinated oaf who would need a surgeon to remove his lips from Williams' ass, had injured his knee. It was a last minute scratch, which was a problem. I knew the plays, so I wasn't worried about that. The problem was that I had never practiced with the starters, only against them on defense. In order for a machine to run perfectly, everything must be geared just right. The only reps that I got before game time, were the five quarter-speed plays that we ran during warm-ups.

Sure enough, quarterback Kevin Casey fumbled the snap on our very first exchange on the very first series of the game. Ferndale recovered.

"What the the fuck kind of snap was that?!" he yelled towards me after we got to the sidelines.

"If you can't snap it right, I'll find someone who will!" Williams added.

Now, I had played center for five years prior to this game and I had snapped the ball hundreds of thousands of times, so I probably had forgotten more about the position than either of those two would ever know about it. During my snap, I always turned the ball so that the laces would land directly in the quarterback's awaiting hands. If I snapped it and left too early for my blocking assignment, the ball would be fumbled and it would be my fault. If I snap it and the quarterback leaves too early, which was what happened on that play, the fumble is the quarterbacks fault. No matter how much I argued, it was my fault. By the way, Casey's dad was the superintendent of the district and was responsible for hiring Williams to begin with. Yes folks, even high school sports are full of backstage politics.

I played the rest of the game without incident. Of course we would always go three and out and would have to punt because Ferndale's defense was phenomenal. They pretty much had their way with us and shut us out by something like 50-0. Our offense had only negative yardage throughout the game. As for the defense, they might as well have just laid down because Ferndale's offense treated them like whores.

By the end of the season, I had played more than enough to earn my letter. You had to play in eighteen quarters, and I played in nearly thirty. Only four other sophomores lettered that year. Naturally, my name was "skipped" during the banquet when the letters were handed out. I had to go to Williams and go through the entire season's stat book and prove to him that I had earned the letter. In the end, he gave me a half-ass apology and reluctantly gave me a letter.

Football aside, my first week of my sophomore year couldn't have been better. I finally, after nearly three years, got my braces off. While I will never admit that the whole time spent with them was worth it, my teeth did come out looking nice. The orthodontist wanted me to wear a retainer full-time for one full year and then just at night from that point on. I wasn't having any of that so I only wore it at night from the start. I was very good about it, though. I wore it every night for about ten years until it got so yucky that I had to throw it away. It's all good—they're still perfect.

If that weren't reason enough to celebrate, Mom took me down to the department of licensing on my sixteenth birthday to take my written test. After I passed it with a 100%, I went up to schedule my drive test for a later date, which was standard procedure. As luck would have it, they had an opening right then and there so I went out to the Explorer and drove the tester around for about ten minutes. When I was finished, he handed me a slip that said "pass" on it and less than twenty minutes later, I was street legal and had my very own driver's license.

I didn't waste any time by signing up right on the spot for a motorcycle safety class to be held that weekend at Skagit Valley College. If I took that class and passed it, all I had to do was go back to the department of licensing, pass their written test, and then I was legal to ride any size of bike that I wanted to.

I took the class that weekend and actually had fun. There were all kinds of people trying to get their endorsements as well—men and women, grandpas and grandmas, and businessmen and scrounges. Even at my age, I was far more experienced than anyone else. I got quite the kick out of watching some of them continuously dump their bikes during their training rides—it reminded me of Dad at Skip's house!

The next Monday, I went down and took my written test. Believe it or not, I missed six questions when you could only miss five and subsequently failed. I don't know if it was the excitement of the Sturgis trip that I was going to be legal to go on or what, but I failed. The question that decided my fate was about alcohol. It was something like, "How many drinks does it take to impair a driver?" The choices were one, three, five, or ten. I chose "one" and got it wrong. I had to wait an hour before I took it again. If I failed this time, I would have to wait until the next day to try it again. Wouldn't you know, it came down to the exact same question. If I got it right, I would pass. If not, I would fail. This time I chose "three" and got it wrong again.

"Bullshit!" I yelled from the testing area as I turned and headed straight for the front counter without taking a number like I was supposed to.

I told the lady what had happened and that something wasn't right, using a few expletives to emphasize my statements. She didn't even argue, she just wrote "pass" on the slip and had me take another picture for my second driver's license in less than a week—only this one meant that I was Sturgis bound!

I was one of the first to get my license in the whole sophomore class, as the majority of my classmates wouldn't get theirs for a few more months yet. I instantly began driving myself to school everyday in the Jimmy. Although I was now legal to ride my motorcycle wherever and whenever I wanted, I had no intentions on riding it to school. First of all, I was the only one in school who had a street bike so everyone would know that it was mine. Combine that with all of the stunts that I had pulled over the years, and it would be an easy mark for someone to get even. I wasn't going to take any chances.

Mom and Dad didn't make me pay the extra insurance premium that it cost to have me on the list of household drivers, but I did have to buy my own gas and keep it spotless on the inside and outside. That wasn't a problem because I wanted to drive a nice looking car. I was welcome to drive the Jimmy until I had enough money to buy my own rig. The only catch was that I didn't get a ticket or the deal was off. I would only get pulled over once in that car for passing in an intersection several months later, but I didn't get a ticket. In fact, I went into my twenties before I got my first one.

I really only drove to school and back home again. I would make two trips to town on football game nights, but only living about three miles from the school wasn't exactly what you would call a major commute and it would still take me a month or two to go through a tank of gas. It wasn't because I was cheap, but I just didn't have the usual teenage driver urge to cruise around town and waste gas and time like some of my peers.

The other thing that new drivers did was crank their tunes as loud as possible. They also had to have the coolest car stereo equipment—the more bass, the better. Some kids would have the same amount of speakers in their cars as a local band would have on a barroom stage in a nearby tavern. They would crank their nigger rap about killing white cops and raping white women so loud that the pavement would vibrate until they were out of sight. Uncool me just listened to my normal southern rock, country, and L.A. metal on the Jimmy's stock cassette deck and I couldn't have been happier. Long before the days of the iPod, I would record my favorite songs on a tape and play them in the car over and over. It's not that I didn't have any CDs because I did—lots of them—it just wasn't my car to alter. In fact, my collection was growing so much that I began listening to them in alphabetical order by artist. That may sound kind of nerdy, but think about it—how many times have you walked up to your CD rack and spent a few minutes pondering what to listen to? With my system, the decision was already made. In those days, it would take me about two months to go through my cycle. Now, with my collection at over six hundred, it takes me a full year.

Despite my uncool approach to music and driving, I did manage to land my first date at the end of football season with one of the team's female managers. Her name was Stephanie and she was a year older than I was. When one of the other managers, who was a senior, told me to ask her to the homecoming dance, I figured that she might be interested in me. I never did ask her to homecoming because I just plain can't dance. I did, however, offer to give her a ride home when her brother didn't pick her up one afternoon.

When I dropped her off, she gave me her phone number, which I probably only used two or three times just because I hate talking on the phone. I just feel it is easier for me to understand something when I talk to someone in person because you know that they aren't being distracted and that you are getting their full attention. Besides, we had enough time to talk before and after turnout everyday.

I'm not sure if we were an official "couple" or not, but she was the first and only girl to ever wear my letter jacket. I was the first in my class to have one after lettering the year before in wrestling. I had the coolest, most original (and eventually most copied) design on the back. It was a half-wrestler and half-football player dressed in our school's colors with each half holding an opponent down on the ground. Beings you could choose the colors of the opponent's uniforms, I chose the colors for our two biggest rival schools, Mount Vernon and Burlington. It was by far the greatest design ever made. If I wanted to, I could even have changed the skin color of the opponent's skin to match the noticeable cultural change in those towns, but I didn't.

Anyway, I let her wear it one night when she was on the sidelines during a game. When she gave it back to me at the end of the night, it was all muddy from the rain and after being bumped into by muddy players. It wasn't her fault, it was mine for letting her wear it in that environment. After that it was off limits, even if Pam Anderson decided to enroll in or school. Well, maybe exceptions could be made!

When the season was over, we made plans to go out on a date without me even formally asking. Now when I said earlier that I was confident in myself and in life, the only exception would be when I was around girls that I was interested in—then I was nervous and shy. I could never get the words out of my mouth because I was so scared that they might say "no" or laugh in my face. I didn't want the embarrassment or the pain of rejection, so I just never asked anyone.

That Saturday when I drove to her house to pick her up, I had to drive with all of the windows down in forty degree weather just to keep from passing out from nerves. I wasn't like this when I took her home in the afternoons, but this time I was a wreck. I didn't know when it would subside, but I figured that it wouldn't get any worse—that is, until I knocked on the door and her dad answered.

"Hi. My name's Eddie and I'm taking your daughter to the movies tonight," I said after he opened the door.

"Oh," he said. "I thought Jim was taking her out tonight."

I felt like I was knee-high to an ant and had nothing to say even if I could.

"Hah! I'm kidding, Ed. Come on in."

After his poor attempt of humor, I literally had to hold onto the chairs and couches while I walked into the living room to keep from falling over. The ten seconds that it took for her to come down the hall felt like an eternity.

I never did calm down that whole night. I barely ate any of my dinner at the Buzz-In Steakhouse, which is not my style. I don't even remember what movie that we saw. In fact, I even managed to doze off in the middle of it. As for a kiss or action of any kind at the end of the night, you can forget about that—how could that happen when a guy only says about twenty words all night? Needless to say, that was the end of my dating for a while. Word must have gotten out about how much "fun" I was.

With the girl scene on hold indefinitely and with two weeks until wrestling started, I spent the next two weekends riding motorcycles with Dad. It wasn't on our street bikes, but rather on our dirt bikes. For the first time ever, we rode them to actual off-road motorcycle trails and would spend hours riding them through the mud. With our bikes not exactly your modern motocross machines, we got stuck a lot. We spent just as many hours trying to climb out of a hole that we got ourselves into as we did on flat ground. With Dad being the lighter one, I did the extra pushing while he was on the bike twisting the throttle. The bikes eventually made it up, but I had a rooster tail of mud constantly hitting me in the face the whole time.

While riding dirt bikes is certainly fun and believe it or not a real workout, I still would rather stick to riding on the highway. By now, I was far too big for my Kawasaki and I wasn't interested in upgrading to a bigger bike because I was saving money like mad for a pickup of my own. I probably should have sold it, but I figured that it wasn't hurting anything to keep it. Besides, I would need it later for something totally different.

CHAPTER 30

In the Spotlight

SCHOOL ITSELF WAS becoming just an afterthought. My grades were still nearly perfect, but my requirements for graduating were getting fewer and fewer. While I still had to wait until eleventh and twelfth grade for a few classes, I was finished with math now and this year was going to be my last year of world history and science, two classes that I enjoyed.

Sherm was the history teacher and he would always somehow segue into wrestling during his lessons. When he was talking about the Roman Empire or something, he would finish off by relating it to great amateur wrestling dynasties like Coach Dan Gable's Iowa Hawkeyes, who won fifteen NCAA team titles from 1976-1997, including nine in a row. For science, I took chemistry and loved it. We did lab experiments where we would change the colors of pennies to gold and silver, freeze certain objects instantly, and use peanuts as torches. I even took a whole pile of peanuts and lit them on fire. Surprisingly, the teacher wasn't mad because I was "experimenting."

As for the rest of the classes, I took weightlifting, auto mechanics, and wood shop. In the latter of which, I began work on a project that would take me two or three years to complete—a solid oak gun cabinet. As I said before, I am a perfectionist and I would take every step necessary to make it a true handcrafted work of art. I started from the absolute beginning with designing my own plans. Every single measurement on the basic plan sheet was altered by me to make it totally authentic. I bought the absolute best lumber, without any knots whatsoever, in order to make it perfect. I'll get back to this later because after all, it was going to be a two year project.

Seeing Sherm everyday since school began in September made it seem like wrestling season started a few months early. He not only talked about it in class, but spent much of the time before and after class looking at the upcoming schedule and penciling in guys who were coming back for another season. Things were certainly changing, as the seniors who fought their way to the podium at the state tournament the year before were gone. What was left was a group of upperclassmen who, with the exception of two, previously only competed at the junior varsity level. The returning sophomores were were once again myself, Troy, David, Matt, and Monte.

Monte actually quit at the beginning of the season. There were all sorts of rumors and stories that were passed around about a locker room argument between him and Sherm. The common denominator in it all was Sherm telling him that he had the heart the size of a pea. Of course that is biologically impossible, it just meant that Monte showed minimal desire, guts, and determination. Sherm was right. Monte had natural talent and a chiseled body but if shit didn't go his way during a match, he would stall for time by untying and retying his shoes, oversell an injury as if it was life-threatening, and storm out of the gym after a loss. As a matter of fact, with the shoe thing happening several times during every single one of his matches, a new rule was created after we all graduated that required all wrestlers to tape their laces together before a match. I call it the "Monte Peterson Rule." That said though, I still liked Monte as a person and always got along with him.

Following his departure, our eighth grade championship group was now down to four. We all made the varsity squad by beating a few freshmen and some of the lackluster upperclassmen. This time around, I wrestled at 178 pounds, a weight lower than I did last year. It gave me a legitimate shot at varsity because Tyler Bridgman was still around at 190 and I wasn't at his level yet. Troy had to beat freshman Jordan Janicki, who was Dad's boss' son. (Jordan would actually become my permanent training partner for the rest of my wrestling days.) David was a shoe-in because when he wanted to, he could beat anyone. For his spot, Matt had to only beat Brad Gates, whose father, Robert, is now President Obama's Secretary of Defense.

I was so excited about making the varsity squad being only a sophomore and in my third wrestling season. Back then, it was unheard of to be in that position without a strong wrestling background. It wasn't because I was good by any means, I was just better than anyone else on the team at that weight and proved it by beating them during challenges.

The first match was in early December at home against Stanwood. I got to the gym around five as the mats were being set up and the spotlight was being raised over the center ring. I walked into the locker room and saw Sherm talking with his cousin, who was the announcer.

"Are you ready?" Sherm asked.

"Yeah, I'm ready," I said before I turned to the announcer. "Hi, my name's Eddie Thramer. When you announce my name later tonight, be sure to remember that the "H" is silent."

"Sure thing, kid," he said. "But maybe you should concentrate on the match instead of worrying about how I say your name."

I didn't answer him and just walked away. It actually pissed me off at first. *What right did he have to say that?* It wasn't until I eventually took his job of announcing two years later that I realized that he didn't mean it in a bad way. He simply meant that I should be so focused on my match that it shouldn't matter what was said on the microphone. As an announcer now, I relay those same words to anyone that comes up to me with pronunciation instructions.

On that night, though, it was different. It was my first big time match in front of a capacity crowd of several hundred and it was about the presentation. I wanted my name said right, my singlet and tights perfect, my socks straight, and my shoelaces even. I even taped my wrists up so that during the course of my match the veins in my forearms and biceps would bulge out

202

more prominently, thus making my muscles look bigger. The tape also helped my grip when I was holding an opponent because my locked hand would be less likely to slip off as opposed to a grip on just my own sweaty arm.

I showered up as the junior varsity matches were going down. As usual, I didn't have any underwear as I put my singlet on after I dried off. I put on a Sedro-Woolley Wrestling T-shirt over my singlet and a Sedro-Woolley Wrestling sweatshirt on over that. Everyone did the same before we left the locker room, including putting our hoods up so nobody could see our faces as we staged ourselves in order of weight behind the curtain.

When the lights in the gym that were on for the junior varsity matches suddenly shut off, leaving only the spotlight, the crowd started clapping and shouting. Then "Firestarter" by The Prodigy started blaring through the speakers so loud that you couldn't hear yourself think. Once the techno beat picked up, we all ran out single-file and circled the mat to the roar of the crowd. We all lined up at the edge of the mat and was introduced to the crowd one by one. Other than rock concerts and big time sporting events, nothing compared to the noise made by the rabid wrestling fans in late-90's Sedro-Woolley.

As the lighter weight matches began, I sat in my chair and began thinking about how I was going to start my match. I wasn't good at shooting in on a leg and the head and arm thing didn't work, so I planned on hooking up, snapping my opponent's head down and taking him to the mat with a front facelock. I would then go around behind him for my two, and then start the process of turning him to his back.

I didn't know it yet, but that night I was going to learn yet another wrestling lesson—planning out your match doesn't work. In football, teams script their first ten or so offensive plays and make adjustments to their game plan based on what happens during those initial plays. In wrestling, you can't do that—you have to feel out your opponent for a few seconds before you know what moves may work against him. It all depends on his strength, his balance, and how he reacts to you. It is sort of like how comedians who ad lib during their shows. Each crowd is different and if they follow a script to a dull audience, they're not going to get the response that they want—they must improvise. Same with wrestling. I learned that lesson in less than a minute during my very first home varsity match.

When it came time for my match, I went out there and shook hands with my opponent. When the whistle blew, I charged right at him and reached over his head to snap him down. While reaching for his head though, I committed the biggest no-no in wrestling by standing straight up during a match. The guy swept my legs and the next thing that I knew, I was on my back with 1:40 left in the first round. I managed to keep my shoulder up for a forty of those seconds, but that was all. The referee slapped the mat and just like that, I started another losing streak.

Thank God my losing streak didn't last as long as the year before. While I did lose the biggest share of my matches, I wasn't getting pinned all the time and I was more competitive. If I did lose by fall, sometimes it would be well passed the five minute mark. During those early varsity matches, going the full six minutes and losing by decision was almost as good as a win for me—just like Rocky Balboa in 1976. I also started studying matches more. I would watch the matches that were on before me and see how their battles developed. I would also watch the junior varsity matches to try and learn from their mistakes.

The majority of the matches that I lost were basically setup by Sherm to go that way. I would be fed to the top upper-weight guy from the opposing school who was usually a state qualifier at least. It makes sense from a team score standpoint to just give them six points by beating me instead of of them earning six against Tyler. At least Tyler could earn points for us by beating one of their guys, that I would otherwise struggle with, and the points would cancel each other out. If both of us got pinned, we were down by twelve points. I certainly understood why I was the fall guy, but it just made it harder for me to try and get better. I still wrestled junior varsity on occasion in order to try and build for the future. I stood much more of a chance in those and won a fair share of them. Although it wasn't the same as winning at the varsity level, a win was a win and I would certainly take it any chance that I got.

One of my few junior varsity matches was a home match against Bellingham. We had a girl wrestler on our team at 122 pounds named Rochelle Faye, whose brother, B.J. (from the food fight), had graduated a year earlier after placing at state. (Their dad was THE most vocal fan that I ever heard. He would stand and yell and stomp his feet, drowning out the other people in the crowd with his famous yell of "BEEEEE-JAAAAAAAY!!!!") She was quite the wrestler in her own right. In the days before women only wrestled women exclusively (where she no doubt would have won multiple state titles), she had to take on the boys. Say what you want about adolescent boys wrestling adolescent girls, but it shouldn't be a problem if you look at it from a wrestling standpoint. I've wrestled Rochelle and, other than smelling like a girl, she was just like competing against another guy. The only humiliation should be for the several guys who lost to a girl, but it was different that night against Bellingham.

Within the first thirty seconds of her match, the guy that she was wrestling sprung a wood in his tights. Now, guys can hide their excited little buddy in loose clothing, but not in a skintight singlet. Once something like that happens, it just doesn't up and go away and the kid did the only thing that he could do—he left the mat during the match and went to the locker room. Of course everyone that saw it began spreading rumors that he and Rochelle went to the back and just hammered the shit out of each other, but obviously that didn't happen. I can't imagine what went on the next day at his school.

Unfortunately, that wasn't the only rise of a wrestler's penis that year. This one was worse. For this one, it happened to a guy on our own team. If that wasn't bad enough, it happened to him in the shower with all the rest of us naked guys. Nobody said a word, but we all got out of the shower right then whether we were soapy or not. He, who will not be named here, got dressed and never came back to the team again. Every time that someone said his name from then on, that was the only image that came to mind. Yuck.

Although that wasn't one of them, there were a lot of funny things that went on during the group showers. We would soap ourselves up and go body surfing on the shower floor from one end to the other. One moron even decided to go feet first and went spread-eagle right into the shower stand and totally crushed his balls.

Another time during Christmas break, we all sang various Christmas songs in the shower as a group for about twenty minutes. We made such a racket that the girl's basketball team, who was practicing out in the gym, walked into the locker room to see what was going on. There we were in all our glory singing "Jingle Bells," "Run Rudolph Run," and "Santa Claus is Coming to Town." They then stripped off all of their clothes and jumped with us for a special holiday orgy. Just kidding, but what a Merry Christmas that would have been!

Speaking of Christmas, Dad and I each got a set of boxing gloves that year. It wasn't so much for us to take out our frustration on each other, but mainly to spar around for exercise. It seemed like every time that we put the gloves on, though, we would always revert back to wrestling and try to put each other in submission holds.

My season ended in controversy at the league tournament in Lynden, a few miles south of the Canadian border. My shoulders were counted to the mat for the fall even though my right shoulder was at least an inch off the mat. The referee was a guy named Greg Knutzen, who was said to always show bias against Sedro-Woolley wrestlers. I figured that was the case that night but after getting to know him better over the years, that couldn't be further from the truth. The fact is, referees make mistakes and you simply can't reverse a call once it is made or try to make up for it by making another bad call towards the other guy just to offset it. Shit happens, but why does it have to be me that it happens to?

Despite my early elimination in the tournament, I felt that I had a decent year. I got plenty of big match experience and earned my second varsity letter in the process. I felt that with another year of learning and getting better, I could make a run for Tacoma come my senior year—then Sherm resigned as coach and I was going to have to start over from scratch.

See, in Sedro-Woolley, if you don't win, you don't have a job. It is kind of shitty because the coach can only get so much out of the athletes that he has. If they have a team full of people that are low on talent, the people don't see that—they only see wins and losses. They love coaches when they win and hate them and will make their lives miserable if they lose. Check recent Sedro-Woolley sports history—it ain't no lie.

I didn't know it at the time, but I would benefit greatly from Sherm's departure. During a trip through Concrete during the spring after the season was over, a short and slightly stocky guy with a goatee and two cauliflowered ears came up to me and asked me if I was Eddie Thramer.

"Yeah, that's me," I said. "Why?"

"I thought I recognized you," he said while extending his hand. "I'm Jay Breckenridge, Concrete's wrestling coach."

"Nice to meet you," I said, shaking his hand.

"Are you wrestling 190 next year?"

"I'm planning on it."

"Great—see you later," he said as he got into his car and drove off.

I had no idea the reason for that conversation until about a month later when he was named the new wrestling coach at Sedro-Woolley.

CHAPTER 31

Pounding the Pavement

THE VERY SAME Friday that school let out for the summer, Dad and I took off on a bike trip over to Uncle Robbie's. It wasn't yet time for the Sturgis trip, but it was the official dress rehearsal—the sneak preview—the last chance to make sure everything was right. Although it was only for the weekend, each guy packed the exact stuff that he would take eight weeks later. The only difference was that Tristan was coming along for the ride.

Tristan wasn't quite ten years old yet but when he was with the rest of the boys, he talked like he was thirty. Just because it was okay, he would say "shit" or "fuck you" in every other sentence.

"Hey, Tristan," somebody would say. "Do you want a pop?"

"Fuck you," he'd say. "I'll get my own."

It's not like he said that kind of stuff in front of people (usually), so it wasn't that big of deal. The other thing that he liked to do was call everyone "fatty" or "fat boy," which was a little ironic considering that he was rather hefty himself. He even called his mom that one night after she told him to go take a shower after he covered his whole body with sour cream drippings following a taco feed.

"Tristan, you need to go take a bath," Aunt Karen said.

"No, I don't wanna," he replied.

"Do it now, Tristan!"

"Shut up, fatty!" he yelled on his way to the bathroom.

You don't want to laugh at things like that, but they made it damn hard not to.

All four us us met about halfway between the two houses in Grand Coulee. We spent the night at a campground that was nearly covered with nothing but seagull shit. The next morning, we got up and headed east towards Montana. We planned on riding around there for a few hours before coming back into Washington around nighttime.

About twenty minutes after crossing the Idaho border, we pulled into a Texaco station in the town of Sandpoint. The gas station was packed so we each had to wait our turn for a pump to open. I snuck into a spot in the second row of pumps on the other side of the parking lot and as I was getting the nozzle ready, I looked up to laugh at the rest of the guys for pulling a fast one. Rob got into the next available one by me, leaving only Dad circling the pumps to find a spot. Just as he spotted one and made his turn to go get it, another car jumped in and stole it. Dad then had to swerve out of the way and lost his balance, causing him to lean just far enough over that the weight of the top-heavy load took over and sent him to the asphalt. I was in the middle of pumping fuel so all I could do was laugh—just like the rest of the people at the station. Rob hadn't started fueling yet, so he jumped off his bike and helped Dad get his bike up. He and Tristan were laughing as well, but Dad, as usual, didn't think that it was funny. I don't think it was so much his bike falling over as it was the embarrassment of it happening in public.

"How the fuck would you like it if your bike tipped over?" he asked as I continued to smile at what I had just seen.

Apparently he didn't have a great memory because shit did happen to my bike. A slight misunderstanding between us on who was supposed to steady my bike while we put on my highway pegs caused my bike to crash to the cement. If that wasn't bad enough, when we were riding dirt bikes a few months earlier, I crashed in a creek and broke off one of my rear turn signals. Of course that was after I caught the engine on fire after using a little too much starting fluid. If I could laugh at my mishaps, why couldn't he laugh at his?

After the comedy show in Sandpoint, we carried on into Montana. The weather started getting rough (where have I heard that before?) so we decided to turn around and head back west. Tristan started getting a little groggy and was trying to fall asleep on the back of Rob's bike, which Rob figured out after Tristan kept clunking his helmet against his every few seconds. Afraid that he was going to fall off, Rob pulled over and tied him up to the backrest. That pissed Tristan off something awful but within a few minutes, he was asleep safely.

That night, we ended up at Potholes State Park, which is southeast of George, Washington (it's true, look it up). There, for the first time in my life, I got myself drunk. It wasn't like I was drinking and driving (or riding), because we were stopped for the night before any beer was cracked open. To keep Tristan from squealing to Mom and Karen, Dad just kept pouring my beer into a pop can. We drank enough that night that we used our fishing poles as guitars to play along to "Urgent" by Foreigner.

I don't know if it is because of the fresh air or what, but no matter how much I drink, I won't get a hangover if I sleep outside. The next morning after my initial tangle with the booze, I showed no affects. The only thing that may lead one to think otherwise was that I didn't strap down my sleeping and bed roll correctly. Two minutes after we left camp, I spilled my load all over the highway at fifty miles per hour.

The dress rehearsal was a success and the wait was then down to just eight weeks. The whole way home, all I could think about was how much fun it was going to be come the end of July. Finally after all the planning, the trip was in sight. Once we pulled into the driveway, however, I had to shift gears and get my mind back on football.

I was home for all of an hour when Mom dropped me off at the high school and I boarded a Greyhound bus bound for Eastern Washington University in Cheney for football camp. It was the same facility that the Seattle Seahawks used for training camp in those days. Unlike wrestling camp, the rooms were much bigger and we only had to have two guys in each room.

The next morning, we had the first of two, three hour turnouts in the ninety-plus degree heat. The only bright side was that we got a water break every ten minutes. Naturally, the water was hot from setting in the mile long hose that stretched across the field. It just wasn't the same as a refreshing swig of cold water, but it was better than nothing.

The turnouts went fine and we all went swimming after the afternoon session. That night, nearly everyone in camp met downstairs to watch *Monday Night Raw*, which was the hottest show on television in June of 1998. Who would have thought that the same guys who bitched about wrestling being a joke would now be on the edge of their seats watching The Undertaker slam Mick Foley onto a pile of thumbtacks?

My season ended, technically before it even began, the very next morning. The worst part was, it didn't even happen on the field. All I did was put on my cleats while I sat on the edge of my bed. Somehow when I leaned over, a disc in my lower back, just above my butt crack, slipped or tore or something. It took my breath away with how bad it hurt. I couldn't bend over, sit, stand, walk, or nothing without being in pain. I tried to play through it, but I just couldn't.

The only coach who would listen to me was Coach Monte Montgomery, who was my weightlifting teacher. When I told him what was going on, he said that I had to live with my back forever and not to ruin it in my youth on the football field. He gave me suggestions on how to manage the pain and told me that I would most likely not see a football field that year.

Coach Asshole/Williams didn't want to hear anything that I said.

"Well if you can't play, I'll find someone who can."

What a swell guy. If one of his favorites got hurt, he would call their house after each doctor appointment just to check on them. He would even stop by their classroom once in a while just to make sure that they were comfortable.

When camp ended and we returned home, I went to chiropractors, physical therapists, sports rehabilitation centers—anything to try and work through the pain, but it just wouldn't go away. No matter what I did, how many ibuprofen I took, how many shots I got, it didn't stop hurting. With the pills, all I could do was minimize it. Not wanting to become reliant on them, I just quit taking them after two or three weeks and just dealt with it. Lifting weights with anything other than my upper body was out, I had to sit down and stand up a certain way, I had to sleep on my back or my belly and not on my side, and I had to keep my shoes tied so that I could just stand there and slip them on without bending over.

As bad as it sounds, Jen had it worse. She actually broke her back and had to wear a hard plastic brace full-time for about a year in order to heal it. That was the end of her gymnastic career after six or eight years. Maybe our bodies just weren't cut out for sports.

Nearly fourteen months after the idea was initially suggested and after a year packed full of countless hours of planning and discussion, the time had finally arrived for the Sturgis trip. I had saved all of my lawn mowing money for the entire summer to be able to pay my own way. I had three hundred dollars in traveler's checks to last me ten or twelve days. At the time, that was plenty for food at five to six bucks a meal, gas at six or seven dollars for a full tank of premium, my share of camping, and any souvenirs that I wanted along the way.

The only thing that I was even slightly concerned with was leaving Tuco for that amount of time with Mom. It wasn't that she couldn't handle him, it just seemed that he would always find a way to take off on one of his jaunts around the neighborhood while under her watch. Although they were now getting to be fewer and farther between after being with us for over two years, he still got that urge to explore now and then. With that in mind, he was the first thing that I asked about when we called home every few days.

On the last Wednesday in July of 1998, I mowed all four of my lawns while Dad was at work to not only get them good and short so they would go nearly two weeks, but to get that last bit of extra cash for the road. I mowed ours first, Dorothy's second, Don Ringhouse's next door third, and Aunt B.'s last. Actually that turned out to be one of the last times that I mowed Aunt B.'s yard before her son, Sam, who had mysteriously shown up after not being heard from for years, took over that and the rest of the household chores to earn his keep.

I had them all done and the bikes pushed out in the driveway as Dad got home from work. We had packed several days beforehand and even had filled up with gas a day or two earlier so that all we had to do was saddle up and go. We had just over three hundred miles between us and the official start of the trip.

We got to Uncle Robbie's house just before dark and stayed up half of the night talking because everyone was too fired up to sleep. After we woke up the next morning, we went out in his shop to take one last glance to make sure that everyone had everything that they were supposed to. We had to have a state map for every state that we would be going to as well as the accompanying tour guide, a small set of tools for each bike in case of a breakdown, cooking gear, rain gear, a portable toilet so Rob didn't have to shit at a public place (which he couldn't do to save his life), and sleeping gear. In the middle of our checks, I somehow managed drop my sleeping bag off of my bike and directly into a drain pan that was full of used motor oil. Although some of my red sleeping bag was then and forever would be turned black, I didn't care—I was on a bike trip!

Uncle Robbie, Tristan, me, and Dad before leaving for Sturgis

Ten minutes after we left Rob's driveway, we pulled into a gas station so we could all fill up for a three hour stretch of non-stop riding. After filling up, Rob decided that he wanted to pressure wash his bike before we took off, which is strange because he isn't the kind to wash his vehicles—ever. It was a good thing that he did, because sitting on the cement by the hose was about twenty dollars in quarters. He didn't share of course, but I wouldn't have either.

We rode all day until just before dusk. Now when it comes to lodging, we are as old-school as you can get. We don't sleep in motels—period, we only stay at campgrounds if absolutely necessary, and we have no family outside the state (except Grandma). Our main source of lodging is just pulling off the highway on some turnout or dead end gravel road just far enough so that we are out of sight of any passing cars. Depending on the weather, we often times just sleep under the stars instead of pitching a tent. Come morning, we pick up all of our stuff and take off without leaving any evidence that three guys had spent the night there. As far as we're concerned, if there aren't any posted signs or fences to cross, we aren't hurting anything doing stuff like that.

It probably wasn't after the first night but one morning while we were packing, I hung a plastic bag full of beer cans on Dad's left rear turning signal instead of walking them to the garbage. He didn't notice because he was already loaded up on his bike. Even if he wanted to, I don't think that he would have been able to see it anyhow with all of the shit that he had stacked up on his luggage rack. Rob and I were laughing like crazy as Dad pulled out onto the highway and led the way like he always did. We followed along and after about three miles, the exhaust pipes heated up and melted the plastic bag, scattering about twenty beer cans along the highway. After hearing the noise, Dad pulled over to see if his bike was falling apart, but instead just saw Rob and I with tears in our eyes from laughing so hard. No surprise here, but Dad didn't find the humor in it.

"How would you like it if I hung shit on your bike?" he yelled as he checked his pipes for burnt plastic.

I wouldn't care. If it was funny (like that was), what harm could it do? It's not like we were going to leave the cans on the road, because I picked them all up and put them in another bag to haul off for real. That burnt plastic that was on his bike would cook off in about an hour, so there would never be any permanent damage. He was just pissed because he was the one that was getting laughed at.

On our second night of the trip, we stopped for dinner at a Pizza Hut in Montana. I don't know what the legal drinking age is in Montana, but I'm pretty sure that it wasn't sixteen. Whatever it was, they must have thought that I was legal because the waitress served us all beer throughout our meal. I was still new to the drinking thing so three beers was plenty beings we had to ride a few miles to get back to our camp spot. Even then, I was a little on the buzzed side. I have to say, though, that was the only time that I drank anything (while underage) before we were done riding for the night.

The next day, we rode just past the Montana town of Crow Agency to Little Bighorn Battlefield National Monument, the sight of Custer's Last Stand. 122 years earlier on June 25, 1876, 260 soldiers and personnel of the United States Army met their demise at the hands of thousands of Lakota and Cheyenne warriors who refused to give up their land and way of life. They had been given that land and permanent government protection eight years prior to that fateful day but after gold was discovered in the Black Hills, which was the center of the reservation, the white men violated the treaty. The government couldn't help as they had promised, so they offered to buy it back. The Indians refused and began leaving their reservation and raiding nearby settlers. The Battle of Little Bighorn was the result of the Army's attempt to force them back.

Although the Indians slaughtered the Seventh Cavalry in a fight that lasted as long as it takes a hungry man to eat a meal, they subsequently lost the war and were soon back on the reservation land. Their leaders, Sitting Bull and Crazy Horse, were murdered by the white men. Sitting Bull was pulled from his bed while he was sleeping, shot in his yard like a mangy dog, and left for dead, while Crazy Horse was stabbed in the back by a soldiers dagger—both cowardice acts perpetrated by a country that clearly has a checkered past.

It was very surreal standing there overlooking the hill and seeing all of the tombstones where men had died during a titanic struggle. We walked on the very ground that staged our nation's most fascinating battle. Taking the whole thing in with an open mind made it clear to see who was right and who was wrong in those days.

We rode our bikes all over the park and walked the trails and took in all of the facts that our tour book provided. One spot in particular, Sharpshooter's Ridge, we found to be the most interesting. It was there that an Indian from 500 yards away shot, one-by-one, three men in a row.

He killed the first two and wounded the third before he was located and killed. He didn't have a scope, a laser, or anything—just open sights. That to me was the coolest part of the entire park.

During another stop in the middle of the park, we all pulled over on the narrow shoulder of the road and lined our bikes up single-file. Rob parked first, I was behind him, and Dad was in the back. After we finished looking at whatever it was that we stopped to see, I got on my bike to take off. My rear tire was in a bit of a hole and in front of me was a few more. I figured that if I backed up a little bit and readjusted my bike, I could avoid all of the rest of them. I dug my heals into the hard ground and with one big tug backwards, I was out. In doing so, however, my rear tire bumped Dad's front tire and knocked his bike over yet again. It didn't go completely over, but it crashed hard at a forty-five degree angle into a hard, rocky bank.

"What the fuck!" Dad yelled as he raced over to pick up his bike. "How fuckin' hard is it to just keep your shit away from mine? Every time you're around me, my fuckin' bike FALLS DOWN! And then you FUCKIN' LAUGH!"

While Dad was going off on his tirade, a park ranger pulled over to see what all of the commotion was about.

"Is everything alright?" he asked.

"It's fine," Dad said. "He's my son, so I'm probably not going to kill him."

That night, we ended up at a campground in the shadow of our nation's first national monument, the Devil's Tower. Standing 867 feet tall with a somewhat level acre-and-a-half top, the Devil's Tower is the result of sixty million years of molten magma being forced into sedimentary rock before cooling underground. According to the Kiowa Indians, however, it came about from seven kids being chased by a giant bear. The kids climbed onto a short plateau and it magically raised into the air. The erosion on the sides of the tower are said to be scratches from the bear trying to climb his way to the top. Before the bear reached the girls, they turned into stars and went to the sky. Those seven stars are what makes the Big Dipper. None of us were around to prove what happened, but the latter is a funner story to hear.

We did pitch a tent that night because a storm was brewing off in the distance. The wind was picking up and lighting started cracking in the sky. It never did rain that night, but the wind blew so hard and so consistently that the tent was laying flat as a pancake for most of the night. It was so strong that I honestly wouldn't have been surprised if one of our bikes (hopefully Dad's) tipped over. The wind didn't die down until just about daylight, when it was time to load up and head into Sturgis.

For most of the previous two days heading east, the motorcycle traffic began increasing to the point where it was equaling (if not surpassing) the automobile traffic. By the time we rode into Sturgis, though, it was all motorcycles. The only cars on the street belonged to the city police.

A few blocks off the freeway, sat Main Street, where hundreds of motorcycles lined each sidewalk. In the middle of the street where the yellow line is, two more rows of motorcycles stretched across the length of the road. There had to be well over a thousand lined up on Main Street alone. Then, you had the people who rode those bikes. Guys with beards that hung down to their balls, chicks wearing chaps with real skimpy underwear, people with tattoos covering most of their body—I even saw a topless gal that had just one tiny, circular sticker covering each of her nipples. As odd as everyone looked, they couldn't have been more friendly. Everyone was always happy to bullshit about anything.

While there are more than a few people (close to 80% actually) who trailer their bikes to Sturgis, everyone rides their bikes around town and the surrounding areas. It is a given that each biker will cruise the gut of Main Street—unless your name is Rob. Whether it was the type of bike that he was riding or just the large amount of people that was around, I don't know, but he parked a few blocks away and refused to ride the loop.

"Fuck him," Dad said as we mounted up and headed for the main drag. "I'm not going to let him stop me from going."

I wasn't either. Yeah, we had Hondas, but I assure you that nobody gave a shit whatsoever. It didn't matter what you rode, where you lived, or how much money you made, motorcycle rallies are for bikers to come and hang out, listen to music, drink beer, and eat greasy and fatty foods. It took a while, but Dad and I cruised Main Street—proud of the bikes that we had ridden twelve hundred miles already just to get there.

Me and Dad on Main Street in Sturgis

Rob was kind of a dick the rest of the day. Granted, there were a lot of bikers on the road and some of them were riding a bit crazy, but he let that stop him from going to see Mount Rushmore and Crazy Horse Memorial. We did manage to at least ride by Rushmore, but only stopped on the road in front of the mountain long enough to take a picture. To be fair, I get pissed off/uncomfortable around lots of people myself. There are times when enough is enough and I will leave to get away from it as well, but not if there are other people with me. If that's the case, then I have to take them into consideration—especially on trips when you visit things that you just don't see all the time. As we rode our way further east, the bike traffic let up and Rob started to get a better attitude.

Starting way back in the middle of Montana, we began seeing signs and billboards that advertised Wall Drug. "Four hundred miles to Wall Drug." "Three more hours until Wall Drug." "Wall Drug is five minutes away." The closer we got, the more frequent and larger the signs became. *Goddamn, this place must be awesome!* Not hardly—all it was was a little strip mall that ran up and down both sides of a street. There was just about everything that you can imagine for sale there, but it was a let down.

We spent that night in a picnic area just outside of Badlands National Park. The next morning, we rode through the park rather quickly due to another round of bad weather. Had it been nice out, seeing the sun rise against the various color layers on the hill and rock formations would have been rather breathtaking. Instead, it was "hurry up and get out of the rain."

The rain is the only downside to a bike trip. You have to be careful about how wet you get during the day, because the last thing that you want to do is go to bed wet. If you can bypass any weather, you do it, but sometimes you can't avoid it—and when it rains over there, man, does it really pour. We rode in the rain for a few days straight, wearing rain gear to try to prevent us from getting completely soaked. I wore this bright orange, three dollar set of gear that covered everything but my head and feet. While there wasn't anything that I could do about my face, I did protect my feet with bread sacks that I slipped over my boots. I may have looked like a giant pumpkin, but Dad looked like Papa Smurf in his blue motif.

As we made our way back into Wyoming, the weather let up. It was never cold, which is why we had the thunder to go with it. Even when it was raining, it was eighty degrees out. When the sun was out, it was nearly a hundred. The air was pretty humid too. When you're used to living practically at sea level, it takes a while for your body to adjust to the elevation changes. Add it all together, and it could lead to a headache and fatigue.

We really got a dose of it when we stopped at the summit of a mountain pass to take a piss and get a drink of water. (That's what is nice about traveling with a bunch of guys—you can stop and piss anywhere. You can even take a dump if you want, which is what I did behind an historical point marker on the way to Devil's Tower.) The humidity up there was off the charts and everyone was a little dizzy because we weren't used to the climate. We stood around and talked for a few minutes but with the lack of shade and with absolutely no breeze, we figured that we should just keep riding.

We all got on our bikes and fired them up to go. As usual, Dad was in front, Rob was in the middle, and I was in the rear. (Wait, that doesn't sound right.) Dad eased forward a few feet and stopped to look for oncoming traffic before he got onto the road. When he put his left foot down to balance his bike and wait for a passing car, he put it right into a deep chuckhole.

Guess what? His bike fell over yet again, giving a new meaning to "pounding the pavement." He let out a yell that would curl your hair as he hit the ground because he wasn't wearing a shirt and the asphalt was about a thousand degrees. Rob thought that the yell that he let out was because his leg was pinned under his bike, so he flew off his bike to help him. Well, he got off so fast that he forgot to put down his kickstand. After he saw his bike start to roll, he reached out and grabbed one of the hand grips, which came off in his hand, sending his bike to the ground also.

Meanwhile, I just sat on my bike and watched it all unfold. I couldn't imagine what the passing cars thought seeing two out of three bikes tipped over right there on the shoulder of the road. I can tell you that I have never laughed so hard in my life. My cheeks hurt and my stomach was cramping because I was laughing so hard. You're not going to believe this, but Dad didn't think that it was funny. He thought that I was an asshole for just sitting back and watching the show. Who knows, maybe if I helped, my bike would have went over too.

Unfortunately, that was the last time that Dad tipped the Gold Wing over. I managed to tip it over myself several years later in the worst possible place—in front of the high school. Luckily, it was on a Sunday and the only person who saw it was Dad, who laughed like crazy by the way. It's interesting how people act when the shoe is on the other foot—myself included.

After the comedy special on the mountain, we made our way to Yellowstone. We cruised along through and camped on a river bank on the other side of the park. Running a little low on cash, we bought a pack of hotdogs for dinner. This wasn't just a regular pack of hotdogs, either. For two dollars, we got a pack of fifty links that were made of who knows what. We ate them for breakfast, lunch, and dinner for two full days until they began to turn green. After we finally threw them out, even the birds wouldn't eat them.

Eleven days after it had began, the trip was over. What we had spent over a year planning, had came and gone. All in all, it was a great time. There were a few bad times, but we more than made up for those with the good times. Afterward, just like a good movie, we were already planning the sequel.

CHAPTER 32
A Country State of Mind

FOR SEVERAL YEARS, Mom and Dad had flirted with the idea of moving. A couple of times each year, the idea would come up and we would all go look at houses. There were even times that things would get serious and we would go to a particular house everyday for nearly a week, only to eventually decide to stay where we were. Having been through the same thing for years, I figured it was just another one of those phases when we loaded up in the car and drove east of Hamilton to look at a house on Pinelli Road that had just three other houses on it.

The house was nice to say the least. It was quite a bit bigger than ours was in town. There were two separate shops on the three acre lot as well as fruit trees, a chicken coop, and lots of nearby trails for riding dirt bikes. The only problem was it was a change—and I hate change. I was always dead-set against any major change and I really can't explain why. Maybe it's the stress of worrying about it, I don't know. As usual, we left and headed for home, talking about the possibilities. It was the same old story that had gone on for years. In fact, it happened so often that I didn't give it much of a thought. I knew that within a week everything would be back to normal.

Just when I thought that I was right, things went down a road that hadn't been traveled the other times that moving came up. This time a real estate lady came to the house and talked to Mom and Dad about putting the house up for sale. Although it was appearing to get serious, I was still holding on to the hope that it was just another phase. Then the for sale sign went up in the yard, indicating that this time it was real.

The next day while Dad was at work and Mom was down at the middle school setting up her stuff for the upcoming school year, the phone rang.

"Hi, is this the Thramer residence?" Somebody asked from the other end of the line.

"Yes it is," I answered.

"Oh great—your house is for sale isn't it?"

"No."

"No? Isn't this the Thramers at 709 Orth Way?"

"Yes it is."

"So you house is for sale isn't it?"

"No, my house isn't for sale—goodbye."

I hung up the phone and figured that I wouldn't hear back from them. I was wrong. After Mom got home, they showed up at the house and stooged me out.

"He said the house wasn't for sale," their real estate heifer told Mom as she pointed her accusing finger at me.

"No," I corrected her. "I said MY house wasn't for sale."

"Oh."

Mom didn't get the joke—neither did they. To me, the whole damn thing was a joke. My laughs ended that night, however, when they made an offer to Mom and Dad, which they accepted, less than twenty-four hours after the house was listed. Now it was for real. The worst thing that I could imagine (at that time anyway) had just happened—we had to move. We were leaving the house that I had spent the last fifteen years of my life, all of the memories—everything. It was now going to be all in the past—and I hated it.

Moving day was scheduled for Sunday, September 13, two days after my birthday. (Why does all the bad shit happen around my birthday?) The only saving grace was that the day before, Dad took me to Seattle to see the WWF, which was going through some major changes. "Stone Cold" Steve Austin and The Rock (you know him as Dwayne Johnson) had taken the places of Hulk Hogan and Randy Savage. The show was aimed more at males under thirty instead of younger children. Now instead of Hogan posing in the ring after a match, Austin cracked open beers and celebrated with a cold one. Even the slender valets were replaced with busty, blonde babes.

Just like at a rock concert, the girls in the audience began to "dress to impress." There was one lady that sat four or five rows in front of us that had absolutely enormous boobs. The guys around us started getting out their wallets in hopes to raise enough cash to entice her to give everyone a peek. There must have been a couple of hundred dollars up for grabs, but she wouldn't do it—bitch.

On Sunday, we packed up everything that we owned and hauled it to our new house. As we put things away and settled in over the next few weeks, my feelings about moving changed. Yeah, the only home that I remember was gone, but so too were the neighbors, the traffic, and the noise of the sirens. It was peaceful there, laid back, and relaxing (aside from all of the countless hours of work that we all did to clear the overgrown brush). It brought out a new state of mind—the kind that I didn't know was missing, and the kind that I will never let go of.

It wasn't all peaches and cream, though. As I was certain of, there were drawbacks. Leaving fourteen miles further away than before meant over thirty miles round trip to school, as opposed to five. That meant more gas and more money for the gas. To cut down on expenses, I made the trip just during school days. If there was a game that particular night, I would just stay in town after school to save money and the miles.

I had a good reason to be conservative. I was still mowing the two lawns in our old neighborhood for twenty bucks each, but forty dollars a week wasn't exactly living high on the hog. I got eight days on a tank of gas so every three weeks, I had to buy two tanks of gas. Luckily gas was cheap, so it only cost about twenty five bucks per fill-up. Combine that with buying stuff that I wanted for myself, and I was going through my income as fast as I was getting it. To make matters worse, mowing season would be over in another few weeks. It was clear that the time had come for me to get a job. In order to perform well at my first regular job, however, I was going to wait until February when wrestling was over so I could be available anytime after school.

In order for me to still have a few extra dollars, Mom and Dad pitched in a few dollars for gas because I had to drive Jen to school. She was on her own to get home, though, because I had sports in the afternoons. I even got conned into driving one of her friends to school too, which was really strange because the two girls rarely ever talked the whole way to school. Oh well, I was still driving Dad's Jimmy after all, and he made the rules.

In the three months since my back injury, it really hadn't gotten a whole lot better. It was a little more tolerable once I began paying more attention to how I lifted things, how I bent over, and how I sat in a chair. It still didn't go away, but it seemed to help. I started stretching several times during each day so that I wouldn't tense up. I stayed away from squats in the weight room and anything else that put pressure on my back—including football.

It just killed me to just sit back and watch turnouts, but I went to each one anyway. I stayed just as long as everyone else, went to every team meeting, and set up all of the equipment each day. On game nights, I ran the chain gang (the group that measures the distance between first downs), took stats, and wiped down balls (footballs, that is). When the games were at home, I would even set up the yard markers on the field. I did anything that I could do to stay involved.

Not that I was surprised by any means but come the end of the season, I didn't even get so much as a participation certificate from Coach Williams, let alone a thank you. That made zero sense to me because just a year earlier when another player missed the entire season due to a broken arm that he got outside of football, he got a letter and an inspirational award. He never came to turnouts, but he did come to the games. The only time I left turnout early was to go to physical therapy. I guess that things were different if you were one of his "boys."

One day when I got home from turnout, Tuco was nowhere to be found. He must have decided to go off on one of his Lewis and Clark-style explorations (while under Mom's watch as usual) now that we lived at a different house. The trouble was, now there were thick, wooded area and wild animals to the north and a very busy Highway 20 and a swift Skagit River to the south. I looked all over the motorcycle and ATV trails that we took him on now that we had our own four wheeler—nothing. After several hours and just before sunset, I found him across the highway near the river. How he made it across during the busy evening commute baffles me, but luck was on his side that day. Following that, he never once ran off again. It only took two-and-a-half years to get that shit out of his system.

Living out there brought some other changes for him. I would still give him his weekly bath, but he would need a few touch-ups now and then to get him through, thanks to his constant tromping through the dirt and mud. Inside the house was mostly hardwood floors, except for the living room and bedrooms, so now he couldn't run his trademark laps in the house without Mom flipping out. He tried to, though. He would try to take off and his feet would come right out from under him like he was running on ice. That wouldn't deter him, he would just get up and try it again.

The biggest change for him, however, was his sleeping arrangements. Finally after years of sleeping with my feet hanging over the mattress and springs stabbing my butt cheeks, I was able to ditch the bunk beds and get a queen-sized bed. Unfortunately, that meant that Tuco lost his bed also—well, not exactly. He just flopped his fat ass up there with me, forcing me to sleep diagonally. Of course the minute that I got up to take a leak in the middle of the night, he would scoot up and lay with his head on the pillow. I would try to get him to move, but he would purposely make himself dead weight. While there were times that I would drag him back down to his spot, I found myself most of the time just sliding in next to him. Man, the things we do for our dogs!

My back was feeling pretty good come the two week break between football and wrestling. While I was healthy enough to play in the meaningless season finale, I opted to hold off and just go full-steam into wrestling season. We had a new coach, a new lineup, and I wasn't going to risk missing both seasons for just one game that didn't mean shit for our hopeless team.

As soon as I walked into the wrestling room on our first day of turnouts, I noticed a big change. Instead of us being on our own to warmup like were with Sherm, Jay was shouting orders beginning at three o'clock on the dot. Anyone that was late had to run two miles before they even stepped onto the mat. With him, it didn't matter if it was a state champion or a third string junior varsity wrestler. If you were late, you ran.

Our conditioning training was not limited to just running and sprinting, Jay had other techniques as well. Don't get me wrong, we still jogged and sprinted until we were weak in the knees, but then he would give us some unorthodox regimens to try to make us not just physically tough, but mentally tough as well. He wanted us to get to the point when we felt that we couldn't continue, to then suck it up, and just keep going. That is why we only had less than twenty kids even finish the year. Fifty started on the first day, only thirty remained come the next day.

After warmups and two hours of drilling and live wrestling, he would start the torture. We would have to carry a guy equal to our own weight piggyback up and down the football grandstands four different times without stopping or setting him down. Other times, we would hold out barbell plates with our hands totally straight and walk heel-to-toe across the length of the football field. The bigger you were, the more weight that you had to pack. When the weather was too shitty for outdoor stuff like that, we would stay inside and jog with dumbbells in our hands for thirty minutes without setting them down.

Although it might sound easy on paper, the hardest thing that we ever had to do was run for one hour with our arms straight up over our heads. It doesn't take long before those same arms feel as heavy as tree trunks once the circulation of the blood starts slowing down. It's kind of like when you sleep on your arm too long during the night and you have to physically move it with your other arm to get it to another position.

There were others as well, but the whole point of it was to get it set in your mind that quitting is never an option. Quitting is for cowards. Quitting is for weak-minded, chicken-shit, poor excuses for men. It may sound rough, but it also builds confidence because if you can take that punishment and make it, what in this world (short of weaponry) can stop you?

In addition to the torture, Jay also had a no-nonsense style of wrestling to go along with it. Wrestling is a physical, contact sport and if you do it within the rules, you can inflict a severe amount of pain on an opponent. It's the simple things, like driving the point of your elbow into your opponents lungs when you are trying to get a hammerlock, pulling a guys head up towards you to block off his jugular while you have him in a front facelock, or by pressing your side into a guys face while he is on back so he can't breathe and literally wants to be pinned. The best part about it is, it's all legal.

Turnouts lasted for at least three hours each night. He would even make us come in early on weekends at around four a.m. to turnout, just so he could find out who was out partying the night before. Partying with alcohol and underage kids wasn't my bag, so I didn't mind. Other guys would be puking at one of the four garbage cans that he set up around the room, before he made them clean them all out. The guys that did indulge in that sort of thing figured that they better stop that shit for a while, and do you know what? Most of them did.

It took me less than a minute to pin two guys and earn my spot on varsity. Being a junior now, I was the one who was now stomping on the younger guys. After two years of paying dues, now it was my turn to have a little success.

Our first match was the Stanwood Wrestle-Rama, the same event that I competed in two years earlier. Like before, it was once again a four-man bracket per weight class. This time, though, instead of just getting a surprise near-fall, I pinned two guys en route to my first high school wrestling tournament title. Granted, there were only four guys as opposed to sixteen, but a tournament title is a tournament title.

The home duel matches weren't quite the same as they were in recent years now that Jay was in charge. He did away with the whole spotlight thing and just stuck with the regular lighting. It was easier for the officials to see pins when there was more light, making it less likely that they would quick-count a guy. The entrance music was still there, though. We no longer had techno music, instead we had Kid Rock's "Bawitdaba" thumping through the system. He was the big shit in 1998 with his blend of rock, metal, country, and hip-hop all rolled into one. While I'm not much into rap, this was different—it was cool and I liked it immediately.

The weight classes even changed a little bit prior to the beginning of the season. Instead of 190, my class was now 189. Unfortunately for this season and most of the next, most of my matches during duel meets were at 215. This was because our heavyweight, Matt Denmark, quit during the season.

Matt never was in shape. He was right at the 275 pound limit during each weigh-in. He worked hard during turnout and matches, but was often distracted by himself. He was so self-conscious about his appearance that he spent most of the time worrying if his boobs were in or out of his singlet during a match. While he was definitely losing interest, that wasn't why he quit. He quit because his dad, who was two hundred pounds bigger than he was, broke his ankle and died during the surgery to repair it. For support, every one of us on the team went to his funeral, far outnumbering the rest of his entire family.

Suddenly, Travis Geiger reappeared. Unwilling to pay any sort of dues, like a vulture, he shows up once the job is already done. Without earning it, he steps right into the heavyweight spot and, much to everyone's chagrin because of how he got there, did pretty well. There were more than a few matches that came down to the team winning or losing based on his performance. Most of the time he came through and saved the day. It made me sick because his work ethic in turnout sucked. He would stop and walk during conditioning and would only try if he was on top during live matches. During drills, he would be dead weight instead of allowing you to practice a move or hold. Plus, he was still into untying shoes and giving wedgies. I'm all for fun and games don't get me wrong, but there is a time and a place—and turnout wasn't one of them. God, I swear he was a third grader trapped in a seventeen year old's body.

Thankfully during tournaments, I didn't have to watch his matches because I was usually wrestling at the same time. That year at the Skagit Valley Invitational, I had one of the highest scoring matches ever to take place in that gym. I reached the semi-finals by beating a guy 23-21. Most matches are lucky to make it into double digits and if on the rare occasion that they make it into the twenties, it is because one of the participants is getting slaughtered. For this one, we were both pretty evenly matched. It was takedown, reversal, escape—back and forth. He had me on my back once during the match to get a three point near-fall and I had him on his back once as well for three points. Other than that, the only other points came in one or two point increments, so you can imagine how physical it was. While it was a great match, I wasn't able to recoup in time for my semi-final match and subsequently was eliminated from the tournament.

Tournaments can be hard for coaches to keep track of how everyone is doing. With six matches going on at once for ten straight hours, it can be rather hectic. Even with our assistant coach, Jack Herd, Jay couldn't keep up with everything, so he brought in a team manager—and I'll be damned if it wasn't Josef.

I hadn't seen much of Josef since his love affair with Mrs. Malcolm went sour in the eighth grade. He couldn't do sports, but he was really into wrestling, so Jay let him tag along with the team. Boy, did he eat it up. He was at every turnout, every weigh-in, every match, and every tournament. He took his job seriously and besides being an annoying pain in the ass, he did a good job.

Jay gave him the greatest gift of his life during a home match against Mount Vernon. For some reason, Mount Vernon never had a full squad and had at least two or three holes in their lineup each year. On that night, they had nobody at 125 so Jay let Josef suit up and take the forfeit. In order for it to be official, he had to weigh-in and be introduced with the team. He stripped himself naked twenty minutes before he had to, just to be sure that he was going to be in line at the scales. He was smiling from ear to ear while he put on his singlet, to the point where I thought that he was going to have to have it surgically removed. When introductions started, he got the biggest pop of the night from the crowd.

When it was time for the 125 pound match, Josef got a standing ovation as he put his headgear on and went out to center mat. The referee raised his arm, signifying the victory, and he went over for the customary hand shake with the opposing coach. He didn't stop there—he went on to shake every Mount Vernon wrestler's hand, as well as the hand of everyone in the front row throughout the circumference of the gym. Check the record books, he is the only wrestler in Sedro-Woolley to finish his career with an undefeated record.

I certainly couldn't say that, but it was a good year for me. I won more matches than I lost for the first time in three years and placed in the league tournament, though not high enough to take that next step to regionals, as they still only took two guys per weight.

A change was on the horizon, however. Before the next school year, all of the schools were going to be reclassified according to size. The smaller schools would compete with the smaller schools and likewise for the larger schools. This would create more divisions in the state which meant that it needed more participants for postseason action. Now instead of two guys coming out of league, it was going to be four—and I was already ranked third in my weight class for the next year's returning wrestlers.

CHAPTER 33

Fast Food Fun

A FTER LAWN MOWING season had wrapped up in November, I had zero income for the next three months. I had stockpiled enough to afford gas, but that was it. If I was ever going to have enough money to buy and support my own vehicle, I had to get a regular job—lawn mowing just wasn't cutting it. I did, however, give Dorothy and Don notice that I would only be able to mow their lawns for one more season, mainly because it was an easy forty dollars a week and they weren't far out of my way.

The first Monday after wrestling season was over, I went out job hunting. Although I really didn't have any interest in the embarrassment that working at a fast food restaurant would garner, I put in an application at every place that was hiring—including them. When I noticed that the majority of the places that were hiring were in fact places of that nature, I figured that was what I was going to end up with. The more I thought about it, the more I changed my attitude towards it. I was only going to be available after school and on weekends, so beggars couldn't be choosers. Besides, this wasn't going to be something that I was going to make a career out of.

While driving along the freeway coming into Burlington, I saw a now hiring sign at a McDonald's that sat just off the interstate ramp. Both the parking lot and drive-thru lanes were full, which is a good sign because that means they do a lot business—the more business, the more need for workers. The building sat in a perfect spot where cars had to drive right by on their way to the San Juan's or Whidbey Island. It was also on the same exit for drivers who were looking to drive through the North Cascades. At the time, it was the only visible McDonald's along the freeway between Marysville and Bellingham. This particular restaurant was just one of 31,000 locations worldwide who employ around 1.5 million people and serve approximately 58 million people per day—talk about job security. Maybe this wasn't such a bad idea after all.

A little off the subject, but that brings me to today's economy and historically high nationwide unemployment rates. Now I know that a McDonald's wage will not support a family, but it is income. There are always going to be people who eat fast food. In fact, studies show that the average person eats at places like that three times a week. Wouldn't it be better to serve hamburgers than to sit home and bitch about not having any money coming in? Come on. It may not be glamorous, but it's a job. To top it all off, I guarantee that a place like that will be one of the last places to go out of business in a struggling economy.

Although those weren't the reasons that enticed me to do so, I figured that it was a good of place as any to fill out an application before I continued with my search. I walked inside and asked to see the manager and within about twenty seconds, a man with a pin-striped shirt came out to the counter.

"Can I help you, sir?" he asked.

"Yes," I began. "I'd like to fill out an application."

"Well today is your lucky day. My name is Gary and I've got a few minutes so if you'd like, I can give you an interview right now."

"Sure, but what about the application?"

"You can fill that out later."

So we sat down and he asked me a few questions and probably three minutes later, we shook hands and he told me to meet him in Mount Vernon in an hour at the corporate office. Once there, he gave me a few pairs of black pants and a few ugly, fuchsia-colored shirts.

"This is your uniform," he said. "Keep them clean and don't come to work with them dirty."

I looked them over and I just had to ask, "Is pink the only color?"

"No," he said with a sly grin. "If you make it to crew supervisor, you can wear purple."

"Oh—swell."

I left the office and went down to the county courthouse to get a food handler's permit. I brought it back to him a little while later and he gave me my first schedule. After a three day training session the following week, I was going to be getting twenty hours of work per week at least. At five bucks an hour, which was minimum wage at that time, I was going to do alright.

As I drove to work a few days later for my first day on the job, I was a little nervous. It wasn't because of the job itself, but rather because of the stupid pink shirt. I had never worn anything like that before. The only time colors like that were worn by guys were when they were purposely looking for attention. I didn't want any attention or need it. I just wanted to do my job, get paid, and save my money. Unfortunately, I was going to have to do so looking like a giant penis.

When I got there, Gary introduced me to the guy that was going to train me, Jon. I already knew this guy—he wrestled for us on the junior varsity squad, but his name wasn't Jon, it was Archy.

"What's with the Jon?" I asked him

"It's my real name," he replied.

Even though it said it on his name tag, I never did call him Jon—just Archy. I don't know how he got the nickname, but that was what everyone called Jon Ballenger. His mom, his dad, teachers, students—everybody. He was a year younger than I was and he had just transferred to Sedro-Woolley from Concrete the previous fall. Come to find out, he lived just across the highway from us.

Although he wrestled on the same team as me, I didn't really know much about him except for his "unique" trait. When you are a wrestler, there is nothing to hide in the group shower area. If you are packing heat or not, everyone is going to know. Nobody will ever admit to being a "pecker checker" but when a 125 pounder is standing there with what appears to be a third leg, how could you not notice? Everyone on the team even gave it it's own name—Hog.

After he trained me for a few days, Archy and I went on to become pretty good friends. For the next two years, we would carpool to work, jog around the logging roads near home together to stay in shape, and help each other with projects around the house. Although he was one to hit the weed now and then, he never did that stuff around me. I didn't want any part of it and he respected that. I didn't hold it against him, either. His parents often left him alone for weeks at a time and he never felt wanted. It was just his way of escaping for a bit. He even came to school drunk a few times but thanks to me, he never got into trouble because I skipped a few classes to take him for a drive and out to breakfast to sober him up. I normally didn't hang out with people like that, but he was different, and we had a blast together at work.

I've always felt that if you can get a good days work in and have a little fun doing it, then the day goes by much quicker and smoother—the less stress, the better. We were the two fastest employees in the grill area. In order to grill meat, fry fish and chicken, toast buns, and assemble sandwiches, it would usually require a minimum of four people. Archy and I could do it with just the two of us—lunch and dinner rush or not. When it was time to fill thirty orders in less than three minutes, we could do it without blinking an eye. Things weren't always a rush, though. Sometimes it was a little slower, which gave us lots of time for goofing off.

We wouldn't play tricks on each other, instead we would save them for new employees and people that we didn't like. All new employees started out cooking hamburger patties on the grill. There were two sizes of patties, four ounce and one-and-a-half ounce. The four ounce patties took 117 seconds to cook, while the smaller ones took just 47 seconds. The lids would pop up automatically when the time expired with the meat at the proper temperature but if some asshole hit the standby button, the lids would stay down until you manually hit the open button. If the griller got busy doing something else, he would lose track of time and pretty soon his meat would be charcoal and he would have to start over. The manager would then yell at him for falling behind.

After the meat was cooked, they were put into trays and into a warmer with a twenty minute time limit. If the time expired, the meat had to be thrown out. There were more than a few times that I started the time over, sometimes two or three more times on top of that, just to avoid wasting meat. Various sandwiches were then made and placed into another warmer for a maximum of thirty minutes. Again, I would start the time over to avoid wasting food. (Or I was just being lazy.)

Shortly after I started, a new system began in which sandwiches weren't made until they were ordered. While the meat was still precooked, customers would get a fresher product and the company would waste less food. Instead of throwing out hundreds of burgers each day, we might have thrown out ten, which were mistakes made by the people in the grill. But most importantly, customers would be eating fresher food—supposedly. If you want to assure yourself that you are only eating the freshest meat on your future fast food visits, order your burgers without seasoning. Trust me, that is the only way that you can eat the freshest, juiciest burger possible.

You do have to be aware of the risks of special orders, though. If you have an allergy to an ingredient but don't specify that as the reason why you don't want a certain thing on your burger, most likely somebody will just remove it and give the same sandwich right back to you. It gets worse. Although I have personally never done it, I have seen people both accidentally and on purpose drop meat on the floor and put it back on the bun. I've even seen a guy wipe the top of a bun against his bare balls just because he didn't like the particular person who was ordering the burger.

Now if you were a friend of the guys in the grill, you might get an extra patty on your burger. If somebody gave me a heads up that they were coming and told me the special order ahead of time so I could look for it, I would hook them up. As long as we were on the same page, they could order it in the drive-thru without me ever seeing them and still get their loaded burger.

All of the guys in the grill (that weren't dip shits) looked out for each other so we could take advantage of the food that we worked with. We had our own signals that we used to tell each other when the coast was clear for us to eat hamburgers while we were on the job. We would fix extra food and give it someone to slip in their pocket and take it in the back to eat it while they were in the walk-in cooler or freezer getting supplies. For the guy that was running the screen and starting all of the sandwiches, he had to hide his in the toaster and just take a bite or two of it at a time.

Although we snuck our fair share of food, we were allowed to eat two menu items each day that we worked. I would usually have a Double Quarter-Pounder and a Cajun McChicken every day that I worked. But with working out all the time, I never gained an ounce. It also saved Mom and Dad money on groceries.

Other things that we did, unbeknownst to the managers, were clocking each other in early and out late and resetting break timers to allow for longer breaks. Some of us had a system that designated one front counter person to clock us in a half-hour before we got there and another person to clock us out a half-hour after we left. We didn't do it all the time and we took turns, so each guy would get an extra hour every pay period. I'm not all that proud of it, but I did it. Besides, how entertaining would this book be if I only talked about each of the hundreds of thousands of burgers that I made?

Two months after I started working at McDonald's, Dad and I were driving into town to go to the grocery store. For the past several months, we would constantly glance at the used car lots while we passed by to see what was out there. On that afternoon, and just out of the corner of his eye, Dad saw a red, four wheel drive pickup parked on the side of a car lot. It wasn't just any car lot, it just happened to be that lot that was ran by my old football coach, Ron Russell.

We whipped into the lot just as Ron was closing up. He hadn't even listed the Chevrolet pickup as being for sale yet because his son had been driving it for a few days while his was in the shop. It was exactly what I was looking for—red, 4x4, extended cab, and in pretty good shape. It had a manual transmission, which was no big deal, but it did have 175,000 miles on it. Granted it was a 1987, but that was still quite a bit. Following a test drive, I asked Ron what he'd let me have it for.

"To you," he said. "Three grand."

"Deal," I said—just like that.

It needed some detailing work and for the next several weeks, I polished it, inside and out, twice-over. The bed looked like a paint can exploded in it, so I had a spray-in bedliner installed. The side rails were a little scratched up as well, so I bought a set of diamond plate rail caps to put on it. I liked the diamond plate look so much that I added four mud flaps and a license plate bracket to match. Papa even gave me a diamond plate toolbox, that he had held onto after selling his Ford Ranger a few years back, which fit perfectly. I finished it off with a bug shield to cover up the rock chips on the front of the hood. To me, it was the perfect truck.

My first pickup

The minute that I bought my pickup, I was on my own to insure it. For ninety dollars a month, I had full coverage. If anything happened to it, it would be taken care of. I didn't know it at the time, but I was going to have to use it a few times down the road.

I had lots of time to work on it right after I bought it because I had a whole week off of school after I was suspended for a week for a "vicious assault." It had been four years since I had gotten into a suspension situation at school, so I guess I was overdue. Not that I never got into trouble, because I did—I just have an uncanny ability to get myself off the hook. This time, though, I couldn't.

A tag-along, habitual liar by the name of Josh Massingale always sat at the same lunch table as me and some of the other guys from football. Why I don't know—he never played a single sport like we did, yet he claimed that he was better and stronger than everyone else. If somebody is going to talk such a game, they would usually at least attempt to back it up. Not this guy—all his mouth ever did was write checks that his ass couldn't cash. Nobody liked him, nobody wanted him around, and I took care of it for good right in the middle of the cafeteria.

Josh was on his usual kick about being the strongest guy around and, as usual, nobody gave him the time of day. Then he went on talking about how his father trained him by carrying around one-inch thick logging cable. Okay, I'll buy that. Some people don't have access to actual weights and thus have to improvise. Kurt Angle trained for the Olympics carrying logs. Brock Lesnar trained for the NCAA Finals by lifting weights that he made out of chunks of steel, concrete, and buckets.

After getting everyone's attention, he then started to lay the bullshit down. It wasn't just a little cable, it was three hundred yards of it. That's nine hundred feet! Just for the sake of argument, let's say that each foot weighs five pounds because it is heavy stuff. That's 4500 pounds! That's impossible for any human being on this planet.

"I'm not kidding," he said. "Dad can do it and so can I."

"I'll bet you a thousand dollars cash that the two of you couldn't even budge it together," I said.

"It's a bet," he said as he stuck out his hand.

But as we stood up and our hands locked in a handshake, he grit his teeth and squeezed my hand. Out of pure reflex, I used my left hand to push his face away from me. In the process, my index finger went right into his left eye socket, clear to my second knuckle. He went to the ground instantly, crying and screaming like a little baby. Within about two seconds, everyone else in the cafeteria ran over to see what the commotion was. Teachers swarmed to see who was hurt and how bad. Once they got him up and hurried him to the office, they wanted to know who did it.

"I did," I said calmly without hesitation.

Not a minute went by before the vice-principal, Mike Schweigert, came to the cafeteria to get me.

"What did you do?" he asked me, knowing that it wasn't like me to get into fights.

"I'll tell you if we go to you office and get away from all the people," I answered.

"Don't worry—that's where we are going."

I went into his office and sat down. He was probably going to go check on Josh, who was screaming from another room, because he said that he would be back in a few minutes. When he returned, he wasn't alone. As customary following a fight, he brought in a police officer.

"Who do you think you are?! Do you want to go to jail?! What business do you have putting your hands on another student?!" he yelled.

"Now just a minute—" I began before I was cut off.

"No. I'll talk," he said as he went on to inform me about what would happen if that kind of thing took place on the street and what would happen if Josh lost his eye.

"I'm not trying to argue with you," I said. "I know what I did."

I went on to explain the whole situation from start to finish, without leaving anything out.

"I didn't aim for his eye on purpose," I said. "But make no mistake about it, I'm NOT sorry for what happened."

That's all that they needed to hear. Just like that, I had to pack up my stuff and go home for a five day suspension. It could have been reduced to three days if I would have written a letter of apology, but I refused and took the two extra days.

After Dad got home that evening, we went down to the school to talk to Mr. Schweigert—not to try and get out of the punishment, but to explain myself better. I mainly wanted him to know that a "vicious assault" would have been me continuously beating the living shit out of Josh while he was already down. While I had a golden opportunity to do that, I didn't.

Once I was done talking, he told me that he admired my honesty. He said that in being so brutally honest about not being sorry is what brought on the bigger punishment.

"If you wouldn't have said that, you may have only missed a day or two."

"But then I wouldn't have told you the whole truth," I confessed.

He smiled. He also went on to warn Dad that Josh's mother was considering a lawsuit. It never did happen, instead Josh was pulled out of school that day, along with his two cousins, and never returned. That's too bad.

I received a hero's welcome when I returned to school a week later. Eleven years later as I write this, I still feel the same way about it. How can I apologize for standing up for myself? What I did was quick and easy—it put an end to a situation instantly before it could escalate into a big brawl. No matter how tough you are are how tough you think you are, if you get it in the eyes, groin, or lungs, then you're in trouble. Is it a cheap shot? Maybe, but where is the rule book in a fight?

As my junior year came to a close, so to did my list of graduation requirements. In composition class, I had to write a paper with a minimum of 2,000 words to complete that course. I wrote it on Harley-Davidson Motorcycles and figured that beings I was into it that far, I might as well write the extra thousand words that would meet the requirement for my senior paper. Then I could kill two birds with one stone. The only thing that I had left to complete in school by this time was the senior-only class called CWP, or current world problems. I would still have a few electives that I had to do, but I didn't consider wood shop and weightlifting actual classes. The way it was shaping up, I would only have to go to school for three hours a day next year from January to graduation in June.

In the same composition class, I wrote two short stories about an amateur wrestler who fought his way from the bottom to a state title. In the second story, I wrote the sequel that had him in college at the NCAA Tournament. While he didn't win an individual title, his performance was enough to secure his team the national title. I was especially happy with the ending because it showed that you don't always have to be unbeatable to be a winner. It just makes it more realistic.

In wood shop, I continued my ongoing masterpiece. It was coming along slowly but surely. The only reason that it was taking so long, besides my excessively compulsive desire to make every square inch of my gun cabinet perfect, was the fact that I only got one semester in the class. Come to think of it, with 45 minute periods, you can't get a whole lot accomplished anyway. After you subtract time for getting started and cleaning up, you're at best looking at a half-hour of work a day. That's just over two hours a week, eight hours a month, or forty hours per semester. Maybe I wasn't doing so bad after all.

After taking a full semester of beginning automotive the year before that consisted entirely of classroom work, I was cleared for the advanced course for eleventh grade. Because it was absolutely impossible for this class to be done in one period, it was a two-period class. Even then it was hard to fit work into a ninety minute window. Remember, with the setup and cleanup, your time is even shorter. The district would actually change the class time to four, eighty minute periods the following year to increase time and learning opportunities for all courses. That would be great for vocational classes especially.

In auto shop, I started working on cars for the first time in my life. While Dad did some work and basic maintenance on our cars at home, I didn't ever help him when I was younger because I was more interested in reading or watching wrestling and football. As I got older and became more interested, I was too busy working to be able to help him when the rare opportunity arose. Besides, we didn't drive pieces of shit that needed constant work, which posed a slight problem for the class itself. Most kids had clunkers that needed an over abundance of T.L.C., so they were always busy. At the time, all my pickup needed was thoroughly cleaned and polished, which was off limits.

Only twice did I bring in one of our family vehicles. I put a thermostat in the Explorer and a catalytic converter in the Jimmy. The rest of the time I worked on vehicles that were brought in by teachers or community members who wanted to take advantage of free shop labor. That may sound good considering today's shop rates of at least eighty dollars an hour, but who in their right mind would really want a high school kid with no experience and a short attention span to work on their stuff? Let's face it—at that age, you're mostly thinking about chicks, food, tobacco products, and beer, and where to get all four of them.

I mainly stuck to oil changes, transmission service, and brake jobs. Over the year, I must have done thirty of each. I did other jobs too that were much more complicated and time consuming. I put new head gaskets on a Toyota, which sucked because you have to take nearly the whole top of the motor off. A couple of weeks later when it was time to put it back together again, some of the parts were moved by another class and I was unable to find some of the bolts. The owner was pissed, but they did sign a "no liability" waiver to earn their free labor. They had to buy just a few mounting bolts, so it wasn't like it was the end of the world.

The lady that brought in a Ford Ranger for a new water pump didn't get quite as lucky. She bought three different pumps and several other gaskets before I was able to install it correctly. I kept putting the gasket on uneven and tearing it when I subsequently tried to adjust it. As for the pumps, I dropped one and cracked it while I ruined the other one by trying to remove another screwed up gasket installation with an orbital grinder—oops.

As for my third elective, weight lifting, I was limited to upper body exercises only because I wasn't going to risk another lower back issue by doing squats or clean and jerks. By the end of the year, I was able to bench press 285 pounds. That was 100 pounds more than my body weight and more than any other guy in the junior class could do. Only one senior had me beat with 305, which was going to be my goal for the following year.

Since we had moved, Dad and I had given up our nightly workouts at the gym—it was just to far to go for an hour workout. It didn't matter much because the place was shut down a couple of months later for a huge steroid bust. To top it off, James (the guy with the giant arms) was arrested for attempting to murder his wife with the hopes of getting her life insurance. Most likely he needed the money because he was getting to deep into the drug distribution business. It just goes to show you what drugs really do for you.

Aside from my electives and composition classes, I also took United States history, making the total time I spent in an actual classroom a mere two hours a day. While I enjoyed both history and writing, I did find my usual time to distract myself and others. This time I did it in a little bit of a more creative way, thus starting the hot new craze of bringing guns to school—as in squirt guns.

For around fifty cents at the dollar store, you could buy a three-inch squirt gun that could shoot about fifteen feet. It took a few days before people found out that it was me. I could shoot someone and stick the gun in my armpit before they had a chance to turn around. The idea took off and soon almost everyone had one. For the first time ever, the school had to put out warnings about consequences for being caught with a toy designed for ten year olds. Like most fads, though, it fizzled out by the end of the year.

As I walked out the door on the last day of school that year, I remember getting really excited about having just one more year left to go in school. It was like getting a shot of adrenaline as it sunk in that by next June, I was finished for good. Finished with school, finished with teachers, finished seeing people that I didn't like—just finished. I was ready to move on, and while I knew what I wanted to do with my life, I wasn't exactly sure how I was going to get there yet.

CHAPTER 34

What You Don't Know Won't Hurt You . . .

I HAD THE SUMMER of 1999 pretty much booked before it even started. Dad, Uncle Robbie, and I had our second motorcycle trip planned to the Grand Canyon and surrounding areas. There was a football camp in late June, fundraisers for wrestling throughout the summer, and I still had to fit in forty hours a week at McDonald's and get my two lawns mowed. The lazy summers under a shade tree were now a thing of the past.

As if I didn't do it enough on a daily basis, I volunteered to cook burgers at the wrestling team's hamburger stand at the week-long carnival in town. Somehow that earned me the nickname of "Carny." It probably didn't help that I had an out of style, long haired look either. What started as a nickname derived from me helping out my team, escalated into rumors of me traveling with the actual carnival. Almost a decade later, some people still call me that when they see me—jerks.

I worked the stand twice during the day leading up to the extremely busy "unlimited rides" Friday night. Dad liked Jay, so he volunteered to help out with the guys during that evening also. I had to work at McDonald's that day, so I made a rare second trip into town just so Dad and I could ride down together. I figured that we would talk about the upcoming bike trip on the way down, but I was in for a big surprise.

We had about an hour before we had to be at the stand once I got home from work. Dad was in the living room without the TV or the radio on, sitting in total silence.

"Hey, are you ready or what?" I asked.

"Come here for a minute," he said. "I want to talk to you."

I had done nothing wrong, so I knew that I wasn't in trouble.

"What's up? We need to get rollin'."

"You might change your mind after we have this talk."

"Okay," I said nervously. "What's wrong."

"Well—" he began, before stalling out into a long pause.

I swear to God the first thing that entered my mind for no reason other than it was in fact my first initial thought was that Mom and Dad were splitting up. From my vantage point, they didn't fight, argue, or anything like that but then again, I wasn't around all the time now that I was working. My second thought was that Papa had died. Less than a year ago, he had a heart attack at home and we had to drive over to Spokane at ten o' clock on a Monday night so we could be at the hospital when he came out of an emergency surgery that put balloons in his aorta. (I even had the audacity to ask Dad if we could wait an extra hour so I could finish watching wrestling.) Papa recovered but didn't take the doctor's advise to quit smoking, leaving the possibility of a future recurrence a near certainty.

Only these two things ran through my head during Dad's long pause. I was right on one of my guesses, but I was still floored when I found out which one it was.

"I should have told you this earlier but over the past couple of years, your mom and I have been slowly drifting apart," he said, trying to fight back tears. "And she wants a divorce."

"What?!"

Even though I guessed it right, I still couldn't believe it.

"Why?"

"She just don't love me no more. There isn't another guy or nothin', she just doesn't want to be with me."

I didn't know what to say. But as we sat there staring at the living room window that ran the entire length and height of the living room, things that I didn't give a second thought to started to make sense. Less than two weeks earlier, Dad rode home on a brand new Harley-Davidson Heritage Softail—price tag sixteen grand and some change. Mom had also opened up a brand new bank account, in her name only, at a different bank. Both of these were no-nos for our family. Mom and Dad always talked about every dollar that was both made and spent. From what I saw, nobody bought so much as a stick of gum without the other one's approval. Come to find out, they had split their savings account in half. Mom opened up her own account with hers and Dad spent his on the bike. They had also split up the cars. Mom kept the Explorer and Dad kept the Jimmy.

Then came the actual household. Dad was going to legally give me the Gold Wing once I was eighteen and legally able to own a vehicle so if things got ugly in court, it could stay with the family. Jen, in turn, got the family computer. As for the house, Dad was the only one who could afford the payments to be able to keep it, thus making it to where we didn't have to move for the second time in less than a year. He volunteered to live in the camp trailer up on the logging roads above our house until everything was finalized. Again, the reason was for Jen and I to avoid moving. They also didn't want it to be a total distraction from everyday life—too late for that.

After Dad told me the news, he said that we could either go to the hamburger stand or we could stay home and finish off all of the alcohol in the house. I took a pass on the latter because I didn't want to start accepting drinking alcohol excessively solely as a reason to help cope with emotional pain. If I was going to drink, I was going to responsibly do it for fun.

A few days later, I packed up my stuff and took a Greyhound with the football team over to Cheney for camp. I left all of the problems at home—out of sight, out of mind. I didn't tell anyone on the team what was happening. It wasn't any of their business in the first place and second of all, they couldn't do anything to make it better anyway—and I didn't want to fuckin' talk about it anyway.

Honestly, I didn't know why any of us soon-to-be seniors even played football. We hated Williams because he only liked the guys that sucked up to him. We screwed around at turnout instead of giving the slightest damn. While we played hard in the games, we mainly looked forward to misbehaving on the bus rides to and from the fields.

Camp was no different. We ran our drills and scrimmaged against other teams during the sessions, but the real fun came in the dorms. Anyone that left their room unattended would have it turned upside down, just like a warden tossing prison cells. Shoelaces were tied together, Icy Hot was smeared into boxer shorts, and that was just for the guys on our own team. As for the players on the other teams, they weren't exempt. We would shit in plastic bags and hang them on their door handles at night. During the meals that took place after turnouts, we would sabotage and hide their equipment that everyone had to leave outside of the cafeteria. We would dump juice and mushy food into their cleats and take their helmets and put them in another team's room.

On the field, I was totally healthy and playing well. My back was giving me zero problems and I had retaken my starting position—sort of. I was moved to right tackle on the offensive line instead of playing center. If we were in passing situations, I was responsible for everything on the outside edge. When we were running the ball, I was used for pulling to the other side of the line to start opening a hole for the fullback and halfback.

While I would have rather played center because I was better at it than tackle and better at it than anyone else on the team, I had to switch spots to make room for Jordan Janicki. Now I love Jordan to death—he was my training partner in wrestling for three years and we have known each other since Dad started working at Janicki Logging in the eighties. Jordan deserved to play on the team, don't get me wrong, but given the fact that his dad was on the school board and Williams was always a kiss-ass to anyone that he felt could save his job despite poor records, it is my belief that Jordan was given that spot to earn brownie points with the higher powers—or maybe I wasn't as good as I thought I was.

Defensively, I was the starting right defensive end. That lasted through camp but ended after the first week of the season when Joey Moore (who no longer wore Steve Urkel's glasses) took my spot because he was simply better than I was. Besides, a competitive high school team should only have players that play exclusively on one side of the ball. That way they are as fresh as possible later in the game when everyone else is tiring. Nobody plays both ways in the pros either, because no man can play that physical of a game at 100% for sixty minutes.

I worked as much as possible when I wasn't doing sports activities. I had to pay Mom and Dad back for the seven hundred dollars that they loaned me to get my pickup, buy gas and insurance, and hopefully have enough left over to spend on something besides bills—welcome to real life. It was clear that I wasn't going to have enough money to go on the upcoming bike trip, but Mom stepped in and helped me out without me even having to ask.

The 1999 bike trip didn't have near the buildup as the Sturgis trip did a year earlier. This time we were heading south down to the Grand Canyon, Las Vegas, and Death Valley. Exactly fifty-two weeks removed from the beginning of our previous year's trip, Dad and I once again rode over to Uncle Robbie's, where we would leave from the following day.

We left Rob's house an hour or so after daybreak. We cruised along Highway 231 for about thirty minutes when, without warning, Rob's bike just up and shut off. He was riding the same Gold Wing as the year before and hadn't had any previous problems with it. For the next three hours, he tore apart his ferring and side panels to check his wires and fuses. A few minutes away from noon, he had it running again—for a while. Every few hours throughout the next week-and-a-half, we would have to stop at the hottest possible spots to work on his shit-heap. It couldn't break down on the cooler summit of the Sierra-Nevada's—it had to be Death Valley or the Mojave Desert and places like that where water don't exist. Because we had so far to go, we were always on the move from daylight until dark with our only stops being the ones to fix his bike.

On the first day, we stayed southbound on US-395 through Washington and a third of the way into Oregon. Towards evening, we rode into the small town of Dale, Oregon. We had gotten gas in Walla Walla a while back and I suggested that we should keep on going for another half-hour to Long Creek, where we could gas and eat all at once before getting another hour of riding in until we had to stop for the night. Dad and Rob didn't want to, but they agreed.

Five miles north of Long Creek, and right on schedule, my fuel light came on. As we pulled into the small town, we noticed that there was only one gas station that right in the center of town. We pulled up to the pumps and there wasn't a sole to be seen, as they had closed an hour earlier. Keep in mind this was 1999—24 hour pay-at-the-pumps weren't around yet. Nowadays, we could have zipped a credit card and been on our way, but this time we were stuck.

"Well this is just fuckin' great," Dad said to me. "Why is traveling with you such a chore?"

Apparently he forgot about his brother's bike problems.

"How far is it to the next town?" I asked Rob as he was studying the map.

"Thirty miles."

There was no way that I could make that. We couldn't go back to Dale either because that was twenty-eight miles. The only thing that we could do was wait until six the next morning when the Chevron opened up again. That problem was solved, but we still had to find a place to spend the night. Dad started up his bike and went to check out our options while Rob and I stayed at the pumps. He came back five minutes later and told us that he had found us a place.

"Where is it—a school yard?" Rob muttered.

"No," Dad answered with a little excitement. "It's at some guy's house and he has beer and barbequed ribs for us too!"

Maybe this was a blessing in disguise. Maybe with this kind of luck, we should spend more time in Las Vegas besides just the overnight stop at Grandma's.

"Welcome to Long Crick, dudes," the owner of the hippie pad said in a slow, monotone voice. "Help yourselves to some beer and ribs, dudes."

I have no idea what this guy's name was, nor did I of the couple of other guys that talked and acted just like he did. They talked almost nonstop, ending each sentence with "dude" or "man." They fed us well, though. We could eat their ribs and drink their beer until we couldn't stand up if we wanted to. We were even welcome to hit their stash of marijuana, which we politely declined.

The party went on all night. Eventually a bunch of girls, who looked to be about my age, showed up for some beer and weed. Not sure what good could come from that equation, we opted to lay our sleeping bags out in their yard that was covered in dog shit and call it a night. Literally counting the minutes until six the next morning, we tried to find any spot that resembled grass and hit the sack. As soon as it even hinted on becoming daylight, we quickly packed up and pushed our bikes down the street to the Chevron to avoid waking our passed-out pals.

After filling up, we continued south on US-395 into Susanville, California, where we chose to go west until we reached Highway 89 and take that south to avoid Reno and Carson City. Besides, that route would take us into the Sierra Nevada's and along Lake Tahoe as well. A couple of hours north of Tahoe, we ran into another gas station issue.

The Shell station in Quincy, California advertised their fuel for $2.49 a gallon for premium unleaded, which was a complete shock for us. That may seem like a steal today, but not in 1999 when gas was just over a dollar a gallon. We paid it to avoid another situation like the Long Creek episode. We even took a picture holding our butts after "getting raped" by the Quincy Shell. Little did we know, we would actually pay a higher amount later in the week.

That night, we ended up on a backroad turnout just south of Lake Tahoe. We no sooner than parked our bikes before I jumped over a couple of downed trees to go and get rid of some bad lunch. Rob wouldn't let anyone else use his portable shitter, so I had to hunch down the old fashioned way. Unlike regular toilets where you can take your time, a wood's squat forces you to hurry up before you lose your balance and fall back into what you just created.

As I was finishing up, I noticed a catalog of some sort sitting off to my right about ten or twelve feet from me. I pulled up my britches and walked over to find a pretty explicit porno magazine. You can come up with your own conclusions as to why a dirty magazine was off the main road and out of sight, but there it was—nearly brand new. I took my new found treasure back to show the guys, where they promptly threw it away . . . . Are you kidding?—we went through it page by page!

The next morning with ZZ Top's "Woke Up With Wood" playing on the radio, we continued to make our way south. We barely cracked the two hundred mile mark that day, as Rob's bike was being especially stubborn. It actually worked out better that way because that would put us riding through Death Valley early the next morning when it was as cool as possible.

That night, we stayed at a campground outside of Lone Pine, California. Beings we stopped much earlier than usual, we bought extra beer to get us through the extra hours. Well, even the extra wasn't enough, as the three of us really tied one on. I don't know how and I don't know why, but the night ended with me and Dad scuffling on the ground and his gun coming up missing.

The next morning, we headed straight into Death Valley. Named in 1849 by prospectors who crossed it during the California Gold Rush, Death Valley sits 285 feet BELOW sea level. Oddly enough, just 85 miles away stands Mount Whitney, the highest point in the contiguous United States. Temperatures in Death Valley range from 86 to 95 degrees—at night. Daytime highs average in the 120's with the highest being 134 degrees, recorded at the Furnace Creek visitor center. At eight in the morning when we went through, it was 122 degrees.

Once inside the park, we saw giant containers of radiator water located in turnouts that were just three miles apart from each other. We didn't need them as we all had air-cooled engines, but just about every container we passed would have a car parked there filling up with water. When it came time for us to get gas, we pulled into the Chevron in Furnace Creek and proceeded to pay $2.99 a gallon for premium. Remember, it was 1999—can you imagine what today's prices would be. The screw job didn't end there, however. The vending machine charged two dollars for a twelve ounce pop, which I gladly paid. To this day, it was the most refreshing two dollars that I have ever spent.

After an exhausting day of endless heat, we ended up at Grandma's house in Las Vegas. Rob and I sat in the house and drank beer while Dad took Grandma for a ride on his new bike and to inform her of his marriage situation. I must say, it felt great to be inside with air conditioning for a change. When they got back, we loaded up in the pickup with her and Milt to go out for dinner at the Gold Coast Casino. Despite living in Las Vegas only a stone's throw from The Strip, Grandma and Milt rarely gambled. Even if they went out to dinner, they would just walk right by all of the flashy slot machines and table games. Think of how hard that would be, as you can even find slot machines in laundromats in Vegas. Unbeknownst to the three of us, the Gold Coast had a dress code for their restaurant. With us being on a motorcycle trip, all we had were jeans, T-shirts, and tank tops. The usher obviously stopped us at the door.

"You gentlemen can't come in here dressed like that," he said.

"Excuse me," Grandma, who use the F-word at least twice to describe a sunset, said firmly, about two inches from his nose. "My boys have driven from fuckin' Washington to see me and HERE is where we're gonna fuckin' eat!"

The usher just stepped aside as we walked in and seated ourselves.

After dinner, we went back to Grandma's and got on our bikes for a ride down Las Vegas Boulevard at night. As cool as it is to do in a car, it is twice as awesome to see it while riding on a motorcycle.

Following breakfast the next day, we said our goodbyes and headed east, crossing the Hoover Dam and cruising right on through to the Grand Canyon. We stopped at all of the scenic points along the south rim for pictures—and to work on Rob's bike.

The only major disappointment of the trip came the next day when we were at Four Corner's National Monument. I don't really know what I was expecting to see, but I figured it would be something cool at least because it is the only spot in the United States that four states come together. Forgetting the fact that it is located in the middle of the Navajo Indian Reservation and there are tons of tables and booths full of Indians selling blankets, jewelry, and pottery at the end of a dirt road, all that was there was a cement platform divided into fourths with Arizona, Utah, New Mexico, and Colorado labeled on the slabs.

As we made our way through Utah on our way home, Dad and Rob kept getting on my case about falling behind as we rolled down the highway. I can't help it. For some reason when I'm riding in the back, I just go off into my own world and forget about keeping up with the pack. I tried to explain it but they wouldn't listen, so I just took off at eighty and made them try to keep up with me. Of course my little temper tantrum caused us to spend the night at a rest area instead of one of the many nice camping spots that I flew by without stopping.

We made it home a few days later, ending a good trip. Not a great trip, but a good trip. It was another example of the movie sequel analogy that I have already used—we set the bar so high with the Sturgis trip, it's almost impossible to match it. It was also the end of an era in a way. While we would take weekend trips occasionally over the next couple of years, often including Papa and Jake who would each have bikes by then, it would be nine years until the three of us went on a bike trip like that for an extended length of time.

As August was winding down, it was two-a-days for football turnouts that occupied my time outside of work. For three hours, twice a day, we would have full turnouts to get ready for the upcoming season. Once school started and with turnouts immediately after, I had to change my work schedule to weekends only. There just wasn't enough time in the day for me to get everything in.

I was never home, which wasn't necessarily a bad thing because I didn't have to be distracted with Mom and Dad's problems. Dad would live in the camp trailer for a few weeks and then it was "Fuck this—she's the one who brought this on so she should leave." So Mom would pack up and go and stay at a motel or at a friend's house. Then they were both home for a few days and the cycle would start all over again.

For the first time ever, I started to frequently hear them scream at each other. As long as I could remember, they had taken their arguments to another room where Jen or I couldn't hear what was going on. Now it was all out in the open. I even heard Mom say the F-word during one showdown that they had early one morning while I was trying to sleep, following a closing shift at McDonald's the night before. From where I sat, however, the heat seemed to go away after a day or so—or maybe it was just wishful thinking on my part.

The previous three months of back and forth squabbles and all-out screaming matches came to an end for good on Saturday, September 11, 1999—my birthday. To me, it was business as usual. I got up, went to town and mowed two lawns, and then made my way to McDonald's for a ten hour shift. Before I left, Mom and Dad gave me a birthday cake and a wrestling tape for a present. Everything seemed to be normal.

Me and Mom on my 18th birthday, before she moved out

Around eleven or so that night when I got home and parked my pickup in the shop, I noticed that Dad's Jimmy was gone. *Well, they are at it again*, I thought. The camp trailer was still there, so I figured that Dad went off to sleep in his car somewhere. When I went up to the back porch and opened the door to the house, Tuco met me at the door as usual. There was a light on in the master bedroom, so figured that Mom was still awake. From the hallway and with genuine curiosity, I asked where Dad was.

"I'm right here," he said.

Confused, I went into my room and started changing my clothes.

"Well, where's the Jimmy?" I asked.

"In the garage."

"Okay—where's the Explorer then?"

"Your mom has it."

Apparently I wasn't asking the right questions.

"So what is it now?" I asked, finally coming into their room to get a legitimate answer.

"She's moved out and living at her friend Mona's house permanently."

I didn't even know Mona and I hated her guts. *She must have been the one talking to Mom and planting the seed in her the whole time.* She was always taking Mom out on the weekends, staying out until the wee hours of the morning, while Dad sat out in the camp trailer. Mona.

Mona. Mona—I hated the bitch and I didn't even know what she looked like. If I ever met her, though, I convinced myself that I was going to punch her in the mouth as hard as I could for starting all of this shit and ruining my summer, my birthday, and my whole fucking family. I didn't care if it meant jail for me now that I was eighteen, I just wanted her to feel as much physical pain as my family was feeling emotionally.

CHAPTER 35

...But What You Do Know Will

I WOULD BE LYING if I told you that the drama going on at home wasn't a distraction to me. As far as school went, that was no big deal because it was almost all elective classes. I lifted weights, worked on my gun cabinet, and only spent just one class period in an actual classroom. After school, it was football occupying my afternoons. As long as I stayed busy, I was fine and didn't give home life a second thought. The problem was, everybody in school knew about it now. I didn't tell anyone about it but in a small school, it only takes one person to push the snowball down the hill—Jen. Everyone showed genuine concern, though, but I just shrugged it off as if it wasn't a major issue so people would leave me the hell alone.

For my final season of football, all of us in the senior class opted to play for ourselves for fun instead of competitively playing for Williams. Don't get me wrong, we fought our asses off during games. In turnout, though, we did nothing but screw around. We knew full-well that you have to practice as hard as you would play in a game, but we didn't care. Williams ruined that with his insistence on running a passing offense that wasn't designed for our running team. In high school, you have to adapt your game plans around the talent that you have. It's not like the pros that can trade for players that are better fit for the system that you are after. *Why didn't that idiot understand that?*

On Mondays after Friday night's game, we wouldn't have an actual turnout. Instead, we would watch the game film from the game that went down three days earlier. Williams would go through each play, pause it long enough to point out what should have happened, and then play it as we all watched to see if we executed it right. To be fair, he would praise the good and scold the bad—unless of course if you were his start quarterback.

In pass protection, an offensive line should be able to buy the quarterback at least three seconds to drop back, read the coverage and his receivers, and make the throw. The line will fall back to form a U-shaped pocket of which the quarterback is to step into to make his throw. If nobody is open, he should scramble or throw the ball away. Our quarterback ran from side to side in the pocket instead of getting around to the outside. When that happens, the defense is going see that he is in trouble and come after him and swallow him in the collapsed pocket. Williams always blamed it on the line like the ignorant fuck that he was.

"You guys need to hold your blocks as long as it takes for him to make the throw. And Ed, you're holding,"

Truth be known, an offensive lineman holds on every single play. The only time that he gets caught is when the defender beats him and he continues to try and stay with him. My grade from Williams was always a D because of my alleged holding. Well, I only got flagged twice that year for holding and my head-up opponents rarely made a sack or an interior tackle.

If you were one of Williams' favorites, he always made excuses for you. We had a set of twin brothers, Roan and Reuben Dreyer, who were athletic as hell but dumb as a couple of posts. During one game in Lynden, one of them was back to receive the opening kickoff but didn't bother picking the ball up after it was kicked. Lynden recovered it in the end zone and had six points before the game clock even started. Williams defended him by claiming to have called for the punt return team to take the field instead of the kickoff return team. Whatever.

During regular turnouts, we would spend most of our time dicking around in between plays and drills. Greg Mahle played wide receiver because he could snag any ball that was within his reach. He probably could have played quarterback if he wanted to because he could hit a dime from a mile away.

"Pick a number, Carny," he would say as we waited for the second string team to finish setting up the equipment.

"Thirty."

He would then locate the guy who wore that particular jersey number and launch the ball, from well over forty yards out, and hit him right in the earhole of his helmet.

"Another one."

"Sixty-five."

Again he would spot the unsuspecting victim and rifle the ball right at him, hitting him in the back, the face, or even the groin. Everyone knew who it was, but nobody ever did anything about it.

Greg and I, along with Jeremy Ellis, Darren Beutler, and Joey, began a five man crusade to get into as much trouble, start as much shit, and have as much fun as we possibly could. Before home games, the grounds crew would paint the lines on the field and set up the yard markers. We would change them all around after they were finished, putting the fifty yard marker on the goal line and shit like that. I even crawled up on top of the grandstands to the announce booth and started saying nasty things about some of the nearby tennis players' girlfriends for everyone within a quarter-mile to hear. I had to run five miles for that one, but it was worth it.

Every week, we would always receive extra conditioning for misbehaving before games. We always admitted to what we did and proudly served our punishments. For away games, we would sit in the very back of the bus and hold up signs to the window that said "show us your tits." We got a lot of laughs from passing cars, but unfortunately there weren't any takers. We probably wouldn't have been caught if I hadn't had the bright idea to show the sign to our cheerleader's van that pulled up behind us at a stop sign. I got another five miles for that one and had to write an apology letter to the entire squad.

Greg actually got suspended for a game for a stunt that he pulled after a game in Ferndale. The cornerback who was covering him all night was always illegally holding him during every one of his routes. During one play late in the game when Greg ran a dummy route, he punched the defender right square in the nuts as he ran by him. Just to make sure that he felt it, Greg hit him in the balls again during handshakes at the end of the game. The Ferndale coach sent a tape to Williams that showed the footage of what happened plain as day. While Greg had to sit out a game, we all had to run laps for laughing at the incident while we watched the game film on the following Monday.

On Thursday nights, following our pregame walk-through, all ten or twelve of us seniors would go out to dinner as a group. Sometimes we went to a guy's house and other times we would go to a restaurant—usually a place that was either an all-you-can-eat, or at least a place that had huge portions. There, we would stuff our face, talk about the game, and have a good time.

One night, we broke our own rules and took along a player from the junior class along with us. Brent Frisbee was over six-and-a-half feet tall and weighed close to four hundred pounds. He was so big that coaches had to special order his game pants. The pants only came in white, so they had to dye them blue in hopes that they would match ours. It didn't work—they ended up more on the gray side. Anyway, the reason we took him was because we wanted to see in person just how much food he could put down at the Royal Fork Buffet. He ate plate after plate, heaping plates, for over an hour. I think he mainly did it for show, but what a show it was!

After dinner that night, we all went out to the parking lot to get in our cars and leave. We were standing around talking when Brent, who we called "Tonnage," started looking a little green in the gills. His eyes then opened real wide as he took a deep breath and blew his dinner all over the parking lot. The worst part was, once something like that happens, everyone else gets queasy. Before you knew it, there was a chain reaction puke-fest happening right in the parking lot.

After our meals, we would all drive back to the school to toss the football around in the empty parking lot. I would always follow my truck behind Greg's rig because he would swerve at every oncoming car to try and get them to drive off of the road. Nobody ever crashed or got hurt, but it wasn't for the lack of trying. It wasn't all that smart, but boy was it funny to watch!

On Friday afternoons before the bus would leave or before we had to report to the locker room, a few of us would go over to Jon Wallace's house, who lived right across the street from the high school. Neither Jon or his parents would be home yet, so we would make a bunch of sandwiches and watch TV. Once Jon got there, he wouldn't get any of the sandwiches because they were all gone. Soon, his mom would get home and she would make us all tacos or hamburgers for dinner, thinking we must be starving after a long day of school.

Once the whistle blew on Friday night, though, it was all business. I came up with a catch phrase, "Who's got sack?!," that we all hollered out to each other as we walked onto the field.

The whole team would yell "We do!" Incidentally, I also used that phrase to dare people to do stupid stuff. It's amazing what guys will do when you question their "manhood."

As hard as we played, win or lose, nobody in the stands except for the parents cared. Unfortunately, high school football games are just an excuse for kids to loiter around with each other. Nobody remembers the score, the big plays, or even the injuries. It was all about hanging out and waiting for the game to be over so the dances could start. I was never into the dancing shit, or homecoming contests, or anything like that. I thought they were all silly and were a waste of time.

That all changed during homecoming week that year. The school always put on dress-up contests, obstacle races, and a lip sync. For my previous three years, I hated them. They weren't even close to being entertaining or funny. Each class would lip sync a corny song and do some circus act in order to try and win. I had seen enough and I was going to get involved to right the sinking ship.

"What are you here for?" one of the class officers said as I walked up to suggest an idea.

"To win the contest," I said.

"With what, a Hank Williams or an Elvis Presley act?"

I don't know what I had in common with Hank Williams, but I did have long sideburns like The King.

"No. I want to take three other guys and dress up like the guys in KISS—real make-up, real instruments, and real leather."

They loved it! We used all of the leather motorcycle pants, jackets, and vests that I had at home for our outfits. I had my face painted just like Gene Simmons painted his. Joey was Paul Stanley, Jon was Ace Frehley, and Darren was Peter Criss. Just for an added element of surprise, we had a girl named Kristine dress up like Britney Spears, who was on fire at the time, to perform with us.

For the act, we had three real electric guitars and a real set of drums set up on the gym floor. To start with, we played the first minute or so of the live version of "Detroit Rock City" from 1977's *KISS Alive! II* album. Even though Paul Stanley is on vocals during the real version, I did it as Gene Simmons because I knew the words. Nobody even noticed the error. After the first verse and chorus, we broke into ". . . Baby One More Time" from Spears' 1999 album of the same name. As Kristine danced around and sang, we all started pushing and shoving each other and doing silly dance moves to try and vie for her attention. Just as predicted, we won the contest unanimously.

After Mom moved out, the divorce proceedings started getting ugly. I'm not going to get into all of it, but let's just say that Dad had enough money to make the house payment and pay the regular bills. There weren't a lot of groceries around. On the nights that I didn't eat at work or on the road, we had deer meat and potatoes and that was it. We had it everyday for almost a year. For breakfast, we had our free chicken eggs. Beggars couldn't be choosers so if I wanted something different, I was on my own to get it.

Dad would go to work early and come home in the evening like he always had. On school days, I would get up at six and watch wrestling for an hour while Jen spent sixty minutes in the shower. Around seven, Mom would always call from her cell phone and wish us a good day. That was pretty much the only time that I ever talked to her. I didn't want to go and see her at Mona's because I was still pissed off at the meddling bitch. Besides, I was busy every afternoon and evening with either football or work.

On a Monday afternoon after a short version of game film (we actually won a game, so Williams didn't have too much to complain about), I went home as always to watch the East Coast showing of wrestling on satellite. It couldn't have been four o' clock and Dad was sitting in the Jimmy at the stop sign at the end of our road. He was never home that early on a Monday—something wasn't right.

"What are you doing home already?" I asked.

"I didn't work today," he answered.

"Your log truck was gone this morning."

"I went on an investigation."

"About what?"

"Well . . . ." he began with that same long pause that he had when he first brought the situation to my attention. "Your mom . . . ."

"Mom, what?" I asked impatiently.

"She has a boyfriend," he sobbed.

"For how long?"

"A long time."

I left him there at the stop sign as I got into my pickup and drove the half-mile up to our house. At first I was irate. Then I was upset. Then I was back to being mad again. I started getting real warm and nauseous when I pulled into the driveway but as I got out to open up the shop door, I just fell to my knees and started crying like a baby. The neighbor guy, Jackie Aldridge, hopped the fence like Carl Lewis and ran over to give me a welcomed embrace. I cried on his shoulder until Dad came back to the house.

After I calmed down, he told me that he went to places where Mom had written checks while supposedly out with Mona, who was never actually involved, to get information. (You can't hide too many things in a small town.) Afterward, he went up to Bellingham where Mom had said that she had checked into a motel during one of her "moving out" phases. They had no record of her ever being there. Next, he went to an apartment complex where all of the calls that she made on her cell phone were traced to. Mom's Explorer was there in a numbered space that coincided with the apartment number. So Dad walked up and knocked on the door, covering the peephole so nobody could see who it was. Sure enough, Mom opened the door. I don't know what was said, and I don't want to know.

Jen got home on the bus a while later and I had to listen to the whole disgusting story again. As hurt as I was, I did find laughter in the fact that I was apparently living with Dick Tracey. But even then, it was just a small, glimmering light in a world that quickly became dark and gray.

The next morning, right at seven, the phone rang. We didn't have caller I.D. or anything, but both Jen and I knew that it was Mom. We both just sat there and let it ring. After a few rings, it would stop for a minute before starting again. Neither of us picked up. It was the best thing to do, because I don't even know what would have came out of my mouth.

It would be several weeks before I spoke to her and even then, it was by accident when I answered the phone expecting it to be someone else. She never told me his name, and I never asked. I told her that I didn't want to see him and that I didn't even really want to see her right away. She bawled and asked me if she could at least come and watch my last few football games of my career.

"By yourself," I said.

She came alright, and so did he. I never saw him because I wasn't going to let staring up at the stands distract me. After the games, I would just go to the locker room instead of hanging around and getting the congratulatory words from the parents. Dad did see him and even tried to start a fight in the parking lot, which some of the players saw. The whole team had his back and said that whenever I was ready, we could all go to his house and make Rodney King's beating at the hands of the L.A.P.D. back in 1991 seem like a birthday party. I respectfully declined. It sounded good, believe me, but I wanted to think things through a little more before I did something that I may regret.

On the last home game of the season, I was faced with a bit of a dilemma. Traditionally, the last home game was senior night, in which all seniors were introduced one at a time at mid-field. That wasn't the problem. Additionally, their parents were also introduced as well and would pose together for a picture along with the coach. Other split families did just fine, but theirs wasn't a fresh wound like this.

Prior to the game, I went into Williams' office and told him that I would like to be excluded from the pregame festivities.

"Nonsense," was his compassionate response.

I called both Mom and Dad and told them not to under any circumstances meet me on the field. Mom cried when she heard me say that. Dad didn't, but I could tell that it hurt him. Still, I thought that it would be in everyone's best interest if the situation was avoided.

During introductions, I was called out to the center of the field. Against my will, I stood at mid-field with Williams for a picture. I was the only senior who didn't bring down at least one parent or family member. By then, the whole town knew what was going on so it wasn't a surprise that I stood out there alone.

I felt a little guilty about it, though. Ever since my first season of football nine years earlier, both of may parents had always been at my games. The only times when the two of them wouldn't make it together were when Jen had a gymnastic meet or if Dad had to work. Otherwise, they were there. It would have only been right if they were there to be with me for the culmination of my career, but I wouldn't have any of it. Besides, this whole thing was Mom's fault and she deserved to be excluded for being such a whore—fuck her.

As for the game, it was against Anacortes. Although we were a sub-.500 team, a victory would put us in the district playoffs. The game was close throughout but unfortunately, the officiating was completely one-sided. I have never been one to blame the loss of a football game completely on officiating, but this was ridiculous. We must have racked up over two hundred yards in penalties, most of which were horseshit calls. The Anacortes players were constantly hitting from behind after the plays were over, holding during pass coverage, and lining up in the neutral zone without being called for it. Late in the fourth quarter, I finally had enough.

After the whistle blew, their defensive end clobbered Jeremy from behind right in front of me. I grabbed the defender by the back of his shoulder pads and threw him to the ground. As I stood over him, I told him that I was going to sodomize him at mid-field if he kept it up. As expected, I got a fifteen yard personal foul for unnecessary roughness. I knew that it was coming because even in an impartially officiated game, the referees always see the reaction.

That was the last play of my football career as Williams pulled me from the game.

"What is your problem?" he yelled.

"FUCK YOU!"

"WHAT?!"

"I'm not going to just stand around like you and let another team push my teammates around!"

"Wanna bet?"

I spent the last two minutes of the game on the sidelines. It was okay—I finally got to tell Williams off.

Football is a game of respect and you have to earn it to get it. Jack Lambert of the Pittsburgh Steelers did the exact same thing to a member of the Dallas Cowboys in Super Bowl XIII. He got the penalty, but there wasn't anymore pushing and shoving after the plays from then on. He was also elected to the Pro Football Hall of Fame in 1990.

Another Hall of Famer, 49er free safety Ronnie Lott, stood up in front of the whole San Francisco team during a film session and ordered the picture to pause. Rookie linebacker Bill Romanowski was shoved on his face from behind after a play was ruled dead. Without hesitation, Romanowski got up and just walked back to the huddle.

"Romo," Lott called out in front of the whole team. "If you ever let a player from the opposing team do that to you again, I personally am going to kick your ass! Football is a game of respect."

Lott had respect. He had the tip of his finger amputated during a game so he could get back on the field and keep playing. As for Romanowski, he went on to be one of the most physical, hardest hitting linebackers of the 1990's. Maybe Williams should have done his homework and learned a thing or two about the non-corporate game of football.

We lost that night, thanks to the refs ruling Greg's game winning touchdown out of bounds. Afterward in the locker room, all of us seniors sat together in the corner and cried. It wasn't the loss that got us teared up, nor was it the officiating. It was the fact that we were done playing a sport that we had grown up together with. We also realized that maybe we could have won that game and lived to fight another day if we had gave everything that we had at turnout instead of screwing off. But now, it was too late.

CHAPTER 36

Another Bad Ending

Not only was my birthday screwed thanks to Mom's impeccable timing, but the holiday season was now fast approaching. According to court papers, Jen and I had to go to Mom's every other holiday. Well, that wasn't going to happen. I had not seen Mom in person for over two months and that wasn't going to change anytime soon. Even if I were to change my mind, I wasn't going to do anything the courts said and I wasn't going to meet her boyfriend under any circumstances—let alone have a holiday meal with him.

I still had no idea what his name was. I hadn't asked Mom during our phone conversations because I simply didn't care. Word did spread rather quickly that he was a milk truck driver who delivered to all of the local schools for their meal programs. Well that made sense. Mom worked at schools for several years and had to to have met him that way. Who knows how long that this was going on behind everyone's backs? Still, as bad as I was angered and hurt, I once again managed to get a laugh out of the irony of the situation. I mean, everyone has blamed the milkman for years!

As Thanksgiving approached, Dad insisted that he was going to try and keep everything the same as it always had been. Ever since I could remember, dinner was at our house with Grandpa and Grandma and Grandma Murrow. If that was what we were used to, then Dad said that was what we were going to do. I'm sure that everyone was just as excited about it as I was.

The night before, Dad, Jen, and I drove down to Tacoma to see a concert at the Tacoma Dome. Money was especially tight by then, so this was going to be everyone's Christmas presents. That was fine with me because it was a show with two of my favorite bands, Lynyrd Skynyrd and ZZ Top.

Naturally it wasn't the original Lynyrd Skynyrd lineup as twenty-two years and a month earlier, Ronnie Van Zant, Steve and Cassie Gaines, and a few crew members died in a plane crash in Mississippi. Replacing Ronnie on vocals was his brother, Johnny. Gaines and Ed King (who was still alive) were replaced by Rickey Medlocke and Hughie Thomasson respectively. Original bassist Leon Wilkeson, drummer Artimus Pyle, and keyboardist Billy Powell rounded out the band. They didn't skip a beat, scorching through "Call Me The Breeze," "Sweet Home Alabama," and a fifteen minute version of "Free Bird."

As for ZZ Top, it was "the same three guys, same three chords," as guitarist/vocalist Billy Gibbons always says. Dusty Hill and Frank Beard (who ironically is the only member without a foot long beard) rounded out the group who has remained constant, without any changes in the lineup, longer than any other band in the history of music. The three rolled through "Sharped Dressed Man," "Legs," and La Grange" to a packed house.

The fun and games were over Thanksgiving Day, as we sat through the longest, most awkward and uncomfortable meal that I have ever eaten in my life. Not a whole lot was said, but what could you say? After it was finally over, Dad decided that we would just do holidays with the three of us from then on. There wasn't any sense of living in the past, it was time to move ahead. No more dinners with Skip and Lisa, no visits from Grandpa and Grandma—nothing. Nobody wanted to talk about the subject that everyone was noticeably dancing around.

I did continue to stop by and talk to Grandpa, who had recently retired from driving, on my own time for a little while. We would small talk for two or three minutes before that same long pause, that always meant something about Mom, would begin. After a few visits, I just got tired of dancing around the subject and quit coming by their house altogether. He took it as me being mad at him and the misinterpretation led to an eight year period where we didn't speak to each other.

Wrestling season began in mid-November after the normal two week break between it and football. I told Dad, Jay, and everyone that would listen that my goal for the year was to compete at the state tournament at the Tacoma Dome. My goal wasn't to necessarily win, but just to qualify for the tournament. From there, anything could happen. I just wanted the chance to compete at the level where only the best in the state could. Jay said that it was a reasonable goal (he would have told me flat-out if it was impossible) but I just needed to wrestle with a little more aggression.

During turnouts, I would train hard as usual. There was always screw-off time, which was encouraged, but it was all business for the most part. The minute that I showed a lack of aggression, Jay would match me up with a much smaller and more technically sound kid to drill with. Usually it was with Andy Andrews, who I didn't much care for to say the least. After a few minutes, I would get pissed off at him and start crushing him within the confines of the rules. Jay would then put me back with an opponent of my own size for me to continue to unload on.

It worked because I wasn't pinned to the mat all season long. I lost matches, sure, but only by a couple of points at a time. Unlike previous years, I was reaching the time limit almost every night. The only time that I didn't wrestle a match for the full six minutes was when I was the one who was doing the pinning. The downside was that I was always giving up twenty pounds or more for each match. We lacked upper weight guys so in order to fill the roster, Jay put me at the 215 pound spot for the whole season. I still made weight at under 189 pounds so I could wrestle at that weight during the postseason.

Twenty or twenty-five pounds makes a lot of difference in wrestling, that is why they have weight classes to begin with. Amateur wrestlers can only bump up two weight classes legally. For example, if a 120 pounder makes weight, he can compete no higher than at 130. If he is overweight, he can compete up to 135. In the lower weights, the separation is only five pounds. As you get to the upper weights, though, the increments increase. Technically with me making weight at 189, I could legally wrestle heavyweight. That means that I would give up nearly one hundred pounds! I did wrestle heavyweight on occasion, whatever was asked of me to give the team the best chance of winning. It wasn't so bad because I could run circles around them until they tired out and became easy pickings.

Despite giving up a bunch of weight, I had some pretty good matches at 215. During our duel match against Lake Stevens in front of two thousand people, I wrestled to a 0-0 draw. It is almost impossible to wrestle a full six minutes without a score and not get penalized for stalling, but we did it. Neither one of us could take the other guy down in the first round. During the next two rounds, we each took turns holding the other guy down on the mat, while at the same time, unable to turn the other guy to his back for any points. No take downs were awarded in the two minute overtime, so we went to a one minute sudden death round.

In sudden death, the match is won by either keeping your opponent down or escaping from the bottom. As the match neared the nine minute mark, he escaped from my grasp to earn the only point and the victory. Couple that 1-0 loss with the 23-21 victory from the previous year, and I have two of the rarest point totals that you will ever see in wrestling.

Another match that I consider to be one of my best ever took place in Bellingham at Squalicum High School. Again it was at 215, wrestling one of their top upper weight guys. I was behind 3-2 late in the third round and I had to win to secure the victory for the team. If I lost, we could still win, but Travis Geiger, the perennial screw-off, would have to score a pinfall at heavyweight.

I was down, fighting to get to my feet, with less than twenty seconds to go. I managed to make it to my feet as we went out of the ring, stopping the clock. As we went back to the center of the mat for the restart, the entire visiting side of the stands started chanting my name, "Eddie! Eddie! Eddie!" Across the gym, the crowd started chanting his. We stood in the circle and each looked up at our own fans. Our eyes then met and we gave each other a slight nod and and even smaller grin as we prepared to collide for the final seconds of the match.

The crowd was yelling so loudly that neither one of us heard the whistle that the referee blew, not two feet in front of us, to restart the match. He had to get right into our faces and yell "GO!!" With an indescribable burst of adrenaline, I shot out of his grip like a cannonball to tie the match at three as time expired.

I was taken down half-way through the overtime period to lose 5-3. Geiger surprisingly pinned his guy to win the match for the team and become the hero as I got lost in the shuffle. It didn't matter, my match had the most crowd involvement of the night—the kind that doesn't happen but once or twice throughout the entire season for the entire team combined. I was so high from that match that I couldn't stop shaking, even after showering and getting on the bus to go home.

I did finally get my moment in the sun and the chance to win a match for my team during a home match against Ferndale. The meet itself started out with us at a six point deficit thanks to one of our freshman failing to make weight. Jacob Evans decided to wait until the last minutes to cut his weight, instead of monitoring it all week. After he stepped off the scale, he just shrugged it off like it was no bid deal. No big deal, my ass—that was an unpardonable sin in the sport of wrestling. You have a responsibility to your team to be in shape and underweight. There is no excuse for not being able to do either one. As he sauntered back towards the lockers, I jumped out of line, grabbed him by the throat, and held him against the locker. I didn't care that we were both completely naked, he needed to know that this was unacceptable.

"Listen, you puny little fuck," I started, not an inch away from his eyes. "If you ever do this to the team again, I am going to see to it that you never wrestle again because I am going to put you in the hospital. I wish that I had as much talent as you but I don't, I have heart instead. But your chest might as well be made of toilet paper because there's nothin' in there but shit!"

His dad was right there watching as I poked at his little chest. He never said a word.

Previously, as per my request, Mom hadn't come to any of my matches with her boyfriend—at least as far as I knew. When I talked to her after the matches the next day, she said that she had been there. I didn't see her, though, nor was I looking for her. By a simple twist of fate, I spotted her in the gym that night during the Ferndale match. Her boyfriend was right by her side.

I never once even tried to picture in my mind what he looked like. It didn't matter to me if he looked like Brad Pitt or Red Fox, he was still a piece of shit that I wanted to slowly tear apart. *I can't believe that she brought him here after I respectfully asked her not to. How hard was it to do what I asked so I could concentrate on my stuff that had nothing to do with her.* That's all I could think about until it was my turn to wrestle.

By that time, we had a one point lead with only my match and the heavyweight match left. I took off my shirt, put on my headgear, and walked out to the center of the mat. I just stood there and stared at my freckle-faced, red-headed opponent as he crouched down into his stance to start the match.

"Get ready," the referee said.

I got into my stance and shook his hand, giving him a little grin the whole time. When the whistle blew, I tied up with him just like I did to start every match. Then I did something that I never did. I grabbed his headgear, spun him around to the other side of the ring, and shoved him into my teammates who were sitting in chairs the chairs along the edge of the mat. When the whistle blew to stop the match in order for us to go back to the center, I shoved him again.

"Knock that shit off or I'm gonna disqualify you," the referee warned.

Jay smiled and said, "Finish him before you kill him."

We went back to the center mat and when the whistle blew for the restart, I tied up with him again. This time I pulled his head straight into mine, splitting his head open slightly. Headbutting is illegal but just like any other illegal blow, if you do it right then you won't get called for it. With him reeling, I quickly took him to his back. For added good measure, as the referee was checking his shoulders, I stuck my index finger inside of his mouth and fish-hooked his cheek. Just for fun, I also stuck my pinky finger into his right eye socket.

The time of the fall—42 seconds.

When I walked over to shake his coaches hand, he asked, "What the hell is wrong with you?"

I just smiled at him and turned to walk back to my team to a standing ovation from the home crowd. I had not only solidified a win for my team, but I had just shown what I was capable of doing if I wanted to. If the state finals were that night, I could have taken on anybody and won, even if it meant walking through hell barefoot to fight the devil himself.

It had been four years since I had a good run of success on the mat and finally I was getting somewhere. It wouldn't last, however, as both my career and my body took a turn for the worse in Chehalis, a town just south of the state capitol of Olympia. With a tournament scheduled to start on Saturday, we left Friday night and spent the night at a Howard Johnson near the school. The next morning, we went to the gym for weigh-ins, pairings, and eventually the tournament itself. Dad said that he would be down there by ten. By eleven, just before my first round match, he still wasn't there.

I actually counted on Dad a lot for tournaments. Throughout each tournament, there are between six and eight matches happening at once. With only two coaches, it wasn't uncommon for them to both be in other guys' corners while I was up. With the rules stating that I had to have a corner man, Dad often times would fill in as a coach during my matches.

Sure enough, both coaches were busy when it was my turn. Dale Wicker, my old coach from our 1994 perfect season in football whose son, Jonny, was now a freshman on our team, sat down in my corner.

"Just go out there and kick his damn ass," Dale said before the match.

"You got it."

After we locked up following the whistle, my opponent tried to put me in the old eighth grade head and arm. I wasn't going to let him take me over so I just held a rear waistlock on him, hoping he would give up and try something else. Instead, he jerked his whole body to the mat. Still locked onto my defense hold, I went with him—landing on the top of my head with my feet straight up in the air like I was a pencil.

"Fuck, I can't move!" I yelled as I laid there on my back.

The referee stopped the match immediately and crouched over the top of me, holding my head.

"Don't move," he said.

I couldn't anyway at that moment, even if I wanted to. It may have lasted six seconds in all (it felt more like six years) before I was able to feel or move anything. At first, my whole body was tingling. Then it started burning. It got hotter and hotter and seemingly thousands of needles were being poked into me from head to toe.

"Can you feel anything?" the referee asked. "Wiggle your toes and move your fingers."

I was able to do it, only slowly.

"We've called an ambulance so just hold tight."

Where was I going to go, stupid?

It didn't take long for the ambulance to arrive. Three guys held me still and rolled me to one side in order to slide the backboard under me. They then taped me to it, making sure that I couldn't move. They then loaded me on a stretcher and started wheeling me across all of the mats, as all of the matches had stopped. The crowd applauded respectfully as I gave them the thumbs up, letting them know that I was okay.

I don't have any idea how far it was to the hospital but at the speed we traveled, it didn't take long to get there. Jack Herd, the assistant coach, went with me. Dad still was nowhere to be found as they wheeled me in for X-rays and CAT scans.

I was still immobilized as I laid in the dark room, waiting for the results. I was starting to get itchy from the sweat and the ever-so-slight friction of the backboard. There wasn't anything that I could do about it. To take my mind off of it, I began to gently flex each muscle from my feet to my head to make sure that I could feel everything.

Thankfully, the tests came back negative. I ended up with a little nerve damage, in which I began twitching when my body relaxed. I also lost a lot of mobility in my neck. Both of them I still deal with to this day. I was placed in a neck collar and released.

As Jack and I headed for his car, Dad came walking from the edge of the parking lot towards us. I told Jack to go ahead and go back to the gym and that I was going to just go home with Dad.

"Are you alright?" Dad asked.

"Yeah, but where have you been?"

"Well . . . ."

Another fucking pause. *How hard is it to just say something and get it over with?*

". . . . I got in a wreck."

"What?!"

Sure enough, the whole front of the Jimmy looked like he had tried to wrap it around a telephone pole. Thinking that it happened while he was on his way to Chehalis, I asked him how it happened.

"It wasn't on the way here," he said as we got into the car where Jen had been waiting. "It was last night."

After the separation, Dad had taken up drinking at bars and driving home drunk like an idiot. I had asked him to stop and be more careful. He either told me that "he would" or that "it was none of my business," depending on the day. If there was ever a reason to quit, he had it right there in front of his face—a wrecked car and an injured son. Sounds like no-brainer to me. Dad just couldn't grasp it.

I had to miss a couple of weeks of action right around the big "Y2K" deal, where everyone thought that the world was going to end on January 1, 2000. It was perfect timing because with the holidays, I only ended up missing one match. Had it happened a week or two earlier, I might have missed five or six. As painful as it was, I'm actually in a way glad that it happened because it opened up a new window of opportunity for me when my wrestling career was over.

For some reason, the guy who did the announcing for the matches didn't show up without any notice. As the junior varsity matches began, the referee had to call them out himself on the microphone. Without asking anyone, I just sat down behind the table and started doing it myself. I went through the whole JV lineup before the athletic director came up to me and asked who gave me permission to do the announcing.

"Nobody," I said. "The announcer didn't show up, so I figured that I would do it."

"Oh. Well, good job—keep going."

I then went on to announce the entire varsity match.

Since then, I have called every single match and every single tournament, including postseason action, that has taken place at that school over the last decade. I even get paid a few hundred dollars a year to work a handful of dates. What could be better? I have the best seat in the house to watch wrestling, follow my alma matter, and get paid to do it! To cap it all off, I have been told numerous times by numerous people that I am the best announcer around. That's fine by me. If I couldn't be the best wrestler, I'm satisfied being the best wrestling announcer.

Following winter break, I was cleared to compete by the doctor. There wasn't a lot of time left before the postseason tournaments began. We had one duel match against Mount Vernon that I didn't have an opponent in my weight class to wrestle. Although my last home match of my career was technically a win, it was by forfeit. It was also senior night with the same parent deal as football. Again, I took a pass on having my parents come out on the mat with me. It was still a little too soon for that.

There was just one varsity tournament remaining in the south central Washington town of Prosser. We took a school bus over Snoqualmie Pass in a miserable snow storm. There was already snow on the ground in Sedro-Woolley when we left, so it was bound to increase at 3,000 feet. It took thirteen hours to make a standard four or five hour trip. Three different times, we got on and off the bus in the freezing cold to help the driver chain up.

As we almost always did when we traveled across the state for matches, we stayed overnight at houses of various other wrestlers. Naturally, the whole team couldn't stay at the same house so we usually split up into groups of two or four. The host families were always well prepared, as we would have as much food and drinks as we wanted and beds to sleep in.

I may have gotten fourth or fifth in the tournament, which was just fine with me because I was mainly focused on building up my stamina again. The two weeks off really had a negative effect on my conditioning. I was now grasping for breath in the third round instead of the normal elevated breathing. If that weren't bad enough, I was also coming down with a cold.

That tournament ended the varsity schedule for the regular season. There was, however, one junior varsity tournament scheduled in Darrington the following Saturday. In order to get a few more matches under my belt before the league tournament, I begged Jay to take me along.

"You don't need it. You're seeded third for the league tournament already and even if you win, you won't gain any ground."

"I don't care. I just want to get a few more matches in because I want to be in top shape."

He agreed and took me along in another shitty snowstorm to Darrington. I got into the tournament as an unattached wrestler, meaning that I wasn't scoring points for any team. While I still could advance as far as anyone else in the tournament bracket, the points I scored didn't count.

I tore through my first two matches, pinning both of my opponents early in the second round. My semi-final match was then scheduled to be against Jordan Janicki, my own teammate. When Jay saw this, he told me to forfeit the match so that Jordan would get the points for our team. Although I didn't like it because I wanted to win the damn thing and I could beat Jordan at any time, I knew the business side of wrestling well enough to know that it was the right thing to do. It was okay anyway, I was just there to get matches.

Following the "loss," I went into the consolation bracket. After yet another pin, I was set up for a third place bout against a guy that I had already beaten earlier in the day. Oddly enough, I had actually pinned the same dude a year earlier to win the Stanwood Wrestle-Rama. I was a lock for third. After this match I was going to be headed for the postseason, ready to start my journey to Tacoma.

Midway through the second round, I was up 15-3. All I needed was just three more points and I would be awarded the match by technical fall. I was back in wrestling shape by then, but the goddamn cold made it hard to breathe. Knowing that if I put him on his back and got any back points at all the match would be over, I went for a quick head and arm. Instead of hooking him, I tripped and fell onto my stomach. He fell on top of me and got two points, making it 15-5.

With his weight on my back pushing on my inflamed bronchial tubes, I opened my mouth to gasp for a breath. His arm quickly came across my chin with a stiff crossface. It wasn't anywhere near as hard as the ones that I threw but after costing myself two points, I was pissed. His forearm went into my gaping mouth and he began to pull back on my head. Out of a little anger combined with the fact that I couldn't breathe, I stiffened my jaw a little bit.

"AAAGGHH! He bit me!" the guy yelled as he got up and jumped up and down.

"What?!" I yelled as the referee blew the whistle to stop the match.

The ref looked at his arm that had intentions on it from my teeth. I don't classify them as bite marks because they were very faint and there wasn't any blood. If I would have bitten him, I would have had a hunk of meat in my mouth and been chewing on it.

"Flagrant misconduct—you're disqualified," the ref stated.

"Whatever, asshole."

I went back up into the stands and told Jay what had happened.

"Flagrant misconduct? You get one if those and you have to miss the next outing."

"But that's fuckin' league!"

"Let's go find the kid and talk to the ref."

We tracked the kid down and he was willing to admit that I didn't intentionally bite him, as long as the match counted. Ten minutes had passed since the incident and there wasn't even the slightest mark on his arm. The three of us went up to the referee and showed him.

"My decision is final. You're done."

I looked at Jay for some help.

"Let's go sit down. I'll try to talk to the athletic commission and explain this."

I was pissed at myself for even getting into the situation. As I took my tights off and showered up, I started calming down. I figured that Jay would fix the problem. *Who would keep a senior wrestler out of the postseason for something that clearly wasn't what it was ruled to be?* The Washington Interscholastic Athletic Association, that's who. They upheld the referee's decision, crushing my dreams of reaching the Tacoma Dome.

Both my wrestling career and athletic career in general ended that snowy day in Darrington. Had I known it would have ended that way, I would have bitten his whole arm off and used it on him like a baseball bat. I would have caused such a scene that I would had to have been arrested. At least then, the punishment would have fit the crime.

I sat in anguish as the kid that I pinned in 42 seconds, in front of Mom and her lousy boyfriend, marched through league and regionals and onto the state tournament. He didn't place, but he was there. I was too—only in the stands like everyone else who didn't make the cut. Not too many days go by that I don't dream about what might have been. I would give almost anything to wrestle another match and right the ship. Even though the last match of my career would have most likely been a loss, it would have been to better man on a bigger stage.

It wasn't much of a consolation prize, but both Troy Hanson and I received the only four year letters given out at the end of the season banquet. Only the two of us started at the bottom and made it through all of the beatings in the first couple of years to have a nice little run at the end. In recognition of our accomplishments at a time when you still had to earn everything that you got in wrestling, the parents and fellow wrestlers at the ceremony gave us a standing ovation.

October 15,2010. Today marks the two year anniversary since I began this project. Over the past year I have almost doubled my output compared to what I did over the course of the first year. I have much more to write about but with it being so much more recently transpired events, I can see this wrapping up within the next year. Hopefully by this time next year, I will be putting the finishing touches on the handwritten portion of this book. We'll see . . . .

CHAPTER 37
Crossroads

S HORTLY BEFORE THE end of wrestling season, the second semester began at school. With me having all but one elective credit and only needed to finish the current world problems class in order to graduate, I only had to go to school each day until lunch time. By eleven, I was free to leave school. I could be at McDonald's by noon and work until nine. By this time I was getting nearly fifty hours a week in at eight dollars an hour. (My pay had increased since I turned eighteen.) Basically I was only going to school to work with wood, lift weights, and spend sixty minutes in a classroom learning about what was going on currently in the world.

Because we didn't have the same weightlifting class, I had stay after lunch in order to take on Jeremy Ellis, who is actually my second cousin, for the senior class bench press title. The whole class gathered around us as we started with around 200 and increased our way up at twenty pound intervals. By the time we each reached the 300 pound mark, we were lifting on pure adrenaline. In the end, he put up 315 while I only did 310. But he weighed 235, while I was only 195. Still, having the best percentage in the school was just the consolation prize. There are stronger people in the world who can press way more than that amount of weight but in 2000 at Sedro-Woolley High, we were the top two in the entire school.

It only took me the first couple of months of school to put the finishing touches on my gun cabinet that I had been working on for two calendar years. Again, it wasn't like I had worked on it for six hundred days straight—I had one semester per year and less than an hour a day to work on it. With it all being out of solid wood, it takes a little longer than those who chose to take the easy route of building with plywood. For me, it was handmade or nothing. The only things that weren't handmade on it were the glass doors, the hardware, and the quarter-inch plywood on the back. I even hand-cut my own crown molding to put on the very top. Every square inch of it was as smooth as silk.

When spring rolled around, I entered it in a woodworking show held at the high school called WoodFest. There, four other local schools would bring in their best work for a competition. My cabinet and I graced the cover of the local paper, the Courier-Times, leading up to the event. To help promote it further, I went to Mount Vernon to talk about it on an AM radio show on station KBRC.

I was shooting for the "Best of Show" award, but all I got was second place in the category of joinery. The best of show was given to a gun cabinet made out of oak-faced plywood. All that guy had to do was cut each piece to length and stain it. They look great, but you can find them in any furniture store. If mine were to be in a furniture store, they would ask twice the price for it. To the naked eye they look the same, but if you lift the two you will find the difference. Had actual woodworkers made the votes instead of the mayor and other community members, the outcome would have been much different. Instead it was the same as a middle-aged woman legitimately picking the winner in a male bodybuilding contest—it doesn't happen.

Handcrafted with care

SWHS students create masterpieces of wood for WoodFest

By Sean Lamphere

In today's modern world where everything seems to be made from a mold and the word handcrafted has been replaced by machine-made, a small group of Sedro-Woolley High School students are bucking the trend.

Using their skills gleaned from teacher Mike Stewart's woodworking class, these students have invested their time and money to create masterpieces from the bare essentials of wood, nails, glue and stain. Some of these projects are small, such as senior Eric Bryant's set of covered boxes, while others are large, such as junior Brooke Armstrong's four-post bed.

But all of these projects have one thing in common — they'll all be displayed at the High School Woodworking Competition held from 9 a.m. to 7 p.m. on April 8 and 9 in the SWHS gymnasium, along side student projects from Selah, Lakewood and Stanwood High Schools.

These student-built projects will be judged in three categories, according to Stewart, one of the competition's organizers. Local craftsmen and woodworking class instructors will judge the student's work on categories of overall craftsmanship, joint quality and surface preparation and finish.

"WoodFest gives the students an opportunity to show what they're good at," Stewart said. The contest is part of Woodfest, a Sedro-Woolley festival running April 8 and 9.

These students have a variety of reasons behind their projects that goes beyond just doing it for a grade or the contest. "It's the satisfaction of knowing you have built something of quality," senior Eddie Thramer said. "I wanted my project to be done right. It's not for a grade but for my own personal satisfaction."

Thramer is in the final touches of building a gun cabinet completely out of solid oak. He started it two years ago after displaying a beginners' project during the last

Photo by Sean Lamphere.

Eddie Thramer shows off the solid oak gun cabinet he'll be displaying at the WoodFest High School Woodworking Competition on April 8 and 9.

WoodFest contest two years ago. "He's spent more time on his project then most students have," Stewart said. "He's also spent more time sanding and working on the finish than most."

Armstrong has created a four-poster bed from poplar and a toy box to go with it. She started the project in September at the start of the school year. She chose to craft a bed because, "I thought it would be a cool project to build." But Armstrong doesn't have strong ties to the bed so she's decided to put it up for sale at the competition. Proposed asking price: $800, "so she can buy a car," Stewart said.

Fellow junior J.J. Lopez also has dreams of selling the 5-foot-tall armoire he constructed out of pine. He's taking the class because he has "always liked working with wood and building stuff," Lopez said. He has taken a woodworking class since middle school and hopes that he'll have the skills needed for a job after high school. "After spending so much time on this project, I'll remember how to build it for the rest of my life," Lopez said.

These students aren't just thrown the wood and told to do with as they will. They actually have to purchase the materials from their own money. Stewart said that the school purchases the wood from a wholesaler and then sells the students the wood

Continued on page A-8

Me and my gun cabinet on the front page of the Courier-Times.
Courtesy of the Courier-Times, a Skagit Publishing Company. Used with permission.

259

The last class of my shortened day was CWP. While it focused on issues going on in the United States as well as other nations around the world, it mainly was for us to open our minds and form our own opinions based on the actions of our country. There were no tests, no homework, and no papers to write. The idea was solely to get students to express their beliefs inside of them that they may not have known even existed.

Less than six months away from that point in time was the 2000 Presidential Election. Bill Clinton had held office for nearly eight years by then and was leaving the White House when his term was up. Vice-President Al Gore was the democratic favorite to try and succeed Clinton. Opposing him would be George W. Bush, son of George H.W. Bush, whom Clinton defeated in the 1992 campaign. With all of us in the class either at or close to the eighteen years of age mark, we would for the first time in our lives be able to vote on political races and laws that would affect our city, state, and country.

In order to find out what political party allegiance each of us had, the teacher, Mr. Heuterman, gave us a variety of topics that we had to respond to with our own personal opinions of each matter. We focused on everything from education to government reform, consumption tax versus income tax, budget surplus, and the military. But what really decided what political party I was for was the social issues. I'm not going to hit on every one, but rather just a few of the big ones.

I'll start first with the death penalty. Washington State does have one. Inmates sentenced to death have a choice between lethal injection or hanging. (Utah still has the firing squad as an option.) It is rarely used, as it takes several decades of review to get it to go through. I feel that if someone commits a murder, they should be sentenced to death—plain and simple. Too many times they are sentenced to life in prison. But since when does "life" really mean LIFE? Most always there are opportunities for parole and here's a surprise—most of them re-offend.

Another popular one is gun control. I myself have several handguns, pistols, shotguns, and rifles. I was raised around them. I think that it is every American's right to bear arms. The only thing is, people that do should not have record of a crime that involved a firearm. While I don't think certified training is necessary, I do believe that some sort of training in handling and firing is. I have no problem letting my kids shoot guns. They, even at a young age, know the damage that they can do and thus are extremely careful and safe. As for requiring all gun owners to have them registered with the government, the last political leader to do that was Adolf Hitler—need I say more?

Next, we have alcohol and drugs. I have no problem with people responsibly consuming alcohol. I do have a problem with those that do and get behind the wheel to drive. I'm not going to lie, I've done it myself a time or two in the past. I told you about the little buzz that I had on our first Sturgis trip and I can still safely say that that was the only time that I have done it on a bike. I've driven home on a bit more of a buzz twice in a car, but it was only a few miles. That's no excuse for doing so, though. Thankfully nothing bad happened. It's hard sometimes to distinguish between "could" and "should." If you even question it, you shouldn't try it—that's how I decide if I drive or not. Those that do and get caught, I believe should have their driving privileges revoked. To me, that's much better than killing an innocent person or yourself. With Dad doing it frequently at the time, it really made it easy for me to form that opinion because that is exactly what I was hoping would happen to him before he in fact got someone else or himself killed.

As for drugs, I cannot, and will not, ever condone the use of illegal drugs. I am proud as hell to say that I have never once tried them, let alone even a regular cigarette, and I assure you that I never will. I'm above that. I'm better than that. But here's where it gets interesting. There is always talk of legalizing marijuana for more than just medical use. I'm actually all for it. (I would still never do it if it was legal by the way.) It is always going to be out there no matter what. Why not make it legal, tax the living shit out of it, and make some money to offset some of these debts in our country?

I'll finish with probably the most controversial topic—abortion. While I will never accept or participate in one, my reasons for being against it have drastically changed since CWP. Originally, I was against it with the frame of mind being, "you do the crime, you do the time." You had sex, got someone or yourself pregnant, now here's your baby—deal with it. You want to be an adult? Good luck. Well, that's not at all fair to the innocent child. A baby shouldn't have to grow up with parents who don't know what to do with them. If there is an unplanned or unwanted pregnancy, the resulting child should immediately be taken from the delivery room and put up for adoption. Both "parents" should unselfishly understand that it would be in the child's best interest.

After putting on paper what was already in my head and heart, I came to the conclusion that I was a republican. That didn't mean that I had to vote for anyone strictly within the party, it just meant that I had conservative views. As it turned out, I didn't even vote in that year's election once November rolled around. Once I found out about the electoral system, I refused.

The presidential position is determined by who garners the most accumulative points that are won for each state. That means that one candidate could win forty or more of certain states and still lose. To say that every vote counts is ridiculous. Let's say that every single registered voter in Washington State votes for Joe Blow, he will then receive eleven points. Then down in California, only one person in the entire state decided to vote. His opponent, Ben Dover, would get fifty-five points and lead 55-11, despite being outvoted 2,463,098 to1. I wasn't going to take part in any of that bogus shit. I changed my mind in 2004 because I figured that I didn't have the right to complain or cheer for decisions made by our national leader if I didn't cast a ballot.

I was pulling in around seven hundred dollars every two weeks on my paychecks by this time. It was easy to do because I made myself available for work everyday after twelve. With that being lunch hour, it was a much needed slot to fill. It was also the time when the opening shift would be getting ready to go home. The only set day that I had off was Monday. By now, I bet you can guess why.

Jen had just recently got her license and was given Grandma Murrow's Ford Tempo after she decided that she was too old to drive. After a year of driving Jen to school in my own pickup for free, not to mention the other year that I drove her in Dad's Jimmy, we worked out a deal that she would drive me to school on Mondays. With me getting out early, I would drive her car home while she took the bus.

On the very first Monday that we were going to try this and less than a week after she got her license to begin with, she pulled out in front of someone and totaled her car. The worst part was, I took all of the impact from the T-bone collision. I didn't care about the glass shattering all over me (some of which got lodged in my ear), it was the jarring of my still injured neck that hurt. It would never completely heal if I kept riding with my sister!

With both Dad and Jan wrecking their cars recently and the old adage of things happening in groups of threes, I had to follow suit. I had a permanent passenger on my way home from work almost every night, thanks to Archy losing his license until he was twenty-one for underage drinking. Not that it was a bad thing that he rode with me, because we had a good time laughing at the misfortunes of others and listening to music on the CD player in my truck. He got a kick out of the "son of a bitch" line in "The Devil Went Down To Georgia" by Charlie Daniels. He would laugh so hard that his Copenhagen would drip out of his mouth and stain his shirt.

Archy, as well as almost every guy in high school, chewed tobacco. Most likely, if you didn't chew then you at least smoked. Not me of course, but once people began turning eighteen, it was if they had to do it now because it was legal for them to do so. I did snort a pinch of that crap up my nose in front of a bunch of people at work, just like it was originally intended for. The only problem was that I used long cut instead of regular, finely-ground snuff. Talk about burn! Archy did it too and his nose started bleeding.

Nose bleeds were nothing new to him anyway. With a nose that made Pinocchio jealous, Archy always had it sticking out there waiting for something to happen to it. Every single match that he ever wrestled in, he bled in. I've even seen him disqualified for bleeding the full five minutes of allotted blood time. Coaches would shove cotton ball after cotton ball up his nose, tape his nostrils shut, but they still couldn't stop his river.

One night, we were driving home from work, two weeks removed from wrestling season, and Archy was in the passenger seat picking his nose.

"Don't pick your nose in my truck, man," I scolded. "I don't want any of that shit on my floor."

"Just a second," he said, still digging in his right nostril.

Seconds later, he pulled out a bloody ball that nearly measured up to the size of a grape.

"What the hell is that?" I asked, not believing my eyes.

"Cotton."

"Cotton?! From wrestling?!"

"Yeah. I was wondering why I couldn't breathe very well lately," he said, as he dropped it into his paper cup that he used for a spittoon.

I didn't know, or care, who bought him his Copenhagen. He never asked me to buy him any until one night after we had just closed down at work. I didn't want to stop at the 7-Eleven because I was exhausted and wanted to just get home. Reluctantly I gave in, knowing that it was going to come back and bite me. I remember thinking, *Now I'll probably get in a wreck or something.* I should have also bought lottery tickets while I was in there because I'll be damned if I didn't call the future again.

It was pretty stormy on the way home. In the dark, eight mile stretch between Sedro-Woolley and Lyman, I was cruising along at just under sixty in the fifty-five zone. There was a car a hundred feet or so in front of me but with the rain so heavy, I could hardly see its taillights. Before I even had a chance to react and hit my brakes, I hit something standing in the middle of the road—hard.

"What was that?" Archy said, as he accidentally dumped his spittoon on the floor.

"I don't know—I think that I just hit a deer."

I pulled over and, sure enough, I had blood and hair everywhere. My front end was destroyed, I had a hole in my radiator, and I was just certain that I had totaled my truck for contributing to the delinquency of a minor. Thankfully it wasn't and it was repaired as good as new. Never again would I buy underage people anything that they couldn't buy themselves.

During the week that it was in the shop, I drove Archy's pickup. I thought that was fair considering all of the miles that I had driven as his chauffeur. It made sense because I took him to school anyway and we always got off work at the same time. The only problem was me leaving school early. It didn't bother him, he just skipped the last two classes of his day and rode along with me.

When I got my pickup back, I changed my driving habits a little bit. I was never one to drastically exceed the speed limit, take turns at higher speeds, or accelerate from a stop as fast as the rig would let me. I did, however, have a bad habit of following too closely to the cars in front of me. While the deer wreck probably couldn't have been avoided, I did adjust my following distance and began driving slower in extreme weather conditions. I was proud of my truck and I didn't want to get it destroyed for something that could be avoided

After over six months of not seeing Mom in person other than from afar at games or matches, I agreed to come up to the apartment in Bellingham on one of my days off. I told her on the phone before I finally gave in that I was willing to forgive—just not forget.

"Mom, I love you. But I will always hate you for what you did."

She didn't like hearing that, but I meant every word. Whatever did or didn't happen between her and Dad was their business that unfortunately trickled down to me and Jen. I just felt that it could have been handled differently and she sure as hell didn't have to move out on my birthday.

I didn't know that her boyfriend was going to be there until I walked through the front door and saw him sitting on the couch watching TV. I know for a fact that she set this up on purpose because she knew that I wouldn't have come over had I known that he was going to be there. Maybe I should have asked.

"Hi, Eddie. I'm Mike Grahn," he said, shaking my hand. "You've just made your mom's day."

I knew that. I knew that it meant a lot to her. She didn't expect me to accept it right then, but just to begin to try. So that's what I did. I was polite, courteous, and surprisingly calm. My anger and terrible thoughts of violence had subsided. While it was certainly uncomfortable, it wasn't too bad and I got through it.

At some point during the hour that I was there, Mike asked me if I was interested in getting a job at the milk company in Mount Vernon that he worked at. I told him that I was, but I had to wait until school was out before I could start. He said to call him a week before graduation to set it up.

After I left, I gave his job offer a lot of thought. I knew that they had trucks to drive there, just like I always wanted to do. While I knew that I couldn't start at that level, I knew that I could always work my way up. I would be much closer to living my dream if I took that job than I would be staying at McDonald's. I wasn't ready to quit McDonald's yet, though. After graduation in a few weeks, I could work both jobs. I could get two paychecks in stead of one!

For the first couple of times that I went to Mom's, I was always more than ready to go home. While I was getting better with it, I still had a hard time being in a house that Mom shared with a man who wasn't my father. What made it easier for me to accept was that I didn't have to live there and have to see it all the time—out of sight, out of mind. At least at home, there wasn't anyone living with Dad. He said that he wouldn't bring another woman into the house until Jen and I were both moved out. That sounded great to me, but it was too good to be true.

Ever since the deer hunting issue in Uncle Robbie's driveway four years earlier, Dad and I had been having a harder and harder of a time trying to get along. I think that part of it was me getting older and testing my limits while the other part was him trying to make sure that I knew that he was still my superior. He was always on my case way more than he was on Jen's and I didn't know why. Jen was the one out drinking with her friends at night. Jen was the one who had parties at home while Dad was gone. Never once did I do any of those things but the minute that I forgot to take out the garbage, the world was over. I couldn't have gotten a worse reaction if I had shot someone. He even took offense to me watching wrestling on Mondays now.

"I pay the satellite bill, I'll watch what I want to watch," he said.

So I paid thirty dollars a month to keep the big dish hooked up to my room while the rest of the house was converted to Dish Network—anything to get him to lay off about the one night a week that I wanted to watch TV.

To be fair, though, I did bring a bit of his anger on myself. I tested my limits by standing up to him when I felt that something wasn't right. I probably even overstepped my boundaries a few times by telling HIM what HE should do. Whether what he was doing was right or wrong, it was none of my business if it didn't affect me. The problem was, his constant drinking affected me so it was my business to say my feelings about it. I just should have done it in a way other than trying to be his parent.

Just as he got on me for petty things, I got on him for probably even pettier things—like his chewing of food. It sounds ridiculous, but my biggest pet peeve is listening to people crunch and chew their food. I just can't stand it, and Dad is the worst. He makes a cow chewing its cud look prim and proper. He uses his tongue as a suction cup on the roof of his mouth with each chewing motion. Who else does that? I think he purposely makes as much noise as possible because he knows that it bothers me. Nobody could be that obnoxious.

With that being said, I think part of the reason that he began bringing a new woman around the house was to show me that he was in charge and not me. Unquestionably, showing who is in charge is the right thing to do from his standpoint. From mine, it made him out to be a liar. He willingly promised something that was entirely his idea and he was now going back on it. It made me think that he only said that to show Jen and I that he was better than Mom and that he put us first, unlike Mom had. He would also go out of his way to say that he would spend the night at her place for more than just a place to sleep. Like I fuckin' needed to hear that! I already figured that it was happening anyway, I didn't want to be told about it. Based strictly on this, it didn't matter if Farrah Fawcett walked through the door, I was already against her. The problem was, she didn't deserve it.

Debbie Ammons, who was the aunt of the kid, Matthew, that killed himself and I wouldn't go to his funeral, had the heaviest load to bear out of everyone. Mom had cheated on Dad. Mike knew that Mom was married the whole time they were together. Dad was turning into an alcoholic. Debbie had done nothing, yet she was the Antichrist. I am ashamed of the way that I treated her at times.

We were having dinner one night after she moved in and Dad for some reason brought up his life insurance. He said that if something happened to him, everything was going to be in my name and I was to split up what was left of the money after the house was paid for. While he was out of the room, I looked Debbie square in the eye and said, "You ain't gettin' nothin'."

She started bawling. It wasn't about the money, it was about me being such a piece of shit for saying such a rotten thing. It took her several days to work up enough courage to tell me that she wasn't in it for the money. (It wasn't like Dad was loaded anyway. Remember, he was keeping the house on a single income and there wasn't a lot to go around.) When she did, I felt just about an inch tall. I still didn't give her the satisfaction of getting an apology from me, though. Debbie, I am truly sorry for that. I don't think that I have ever said something so hurtful to someone who didn't deserve it as what I said to you. I'm sorry.

I'm sure that there were other things that might have made her think that I didn't like her. I don't remember any off hand, but there is no way that they compare to what I said to her that night at dinner. She should have slapped me across the face as hard as she could. I'm glad that she didn't because I wasn't yet man enough to take something like that. If it were to happen today, I would take it for what it is—a reminder that she deserves respect. If it happened in the year 2000, I would have hit her back and caused a huge problem that would likely be beyond repair. Nobody needed that, times were tough enough already.

It had been two years since I had gone on my first real date. I did take a girl named Adrienne Howard to her junior prom and my senior ball within a six month span of each other, but she was never my girlfriend. We went to dinner each time and stumbled through a handful of dances (mainly because I was blessed with two left feet). After the senior ball, we went to a guy's house (who will remain nameless), whose step-mom was a teacher in the district. When she exchanged beer for car keys, we checked out. I wasn't going to get involved in that and I wasn't going to let Adrienne either.

That is pretty much how most weekends were spent for other people my age—drinking. I wasn't into that scene and I stayed away from girls that were. I didn't want to start a serious relationship with a girl that nailed a different guy each week following a party with loads of alcohol on the menu. I didn't need someone who was only using me to get back at someone else for what happened the week before. (For you idiots that got a piece of the hot chick in school, that means you.) Count me out.

Not every girl was that way, thank God. There were just as many girls by contrast that didn't partake in such activities. The only problem with them was that they hardly ever spoke. Either they were too shy or just plain uninterested, but it's hard to pursue someone who just sits there and tries to blend in with the wall. So I was pretty much convinced that I wasn't going to have a girlfriend in the near future. I didn't like what was on the menu at Sedro-Woolley High School, so I went hungry.

Going without a girlfriend in school also meant going without sex. Most of the guys had gotten some at least once. Those of us who hadn't were thought of as uncool and were teased for it. I didn't care, I had nothing to hide. I was going to save it for a girl who had also been waiting for just the right time. I didn't like the thought of sticking my penis into the same spot as another guy had done before me. If I had to wait a while, then so be it.

Unfortunately, my mind and body weren't on the same page. As does a female who starts her period, once a male reaches a certain age, his internal clock lets him know that he is now able to reproduce. Much like a female who menstruates, we too must discharge the unused built-up product—only at a more frequent rate.

I was eleven the first time that it happened to me. I thought that I had pissed the bed in the middle of the night when I woke up with wet shorts one morning. When I took them off to put on new ones, I found out that the oily substance wasn't urine. While I was relieved that I didn't have to start wearing diapers again, I was embarrassed that I had ejaculated in my sleep. I knew that it was natural and unavoidable, but I still didn't want anyone to know about it. Every few weeks when it happened, I would rinse out my shorts and run them through the dryer for a few minutes. (I forgot about the sheets—oops.)

As for the manual way, you know, the old "five knuckle shuffle," I went almost into my twenties before I did that. All of my nighttime messes could have been avoided if I would have tried it, but I couldn't. It wasn't because I didn't know how, but because it was stereotyped to be something that only queers did. I found out that it was okay to do, as well as healthy, when a doctor advised me to give it a try.

I thought that I had hit myself in the nuts at some point and didn't realize it at the time while I was at work one day. It kept hurting more and more so I was constantly reaching down while I was at work to adjust myself and to make sure that one of my guys hadn't gotten twisted. (Yes, I washed my hands again before I started making burgers—I think.) When I found out that wasn't it, I figured that something had to be wrong. As soon as my shift was over, I went the emergency room.

After feeling my balls for a few uncomfortable seconds, the doctor sat down in the chair and scratched his head.

"What is it?" I asked anxiously.

"Well," he said. "Perhaps you should watch an X-rated movie when you get home and see what happens."

I knew exactly what he meant. If I wasn't having any sex, then it was something that I had to do—unless I wanted to do extra laundry. Someday my time would come, (Yeah, I went there) but I still needed the right girl. Although it turned out that she wasn't, I thought that I had found her right about a month before graduation.

A couple of days a week, a curly-haired brunette named Holly Robbins worked a four or five hour afternoon shift at the restaurant. Instead of working back in the grill like me, she exclusively worked the front counter. Our only interaction while on the clock was when there was a discrepancy on an order. During breaks, however, we would talk in the break room.

One night, she asked me for a ride home because she didn't have a car or a license and her dad had to work late. She only lived five minutes or so away and we got off at the same time, so I told her that I would be happy to. On the way home, we talked about how old each other was, what we liked to do, and other basic small talk. I found out that she was a junior, fourteen months younger than me, and went to Burlington-Edison High School.

"Can you take me home tomorrow too?" she asked as I dropped her off at her house.

"Sure."

"Oh, here's my phone number. Call me if you change your mind."

"Okay."

"You can also call me to talk about other stuff if you want."

"Alright."

She got out and shut my passenger door (way harder than I would have liked) and walked up to her house. Before she walked inside, she looked back and gave me a smile and a wave.

I called her the next day and we talked for a little while before I had to leave for work.

"Are you dating Adrienne?" she asked.

"No, I just took her to the senior prom because I wanted to go and asked her to go with me, just like she had asked me to go to her prom. We just went with each other as a favor to the other person."

"Oh, so you don't have a girlfriend?"

"No."

"Do you smoke or drink."

"No and no."

I didn't go into the few occasions that I would drink on motorcycle trips, but she was referring to the weekend party scene. For that, I didn't do.

"Do you want to meet my parents?"

"Uh—sure."

I never did formally ask her, nor was I formally asked, but we began a steady relationship right away. I wasn't opposed to it. She was against smoking and drinking and staying out all night, so I couldn't complain. In fact, I was ecstatic! I had a girlfriend! I just had to meet her parents now.

Sure enough, her parents didn't like me based on on what they heard from their daughter. I was a wrestler who bit somebody in a match—strike one. I was a few weeks away from graduating high school—strike two. I wore leather jackets and rode a motorcycle—strike three. I never had a chance. On the outside, I was every mother's nightmare. But they didn't know the whole story and I really don't think that they wanted to find out either.

The fact that I was nervous didn't help my cause. When Holly introduced me to her mother, Robin Robbins, I started snickering a little at her name.

"What's so funny?" she asked, rather irritated.

"I just never heard a name like that," I honestly replied.

Trying to keep my head above water, I quickly changed the subject to her house.

"Your house is real nice," I said.

"Thanks," she said, turning back to her TV show.

Boy, she was making it hard. Grabbing for straws, I commented about her decorations and how my mom did the same kind of stuff to her house. She just nodded her head, without saying a word or taking her eyes off of *Oprah*. I pried my foot out of my mouth and excused myself from the room.

"What's wrong?" Holly asked me once we got into the next room.

"I can't talk to somebody who doesn't talk back in return."

"Mom just doesn't like to miss *Oprah*."

I'm sure that there was more to it than that. I know that it isn't polite to laugh during introductions but had Holly warned me that her mom had a funny name, I could have held back my childish sense of humor.

"Let's go out in the garage and meet my dad."

"His name isn't Rob or something like that is it?" I joked.

"No, it's Randy," she answered, not getting my joke whatsoever.

Her dad was working on his pickup's engine when we walked out into the garage. On the radio, KISS was singing "Rock And Roll All Nite."

"Alright, KISS—I love these guys," I said as walked towards the front of his truck.

"Well, I hate them. Holly, change the station," he snarled.

I thought it best not to mention that I was going to their concert in a few weeks.

"So you ride motorcycles, huh Eddie?"

"Yes. I've been to Sturgis, the Grand Canyon, Death Valley—all over on it."

"One of my friends died on a motorcycle."

Of course I had nothing to respond with, but he was going to look at me until I said something.

"What's wrong with your truck?" I asked, trying desperately to just have a basic conversation.

"Nothing."

If I had a gun in my hand, I would have shot myself on the spot. There was no way that this was going to work out. But I wasn't a quitter, I was going to give my best effort to make something out of this situation. I wasn't going to let her talkative parents ruin our new relationship.

The next weekend, Holly and I went out to dinner and to see a movie. I don't really remember, but I think that we went out for Chinese food. As far as the movie, I couldn't tell you what it was. I did manage to stay awake, though. I even had her home by nine, thirty minutes before her curfew.

As we pulled into the driveway, I noticed her looking at every window at the front of the house.

"What's the matter?"

"Nothing." (I wonder where she got that from?)

She turned and sat sideways on the seat, staring at me.

"What?"

"Well?"

"Well, what?"

"You're supposed to kiss me before you drop me off."

Now it made sense as to why she was checking the windows. I had absolutely zero experience kissing girls, but I gave it my best shot.

"I'm not your grandma," she said, clearly unmoved by my performance.

"I just need more practice," I said with a wink.

She smiled and got out, slamming my door as usual. I was going to have to start opening and shutting the door for her if I wanted to keep it on its hinges.

For the next few weeks, we saw a movie and had dinner before 9:30 every Saturday. I knew that she could stay out until midnight if she was with her girlfriends, but I didn't let it bother me. I also didn't let it bother me that I paid for every single thing that we did. As far as I knew, that was how it was done.

As for the kissing, I got better. Honestly, I don't think that I was the problem. I had no plans on ramming my tongue down her throat on the first kiss, so I didn't really know what the big deal was. All of that would come in time but for now, it was just the basic package.

On Thursday, June 8, 2000, I woke up at my usual time of six, had a quick breakfast, and turned on a wrestling tape for an hour or so until it was time to go to school—for the very last time. That evening, I was set to don a royal blue cap and gown and march the aisle for graduation to the tune of "Pomp and Circumstance." Before the festivities officially began, the entire class had to be to school at regular time for rehearsal.

As I got into my pickup to head for school, I called Mike on my new cell phone and asked to talk to his dad, Gary, about the job working at the milk company. Gary got onto the phone and said that if I came in for a quick interview, I could start as soon as Monday. I was beyond excited, mainly at the perfect timing, when I hung up the phone and changed course to go to Mount Vernon. I never did make it to rehearsals, I wonder how they went?

I pulled up to a dumpy, broken-down old building, that looked a lot like The Alamo from the front, that sat just off of the bank of the Skagit River in south Mount Vernon. At least The Alamo had an excuse for its appearance—258 Texans held of 2400 Mexicans from February 23 to March 6, 1836 before their eventual demise in the most famous battle of the Texas Revolution. *What was the excuse for this, or did I even have the right place?* The Darigold trucks out in the truck yard alongside the building answered my question. I instantly started having second thoughts. *How could a company have a future in a shithole like this?*

I walked through the front door and asked a fat, grumpy-looking old lady with a giant mole on her eyelid that looked more like a potato, where I could find Gary. Instead of answering me verbally, the hag, who went by Myna, just pointed toward a small office that looked like a closet. I thanked her and knocked on the door.

"Not now, dammit. I'm on the phone!" hollered a grouchy voice from inside.

I took a step back and thought very seriously about getting in my truck and getting the hell out of there. Mike then came up from behind me wearing a heavy-insulated suit and led me into Gary's office—without knocking.

"Goddammit, Mike—I'm on the fuckin' phone!" yelled a man who resembled Mr. Clean.

"Eddie is here for his interview," Mike told his dad.

"Oh, okay," Gary replied as he hung up the phone.

Gary and I talked for less than five minutes. I liked him because he sort of reminded me of a coach. He told me that he was the majority owner of a company called Dairy Valley Distributing. He and his partner, Gordon Mills, each had two sons that worked for them. They had just four other employees, who were not relation, to round out the company. Each guy drove a truck and delivered milk to local convenience stores and schools from north of Seattle clear to the Canadian border. I was going to be hired as the truck loader for around nine dollars and hour.

Although I was more than happy to have a higher paying job, I wanted Gary to know that my only reason for starting here was for the opportunity to drive a tractor-trailer.

"I can't tell you when it will happen but if someone quits or we have the need to add routes, you will be the first in line—if you are a good employee. If you commit to us for three years, we will train you to drive truck, pay for you to get your license, and have you prepared to make the transition when the time comes."

I was in. I am big on word-of-mouth agreements and take them just as I would a contract.

"Do I have to be a certain age to drive on my own like I would have to be for other companies?"

"I don't give a shit about age—I just want good workers."

I was dancing in the street! Most companies set a minimum age of twenty-five before they would let a guy drive. I was going to start training to drive now! I ended the interview by asking him how secure a job in this business would be.

"If you're good," he said, "People are always going to need milk."

That was good enough for me. I told him that I would see him on Monday and took off to get back to the school. Already over an hour late, I figured that a couple of more minutes wouldn't hurt so I stopped at McDonald's to tell them the news. I wasn't going to quit entirely just in case something went sour. I instead changed my schedule to work just two nights a week for five hours at a time, unloading their delivering truck from Golden State Foods. No more burgers to cook, sandwiches to assemble, or working with handicapped grill employees.

At around ten o'clock, I pulled into Sedro-Woolley High School for the last time as a student. I turned the engine off and sat back in my seat to reflect a little bit. I thought about running after Mom on my first day of kindergarten, how much fun that I had in Mrs. Brooks and Mr. Prange's classes, and all of the football games and wrestling matches. After the sun set tonight, it would all be over.

150 kids graduated that night. Just five years earlier, our class was 300 strong. *Where did everybody go? Did I even care?* As I sat next to my good friends Joey and Greg for the duration of the ceremony, I knew that I was ready to put it all behind me and to move on to the next phase of my life. My childhood was over now. I had made the decision in ninth grade that I was going to decline the opportunity to further my education and instead pursue my dream of driving trucks. Just four days after receiving my diploma, it would be time to begin that journey.

PART III

BECOMMING AN ADULT

CHAPTER 38

Oil and Water

SHORTLY AFTER GRADUATION, Dad, Debbie, Jen, and myself went over the pass to George, Washington to see KISS at the Gorge Amphitheater, right on the banks of the Columbia River. Whether it was a graduation present or not, it was the only real family outing that the four of us ever went on as a unit. Rather than revel in the significance of that, I looked more at it as a carpool to see a concert.

Dubbed the Farewell Tour, KISS set out in 2000 to tour the world one last time after a thirty-five year run. They must have changed their minds since then because they still record and tour to this day. However, Paul Stanley and Gene Simmons are no longer joined by Peter Criss and Ace Frehley, as they were replaced in the early part of the new millennium. So essentially we did see one of the last performances of the original band.

Skid Row and Ted Nugent opened the show. After the sun set behind the river, KISS hit the stage with more fireworks than a Fourth of July celebration. Known more for their theatrical stage performances than their singles, they didn't disappoint. Stanley flew through the air on a zip line during "Love Gun." Simmons ascended from the stage screen and blew fire from his mouth during "God of Thunder," Criss played his drum kit upside down during "Black Diamond," and Frehley set his guitar on fire during "Firehouse."

The only low point of an otherwise great night was when Dad said that it was time to go after they performed "Beth" and left the stage. I knew that they weren't going anywhere until they played "Rock And Roll All Nite" but Dad insisted that it was over, so reluctantly I went along with it. Sure enough, they came back and scorched through a ten minute version of their classic rock anthem. By then we were already in the Jimmy, so we just rolled down the windows to listen to it.

As I said, it was our only real family outing that we went on. We still ate dinner at home as a family as often as everyone's schedules allowed. We celebrated holidays together also, so it wasn't like we were always doing our own things separately.

One thing that I did not get into (that Dad always bitches about) was participating in family functions with Debbie's entire family. They both insist that I don't like her family and thus will not have anything to do with them. Not true. While they may not be people that I would want to hang out with, I don't dislike them for any reason. Just because I don't want to be involved in family functions doesn't mean that I am avoiding them. I have actually volunteered to help Debbie's mom move furniture and even helped one of her brothers get his log truck out of a ditch. I wouldn't waste my time on that shit if I disliked somebody.

The real reason that I don't participate in their family functions is the fact that I am not part of their family and they aren't part of mine, just like Mike's family isn't my family. I don't do dinners and functions with them either. My relationship with his family is strictly on a business level, which is the way that I want it. How would it look if I went to a bosses house for a family dinner?

Dad also complains that me not being involved takes away from his time that he gets to spend with me. That may be true, but how much time could he possibly spend with me when there is a houseful of guests? You can't just ignore other people and devote most of your time to one person because people will get offended. Besides that, Dad acts different when he is around them but he won't admit it. I would rather hang around the Dad that I know from motorcycle trips and hunting camps, minus the bitching about tipping over his bike or shooting a deer's leg off.

Last but not least, I don't go to their family dinners because they have them every other week it seems like. They have one for everyone in the family's birthday, including the pets. (I think that next week they are set to celebrate the anniversary of when one of the kids' chickens laid its first egg.) To top it all off, they have to eat at 2:00 in the afternoon—sharp. It would be a cardinal sin if dinner was served at 2:01.

Mom, on the other hand, went months before I even ate a meal at her house. She also went over a year before I spent a holiday with her. I wasn't going to open up and do any of that until I was ready. For a while, I didn't even want to meet Mike's five year old son, Nicholas. At first when Mom told me that his birthday was either the day before or the day after mine, I just said, "Who cares?" I quickly changed my attitude about that—a five year old didn't deserve to be treated like shit for something that wasn't his fault.

I eased into the whole thing better after getting the job at Dairy Valley and working a little bit with Mike. It didn't mean that I liked him any more or any less, it just meant that I got to know him better. When I first started, I rode along with just about every driver to give them a little help on their routes. I just had a little more that I could talk about with Mike, after the initial uncomfortable feelings went away.

I rode along with the drivers to not only give them some help, but to learn the business of selling milk as well. With a dated product, you can't give a customer too much or it will expire and the company will lose money by having to replace it for free. You also don't want them to run out so they don't get pissed off and go find another supplier. The idea was to find the happy medium, something that I picked up on right away.

My main goal was to simply drive, though. At the time, all I was worried about was driving and getting better at that, rather than learning how to sell milk correctly. Within the first three months of my employment, I was able to take my test and get my commercial driver's license. I even got the best driving score of the summer according to the instructor, not bad for someone who still hadn't reached their 19th birthday.

I was putting in well over forty hours a week at Dairy Valley throughout the summer. I would start at four in the morning and get off at around three in the afternoon. I got Wednesdays and weekends off to break up the monotony of working such long days. As planned, I also kept my job on Tuesday and Friday evenings working at McDonald's unloading their delivery truck and stocking the product in the restaurant.

By this time, both Archy and I had other jobs so unloading the truck twice a week was all we did. We quickly found out that Golden State Foods had a contest in the Washington, Oregon, Idaho, Montana, and California region each month to determine which store had the shortest combined delivery time. With both of us being natural competitors, we had to try to get on that list. We did it for five months in all and ranked sixth, first, first, first, and first respectively, unloading five to six hundred cases in less than thirty minutes on average. Although we worked there for about six hours a week, we were happy just to hang on to that fun stage that we had over the previous eighteen months.

Our employment at McDonald's finally came to an end after we were simultaneously fired for a stunt that the regional manager didn't find all that funny. Each year, McDonald's sells "helping hands" that customers can buy for a dollar, put their name on it, and hang it up in the lobby. All of the proceeds are said to go to Children's Hospital, but I have my doubts because I know for a fact that they had no way of tracking how much they sold. Archy and I each bought one, wrote our full names on them, and hung them up in the lobby. The only problem was that instead of the hand extending all of its fingers, we taped four of the fingers down so that only the middle finger was standing tall. We were fired the very next day when they were discovered.

The truth was, they could have fired us months before that if they could have proven that we were responsible for some of the things that went down. One night during the dinner rush, I was washing my hands in the back by the office. In the office was the master control for the radio that played music quietly in the lobby. I could barely make out that it was ZZ Top's "Sharp Dressed Man," so I reached in and twisted the volume to full power. It scared the shit out of all of the customers and employees at once. After about ten seconds of a full-on rock concert, I shut it down and went back to washing my hands.

"What the fuck was that?" Paul, the on-duty manager who was in the back room taking inventory, asked.

"What was what?" I asked in return.

"That music."

"I didn't hear any music."

He just pointed at me and walked away without saying another word.

If that could have gotten me fired, these next three situations could have also landed me in jail. While Archy and I were in the parking lot talking before our shifts were set to start, a female customer who was our age and pretty well-developed to say the least, pulled up to place an order. I don't remember if it was Archy or me who asked, but one of us asked her to take off her shirt and show us her boobs. Without batting an eye, she whipped off her top and shook her naked breasts in each of our faces.

After she put her shirt back on, she said, "Now let's see your guys' dicks."

Now one thing that you will never hear out of my mouth is that I am packing heat. At the same time, I'm not embarrassed about it and wouldn't care if someone saw it—except this time. Remember the stories that I told you about Archy earlier? Even the Space Needle looks small compared to the Sears Tower. Luckily, the sexual excitement got my blood flowing a little bit. While it wasn't in complete "happy mode," it still had a good showing. Too bad Archy had to have his hang down to his knees. We zipped up our pants, she nodded her head in approval, and we all went about her business.

A few months earlier, Travis Geiger of all people got a job with us. On his first week, he had bathroom duty where every hour he would have to clean the men's room. Just before his two o' clock cleaning, Archy and I each went in and shit on the floor next to each of the two toilets. Travis had to clean it all up. He quit not long after that—darn.

The next scheme didn't involve Archy at all. In fact, it didn't directly involve me either. Don't ask me how I found out, but my pickup's toolbox key also fit the cash registers. I never once worked a register, so it wasn't like I had access to them to make the discovery. Anyway, only a few people knew about it and one of the guys (there is a reason that I'm not going to tell you his name) asked to borrow them one day. Knowing better, I gave him my keys at the start of his shift. A few hours later, he brought them back to me along with a twenty dollar bill.

"What's this for?" I asked.

"I figured that you deserve ten percent.," he said.

For all of you math majors out there, that means that he took two hundred bucks. I didn't tell on him because he was a friend of mine (not to mention I was an accomplice), and I don't apologize for not doing so either. But I kept the twenty, and for that I do.

By winter, Holly and I had been dating for eight months. I made as much time for her as I could. I worked all day during the summer months on routes as I trained to get my license. Come fall I was confined to the dock, loading trucks in the afternoons and evenings. In the summer, I went to Holly's after work for a little bit to see her in the afternoons. When I was loading, I went to her house before I went to work to see her after she got out of school for an hour or so. On Saturdays, we would go out to whatever movie that she wanted to see. She always wanted to go to the theater to watch the newest (and often stupidest) releases each week. While I did enjoy *The Patriot* and *Meet The Parents*, I could have gone without all of the others like *Joe Dirt* and *Road Trip*. I sat through them because I didn't want to start a fight. So basically I was becoming a hen-pecked boyfriend, doing whatever the boss wanted me to do.

Not everything that we did was against my will. I even got her on my motorcycle and took her to Ross Lake, halfway up the North Cascades Highway. We went to the water slides at Birch Bay and had a blast. I even trained her to drive a car (not mine) so she could get her license. Even if I had to sit through a stupid movie every week, I was happy to have a person of the opposite sex to spend time with.

Around Christmas, I felt that our relationship had reached the point where we could begin to think about having sex. She had made it clear back in April when we started dating that she didn't want to be pressured into it and I was more than cool with that. In the meantime, we did almost everything except closing the deal. After several months of that, I asked if we could take the next step.

"No," she said sternly.

"Okay, but how come?"

"Because I still want to be a little girl."

It wasn't just that particular answer that made me realize that despite being only fourteen months apart, I was miles ahead of her. I had a good paying job and was saving for my future while she pissed away money on clothes that she never wore. I took pride and great care of my bike and truck while she drove her car like a maniac to try and beat the car beside her. (She actually thought that her Ford Tempo was the fastest car on the planet.) But it was the way that she reacted when I bought her a Christmas present that showed me the writing on the wall.

I had put a lot of thought into buying her a special gift. After weeks of deliberation, I settled on buying her a camera. I thought that it would be cool for us to take pictures of the places that we went and the things that we did together. Whether we would be together for ten more months or ten more years, we could look back and have pictures of us together.

I went over to her house on Christmas Eve to give her the gift that I was actually quite proud of myself for coming up with. We had to make it quick because they had company coming over and I wasn't asked to stay. I opened my gift first, which was The Beatles' new compilation album called *1*, that had just come out on CD. She hated my music, but she bought it for me anyway. I just wasn't allowed to play it around her because it wasn't "real" music. She was only into every flash-in-the-pan artist that was enjoying their fifteen minutes of fame. I thanked her and gave her a kiss, which was okay to do as long as her parents weren't looking. Was this a third grade romance or what?

I was really excited when I handed over her gift. To me, this was what Christmas presents were all about—giving someone a gift from the heart and watching their eyes light up. Her eyes lit up alright—with rage.

"A camera?" she said with a bitter tone.

"Yeah, so we can—"

"A camera?" she interrupted.

"I thought—"

"Take it back and just go."

"What?"

"You heard me! Leave! And take this with you!" she yelled, throwing the camera at me.

I was dumbfounded. *How could anyone be so rude?* Most people at least fake that they like it. I've never even seen a child act so ungrateful.

I called Mom to try and see if she could help me understand what the hell was in her head.

"I think that she was hoping for a little ring," Mom said.

"I don't want to get married!" I said quickly.

"Not an engagement ring, just a smaller and less expensive ring that she can show off. She probably thought that it was time for one."

I had no idea. As far as I knew, you only gave a ring to somebody who you intended to marry. I was taking baby steps for two reasons, not to scare her off and mostly because I was new to the game. I had just started saying "I love you" because I thought that I should. I really didn't mean it because I hadn't actually found love yet. The only time that she said it to me was in person when nobody else could hear it. Over the phone it was always just "you too," in case her parents were listening.

A few weeks later, I took her to pick out a ring in order to make up for the "shitty" present. Her eyes lit up when she saw a two hundred dollar ring that she said that she just couldn't live without. I shouldn't have done it and I regret doing it, but I bought it for her on the spot. She acted as if she had just won the lottery, calling her friends (not her parents, of course) and telling them the news.

Things were okay for the next few months. We took a ferry ride to the San Juan Islands and walked around Friday Harbor. We went to less and less movies and did more and more recreational activities, like hiking on nearby trails.

The beginning of the end came when she told me that her family was thinking about moving to California.

"I want you to come and live down there also," she said.

"No way, I've got a good job here. I'm saving money like crazy for my future. I'm not moving. You're eighteen and going to be graduating soon, why don't you just stay?"

"I'm never leaving my parents. I'm going to live with them forever because they said that they will support me for the rest of my life."

"Well, maybe we just aren't meant for each other."

"Maybe we're not."

I wish that I would have ended it there. Instead I kept pushing on, insisting that we could get through this little issue. I still wasn't wanting to quit because it just wasn't my style.

I finally had enough when she got pissed off because I came to her house to pick her up with Tuco in the back of my truck.

"I don't want this dog around my cat," she said. (She liked him any other time.)

"But we are leaving," I told her.

"I don't care, he's killed cats and I don't want him killing mine."

"He ain't going—"

"Take him home. Plus only rednecks ride around with dogs in their trucks and I refuse to be seen like that."

"You know what? Tuco is my dog and at least he appreciates this redneck!"

I got in my truck and went home. I called her the next day and gave her an ultimatum.

"If you're not going to let me be myself, we don't need to see each other."

"What do you mean?"

"You know what I mean—the ball is in your court."

"Yeah, then I want out!" she yelled as she hung up the phone.

I sat the phone on the hook and let out a sigh of relief. I was happy that she said that because I wasn't going to quit on it, although I should have parked my pride and done it anyway. I vowed to myself right then and there that I wasn't going to do anything for another girl, within reason, that I didn't want to do.

Holly wasn't for me. I thought that I wanted an innocent girl like that. Although our values were one in the same, we were miles apart in maturity. While I could still act like a teenager, I was a working adult now. With the exception of still living at home, I had bills to pay just like a thirty year old would. I needed someone like that. But for now, I was happy without the ball and chain.

CHAPTER 39
Achieving My Goal

A s promised, I was trained to drive a truck and was able to get my commercial driver's license during my first few months of working at Dairy Valley. During the busy part of the summer, I rode around with almost every driver to learn the business. When business slowed down in the fall, I was confined to the dock where I loaded trucks in the afternoons and evenings. I would start at noon and be off at around ten at night.

I only loaded four days week, but I worked six. Gordon's son, Casey, who was in charge of ordering and receiving orders and rotating stock, did a lot of lollygagging around the dock in order to fool his dad into thinking that he was overworked. On the two days that I didn't load, I would do his physical work so he could concentrate on writing orders. I also rode along with drivers when they were broke down or were sick. On average, I would go out on a route about once a week. Once finished with the route, I would then do my regular job of loading trucks. Before I started loading, I would usually have to rotate product for Casey because he was behind on his orders.

I didn't have much use for the whole Mills Family. Casey was a nice guy but a slow worker. Jason, Casey's brother, did things on the job that truck driver's shouldn't do and I had proof. Although it may or may not have given me the opportunity to take his job if I told Gary, I didn't because it wasn't any of my business. As for Gordon, he thought his kids were perfect and constantly belittled other employees behind their backs. No telling what he had to say about me when I wasn't around.

Even though I got along better with the Grahn Family, they had their faults too. Mike's brother, Corey, is a nice guy for the most part but if something doesn't go his way, he will take it out on everybody—kind of like Jekyl and Hyde. Over the years he has been difficult to tolerate at times, but I know that it will pass quickly. On the occasions that I call him out on it, he will back down in a hurry. As for Gary, he too is a good guy. The only issue that I ever had with him was when he blamed me when he wrecked a truck.

One afternoon while I was loading, the Mount Vernon Wal-Mart needed a special delivery. I pulled the order but forgot a few items, so we had to go back to the dock to get the rest of it.

Gary, who was doing the driving, backed into another company's truck as he was backing back into our dock and smashed up its front end.

As soon as it happened, he looked at me and said, "Now goddammit, this would have never happened if you hadn't fucked up the order."

I had nothing to say to that ridiculous comment. If that same thing happened today, I would no doubt tell him (respectfully) to fuck off.

The four other guys on the payroll who weren't related to any of the owners, were Randy, John, Dave, and Kenny. Randy quit not more than a couple of weeks after I started. Corey and I cleaned up his cab-over Kenworth before we started driving it. It took us several hours to fill three Hefty trash bags full of garbage and two, five gallon buckets full of pure cigarette ash out of that piece of shit. Dave was much cleaner, but he too quit a few months later.

Out of the four guys, John had been there the longest. In fact, he still works there now and is the only guy ahead of me on the employee seniority list. Although he has since changed a lot, when I first started he would call in sick like clockwork every fourth Friday. I would then have to be the one that would get woke up with about two hours sleep and drive the truck, while Gordon told me where to go and what to do. For that reason, I really didn't care for him at the beginning.

I liked Kenny the best. He talked like a cross between a hillbilly and a surfer (if that's even possible). He was the slowest worker out of everybody, but was still liked by everybody. He was the one that I rode with the most, as he was the most experienced driver to teach me.

Every company has that one guy who complains about everything, and Kenny was ours. Most people hate crybabies and whiners on the job like that, but he did it in such a way that it was highly entertaining. I don't know if it was the way he talked or what, but I couldn't wait until the next work day to hear him bitch about being overworked and under payed.

When he got on the kick about how it wasn't fair that the owners of the company made more money than him, he would say shit like, "Man, those fuckers get to come to work every day, tell us what to do, and then go back home to their mansions. We come to work, get bitched at, and go back home to our huts."

He also let everyone know that he was the oldest guy on the crew. Although he was just forty years old, he would try to make it sound like he should be drawing social security by constantly saying, "Man, I'm the oldest motherfucker here, I've got the biggest fuckin' route, and I get the smallest fuckin' paycheck."

After riding along with him for a while and noticing that the tiniest things would be enough to set him off, he quickly became a mark for a few of my pranks. It was like picking on Joey or Brent when I was younger—their reactions are what made it all worth while. Beings he was always bitching about working way more hours than anyone else, anytime that I could get him to believe that somebody put in less than ten hours, he would absolutely have a heart attack. He called Casey on the radio one day while he was on his route and we were back at the dock. When he asked to talk to me, I told Casey to tell him that I had just left for the day.

"What?! Man, that motherfucker gets to work half-days while we're all out here bustin' our asses and puttin' our fuckin' hours in."

I nearly pissed my pants when I heard him say that.

During the winter while I was working the dock, we got a few inches of snow during the day. Gordon asked me to shovel out the dock spots so the drivers didn't get their trucks stuck when they came back that afternoon. I did what I was told, but I dumped all of the snow in front of Kenny's car. I went home before I got to hear his reaction, but I'm sure that he at least said "man" or "fuck" a couple of times during his tirade. He said those words so much that we actually nicknamed him "Man Fuck."

My absolute favorite trick came when he put one of those self-extinguishing ash tray/cigarette butt collectors in the cup holder of his truck. With the cup holder being on top of the dashboard, he would just reach up and stick his used cigarette into the small hole of the cup while he was driving. He couldn't see the hole, but he would just wiggle the butt around with his finger until it slid down. After I discovered that, I shoved about eight or ten matches into that hole after I finished loading for the night. The next day, he left the yard with his four packs of cigarettes that he would puff on all day long. After finishing his first one once he got on the freeway, he went to stick the smoldering butt into the hole. Feeling that it was plugged up, he pressed down on it harder with his finger. WHOOSH!! The matches ignited and he not only burnt the shit out of his finger but, according to him, he almost drove his truck into the ditch. Beings I wasn't at work yet, all he could do was leave me a nasty message on my cell phone.

"Hey Eddie! Man, this is fuckin' Kenny! You pull that fuckin' shit on me again, man, and you're fucked!"

I played that message back three times a day for a week before I finally deleted it.

Kenny don't work with us anymore, but we still tell stories and laugh about his antics at least a couple of times a week.

Work wasn't all fun and games, though. By March, I had been loading trucks for seven months. That part wasn't bad, but it was the extra shit that I did so that Casey would be able to lounge in the office with his dad that got me irritated. I was actually to the point where I had applied for another job and was practically hired, before I called them back and told them that I had changed my mind. I wasn't ready to give up on my driving dream just yet.

The noon to ten hours that I worked sucked. I would get home at 10:30 and watch wrestling for a few hours in order to wind down. For something to do, I started logging down the matches and the amount of minutes that I had on each tape into a notebook to find out the total amount of wrestling that I had on video. I finished at 4,492 matches and 65,839 minutes. As of 2010, it stands at 10,186 matches and 177,892 minutes—the equivalent of 2,964 hours and 52 minutes. If I were to play all of my tapes and DVDs back-to-back, it would take 123.5 days straight.

On April 1, 2001, I finally became a full-time driver. At nineteen years old, I had reached my childhood goal of of becoming a truck driver. I didn't shoot for the moon and try to become something that was practically unachievable. Instead, I set a reasonable goal and achieved it. I knew inside that I could be anything that I wanted to be. I guess that I'm just a simple man—I wanted to drive trucks.

By the time that my one year anniversary rolled around in June, I was bringing home a thousand dollars every two weeks. After my cell phone, insurance, satellite, and grocery bills were paid, I was banking around sixteen hundred a month. Combine that with what I had saved over the previous few years, and I had almost fifteen thousand dollars to my name. With the money being so good, I figured that it was time that I bought a new motorcycle.

On July 29, 2001, I bought a brand new Harley-Davidson Road King Classic right off the showroom floor in Bellingham. I had actually been planning on waiting for a 100th Anniversary model in 2003, but I was advised by Uncle Robbie's best friend, Brad, to get one now because I could be in a different position in two year's time. (Boy, was he right.) Even though I was only nineteen, the owner of the bike shop bought me a couple of beers at the bowling alley next door after we signed the papers. Talk about a bonus!

A few days later on a Tuesday afternoon, I rode up on the back of Dad's bike to pick it up. We then went from Bellingham straight over the pass to Rob's house to show it off. We spent the night and I rode home the next day, as Dad went off on a week long bike trip on his own. When I parked it in the garage at home on Wednesday night, I had eight hundred miles already on it in just over twenty-four hours.

Although it was over a month until my birthday, Dad gave me an early gift after he got back from his trip. It was a personalized license plate that read "KING ED." Even though it costs me twice as much as a regular plate each year to renew it, I do because it was my very first brand new vehicle that I bought on my own.

Now that I had a Harley, I had to part ways with my Magna. As promised, I called up Skip and offered it to him first. He thanked me, but he wasn't interested. Instead, I sold it to a guy that Papa worked with in Spokane for exactly what I payed for it several years earlier.

Around this time, Dad began charging me rent to live at his house. With me making plenty of money and him only charging me a hundred bucks a month, I wasn't opposed to it. It did catch me off guard a bit because he started it just after I spent my life savings on my Harley. When I asked him if he could wait until payday, he told me to "forget it." Beings I didn't have the money, he said that he would take my old Kawasaki in exchange for the first month's rent. I knew that it wasn't worth the $300 that I paid for it in 1994, but I did feel that it was worth a bit more than a hundred. Dad wouldn't budge, so I signed the title over to him. The very next weekend he gave it to Debbie's brother, leading me to believe that he had the whole scheme cooked up for a while.

The only other thing that bothered me about my "landlord" was the fact that he never once charged Jen any rent when she got to be my age and still lived at home. He argued that it was because she made less money than me. That was certainly true, but I never did the shit that Jen did like throwing all of her parties when he was out of town.

Not that Jen was a bad person, but she was very much into the weekend party crap that I didn't do. To her defense, she didn't do anything that the other kids wouldn't do also, as most high school kids are just that way. There were times that I would be on my way to work at two in the morning and I would pass her on the highway. I would call Dad and wake him up, not to snitch on her, but to protect her from doing stupid stuff. Let's face it, how many good things can happen at that hour of the night?

"That's not her," he said. "She's spending the night at a friend's house."

"Bullshit. You don't think I know Jen's truck when I see it?!"

I think that the only reason that Dad would get up and go after her was to try and prove me wrong. Unfortunately for him, that never happened. Jen never has said anything to me about calling in on her. I hope that she would realize that I only did it with her safety in mind like a big brother should.

September 11, 2001. The mere mention of that date strikes fear, anger, and heartache into every American. Although it happened on my birthday, ruining yet another one, this time it wasn't about me. Nineteen al-Qaeda terrorists hijacked four separate commercial passenger airplanes and crashed them into the Twin Towers of the World Trade Center in New York City and the Pentagon in Arlington, Virginia. The fourth was on course for Washington D.C. before passengers attempted to regain control, causing it to crash into a field in Shaksville, Pennsylvania. Four flights, no survivors. Both of the Twin Towers collapsed shortly after impact, killing thousands of people inside. Including the nineteen hijackers, 2,996 people were killed, making it the largest assault ever on American soil.

Everyone remembers where they were when certain tragedies in American history took place. From John F. Kennedy to Dr. Martin Luther King, Jr. and from John Lennon to Elvis Presley—people remember exactly what they were doing when they got word of what happened. 9/11 is no different. Alan Jackson asked, "Where Were You When The World Stopped Turning?" in his 2002 single. I was at work like most people.

It was a clear and warm Tuesday morning. My route took me down to Marysville and Everett, as it did every Tuesday and Friday. I had a radio in my Freightliner truck but at the time, I only played cassette tapes of my favorite prerecorded music. I didn't like the fact that I mostly heard commercials between stops so I figured that if I wanted to hear some tunes, I better bring my own. After this day, though, I decided that I should be aware of what was happening around me by listening to the news at least once during the day.

At 8:46 a.m. eastern time, American Airlines Flight 11 crashed into the north tower of the World Trade Center. At that same time, 5:46 a.m. pacific, I was delivering to a Shell station just north of Marysville. The owner opened at six, but always got there at 5:30 to turn on the coffee, the gas pumps, and things like that.

As I walked in my second of five or six stacks, he said, "A plane just hit the World Trade Center."

"Really?" was all I said, somewhat confused.

"Yeah."

I wasn't too concerned at first. For all I knew, it could have been a tiny plane that just clipped the top of the building. Although rare, it does happen. The news didn't say how big the plane was or how bad the wreck was, so I kind of just brushed it off and went on about my business.

Seventeen minutes later, United Airlines Flight 175 hit the south tower. By then I was at another stop and delivering their order. Like me, the lady at that store just cranked the tunes while she worked so I wasn't aware of what had happened.

Within the next hour, American Airlines Flight 77 hit the Pentagon and United Airlines Flight 93 crashed into an open field. When the fourth plane went down at 10:03 a.m. eastern, I was just pulling up to another store, a few minutes behind my seven o' clock drop time.

The lady who was in charge of the receiving, who otherwise never really spoke much, ran up to me and said, "Did you hear about the plane?"

"Yeah, the one that clipped the World Trade Center, right?"

"Not just one, but two planes hit!"

"What?!"

She quickly went back into her office. As soon as I heard that two planes hit, one for each tower, I knew that something real bad was happening. I still didn't know just how bad everything was, though.

Not a minute later, she was back.

"A plane just hit the Pentagon!"

With a mixture of anger and shock I just yelled, "What the fuck is going on?!"

I know that it really isn't the greatest thing to use that sort of language around women, but this was different. This wasn't the time to worry about etiquette and manners, this was an attack on our country.

I was finished for the day around 11:00 a.m., just under five hours after the initial crash. I still didn't completely know the severity of what was happening until I got home and turned on the TV. (Jen was at school and Dad was still at work.) There sat Peter Jennings at his ABC News desk. The collar of his shirt was unbuttoned and his tie was loosened, something that normally would never happen. But this wasn't normal. I sat there in the exact same spot for the rest of the day. I saw the actual amateur videos of both planes crashing into the towers. I saw both of the giant structures on fire. I watched people jump to their deaths from unbelievable heights. Then, I saw both buildings collapse. Although I saw the footage over and over, I still couldn't believe what was happening.

Needing fresh air, I went out for a walk towards the highway with Tuco. *It must be nice to be an animal and not have to worry about shit like this.* To him it was a great day, getting to go for a walk on a sunny afternoon. Once we got to the stop sign, we stopped for a minute to watch the cars go by. Off in the distance, I saw a semi truck coming towards us. As he got closer, I could see that he had a giant United States flag whipping behind him in the wind. From the edge of the road, I gave him a thumbs-up as he drove by. He acknowledged me by hitting his air horn. We didn't know each other. Aside from driving trucks, we may be polar opposites. But on a day of horrendous tragedy, we were the same—proud of our country, proud to be an American, and we weren't going give whoever was responsible for all of this the satisfaction of letting them know that we were scared. On that day, everyone across the country were united as one. White, black, bankers, killers, lawyers, the homeless—everyone became one. As great as it was, it's too bad that an event like 9/11 has to happen for everyone to come together like that.

After working at Dairy Valley for over a year, I earned a full week of paid vacation time. Their vacation plan is a great one—one week after a year, two weeks after two years, three weeks after five years, and four weeks after ten years. The only drawback was, at the time, nobody was allowed to vacation between May and September because it was our busiest time of year. Although that has since changed a little bit, back then summer motorcycle trips were not possible.

When it came time for a motorcycle trip a year earlier in 2000, I had just started on the job and didn't feel right about asking for time off. So I stayed home while Dad went for a week. With no vacations allowed in the summer, I also missed out on the 2001 trip, which started the day that I bought my Harley. The first opportunity I could get to take a week trip would be on the last couple of days of September and the first few days of October. The weather around that time is either really good or really bad, with not much in between. I didn't care—rain or shine, I was going on a bike trip.

I spent a lot of the previous summer looking at maps to decide on a specific destination. I had done the Montana and South Dakota thing as well as the California and Nevada route. I wanted to go somewhere that I had never been to. If I left on Friday afternoon after work, I would have nine days until I had to be back for work on the following Monday. My choice—Texas.

Ever since I thought of the idea, I had asked Dad if he was wanting to come along. He never gave me a definitive answer until a few days prior.

"Texas is a long ways away, you know?"

"Yeah, Dad, I know. But that is where I'm going to go."

"Okay, I'm in. But we've got to go over the Rocky Mountains twice to get there, what about the weather?"

Not a day went by that I didn't watch the national weather reports during the month of September to learn about the temperature trend in those areas. Still having the big satellite dish because I was the one paying for it, I could also watch the local news in Denver every night. Luckily, the whole nation was having a late summer.

"The weather will be fine," I said with confidence.

Of course I didn't know for sure but if I told myself good news enough times, I could start to believe it for the truth.

In order to reach Texas in the time that we had, we would have to at times ride over six hundred miles a day and stick to interstates and U.S. highways. My plan was to hit Oregon, Idaho, Utah, Colorado, Kansas, New Mexico, Oklahoma, and Texas. With the exception of Kansas, we hit all of them—over four thousand miles of road traveled in all. As luck would have it, we wouldn't hit any rain until we got back into Washington on the way home.

With anticipation burning inside of me throughout the day, I flew through my route on that Friday and got home as fast as possible. Friday was usually a short day so I was generally home before noon. It normally would be several hours before anyone else got home but on this particular day, Dad beat me home.

"What took you so long?" he asked as I pulled into the driveway.

I just smiled and ran in and took a quick shower and packed the last of my things like deodorant, contacts, tooth brush, and a comb. I never usually packed a comb, but I did this time because of my goatee that I had been growing for a few months. With all of the wind blowing in my face for a week, I had to keep it brushed or else it would look even stupider than it already did.

The reason that I started growing it in the first place was because I was through dating Holly. She didn't like me having facial hair because I "looked old." Like a good little boy, I did what I was told. While I may have worn the pants in that relationship, she told me which ones to wear. I wasn't going to do that shit again for any girl. As for the goatee, I grew it out just like a wrestler named Jim "The Anvil" Neidhart did during his career. "The Anvil," who got his nickname for throwing a one hundred pound anvil ten-and-a-half feet, grew his out to a point several inches off his chin.

After packing our stuff, we hit the road. We rode over Snoqualmie Pass and got on Interstate 82 in Ellensburg, en route to I-84. Shortly after crossing into Oregon, we ran out of daylight. Just outside of Hermiston, we pulled up to a truck stop to spend the night.

We had just started pitching our tent when someone came up to us and said, "You guys can't sleep here."

"Why not?" I asked, pointing at all of the trucks. "These guys are."

"Yeah, but they're in trucks, not tents."

Rather than argue, I started packing up our stuff while Dad jumped on his bike and went out looking for a different place. A short time later, he came back and said that he had talked to a farmer that lived nearby and he said that we were welcome to spend the night in his pasture. We had stayed in worse places, so it sounded fine to us. Other than the fact that it frosted that night, we were in good shape.

The next day, we spent a little extra time at the first cafe that we came to in order to warm our chilled bones. Once the temperature got above freezing again, we got back on our bikes and continued down I-84, through Idaho and into Utah. Night fell just as we got into Salt Lake City but we didn't plan on stopping until we got out of the capitol city, especially now that traffic had became so congested. We were stuck behind a Chevrolet Cavalier that had three old grannies in the backseat. Dad said that it was like following a herd of sheep.

We got off the freeway just north of Provo. The gas station that we pulled into to fuel up was just getting ready to close. Out of either kindness for his fellow man or out of the laziness of not wanting to go out to the dumpster, the station attendant gave us each a couple of hot dogs for free. After eating our gourmet meal, we went across the street to the K.O.A., whose office was closed for the night already. Undeterred, we threw our stuff out on the ground and slept there for free.

The next day, we took U.S. Highway 6 into Grand Junction, Colorado, where Dad's mom and Milt had moved to a few months prior. They were now living with Dad's sister, Lorie, and her new boyfriend, Rod. For some reason, Dad kept calling him Rob. After a couple of

Budweisers, Grandma did too. After a few more, she started calling me "Beaver," thinking that my goatee looked more like a woman's pubic hair design.

Knowing that we would be coming back through town on our way home, we checked out early the next morning without waking anybody up. We went east on U.S. Highway 50 through Montrose, where Dad lived for a while as a kid. After a quick but extensive search, he managed to find the house that he had lived in over three decades earlier. From there, we bundled up and headed over the Rocky Mountains.

Two-thirds of the way between Gunnison and Salida, sat Monarch Pass. Standing 11,312 feet above sea level, Monarch Pass is the highest mountain summit that I have ever crossed. Miraculously with it being October, the roads were spotless, as the snow had yet to come in for the season. While we were taking pictures, though, we did begin to feel the smallest and faintest of snowflakes.

Me on top of Monarch Pass

As crazy at it may sound, we weren't the only bikers who were shivering at the top of the Rockies. Another guy, who looked like Jerry Garcia of The Grateful Dead, had his bike loaded down for a big trip like us. Instead of a windshield, however, this guy had a rolled up tarp and his sleeping bag between his handlebars. Snickering at the looks of him but not giving it much more of a thought, we just waived as we took off down the mountain in search of warmer temperatures.

Once we got into Pueblo, all of the mountains were in our rear view mirror and there wasn't so much as a mole hill coming up from the ground. Officially in the Great Plains, the only thing that surrounded us was grass—and an awful smell. As we rode through tiny little towns along the Arkansas River, the smell grew worse. Then just outside of La Junta, we came upon the largest collection of cattle that I have ever seen. There had to be a quarter-million head if there was one. From the first cow to the last, the herd spread along three miles of highway. We stopped to try and take a picture, but it never did turn out.

We kept rolling along, heading for Dodge City, Kansas as planned. With it getting near dusk and with still over a hundred miles to go, we turned and headed south out of Lamar, thirty minutes from the Kansas state line. After seeing deer and antelope for much of the afternoon, we figured that it would be safer to find a spot right away and not take any chances.

Just after dark, we came into Springfield, about thirty minutes north of Oklahoma. We pulled into a gas station to top off and ask around if there were any nearby campgrounds. As we were fueling, the same biker from Monarch Pass, who we began calling "Monarch Man," after leapfrogging him at roadside piss stops all day long, pulled up alongside of us. Believe it or not, he too was headed for Dodge City. The problem was unlike us, he took a wrong turn without realizing it and ended up right where we were—fifty miles off of his course. On his way to Joplin, Missouri and already a few days behind, Monarch Man just saddled up and headed east into the darkness.

After our gas stop, we rode about two blocks past the gas station to an R.V. park. Although it was against the rules because we didn't have a camp trailer, the groundskeeper said that we were free to spend the night for ten bucks apiece. As it turned out, it was the only night on our trip that we had to pay for camping. With it being a nice, warm night, we just threw our bags out on the ground and slept under the stars.

Right around dawn, I was somewhat awoken by a dog licking my face. Still half-asleep, I yelled at whom I thought was Tuco to stop. I was used to being licked in the middle of the night or early in the morning if Tuco had to go outside to go to the bathroom, so I didn't think too much of it. When it happened to Dad, I realized that it wasn't Tuco and I wasn't at home.

"Get out of here, you bastard!" Dad yelled after the dog swiped its tongue across his face.

With the puppy not being very old, he didn't listen. He started running around, grabbing our boots, and having the time of his life. After a few minutes, his owner called for him from across the park and he took off towards him—with my hat still in his mouth.

Once we packed up, we headed south into Oklahoma. We stopped for breakfast in Boise City at a little cafe. Combine the time that it took for us to eat our meal with the amount of miles that we rode, we were in Oklahoma for a total of ninety minutes.

Continuing south on U.S. Highway 287, we pulled into Amarillo, Texas less than two hours later. We stopped at the local Harley shop to buy a couple of T-shirts. When the owner heard that we had ridden all the way there from Washington State in October, he actually gave us a pretty healthy discount. Not too many knuckleheads would even dream of riding that distance in such a short time during that time of year. You either have to be tough or stupid—the jury is still out on that one.

Now that we had reached our destination, Dad and I jumped on I-40 and started making our way back west. We rode halfway through New Mexico into Albuquerque, where we turned and headed north back towards Colorado. An hour or so north of Albuquerque, we stopped alongside the highway for the night.

Over the past several months since I started running a route, I was used to getting up before three every the morning. Even on the weekends, I would wake up at that time to at least take a piss before going back to sleep. Unfortunately, sometimes I couldn't go back to sleep. Laying there and listening to Dad snore made it impossible to get back to sleep that night. I ended up needling him until he got pissed off and got up. With neither one of our cell phones in service, we couldn't see what time it was when we packed up camp and hit the road. At the first gas stop an hour later, we found out that it was just four a.m.

Thankfully, Dad's anger was thwarted by the fact that it was getting abnormally colder outside. Just the night before it was seventy-plus degrees and we were cruising in T-shirts. Now it was all we could do to move our frozen hands. Knowing that we were taking U.S. Highway 550 north back into Montrose, we didn't even bother looking at the map's specifics. If we had, we would have seen that we were going to cross the continental divide and thus may have waited until it warmed up before crossing. As it was, we crossed just before the sun came up.

By the time we got into Cuba, New Mexico, it was twenty-two degrees and snow was lined up along the streets. With both of our faces beet red and with snot frozen to our mustaches, Dad and I spent the next five minutes trying to get our hands warm by our engines just so we could use our fingers to undo our helmets.

After a lengthy breakfast, we got back on the road and continued towards Grandma's. After riding through the scenic town of Durango, Colorado, we rode over Red Mountain Pass, itself standing over 11,000 feet. We got into Grand Junction in the evening and spent the entire next day at Grandma's not only visiting, but doing complete services on our bikes.

On Friday morning, we took off and headed for home. We rode the same route back as we had going down. By Sunday, we were back home with an extra four thousand miles on our odometers. That trip itself not only logged the most miles, but it marked the first (and likely the only) trip that Dad and I took on our bikes for that amount of time together without anyone else. Unlike prior trips, there was no arguing, fighting, or complaining. Other than a few bad meals and some bitter temperatures, it may have been one of my smoothest trips that I have ever taken.

CHAPTER 40

Sharon

I T SURE FELT good to go on a bike trip again. Missing out on not just a bike trip in 2000 but a plain vacation in general, wasn't a good thing. Even though I was new to the work force, I knew that just making money wasn't the only thing in life. What good is having money if you don't take the time to enjoy it once in a while? Starting in 2001, with the only exception being in 2003 for reasons which I will explain later, I have taken at least one big trip each year. It's sort of like my Christmas in a way—I look forward to it all year long.

With my body and my mind refreshed, I returned to work during the second week of October. As always when I go on vacation, I spent the first week that I was back fixing the mistakes made by the person who covered for me. It isn't necessarily the fact that they are doing it wrong as much as it is the fact that they just do it different than me. But everyone has their own way of doing things, I guess.

By this time, I had been running a particular route for six months. I got along with almost all of my customers that I delivered to. One thing that I learned pretty quick was that you can't please everyone no matter how hard you try. There are some people that have it out for you from the start, just because you're not who they are used to. For me, that person just happened to be the former owner of Dairy Valley.

Jay, now the owner of a grocery store in Lake Stevens, and I never got along. I did everything that he asked me to do, but it still wasn't good enough for him. I simply wasn't his favorite guy, but Kenny was. Long story short, he bitched to Gary so much about me that I was taken off of that route and put onto another. Before that went down, though, my life took an unexpected turn.

Ever since the debacle with Holly a few months earlier, I hadn't had any desire to date any girls. (And no, that doesn't mean that I was switching sides.) I was plenty happy just working everyday and doing what I wanted to do on my days off. I didn't have to sit through stupid movies or eat shitty food at lousy restaurants and most importantly, I didn't have to have anyone dictate what I did. Although I would see and talk to girls either at work or out and about sometimes, I didn't have any intentions of going much further than "hello."

After getting used to being around some of my customers, I could relax a little bit and be myself a little more instead of posing like a professional salesman. For me, it's easier being myself around girls. When I was younger, I was shy and awkward around any girl. But now I acted naturally, being my charismatic self. To this day, I've never had a female customer complain about me (who wasn't just a bitter bitch anyway).

Dealing with guy customers, on the other hand, can be a different story. I am not going to be fooled by any shady guy at any time—I can look right through them. While I will try to work with them, there is a point when I put myself ahead of the company. Even though the bosses frowned on it at first (and sometimes still do), they understand that I am not the kind of person who gets pushed around. People will lie and do anything to get something for free, but it's funny how they will cower if you call them out on it.

Anyway, back to the girls. One of the girls that I could talk to a little bit worked at a Lake Steven's convenience store called Norm's Market. It's not like I had much more than a two minute conversation with her twice a week, but I did at least take a little extra time to talk about more than the basic customer service chatter. It couldn't have been too deep, because I didn't even know her name yet.

I did know the obvious, however. She was about a foot shorter than I was and had blonde hair. It didn't look bad by any means, but I have been around bleached hair enough to know that blonde wasn't her natural color. On a scale of one to ten, she was probably a low seven. That may sound bad, but how many tens do you know that haven't had any cosmetic work done? To put it in more perspective, Holly was a pretty girl (when she wore her hair right) and checked in at a solid five. (Incidentally, Holly looked like Slash from Guns n' Roses when her hair was down. No surprise here, but neither her or her family thought that it was funny when I called her that.)

Shortly after I got back from vacation, I shaved my goatee off. She commented on it the next time that I saw her by subtly asking, "No more goatee?"

For no other reason other than it was the first thing that popped into my head, I responded with, "No, I was having trouble getting dates."

Without batting an eye, she said, "Why don't you try asking?"

I know that I just got finished telling you that I was natural and charismatic around women, but that was forgotten on the spot after that comment. I just stood there speechless as she turned away and went about her work. I pondered it for a few minutes while I finished my delivery. *Was she serious? Or was she just fooling around?*

It took a little courage, but I went up front as I was leaving and asked, "What did you mean back there?"

"You know what I mean."

"Oh—yeah."

I couldn't say anything else—I was frozen. She just stood there like "What are you waiting for?" Finally, she took out a piece of paper and wrote her phone number on it.

"Here," she said. "You can call me."

"Okay," I said "But what's your name?"

"Sharon."

"I'm Eddie."

"I know."

"Oh."

"Wait," she said, as I turned to leave the store. "I need to tell you something."

"What?"

"I'm kind of scary—"

Now I didn't know what the hell she meant by that. Two things went through my mind—I don't know why, but my first thought was that she was going to tell me that she had a penis. The second, and more practical, was that she had some sexually transmitted disease. Needless to say, I was relieved when she finished her sentence.

"I have a kid."

"You do—alright! How old?"

"Two. I have a little girl."

I wasn't really surprised because I figured with me being twenty years old and in the kind of work I was in, I was going to meet older women. Most likely, they would have kids already so it wasn't really a shock to me at all. While Sharon was the exact opposite of my dream girl, the cute and innocent thing didn't work out for me very well. This was the kind of person that was closer to what I was after, I just didn't know it at the time.

Ironically, this was yet another case of the old "milkman" stereotype. I guess there is much more to it than the punchline to a joke. Unlike the situation with Mom and Mike, Sharon wasn't married, nor was she seeing anyone. Her and the father of her daughter were never married and been split up for a while. I wasn't going to be stepping on his toes because he didn't want anything to do with the child and for the longest time denied that she was his. Although paternity tests proved otherwise, he still wasn't in the picture.

After I left the store to continue with my work, I started having second thoughts. It wasn't at all about the kid thing, but rather the fact that Lake Stevens was seventy miles from where I lived. With my hours and her schedule, we would only see each other once a week. She didn't even have a driver's license, so I was going to have to be the one who did the commuting. While I was a little concerned, I figured that I would go ahead and give it a try.

Once I got finished with work, I called Mom to tell her about Sharon. I wasn't sure how she was going to take the whole kid thing, but she was surprisingly excited for me. When I told Dad, he too responded in a positive way.

I called Sharon once I got home from work and we kind of compared our work schedules a bit to see when we could have our first date. We decided that on the upcoming Saturday, we would go out for dinner. I figured that I would talk to her next once the weekend came, but instead she asked me if I could come over on Tuesday night and she would fix dinner.

"I hope you like spaghetti," she said.

Well, I don't. I'll eat it, but I honestly could go the rest of my life without it and it wouldn't hurt my feelings. I will never order it at a restaurant and I will never request it for a family dinner.

If I must eat it, I would prefer that Gladys be the one that would make it. She makes her own sauce and doesn't use any of that canned crap. Mom made her own sauce too, but it was so runny that you would have to build a dam with your noodles to keep it from flowing off of your plate.

I was pretty excited throughout the next day. I wasn't sure what to expect when I got there, but I was happy to be away from the high school dating fiascoes. This time I wouldn't have to deal with parents, curfews, or any of that stupid shit. After work, I showered up and took the hour-and-a-half drive down to where her apartment was in Lake Stevens, which was only about two blocks away from the store where she worked.

When I knocked on the door, I was floored when a guy answered it.

"Uh—I must have the wrong apartment," I said after I picked my jaw up off the deck.

"No,no,no. You're looking for Sharon, right?" he asked, scratching his head like he had just woken up.

"Yeah," I answered, still confused about what I was seeing.

"Come on in," he said. "She'll be home in a minute."

I walked through the door and nearly fainted at what I saw. There was a futon spread out in the middle of the living room with clothes piled up next to it. The kitchen had a refrigerator and an oven, but you couldn't get to them. The only bedroom was filled with shit, except for a small area where somebody could curl up and go to sleep. The whole place couldn't have been two hundred square feet. I just sort of leaned against the wall as he sat down and started laughing along to an episode of *Seinfeld*. After about a minute (which felt more like a week), he jumped up and headed out the door.

"I'm late for work—I gotta go. Help yourself to whatever you want," he said as he shut the door behind him.

Who was this guy? Sharon hadn't said anything about living with anyone else. *What the hell was going on?*

Just then, she came through the door.

"Hi, Eddie," she said. "Travis must have let you in, huh?"

"Yeah, I guess—he didn't say his name."

"It's Travis—he's my roommate," she said, without skipping a beat.

This smelled a little funny to me. Had it been milk, I wouldn't have put it on my cereal. I had only known of one person to live with the opposite sex in the same apartment and that was Jack Tripper on *Three's Company*. But that was Hollywood, this was reality. I was still new to this adult thing, so maybe it was normal after all.

Come to find out, it was. Neither one could afford a place on their own. Splitting the rent in half, the two could each have a roof over their head. As for the sleeping arrangements, she slept in the living room with her daughter and he slept in the bedroom. I didn't ask if it was or wasn't, but their relationship seemed to be platonic. After getting to know Travis, who was more like an annoying cousin, I figured that Sharon had to be telling the truth. She cleared her way through the house and pushed a big pile of junk from the stove to the floor in order to start fixing dinner. She wasn't acting at all embarrassed of the appearance of her place. While it wasn't in any way what I was used to, I too ignored it and began concentrating on what I had came to do—getting to know Sharon.

She had just turned twenty-five, two weeks earlier on September 30. (Having the same birthday month was pretty much the only thing that we had in common.) Her daughter, Katelynn, was staying at her Aunt Tonya's house for the evening. Tonya, whom Sharon called "mom," had raised her since she was a teenager. She didn't get into any specifics as to why that was and I didn't ask.

We ate dinner while standing in the kitchen, as she had no dining room table or chairs. Of course, clumsy me had to drop my plate of spaghetti all down the front of me. When I initially lost control of the plate, I tried to pull it back into me instead of keeping it out in front of me. Sure enough, the whole plate emptied on my pants. I had no choice but to let her wash them right then or else my forty dollar jeans would be ruined and my pickup would smell like spaghetti forever. I finished the rest of my meal in my boxer shorts with a bib on.

Once my pants were dry, we called it an evening and I went home. I did give her a customary kiss before I left and told her that if she was still interested in our Saturday plans, I would try not to be as clumsy in public. She said that she would take a chance and give it a try.

Forgetting about the appearance of her house, which didn't bother me too much because I wasn't the one who had to live in it, the only thing that I didn't like about her was her smoking. I just couldn't stand the smell and after our little kiss, I couldn't stand the taste. She was very courteous about it, however. When the time came for her to smoke, she would go outside and do it away from me.

When Saturday rolled around a few days later, I went back down for our first real date. This time, Katelynn was there for a little while before Tonya could get there to pick her up for the night. She was a typical two year old—into everything, always moving, crying when something didn't go her way, and always jabbering. She didn't talk to me or her mom as much as she just talked to herself and the things that she could touch or pickup and carry around.

After Katelynn was picked up, Sharon and I went to Everett and had dinner at Applebee's. I don't remember why we decided on going there, but I wish that we hadn't. The food was terrible and to this day, I haven't ate at another one. On the positive side, however, I managed to eat a meal without spilling it all over me.

Once dinner was over, we went back to her apartment and watched TV. When we didn't find anything good on, we turned on the radio and talked instead. We talked for several hours about everything from work, motorcycles, kids, wrestling, movies, and music. Strangely, I delved deeper into my life than she did into hers.

As the night continued on, one thing led to another and, you guessed it, we had sex (even after she got finished laughing at the size of my little buddy). I didn't plan on that happening at all and was thus unprepared as far as protection went. She, on the other hand, was prepared and had all things covered—if you will. Now to me, a girl having a supply of condoms doesn't sound all that great, but at least she's responsible.

I couldn't complain too much about losing my virginity. It was fun and it gave me a feeling that I had never experienced before. I lasted about two minutes once we started the main course, which I don't think was too bad at all for my first time. Sharon got what she was after in the same amount of time, so we both won—kind of.

As great as it was to get off of the virgin wagon, I had a little bit of regret. I had only known her for five days and this was just our second evening together. It totally went against what I was wanting my first time to be. Even now I regret it—not with it being with Sharon, but because of how soon it happened.

I didn't realize it at the time, but she had a harder time with it. I didn't mean anything by it, but I went home afterward. She had asked me to spend the night, but I declined simply because her house was such a dump. I had every intention of seeing her again and even told her that I would see her on Tuesday. It wasn't until I got to understand women a little better that I figured out why she was hurt. Here she just gave her body to a guy and he then drives off into the night. She must have felt worse than a whore—at least whores get paid for that. Needless to say, I started dealing with her messy house and spent the night on weekends after that. It was also a bonus in the sense that we could spend two days together instead of one.

I liked spending time with her. She didn't bitch about the music that I listened to or make fun of my interests. She thought that it was great that I had a dog for a best friend. She even treated my pickup with respect by not slamming my doors and fingering up my windows. Aside from going to Applebee's, we hardly ever went out to dinner. Most of the time she cooked and we ate at her place.

Every other weekend, I would go pick her up, and sometimes Katelynn too, so she could stay with me at home. I don't really know how Dad felt about her staying in my room, but he allowed it after I asked him. He reacted much better about it than I did when Debbie started spending the night in his room a year or so earlier.

Things were going pretty well until around Thanksgiving when she dropped a huge bomb on me when she finally let me in on her life prior to meeting me. I could sense the uncertainty in her voice as she began to open up to me.

"I need to tell you the truth about me," was what she led off with.

I could have never imagined what I was about to hear.

Sharon had never met her biological father. Much like Katelynn's father, he too denied her as being his own. Her mother, Debbie, went on to marry a man named John Anderson (not the country singer). Together, they had a son, John Jr. According to Sharon, her step-dad gave her nothing but verbal, physical, and sexual abuse for many years while her mother was battling a brain infection. At thirteen, she moved in with Tonya.

Once in middle school, Sharon succumbed to peer pressure, as would any kid who had parents that treated them like hers did. At fifteen, she had her first child after being raped at a party one night. As soon as she gave birth to the child, he was immediately taken away and put up for adoption. She attempted to go back to school but was treated as an outcast, so she quit.

By eighteen, she was married and had another baby. Her husband got her heavily into drugs and spent more time beating the shit out of her than anything else. He spent months at a time in jail for dealing drugs and for burglaries, while she tried to care for their child. In order to save what was left of her life, she signed over custody of the kid and left them and the drugs behind.

Soon, she met another guy, Katelynn's father, Dan. Shortly after Katelynn was born, they split up, leaving her as a single parent who was solely in charge of seeing that her daughter had food and a place to stay. She didn't receive any child support until she was able to prove that Dan was the father, leaving her paycheck as the only way of supporting herself and her kid.

If you just look at the obvious part, three different kids from three different men, you will likely think of her as a bargain-basement slut or something even worse. But if you look at the broader picture, you will see a girl who had the worst possible luck and who is constantly trying to better herself, all the while looking for the family life that every young girl dreams about. Unfortunately, she met the wrong guys and they took advantage of a person who wants nothing more out of life than to make people happy. She had spent all of her life starting over, unwilling to quit on the shitty hand that she was dealt. How many people do you know like that? And better yet, are they even still alive?

Once I heard all of this, I was blown away. I'm not going to lie, it hasn't been an easy thing to deal with. Any other guy would have ran from it. But not me. I'm not a quitter. I wasn't going to be just another statistic. I was going to devote myself to righting the ship that was slowly sinking. I want to be clear about this—my decision to continue the relationship was not out of guilt or pity. I continued it because I found out that we were the same, just on opposite sides of the spectrum. No matter what gets thrown our way, we adapt, improvise, and overcome—and she was heads and shoulders above me. If she could get through that shit, then the two of us together would be unstoppable. Our first test was right around the corner.

CHAPTER 41

Leaving My Family To Start My Own

Since Sharon and I began seeing each other, we spent all of our weekends together. Additionally, we would see each other once or twice a week if her work schedule coincided with my delivery days. Just after Thanksgiving, however, I was pulled from that route to start delivering to the Sedro-Woolley, Mount Vernon, Burlington-Edison, and Bellingham School Districts. Regardless of why I was switched, the fact remained that I was finished on that route. It now meant that I had even less opportunities to see Sharon. Instead, all I got to hear was gossip from Kenny about what kind of person that Sharon really was.

I already knew the story, though. As I said earlier, just given the facts, Sharon was frowned upon for what went on in her past. From her boss' point of view, that he also shared with Kenny, Sharon just nailed every guy that she could to get herself pregnant and thus force him to stay with her. First of all, it wasn't any of their business to begin with. Second, it is impossible to educate close-minded idiots, so they wouldn't know better anyway.

It was extremely difficult for me to hear things like that even though that I knew the truth. For several months, it bothered me every time that the thought crossed my mind. I believed what she said to me but with the facts being what they were, I still had a hard time looking past that in order to remember why that it happened. It didn't happen overnight believe me, but eventually I forgot about it in order to focus on our future, or else there wasn't going to be one.

As for my new route, I didn't care for it too much at all. I was now driving a smaller, boxed truck as opposed to a tractor-trailer. Instead of seeing Sharon once or twice a week, I had to see nearly fifty middle-aged, nagging, and often bitchy lunch ladies. On a positive note, I did get to see Mom a couple of times a week. (And no I didn't include her in the previous category.) I had to get used to the change if I still wanted to run a route. I did and would spend the next two-and-a-half years dealing with it, all the while waiting for my opportunity to drive a real truck again.

Back at home, things between me and Dad were getting worse. It was just as much my fault as it was his, but there wasn't going to be a winner in the constant power struggle. He made it clear on a daily basis that it was his house and not mine. While I was aware of that, I reminded him that I was paying to live in his house while Jen and Debbie didn't have to. Out of protest, I stopped mowing the lawn and helping him with the chores. Honestly, I was expecting him to get in my face over it so we could fight it out once and for all. It didn't happen. But to even hope that it would meant that it was time for one of us to leave.

I was twenty years old by this time and made more than enough money to support myself. It wasn't healthy for me to have somebody telling me what to do when I was old enough to make my own decisions. At the same time, it wasn't healthy for Dad to have a cancer in his house disrupting his developing relationship with Debbie. Combine that with the opportunity to further my relationship with Sharon, and she and I moved into together just after New Year's Day in 2002.

We rented an older, double-wide mobile home just east of Lyman on a half-acre lot. Both the house and detached shop had been slightly neglected over the years. The buildings could have used a paint job to cover up the poop-brown color that they currently had on display. The inside was nice, but it showed its age. There was mold on the windows, leaks in the roof, and divots in the floor. That being said, for $775 a month and a chance to not have to answer to a higher power, I was going to be living the life of luxury.

It took a while to sell Sharon on the idea of moving up here. While she was all for us moving in together, she would have preferred that I move down to Lake Stevens or Everett. I flat-out refused to move to the city and I told her so. With me not ever having lived in a city, I wasn't going to try to adapt to both that and living with a woman at the same time. It's not just me—how often do you see somebody from the country up and move to the city? It's pretty much the other way around, right? It is a culture shock that people like me avoid like the plague.

Knowing that we could live pretty well on two incomes, Sharon got a job at the Lyman Tavern as a bartender. While it may not be the most glamorous job in the world, it helped pay the bills. And although she had to dress slightly provocative and deal with drunks trying to grab her on a regular basis, she raked in more than twice her pay on tips alone.

The week before we were scheduled to move in, Dad and I each took a car load of Sharon's stuff out of her Lake Stevens apartment and stored it out in the shop. She didn't have much other than a few boxes of clothes, that futon, a table, a shelf, and Katelynn's stuff. I also loaded up the 27" TV that her roommate was renting because I had to cover his last two week's rent when he claimed that he was out of money. He said that he would pay me back but then stopped returning my calls once I made the second payment. Let that be a lesson—don't make deals with anyone (especially me) if you don't intend on following through with your end.

After one final week of living at Dad's, we moved into our rental the following weekend. Dad helped us both load up at his house and unload at our place, but I think the only reason was to get me out quicker. (Just kidding—I think.) Everything went fine until the very end.

I always intended on taking Tuco with me when the time came for me to move out. After all, he wouldn't have been in the family in the first place if it wasn't for me. I spent the most time with him, fed and bathed him more than anyone else, and even bought all of his food and paid his vet bills over the past couple of years. It was only right that he go with me because he was mine.

"The dog stays with the family," Dad said.

"What?!"

"You heard me."

"Why? He's my dog!"

"No, he's a family dog and he stays with the family."

I couldn't believe it! Out of one last show of authority, Dad was taking my best friend away from me. Why didn't he just take a stake and jab it in my heart? I wasn't taking Debbie or any of his stuff with me, so how was this fair? It was hard enough emotionally to leave home and now I had to leave my buddy behind also? I was so sick of him that I went along with it, anything to just get out of there for good. But shame on you, Dad. Shame on you for costing me a few months of time with my best friend that I can never get back. That's a wound that you inflicted on me that will never heel. I forgave Mom for what she did, but I will never forgive you.

A few months later, Dad did give him back to me, but it wasn't out of the kindness of his heart. To be fair, Dad doesn't have a set work schedule and therefore often times doesn't come home until late. When he gets home, he may not have enough time or energy to spend with Tuco, who had been cooped up in the house all day long. Bored and angry, Tuco tore up every blind in Dad's house. Dad, in turn, gave him to me—along with a $300 repair bill.

"What's this?" I asked as he gave me a receipt from Home Depot.

"Your dog caused it and you're paying for it."

I didn't even bother arguing. If that's what it took for me to have my dog back, it was worth it. The other reason that I paid for it was because I didn't want to make things any worse between us than they already were. I regret it, though. If I had to do it all over again, I wouldn't have gave him the money. It was his idea to keep him in the first place and I believe it was him that used to say, "If you shit the bed, you must sleep in it."

The irony of it all was that Tuco never once tore anything up when he moved in with me. I could leave him just as long or longer and he wouldn't mess with anything in the house. It sounds to me like he either didn't want to live at Dad's or he just wanted to be with me.

As I said, I didn't need this extra shit on my mind when Sharon and I moved in together. It was going to be hard enough to be the head of the household, responsible for a woman, and responsible for a child. Although it was unofficial, I had to get used to being married and raising children and I didn't have time for on-the-job training. It is like playing stud poker—you play with what you are dealt.

We spent our first night at our new home unpacking and putting things away. Aside from the Tuco situation, Dad was very generous. He gave us a set of dishes, pots and pans, a dining room set, a refrigerator, and a washer and dryer. Before you start to think of him as a saint, they were all just collecting dust out in the shop. Regardless of their condition, we were glad to have them and I thanked him for his generosity. The oddest thing that he gave us, though, woke us up the next morning.

Dad had raised chickens at his house every since we moved to Pinelli Road. He primarily raised Rhode Island Reds but lately had been starting to raise Araucanas, which originated from Chile. By accident, one of the Araucana chicks (that he had hoped would all be hens) turned out to be a rooster. He turned mostly white, so we named him Whitey. The problem with Whitey was that he had an odd sounding crow. Worse yet, he would do it in the middle of the night. On two occasions, Dad shot at him with a .22 from inside the house. Whitey wasn't hit but he did runoff and was gone for a few days before he would come back.

I hadn't been away from home 24 hours when I heard that familiar crow.

"What is it?" Sharon asked as I flew out of bed.

"It was a rooster," I answered.

"In the house?" (I swear that she asked me that.)

"No, he's outside."

"But we don't have any chickens."

"I know."

"Is it the neighbor's?"

"I don't know."

I got up and looked out the window and there stood Whitey in my front yard along with an Araucana hen.

"We have chickens now," I called back to her.

"What?!"

"Whitey's here."

"Ugghh."

"Come on, chickens are great."

"I don't want to listen to that every morning."

Dad did it as a joke. I called him up to thank him because I actually liked Whitey. He followed me around while I was outside doing work, just like a dog would. Both him and his woman slept twenty feet off the ground in the top of a tree alongside our driveway. They stayed until Tuco moved in and he decided to have the hen for lunch. Whitey stayed for a while after that but kept his distance. Soon, he went over to the neighbor's house a couple of hundred yards away during the day and started spreading his seed and creating Little Whiteys. He would still come back at night for a few months, but eventually he moved away for good.

The next night was my first night of being a dad. Until now, Katelynn had little if any structure or routine in her life. It wasn't anybody's fault, but it was true. Katelynn slept with her mom every night, she watched Disney movies all day, she wasn't potty trained, and she cried all the time. With Sharon working until one in the morning every night, I was going to be the one that would spend the majority of the time with her because I was off early and only worked four days a week.

Before anything got started, I told Sharon that I only wanted Katelynn calling me Eddie. I didn't want her to call me dad because if something happened, I didn't want her thinking that I was her father and that I had left her. It would be bad enough someday when she found out the truth about her real deadbeat dad. She didn't need any more confusion.

Katelynn's dad still wasn't in the picture. He did find out that Sharon was moving and that Katelynn was obviously moving too. He wasn't happy because he now had to drive further to see his kid (when it was convenient for him), instead of having his mom transporting her for him. He was also mad because he now had to start paying child support for someone who he denied was even his. It's funny because he did the exact same thing to another child that he fathered. Funnier still, he calls Sharon a whore for having different children with different partners. What a hypocrite.

Sharon had no intentions of keeping Katelynn from seeing her father. The opportunities were there, he just wouldn't take the time to see her unless someone that he knew was coming up our way. He never called his daughter, sent her letters, or anything like that for more than a year. Boy, I wish I had such a loving father, don't you?

Anyway, I had it all planned out as I dropped Sharon off at work for her Saturday night shift—I was going to put Katelynn to bed after we ate dinner together at the table and took turns sitting on the toilet to try to go to the bathroom. I was confident that things would go great. They went over like a lead balloon instead.

As soon as Sharon got out of the truck, Katelynn started bawling. *No big deal.* I figured that it would be fine once we got back home. Nope—she cried harder and louder instead. I tried holding her—nothing. I tossed her up in the air and caught her like she loved to do. She stopped just long enough to catch her breath before she started in again. I made her dinner—nothing. She even cried while she was playing with her toys.

After a five hour run of continuous crying, she fell asleep on the living room floor. I planned on just leaving her there while I relaxed and watched some TV. A peaceful hour went by and then she woke up crying, seemingly right where she left off.

"Katelynn, why are you crying?" I asked.

"WAHH! WAAH!"

I did somersaults, talked in funny voices, did handstands—anything to get her to laugh and to take her mind off of crying. She would acknowledge me for two or three seconds and give me a little giggle. It was short lived, because it was back to crying in her next breath. By now, though, she wasn't even shedding tears.

Sharon called me at about 1:30 in the morning and said that she was ready to be picked up. My plan was to have Katelynn in bed and just leave her home for the five minutes that it would take to go pick her up. Well that wasn't going to happen, so I just loaded Katelynn into the truck while she kept on crying.

"Why is she still awake?" an irritated Sharon asked when we pulled up to get her.

"She hasn't stopped crying since you got out of the truck."

"Why?"

"If I knew, she probably would have stopped, don't you think?"

"Oohh—it's okay, baby," Sharon coddled. "Mama's here."

Of course Katelynn shut up on the spot. *This was going to be fun.* Sharon had babied the child for so long that it was going to take forever to to figuratively get Katelynn off of her tit. Even worse, as long as Sharon continued to give in to her, it would slow any progress that we would make. But I had four nights a week when Sharon wasn't home to do it the hard way. If it killed me, I was going to get Katelynn to sleep in her own bed, go to the bathroom in the toilet, and to stop crying for no reason.

The crying when we dropped Sharon off at work eventually stopped. Once we got home, I just put her in the corner and told her not to come out until she was finished. At first she would try to come out and I would put her right back, telling her that she could only come out once she stopped her crying. Sometimes I would even sit behind her to make sure that she wouldn't escape. I wouldn't let her eat, play, or anything until she quit. It worked, but it took a few days. She still would cry over any little thing, but at least she wouldn't cry just because we dropped her mom off at work.

The most important thing to me at the time was to get Katelynn to sleep in her own bed. She had her own room at this house and her own little toddler bed so there wasn't an excuse for her not to. Unfortunately, she had slept with her mom all of her life and that was what she was used to. That was just as much Sharon's fault because she was certain that her daughter was going to stop breathing in the middle of the night and die. She told me that if they slept together, then it wouldn't happen. Please.

Beings I wasn't getting much help from Sharon, I again took it upon myself to work on it while she was at work. At first I just shut her in her room at 8:00 and let her cry herself to sleep. Relentlessly, she would wake up right where she left off. Seriously, if she fell asleep at "waa," she would wake up with "aahh." This was clearly not going to work because she would start to associate going to bed with something like a punishment.

Plan B called for me giving her what she wanted—in a way, of course. She refused to go to bed, so I wouldn't let her go to bed. She wanted to watch a movie, knowing that she was used to falling asleep that way—not happening. She wanted to set in my lap, knowing that she was also used to falling asleep that way—not a chance. It wasn't because I didn't want to snuggle, but it just wasn't the right time for that. Any other time I was all for it, but not at bedtime. The only thing that I let her do was stand up.

Now you may think that something like that is abusive, but it wasn't to me. She had gone two-plus years in the wrong direction and had to go all of the way back and start down the right path in a fraction of the time. I wanted her to know what getting tired really meant and what needed to happen in order for it to go away. She needed to know that sleep wasn't a bad thing, it's a good thing. I figured that having her standing still would have her begging for her bed—no such luck. She would fall asleep standing up, fall down, and jump right back up. She would absolutely refuse to give in and go to sleep. I would ask her every ten minutes if she was ready to go to bed and she would just shake her head from side to side, letting me know that she wasn't going down that easy. For a couple of weeks, she would stand up in the same spot from eight o' clock until when Sharon was off at 1:00.

For my third plan, I went away from being a drill sergeant to a kind, nurturing, and compassionate man. I bought her a book called *The Puppy Book* and I would put her to bed at 8:00 every night and spend five minutes or so reading it to her. Once it was done, I would tell her that I was going out to watch TV for a while and then I was going to bed. I also told her that her mom would be here when she woke up in the morning.

Two days was all it took. I only had to take her back to her room a few times, reread the story, and go through all of the same routine again to help drill it into her mind. Soon, even at two or three years old, she could recite that entire book, without missing a word, just by looking at the pages. When Sharon was home, we would both do it together as a family. It took about two months in all, but she eventually got it all figured out.

Staying asleep was the new problem. If she took a nap during the day, she would be up at midnight and not want to go back to sleep. If that happened, then we tried to redo the whole bedtime thing all over again in the middle of the night. At first she would wake up and get her attention by doing, what else, crying. I could get her back to sleep much quicker if I went in alone but if her mom was home, you could at least double the amount of time that it took. Once she got older, she would just get out of bed and walk into our room. Usually I would hear her and just point for her to go back to her room. Again, it would take a little bit more if her mom woke up too.

Katelynn got much better at the whole thing once we cut out the naps. She would sleep through the night and be bright and cheerful in the morning. On the days that I was home in the morning, I would fix her cereal and we would watch cartoons together. On the days that I was gone, Sharon would turn the TV on for her and go back to sleep for a little while because she had just been home from work for a couple of hours. Once in a while, she would get into mischief while Sharon was still in bed. It wasn't all on Sharon, because sometimes I slept through it too.

One morning, Katelynn got up and decided to get into the vapor rub. She stripped off all of her clothes, except for her underwear, and rubbed it on every inch of her body. While I had used the vapor rub on her before when she had a sore throat, I think she mainly did it to look like the wrestlers that we watched on TV, who would oil up with baby oil during interviews to make their muscles look bigger.

Although it seemed like an eternity, the sleeping problems were solved in a few months. The next order of business was the potty training. Until that point, Katelynn hadn't been consistently worked with to get her out of diapers. Sharon and I started having her sit on the toilet first thing in the morning and at each hour throughout the day as well. She would sit down on the pot, sing, talk, and do anything but go to the bathroom. After four or five minutes, she would pull her diaper up and fill it—every single time. Sharon and I tried rewards of ice cream, candy, money, actual underwear, and even her favorite movies—nothing worked. *How was this happening? I graduated with a 3.87 grade point average, eleventh highest in my class, and I couldn't outsmart a two year old.*

Finally I figured it out. She only went to the bathroom when her diaper was on, so I removed the diaper. I had tried that before by letting her wear real underwear, but that only made the messes bigger. Ever the unorthodox one, I just let her walk around in a T-shirt without any pants on. Again, there might be people out there that think that is abusive, but it worked—instantly. As soon as she had the urge to go and realized that she didn't have anything to catch it or absorb it, she rushed to the toilet. Two days of no pants, or no security as I call it, she was potty trained except for the usual accidents that are to be expected.

Despite all of the struggles, Katelynn and I had a great time together. Because Sharon was gone half of the nights each week, we would eat dinner together, watch TV together, play outside together, and do chores together. Wherever it was that I went, she would come along with me as my sidekick. I took her to work with me in the big truck, just as my dad did with me when I was her age, and we delivered schools, or stores, or whatever I was doing at the time. I treated her just like I would have treated my own child and nobody can ever deny that—ever.

Me and Katelynn vacuuming our living room

Once her real father appeared a year or so later, he suddenly felt that he was entitled to time with her because she needed to spend time with her "actual father." While that was true and we always told Katelynn about his existence, his only reason of seeing her was out of a combination of jealousy and guilt. To me, it was like a kid in school who wouldn't share his toys—Katelynn was an object that he had a right to and shouldn't have to share because she was all his. Well Dan, fathering a child makes you a dad about as much as standing in a garage makes you a car, and part-time parenting won't get you there any quicker.

Sharon continued to work four nights a week until two in the morning when the bar closed. She still wasn't driving so if I didn't transport her, one of her coworkers would so I could stay home and not have to interrupt Katelynn's sleep—or mine for that matter. When she was home she made dinner and all that housewife stuff, but she spent so much time sleeping that she didn't do very much housework. Again, it wasn't her fault that her hours were the way that they were, but I had a job too. *Why should I be the only one that does the work?* Things were pretty tense between us for a long time over that. I know that it may sound piddly, but any stress that builds over time isn't good. If I didn't say anything, it would explode someday and be much worse.

The other thing that I was on Sharon for was her smoking. In fairness, I have never done it and thus don't know how hard it may or may not be to quit. The thing was, she would say that she didn't smoke, yet I would find cigarette butts all over the house and in the backyard. It wasn't the smoking that was bothering me then, it was the lying. If she lied about that, what else could she be lying about? The possibilities were endless and with me always thinking the worst, it wasn't a great recipe. *Maybe she had a thing on the side with one of her customers?* I was underage so I couldn't just pop in and check on her, but to even think that I had to wasn't healthy. It was all stemming from a lie.

It didn't help matters when a guy called the house one night and expressed his undying love for her. I was furious. I yelled and swore at Sharon, who didn't deserve it, and just went nuts. Then I calmed down when she explained to me that he was just drunk. Even I knew from my few experiences with alcohol that it screws with your head. The guy could have very well had the hots for her, had a little liquid courage, and figured that he would give it a shot. Or they did have a thing on the side, which I refused to believe but would be lying if I said that I didn't think about it.

It was a blessing in disguise when she was let go over the summer. While we didn't have near the income, we still had enough money to do just fine. Plus, you can't put a price tag on piece of mind. No more smoke, drunks, or questions surrounding them. To me, that was worth much more to our family than two paychecks. We got to spend more time together, get to know each other better, and become closer.

We still had our moments, though. When we first got together, Sharon was on medication for mood stabilizers, stemming from the shit that had taken its toll on her brain from her past. Stupid me thought it was a silly excuse to take pills and that she should use her will power to get over it and to not have to rely on drugs. Well that was a bad idea. While she quit them because I asked her to, she was a head case. That's why I had to work with Katelynn while she was at work, why she fought with me about housework, and why she freaked out every time that Katelynn farted and then insisted that she go to the doctor. Once I became educated first hand, I learned that there was a difference between recreational and prescription drugs. While I had a relatively easy life, she had the polar opposite and needed help through it both emotionally and medically. Needless to say, she got back on her pills and we have been fine (with the occasional hiccups) ever since.

Once schools were out for the summer, I started delivering up to Vancouver, British Columbia, Canada five days a week to the loading docks where the Alaskan cruise ships docked. It was, and still is, big business for Dairy Valley to be the dairy supplier for the cruise lines. While our routes paid the company's bills, these deliveries are what makes the profit. At first I didn't mind making the deliveries. It was a change of pace and I didn't have to rush all the time in order to get the schools delivered before they started serving lunch. I was back to driving a tractor-trailer, which was very important to me, and I didn't usually have to start work until six or seven in the morning.

The trouble was, I was no longer in control of when I was done for the day. With a route, I'm finished when all of my deliveries have been made. When dealing with longshoremen, who live and die by the union, you're done when they decide to unload you. They were always checking their watches and making sure that they didn't work into their coffee or lunch breaks. Worse yet, they wouldn't even start on unloading a truck if they thought that it might come up against their break. That means that a fifteen minute break could mean an additional hour of wait time, which is nothing compared to waiting for them through their lunch break at 1:00. If I wasn't unloaded before lunch, most likely I would be there until 3:00 and would then have to fight traffic all the way home.

Then, of course, there was crossing the border twice a day. Crossing into Canada was nothing, all I had to do was show my I.D. and get my papers stamped. Coming home into my own country was a different story. I was constantly interrogated, searched, and even X-rayed just to return to my native land. While I understand and agree with the reasons for doing so, especially after 9/11, I would think that they would cut me some slack after seeing me five days a week. Unfortunately, the frequent travelers are the ones who smuggle the most stuff in thinking that they can get away with it.

Aside from the monotony of the border and the traffic, I never knew what I would see driving in the northeastern section of Vancouver. I would see hookers on every street corner, hundreds of homeless people huddled into every nook and cranny that they could find, and people doing drugs right there on the street. One day in the span of about two blocks, I saw an ambulance crew pull a sheet over the face of a guy who had just checked out and a policeman jump out of his car while driving through an intersection and proceed to beat the shit out a guy with his nightstick. Shit like that was typical in the areas that I had to drive through to get to the ships.

On certain days that I knew would be a quick trip, which was usually on Sundays, I would take Sharon or Katelynn with me. Usually it was Katelynn, due to Sharon's work schedule while she still had her job. Just like I did all those years ago with my dad, the two of us rolled up and down the road, laughing and carrying on, and listening to our favorite songs on the radio. It wasn't often, but each time that I heard Bon Jovi, Bruce Springsteen, The Georgia Satellites, Billy Joel, or any of those guys that I remembered listening to in Dad's truck, I smiled to myself and realized that I was coming full circle.

I was also saddened in a way because I no longer had that kind of relationship with my dad. Sure things were getting a little better between us now that I had moved out, but it was nowhere near back to how it was when I was riding in his truck and worshiping the ground that he walked on. I also knew that someday Katelynn and I would go through the same stuff, so I should enjoy it while it lasted.

For now, though, Katelynn and I were great buddies. For her third birthday, which is on July 16 by the way, Sharon and I got her a pink bicycle with training wheels. She never even had a tricycle before, let alone a place to ride it, but with where we lived now, she could burn up the asphalt all day long.

Beings she liked bikes so much now, I also began to ride her up and down the road on my Harley. She wasn't old enough yet to legally be on the highway, so we just went up and down the back roads. I would have hoped that Sharon would have wanted to ride with me as well, but she was scared to death to even try it. In the two times that I have had her on my bike since I have known her, we have traveled a grand total of a quarter-mile. She would rather hold a lit match and jump into a pool of gasoline. I wish that she could get past her fear or whatever it is that she doesn't like about them. I would love to be able to take weekend trips or even day rides with her. Instead, I take the kids—at least they enjoy it and aren't afraid of it.

For the entire month after Katelynn's birthday, we had something going almost every weekend. In early August, Jen and I went to the Skagit County Fair in Mount Vernon together to see Aaron Tippin, who is one of my favorite country singers, as he put on an outdoor concert. Sharon didn't get to go because she was sick or something, so I took her to see him a few years later when he came back to town to play at the Skagit Valley Casino in Burlington.

Three days later, all three of us went down to Seattle to see *Monday Night Raw* at the Key Arena, while Katelynn spent a few days at Mom's. Now called World Wrestling Entertainment (WWE) after losing a lawsuit to the World Wildlife Federation, the company was in a bit of a retro period while still transitioning to new talent. Even Hulk Hogan and Ric Flair were back to wrestle The Rock and Steve Austin in matches that nobody thought possible before.

In reality, wrestling was down considerably after it plateaued before the new millennium. Ted Turner sold Vince McMahon World Championship Wrestling, which also included wrestler contracts and video libraries. While it was great to watch the best talent in one show, there wasn't any competition to keep the product at a high level. It would be like only having NBC instead of also having ABC, FOX, and CBS to to choose from.

The very next night, Sharon and I went back down to Seattle to watch another WWE event that was going to be taped and aired at a later date. While I can't tell you who wrestled that night without looking it up, I can tell you that while we were there they announced that WrestleMania XIX was coming to Seattle on March 30, 2003 at SAFECO Field. Tickets weren't on sale yet, but I told Sharon right then and there that we were going to go at all cost.

At the end of August, Sharon and I again dropped Katelynn off at Mom's and drove over to the Gorge for Sharon's first concert. Heavy metal legend Ozzy Osbourne had lately been putting on a traveling music festival called Ozzfest, which showcased himself and various other heavy metal bands in the music world, and he was stopping in Washington. A sixty dollar ticket bought us twelve hours of live music—more (head)bang for your buck.

Neither one of us had clue about who anyone was until the last three acts. Tommy Lee, best known for being the drummer for Motley Crue and having made a sex tape with Pamela Anderson, was at the time in another band called Methods of Mayhem. When he played his guitar and sang, he was actually booed and had chants of "play the drums" directed towards him. The jeers did turn to cheers when he brought out a portable video camera that instantly projected his video onto the big screen that was behind him. He called it the "tittie cam" and asked for chicks to show them off and be on TV for us all to see. Thanks, Tommy!

The next guy that we were familiar with was Rob Zombie. He had previously led the band White Zombie before going solo and eventually into directing horror movies. The coolest thing about him was his banter towards the crowd that reminded me a lot of a wrestling promo.

"HOW THE FUCK ARE YOU!!" the dread-locked singer yelled.

The crowd went nuts.

"Thanks for coming out and sweating your asses of to listen to our shit tonight."

Everyone began to cheer even louder.

"And everyone of you needs a fuckin' shower!"

Everyone then started booing.

"Gotcha fuckers," he laughed, breaking into his first song.

Once he was finished and after ten hours of sweating in the heat, Ozzy came on and played a two hour set. After spending his whole life doing every conceivable drug, you can't understand a word that he says if he is asked a question on the spot. However, if he stands still and plays the same songs that he has played over the last thirty years, he is completely understandable. He played "Iron Man" and "Paranoid" from his Black Sabbath days and everything from "Suicide Solution" to "No More Tears" from his solo albums.

Late in the evening, I even ran into my old pal Joey Moore on the way to the bathroom. While I knew that he was coming, it took me all day to find him in the sea of humanity. He had actually been the one who had tipped me off to the tickets in the first place.

In the two years since graduation, he was pretty much the only person that I talked to on a regular basis. We would call each other and bullshit about wrestling, as we were most likely the two biggest fanatics in Washington State. He also told me one day that if Dairy Valley was ever hiring, he wanted me to call him so that he could come in and apply.

I've always been leery of recommending someone for a job or anything in general because if they fail, I think that it will make me look bad. But I had known Joey forever and aside from Archy, who had since fallen off the radar entirely, he is the only person that I would put my stamp of approval on. Not much later, a job did open up and he got it. I was right because he has been working with me ever since.

In October after cruise ship delivery season ended, I took my two weeks of vacation before I went back to delivering the schools. Throughout the summer, Sharon and I had kicked around the idea about the three of us taking a family trip. With me being the only one that was bringing in a paycheck, we had to go easy on the amount of money that we were going to shell out. Instead of doing a bunch of different things, we could really only afford one, so we chose Disneyland. Even if it was an option that we could afford, I still would have passed up on flying for driving.

For me, that's half the fun of the entire trip. While I still preferred traveling on a motorcycle, this was going to be my first major road trip on four wheels as the head of my own family.

Taking my pickup wasn't an option because we would have had to pack our luggage in the back seat with Katelynn to keep it dry if we came to any rain. Instead, we took our new GMC Jimmy that Sharon and I had bought a few months earlier. It wasn't really new—it was a 1997 with just one owner and it had nearly eighty thousand miles on it. It was a white, four-door 4x4 that was perfect for our little family.

The Jimmy was actually my third car that I ever bought. Two years earlier, I bought Debbie's 1990 For Thunderbird for a commuter car to save miles on my pickup. After a month, I blew the headgaskets, which Dad and I replaced, and it never ran the same again. Including all of the money that I put into it for engine work, brakes, rotors and drums, and tires, I paid nearly four thousand dollars for that car. I sold it for twelve hundred. It was a lesson learned, I guess.

Before we even left, I had done some investigating on the phone and bought us a room for three nights at a Best Western a few blocks away from the park itself. It came with a shuttle for the three of us to get back and forth and two, two-day passes to the park. (Although Katelynn was three, I was going to say that she was only two so I could get her in for free.) No it wasn't the Hilton or any of those upper-end places, but it was good enough for us because it worked within our means. We were a family that was just starting out and if that's all we could do, then so be it. At least we were taking a trip.

After spending the money for our time in Anaheim and adding up my estimates for the cost of gas and food, extra nights in a motel on the way down were out of the question. Instead, we packed our camping gear so we could stay in a much cheaper campground. I seemed to have forgotten that it was nearly Halloween and it could get cold at night—oops.

We left home at two in the morning on a Saturday to begin our twelve hundred-plus mile drive. The reasons that I like to leave that early are because we can get through Seattle without the nasty traffic slowing our roll, and because I can get the majority our driving done on the first day. That way we could check into our room in Anaheim early and get rested up for Disneyland. But the main reason is so I can get as many miles out of the way as possible before the girls woke up and all I would hear was "I'm hungry" and "I gotta go potty." After all, it hadn't been that long since I had to listen to that on road trips with Mom and Jen.

I managed to knock off nearly 250 miles before both Sharon and Katelynn simultaneously woke up in Portland, Oregon and wanted to stop and eat and go to the bathroom. Although by this time Katelynn was out of diapers, she still had to be told to go to the bathroom or else she would gladly go in her pants. I had already planned on stopping every hour to prevent such occurrences and actually considered myself lucky to have made it as far as we did before it started.

After breakfast, I spent the next hour trying to get back on the freeway. For some reason, the signs that directed drivers to the interstate weren't very clear. Usually they will read "North I-5" or "South I-5." Sure enough, I got on the northbound lane and had to cross back into Washington before I could get off and turn around. Once I did that, I again got on the wrong road and ended up on the campus of Lewis and Clark College and spent the next ten minutes trying to find my way out of there. As pissed off as I was, I had to laugh because now I knew how Dad felt when he used to get turned around on trips and had to listen to Jen and I giggling at him from the backseat.

Following our extended pit stop, we spent the rest of the day driving and stopping, driving and stopping, and—you get the picture. As we pulled into Stockton, California in the evening to have dinner at McDonald's, I figured that it was time that we should start looking for a place to camp for the night. The people at the McDonald's didn't have any idea about any campgrounds so I went to the building across the street to ask them. Sharon had the creeps and didn't want to stay in the car so she and Katelynn went in with me. As we walked up to the door, some guy gave us a very funny look as he made his way out of the building. I never thought anything of it as the three of us continued inside. Once we passed through the second door, I knew exactly why he looked at me the way he did—we were in a porn store with a three year old girl! Embarrassed beyond belief, we just got back into the car and got out of town as quick as possible.

A short time later right around dusk, I saw a campground sign on the freeway that said one was just five miles off of the interstate. We found it without any problem and decided to spend the night there. Nobody else was around so we just "ignored" the pay station and pitched the tent for a free night's lodging. When we woke up the next morning with a thick layer of frost lining the outside of the tent and a car thermometer that read 27 degrees, we knew why we were the only ones there. I heard about that the rest of the way to Anaheim.

"So help me God, I'm never going to go on another trip with you if you ever make us camp like that again," Sharon said about thirty times throughout the rest of the day.

Once we got to our room that afternoon, we went to the grocery store to buy cereal and snacks so we could save money on restaurant food. We had a small refrigerator in our room so we could even buy milk for the cereal and lunch meat for sandwiches. Again, it may not be everyone's idea of a vacation, but we were on a budget. If we could eat our stuff from the room for breakfast and lunch, then all we had to buy was dinner.

For the next two days, we were in Disneyland from open until close. Sharon wasn't the kind for rides so it was up to me and Katelynn to ride every ride that she could go on. I even managed to sneak in Space Mountain and Thunder Mountain Railroad while the girls took a few pictures with some of the characters. As much fun as I had there as a kid, it was twice as much fun doing it as an adult. Watching a kid have the time of her life was absolutely priceless.

We packed up and headed for home on Wednesday morning. I managed to get myself lost again in Hollywood attempting to find the Harley-Davidson shop to buy a T-shirt. While I was looking for a dealership, I should have been looking for a Harley clothing store. I never did find it, but we did drive into Warner Brothers and Universal Studios trying to find our way out of town. The security guards didn't find the humor in my directional errors.

We spent so much time trying to find our way out of town that we ended up wasting most of the day. As luck would have it, we were right back at the same campground by nightfall. I managed to convince Sharon to camp one more time because there was no way that it would get down to 27 degrees again, as it was just a freak thing. I was right, it was 25 degrees the next morning instead—oops.

The next morning we picked up a girl in Lodi, California to give her a ride back to Lyman. It wasn't some random hitchhiker or anything. What happened was while Sharon was still working, she had offered to one of her bar customers that we could pick her up for her in order to save her a trip down there. She was a nice girl but didn't like Lyman so she moved back to Lodi a short time later.

With all of the stops that I had to make to accommodate three girls now, we had to spend one more night on the road. Sharon put her foot down on the camping so I had to spring for a motel in Portland. Wouldn't you know, I got lost the next morning on the way to the freeway and ended up at that same goddamn college.

The three of us had such a wonderful time on our trip that we could hardly wait until our next one. While we eventually would take another trip, it would no longer be with just the three of us because while we were at Disneyland, Sharon and I gave new meaning to the phrase "Happiest Place on Earth." Right or wrong, like it or not, and ready or not, we were going to have a baby of our own.

CHAPTER 42

THE Most Stressful Nine Months

Obviously we didn't know right away that Sharon was pregnant. While she may or may not have known towards the end of November, I wasn't told about it until early December. The only reason that I say that is because I have been told that women know when they're pregnant, and I don't mean by the obvious missing of their period—they feel it. At least that's what I've been told, but who knows?

Before we even knew that Sharon was pregnant, November was a month chock-full of unexpected expenditures. Somehow Sharon had forgotten to mention to me she had accumulated a little bit of debt over the course of her life. By the time everything was paid off, I had shelled out nearly four thousand dollars for shit that I didn't have any part of. While I certainly wasn't happy about it, I paid them all off. I didn't do it because I felt obligated to do so, I did it because it had to be done. The longer you wait, the worse it gets.

As stressful as that was, the trouble that we had with Katelynn was much greater. Between Sharon's insistence on unnecessary trips to the doctor and the emergency room as well as the necessary ones, we had to be at the hospital for that child at least every other week. Every third or fourth trip was legitimate. All inside of a month, she had a tonsillectomy, an abscess on her gum, four teeth pulled and some crown work, and a cut labium that resulted from her falling out of an apple tree. Luckily she was covered by welfare and we didn't have to pay a thing.

The one bright side of the month was when Sharon and I and Dad, and Jen went to the Tacoma Dome to see Guns n' Roses, my all-time favorite band. Thank God the tickets had been purchased three months earlier or else I wouldn't have been able to afford it. The only thing that would keep us from seeing the show would be the volatile Axl Rose, who skipped the previous night's tour opener in Vancouver, B.C.

As a result of constant fighting for control within the band, Guns N' Roses split up in the mid-90's. Axl had everyone sign over their rights so that he would have complete control of everything. New members came and went, unable to deal with him. With the exception of internet rumors, the band was out of the public eye for several years.

Out of nowhere, Gn'R returned in late 2000 with the promise of a new album (which didn't come out until 2008) and an accompanying tour. Two years later, the tour was announced and we all bought tickets when we found out that they were coming to town. Knowing Axl's history, I wasn't going to get my hopes up until I saw him on stage.

After a shitty opening set by some band called CKY, the lights went down and a train whistle blew, indicating the start of "Nightrain." Once the music started, he hit the stage with his trademark headband and nut-hugging bicycle shorts. The band scorched through "Welcome To The Jungle," "Sweet Child O' Mine," and all of my favorites. From where we sat, ten rows up from the right side of the stage, I could see that he had a teleprompter (like you would read while doing karaoke) there to remind him of his lyrics. At first I was a little disappointed but after I heard an interview with Billy Joel about the subject, I found that most singers in fact use them as a backup. Joel referred to it as his "security blanket."

Only Axl and keyboardist Dizzy Reed remained from the band's original lineup. (Reed technically wasn't an original member but he had been around since the late 80's.) Gone were Slash, Duff McKagen, Izzy Stradlin, and Steven Adler. In their places were Buckethead, Tommy Stinson, Richard Fortus, Robin Fink, and Bryan "Brain" Mantia. It didn't matter, they sounded just as great to me.

Buckethead, the lead guitarist, was not quite as good as Slash (nobody is), but he was close. Wearing a hockey mask and an empty box of Kentucky Fried Chicken for a hat, he tore through the solos of "November Rain," Knockin' On Heaven's Door," and "Rocket Queen" without missing a beat. During an extended solo he even played the *Star Wars* theme and the "Star Spangled Banner."

I was thrilled beyond belief to see my favorite band. The guy next to me missed the entire show because he had drank himself into unconsciousness. I never could figure out why people would want to do that to themselves and miss something so cool. I don't see anything wrong with having a few drinks, but you miss too much if you overdo it. I learned my lesson after hitting the whiskey too hard and missing an NFL playoff game that I really wanted to see. Since then, a few drinks (if any at all) is fine but I don't want to miss anything big that doesn't happen everyday, especially a concert like that.

Now that I was twenty-one, I did drink a little more than just on motorcycle trips. While doing so, I still knew better than to drive afterward. Dad got himself busted one night and had to get one of those "blow-and-go" things just to drive his car. He even had to get one for his motorcycle. The funny part was two minutes after you get going, you had to blow again and watching Dad try to steady his bike as he rode down the highway and blow into his machine was a real gas. It finally taught him the lesson that I had tried to warn him about (and eventually gave up on) over the past couple of years.

A few weeks before Christmas was when Sharon told me what was happening inside her.

"I think I'm pregnant," she said with a great deal of uncertainty in her tone.

"Are you sure," I said. "How?"

She looked at me like I was an idiot because she thought that I meant "how did it happen?"

"No, how do you know?"

"I just do."

I got real nervous. It wasn't because she was pregnant, it was because I had to tell my parents. Even though we lived on our own and were raising a child, I still cared deeply about what my parents thought of me. I wanted them to be proud of me and I thought for sure that it was going to be impossible for that to happen if this pregnancy thing was true.

It wasn't so much Dad as it was Mom. For some reason, she and Sharon didn't hit it off very well at all. I think a lot of it was Mom having a hard time coming to terms that I had a new dominate female in my life. I really dreaded telling her, but we were getting a little ahead of ourselves—she still needed professional confirmation.

"Yep, you're pregnant," was all the nurse said at the doctor's office.

"You're mad," Sharon accused.

"No, I'm not mad," I argued. "I'm just shocked."

"Why? I told you that I was."

"I know."

"Well?"

"Well, what?"

"We're going to have a baby."

Now I had to tell everyone.

I figured that I would start with Dad because it would be a little easier, so Sharon and I went up and told him together. I went about it wrong by telling him with my head down in a cowering way. I should have told him like I was proud of what was happening, but I didn't.

"Sharon is pregnant," I said quietly with body language like a dog that was waiting to be scolded.

"Oh really?" he said, not too surprised. "How do you feel about that?"

"I don't know."

The truth was, I was happy because I always wanted my own child. I was just ashamed of myself because I had always wanted to be married first. It was my own fault because we had stopped using protection a while ago. While we were still careful to not let any live rounds go where they shouldn't, it happened anyway.

Seeing that I was down, Dad started giving me some much needed encouragement about the situation. Within a few minutes we were laughing and looking ahead to all of the joy that a newborn child would bring. Not that I wasn't happy with Katelynn, but I missed all of the baby time because she wasn't mine.

Then I got nervous again when he said, "Did you tell your mom?"

Damn. For a moment I forgot all about her.

"She's going to find out, you know? You better be the one to tell her."

I knew that he was right, I just didn't want to do it. Reluctantly, I picked up the phone the next day and asked her to come over on Wednesday after she was off work so I could talk to her about something. I asked Sharon to go to her friend's house so I could tell her alone because I had no idea what her reaction would be.

"What is it, son?" she asked as she walked through the door.

"Well," I began. "It's about me and Sharon."

She later told me that she thought I was going to tell her that we were splitting up. You can imagine the look on her face when I told her the real deal.

"Sharon and I are going to have a baby."

Her eyes instantly became the size of watermelons.

"What?!"

She wasn't mad, she was just surprised because like I said, she wasn't expecting me to say that. For whatever reason, whenever Mom hears potentially catastrophic news, she instantly gets the runs. She no sooner than said "what" before she ran off to the toilet. After she was finished, she would come back, say a few words, and she was back on the pot. I eventually had to finish the discussion from the outside of the bathroom while she was taking care of business inside.

It wasn't as bad as I imagined. I was questioned a little bit about our judgment from both Mom and Dad but for the most part, I got the support and encouragement that I was after. No longer was I nervous—I was proud. *I was going to be a father!* But the father of what? A boy? A girl? I had enough estrogen in my house already so I was pulling for a boy.

After everything was starting to settle down, Katelynn once again found her way back to the emergency room. I wasn't even home at the time because I had driven over the pass to Leavenworth to have dinner with Papa and Gladys for Christmas. While I was there, I was going to tell Papa that he was going to be a great-grandfather. Dad, who went over there in his own car, had news to tell him too—he and Debbie were getting married. We joked that if those two bombshells didn't kill him, then nothing would.

After we told him the news and right as the waitress was passing out the menus, my cell phone rang with an hysterical Sharon on the other end.

"GET HOME NOW! Tuco bit Katelynn in the face! I called an ambulance! HURRY!"

"WHAT?!"

"Her face—it's bleeding bad!"

Something didn't add up—Tuco had never, and I mean never, bit a human. He may latch on to an arm while he was wrestling, but he would never bite a person. He would fight a dog, kill a rabbit, kill a chicken, and I even watched him attack and kill a deer in my front yard, but he would not hurt a person.

"If you told 911 that it was a dog bite, they are going to send animal control over. DO NOT let them take my dog."

"I won't, just get over here!"

Easier said than done because I was three hours away. Thank God everything had calmed down once I got home. Katelynn had a stitch of two in her lip and the doctor said that it certainly was not a dog bite. What happened was, Katelynn was in her room singing Christmas carols in Tuco's face. His main display of affection was extending his paw forward and to either show his appreciation or to get her to shut up, he pawed her face. Katelynn screamed and Sharon came in and saw blood, so you can see how it was misconstrued.

Christmas came and went without anymore strange shit going down. For the first time since I was younger, I enjoyed myself and even found myself believing in Santa Claus again. Seeing Katelynn open her present that the fat guy in the red suit left her brought a lot of joy to my heart. Just seeing the smile on her face and hearing the excitement in her voice brought back memories of when I was her age and when I actually gave a damn about the holidays.

Sharon, me, and Katelynn in our first family picture

Everyone has a few select things that they simply must do or see before they die. Some people want to go into space or some farfetched shit like that. For me it's pretty simple—I want to set foot in all fifty states (I currently have twelve to go), someday I want to see a 49ers game at Candlestick Park (which I will do on my thirtieth birthday on September 11, 2011), and I want to go to WrestleMania. I figure that if I aim small, I miss small. One of my three wishes came true on March 30, 2003.

Jen and I went up to a ticket outlet in Bellingham on a January morning and stood in line for five hours until the doors opened, just to be the first ones with the opportunity to buy tickets for WrestleMania XIX at SAFECO Field when they went on sale to the public at ten a.m. I tried all week on various radio stations to win the tickets but was unsuccessful. I knew the answer to every question that was asked on air, I just couldn't get a line through. Alas, I had to buy them. 54,097 tickets were sold in a matter of minutes, selling out and setting the attendance record at the home of the Seattle Mariners. I bought six tickets, forty rows from the ring (the best available), for $75 bucks apiece at 10:03 a.m. At 10:04, I had the tickets in my hand. I didn't even know who was going to be wrestling that night, and I didn't care—I was going to WrestleMania!

In the next two months, the matches were announced as the storylines unfolded on TV. They could have been the worst performers to ever suit up and it wouldn't have bothered me. This was the biggest show of the year in the form of entertainment that I grew up on. Think of your favorite team, television show, or band at their absolute peak and you get to watch it unfold live and in person—that's what it felt like to me. On the Sunday of the event, myself, Sharon, Dad, Jen, Joey, and the teenage son of one of Sharon's former coworkers, all carpooled down to Seattle. Over the course of four hours, ten matches took place. Though they were all good, only a few stood out above the rest due to their significance.

The main event for the World Heavyweight Championship was contested between Kurt Angle and Brock Lesnar. Everyone knows that this form of wrestling has predetermined outcomes that are performed by highly skilled athletes and entertainers, some of whom don't know a wristlock from a wristwatch. These two men were different. Lesnar once won the NCAA Finals, while Angle won a gold medal in the 1996 Olympics in Atanta in freestyle wrestling. Lesnar won the match, despite knocking himself unconscious when he landed on his head after doing a flip off the top turnbuckle. The impact echoed throughput the building and it gave me sick feeling in the pit of my stomach. Wrestlers are trained to fall, but accidents happen. Having watched this forever, I can tell if something isn't right and this was it. He finished the match but spent the next few days in the hospital.

The match before that was between The Rock and "Stone Cold" Steve Austin, arguably the two performers that were most responsible for bringing wrestling to it's peak in the late 90's. It was a classic between two pros but it wasn't until the end that I understood the significance. While Rock went on to wrestle a couple more matches before jumping into making movies, this was Austin's final match ever.

To you, it would be like seeing Hank Aaron's 755th home run or The Beatles final concert. While those guys may or may not have been the very best at what they did, you can't mention the history of their trade without talking about them. I was thrilled to be able to see it in person.

The biggest match of the night (and most nonathletic) was between Hulk Hogan and Vince McMahon. Both men beat each other to a bloody pulp but again, it was the significance of the match that stood out. Although not a wrestler, McMahon as a promoter was responsible for starting the event in 1985 as well as for putting out all of the tapes, toys, and magazines that I had grown up on. In Hogan, you had the greatest professional wrestler ever and my childhood hero competing in what would be his final WrestleMania match. So in the match, you had two of the three most inspirational human beings in my life performing right in front of me. To top it off, "Rowdy" Roddy Piper got involved in the match and it was like taking a trip in a time machine back to 1985. I was like a kid in a candy store or better yet, I was myself at five years old, in front of the television watching wrestling, and playing with my wrestling figures. It was a dream come true for me and I got to see it in person with the mother of my child (who was getting noticeably larger), my father, my sister, and my best friend. Who could ask for more?

I know that I have talked about professional wrestling a lot in this book and if you're still reading, I appreciate your patience. It has been a part of my life as long as I can remember and has influenced me, outside of my family, more than anything else. It taught me self-confidence and the importance of being myself and believing in myself. It wasn't D.A.R.E or anything that told me not to do drugs or to drink and drive, it was Hulk Hogan. Believe it or not, it has even had an influence on my announcing for high school wrestling. I can honestly say that if it wasn't for wrestling, I would not be who I am today. I hope now you can understand why it has taken up so much of this book.

Throughout Sharon's pregnancy, we went to the doctor every few weeks for checkups. Beings she didn't have any insurance, D.S.H.S. paid for her entire pregnancy so it never cost us a dime. Before you think that I pulled some sort of scam, it was all legal because we weren't married. I also didn't feel bad about doing it because I looked at it this way—I'm going to give thousands of my tax dollars to the state for things like that in my lifetime, so why shouldn't I get a little use out of my own money? Once the child was born, I would have it on my insurance plan. When the time came for me and Sharon to get married, she would be on it too.

We had actually kicked around the idea of marriage enough to where I bought her a ring. Unlike the ring for Holly, I didn't buy this one out of guilt, I bought it because I wanted to. Once we found out that she was pregnant, we opted to put off the wedding plans until after the baby was born. I'd be lying if I told you the main reason wasn't the fact that I would then have to pay for the pregnancy bills.

Speaking of marriage, both of my parents got remarried around this time. Before moving from Bellingham to Mount Vernon, Mom and Mike got married in Las Vegas. I wasn't invited and I wouldn't have gone even if I had been because at the time, I was still a bit bitter about what had happened. I was, however, invited to Dad and Debbie's wedding, but was rather insulted when I was asked to be an usher along with one of Debbie's nephews. Dad selected all of Debbie's brothers as groomsmen. Perhaps if I had been nicer to her at the start, I would have gotten the honor. Nonetheless in order to get even in yet another childish way, I wasn't going to include him in my wedding when it was time. Although we had our issues, I still would have wanted him to be my best man. This proverbial slap in the face ended that thought for good.

It wouldn't have been a good time for Sharon and I to get married anyway. She was a storm of mixed emotions that would twist and turn in the blink of an eye. One minute she was my best friend and the next she was crying and hated my guts. She even fired that phone at me from across the room while my back was turned. Just before impact, she called my name so that I would turn around just in time to take it right in the face. Every couple of weeks, she would get pissed off over something stupid and want move out and never let me see my own child. I told her to "go ahead because the child probably wasn't mine anyway." I knew that I was only throwing fuel on the fire but I still said it in order to fight back against her verbal tirades. Needless to say, marriage wasn't necessary until we got through that period of immaturity.

When we weren't arguing about each other, we were arguing about what the baby's name would be. I was just dead-set on it being a boy so I wanted to name him Andre, after Andre The Giant. Sharon hated it, as did the rest of my family, but I wouldn't let it go. She wanted to name it Raymond, after her grandfather, but I refused. We eventually settled on Harley—then we found out it was going to be a girl.

At first I was devastated. I wanted more than anything to have a son of my very own so he could do the same things that I did when I grew up. We could ride motorcycles together, wrestle together, and be best buddies. I wanted my last name to be passed on to another generation so it could continue through the years. But then I realized that a daughter could do all of those things as well.

Now that we knew that it was going to be a girl, we had yet another reason for argument. One way or another, Sharon was adamant about getting her grandfather's name into the equation. I finally agreed on Rey as the child's middle name just to shut her up. (In the ultimate act of defiance, I had the nurse change it to Nicole while Sharon was still under anesthesia following surgery.)

As for first names, we argued about that up until June. Night after night, we would spend hours saying names one after another, only to have the other person hate it. The only name that we could somewhat agree on was Cheyenne, but I didn't really want that either. The more I thought about it, the more I wanted her name to start with an "E" just like mine. Then out of nowhere, I had it—the perfect name.

"We'll name her Elizabeth," I said to Sharon confidently.

"I love it!" she replied.

Just like that, we had a unanimous winner. Had either one of us just said it earlier, we would have saved ourselves hours of bickering and flat-out screaming back and forth. Elizabeth—perfect—now we just had a few more weeks to wait.

Right around income tax time, Sharon and I decided to buy our own house. Other than we were going to have a baby coming soon, the time was perfect. The housing market and interest rates were at record lows and I could put a $6,000 down payment on a $140,000 home on my income alone. I didn't even have to have Sharon on the loan to qualify. It's a good thing because with her credit history, it would have only worked against me anyway. Over the previous fifteen months, I had grown increasingly tired of the renting racket. No question about it, we made the right decision to rent first while we began traveling the sometimes bumpy path of our relationship with each other. The problem with renting was that our landlord was a complete idiot.

Rande Taylor was a single guy, who had probably never even had a girlfriend, and was in his early fifties. While he answered the phone on the first ring when I called on the house at the start, I only talked to his answering machine after the papers were signed—and you could just forget about getting a call in return.

Upon moving in, we made a verbal agreement that he would get electricity installed in the shop if I, in turn, dug the ditches for the conduit. Not two weeks after we moved in, Dad came down and the two of us dug a fifty-foot long and two-foot deep ditch. After nearly a full year went by, I finally filled the ditch back in when Rande told me that he changed his mind because it was too expensive.

Obviously without electricity in the shop, it had a manual garage door. It was no big deal to lift it on a regular basis to get out my pickup or motorcycle until the day that the spring broke. I called Rande every day for almost a week and left a message on his recorder, telling him what was wrong—nothing. Finally I called him at 5:00 in the morning, woke him up, and chewed his ass out.

"Well, I've been busy," was all he could say.

Fed up with waiting, I called a repair man and just took the amount that I paid him off of Rande's rent check.

"Hey, you shorted me rent," he said on his only call that he ever made to the house without me calling first.

"No I didn't," I argued. "Look in the envelope and you'll see an invoice from the garage door repair."

"Oh. Why did you do that?"

"Because you didn't and I'm tired of leaving the door open so all of my shit is in plain sight."

"Well you should've called me first."

Click—if I had stayed on the line I might have been evicted after the things that were fixing to come out of my mouth.

Only one time did he ever call me back on the first day that I called him—when the ceiling opened up in the kitchen after years of water damage from a leaking roof. With the amount of water that was coming through the ceiling, you would have thought that the plumbing was ran through the trusses instead of under the house. Our faucet didn't even have that much water pass through it as fast as this water was flowing. Luckily, the hole was directly over the kitchen sink so the rain water just ran down the drain. Within two days, we had a new roof. Funny how when something that could potentially affect him went wrong, he had it fixed just like that. That was the end of the line for me because I knew that he had been dodging me on purpose all along.

In the span of about two weeks, I went to the bank for approval on a home loan, hired a real estate agent, and bought our first house. I called Rande at 4:00 a.m., just to be sure to talk to his worthless ass in person.

"I'm moving out in mid-May so you won't be getting your April rent because I prepaid you my final thirty days when we signed the lease."

"Well I want you guys as tenants."

"Sorry—we're gone."

"But we had a two year lease."

"And you didn't live up to our other agreements at signing."

I didn't get my deposit money back but for $500, I was okay with just putting that experience behind me.

We bought the first house that we looked at, which may sound like a dumb idea. It really wasn't because going in, I knew that I only had a certain amount of money that I could be approved for, I wanted a two-car shop and I wanted a little property. Out of what was listed at the time, I only had four options. It just so happened that the first one that we looked at made the most sense. It had the most room, the most property, fewest neighbors, and was the closest to where we already were.

The six year old manufactured home was on a developing subdivision in Concrete, seven miles east of where we already lived. It was one of only seven houses currently in a development that each had full, one acre tracts. The backyard was full of cedar and pine trees, giving it a park-like atmosphere. Next to the house was a detached shop (with electricity) that could fit both vehicles, my motorcycle, and our other outside things. The house itself was three bedrooms and two full baths and had covered front and rear porches. While it was actually smaller than the one that we had rented, it was much newer, nicer, and cleaner than Rande's dump. Most importantly, it was ours for only $300 more a month than what our rent was. Now, WE were the landlords, WE were in control, and WE called the shots.

Just before Memorial Day, I brought home a tractor-trailer from work and we filled it with all of our stuff. What we had done with pickups not even two years earlier now took a 30' trailer. In addition to everything else, we now had our own furniture, a riding lawn mower, a barbeque, an outdoor picnic table, and a swing set for Katelynn.

After getting unpacked, Sharon, who was now tipping the Toledos at nearly two bills, began doing all of the decorating in Elizabeth's room. Although we still had several weeks to go, she had a crib set that Mom had bought us, a changing table that was stocked and ready to go, a cradle, a motorized swing, and a play pen. Oddly enough as I write this, I don't think we ever had a plan as to where Elizabeth was going to sleep if we had stayed in Lyman. I'm pretty sure of the answer, so I'm glad that it worked out the way that it did.

While Sharon handled the inside duties (as much as she could anyway), I was in charge of the outside. I broke in my new riding lawn mower on the fourteen inches of grass that the previous owner had neglected to cut before he left. Dad came over the following weekend to help me build an attic in the shop and to give me a hand building a chicken coop so that I could have chickens without them being an extra meal for Tuco.

For the next two months, I spent every afternoon after work caulking and putting two coats of paint on the house and shop. On my days off, I worked out there from daylight until dark. Having remembered watching Dad spend all summer on a couple of different occasions painting over various color patterns on our house as a kid and seeing how much trouble that it was, I told Sharon that she could pick the color. The only catch was, she better like it because I wasn't going to ever change the color. She chose white with green trim, ironically the same colors that we had on the house at the time we moved out of Orth Way.

Just like the way that Dad had done it in the past, I too painted the entire place by hand. I didn't use a sprayer or rollers, I instead used disposable pads. They are much more time consuming because they force you to go slow but in doing so, it allows you to do a much better quality of a job. The paint goes on more evenly and will look better over a longer period of time.

While I hate painting, especially after that, at least it kept me out of the house and away from Sharon's mood swings as she approached her due date. I recently read that two out of the three most stressful times in one's life are moving and having a baby. You can imagine how much fun it was at times, as we did them both at once.

CHAPTER 43
Elizabeth

ON THE MORNING of Friday, July 25, 2003, Sharon and I woke up before dawn and went to the hospital for the big moment. Since she was having a cesarean section, we had everything scheduled ahead of time so we didn't have to deal the any of the "any minute now" crap. Besides, we didn't have a choice. After Sharon nearly bled to death delivering her first child, a cesarean was the only option after that. It also made it easier for me with work and I could take three days off before going back on Monday.

After weeks of pleading my case, Sharon agreed to have a local anesthetic to keep her awake during the birth. Had she not agreed to do so, I wouldn't be allowed in the delivery room and thus would miss the birth of my only natural child. I say "only" because the doctor had recommended that she have a total hysterectomy following the birth. So this was going to be it—a once-in-a-lifetime moment that would never happen again.

Both Mom and Sharon's mom were at the hospital before we got there.

"Where have you guys been?" they both asked in unison, not happy with our tardiness.

We all went up to the pre-op room and Sharon got into one of those world famous hospital gowns with the open back. They checked her vital signs, blood, and all that crap and by 8:00, we were in the very room where Elizabeth was going to come into the world. I even had to put on a mask, hairnet, plastic covers on my shoes, and a green suit just like the doctors so I wouldn't "contaminate" anything. Both of our moms and Debbie, who had shown up also, waited outside of the room where the babies were measured, weighed, and cleaned to be amongst the first to see Elizabeth in person.

As much as I would have liked Dad to have been there also, there was enough people there already. Even Katelynn wasn't there, as she left the day before to go to her grandma's. Not that Sharon and I didn't want her around, we just felt that it would be easier without her. Besides, she would get to see her new sister soon enough.

By 8:15, Sharon was numb from the chest down. I sat right by her and held her hand as the doctor, who talked just like Winnie The Pooh, came into the room and immediately started doing his thing. To avoid getting any germs into Sharon's open belly, there was a small curtain that was placed just under her boobs. It also prevented her and I from seeing what was happening. I did it anyway, though.

"Get back!" Dr. Pooh yelled.

I did, but not before I saw two little feet poking out of her mother's belly. Unfortunately, I also caught a glimpse of the placenta and nearly gagged. *Maybe the curtain was necessary after all?*

Once Elizabeth was completely out of the womb, Dr. Pooh lifted her up in the air for me to see and to hand her off to the nurse who was going to cut the umbilical cord. Sharon got to see her for a quick second before she was wheeled into another room for her hysterectomy.

"Does she have all of her fingers and toes?"

"Yes, she's perfect," I assured her.

She was, too. At 8:25 a.m., the most beautiful and precious thing that I had ever seen took her first breath of life. She was seven pounds, eleven ounces (just like I was) and had gorgeous sapphire eyes and a full head of dark hair. In my first twenty-one years, I had read over 200 books in a single summer, played on a football team that won a game 82-0 en route to a league championship, and battled adversity in the world's most physical and demanding sport, but this was my greatest achievement. I was the proudest father in the world as I looked at my baby girl. I, like all fathers, wanted a son—at least that was until a daughter came along and stole my heart.

The nurses wrapped her up and I took her into another room to give her a bath. I dried her off and put her in a set of pajamas along with a matching stocking hat. The mothers, who had gone to eat thinking that it would be a while, just happened to glance over and see us as they paced the halls. As soon as they saw us, I popped off her hat so that they could see her hair. They all melted.

Once the cleaning was all finished, Elizabeth went up to the room where Sharon would stay for the next couple of days. As a new dad, I got to sleep in the second hospital bed in the room so we could all stay together as a family until we went home on Sunday. I held her in my arms the whole time as I waited for Sharon to come out of surgery. As per her request, I didn't let any of the mothers hold the baby until Sharon got to first. While they may not have liked it, they understood it and did it anyway.

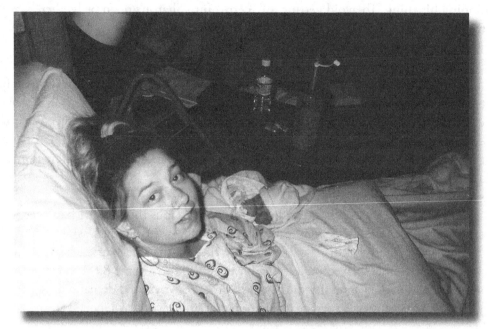

Sharon and Elizabeth on the day she was born, July, 25,2003

After Sharon got out of surgery, she was pretty much immobile. Elizabeth had to be handed to her for feeding and things like that—that is of course if you could pry her out of everyone's arms, as Dad, Jen, and Mike had all shown up by then. Elizabeth did nothing but sleep the whole time. She had a small little cradle between our beds (not that she spent that much time in there) so that when she woke up, we were right there. I was up every few hours to pass her to Sharon so she could nurse. Afterward, I would change her diaper if necessary. Thankfully at this time, her poop had no order to it and looked more like a scoop of roofing tar. Boy would that change!

We went home on Sunday morning after all of the paperwork was completed. By now, Sharon knew about my switcharoo that I did on Elizabeth's middle name. Surprisingly, she wasn't really all that mad and only brings it up now as a joke. Beings I was going back to work the next day and Sharon was going to be bedridden for at least a week, Mom stayed at our house for a few days. It was a good idea because it hadn't been that long since Mom had the same surgery and she remembered that it took Jen and I to care for her while Dad was at work. The only difference was, there was a baby added to the equation and load was a little greater.

As soon as I got home from work each day, I would play with Elizabeth as much as I could. She was so little and helpless that I began to affectionately call her "Wimpy," a name that I still call her today. She doesn't seem to mind as long as Katelynn doesn't call her that.

As for Katelynn, she came home a week or so after we did once Sharon was able to get around a little better. It was slow going for a while, as it took both me and Katelynn to help her off of the toilet, but the big sister would do anything to help. She was happy as can be to not only help, but to have a little sister to hold and love. Knowing that this was a time when when an older child could begin to feel left out, everyone did their best to include Katelynn. If Elizabeth was given a gift, so was she. Elizabeth may have been held more, but Katelynn could do so much more—like anything physical.

Once Sharon was back on her feet, Mom went home and we were on our own as a foursome. Elizabeth, whom we mostly called Lizzy for short, was doing great for the most part. She slept, ate, slept, and shit, pretty much in that order, all day long. The only trouble was that her belly button continued to ooze, so we took her to the doctor.

We had actually gone to the doctor several other times for stupid things that only Sharon understood. I tried to tell her that it was now costing us money each time that she wanted to take her in following a fart, but you try telling a woman fresh off of a hysterectomy and see where you end up—you'll be at the doctor's office with me.

This time was different, though. We took Lizzy in and the doctors took one look at her bellybutton and left the room. I figured that they were fixing up some sort of antibiotic for something but they instead returned with directions to Children's Hospital in Seattle. I never felt so helpless in my life. Here was my smiling baby girl in my arms and they were telling us that they couldn't do anything for her. I stayed calm and positive in front of Sharon, but it was hard.

We left the doctor's office and picked up Mom on our way down to Seattle. I was glad that she went because I needed someone to help me with Sharon, who was doing well so far. But I knew that she could blow at any minute, worse than what Mount Saint Helen's did in 1980.

After ultrasounds, MRIs, and an overnight stay as a precaution, it was nothing. What they had feared was that her bellybutton excreted waste (like a second butthole) due to her intestinal track splitting into two paths. While she could be fixed if that were the case with extensive surgeries, thankfully it wasn't. I'll tell you what, though, it sure put everything into perspective.

We thought that our world was crashing down when it was nothing more than a false alarm. The other kids and their parents who were there weren't so lucky. I saw bald kids with bright yellow skin, kids with thirty tubes coming out of their bodies, and was in the same room when I heard a doctor tell two parents that their child was now terminal. It was the saddest, most depressing place that I have ever been, yet we felt like we were the luckiest people on the planet. Parents of those children, and the kids as well, are a hundred times tougher than I could ever pretend to be.

Following that eye-opener, the only other potential hospital trips were caused by me being a fool. One time, I was carrying Lizzy in my arms in the living room and tripped over Tuco, who was sprawled out on the floor, and she flew out of my arms like I had just fumbled a football. As luck would have it, she landed right in the recliner and started giggling. I started laughing too, but Sharon didn't get the joke. During another show of stupidity, I waved a clean baby wipe over her face while I was changing her and accidentally brushed it across her eyeball. Boy, you have never heard a child scream so loud in your life. We were actually packed up to go to the hospital until I came clean and told Sharon what "might" have happened.

It may have been a dumb thing to do, but I was really only trying to do whatever I could to take my mind off of the now putrid diapers that I had to change. In order to keep from gagging, I would tie a shirt around my face to protect my nose from getting a whiff of what Lizzy had cooked up. Sharon thought I was overreacting but it was legitimate—I have a weak stomach when I'm face to face with shit, even my own. Sharon still thought of it as an excuse to not have to change diapers.

Aside from driving Lizzy to the doctor and hospital, we did take he other places, believe it or not. In late August we went to a Thramer Family reunion in Burlington, where she was welcomed as the newest member. Papa even came over, giving us the rare opportunity for a family picture showcasing four generations.

Four generations: Me, Dad, Elizabeth, and Papa

By September, Lizzy got her first tooth. As it turned out, she wouldn't get her second one for over a year. Man, did she ever make use out of the one that she had, though. She would literally peel carrots with it once we started her on solid food, and also use it to scratch her hand.

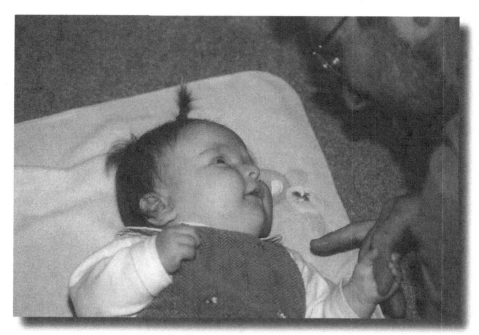

Elizabeth holding my hand

By mid-September, the focus was off of Lizzy and onto Katelynn, who was getting ready to begin preschool. She was now four years old and ready to begin her educational career. Since we lived inside of the Concrete School District, she went to school there.

The only trouble that we had with Katelynn in school was her going to the bathroom in her pants. While she knew better, she did it anyway. She claimed that she didn't know that it was happening, but I think that it was simply her being to lazy to get up and go—much like I used to do while playing in the sandbox when I was her age. In order to keep Sharon (who had finally gotten her driver's license) from making another trip up to the school everyday, we kept an extra set of clothes up there just in case. In fairness to Katelynn, she wasn't the only one who it happened to.

Unlike when I went to preschool, Katelynn went everyday. She was out by one, though, so it wasn't like she went a full day or anything. The reason that it had changed since I had gone was because kindergarten was now an all day, everyday affair and they were transitioning the kids so that they would be ready for the big change. They spent most of the time focusing on the alphabet because by kindergarten, they would be learning to read.

Me, Elizabeth, Sharon, and Katelynn in our living room

As quickly as it had turned from her to her sister, the focus was back on Elizabeth by autumn. It was her first Halloween, her first Thanksgiving, her first Christmas, and all of that. While it was special, I was happy once they all came and went and ended all of the sentimental bullshit. Now we could put the newborn stuff behind us and get on with raising our family. Like I said, it was special, but you can only squeeze so much toothpaste out of a tube. Celebrating everything multiple times because everyone wanted their share was too much.

CHAPTER 44

Cold Feet

I T WASN'T VERY long after Elizabeth got her first tooth before she began crawling. At first, she would either scoot herself across the floor or do log rolls clear across the room to get where she wanted to go. Once she got the crawling down, we started holding and steadying her arms while she took a few steps. We then would let go and let her try to do it on her own. She would get one or two steps in before she would either fall on her butt or flat on her face.

Whether it was scooting, rolling, crawling, or walking, she did nothing without being accompanied be her pacifier, or "binkie." She had to swing with it, play with it, sleep with it, and do everything else you can think of, besides eating, with it. I'm sure that if she could have found a way to eat with it, she would have. We even kept a stock of them just in case she lost one, which she did on a regular basis. When that happened, you might as well have been cutting off her air supply because she would act like she was dying. Come bedtime, she had to have it in or else you could forget about her going to sleep. Once she did have it in place, she was out like a light. If it fell out during the night, she was most of the time able to find it in her sleep and put it back in. If she couldn't find it, she would cry or make some sort of noise until somebody came in and put it back in her mouth. That damn pacifier was the only thing that kept her sleeping through the night. She was a hundred times better than Katelynn was when I met her.

I was against the pacifier thing from the start as I knew that she would grow to depend on it for everything. Sure enough I was right. She had it at night until her fourth birthday when I made her throw it in the garbage so she could open her presents. She did it and never said another word about it. I just wish that we could have done it sooner.

Every child has that one security thing that they have to have, though. For Katelynn it was a sippy cup full of milk. She packed that around for years. It couldn't be full of something easy like juice or water either, it had to be something that you had to keep cold and fresh. We always had to watch her and put it in the fridge every little bit to try and keep it cool. One time, everyone lost track of it and it ended up behind the couch for a few days. When Katelynn found it, she immediately took a swig out of it before we could tell her not to. She didn't throw up (or seem to mind for that matter) but I wanted to after seeing it.

By spring, Lizzy was big enough for her first motorcycle ride. Before you go thinking that I put my daughter's life in danger, all I did was putt her up and down our street in first gear. Katelynn, on the other hand, got to try out the highway. While she wasn't at the legal age of five yet, a three mile trip down to Dad's house on occasion was a good training lesson.

They both loved it, especially when all three of us rode together, but we had too many limitations on what we could do. With that in mind, I convinced Sharon to let me buy a four wheeler. Then I could ride both kids on the street, in the yard, and in the undeveloped lots in our neighborhood. When it snowed, I could drag them both on inner tubes, just like Papa used to do when I was younger. She was all for it, so I went and bought a brand new one right off the showroom floor.

About two weeks after I bought it and before I even made my first payment, I took it over to Dad's to ride it on the trails above his house. He got his out and the two of us rode around just like we did on our dirt bikes a few years earlier. Before we called it a day, we decided to see how much guts each other had by doing steep hill climbs.

After a few successful attempts, we each went down the steepest hill that we could find just so we could turn around and climb it back up. Dad went first and made it up to the top and out of sight. I then hit the gas and made it two-thirds of the way up before I hit a rock, which caused me to do a wheelie, and went over backwards with the ATV landing on my lower leg. Luckily, I created separation and didn't go all the way to the bottom of the hill end-over-end with it. Although it hurt like hell, my leg wasn't broke. My four wheeler was going to be a different story, as it had done four or five barrel rolls and landed with a crash out of sight.

Dad heard me holler and came sliding down the hill. He asked if I was alright, which I was physically, but I was distraught over what I was certain was the end of my new ride.

"Where's your four wheeler?"

"Down there somewhere, I heard it crash into a rock or a tree—it's gotta be ruined. Sharon's gonna kill me."

Dad continued down the hill and shouted up the surprising news that it was okay. The loud crash that I heard was a weld on the chassis breaking after it T-boned a tree at a 45 degree angle. Had it taken another half-roll, it would have hit the tree with the gas tank and surely would have been destroyed. Other than being scratched up (which was eventually going to happen anyway) and having a broken weld and a little bend on the handle bars, it was fine.

That pretty much ended the hill climbing. I still rode it on trails once in a while, but I mainly kept it at home to ride around with the kids. I also used it a lot around the property packing down snow, choking and dragging large branches that fell during wind storms, and pulling a trailer full of brush and dirt. Besides, I had prove to Sharon that it was both fun and useful to own one.

A month or so later, and after I was able to make my first payment on my now "well-used" ATV, I celebrated my first Father's Day. Again, I'm not one for holidays and birthdays and I haven't really acknowledged another one since, but the 2004 Father's Day was special to me.

It wasn't about the gifts so much as it was about Elizabeth trying to tell me "Happy Father's Day." She was able to say a few words, some better than others, and she was able to tell me, "P-far-day," which clearly meant "Happy Father's Day."

The physical gifts were good too. Sharon bought me the latest Hank Williams, Jr. album *I'm One of You.* What's so cool about that was the fact that she doesn't like Hank Jr. at all, but she knows that I do. While there are certainly better albums out there, that one holds a special place in my heart each time a hear it.

Keeping with the music theme, Mom bought me tickets to see Dwight Yoakam at the Skagit Valley Casino. What was unique about this show was that there was never more than three guys on the stage at once. All of the guitar work and singing was done by Dwight. There were just two other guys in the band that played a cello for bass, drums, steel guitar, or fiddle, depending on the song.

Once Father's Day had come and gone and just after the fireworks went off on the Fourth of July, Sharon and I had our own fireworks going off between us. All couples have ups and downs and have their share of times when things don't look to good. You have your threats and things, but most of the anger blows over and the situation gets solved between the two. This time, however, we had actual plans of splitting up for good following a series of events.

To begin with, I have always had a habit of keeping my feelings to myself until they explode like a balloon that gets that final volume of air that exceeds its threshold. I let shit stack up until even the smallest thing causes me to go off. Sometimes it takes a few months, but this time it took almost three years.

Since Sharon and I moved in together, I had the stress of living with a woman and a toddler. Both are hard enough on their own but both at the same time is extremely tough, especially if it's your first time out. Throw in the different philosophies in parenting and you're going to have your share of issues and added stress.

As I said, I dealt with my stress by keeping it to myself. Sharon dealt with hers by smoking. It wouldn't have been so bad if she didn't lie about doing it all of the time. Now instead of just ignoring it, I would make an effort to catch her doing it. I would check her receipts, check her pockets, and check the car for ashes. Anytime I caught the slightest odor of smoke, I was all over her.

Forgetting that I hate the smell of cigarette smoke and that smoking will eventually kill you if nothing else does first, the biggest problem was the lying. *If she lied about this, what else has she lied to me about?* With as much time as I spent working on my own and with unlimited time to think and stew over it, I drove myself nuts. Believe me, it's not a healthy thing. Instead of just loving her for who she was, I became obsessed with catching her in a lie.

To top it all off, it had only been five years since I watched my parents go through this with each other. Although Mom had gotten remarried without much of a glitch, Dad kicked Debbie out two or three times before they finally married. I didn't want that in my life, I wanted to be in a stable relationship before I got married. But I couldn't marry a liar. If I did, we would surely get a divorce and I would have to say goodbye to my house, my Harley, my kids, and everything else that I had.

335

The bottom line was that I was scared of failure like I always had been. In school, it was taking algebra tests not to get lower than a B and second guessing myself when I should have just relaxed and answered questions like it was a regular assignment. In wrestling, I was so worried about losing that I would forget to use my strength and knowledge of a few good holds (which is all I really needed to win matches) and I would lose to a guy that I had no business losing too. Now, I was going to split up with the mother of my only child and the only woman outside of my mother that could ever put up with me, just because I was scared of getting a divorce.

The problem was, I didn't know that was the reason. I was so overwhelmed with the stress from Sharon's smoking, her thousands of dollars racked up in credit card bills because she was uneducated in interest, and even my parents divorce from a half-decade ago, that I somehow talked myself out of being in love with her. I tried to keep it all inside until the shit finally hit the fan one night around nine o' clock when I got a phone call from another woman. Before you get the wrong idea, let me explain.

At one of my stops, there was a girl a year out of high school that was going to go to college in Iowa in a couple a few weeks. Rather than flying, she was going to to drive herself there on her own. Having just taken a trip to Montana on my own on my Harley, I knew of some good and safe places to stop for gas and lodging between long and dark stretches of highway. I gave her my cell phone number, a few of my maps with the best route highlighted and the best towns for stops marked with an "X," and told her to call me if she had any questions. I never gave it a second thought until my phone rang on one of the few nights that I forgot to turn it off.

Sharon went ballistic without even listening to what I had to say. She threw all of my clothes out in the yard, cussed me out, and threatened to cut my dick off. While she did have a track record of that happening to her in the past, I wasn't like that—I'm Eddie Thramer and I know better than that! But that was it—I told her what was on my mind at the worst possible time.

The next day she calmed down, but the two of us decided to end it. I was going to let her have sole custody of Elizabeth because I would in no way try to take another child from her. I cared for her too much and I honestly don't think that she could have that done to her again and live through it. I would keep the house and my truck, while she kept the Jimmy and I paid for her to live in a low income apartment. Just before we signed papers on the apartment and got things packed, Debbie saved us from making the biggest mistake of our lives.

Having to deal with the emotional stress brought on by Dad and probably even the anguish that Jen and I unfairly brought upon her a few years prior, Debbie had some psychological help from the pastor at her church. Now I'm not much into buying what a preacher says just because he leads a group of people as if they were sheep, but you can't dispute a man who has degrees in psychology hanging on his wall that proves that he knows what he is talking about. Although we didn't belong to the church, Billy Farrar offered to have a visit with Sharon and I after Debbie told him our story.

It was during the two hour talk with a guy whom I had never met that I realized that I was just scared of failure. I mean this guy had me pegged—he told me that I was a perfectionist, a charismatic leader, and a man of tremendous will (things that I already knew) just by listening to me talk. He had Sharon down too. He said that she would do anything to please people that she loved and all she ever wanted out of life was to be loved in return. Yeah, she smoked when she was stressed, but she was embarrassed about it and scared of rejection so she kept it from me because I might just think of her as less of a person.

Rightfully so, he spent more time convincing me to convince myself rather than worrying about Sharon. He knew that Sharon was in it for the long haul. He also knew that I was too if I could just see inside my soul. In a polite, preacher-type way, he basically told me not to be an idiot and piss away a good thing because of what happened to other people in my life. I wasn't Mom. I wasn't Dad. I'm Eddie Thramer. I'm my own person and I go where I want to go in life. The funny thing was that it was inside of me all along, I just didn't get it. He said that if I was a little looser and not so uptight, Sharon might not smoke to relieve stress—no stress, no smoke. Who cares if the laundry didn't get folded or the dishes didn't get put away? If it bothered me, I should do it myself.

The last thing that he said to me was that people were always going to be afraid of me. They wouldn't be afraid for their safety, but they would be afraid of whether or not they were accepted by me. He said that I have such a strong leadership aura that people sometimes walk on eggshells around me. As good as it may sound, it usually works against me, especially at home with Sharon and the kids.

We left our session feeling pretty good about ourselves. Billy didn't take any money from us or a payment of any kind. He said that if we understood what he was saying, then he had his compensation—and we did understand. We had a good thing going and we were more than capable of handling our adversity with what we had inside of us.

Now I'm not going to say that we never had another argument because that would be a boldfaced lie. I will, however, say that we have been nowhere near the point of no return like we were that summer. I've lightened up (sort of), Sharon eventually quit smoking entirely, no phones have been thrown, no more clothes have been tossed out in the lawn, and no more holes have been put in the walls. While we will always have our occasional disagreements, we always work them out by understanding where each other is coming from.

At the end of July, Elizabeth celebrated her first birthday. She got her presents and cards and such, but her favorite gift was her very own cake that Sharon had ordered for her and her alone. We all ate from a different cake like civilized humans but Lizzy, on the other hand, used her hands and her face to demolish a cake that was the size of a dinner plate on her own. While I thought of it mostly as a complete waste of food, it was highly entertaining seeing her purple-frosted face.

Aside from the frosting, seeing Lizzy with purple around her mouth was nothing new. After having that stupid pacifier in her mouth all of the time, she would often get an outbreak of oral thrush, which is essentially a yeast infection. In addition to taking antibiotics, the doctor also swabbed her mouth with a purple substance that took a week or so to wear off. Sharon also had to use the purple paint on her nipples while she was still nursing our purple monster. She didn't think it was all that funny, but I did.

Thanks to Lizzy's generosity, I managed to have a bout with it myself in early October when we went on our first family vacation as a foursome. It didn't come on right away, but it would make its presence felt soon enough. It really pisses me off too—getting sick or something like that while I am on a trip. For me, it's the best part of the whole year and to have it impacted with an illness really sucks.

It had been three years since Dad and I had taken our motorcycle trip through Colorado on our way to Texas. Ever since then I had told Sharon about the sheer beauty of the Rocky Mountains and how the autumn sun glistens off of the streams and rivers. It was easy selling her on the idea of going there. To add to it, I also planned for us to go see the Grand Canyon, Hoover Dam, and Las Vegas. Yeah, I'd seen them all before, but now I wanted my family to experience them too.

Following our frozen camping adventures in California, I was forbidden to even touch the tent and sleeping bags when we loaded up the Jimmy the night before we left. Sharon said that if we didn't stay in motels at night, then she wasn't going. There wasn't even an argument to be had. I knew that she meant business on this one, and she was right.

Knowing that we had to find a motel every night and remembering all of those no vacancy signs that Dad drove us up to a hundred times before we finally found something, I decided to make reservations in the towns that I estimated us ending up in on each of our ten nights on the road. To save a little money, I reserved rooms at the cheapest places that I could find in each state's travel guide. While they all weren't too bad, one in particular was—and it of course had to be our first motel of the trip.

After driving over 900 miles through Washington, Oregon, and most of Idaho since 2:00 that morning, we pulled into Burley, Idaho off of Interstate 84 to check in at our first motel, the Lamplighter Inn. Well, it sounded good when I read about it in the travel guide, but Sharon didn't think of that as much of a consolation. The welcome sign was only half-lit when we pulled up to a place right smack in the middle of the shittiest part of town.

"Maybe it's better on the inside?" I suggested as I returned to the car with the key.

"How much did you pay for this room for tonight?" Sharon asked.

"$19.95," I said, knowing that I shouldn't even have been speaking.

She never said a word, she just stared holes through me and left me feeling like a piece of Swiss cheese.

I opened the door to the room and reached for where you would normally find the light switch—nothing. After looking around a little more, I saw a single light bulb on the ceiling and a two-foot chain hanging down from it. I just smiled and reached up and gave it a pull. Instead of lighting the room up, the whole fixture fell into my hand. I gave her another innocent smile, but she wasn't amused.

The bathroom light did work at least so we were able to brush our teeth and get ready for bed. The TV didn't work but that wasn't such a big deal because we were exhausted from driving all day anyway and we really only wanted to just go to sleep. We all got into bed and I assured everyone that tomorrow would be better.

I no sooner than laid down in bed when I felt something poke me right in the left kidney. I figured that it was just a spring that was poking me as I continued to adjust positions. Then I felt another jab a few inches apart from the first one.

"Goddammit! What the hell is poking me?!" I hollered as I jumped out of bed.

I went into the bathroom and switched on the light so I could try to see what was up with the mattress. When I walked back to the bed and began feeling around, I found something that shouldn't have been there—a headband.

"Honey, is this yours?" I asked, even though I already knew the answer.

Sharon still wasn't speaking to me so she just shook her head.

"Katelynn?"

"No."

It wasn't Lizzy's and it sure as hell wasn't mine. I went to the office to show them the buried treasure that someone had left behind, but the door was locked up. Feeling dejected, I went back to the room and asked forgiveness from my family for my thriftiness.

Following our night in what Sharon dubbed as "Headband Land," we stuck to Motel 6s from then on. They were cheap but clean, and always had two beds. I could still save a few bucks a night by saying that I was a single parent with two kids, who stayed for free. It may not be the most honest thing in the world, but it adds up to a free night over the course of the week with the money that I save by not mentioning Sharon.

The next morning we went down through Utah and into Grand Junction, Colorado to spend the day and night and Grandma and Milt's house. After Grandma heard about our plans for the rest of the trip and how we were going to end up in Las Vegas, she offered to put us up at her time share at the Greek Isles, just off of The Strip. We couldn't possibly turn that down after our experience from the night before.

After our visit, we went over the Rocky Mountains on two separate highways and ended up (as planned) for two nights at a lodge in Cortez, Colorado. The reason that I booked two nights was because we were going to spend an entire day at Mesa Verde National Park, exploring the cliff dwellings built and lived in by the Pueblo Indians seven hundred years earlier. Say what you want to about technology of today, but those guys were in a class of their own. Structures that are still standing today range from single room houses to Cliff Palace, which has more than 200 rooms.

On our second night in Cortez, I started really noticing how much my throat was hurting. It wasn't like a sore throat that only bothers you in the morning and at night, it was constant. It hurt to talk, swallow, and even breathe. I bought a pack of cough drops and a bottle of Chloraseptic to try and numb it. Every five minutes I would spray three squirts of the medicine at the back of my throat, all the while continuing to suck on cough drops.

By the time that we got to the Grand Canyon the next day, I had to go to the doctor. I had a 103 degree temperature and was freezing cold in the deserts of Arizona. Believe it or not, they actually had an urgent care place inside the park. The doctor said that it was strep throat and wrote me a prescription for some antibiotics that I would have to pick up sixty miles away in the town of Williams. Lucky for me, that was where we were planning on spending the night anyway. I started taking the pills right away and continued with my Chloraseptic and cough drop routine. I figured that I should be getting better right around the time we got home.

The first stop on our next day of travel was at Hoover Dam. Unlike when I was there in 1999, this time we spent a few hours there and took the tours down inside the power facility and watched a number of educational videos. While it was information that I already knew for the most part, the girls got a big kick out of it, which made it all worth while. Still, being inside and seeing all of the generators which power Las Vegas was amazing.

After the tour, we drove an hour into Las Vegas and checked into the Greek Isles for the next four nights. Gone were the inoperable TVs and light switches and in were the queen-size beds and easy chairs. We had a sliding glass door that led right into the pool area and we didn't have to worry anymore about surprises in our sheets.

We spent the next three days taking in all of the family activities in Vegas. While it is still primarily an adult destination, Las Vegas is billed as the "Family Entertainment Capitol of the World." Whether it was the acrobatics at Circus Circus, the pirate show at Treasure Island, the lions at MGM Grand, or the magic shows at Excalibur, we did it all and had the time of our lives.

At night after the kids went to bed, Sharon and I did take turns playing a few machines down in the casino. We're not much for high-stakes stuff, so we could usually be found around the nickle slots. You don't win much, but you don't lose very much either. It can still be a lot of fun and you don't have to worry about how your life hangs in the balance of one spin of the wheel.

This one hag that was sitting at the machine next to me dropped in a twenty dollar bill as soon as she flopped her fat ass in the chair. Within minutes, her twenty was all gone. She threw in another twenty and it was gone in an even shorter amount of time. Then another twenty—same thing. On her fourth twenty that she dropped in, she hit a sixty dollar jackpot. If you would have been standing on the other side of the room, you would have thought that she had just won a million dollars by the way she was shouting and screaming with joy. I just shook my head as the moron picked up her sixty dollars, twenty less than what she started with, and strutted across the room like she was Donald Trump.

When we had all of the fun that was to be had, We drove the 1,400 miles home straight through. We stopped for gas, food, and to piss and that was it. The girls were unbelievably good travelers. They didn't bitch or anything, mainly because they were exhausted and slept the whole time. Twenty-two hours after we left Vegas, we pulled into our driveway—not too bad if I do say so myself.

Beings I was still on vacation from work for a few more days, I took the time to go to my doctor to find out what was really wrong with my throat that hadn't gotten any better. After looking inside of my mouth, he discovered a hole in my throat lining.

"You got a yeast infection called thrush," he said. "But it's really bad."

I told him that I must have gotten it from my daughter and asked if I too was going to have to have my mouth painted purple.

"No," he said. "You only have to take one pill and it will go away, but you're going to laugh when I tell you what it is."

"Really?"

"Yeah. It's a woman's vaginal yeast infection tablet that they use when the cream doesn't work."

Great.

At least it worked. For seventeen dollars (even after insurance) for one tiny pill, it damn well better.

Lizzy never got it again. After that, we started washing her pacifier in the dishwasher every couple of days and began replacing it on a regular basis.

Shortly before the beginning of 2005, I was happily removed from running the school route at work and started running driver relief when guys were sick or were on vacation. Although I had to work the dock twice a week if I wasn't on a route, I did get a pay raise for taking the position. It wasn't as much as I had asked for, but it was sufficient.

I only did it long enough for two guys to take vacation before I told the bosses that I was no longer interested. The problem was, guys would be in such a big hurry to take their time off that they would do a half-ass job on their routes for their final few days. They wouldn't check for short-dated product, wouldn't pick up any empty crates, wouldn't update their par sheets for each store, and would even skip certain stops altogether. What did they care—they were on vacation.

That pissed me off so much that I asked to go back to schools where I could do my own shit and not have to screw with picking up the slack for my loser coworkers. I mean I liked them and all, but their work ethics sucked. Not only do I never do that shit to anyone else when they had to cover for me, but I also make it a point to make things as simple as possible so that even guys with an IQ in the single digits can dandle it. I tell them exactly what to take out on the truck, exactly what to leave in each store, and everything else short of driving and wheeling.

With that, I was back on the school route again. I did, however, keep my new salary to the chagrin of some. This run on the schools only lasted a few weeks before a new drug policy sent a few guys to the unemployment line and subsequently changed the company from top to bottom.

Three guys got popped from a dirty piss test that we all had to take one after work one day without any notice that it was coming. Coincidentally, Jason was terminated shortly thereafter, causing even more of a rift between the two co-owning families. Since Gary had the ultimate say, he sent all of the Mills' Family to the unemployment line before long. I can't say that it hurt my feelings all that bad.

With all of the corporate unrest, several guys came and went over the next little while. I took over for a guy that ran a route strictly in Whatcom County when he too decided to leave. As of this minute, that was nearly six years ago and I'm still doing that route today. I was back to driving a tractor-trailer, I didn't have to deal with bitchy lunch ladies, and I didn't have to deal with Koreans who couldn't speak any English. I couldn't have a better job! To top it all off, I was now second in seniority in less than five years on the job!

CHAPTER 45

Sacrifice

IN THE WINTER months of 2004 and 2005, Tuco started showing symptoms of arthritis. Since the situation with him and Katelynn, I had him sleeping outside just in case. He didn't mind it at all in the warm summer months, but the winter was different. He was under the cover so he stayed dry, but the creeping in and out of his doghouse on bitter cold days was causing him to whimper in obvious pain. I took him to the vet and they put him on some arthritis medicine. It was sixty bucks for 200 pills, but I happily paid it because it worked. He was still a little slow getting up, but he didn't make a sound while doing it anymore. To make it easier on him even more, we let him back in the house.

Knowing that he was getting up there in age and that the day that I was dreading was now much closer than it was when he followed me home from school so many years earlier, I decided that it was time to get another dog. Not only would it be good for Tuco to have a buddy, it would be a good transition for us. With any luck the new pup would learn from his mentor and when the day did come, we would all still have a dog and it may not be quite as painful like it is when you lose the only one that you have.

After Christmas, Sharon, the kids, and I went to check out some dogs that were advertised in the paper. Not only were the puppies not what we were after, but the whole place was a dump so we basically just drove right on by. On the way home, Sharon asked to go to one more place on the south side of the Skagit River where they were selling a litter of Golden Retriever and Labrador mixes. Even though the place was a farm, it was much cleaner than the first place was.

The owner of the farm took us out in the barn and showed us the eight week old litter of little black pups. She said that only the males were for sale, which was what I was after anyway. We settled on a mischievous little rascal that was goofing off while his brothers were all huddled around each other. He had a mind of his own and a great personality compared to the rest. I paid the lady a mere $75 and took home a puppy that was even smaller than a football. Based on the five minutes that I spent watching him play around, I named him Slick.

Having Slick as a pup showed me what I had missed out on not having Tuco as a pup. Seeing those huge feet and watching him grow into them was as cute as it gets. He would try to walk down the porch steps but would end up just tumbling down them instead. When he would attempt to run, he would end up tripping over his own feet and would roll to a stop.

Tuco liked him from the start, which was certainly a good thing. He had never really been around other dogs before for an extended amount of time, so I wasn't really sure at first how it was going to work. As long as Slick didn't touch his tennis ball, bone, or eat out of his dog food bowl, everything was cool. Even then Tuco would just growl at him rather than try to take his head off. They played together constantly, starting out gently and progressing towards a little rougher form as Slick got older.

Tuco and Slick

Both of them lived in the house, which got increasingly more crowded as Slick got bigger. Shit was always getting knocked over because of them wrestling and running around in the house. While they were told not to, they would still do it if you didn't send them outside once they got that initial look in their eyes.

As if two dogs weren't already enough, Sharon decided that she wanted a dog for herself to sit on her lap and to snuggle with. She told me to go to hell when I told her that the boys would be happy to do that. On her own, she picked out a little white Maltese that would only grow to be a whopping five pounds. Once I agreed on her getting it, she informed me that she cost $800—over ten times what Slick had cost! She got it anyway, but I made her talk them down to $600. While it was still high, I was much happier with that price. Lilly, as she named her, wasn't much bigger than a rat. Just like that, we had almost as many dogs living in the house as we did people. Oh well, at least they all got along. Better yet, Tuco was showing more energy than he had shown in recent months.

Not wanting to be outdone by his younger pals, Tuco kept up with them step for step. He played fetch more than he had in quite some time (probably just to keep the ball away from Slick), he began pestering our chickens from outside the fence again, and he even chased down and killed a few wild rabbits. He even managed to kill a cat and aided me in killing one as well.

To begin with, there were a lot of stray cats running around our neighborhood. I figured that they belonged to somebody, but nobody around would take responsibility for them. Once they started getting into my chicken coop, I thinned them out my way. Most of the time I would have Tuco chase them off. Very rarely would one come back but if he did, I would shoot him with my pellet gun. I didn't shoot to kill them, just to warn them.

Two cats just couldn't take the hint. The first one Tuco caught and killed on his own. After chasing a second one up a tree, he stood at the base of it and just barked. No way was the cat coming down, so I grabbed my pellet gun and shot him as he was clinging to the bark. He fell to the ground with a thud and that was the last of my cat problems.

Although Tuco had killed chickens, rabbits, cats, and even a deer, he wasn't a vicious dog. He didn't fight other dogs outside of the occasional initial meeting of two territorial canines. He and all of the other neighborhood dogs got along great. Though none of the dogs were permanently loose, they all came out to play on a regular basis. No owner, myself included, had a problem with it.

That all changed when Tuco and a neighbor's Rottweiler got into a pretty good fight. I don't know what caused it because the two had gotten along with each other for two years so far, but they went at it nonetheless. Both me and Shawn Duffy, the Rottweiler's owner, took our dogs to the vet and got them stitched up. To us it wasn't a big deal, but we decided to keep our dogs on our own property unless we were going to be with them. If I saw Shawn ride his bicycle down the street with his dog, Jack, I would make sure that Tuco stayed in the yard. When I would ride four wheelers down to his end of the street with my dog, he would keep Jack in his yard. It all went fine for several months (we even joked about how they ran around with those cones on their heads following their trip to the vet and how they were always knocking stuff over in the house) until all hell broke loose.

A couple of days after my birthday (imagine that), my whole crew loaded up on four wheelers (I now had two after buying one of Papa's) and went for a ride on the trails that we had started carving in the vacant lots. As usual, Tuco went along with us. For whatever reason, Slick decided to stay at home on the porch, where we had purposely left Lilly tied up to. Shawn and his wife, Darcy, were gone and Jack was locked up in their house.

After not more than five minutes of riding, the four wheeler that I bought from Papa started to act like it was running out of gas. I had been having trouble with its carburetor recently, so I had my screwdriver with me just in case I needed to do another adjustment. While I was knelt down and tinkering with it, Shawn and Darcy pulled into their driveway which was directly across the cul-de-sac from where we were. Tuco was lying next to me taking a breather after chasing us along the trails. Katelynn was on my four wheeler waiting patiently as Sharon and Lizzy were sitting on the one with the troubled carburetor. I had Sharon fire it up as I put the screwdriver back in my pocket and got ready to go again.

When I stood up, I saw Jack running towards us with neither Shawn or Darcy in sight. I crouched back down next to Tuco, who was still sprawled out, hoping that it would deter him from jumping my dog. I turned towards Tuco, away from Jack, and within a second, Jack was on me. I immediately turned into him and and stuck my right forearm out parallel about six inches away from my face, essentially giving up my arm to protect my face. Jack clamped down, putting four deep holes into my arm just below the elbow joint. Knowing that it was going to continue, I kept my arm there anyway so he wouldn't get to my face.

As soon as Jack latched on, Tuco jumped in and went after his much larger opponent. Jack released my arm and took a second bite into my wrist before Turning towards Tuco. The two then went at it violently right on top of me, making it impossible for me to stand up and get away. The girls were screaming at what they were witnessing, causing Shawn and Tom, another neighbor, to run over and see what was happening.

When the dogs fought their way back towards the bushes, I was finally able to get up. With a massive puddle of my own blood next to me, I jumped up to try to stop the dogs along with Shawn and Tom, who had made it to the scene. Jack got the upper hand and latched onto Tuco's throat and put him to the ground. Shawn and Tom grabbed onto Jack's hindquarters and tried to pull him off of my motionless dog. Seeing what was happening and knowing what the final result was going to be if I didn't do something, I went straight into Jack's mouth. I stuck both of my hands inside and tried to pull apart his jaws. I felt Jack bite down onto my fingers and I knew that they were going to be completely ravaged, but I continued to try prying his mouth apart. I couldn't help but notice that my arm was literally pouring out blood, just as if it were a faucet, while my muscles were strained. Normally you only see that in the movies, often questioning if it is really something that happens in real life—it does.

Knowing that seconds were now precious and the prying wasn't working, I reached into Jack's mouth one last time, grabbed onto his tongue as tight as possible, and pulled it as hard as I could. He let go and Shawn and Tom took him back to the house. I rolled over next to Tuco, who was still alive but in bad shape, and just laid next to him. I was exhausted. I had lost so much blood by that time that I couldn't even speak. I was getting lightheaded and the whole area was spinning in my head.

The entire fight lasted less than a minute, but it felt like an eternity. The girls saw everything right in front of their faces and were screaming in fear and sorrow. As bloody as I was and with two hands that looked like they had been caught in a set of turning gears, I didn't feel any of it while it was happening. I don't regret it for a second because it saved Tuco's life, who had just sacrificed himself in order to help me. The only regret that I have was forgetting that I had that screwdriver in my pocket the whole time.

345

Sharon ran off to call 911 so they could do something about my bleeding. More worried about Tuco than myself, I told her as best as I could to not worry about the ambulance and to load up the dog and to take him to the vet immediately. She called them anyway, as well as Dad, before she went to the vet.

Shortly before the EMTs arrived, Dad and Debbie came racing over in Debbie's van. Dad got a few tears in his eyes when he saw me in completely blood-soaked jeans and a T-shirt wandering back towards my house. I too started crying a little bit because the adrenaline was quickly wearing off.

When the ambulance got there, they wrapped my arms and hands with gauze and asked me to get into the vehicle so they could take me to the emergency room. I refused for two reasons—I will never get into another ambulance as long as I am able to move on my own, and I knew that the bill would be outrageous if I did. I kept my pride and my money and had Dad take me instead.

Before we went to town, the sheriff came and wanted to take Jack away. Shawn, who had only come to check on me once the sheriff came over, threw a fit and told them that they had to take Tuco too. Tuco was already on his way to the vet anyway, but he persisted. For some reason, the sheriff backed down and didn't take his dog. Shawn then went back home, without so much as even asking how I was doing. As far as I'm concerned, he only stopped by in the first place to make sure that there wasn't going to be any trouble with the law.

Dad took me to the emergency room were I got twenty or so stitches and a few shots. I don't remember to much else. Everything was kind of a blur, but I do remember Mom showing up in hysterics and Dad having to calm her down. Once they gave me an IV, I came around a little bit and remembered that Tuco was hurt too and that I still didn't know how he was.

Come to find out, Sharon had taken him to the vet and got him all stitched up. The doctor did tell her that one of his throat wounds was a hair's width away from being fatal. That alone made me happy with the decision that I had made and well worth the pain that I was going through.

Obviously I wasn't able to work for a few days, so I had plenty of time to call animal control and make sure that Jack was going to be dealt with before the same thing happened to someone else. They said that beings Jack hadn't been taken at the scene, I would have to take legal action to make it happen. No problem—I had a lot of doctor and vet bills that were going to have to be paid anyway. Just for the record, I only went after that and the reimbursement for my attorney fees. I didn't ask for it, but was also given an extra five hundred bucks by the time it was all said and done. Believe me, I can think of a million better ways to pocket $500 than going through that hell.

Jack was gone a few days later, pretty much turning that end of the neighborhood against me. Shawn even had Tom come and testify against me in court. He, in turn, looked like nothing but a fool when he had to answer questions about "which dog left their yard to attack another dog and a human?" He also didn't have anything to say when the judge told him and Shawn that what happened to me could have happened to my kids, their kids, and anyone else.

Not two days after looking ridiculous in court, Tom and his family were out on a family walk and subsequently passed by my house. They had never done that before, so I knew that something was up. Well, he went fishing and caught a sucker as he hollered and kicked at Slick, who was minding his own business and just wagging his tail at the edge of my driveway.

"What is your fuckin' problem?!" I yelled as I walked towards him.

"Your dog could hurt my kids!" he yelled back.

"He hasn't moved, you stupid motherfucker!" I replied, getting right in his face.

"What are you doing?"

"What does it look like?" I said, shoving him back about three feet. "If you gotta problem with me, let's finish it now. I'll kick your ass and then I'll slap your wife and kids around too!"

Of course I didn't mean that. I was just doing all I could to entice him to want to fight me.

"Let's call the cops," he told his wife after I shoved him. "He just assaulted me."

With that, he turned and left. Sure enough, the sheriff pulled up to my house a few minutes later. I wasn't arrested, but I was cited for third degree assault that was punishable with up to a year in jail. Luckily I already had a lawyer, so he took care of it for me. I did have to pay a fine, however, and go to an anger management class.

Following the dog fight, I healed up pretty good. I couldn't bend my fingers for quite a while and thus had to have someone ride with me at work to do most of the labor. I had to make several additional trips to the doctor because my right arm kept swelling up to over double its size. It was cool having the arm the size of Hulk Hogan's, but it would have been better if I had a left arm that matched.

Tuco, on the other hand, was a little slower to heal. After a couple of days, I took him back to the vet because of lumps that were in his throat near his puncture wounds. The vet said that those lumps didn't have anything to do with the dog fight—Tuco had cancer. My heart just sank as I heard them tell me the news. To make that day and the whole past week worse than they already were, they topped it off by saying that he had only three months to live at the very most.

CHAPTER 46

Viva Las Wedding

Following Tuco's terminal cancer diagnosis, I was left with very few options. I could just do nothing and watch it overtake him quickly, I could (believe it or not) spend thousands of dollars on radiation and have it take him anyway, or I could spend twenty dollars a month for a type of steroid that he could take once a day with food. The steroid would temporarily shrink the tumors and get him to revert back to his younger days until the cancer eventually came back and finished him off. For me it was an easy choice.

Within a few days after getting the steroids into his system, he was behaving like he did when I first got him. He had unlimited energy, a ferocious appetite, and he was moving around without any arthritis pain whatsoever. He was acting so good and so full of life that I thought that he had been misdiagnosed. Too bad the vet told me beforehand that things would go down exactly like they were happening once he started the pills.

Once Tuco found his fountain of youth and after all of the legal stuff had settled down, Sharon and I could concentrate on our wedding plans that had been working on after our little bump in the road the year before. With neither of us (especially me) wanting or being able to afford a regular wedding with all of the grandeur, we decided to get married in Las Vegas. No reception, no churches, just an "I do" and it's over. It wasn't quite on the drive-thru chapel level, but it wasn't too far off—perfect for my taste. We didn't need all of the hoopla, as the end result would be the exact same anyway. We were going to be down there for a week, along with the two neighbors that did like us, Dustin and Jana Engler, and anyone else that wanted to come were welcome. It may have hurt the feelings of my parents and cost them a little money, but it was what we wanted to do.

The week before we were to leave, the guys at work took me around town for a bachelor party. Dad came along too as we had taxis take us from bar to bar, so we could drink like it was going out of style. We ended up at a western bar where we rode a mechanical bull for what seemed like hours. By the end of the night, the inside of everyone's legs were purple and blue.

It wasn't the hangover that hurt, it was the rest of our bodies from getting destroyed from an unforgiving beast.

The following Saturday, the four of us loaded up in Jana's little Dodge Neon for the big drive down to Vegas. Due to the recent hike in gas prices, we decided to take their car to save on fuel as opposed to taking the Jimmy. To make up for putting the miles on their vehicle, I paid 75% of the gas. We planned on it taking two days down and back, leaving us one full week in Sin City.

Although this was going to be our annual family trip, the kids weren't coming along. I felt bad in a way because I never want them to miss out on any trips. Granted they weren't missing any of the bright lights because we were just there a year ago, but I still felt guilty. We did almost everything as a group.

Sharon and I could probably count on a single hand how many dates we have had with each other without them. It wasn't like we never got rid of the kids, it's just that we usually stayed home when we did. Going to the movies was out of the question because I did too much of that before I met her, plus I can't stand to listen to people crunch their popcorn. (I swear that some people had rocks in their buckets.) Instead, we would save up and do something really cool like going to a concert.

Aside from the Dwight Yoakam show a year earlier, we had just recently went to Auburn, a town outside of Tacoma, to see Motley Crue at the White River Ampitheater as part of their Carnival of Sins Tour. The group had recently reunited with all four original guys and were filming parts of the show for an upcoming DVD and a live album. For those who are wondering, Tommy Lee did break out the "tittie cam" again. I wasn't opposed to it.

For the trip, we left the kids at Mom's and Dustin and Jana left their boys, who are close to the girls' age, at his parents' house. Mom and Jen were going to fly down for a few days, as were Dad and Debbie. Mike, on the other hand, stayed behind because he was the one that was going to run my route while I was gone as well as watch the girls while Mom was down with us. As we did the year before, we stayed at the Greek Isles in Grandma's time share for the duration of our time in town. With her time share, I think that I was out about $200 for seven nights. Dustin and Jana stayed in the same building a floor or two above us. Mom and and Jen stayed at the Flamingo a mile or so south of us and Dad and Debbie stayed a few blocks from us at the Sahara. It may sound silly that everyone stayed at a different spot, but it all depends on the travel package that you get. Each of them are different and you can save money based on where you stay and the time of your flight.

The four of us got down to the hotel in the early afternoon on Sunday and checked in. We didn't have anything planned for that day so we just ate dinner and played a few slots at the hotel's casino. We didn't win anything but we got to drink for free, which is an awfully nice treat that all of the Vegas casinos offer as long as you are gambling. It doesn't matter if your betting a hundred dollars or a penny, you can have any drink that the bar offers at no charge.

On Monday, we had to go to the Clark County courthouse to get our marriage license. After that, we got suckered in to watching a couple of presentations on time shares. While we had no intentions on buying one, we did it anyway just for the free gifts. One of them gave each of us a hundred dollar bill, which more than paid for the gas for our entire trip, and the other one gave us four dinners and four show tickets.

That night, we used the show tickets to see the American Superstars Tribute at Stratosphere Tower. The show featured Elvis Presley, Tim McGraw, Christina Aguilera, and Michael Jackson—sort of. They were actually very talented impersonators that not only looked like the real people, but sang and moved like them as well. While I'm not much into any of the latter three, they were excellent at what they did.

With Elvis having died nearly thirty years earlier, this was the best hope that I had of seeing his energetic stage performance that he had in his heyday. This dude moved and shook just like The King and the women in the audience responded just like they did three decades earlier. As luck would have it, I managed to get him and Sharon together for a picture after the show. Sharon couldn't have been more giddy if he had been the real deal.

Either late that night or early the next morning, my family showed up on separate flights for Tuesday's wedding. While it was nice to have them there, I felt bad because Sharon's mom didn't come down to see her own daughter get married. She said that it was the money that was holding her back, which was bullshit because they will spend any amount of money on their son. Based on how her parents treated her in the past, I can't say that I was surprised.

Everyone met at our hotel early on our wedding day. The actual wedding was later in the evening, but it took several hours for a hairdresser to do Sharon's hair and put on her make-up. I don't think they worked straight through, as there was a fair share of alcohol consumption going on, but she looked amazing by the time that she was done. Earlier I told you that she was a about a seven, well on this day she was a ten. I'm here to tell you that she was the most beautiful person that I had ever seen and within hours, on Tuesday, November 8, 2005, she was going to be my wife.

Sharon on our wedding night

While the girls were upstairs in the room, Dad, Dustin, and myself were down in the casino taking advantage of the free drinks. By the time the limo arrived to take us all to the chapel, we were all feeling pretty good. When we got to the chapel, I realized that I didn't have any dress shoes. While it wasn't as bad as the time that Dad drove clear to Disneyland in his slippers, it was close. I had a brand new pair of Levi's and a button-up dress shirt that I call my "Rock shirt," as it looked just like the one that The Rock wore to the ring to mouth off to a jabroni. I looked pretty slick if it weren't for my white tennis shoes. Luckily Dad brought his black boots, so I borrowed his. Too bad they were two sizes smaller than what I wore.

Our wedding crew from the left: Jen, Mom, me, Sharon, Jana, Dustin, Dad, and Debbie

As soon as Sharon and I started saying our vows, we both started crying like babies. Maybe it was the culmination of several years of high and lows and the stress and peace that comes with raising kids and building a relationship at the same time. Maybe it was the one moment that we finally realized that there were not two people on the planet who were more meant for each other. Maybe this was what we all wanted from the start. Maybe it was all of the above but whatever it was, it was something very special.

With the tears flowing, I managed to mess up the vows for everyone to hear and laugh at. When the line came along about "to love and respect," I repeated it as "to love and expect." I didn't even know that I did it until afterward when I asked why everyone was rolling with laughter.

Right before the "I do," we exchanged our wedding rings. She had long since been wearing hers, so it was nothing new. I wore mine for that night and then didn't wear it again. While I had always intended on not wearing it just because I didn't want it getting snagged on something at work and having my whole finger ripped off, I couldn't have even if I wanted too because it was stolen by a babysitter a short time after we got home. I since then have gotten a wedding band tattooed on my finger instead. Most people scoff at it, but I don't think they are as secure in their relationship as I am. I'm proud of it because it's not something that you can slip off to put on a single's act—it's there permanently.

After the ceremony, we had to walk back to our hotel. Before we did, though, Dad wanted to go to Stratosphere Tower to ride the thrill rides. Oh yeah—those rides—they are ON TOP OF THE TOWER!

Stratosphere Tower is a free-standing concrete structure that was originally planned to be taller than the CN Tower in Toronto. Due to its close proximity to the airport, it was reduced to a height of 1,149 feet. By contrast, Seattle's Space Needle is 605 feet tall. At the top of the tower sat the world's first, second, and third highest thrill rides. The High Roller was a roller coaster that cruised around the top of the building. The Big Shot was a bench that suddenly shoots you up the needle as if you were launching into space. The X-Scream was a rail car that literally drives you over the edge of the building and stops, leaving you staring down at the ground below. For a mere twenty dollars, you could ride them all.

Dad and I did them all. As God as my witness, I have never been so scared in my entire life as I was when I rode those rides. The roller coaster was like a country drive compared to the other two, with the X-Scream being the scariest of all.

We got loaded into the car of the X-Scream and without so much as a warning, we drove straight over the edge and stopped. My heart was jumping out of my chest as we sat there at a 45 degree angle and looked at the tiny lights 866 feet down from us. I held on for dear life, which wouldn't have done any good if the ride broke free. Incidentally, a few weeks after we did it, the ride broke down and the people that were in that same position, staring at death, were stuck there for nearly two hours. We were only hung out there for ten seconds, but it seemed like an eternity. I couldn't imagine how those other guys felt.

Within a day or two, the rest of the family went back home. We still had several days left, so we spent one of them taking a bus trip to Hoover Dam and the Grand Canyon. By now I was tired of seeing the same old dam and the same old hole in the ground but Dustin and Jana hadn't seen it, so we went along anyway. Across the aisle from us on the bus was a huge lady that had to weigh every bit of 300 pounds. Next to her was her son, who might have weighed 75. I felt sorry for him because his mom took up half of his seat. Since it was a couple hour ride, we were allowed to bring food and before we were even out of town, Fatty opened up her bag and gave the boy an apple, an orange, and a banana. For herself, she hauled out and inhaled six McDonald's breakfast sandwiches in less than the time it takes to say the Pledge of Allegiance.

When we got back that night, we all went to the Rio for a topless show called Erocktica. It was more than just half-naked women, it was also a concert with acrobatics. For some reason, Sharon and Jana were bickering back and forth. Sure enough, it all exploded and Dustin and Jana left us at the Rio, several miles away from from the Greek Isles. After a thirty dollar taxi ride, we got back to the hotel so I could be the mediator between the two girls. Not only did I not want them to stop being friends, I wanted a ride home! They ended up reconciling a little bit—enough to get us back home. Their friendship was soured for a while but it eventually blew over. It must be a girl thing or something.

By Christmas, the end of the three months that the vet gave him to live, Tuco was still doing well. He was still eating like a horse and continued to thrash around with Slick on a daily basis. The problem was they liked to wrestle in the house, which was getting much smaller with two growing kids and two full-grown Labradors. If it wasn't for Tuco being sick, I would have made them outside dogs.

He wasn't a bad dog as much as he was a sneaky dog, but Slick certainly had a way of living up to his name. During the holidays, Sharon made two huge pumpkin pies and let them set out on the counter to cool. While we were in the living room watching TV, Slick quietly got up and went into the kitchen where we also kept all of the food bowls. Instead of eating his own food, though, he ate the middle out of both pies. Unfortunately, nobody noticed it until the next morning—the day we were to eat them.

A few weeks later following a pretty bad snow storm that dumped over two feet during a single day, I was out shoveling the driveway in hopes of being able to park my truck that was currently stuck out in the street. I had the shop doors open so I could listen to my music like I always did when I was outside. After tiring out, the boys went into the shop to get out of the cold. Tuco laid on the cement next to the space heater, while Slick decided that he was going to lay on top of my Harley. I didn't notice it until I walked in there and saw him getting off of it. If I would have been able to catch him . . . .

The snow took several weeks to melt off but by the end of January, it was finally gone. A few weeks later on February 5, 2006, Seattle was at the forefront of the sport's world. It was on that Sunday in Detroit, Michigan that the Seattle Seahawks played the Pittsburgh Steelers in Super Bowl XL—and it made me sick as a sport's fan.

It wasn't the fact that the Seahawks were in the Super Bowl that bothered me. While I root for the 49ers, who haven't so much as sniffed a playoff birth in almost a decade, I like the game enough that I don't care who plays for the championship as long as it is a good game. The only team that I root against no matter what is the Dallas Cowboys because they cost my team at least two more Super Bowl appearances in the 1990's. What did bother me, however, was the way that all of the people in the area were now giddy over the Seahawks all of a sudden.

Up until their playoff run, you were lucky to see a handful of people in an entire month wearing a Seahawks shirt or hat out in public. I only know of two people who are die-hard Seahawks fans, as I am with my team, that watch every snap of every game like their lives depended on the outcome—Joey and Josh Williams, the habitual liar. Now everyone was donning the blue and green, including people that didn't even watch football. The local radio and TV stations were now spending a great deal of time talking about "our" Seahawks when before they wouldn't even report the score unless they won. What it is, is the classic example of "fair weather fans," and nobody is worse than the so-called fans in Seattle.

Seattle as a city didn't have any professional sports franchises until the 1970's. Towards the latter part of that decade, the three major sports awarded expansion teams to Seattle in their respective sports. Football had the Seahawks, baseball had the Mariners, and basketball had the Supersonics. As of this writing, only one of them has won a world championship—the 1979

Supersonics. Only one other Seattle professional sports team of any kind has won a league championship and you would have to go back all the way to 1917, when hockey's Seattle Metropolitans became the first American team to win a Stanley Cup.

Needless to say, Seattle fans haven't had a lot to cheer for. Most are fans of other teams for various reasons. But once the Seahawks started winning, everyone became a fan. They all had their jerseys, hats, bumper stickers, and little flags for their car antennas. I'll give them a little credit because although the Steelers won 21-10, they still displayed their apparel throughout the offseason and into the following year. Their home games were always sold out and take it from me, Qwest Field is the loudest place that I have ever been in my life. But by the time that the Seahawks turned in a 4-12 and a 6-10 season in consecutive years, most of the clothes were put back in the closet and the attendance in the stadium went down.

Don't think that it's just about the Seahawks, either. The Mariners had a good run in 1995 and in 2001 but other than in those years, good luck finding anyone with a Mariners shirt. As for the Supersonics, they left for Oklahoma City after the Seattle voters didn't approve a new facility for them following a couple of terrible seasons. The prosecution rest, Your Honor.

CHAPTER 47

Saying Goodbye

B Y APRIL, TUCO's health began deteriorating once again. The tumors that had been shrunk by the steroids had resurfaced, as cancer once again overpowered medicine. It had been seven months since the vet gave him his death sentence and he had more than doubled what they gave him. Just after his tenth anniversary of being in my life, I called the vet and asked him if it was time for me to bring him in.

"Has he stopped eating?" the vat asked over the phone.

"No," I said. "He still eats but not as much as before."

"Well, when he won't eat a cheeseburger, then it's time."

While it was a relief that he was going to be around a while longer, it was still only putting off the inevitable. I was going to wait a bit longer but when I saw the first sign of him suffering, I was going to take him in—he didn't deserve to live in pain because I selfishly would not let go.

I had been prepared for the day, after the initial shock wore off. Back in October, I actually paid the money for the office call and the euthanization for when the day finally came. I also opted for him to be cremated and have his ashes returned to me for not much more money than a basic disposal of his body.

People may laugh and joke about having a pet's ashes displayed in an urn at one's house. While I won't do it for every dog that I'll ever own, I felt that it was necessary for this situation. By the time he were to pass away, I would have had him for ten years. In that ten years, I had started and graduated high school, learned to drive and bought my own cars and motorcycles, started working for a living, bought my own house, had a baby girl, and got married. Outside of being born and dying, he had been a part of every major milestone in my life. He had been a shoulder to cry on when things were bad as well as a friend to celebrate with when things were good. At times, I was closer to him than I was with my own parents, Sharon, or any friend that I ever had, so it was only logical that I have him with me forever.

A couple of weeks after talking to the vet, he stopped eating his dog food. One afternoon, I cooked him up a cheeseburger and he practically inhaled it. Afterward, I went to the store and bought a few packs of ground beef for his new diet. As long as he was eating, I didn't care what it was or what it cost (within reason).

On May 15, he ate his last meal because the next day, he didn't want to even look at food. On that afternoon, I called up the vet and made the appointment for the following day. For the rest of the day he had really bad diarrhea, so bad that he was literally shooting liquid out of his ass. It was not only painful for him, but it was painful for me because I knew the cancer was eating him up.

That night while Sharon and the girls were in town doing something, the two of us just sat in the living room and watched wrestling together like we always did. I watched a tape of bloopers and funny moments and tried to laugh but it was hard, knowing what I had to do the next day.

On the morning of Thursday, May 18, 2006, I woke up and went to work as usual. Normally I keep a steady pace that some misconstrue as rushing or racing through my day. On this day, though, I had no desire to work at my regular pace. Instead of a paycheck at the end of the day, I was going to see my best friend die in front of me.

That afternoon after I got home, the two of us sat together on the front porch and looked aimlessly towards the mountains. I put the last decade in rewind and thought of all the fun that we had together wrestling, playing ball, and swimming in the lakes. While I was lost in my time machine, Tuco just got up and went and sat by my truck in the driveway. To me, it was his way of saying that it was time.

I don't remember where the kids were, but Sharon and I loaded him up in the truck and headed to town. We drove by where the two of us first met on my way home from school that day. We even drove down past the old house on Orth Way where he was first introduced to the family. While he set up in the bed of the truck so he could see, he no longer jumped from side to side and barked at the oncoming rigs.

I pulled up and backed into a parking space on the side of the clinic before going and checking in. They looked at me kind of funny when I didn't have Tuco in the building with me.

"I want the procedure done outside—not in here."

They agreed—they didn't have a choice. Tuco had spent far too much time in the vet over the last year and I was not going to let him take his last breathe of life in a place that he only went to when he was injured. He was going to die with dignity, in my truck, and by my side.

Even Mom and Dad showed up as the vet was inside and getting his things together. It was only right—they too had been a big part of his life. Mom took him everywhere that she went in the Explorer, while Dad did the same when we would go to Papa's. Before I was financially responsible for him, they were.

After a few minutes of very little talking (what could you possibly say?), the vet came out with a long cart, a clipper, and a needle and vial. He shaved a little patch of fur off of Tuco's right leg as my pal rested his head in my lap. Next, he reached for the needle and stuck it right into one of Tuco's main arteries. He then slowly injected the phenobarbital into his veins, causing him to slowly close his eyes. Once the shot was finished, so too was the life of my very best friend that I would ever have.

"That's it?" I asked.

"That's it," the vet confirmed.

I helped him load Tuco's limp body out of the bed of my truck and onto the cart. I pulled the sheet over his body and watched him get wheeled into the building.

Did I cry? Of course I did. I didn't sob uncontrollably, but I had to wipe my eyes frequently. I'm doing the same while I'm writing this. It's hard to think about watching your best friend die, no matter what kind of creature he is.

There isn't a day that goes by that I don't think of him. More so now, as I have recently just had his name tattooed on (of all places) my throat. Believe me, it is the first thing that people notice. Usually people just ask if it hurt (which it surprisingly didn't), but other people ask what it means. While I always tell them that it is my dog's name, I rarely tell them the reason why it is in such a blatant spot.

It's a simple explanation—Tuco jumped in to protect me when I was getting attacked, even though he was in poor health. I then did everything that I could to get the Rottweiler off of his throat before it killed him. While I was successful, Tuco had marks on his throat that he would have for the rest of his life because he sacrificed himself. The least I could do is return the favor.

It was tough for a few weeks getting used to life without him. To try to make me feel better, Sharon bought me another dog for Father's Day. He was a purebred Golden Retriever that I really didn't want, but kept anyway. I named him Duke, which was John Wayne's nickname. It was actually started because of a dog that he was always seen with in his early days.

In the months that followed, Slick took a serious turn for the worse and wouldn't eat. I took him to the vet, who was now renovating their building with the help of all of my money that I had given them recently. They figured it on being some sort of blockage in his digestive system and I could either spend $800 on a surgery or spend $100 and have him put to sleep. It wasn't my first choice, but I couldn't put the kids through losing another pet already. I chose the surgery that would hopefully discover something in his digestive system that he had swallowed, instead of something that he had growing inside of him. If he didn't have an object in there and had a tumor instead, I told them to just put him down. As luck would have it, they removed a stuffed animal and he was as good as new the next day.

It was during his few days in the hospital, however, that he once again lived up to his name. On three occasions, Slick managed to open up his kennel and wander around the back of the building. At first they put him back into the cage but after the second time, they figured it was a faulty cage and moved him. When he broke out a third time, they gave up and just let him wander around on his own. "Houdini," as they began calling him, after the legendary escape artist, Harry Houdini, was unable to be confined in a cage.

I was happy with my decision of letting Slick live. He is a great dog, mellow as can be, and would never fight another dog. He's tough as hell because not only did that blockage not kill him when the vet said that it should have, but I just recently ran over him with the four wheeler after hitting him head-on. You would have thought that I missed him almost completely because all he had was a busted lip. He was awful stiff for a few days and has since avoided the ATV at all costs, but he made it.

CHAPTER 48

Passing it Down

W ITH THE KIDS getting older and spending five days a week at school (Lizzy included, as she was now in preschool already), Sharon began to grow tired of being at home all of the time. She wanted in a big way to go back to work, knowing that a second income would be great for our growing family. By summer's end, she had a nearly full-time job working at Old Navy, a clothing retailer that had a store in Burlington. She would work there for a year or so before getting an assistant manager position at a shoe outlet store called Nine West, which was just across the street.

Now that we had two vehicles going to town on a regular basis and with the cost of gasoline beginning to go up, we decided to trade in the Jimmy for a more fuel efficient car. For the Jimmy and a couple of thousand dollars on top of that, we bought a silver, 2005 Chevrolet Malibu with a mere 30,000 miles on it. Rather than getting seventeen miles per gallon like the Jimmy got on a good day, the Malibu got nearly forty—more than twice the mileage.

Not long after getting the new car, we were ready for our next family trip. Although it had been just four years since we were there before, we opted for a return trip to Disneyland. It made perfect sense to do so as Lizzy was the same age as Katelynn was when we went the last time. She could do all of the kiddie rides that her big sister got to enjoy before she was born, while Katelynn was now ready to hit the cool rides with me.

As usual, we left somewhere in the middle of the period between dusk and dawn, driving more than 800 miles on our first day. Our first stop was San Francisco, which was not even really on our way. The only reason that we went there was because Katelynn wanted to go across the Golden Gate Bridge. She got the idea from the intro to *Full House*, which we had started watching on DVD.

"Hey Eddie, where's that bridge at?" she asked out of the blue one evening as we watched the show.

"San Francisco."

"Where's that?"

"California."

Her eyes lit up immediately.

"Can we drive on it on our way to Disneyland?"

"Sure can."

Other than seeing Alcatraz, we did the whole San Francisco deal while we were there. We crossed the bridge twice (one of which cost a toll of five bucks that I should have taken out of Katelynn's wallet) and spent the rest of the time walking along Fisherman's Wharf. After a few hours, we headed back to I-5 and eventually ended up in Santa Nella at a Motel 6 for the night.

The next morning, we packed up our stuff and headed to the car that had since been completely covered with bird shit. I'm not talking about ten or twelve piles—I'm talking COMPLETELY covered. It was if a septic tank emptied its whole load on our car. There was so much that I had to use the little ice bucket from the room, fill it with water five or six different times, and rinse the door seams so we could get in without it pouring into the car. Obviously our next stop was the car wash, which we usually hit on a trip at least once. But we never did it on just the second day, though.

Following a thorough cleansing, we headed down to Hollywood to see Grauman's Chinese Theater and to stroll down the Walk of Fame. While on our walk that honored every major star in entertainment, we finally found that illusive Hollywood Harley-Davidson that we couldn't find to save our lives four years earlier. Come to find out it was nothing more than a clothing store on Hollywood Boulevard. While seeing all of the stars on the sidewalk was cool, there were far too many homeless people standing around and begging for change for us to want to stay more than a couple of hours.

Grauman's Chinese Theater was much better. At the front of the very building where major motion pictures have made their premier since 1926, sat many concrete panels where some of the biggest names in Hollywood have carved their names or stuck their hand and foot prints in. Everyone from Julie Andrews to John Wayne to my main man Clint Eastwood have left their permanent mark in the cement for all to see.

Me in Hollywood outside of Grauman's Chinese Theater

When we were finished with Tinseltown, we made our way into Anaheim and checked into a Travelodge for the next the next four nights. This time around, we bought a three day pass for Disneyland and the California Adventure theme park across the street. During the three days, we could stay from open to close and jump back and forth between the parks. To save a few dollars like we did with Katelynn the last time we were there, I got Lizzy in for free by saying that she was two.

For three non-stop days, we rode every ride that we came across at least once and sometimes up to three or four times. Now that Katelynn was bigger, she got to ride Space Mountain and all of the other cool rides. She was a bit apprehensive about even getting in line for some of the rides but if I didn't let her in on the specifics, she was willing to try. She may not have done them a second time, but she at least did them once.

On the last day, Sharon and I had a surprise waiting for the girls. Disneyland had recently started a new deal where you could have a meal with some of the characters. Of course it was outrageously priced, but seeing the look on the kids' faces made it worth while. Elizabeth in particular, who was at the time really into Cinderella, was amazed to see her hero come up to her while she was eating dinner.

The kids were exhausted after three full days in the park. We still had plenty more trip to go, though. After we left Anaheim, we spent the entire duration of the day driving. It allowed the kids to rest up a bit as we made our way north for the second half of our vacation.

Before ending up in Fresno for the night, we went into Sequoia National Park to see some of the redwood and sequoia groves that California is famous for. Among them, the General Sherman Tree, which is the world's largest living tree. Standing 275 feet tall with a trunk circumference of nearly 103 feet, the General Sherman is estimated to be 2,200 years old—and still growing. Each year it is said to grow enough wood to make a 60 foot tall tree of normal proportions. To say that this and the other giant trees are amazing is a gross understatement.

The next day we went into Yosemite National Park, which was new territory for everyone. While I had seen everything that we had done on most of our previous trips, it was rare that we all experienced something new as a group. I anticipated more of a Yellowstone-type of place, rather than the vast geological landscape that it turned out to be. While you can see a great deal of rock sculptures that were naturally created by glaciers that once moved through the canyon as you drove along the road, the true beauty of the park would have to be seen on foot on the hundreds of miles of hiking trails.

After overheating the brakes to the point where they stopped working while going down the steep elevation drops, we pulled over to let them cool. Just by chance, we saw a black bear taking a stroll a hundred yards or so down the hill. It was the first time that the girls saw a bear in person, so you can imagine their insecurity. When Sharon farted while leaning across the seat to get the camera, they forgot all about their fears and laughed at their mother, who wasn't amused. For the record, that was only the second one that I ever heard her do and she hasn't done it in my presence since—that's what she says anyway.

Lake Tahoe and Lassen Volcanic National Park were next on our list. While the snow that began falling in the Sierra's didn't affect the driving conditions at Tahoe, it did lead to Lassen's closure. We were forced to bypass it and we headed north up US-395 through Oregon, where it continued to snow pretty heavily. It was early November so it wasn't surprising that we had snow, but it made Sharon nervous throughout the hundreds of miles that we had to continuously drive in it. It was during that stretch that we decided that we were going to start taking our trips a little earlier in the year, around her birthday, to avoid any snow and still have some of that warm, early fall weather. After a brief stop at Crater Lake in the southern part of Oregon, we drove a little further and parked for the night to let the storm pass.

That night, we started talking about how much the family was growing and how we were beginning to outgrow our house. Even though the big dogs were now living outside permanently, it was still getting too small. Although I knew that we were going to have to do something soon, I wanted to take care of paying off her car and replacing my pickup, which was approaching 300,000, with a new one first. Once that was done, which we figured would take at least three years, we could start looking for a bigger house. I had to explain to her that a bigger house comes a bigger payment and we likely couldn't afford that while having a car to pay for on top of it.

While she understood my reasoning, she didn't anticipate me dropping over $20,000 on a brand new, red, 2007 Chevrolet Colorado, which was basically a twenty years newer version of my S-10. She wasn't real happy with me (probably because she only got a used car) but she went with it. If I had to do it over again, though, I wouldn't have bought a brand new one. The reason that I did was because it was exactly what I was looking for and they took my truck in on trade for exactly what I paid for it.

In early 2007, Jen and Joey dated each other briefly. What happened between them is their business, but it didn't last long to say the least. One night while they were either still dating or had just split up, all of the guys from work were at a bar in Burlington to celebrate somebody's birthday. After a great deal of alcohol had been consumed, Jen shows up and confronts Joey. The two bickered back and forth in the bar and then went outside together. For some reason, I followed them out.

When we got out there, Jen had two guys waiting for what I can only assume was a setup from the start. The two guys got in Joey's face and told him to stay out of Jen's life or else they were going to do something about it. Joey wasn't really happy to hear that so he just kicked one of them right in the nuts. Before the other guy could jump Joey, I hooked him in a full nelson and drove him face-first into the ground. Joey then put the boots right to his unprotected face before all of the commotion emptied the bar. Beings the two cowards took off on their own with their tails between their legs, nobody called the police.

A few weeks later after our little brawl, Joey and I went up to Bellingham to the Mount Baker Theater to see "Rowdy" Roddy Piper tell his life story to a room full of wrestling fans. In reality, it was just another stop on a tour for him to make money by selling his books and T-shirts. It's not just him that does that, as every significant sports athlete that is physically past their prime does it for as a way for them to not only make money, but to keep their face in the public eye. It's smart business for an independent contractor if you ask me. For twenty dollars, I got to listen to him tell his story (which I could have listened to for many more hours on top of that), I got a signed copy of his autobiography, and got a picture taken with him.

Me and "Rowdy" Roddy Piper

I managed to catch him by bit of a surprise when we met in person and I showed him a video sleeve of his Coliseum Video form 1985.

"Wow, how long have you had that?" he asked as he looked it over.

"Fifteen years or so," I replied. "Don't you have one."

"No," he said. "I don't keep nothing."

"Why not?"

"Well, I've been in the business for thirty years. When your character is licensed to a company, they can sell whatever they want and whenever they want. Most of the time I don't even know that I have a new shirt until they say 'Hey, put this on before you go to the ring.' If I kept every little toy, video, poster, or shirt, my wife would throw me out of the house."

I totally understood. While I've never been anywhere near the recognizable star that he is, I wouldn't want to have tons of stuff with my name on it or to sit around and watch videos of myself—you're your own worst critic. It's the same as musicians not listening to their own music because they have to play it all of the time. It made perfect sense.

We talked not much more than a minute or so but for a guy that plays such a despicable role on TV, he was just the nicest guy. He actually had just been diagnosed with cancer (which was probably the reason for him going out to make a few dollars) and the doctors only gave him a fifty percent chance to live. Well he was one of the lucky few, because he beat it.

During his speech, he brought out his special guest, "Mean" Gene Okerlund, the man who was responsible for interviewing all of the big name wrestlers before their matches back in the day. While he didn't talk near as long, he told a few funny stories and posed for pictures as well.

In the spring after Katelynn got home from school one day, she asked me if she could sign up for baseball. She was now in the second grade so the timing was perfect for her to get into it. I signed her up and after the league president read that I was interested in helping coach, he gave me a head coaching spot for the Birdsview team, whose practice field was a quarter-mile from my house. I got all of the team's information and went about calling their parents to tell them my practice schedule and plans for the season. I was going to have three, ninety minute turnouts a week to teach the kids how to properly play baseball. My big thing was going to be making sure that they threw and hit with the right form so they would be prepared for future seasons.

I had been in touch with every parent except one, who wouldn't return any of my four phone calls that I had made over the course of a week. Sharon figured out why while she was looking at the information sheets on the players. One of the kids was the son of the Tom, the guy that I shoved and tried to get him to fight me a while back.

"What are you gonna do?" she asked.

"I'm going to see if his kid is going to play for me or not."

A day or two later, I was outside and happened to see his truck pull out of his driveway down at the end of the street. We hadn't spoken to each other or even acknowledged each other in the slightest way since the incident in front of the house—no waves, no nods, just a look straight ahead if our paths happened to cross. As he was coming down the street, I walked right out into the middle of the road, forcing him to either stop or commit vehicular homicide.

When he rolled down his window, I asked, "What's your last name?"

"Bass," he answered. (Dustin and Jana call him "Tom Ass" instead of Tom Bass.)

"I thought so. Your son is on my baseball team."

"Oh yeah, I've been meaning to talk to you about that (I'm sure he was). I think we are going to put him on another team. I think that he should be at the next level."

"Okay, let me know so I can save him a spot or move on without him."

"Sure thing," he said as he drove off.

I gave him a few days and when I still hadn't heard anything, I decided to take it upon myself to see if he was in or out.

"Yeah, he's in," he said. "Do you need an assistant coach?"

I'm sure that the only reason that he wanted to was to be sure that I wasn't going to mistreat his kid, but I gave him the benefit of the doubt. Yeah, we had our problems, he cost me a bit of money, and I had to take an anger class, but I'm big enough to put our differences aside and be professional. It wasn't about us and what we thought of each other, it was about the kids and getting them to learn how to correctly play baseball.

"Not anymore," I said, reaching out my hand. "We start Monday."

When we all gathered as a group for the first time at the first turnout, I saw that my squad was mostly comprised of girls. That wasn't the bad part—nobody even knew how to throw. Even though all of the kids just wanted to bat, we spent the entire first day working on throwing—step and throw, step and throw. The same went for batting—step and swing. After a week or so, everyone had it down pretty well.

During turnouts, I would split them into two groups and would have them scrimmage most of the afternoon. The kids got an early taste of competition while working on hitting, fielding, and throwing at the same time. Afterward, I ran conditioning games that raised their heart rate and still gave them a chance to goof off at the same time. Without them knowing it, I was getting them into shape and teaching them the fundamentals of baseball.

Every kid had to be handled differently. Some liked to lose focus and daydream, some liked to be disruptive, and others actually wanted to get better at what they were doing. The kids that were disruptive and lost focus would run extra bases as a punishment. After a while they got the idea that I was in charge and they were to do what they were told.

Out of everyone, Katelynn probably got the toughest treatment. It wasn't because she goofed off or daydreamed, it was mainly to show the rest of the players and parents that I didn't play favorites. I had stopped playing baseball because my coach put in his uncoordinated, string-beaned goof of a son to play my position when he wasn't even close to my level, and I wasn't going to let the other players get the same feeling that ruined my last year of the sport.

Before our first game, I drew up a batting lineup that had our five best hitters going first and the good and not-so-good batters alternating the rest of the way. I kept it the same all season so the kids would easily remember who they were after. I pitched to each of the kids during both practice and the games so they would have consistency and before long, the not-so-good hitters stepped their game up and we hardly ever suffered a strikeout.

The team was called the Rockhounds and we finished in first place with seven wins and only two losses. Both losses were on those days when the kids just didn't have their heads in it. When they were on, though, they were unbeatable in their age group. They weren't the best athletes, but they worked harder and practiced more than any team in the division. We more than doubled the points of our opponents in the games. We didn't do that on purpose, we were just that much better than our competition.

During one of the games against a team that was coached by Judd Wilson, who was at the time the mayor of Concrete, he accused me of being too aggressive with my players. They even tried to change the rules as the game went on, causing the parents of my kids to get angry as well. So naturally I ran up the score against them on purpose to show him that we were better than his group. He actually had his team quit and leave the field during the game, knowing what I was doing in retaliation to his rule improvisation.

"You're a real son of a bitch," he said to me quietly after his surrender, where he knew that I was going to be the only one to hear him.

"You're right," I said with a grin. "And I'm also a better coach than you."

I didn't know he was the mayor of town at the time. That night, I got reamed by the president after Judd had called and whined about the situation. It was obvious whose side he was on so I knew that it was going to be the end of my coaching career in Concrete until those two weren't around. It didn't matter that all of my kids' parents were defending me, I couldn't beat those two off the field.

Although I only coached one season, I couldn't have had a better time. I got all that the kids had in them, as they improved beyond my wildest expectations. They learned the fundamentals, how to compete, how to be a team player, and how to win. It gave me an opportunity to coach, something that I always wanted to do, and it allowed me to pass down a little of my work ethic and competitiveness to a younger group.

Even Tom and I got along great. In fact, while I wasn't welcome to coach anymore, Tom was. Katelynn spent the next season on his team. He ran his turnouts the exact same way as I had when I was in charge. The only problem was, he put up with too much crap from the poorly behaved kids. He allowed them to take control and cause the rest of the team to lose focus, resulting in numerous losses in games. If he would have been a little tougher, they would have done much better but then again, he too might have been accused of being too aggressive.

Things had certainly changed since I was being coached as a player. Now, things that used to be done back then aren't tolerated in any way anymore. You can't swear, work them too hard or too much, and apparently can't play to win. It's funny (or sad as far as I'm concerned) to see how sports have changed so much in one generation's time. It will be interesting to see how much more politically correct and "pussified," as I like to call it, that all sports will become in the future.

It was hard to believe that Elizabeth was in preschool already. The learning to walk, talk, and use the toilet seemed like it had just happened. Now she was four years old and was developing a personality that resembled mine. She was mischievous, creative, and tough when it came to pain. Although she was a lot like me in many ways, she was still her own person with a mind of her own.

Katelynn was becoming a different person altogether, even compared to when I met her. Her dad had recently been married and thanks to his new wife, who I actually like, decided that he should be a consistent part of Katelynn's life. She was now going down to spend time with him on most weekends and school holidays, as well as the majority of the summer. He took her to fairs and movies, bought her anything that she wanted, and had a pretty long leash on her. Though it was nothing more than him feeling guilty and making up for all of their lost time, it was at the same time hurting our family. She started arguing with us, whining to try and get her way, being lazy when it came to school work—all things that she knew better than to do. What I assumed to be a phase, was just the beginning of a rough period that has been very difficult on me, but I'll get back to that in a bit.

In the meantime I want to stay positive because at the time, we were still a close foursome. A few days before Sharon's birthday, as she had requested, we went on our family trip. While this trip was again going to be my second or third go around on almost everything, it was going to catch everyone else in the family up with me. I wanted to have them see what I have seen and to experience everything that I had done in the past without them before we did new things together. After this trip, we would have pretty much the entire country west of the Rockies covered.

After leaving in the evening on Friday, we drove through the night hoping to arrive at Lewis and Clark Caverns, an hour east of Butte, Montana, in time for the first tour of the day. Just after Missoula, I switched places with Sharon so I could get a quick nap. I no sooner than dozed off before Sharon woke me up because there was a blizzard in Butte. I couldn't do anything but laugh at our luck. We even left early this year to avoid it, but it wasn't to be. The funniest thing was, it was still September!

"I thought that I told you that I didn't want to vacation in the snow anymore!" an irate Sharon yelled once she pulled over so we could switch places again.

"I thought that we would be safe in September," I said, honestly believing that.

We stopped for breakfast in Butte at a Perkin's Restaurant, a place much like Denny's. It wasn't our first choice but all of the other cafes were apparently opening late due to the weather, so we had to settle for it. The food sucked and the service was even worse. Our orders were wrong but we couldn't tell the waitress about it because she never came back to our table to check on us. So we ate the food that we were served and left—without paying.

Although later than we had hoped, we still made the caverns in time for one of the earlier tours. The kids had a ball, strolling in the dark, damp caves and seeing the different formations of the stalactites and stalagmites inside. Other than the half-mile hike through the snow just to get there, Sharon liked it too.

Afterward we drove into Billings, away from the snow, and got our motel for the night. He had hoped to be there in time to go to Zoo Montana, but the weather slowed us up too much. Instead, we drove out to see Pompey' Pillar, the only place that proved that Lewis and Clark actually came through the state of Montana. Nobody was all that impressed after seeing a rock with a guy's name on it, so we went back to the room and turned in early.

We headed east to see Little Bighorn Battlefield after we got up the next morning. Unlike the previous time that I was there with Dad and Uncle Robbie, we spent several hours there. We watched films and presentations and even took guided tours over some of the area. It really helped to enhance the understanding of such an historical place. We were still free to wander away from the group on our own, so I had to take the girls to the spot where Dad (or I) dumped the Gold Wing. (Speaking of the Gold Wing, I forgot to mention that I gave it back to Dad after the divorce was settled. He then gave it to Papa to ride for a couple of years before getting it back again. He finally sold it to a vintage bike collector for what he paid for it when he bought it.)

By the end of the day, we ended up in Gillette, Wyoming, probably the most overpriced place in the world given its location. Located out in the plains with nothing surrounding it but land that could only be used for a backdrop in a western movie, Gillette is the only place for lodging on I-90 between Sheridan and the South Dakota border. Knowing that, they charge nearly a hundred bucks a room per night at all of the six motels in town. I was able to get one for eighty, but I had to lie through my teeth about crossing the country to see my dying mother to get them to show me any mercy.

Following our expensive night of accommodations, we went a little ways north to Devil's Tower. Again unlike before in 1998, we spent an extended period of time there hiking the trails around the tower itself. Come to find out, you could actually get a permit to climb to the top of it if you wanted to. While it isn't something that I will ever do, thousands of people do it each year.

Next, it was on to Sturgis, South Dakota, home of the Black Hills Rally. It had been nearly two months since the annual rally brought in its usual 250,000 people but in early October, it was almost a ghost town. All of the shops and things were open and selling discounted items, but we were the only customers around. I actually enjoyed it, as I could for the first time visit the National Motorcycle Hall of Fame without having to take a number and come back at a specific time. Nobody else but the four of us were there and I was able to take my time looking at vintage bikes. Still, it wasn't the same as when the bikes are handlebar to handlebar in four rows down Main Street. We finished the afternoon by going to Wall Drug and driving through the Badlands, which we did at dusk for an chance to see some really cool scenery. The kids went nuts as we drove by a bunch of deer, but they knew that we would be seeing much more once we got to Yellowstone.

After spending the night in Rapid City, South Dakota, we went on to Mount Rushmore first thing in the morning. In 1998, I had only just ridden by it long enough to see that there were face carved in a mountain. Had I not known who they were already, I wouldn't have had the time to identify George Washington, Abraham Lincoln, Theodore Roosevelt, or Thomas Jefferson, as Rob didn't want to stop. This time I was in charge, and I could take as much time as I wanted to take.

The four of us spent a couple of hours there, watching videos and listening to tour guides. Come to find out, the man who was in charge of the sculpture, Gutzon Borglum, was the one who chose the four presidents for the memorial to begin with. The project began in 1927 with 400 workers and a plan that would have each carving go from the head to the waist of each president. However in 1941 due to the lack of funding and the death of Borglum, the project ended prematurely with the results of which being what is on display today.

A few miles down US-385 sits a much more amazing sculpture that will be (if completed) 641 feet wide and 563 feet tall, dwarfing Mount Rushmore. Crazy Horse Memorial is the still under construction sculpture of Crazy Horse, the Oglala Warrior who was stabbed in the back by a United States soldier outside of a courthouse when he was in his early thirties. In his life despite his age, he was a veteran leader in the Great Sioux War from 1876-1877 and the leader of the Fetterman Massacre in 1866.

In 1948, the elders appointed Korczak Ziolkowski, who had worked on Mount Rushmore, to create a memorial for their leader. Ziolkowski promised to work on it on his own and with the help of his ten children and to never take any federal money to help the project, as it was the United States' fault that Crazy Horse was murdered to begin with. He twice turned down ten million dollars in federal and state funding to keep that promise.

He worked on it everyday until his death in 1982. Now his children are in charge, working seven days a week with their own equipment and materials. The only money that they make to fund their project is what they get from the entry fees that visitors pay to see the memorial. With so few workers and so little money, it isn't a shock that only the face has been completed. Eventually, the whole upper torso of Crazy Horse with his arm extending in front of him, the head and front shoulders of his horse, and a giant tablet with a scripture on it will be protruding from the mountain. Sadly, most of us won't live to see it.

We made our way back into Wyoming later in the day and spent the night in Casper. The next morning, we headed west into Grand Teton National Park and ended up in Jackson early in the afternoon. Rather than going into Yellowstone then, we opted to get a good night's sleep and enter the park first thing in the morning for what was going to be my fourth time going through Yellowstone. It was going to be much different this time, however, as almost the entire park was now blanketed with snow after an overnight storm.

Sharon was pissed off again about what was on the ground.

"Why didn't we leave earlier?" she hollered as we cruised along at all of fifteen miles per hour.

"We did leave earlier," I told her.

"I know, but this isn't fair."

It wasn't, but as I said, it was a new experience seeing Yellowstone in the snow. The flakes stuck on the antlers all of the enormous bull elk as they walked along the banks of the Yellowstone River. Not many other people were visiting the park due to the weather, so we could stop in the middle of the road and look at the snow-covered buffalo as they made their way across the white plains.

We stayed two nights at Mammoth Hot Springs Hotel, which sounds fancier than it really is, but it wasn't a dump either. I never stayed in a lodge in Yellowstone before so again it was a new experience. It was a lot like football or wrestling camp in a way, as we were only in our rooms to sleep and were otherwise gone for the day. For our meals, we would go to the food hall across the street for buffet breakfasts and dinners.

The trouble was, we had taken Lilly with us this time and there weren't supposed to be any pets in the building. I had no trouble sneaking her in, but keeping her quiet was a different story. She had a barking fit one night as the elk were literally right outside of our window bugling and carrying on. They did it all night long and the next morning we found out that two bulls had a fight overnight that left one of them dead. With it being a national park, I was curious what they did with the meat and carcass. A ranger in the the area told me that when that happens so close to a populated area, they haul the animal off to another area where the animals can eat it. I wonder if he's full of shit and they don't just split it up and take it home?

Throughout our two full days, we drove every road there was to offer in the park and hiked a few trails when it wasn't snowing. Twice we had to go back to the car early as Elizabeth fell in the mud and we had to get her clothes changed. From then on, I gave her piggyback rides to prevent us from wasting time going back and forth to the car as well as spending a fortune at the laundromat.

When we saw all that there was to see in Yellowstone, we headed for home. We spent two nights at a motel in Kalispell, where we spent a full day going to the movies and going to parks to let the kids go wild and burn off steam from riding in the car for so long. They did great, though, and I've got to say that with all of the miles that we have driven over the years, I couldn't have three better passengers.

Our last night of the trip was spent at Papa's, as I couldn't go through his neck of the woods without stopping or we would be pissed. The one time that I didn't stop when I went by, he found out and bitched at me about it for five minutes straight.

"What the hell's wrong with you?" he would say. "Ain't you got the decency to stop and see your grandpa when you go through town?"

Well after that ass chewing I sure did. Whether it was with my whole crew, on a motorcycle trip with the guys from work, or on my own, I made the time to stop in if I was within an hour or so from his place. I'm glad that I did, because I didn't know that he wasn't going to be around a whole lot longer.

CHAPTER 49

Money for Nothing

B Y THE EARLY part of the summer of 2008, Katelynn had finished up the third grade and Elizabeth had completed preschool. Given the fact that Concrete didn't technically offer it, we had to pay for her to go to what they called "head start." For eighty outrageous dollars a month, she got to go to school for four hours a day to begin her educational career. The district did throw in the meals and bus transportation as part of the package, but it was still a bit much in my mind.

At one point during the year, Elizabeth's bus got into a little fender-bender after someone pulled out in front of it. Nobody was hurt and most of the kids on board weren't even aware of what happened but when I heard about it from another parent rather than from the district, I flipped out and stormed right into the superintendent's office. We already knew each other because she was the mother of the girl that I had to take to school along with Jen when we first moved up-river.

"I heard that my daughter's bus was in a little wreck today."

"Yeah it was," Barb Hawkings said with a little smile.

"And?"

"And, what?"

"And why wasn't I notified?"

"Well, it wasn't that big of a deal."

"The hell it ain't," I said, raising my voice a bit. "If something happens to her on your watch and I'm not told about it, it is a big deal."

"We treat each incident on a case by case basis, and we didn't feel that it was going to be an issue."

"I don't care if all of the kids thought that it was funny, I want to know what happens from now on—got it?"

"Yes."

I probably overdid it a little bit, but I still think that I should be told of things like that. If they have a sex offender that moves within the district, sometimes even many miles from the school, they send home letters. If someone makes a bomb threat, they send home letters. Those two are just potential problems to where a wreck actually happened. I'm not saying that the local news should know, but a little information to a caring family would be appreciated.

Even though Katelynn was gone for the summer, we still had Lizzy around while Sharon and I both worked full-time. I had my usual three days off every week so we really only had to worry about having somebody watch her four days a week. Sharon would usually drop her off at Mom's until I got off and could pick her up on the days that our schedules didn't allow an easy transition between us.

Every couple of weeks, I would take Lizzy to work with me on Fridays because they were my lightest day. She got to be quite popular at several of my stops as they all knew her by her name. Some of them even gave her donuts or cookies each time they saw her. I'm not sure that she wanted to go with me so we could spend time together or if it was to sit around and eat junk food while I worked, but it was fun to do it together anyway.

One Friday after work in June, all of the guys loaded up in two cars and headed for Tacoma for a double bachelor party. Both our truck loader, Gerald, and Joey were going to be married in the coming weeks (not together, by the way). To celebrate, or as an excuse to get as drunk as possible, we all stayed in a suite at the Emerald Queen Casino and had tickets to a concert.

It had been almost a year since my last concert when Sharon bought tickets for my birthday to see Def Leppard, Foreigner, and Styx at the White River Amphitheater. Although neither of the three are anywhere near my favorite band, it was a good show and I came away knowing that I could have a good time as long as I liked the music that was playing.

If I didn't like the music or any of the songs, it might be a different story. A while earlier when Sharon and I went and saw Heart, they played just two of their most popular songs while they filled the rest of their set with songs of their newest record. With bands like that who were popular thirty years ago, you have to play the music that people want to hear. Sure you can throw in some new stuff to try to get people interested in your new record, but we want to hear the tunes that made you popular to begin with. Most artists and groups get it, but Heart didn't.

The artist that we saw for the bachelor party, Paul Rodgers, did it the right way. Rodgers was the front man for Free prior to his days in Bad Company. Once they disbanded, Rodgers went solo before becoming the new lead singer for Queen, almost twenty years after the death of Freddie Mercury. During the show, he played all of the best songs from all three bands for a room full of people that didn't set down for the entire show.

When the show was over, we all went back to the room for the second half of the night's entertainment—the strippers. It doesn't take a Rhodes Scholar to know that most bachelor parties involve strippers. Other than mine and Dad's, every one that I have ever been to has had naked chicks of some sort. What I could never figure out was why all of the guys lied about it to their wives. Oh well, it's none of my business.

The last bachelor party that I went to that had a stripper was when Greg Mahle got married (for about a week). The girl that was there wasn't all that pretty to be polite, but she would give lap dances to anyone with money. She even did this thing where I guy would lay on the floor with a dollar rolled up in his mouth and she would squat over him and pick it up with her snatch. While I watched it, I wasn't going to get involved. I wasn't scared of Sharon or anything, but this particular girl had an odd odor coming from her the minute that she dropped her pants. Maybe it was because I had a girlfriend and access to that sort of thing whenever I wanted and they didn't, but those guys couldn't get enough. She even said that she would go all the way with anyone in the room, either in a bedroom or right out for everyone to see, for a hundred bucks. Between all of us there, we managed to raise the bounty for the only virgin in the group. Although drunk, he still had enough sense to pass.

I told Sharon about all of it when I got home from Greg's, as I did the time when I went up to Vancouver to get a work pass for the loading docks and stopped off with the guys at a strip club for a lunch time lap dance. That one I felt guilty for because the naked girl was grinding near me instead of someone else but when I told Sharon, she wasn't angry because she knows that there is only so much that can happen. Now if anything further would have happened, she would have had me castrated.

Even if I didn't plan on telling her, she would find out anyway with my luck. Then she would be pissed that I was doing something behind her back. I can't do that—I have to be honest with her because I would want the same in return from her. If the other guys don't tell their wives, that's their business, but I'm telling mine before she hears about it from somebody else.

Anyway, Sharon was the only wife that was prepared for the fact that there might be strippers at the party. Sure enough, there were two much better looking girls there than the one that was at Greg's. These girls did the exact same trick that the other girl did and even took it a step farther by giving everyone what they called a "beaver bash," where they sit on each side of a guy's head and take turns pounding their crotches into his head. It's funner to watch it than it was to receive it, as heads were treated like paddle balls.

Before their grand finale, which was screwing each other with vibrators, Joey and I left to go talk in another room. With him getting married, he was feeling guilty about what was going on. I told him to tell his bride-to-be if it would make him feel better and that I was planning on telling my wife when I got home.

"Would you be mad if she saw a male stripper and got dances from him at a bachelorette party?" I asked.

"No, not really."

"That's because you trust her. If she trusts you, then she'll understand."

Whether he told her or not, I don't know. I told Sharon everything when I got home the next day. She wasn't overly excited to hear about it by any means, but she trusted that what I was telling her was true. It was probably a little easier for her to digest knowing that those sort of things only happen sporadically. Now if they were happening on a weekly basis, I would probably be divorced, castrated, or both!

It had been eight years since I started working at Dairy Valley by the summer of 2008, and in that entire time I was not allowed to take a summer vacation, thus missing out on numerous motorcycle trips. Although I had done weekend trips with Dad and Uncle Robbie and even Papa and Jake, who each had bikes by this time, I always had to miss out on the big trips due to work. In fact, it had already been seven years since Dad and I went to Texas in 2001.

While missing trips was mostly because of work, my growing family had something to do with it too. But now the kids were getting older, Katelynn was gone all summer, Sharon was working full-time, and Lizzy was always wanting to go stay at Mom's (or Grammy's, as Lizzy called her), allowing me chances to go on rides like I did before I was a husband and a father and not having feel guilty about doing it. Instead of riding just back and forth to work on my bike, I could go back to putting some serious miles on it.

The "no summer vacation" policy was temporarily lifted over that summer. As long as there were extra people, which there were once school deliveries were done for the year, people were allowed to take a week off during the summer according to seniority. Beings I was number two and the number one guy, John, usually took his vacation in pay, I got the first choice of weeks. I selected the first full week of August, the week of the Black Hills Rally in Sturgis.

I called Dad and told him the news and that I was planning on taking a bike trip to Sturgis, exactly ten years after our inaugural trip in 1998. By telling him my plan, I was also in a way asking him if he was interested in coming along. I didn't just flat out ask him because I figured that he would decline, and you can only be rejected so many times before you stop trying. While I would have liked the company, I wasn't going to let it prevent me from going just because he wasn't. After talking to him, he sort of him-hawed around about the idea for a few days. But after talking to his brother a little while later, they both decided that they wanted in on it. Maybe it was the nostalgia of it being ten full years since our first trip there, or maybe it was the fact that it had been nine years since the three of us took a trip as a group, but for whatever the reason, we were going to team up to ride again.

A lot had changed in the ten years since our initial cruise. Forgetting all of the personal stuff, we were all ten years older, which meant that we had now missed nearly a full decade of rides. At that rate, we might get in only one or two more in before Dad and Rob reached their seventies. Since our last trip, Dad and I no longer spent every day together, which meant that we were no longer constantly at the other guys' throat and fighting all of the time. Finally, we all had upgraded our bikes to newer models which meant that we should no longer have to spend good chunks of our trip making repairs and adjustments.

Just like a decade earlier, Dad and I left his house after he was off work in the afternoon and rode over to Eastern Washington. Rather than going to Rob's house like before, we spent the night at Papa's house before Rob joined up with us in the morning after daylight.

After Rob took a few minutes to have a cup of coffee to warm up following his hour ride in the moist fog, we pulled out of Papa's driveway in our typical formation—Dad in the front, Rob second, and me in the back. Once I got through my gears, I pulled up alongside Rob to let him know that his taillight wasn't on.

"Hey, your taillight's not on," I hollered at him.

"FUCK!!"

Judging by his reaction, I figured that it was a little more than just a dead bulb. If it was just a bulb, He probably would have just said "Goddammit." Instead I watched his head bob back and forth as I dropped back, likely cussing his bike out.

We pulled into a Shell station, exactly two miles from Papa's house, where we shut our bikes down to find out what was wrong with Rob's bike.

"This motherfucker," Rob said of his bike. "It is fine all fuckin' year until it's time for a fuckin' trip and then it fuckin' breaks down—fuck!"

Dad and I did all we could do to not burst out into uncontrollable laughter at the combination of Rob's tirade and the irony of yet another pit stop on a bike trip.

Rob tore the front headlight assembly off of the front of his bike right in the parking lot. He checked all of the wiring and the fuses. The wiring was good, but one of the fuses was out. The bad one was a high amp fuse which the Shell didn't carry, so he had to go further into town to the Napa store to get one. Of course they didn't open until 9:00, so we had to wait almost two hours before he could get what he needed. Once they did open, Rob got what he needed and we were off—nearly three hours later than we had hoped to be leaving town. It was just like old times.

Once we officially got on the road, we dropped down into Coeur d'Alene to get on I-90, twist on the throttle, and make up some time. By the time we got into Montana, Rob's light was out again. Just like before, the fuse had blown. Rather than hunt for another fuse, he opted just to run without a taillight until we got to the next Harley dealer that was a few hours ahead in Belgrade, which just happened to be where he bought his bike to begin with.

After we got into Belgrade, Rob marched right into the bike shop and into the service department. They remembered who he was from a few months earlier when he bought the bike, probably because they didn't get a lot of people from Washington coming over to buy their bikes.

After Rob explained the situation to them, the service guy said, "It looks like you're overloading your fuse."

"No shit!" Rob yelled. "Why?"

"I don't know," the guy replied.

The bike itself was a former police bike which officers ride for just one year before our tax dollars buy them new one. Their used bikes are then stripped of their sirens and flashing lights by local dealers and then resold. Rob insisted that they were responsible for it beings he had bought the bike from them. As it turned out, it was actually Rob who caused it by installing an alarm on it. We didn't figure that out until two days and twenty fuses later.

We spent the night in Livingston at a campground that charged us by the person rather than by the site like normal people. With it getting near dark and with Rob at the time still without a taillight, we just bit the bullet and forked over their ridiculous fee.

The next day, we spent more time messing with his bike in the hot and dry climate of the Crow Indian Reservation in the southeastern part of Montana. We rode the same path as we did in 1998 along the way to the Devil's Tower, where we spent that night in the same campground as we did the first time around. This time there wasn't any wind, but the rates had nearly doubled for camping giving us a two-night streak of getting hosed with camping prices.

In the morning, we rode the hour into Sturgis where we spent an hour or so riding Main Street and getting our T-shirts. Although this time he actually rode through town instead of waiting for us near the freeway, Rob didn't seem to be too enthused about much of anything. Come to find out, it wasn't just his taillight that was putting him in a shitty mood. He and his working buddy, Brad, were making payments on their own semi truck that they leased to a company and hauled lumber for them. The truck took a shit at the same time that the company that they ran for wanted to cut back on their loads. Brad, who had no idea what to do, called Rob each day with more bad news. Rob wanted to go home, but we convinced him to stay.

Once out of Sturgis, we rode up US-85 into North Dakota as per my request. None of us had ever been there before, thus making it the first new land that we had seen on the trip so far. We spent the night in the Theodore Roosevelt National Park for free (finally), before getting on US-2 in Williston, North Dakota and heading west towards home.

Now that I have been to North Dakota, I will not be going back. Each time that we stopped for gas, to piss, to take a picture, to eat, to drink, to fart—whatever—we were instantly attacked by bugs. Big ones, small ones, fat ones, long and skinny ones, multicolored ones, and any other kind of insect that you can imagine, were all over us. Even bug repellant wouldn't keep them away. The only thing that stopped them seemed to be the Montana state line, as they seemingly eased up once we crossed it.

After riding through hundreds of miles of grass and dirt without seeing so much as a slight bend in the road, we came into Havre, Montana, a town that is basically the halfway point of the state along US-2. Havre was also the first town that we had seen since North Dakota with more than a gas station in it. With it being a Tuesday, we were all plenty sweaty and dirty with road grime that we all needed a shower. We stayed at a Good Sam's RV park that we could both clean up and camp at. Although it was a little spendy, it wasn't anymore than we had paid for each of our first two nights and it came with a shower.

Once we all got cleaned up, we went into the store which also had a casino and a bar in it. We sat down in the air conditioned room for a couple of beers and to just relax, really for the first time on the trip. Rob's bike was working right by now and he wasn't thinking about his troubles at work. The bugs were gone, the air was cool, and the beer was cold, so we just soaked it up for the rest of the afternoon.

A couple of hours later we were still at the very same table, throwing back the beers quicker than the Native American bartender with no teeth named Dave could serve us. In fact, the three of us ran his bar cooler dry not once, but twice! We didn't have any help either, because we were the only three in there from the time we got there until closing time. After closing time we went across the street to another bar for a few more before stumbling our way back to camp. By this time we had consumed so much beer that we just laid on the ground next to our bikes and sleeping bags, rather than crawling in them. As for the next morning, well you can just imagine the hangovers that were going on.

While still in a bit of a haze for much of the next day, we continued east out of the plains and into the beauty of Glacier National Park. For all of the times that I had been close to it on both motorcycles and in cars, I had never actually gone through it. To say it was beautiful would be like saying that I am just a casual fan of wrestling. The trees, the creeks, the streams, the waterfalls, and the local wildlife altogether made for the kind of scenery that you only see in magazines rather than in real life. Following a night's stay at an abandoned campground near Libby, we rode back to Papa's house where we split up and headed home.

Sadly, it has been the last trip to date that the three of us have been on. While Rob's work troubles passed, new ones arose and he hasn't been able to take the time to go yet. When I got home and Sharon asked how it went, all I could say was "good." There was no fighting like we had done before. Nobody had their bikes tip over to get them pissed off. Other than just that day where Rob was visibly down, everything went great. It may have had the least amount of drama and funny stories, but it is safe to say that it may have been the best trip that we have had as a group.

Perhaps the most important part of the trip, for me anyway, was during just a random thought while cruising down the road that got me to think about what all had transpired in my life since 1998. Yeah, ten years had gone by quick but so too had my whole twenty-six-plus years on this Earth. *What if I crashed my bike right here in the middle of nowhere?* Sure Mom and Dad and Sharon know almost everything about me, but maybe they don't know the reasons why I am the way that I am. Then there is Elizabeth. She may have been five, but she wasn't yet old enough to understand or even care about everything about her dad. If I died, she may not ever know—same with Katelynn. It was with those five in mind and for anyone else that would ever be interested that I decided to write a book about my life for both everyone's information and their entertainment. I didn't, however, plan on it having the ending that it is fixing to have.

Following Mom and Dad's divorce nearly a decade earlier, I stopped going to visit Grandpa and Grandma because all they wanted to do was rag on Mom. Of course I didn't care for her decision either but most importantly, I didn't want to keep talking about it. As I said, after that awkward Thanksgiving in 1999, I distanced myself from them just to avoid talking about things that weren't any of our business. I still sent them Christmas cards each year, but I purposely waited until a day or two before so they wouldn't have time to return the gesture prior to the holiday. I only did that to prove to myself that if I didn't make the first move, nobody would. I continued with that for five years or so until the cards started coming back to me because they had moved.

In the ten years that had gone by, I had only seen them twice. The first time was at the store in Lyman after Sharon and I first moved into that rental dump. I invited them over and they stayed for about ten minutes and left. I figured that was a good start on making up for lost time, but they didn't seem all that interested. While it was hard to communicate because nobody really knew what to say, I tried my best to continue with basic small talk to avoid any periods of silence.

Two years went by until I saw them again. This time they had written a letter to Mom, whom they hadn't seen or spoken to either since she moved in with Mike, and asked everyone to meet them for dinner—everyone being Mom, Mike, Jen, and me and my family. The only stipulation was that everyone forget about all of what was said in the past and that everybody just start over. It sounded fine to me because by that time, the stupid battle of stubbornness was really the only thing that brought back memories of Mom's affair anyway.

To the best of my knowledge, everything went fine. We ate dinner and talked for a few hours like nothing had ever happened. From where I sat, everyone got along fine. Then a few days later, Mom sent Grandpa a Father's Day card that he returned to her with a nasty note about how she had ruined their lives. Although that was none of my business and I probably could have continued a relationship with them on my own, I just didn't want to deal with more badmouthing of Mom. *If I could get over it, why couldn't they?* To avoid all of the extra drama in my life that I didn't need, I washed my hands of the situation completely, save the Christmas card deal.

Once they had moved, I had no idea where they had gone. Their phone number wasn't in the phone book and I had no way of finding them even if I had wanted to. They didn't have any friends that I knew of so I couldn't ask around to find out. They broke off all communications with their oldest daughter, Sheila, twenty years earlier for her choice in husbands, so I couldn't rightly go and ask her if she knew anything. For all I knew, they could be living in Florida or even dead. While I certainly didn't want it to be the latter, I guess it didn't bother me enough to call the FBI.

Come to find out, they had moved into a huge house not more than a half-mile from Mom. At first, Mom would occasionally see Grandma walk by her house or the two of them drive by in a car together. Mom didn't put two and two together right off, as she just thought that they were driving by to spy on her. That was their style, as I saw them drive by me at work once in a while in places that they really had no business being at—like schools in Bellingham. Eventually, Mom stopped seeing Grandma walking by her house and only saw them drive by sporadically.

In the spring of 2008, Mom had found out that they had indeed moved into the same neighborhood but when she went up to their front door, she was asked to leave by a weak sounding lady on the other side. Mom persisted and the two finally let their daughter inside. Mom saw her mother in person face-to-face for just the second time in nearly ten years, seeing a lady that was a shell of her former self. Grandma was now in the late stages of Amyotrophic Lateral Sclerosis (ALS), which is also known as Lou Gehrig's Disease, that basically causes complete muscle atrophy until you die. Think of how Mom felt—her parents disowned her for the better part of ten years and now that she was going to try yet one more time to have a relationship, her mother was clearly dying.

When I heard the news, I pretty much wanted to stay away for the kids' sake. Who's to say that after introducing them to their great-grandparents and even their great-great grandma (Grandma Murrow was still alive and well into her nineties), that they wouldn't up and do their same disappearing act like before? Even if they did stick around, Grandma was going to be dead within a few months and they would be upset because they had basically just met a great-grandparent in time to watch her die. I didn't want to, but I gave in.

After everyone got acquainted/reacquainted, I took Grandpa out to the front porch of his house and laid everything out on the line. I told him that I had no problem forgetting about everything that both was and wasn't any of my business and starting over, just as long as he wouldn't turn his back on any of us again. He agreed and has kept his word ever since.

I few days before my birthday (I swear I'm not making this up) on September 5, 2008, Grandma died with everyone in the family but me by her side, as I had just left to go to work. We had spent the night at their house along with Mom, Mike, and Jen, knowing that the end was near. It wasn't a planned thing obviously but when it came apparent that every breathe that she took was a struggle and that they were several seconds apart, the writing was on the wall.

The real shock came when Grandpa showed up at our house in the evening prior to Grandma's death. I met him out in the driveway and he gave me a check for $40,000 and two receipts showing that he had started a $10,000 savings account for each of the girls.

Clearly dumbfounded, I asked him, "What's this about?"

"You know that I have saved money all my life and now I want to spend it. I'm giving this money to the girls and you get this money to buy yourself a bigger house."

I was floored.

"I can't take this," I said, truthfully meaning it.

I didn't earn it and, although mostly no fault of my own, I hadn't had anything to do with them for ten years.

"Sure you can," he said. "You're my grandson and I want you to have this and a comfortable life."

I thanked him and put it in my pocket as he drove off. He no sooner than left the driveway when Mom called and said that Grandma wasn't going to make it much longer. I just hoped that she lasted until Grandpa got back or I was going to feel even worse about the money than I already was.

After she died, I wrestled with the money business for weeks. He wouldn't take it back (believe it or not, I tried), which gave me a huge feeling of guilt. It wasn't like I had just ripped somebody off by selling them something for much more than it was worth (I didn't mind doing that), this was different. *Why would anyone give someone that amount of money after such an estranged relationship?* Guilt, that's why. They felt guilty after all of the lost time. For ten years they lived in exile, taking away ten years of family bonding that cannot be replaced. They finally returned, and not on their own accord, just in time to have their daughter watch one of them die a slow and miserable death. Can you imagine how that made my mother feel? So they do what makes most everything go away—solve it with money. Trouble is, money doesn't make EVERYTHING go away.

Once I realized that I was going to have this money when they both died anyway and that Grandpa would rather be alive to see me enjoy it, I did with it what I had been given it for—kind of. I put thirty grand into a high interest savings account and used the other ten thousand to pay my pickup off. The only reason being was that I could in no way afford a bigger house while still being under a car payment. With no other debts, I could get approved for a larger loan. Although it didn't concern him, I did feel somewhat obligated to tell Grandpa about my plans. It took me over six months of skimping on everything to return that money to the savings, but I vowed that I wouldn't buy anything until I had the $40,000 in the bank to do with it what it was given to me for—and when I set out to do something, I don't quit until it is done. Little did I know that Grandpa was going to shell out a second inheritance later on, but I'll get back to that.

After covering all of the states west of the central time zone, it was clear that our next trip was going to involve some airline travel to knock off a lot of previously covered ground and to allow more time for new adventures. On a Thursday afternoon in late September, the four of us boarded an airplane for the first time collectively, as well as individually, to fly to Nashville, Tennessee for our tour through the southern states. Six hours later, counting a stop in Denver to switch planes, we touched down in Music City where the recorded voices of George Strait and Reba McEntire welcomed us at the terminal gates. After picking up a rental car, we drove ten minutes to our usual Motel 6, where I had reserved three nights in order to spend two full days in Nashville.

The next day we drove into downtown where we spent several hours at the Country Music Hall of Fame. There, they had a museum full of guitars and other instruments in addition to stage outfits worn by everyone from Johnny Cash to Hank Williams, Patsy Cline to Loretta Lynn, Garth Brooks to Alan Jackson, Reba McEntire to Tanya Tucker—anyone who had left the slightest mark on the country scene. They even had a display of every gold and platinum record of the country music genre that covered just about every wall in the building.

As part of the tour, we took a shuttle to RCA Studio B where Elvis Presley recorded several of his earlier records, as did various other artists from the 50's through the 70's. Although it is still used today on occasion, Studio B is mainly used now for tours. In fact, one of my Marty Stuart albums, *Ghost Train*, was recorded there and there are pictures of the recording sessions in the liner notes. I think it's pretty cool to have been in the same place as where something like that was made.

Following the Hall of Fame, we went a few blocks over to the Ryman Auditorium for a tour of the building that was the original site of the Grand Ole Opry. While we were there, I recorded perhaps the worst version of "Heartbreak Hotel" ever put on tape. Sharon and the girls did a bit better when they recorded "Walking After Moonlight." Although both of them certainly leave something to be desired, it did give us a once-in-a-lifetime opportunity to record a song and take them home on a CD. Too bad we won't ever let anyone listen to them.

The next night, we went to a concert at the Grand Ole Opry, which was now held at a newer venue in the northern part of the city. I was probably more excited for the kids than I was for myself, as they were going to see their first concert at the most historic of places. While it was more of a musical variety show than it was a full-on concert, it was still two hours of great entertainment that was going to be nationally televised on Great American Country. We saw Little Jimmy Dickens (whose guitar was bigger than he was), a jug band that played tunes using only moonshine jugs and mason jars, and various bluegrass performers, including Ricky Skaggs.

The person who I was pumped to see was Marty Stuart, as he was one of the two guys who turned me on to country music. He played several of his best tunes as we sat in the second row, right in front of the stage, and sang along to "The Whiskey Ain't Workin'." Though I think he is a pretty good guitar player in his own right, it was his picking on the mandolin that in my opinion makes him the best in the business on that particular instrument.

Another guy that was there, Keith Urban (perhaps you've heard of him), I had no idea was going to be there. Now I've seen a lot of shows over the years, but I have never heard the chicks go as crazy as they did when he hit the stage for his set of songs. Girls were running over each other in the aisles to try and get a picture of this guy and if it wasn't for us being in a roped-off section, they would have been in our laps. Elizabeth, now five, fell in love with him on the spot, proclaiming him as her boyfriend.

After the show, I had the hardest time finding our way back to our motel. The freeway system in Nashville resembles a dartboard, as each of them circle the city with roads that lead you to another circle inside of that and so-on. I thought that I was taking the right roads but before I knew it, I passed LP Field, where the Tennessee Titans play, four times. What should have taken us ten minutes took us two hours instead.

We drove up into Kentucky the next morning, just to say that we have been there, before heading west across the state to Memphis. As nice as Nashville was, Memphis was the exact opposite. It got worse the further we went into town with graffiti covered signs, trash on both sides of the road, and broken down cars strung out everywhere. But we didn't come there to see the town itself, we came to see Graceland, the home of Elvis Presley.

Me, Katelynn, Sharon, and Elizabeth at Graceland

We bought our tickets across from his estate, allowing us to take an enhanced tour throughout the house and outbuildings. We spent hours listening to music clips and stories about his life as we walked through his house. It may sound silly, but they did it in such a way that you could actually feel The King's presence as you walked in his house. It was so much so that I cried as I passed the piano outside his racquetball court, where he played for a few minutes on the morning of his death. The racquetball court was now a display of all of his records and awards and there was a video of him on stage and singing the last part of "An American Trilogy" to a crowd that was playing on a large screen. While I don't know if they play that two minute clip over and over or if we just hit it at the right time, but Sharon and I both sobbed like babies at the impact of it all.

After Graceland, we drove into Arkansas to spend the night. We ate dinner at a Cracker Barrel, which had quickly become our favorite place to eat since we arrived in the south. While they are a national chain, the closest that they get to us is Missoula, Montana or Boise, Idaho. Although I had recently dropped over thirty pounds to get back to my wrestling weight of under 200, I forgot all about my diet plans and splurged when I went there.

I honestly didn't notice myself bulking up to 230 pounds. While I certainly wasn't fat by any means, I wasn't exactly in the best of shape. I got a lot of exercise at work, but I ate a lot of junk food and greasy shit because it was quick and easy. At one point I started having stomach issues that I took several inconclusive tests for, before I changed my diet around and started exercising more to help them go away without paying outrageous hospital bills. Within months, I was down to 195 and have kept it all off ever since.

In addition to the exercise that I get at work, I do at least an additional thirty minutes of cardio when I get home everyday. I eat in much smaller portions, with an extra emphasis on getting enough fiber. If I drink any pop, it is only diet. I buy the reduced fat option for most foods, but not all. The main thing is, I cut out the junk food and will only have dessert twice a week. I also don't eat past six in the evening so my food has a chance to digest before I got to bed, rather than having it form a cement block in my stomach. Since I changed all that around, I haven't had any stomach issues and have been much more energetic.

As for our nightly meals on our trips, we all try as best we can to collectively agree on a place. Each person, however, gets one pick that nobody can bitch about. Sharon usually gets two picks because we are always gone on her birthday, one of which is generally an Olive Garden. Lizzy always picks McDonald's and I normally like to try a non-franchise cafe or diner because with them being locally owned, you always get better food and bigger portions.

When it came time for Katelynn's pick a few days earlier while we were still in Nashville, she chose a Rainforest Cafe, a themed restaurant with animotronic elephants, monkeys, and other jungle animals that make obnoxious noises during the meal. It was kind of interesting inside, and certainly different, but the food was terrible. Ranking somewhere between a school lunch and a basic fast food joint, the meal was a complete letdown. To make matters worse, it cost us $70! It wasn't Katelynn's fault, but it made us think twice before letting her chose again. Now, where the hell was I before I got off on the food topic? Oh yeah—Arkansas.

The next two days were both driving days as we drove through Louisiana, Mississippi, Alabama, Georgia, and South Carolina. While in Louisiana driving along areas of swampland, we had to stop in the middle of the highway in order for an animal to cross. Around home we usually get dogs, cats, rabbits, deer, elk, and an occasional horse or cow, but in Louisiana, we had to stop as a large turtle was taking his sweet time crossing the highway. With absolutely no other traffic on the road combined with the traveling speed of the amphibian, we had plenty of time to get out and check him out.

During our drive, well inland from the Gulf of Mexico, we spent the night in both Montgomery, Alabama and Greenville, South Carolina. The path that we took was quite scenic but the most obvious part of that swing was that we were now in the major minority amongst an overwhelming population of African Americans. I don't want to sound racist whatsoever as this isn't about that sort of thing, but it is a major culture shock when you don't see that many colored people where you live and once you're down there, that's all you see. As for everyone in every town, they couldn't have been nicer people. It was very clear that they had no issues with the skin color of obvious tourists—it didn't bother them and after the initial shock, it didn't bother us.

After our night in South Carolina, which was Sharon's birthday, we drove into North Carolina to a small town off of I-40 called Maggie Valley, just outside of Great Smoky Mountains National Park. It was there that they had an amusement called Ghost Town in the Sky, where I had purchased tickets for several months earlier. Beings we had nearly 2,000 miles that we had to travel on this trip, I had to hold some sort of carrot over the kids' head or I might regret it. With all of the anticipation built up to ride roller coasters and eat cotton candy, you can just imagine the heartache that they had when we pulled up to the empty parking lot of a park that was only open on Fridays and Saturdays at that time of year.

The kids needn't worry, however, as I had already improvised a backup plan. I went to the office and got my money back for the tickets and kept in mind that they would be open two days from now. We then drove through the Smokies and into Pigeon Forge, Tennessee which, by the way, just happened to have Dollywood, Dolly Parton's theme park. Of course, they too weren't open until Friday.

Now I really had a problem. We had to be back in Nashville to fly out at six a.m. on Saturday morning. We could still do either park on Friday, but we would have to drive 350 miles as soon as the park closed to get to the airport in time for our flight. It wasn't a big deal, it just meant that we would have an extra four hours or so to spend at the airport. After clearly laying out the scenarios to the group, they agreed to the plan.

We booked two nights at the Best Western in Pigeon Forge and spent all of Thursday doing everything from miniature golf and arcade games to spending hours in the indoor swimming pool. Come Friday, we got up early and drove back through the Smokies (again) and back to Ghost Town in the Sky. Once at the gate, I gave them the exact same money that they had returned to me for tickets that I had previously purchased without reading the park hours. Lesson learned, I guess.

Ghost Town in the Sky had the most unique entrance to a park that I have ever seen. In order to get to and from the park from the parking lot, you had to get on a chairlift (like a snow skier) and ride about a half-mile to the top of a plateau. Every bit of ten minutes later, we got off the chair and set foot into a western-themed amusement park.

In addition to the rides, they had an old west-style town that was straight out of a John Wayne movie, where they had guys perform five or six different gun fights and shootouts throughout the day. Each of the twenty or so performers wore the complete cowboy get-up, including shooting real guns (with blank cartridges) at each other. It was like being on the set of a movie, watching stuntmen fall off of balconies and onto a four-foot thick chunk of foam, getting thrown through windows, and being shot while pursued by the law.

After the park closed, we all headed back down the chairlift to the car. Sharon, who nearly hyperventilated on the ride up, opted to take a van on the secret road down the hill instead of doing it the cool way. Either she is afraid to do anything fun or she truly is scared of thrill rides and heights, but but she isn't one to do much more than watching people at amusement parks. It's okay, because me and the girls are more than happy to make up for the fun that she misses out on.

As agreed to by everyone two days earlier, we buckled in for the seven hour drive through the Smokies (yet again) and most of the way across Tennessee and back into Nashville. As warned, we had about four hours to kill before we could even check in for our standard two hour wait before takeoff. The kids and I had no problem stretching out on the floor or along the benches to snooze, but Sharon refused. Instead, she angrily waited with gnashed teeth and clenched fists until check in. Once on the plane, she expressed her displeasure until we landed in Denver for a quick layover. The stop only gave her enough time to reload so she continue her diatribe all the way to Seattle.

CHAPTER 50
October 15, 2008 to May 18, 2011

I T SEEMS LIKE a long time ago since that fall day in the garage when I began this project—thirty months to be exact. Obviously having a full-time job, being a married father of two, having multiple projects going at once, and still being able to find time for myself, I haven't been strictly dedicated to this writing deal. I try to set aside at least one day each week when nobody is home so I can sit down for six or seven hours and hammer out some pages without any interruptions. The problem is if I am running out of time, I will stop writing in order to not have to carry a topic over for a few days because it could be a week or two before I am able to get back to the table. When that happens, my six hours drops down to four.

When I first started, it was really slow going. I still watched football when it was on TV as well as wrestling on Monday nights. That may not seem like much, and it really isn't, but when I would want to watch some of my wrestling tapes and DVDs a couple of times a week at times when I could have been writing, I realized that I had to make a change. It was hard, but I have completely stopped watching anything out of my library, save the new ones that I get every couple of months (I have to make sure that they work, right?), until I finish this son of a bitch. Hell, it kind of reminds me of one of Mom and Dad's old punishments.

Before I started my self-imposed punishment, Joey and I went down to Seattle the day after Valentine's Day in 2009 to see a WWE pay-per-view event called No Way Out at the Key Arena. It had been nearly six years since WrestleMania XIX, and this was the first pay-per-view event in the Pacific Northwest since. Naturally, we had to go.

Although Joey was now married himself, anytime there was something huge around that involved wrestling, him and I would skip out of the house and go and take it in. The problem was that with our work schedule of starting at three in the morning or even sooner, we had to miss out on certain things unless it fell on a weekend or a Tuesday night. But even at a Tuesday night event, like when The Rolling Stones played at Qwest Field, we were falling asleep in our chairs while Mick Jagger and Keith Richards (who looked like corpses) hobbled around the stage. We felt bad for not getting everything out of it that we should have, but we were exhausted from working a ten or twelve hour day.

No Way Out was on a Sunday and even with traffic, we would be home by 10:00 easy because the show wouldn't go past eight o' clock or WWE would be fined by cable and satellite providers. Much like a musician who will cut a song or two and edit others to stay on schedule, wrestlers will get a signal from the referee or an official at ringside to finish up their match immediately so they don't commit the cardinal sin of getting pulled off the air before the match is over. That happened in the old WCW days one time, causing such an uproar that Ted Turner had to refund everyone's purchase.

As for who won that night and who even wrestled to begin with, I couldn't say unless I went back and watched the DVD again first. By now, all of the wrestlers that I had grown up watching were gone, as were their first set of successors. If it wasn't for me being such an avid fan and a collector, I probably wouldn't even watch the new stuff—give me the old 80's and 90's stuff any day. Much better than the event itself, which is why I'm even talking about it to begin with, was what happened on the day before the show.

Mom and Mike called me from an airport in Los Angeles, where they had just changed planes on the way home from Mexico.

"Guess what, son?" she said when I answered the phone. "We are on the same plane as the wrestlers."

At first I didn't quite understand her because she sounded like she may have either had a few on the plane or was still a little hungover from their time south of the border.

"What are do mean?"

"The wrestlers who are wrestling in Seattle tomorrow are on this plane."

That made sense—they had just done a show in Los Angeles on Friday and were traveling on Saturday for Sunday's show.

"Well that's cool," I said, totally jealous.

"I'm gonna get you an autograph from the biggest one—Eddie, he's huge!"

I didn't really know who she was talking about but I told her not to worry about it. I didn't want her getting yelled at by a guy who was probably tired of being hounded for autographs and pictures wherever he goes. She didn't listen and did it anyway.

Mike took it a step further.

"I'm gonna hand him my phone," he told me. "And you can talk to him—he goes by The Big Show."

"No, Mike—don't!"

It's not that I was afraid to talk to him by any means, I just didn't want him getting pissed of at some guy who was sticking a phone in his face. Let's put it this way—I would never want to be a celebrity because I would never be left alone, and I like being alone and not having to talk to people outside of my family. This guy, The Big Show, whose real name is Paul Wight, is over seven feet tall and weighs 500 pounds—a modern day Andre The Giant. If he got irritated, he could just flick Mike into unconsciousness—and Mike's no midget.

Sure enough, I heard Mike on the other end of the line hand him the phone and tell him that his biggest fan, Eddie, wanted to talk to him.

"Eddie," Big Show began.

"Hey, Big Show," I said. "Sorry about these guys bothering you."

"It's no bother," he said.

"Well, I'm gonna be in Seattle tomorrow to watch the show."

"Well look for me, I'll be the fat guy in black tights beating up somebody half of my size."

"Alright, I look forward to it."

"Take care now," he said as he handed the phone back to Mike.

It wasn't anything spectacular in terms of a conversation and it may have only lasted fifteen seconds but the point is, he took the time to do it when he didn't have to. Odds are, you won't see a football player or any other highly paid professional athlete or actor do that because they get paid millions of dollars no matter what. Wrestlers, on the other hand, are independent contractors and make the majority of their money off of their own merchandise. The more popular they are amongst the fans, the more cash they bring in for themselves and the promoter. He who draws the most money gets to be in the main events and win the most championships. Although it made my day, what Big Show did is no different than me talking to a potential account at work—it's good business.

Come March after Sharon and I pinched every possible penny that we could, we had returned the ten grand that we borrowed from ourselves to make it a full $40,000 in the savings again. Out of the blue, Grandpa came up to the house with yet another check—this time for $50,000!

"Why more?" I asked.

"Because now you'll have enough for a down payment on just about any house you want."

True—$90,000 would be hard for any bank to turn down. Still I didn't want to just rush into something, so I put the money in the bank and went down to a mortgage company and got myself qualified for a home loan.

I wasn't really in a hurry to jump into another house just because we had the money, but Sharon and I were tired of living on Willard Lane at that point. More and more people were moving in and the peace and quiet that once was there was now a thing of the past. Neighbors bitched about the music the I listened to in the shop and even called the sheriff about my dogs barking, when it wasn't them in the first place.

One evening just as I was getting ready for bed, Slick and Duke started barking from their large kennel in the back of our property that I had built for them in order to get them out of the house. I came out into the living room and saw the sheriff sitting in his car in front of my driveway with his dome light on. With just my boxer shorts on, I walked outside to settle this matter once and for all.

"Is there something I can do for you?" I asked in an angry voice.

"I'm getting complaints about barking dogs," he said.

"Well my dogs are barking right now because you are parked in front of my house with your dome light on. Before you got here, they were sound asleep."

"I was told they have been barking all day."

"My dogs?"

"Well, someone's dogs."

"Everyone on this street but that dude over there (pointing to the house right in front of mine) has dogs, so who says that mine are the ones that are barking? It's that old guy calling isn't it?"

"I can't tell you who is calling, sir."

"Well it ain't my dogs that are the problem, so I would appreciate if you moved away from my driveway so my dogs will shut up and I can get to sleep."

I was so damn tired of the shit going on in the neighborhood involving dogs. I was always the bad guy, but it was never my goddamn fault.

After that went down, Sharon and I started really looking for houses. We didn't physically go to look at any just yet, but we scoured over books and magazines to see what was out there for the money that we had to spend. We hired a real estate agent (who supplemented her income by selling sex toys on the side) and told her to stand-by for when the time was right. In the meantime, we put new carpet in our house and painted the interior to freshen it up and prepare it to be put on the market.

Sharon was constantly pointing out houses to me but I shot them all down. I didn't want a fixer, I wanted quality. I wanted seclusion from neighbors because I was sick of having them, I wanted property, and space for all of our shit so that our house didn't look like a cluttered dump. She wanted desperately to go and look at certain houses, but I didn't want to end up settling on something just because Sharon thought that it was cute. Knowing that she likes almost everything she sees that is nice, I knew that it would be the best if we waited for the perfect house—in my eyes especially.

Then, we found it—the perfect house. A 1400 square-foot house with an attached garage as well as a 900 square-foot detached shop, on two acres of land that was completely secluded by cedar, fir, and maple trees on Healy Road, directly between Lyman and Hamilton. (It wasn't even a mile from where we rented that hole on Burrese Road) It was a stick-built, three bedroom and three bath home with hardwood floors, a covered, full-length front porch, and even a finished and carpeted loft—perfect for a trophy room where I could display all of my wrestling memorabilia. The only work that it needed (and it was a lot of it) was clearing the brush that had overtaken a majority of the property. It was priced at $390,000, which was very high but I was qualified for given the size of my down payment. I didn't even need to have Sharon on the loan (credit problems never go away) for me to get an interest rate of 4.75%.

As soon as we looked at that house we wanted it. We put an offer in on it that day that was contingent to the sale of our house, that we listed at the same time as we did the paper work. Unfortunately the owner of our dream home declined our contingent offer, which meant that our house would have to be sold in order for us to do business with her.

We listed our house for $150,000, nine or ten grand more than what we paid for it six years earlier. The first people that looked at it on the very same day that it was listed gave us an offer of $140,000. At my insistence, Sharon and I took the chance of a lifetime and counter-offered with our original asking price. It had only been one day and I wasn't going to cost myself ten thousand dollars by being in a big hurry. We never did hear back from them.

A few days later, six days after we put it up for sale, a full-price offer came in. Just like that, even in a down economy, our house was sold. Once the papers were signed, Sharon and I put in another offer on our dream home for $380,000. Sold—the house was ours.

Our little gamble had payed off. We took the equity that we had in our old house and bought all new furniture (that's ALL new furniture) for our new house. I sold all of our old furniture to the guy that had bought our old house for a mere hundred bucks. He got the better end of the deal by far, but he was splitting up with his wife and he was getting nothing and beings I had seen how hard a divorce can be, I helped the guy out. If that weren't reason enough, it also saved me from having a garage sale. He got our kitchen table and chairs, couch, futon, china hutch, computer desk, other cabinets, and even a bed and dressers for his two girls when they came to visit. He couldn't have been more grateful.

We moved in during the first part of June. It marked the fourth move for me in an eleven year period. This was going to be the last one, though. I know that you can't predict the future and you never want to say never, but I don't plan on moving again. If we do stay here, it will be paid for when I'm 57, just about the time that I'm not going to want to work all of the time. I plan on staying here until I die. Dad says that I'll move again so if nothing else, I'm going to stay here just to prove his ass wrong.

I don't miss Willard Lane for a second. We are so secluded here, I could step outside with my ball bag hanging out and nobody would ever see it(and not just because it's small either). I can play my radio all I want, as loud as I want, and as long as I want, and there ain't anyone who can bitch about it. Though it wasn't my dogs that caused the commotion in the first place, now they can bark until their voice box falls out for all I care.

Since we moved, we still go back there once in a while to Dustin and Jana's for barbeques and things like that. If you can believe this, even Shawn, the owner of the Rottweiler, and I began talking to each other during some of those parties. While the dog subject is never mentioned, we are courteous to one another and have even played cards and video games together on the Nintendo Wii, the modern version of the old Nintendo. I had so much fun doing that, I had to buy one for my family so the girls could have the same kind of fun that I had playing when I was younger with my dad.

Now that we lived in Lyman (again), the girls were going to start going to school in the Sedro-Woolley School District. They would go to elementary school at Lyman Elementary, where there is one class per grade level through the sixth grade. Once elementary school is finished, they will spend two years at Cascade Middle School (the same one that I went to), before finishing up at Sedro-Woolley High, where they will become the third-straight generation of the Thramer Family to graduate there.

Living a little closer to town also started saving us on gas, which has ranged from three to four dollars a gallon in recent years due to the ongoing feuds in the Middle East and the oil investor's speculation. We pay less for electricity than before and we have had (knock on wood) no major repairs like we had on Willard Lane.

Every person that has seen our house has only the best things to say about it. While everybody always compliments other people's homes, you can certainly notice it when they really mean it. Although on a much larger scale, it just looks like an old country cabin that you would have seen on a farm a hundred years ago. We have a large garden area, cherry, pear, apple, plum, and peach trees, and several large flower beds. We have our chickens, which I just can't live without, and a huge dog kennel that I built for the boys that is mostly covered so they can either get out of the rain or bathe in the sun when nobody is home. They are loose all of the time when we are outside because they have absolutely no distractions or reasons to run off the property. Hell, I even had enough room to build our own four wheeler track, every bit as cool as the ones that Papa built at his place years ago.

I'm telling you, we couldn't be happier. Everything has its place, unlike our houses before. I remember when we moved to Willard Lane and having to haul a thirty-foot trailer load of stuff. This time it took three loads—and that didn't even include any furniture! We had more than doubled our stuff in six years time but with a house like this, you'd never know it. Sharon's car, her scrapbooking desk and supplies, and our pellets for the stove are all that is in the huge garage. Out in the shop is my truck, my Harley, riding lawnmower, two four wheelers, and all of my tools (which was a ton after Grandpa gave me all of his). Even with all of that, I can still have enough room to have a convention in there—it's huge! I even have a large storage room in there for our camping gear, my reloading shit for my guns, painting and cleaning supplies, and so much more.

After several days of unpacking and settling in, I started the three month project of clearing all of the years worth of neglected brush that had overtaken the perimeter of the property. (The reason it was so bad was because the previous owner's husband had cancer and subsequently died during the last year that they lived here.) Without exaggeration, I bet that I have burned six dump truck loads of brush by the time that it was all said and done. I never minded it for a second because there is such a special feeling of satisfaction in maintaining something that is special to me. Whether it's working on my cars, my bike, or my house, the feeling that I get when I am done makes it all worth while. Obviously with all of that work that had to be done, you can imagine the miniscule amount of writing that I was getting accomplished.

Once I quit for the day, I would often just set on the porch and admire what we had been lucky enough to get. I still had a small feeling of guilt inside of me because I wouldn't have this place if it weren't for Grandpa's help. Although I didn't ask for it, I got it nonetheless and it somewhat ate at me for a while that I didn't get it on my own. Grandpa and Mom could say whatever they wanted to try and ease the guilt, but it was something that I couldn't get over.

That finally changed while I was on a motorcycle trip in Eastern Washington with a couple of guys from work. We just happened to be passing by Papa's and I told them that I better stop in for a bit. I gave them directions to the nearest saloon a few miles away and told them that I would meet them there in about a half-hour. I then dropped in on Papa and visited with him for over two hours. In that time, I told him about the house and how I was feeling guilty about it.

"Let me ask you this, Ed," he said. "If you had money and you knew you were going to check out sooner than later, would you fix your family up if you could?"

"Yeah."

"Would you want your kids to feel guilty?"

"No."

"Why?"

"Because I can't take any of it with me, so they should have anything that is left over."

"Exactly. Unfortunately most people ain't lucky enough to have any money at the end of the line. You shouldn't feel guilty, Ed. He may have put the money down for you, but you make the payments and you do the maintenance. What happens in the future is up to you."

I knew all of this, I guess that I just needed a person who wasn't directly involved to say that in order for me to accept it.

As I was getting ready to leave and finally meet up with the guys, who were by this time sure to have a good buzz, Papa told me that he was coming over to Dad's 50th birthday party the following weekend and not to tell him about it. He also said that he would stop by and check out the house.

True to his word, he and Gladys stopped by for a while the next weekend and, just like everyone else, they thought it was perfect. The funny part was that Dad still didn't know that he was coming to his party and was actually pissed at Papa for not having given him a definitive answer when he invited him several weeks earlier.

"My fuckin' dad," he said in disgust. "I go and help him with all of his shit and go to important things for him, but he won't even come to my fiftieth fuckin' birthday."

You can imagine the look on his face when Papa pulled up to his party. While Dad was busy taking his foot out of his mouth, I couldn't help but laugh at the fact that I knew that he was coming for the past week.

Not long after Dad's birthday party, he got into a head-on crash on the highway in one of his company's trucks. The truck wasn't as big as his log truck was, but it was still a commercial vehicle and the person that he hit was driving a small car. It wasn't his fault, as the girl who was driving the car pulled directly out in front of him to pass another car. Unfortunately while Dad walked away being just sore, she died on impact, giving him that permanent scar that anybody who makes their living on the road fears the most. He made it through with the help of a little counseling, which was given to him by the same guy that helped Sharon and I with our troubles. Luckily, Dad was strong enough to pull through it. It isn't uncommon for drivers in his position to quit driving completely after something so traumatic. A select few even take their own lives because they can't stand the pain.

Following Dad's wreck, he took me up on my invitation for an encore trip to Sturgis. He had previously declined, but had since changed his mind after what had transpired. Uncle Robbie was out this time around because he couldn't get that time off. In his place, who was I'm sure the one who ultimately convinced him to go, was going to be Jen.

I didn't really have any objections to it at the start because it meant that I didn't have to go alone. This was going to be my third go around at the world famous rally and this time by God, I was going to spend a full day and night there. I didn't give a damn about cruising the main drag or buying shirts, this time I wanted to go a mile outside of town to the Buffalo Chip, where the party goes down. Beer, burnout contests, motocross stunts, topless chicks, and music—the complete rally experience and the one part of Sturgis that I hadn't done yet.

Staying at the Buffalo Chip is actually a pretty good deal. You can forget about staying in a motel anywhere near the Wyoming and South Dakota border towns during rally week, as you couldn't afford a room even if they weren't sold out. Any other camping there was around was every bit of thirty bucks per person. At the Buffalo Chip, a night's stay is around fifty bucks. But the best part is, you get to see a free concert—and I don't mean some bar band bullshit. Through the years they have had Lynyrd Skynyrd, Aerosmith, Kid Rock (who I unfortunately missed out on a year earlier), Motley Crue, Travis Tritt, and any other classic or southern rock act that you can think of play there. Let's put it this way—Elton John got booed off the stage one song in during his only show there—they don't mess around.

Since I was going for sure before Dad and Jen decided to join in, I had already bought my pass ahead of time on the internet. Once I found out that they were going, I had to buy a couple more, which wasn't a big deal. They paid me back and we were all set to go on what would turn out to be my least favorite trip ever. I would say the worst, but I don't think that I can ever put "worst" and "bike trip" in the same sentence.

I want to preface this by saying that it didn't have as much to do with Jen, the person, as it did with Jen, the woman. In fairness to her, it would have been the same with any other girl, including my own kids. I go on bike trips to hang around the boys and totally get away from girls completely. I have to live with them every day of my life and while I love them to death and will do anything for them, I need to get away from them once in a while.

The trip didn't start off too bad. We all met at my house and took off on a Friday afternoon. Jen hadn't been on a ride of that length before and because of that, her body wasn't used to it and we had to stop much more than we would normally have. That wasn't a big deal but it cut down on our daylight hours, which meant that we would have to ride in the dark for a little bit in order to make it to Papa's that night. While it is a bit dangerous to do so over there with all of the deer, Dad and I had done it many times, were used to it, and knew to be as careful as possible. Jen hadn't done it before at all. Though she was nervous, Dad was more worried about her than I think she was.

It didn't stop there. Dad slowed down coming out of every single turn throughout the trip just to be sure that he saw Jen make the corner as well. He wouldn't pass anyone on the freeway unless Jen could pass at the exact same time so that she wouldn't be stuck behind a car and out of his sight. He filled her gas tank for her, checked her oil for her, and everything else except for wiping her ass for her. It wasn't the fact that I was jealous because he never did any of that for me, it was just the way that it seemed like she needed a babysitter that was irritating me. The way I see it, if you can't do those things on your own, you shouldn't have a bike.

We spent the night at Papa's and left his place around seven the next morning. Although we didn't have near as long of a hangup as we did the previous year with Uncle Robbie's electrical mess, we did get a bit of a late start because Jen wanted to take a shower. While we had only been on the road for one day and it was unnecessary to do so, I understood her wanting to take one beings the option was there. Let's face it, it may be a few days between showers when you're on a road trip and camping on the side of the road.

Our ride on Saturday, which consisted of nothing but I-90, was again constantly slowed by the third member of the group. Just like we did with Rob and his bike troubles, we were always pulling over for Jen to fiddle with her contact lenses. I did sympathize with her to an extent because I had the same problem during my contact wearing days. I did, however, scold her for not planning ahead and bringing her glasses for backup. To tell you the truth, it wouldn't have been a big deal if we didn't have to be in Sturgis on Sunday for the concert. With it two days and 1,200 miles from home, we had to keep a steady pace or we'd be screwed.

Compared to the year before, we actually made better time with all of Jen's stops than we did with all of Rob's, but just barely. In '08, we made it to Livingston, Montana for Saturday night. This time, we made it a whole forty miles further to a town called Big Timber. But when it came time to park for the night, just any old stop wouldn't cut it. Instead, Jen had to have a full-service campground at twenty bucks a head so she could take another goddamn shower.

Now I was starting to get mad. It didn't help that I was suffering from a little constipation, which was my own fault for not eating enough fiber before I left. When I get that way, I won't eat for a little while and when I do, it is only fruits or vegetables in small portions. Just because I couldn't eat didn't mean that they had to go without, but yet they got upset when I didn't give them any meal ideas. They just couldn't get it through their heads that I would eat when my body said I could. After a salad, a bowl of baked beans, and an early morning shit, I was as good as new.

The next day we made it into Sturgis with a little (but not a lot) of time to spare. Because Jen had never been into town, we cruised the gut as usual and got our shirts and hats and shit. Come the latter part of the afternoon, we made our way over to the Buffalo Chip to get our bracelets that allowed us access into the camping and concert areas.

The Buffalo Chip is nothing more than a ten acre field. Hundreds of RVs are lined up in one section and the other area is for bikers and tents. While there are dozens of outhouses, there aren't any real toilets, much less showers, which really pissed Jen off. I really don't know what she was expecting—this was a motorcycle rally and the people that go to them are not concerned with cleanliness. The only permanent buildings and real toilets were in the concert area, where they had the stage and a few bars and BBQ booths (that couldn't be classified as restaurants) where people could eat and drink.

Once in the concert area, I went and sat down in the grass in preparation for the show. Playing that night was going to be Creedence Clearwater Revisited, which was Creedence Clearwater Revival minus the late Tom Fogerty and his talented brother, John Fogerty. They were opening for the band that I was the most interested in, George Thorogood and the Destroyers. Dad and Jen took off to go and have a few beers while I saved our spots. I didn't mind, as I don't drink a lot of beer very often to begin with—especially when it is as hot as it was in South Dakota that night. In fact it had been one year since I had been completely drunk, following of course the night in Havre.

An hour later, right before CCR took the stage, Dad and Jen came back with a pretty good buzz. I didn't care that they were drinking whatsoever, but I didn't want them stumbling into me and talking to me while I was trying to listen to the music. I said it before—I go to concerts to listen to the bands and not to see how drunk I can get.

By the time CCR was done, Dad and Jen were hammered. Much like me, Dad gets happy and a little goofy when he gets going. Jen, on the other hand, gets mouthy and starts thinking that she is tough, and a motorcycle rally is not the place for people to cop an attitude. When some lady came around and danced with Dad for about ten seconds, she stood up like she was going to start something. I sat her back down and told her to back off.

"I'll kick her ass," she said with a slur.

"No you won't. You start fighting and this place is going to come apart. I'm not interested in getting into a huge brawl. Most people are carrying guns and this is not the time to start acting tough."

"Why don't you ever have fun?"

That was it. Before George Thorogood hit the stage for his set, I planned on leaving in the morning without them. Had it not been for my headlight burning out before we parked that afternoon and having to wait until the morning to buy another one, I honestly would have left as soon as the show was over. I did my best to ignore them the rest of the night so I could watch my favorite electric slide guitar player do his thing. (Eight months later when he came to Bellingham for a show at the Mount Baker Theater, I went and saw him again with Sharon to enjoy the things that I missed.)

After the show, they both passed out as soon as they got back to the bikes. I set my phone alarm to be up four hours later so I could split while they were still asleep. When the alarm went off, however, I just couldn't bring myself to doing it. As fed up as I was with Jen's behavior at the concert and with the constant maintenance that she needed, I just couldn't do it. Instead, I broke the news to them as soon as I got up. A couple of hours later and after I bought my new headlight, I struck out on my own. Even though I told them that I was going to ride around Wyoming for a few more days, I just headed for home. To me the trip was a failure, much like a sequel to a successful movie (I told you that I'd use it again). I didn't try to salvage something that just wasn't there. I felt it would be better to end it now and have a fresh start next year than it would be to go down with a sinking ship.

I got a little teared up as I crossed the state line into Wyoming, thinking about having left behind my own family. With nothing but 1,200 miles of thinking ahead of me, I had time to analyze everything. *Did I just not fit in anymore with my own family? What would happen when my kids felt that way about me? Did I overreact? Is it all of the above? Is it none of the above?*

As I rolled along into Wyoming, I got to feeling better. I didn't just dwell on what had happened and I started thinking about the positive things in life—my wife and kids, our new home, and our upcoming family trip. In all, I spent two peaceful nights on the road by myself, one of which was right next to some railroad tracks. (In case you're wondering, the train did come racing along in the middle of the night causing me to shit my pants.) While I was alone, I enjoyed the company that I had for the first time on the entire trip.

For our annual family trip, we had to again take to the air in order to bypass previously traveled roads. This time around we were going to go to Washington D.C. and the surrounding areas, including New York City. After seeing and experiencing the East Coast, I'm certainly thankful that I live where I do. The toll roads, the traffic, the people—I was completely out of my element.

We flew out of Seattle just before midnight on Friday, September 25. Four hours later we stopped in Detroit, Michigan for an hour or two before we took a short flight into Pittsburgh, Pennsylvania, which was the cheapest city around for us to fly into. We saved nearly two hundred bucks per ticket landing in the Steel City compared to Washington D.C., Philadelphia, New York City, or even Boston. It wasn't necessarily out of the way either, as we planned to visit Ohio, Virginia, and West Virginia anyway.

Things didn't really get off to the greatest of starts. Before leaving Seattle, the Northwest Airline flight attendants asked us that we drop our bags below deck rather than carrying them on due to an overcrowded flight. I didn't really want to but the only reason that I did was because very few others were volunteering. The longer they sat and screwed around, the longer things were going to be delayed. Sure enough, we were one bag short when the carousel stopped turning at Pittsburgh International. The bad news was that it was all of Lizzy's clothes and toys for the whole week. The good news was that it landed in Toledo, Ohio and they could have it to us that night. Can you imagine if it went to London or Paris instead?

Once we straightened out the mess and got our Toyota Rav 4 rental car, we split out of Pittsburgh and headed north towards Lake Erie. Not far out of town, we ran into our first of an eventually astronomical amount of toll roads. Around home, we have a few toll bridges in the Seattle area that I have absolutely no need to cross. The only toll I had ever paid was the five dollars that it cost to cross the Golden Gate Bridge. This one in Pennsylvania on Highway 60 was a mere seventy cents, but that was just the beginning.

Before crossing into Ohio, we stopped in a little town called Sharon (It's true, look it up) to visit their Harley shop that I had discovered in one of my atlases. I bought a T-shirt that had both a motorcycle and my wife's name on the back and after I told the story to the sales clerk that we came all the way from Washington State to get one, he tossed in two free shirts for the kids. After we got our "personalized" souvenirs, we headed for Cleveland.

Following our visit to the Country Music Hall of Fame a year earlier, it was only fitting that we visit the Rock and Roll Hall of Fame this time around. But unlike the shrine in Nashville, this place wouldn't allow us to take in our video camera or our brand new digital camera. That pissed me off and I never really let it go throughout our tour, which didn't make for a pleasant afternoon. Some of the exhibits were cool, but it really wasn't I thought it would be.

As evening was settling in, we headed south down I-77 into Canton, Ohio to spend the night and retrieve Lizzy's bags that I had the airlines ship in form Toledo. Following Lizzy's reunion with her clothes and Night-Night Bear, her version of Radar (whom I still don't have by the way), we turned in early in order to get our bodies adjusted to the eastern time zone.

The next morning we drove about a mile to the Pro Football Hall of Fame, where we were the first ones through the door when they opened for business. With it being Sunday, they had TVs throughout the facility tuned into pregame shows so the visitors could listen in while viewing the exhibits. Now I'm not going to pretend that Sharon and the girls like football even a fraction of what I do, but I will say that they enjoyed this more than any other museum/hall of fame that they had gone to. They got to kick field goals, throw passes, and run around in designated areas while learning about the history of the game as well.

As for me, I was in heaven. I saw Jim Thorpe's jersey, Bronko Nagurski's ring (that you could shove a golf ball through), Johnny Unitas' cleats, the ball that Joe Montana threw to Dwight Clark to get the 49ers to their first Super Bowl, the ball that Jerry Rice scored his 208th and final touchdown with, every Super Bowl ring ever made, the actual Vince Lombardi Trophy, and the bust of every enshrined member of the Pro Football Hall of Fame. Seeing the bust room wasn't quite on the level of Elvis' racquetball court/record museum at Graceland, but it was damn close. Rumor has it that they all talk to each other when the lights go out at night. What I wouldn't give to hear some of those stories!

We spent the rest of the day on the road traveling through West Virginia and into Virginia. After spending the night in Covington, Virginia, we went north on I-81 through Maryland and Pennsylvania before jumping on I-78 into New Jersey. An hour or so east of New York City, we turned north on I-287 until it turned into the New York State Thruway at the state line.

The New York State Thruway is the same as a freeway with one catch—you can't get off very often. More like a giant NASCAR track complete with actual pit stops where drivers can only get gas, eat, or go to the bathroom, the Thruway can go for hours between regular exits. You punch a ticket when you get on and present the ticket to a toll booth when you eventually get off. How much you pay is determined by how far you drive. It cost me twenty bucks to run it to Albany. I can't imagine driving through until it ends east of Buffalo and paying those dues.

The whole pit stop situation gave us a problem. After drinking a bunch of Diet Mountain Dew, I had to piss more often than there were pit stops. I had to make more than one dive off the road to piss while other cars cruised by and honked at me, knowing what I was up to because I was in plain sight. I'm not the only one who has ever done that because there was lots of other "evidence" of others having been there before me.

We spent that night in the state capitol of Albany. While in the motel after the kids went to sleep, I turned on wrestling for a little bit. Come to find out, they were only a few blocks away from us at the Pepsi Arena. I had no idea! I, of all people, should have known and we could have gotten tickets. It probably wouldn't have been much fun if we would have gone, as the kids were out like a light before the show even started that night.

The next day we drove through some absolutely beautiful countryside along the southern part of Vermont and lower New Hampshire, ending up in Kittery, Maine. Those areas resembled home quite a bit with the fall foliage, mountain areas, and coastal access that were all within an hour of each other. There wasn't a lot of people, like we had seen earlier and were soon to see again in exponential amounts, making it enjoyable. We even stopped at a beach and jumped in the Atlantic Ocean for a swim in the saltwater.

Following our invigorating dip, we headed south on I-95 through Massachusetts, Rhode Island, and into Connecticut. We spent the night in Branford, along the Long Island Sound, before going into New York City the next day. Just before leaving Connecticut, however, we had to make a quick stop in Stamford to take a picture of the WWE Headquarters building that was just off the freeway. Once we crossed the state line into New York, we drove into Yonkers so we could get off the freeway and run Broadway all of the way down into lower Manhattan.

At the very first stop light that we pulled up to in New York City, we were treated to a unique show. Directly in front of us at the light was a small box truck that was used for delivering furniture. While we were stopped, the truck kept flashing its reverse lights off and on again, over and over. I figured at first that the driver was having trouble with his transmission, but then the truck started rocking from side to side. As I started to pull out to go around him because the light had turned green, I saw a guy jump out of the truck on the passenger side. As soon as I passed the truck, I turned around and saw the other two guys that were still in the cab having a fistfight inside the truck. I couldn't believe my eyes—we had been in New York City for less than a minute and I had already seen a brawl.

As we made our way down Broadway, we were the only vehicle in sight that wasn't a yellow taxi. Nobody paid attention to stop lights, signs, or nothing. They just flew down the road bumper-to-bumper, weaving back and forth between lanes. The only way to get anywhere was to drive like an idiot like they did, so Sharon covered her eyes and let me take on New York City's taxi morons. Even while battling for lane position, I was still able to take in the amazing skyline. If you have never been there, just imagine walking in a narrow closet with a ceiling that seems as if it is a mile above your head.

I did alright, though. In the midst of all of the challenges that made driving through Seattle seem like a country drive, I managed to cruise us through Times Square and take a picture on the front step of Madison Square Garden. In addition to that, I also stopped the car in the middle of Broadway, ran into the Harley-Davidson store to buy a T-shirt, and got back in the car before I could be spotted by the cops that patrolled the city on horseback. It was the only option that I had if I wanted a New York City Harley shirt. There are no parking lots—you either take a cab to where you want to go, or you walk. People like me who drive a car where they wanted to go everyday don't exist around there.

At the end of the line, we crossed the Holland Tunnel into New Jersey. For some reason, I didn't end up paying to cross it. If I missed the toll area, it was an honest mistake. The only thing I could think of was that only people coming from the New Jersey side had to pay. I must have been right because I never heard anything out of the rental car company, as I'm sure I would have if they would've had surveillance pictures and a traffic ticket sent to them.

Our next stop was a tour of the Statue of Liberty, as per Katelynn's request. We didn't go inside the statue because we would have had to buy additional tickets a while beforehand in order to do so. We did, however, take a little boat ride to Ellis Island and Liberty Island and spent several hours learning about the immigrants that came over and what just the simple sight of the Statue of Liberty meant to them—things we take for granted all of the time.

As we made our way out of New York "Shitty," as I began to call it, we paid a fortune in tolls as we came into and out of Philadelphia, where we stopped to see the Liberty Bell and Independence Hall. Like I did when we were in Nashville, I had a hell of a time trying to find the right road that would take us through Delaware and into Maryland and we subsequently passed Veteran's Stadium, where the Philadelphia Eagles play, three times. Only this time, it cost me money as well as time—as in five dollars each of the three times that we crossed over the Benjamin Franklin Bridge. Even after crossing through the same booth with the same guard twice earlier in a matter of twenty minutes and him knowing good and well that I was lost, the son of a bitch still made me pay a third time—prick.

That night we ended up in College Park, Maryland, thirty minutes out of our nation's capitol, where we booked three nights at a Clarion Inn, complete with an indoor pool and continental breakfasts. We spent the entire day on Thursday in Washington D.C. visiting the Lincoln Memorial, Washington Monument, Vietnam Veteran's Memorial, the Smithsonian, Botanical Garden, the Capitol Building, and the White House. Other tourists within the sound of my voice didn't think it was funny when I referred to the White House as the "Black House," due to President Obama living there. Some people just take things too seriously.

When we got back to our room after a long day of walking that added up to every bit of six miles, we sat back as a group to go over some of the pictures that Sharon had taken on the digital camera that day. The only problem was, we couldn't find the camera of which to view said pictures. We searched the room, hotel lobby, and even the restaurant where we ate a few hours earlier—nothing. Somewhere out there is a guy with all of our pictures from our trip (over four hundred to be exact) on a camera that he bought for cheap in a pawn shop. I'm not mad at him, it's the asshole with a pocket full of cash after hocking my wife's camera that I want to chat with!

Exhausted from all of the miles on the road and the rat race that is the East Coast, we spent all of the next day doing things in town. Not only did we go to a movie, but we played a few rounds of miniature golf as well. Afterward we went back to the hotel room and swam for a few hours, finally relaxing after a week of rushing to see all that we could see and doing all we could do. We went to nearby Largo on Saturday, where we spent the full day at Six Flags America. Much like Ghost Town in the Sky, it was the big reward for the kids after what turned out to be just short of 3,000 miles on the road. Unfortunately with Six Flags only being open on weekends just like Ghost Town was a year earlier, it meant that we had to drive back into Pittsburgh to catch our early morning flight as soon as the park closed. Only this time I had to spend the money on a motel room for a mere five hours because if I didn't, Sharon promised to remove a very vital part of my body—whatever that meant.

Towards the end of fall, not long after the one year anniversary of the beginning of my writing project, I was sitting out in the living room watching wrestling while Sharon was at work and the kids were in bed. Right in the middle of a good match, the phone rang, it was Dad on the other end of the line.

"Hey," he began just like he always did when he called me.

"Yeah."

When he didn't say anything after a second or two, I knew something was wrong.

"What is it?" I asked, sensing something pretty bad.

"Just give me a second," he began, starting to choke up. "Gladys called—Dad's got lung cancer."

"How bad?"

"He's had it for a while. He's in the late stages. Doctor's are giving him three months."

If I felt bad, think of how Dad felt. His father had three months left and he lived nearly four hundred miles away. Dad couldn't up and quit his job or take any sort of sabbatical to spend the next three months with him. The best that he could do was go over there every other weekend. The worst part was when it came time to say goodbye and come back home, he never knew if it would be the last time that he would see his dad.

Upon hearing the news, we all decided to spend Christmas over at Papa's. Although the circumstances sucked, it was a pretty cool throwback to the days of old when we would go over to their house on Christmas Eve along with Uncle Robbie and his crew. It also marked the first time in over a decade that Dad, Jen, and myself were together for the entire Christmas holiday. If you top it off with Sharon and Elizabeth being there too, it made for a once in a lifetime holiday experience. The only things missing were Debbie, who opted to stay home to be with her recently widowed mother, and Katelynn, who went to her dad's.

Given the situation, there weren't any big gift exchanges. The only person who opened presents was Elizabeth, who Santa Claus had tracked down even though she wasn't home for Christmas. We did, however, have a giant Christmas dinner that would have probably fed a small army. After dessert, we played a seven hour marathon game of Uno.

As for Papa, he slept quite a bit. He would be up and talking, though in a much softer voice, and would try to be a part of everything. Unfortunately he tired easy and had to snooze either in his chair for thirty minutes or so, or he would have to go into his room for a much longer nap. It was tough to watch but it was even harder for him, knowing that he was running out of time. In fact he would even tear up when talking about anything in the future, something that I only seen him do once in my life before, knowing that he wasn't going to be around to experience it.

After his initial diagnosis, he went through all of the radiation treatment and began a twice weekly session of chemotherapy. Papa lost a lot of weight over the first couple of months, probably over a hundred pounds, but it really only put him back to around average given his size. In times like these, I guess it pays to have a little extra poundage. When his three months that the doctors gave him came up, he was still hanging in there and doing alright.

Dad would call me, or I would call him, when he was over there for his bi-weekly visits so I could talk to Papa. I might have rode along with him once, but I usually opted to stay home to allow him some one-on-one time with his dad. I didn't call Papa on the phone so much unless Dad was there because his chemotherapy treatments would put him down for several days at a time and I didn't want to disturb him. At least when Dad was there, he could give me an update if Papa was sleeping.

One night in late January, Dad called me from Papa's with an entirely different critical report. It seemed that Aunt B. had fallen down while at a routine doctor visit and was in a coma. To take it a step further, her will stated that if she was ever in that state, the doctors must pull the plug on her.

I just started chuckling. It wasn't funny by any means, but the timing of it all gave me no choice.

"Jesus Christ," I said to Dad. "Have you noticed that everyone is dying at once."

"Yeah," he said. "Who the fuck is next?"

Sure enough, he called me a day or two later on January 31, 2010, to tell me that she was dead. Although I hadn't seen her for a while and really only just sporadically since I stopped mowing her yard, I was asked to be a casket bearer at her funeral, as was Dad, to represent the Thramer side of her family.

Now that Aunt B. was gone, so too were all of my other previous lawn mowing employers. Everyone on Orth Way whom I had worked for was gone. Hell, even Ron Russell, my old coach, died around the same time. When I went to his service, as did several other of his former players, I saw that they had a little display of some of his sports memorabilia set up. Among them was a plaque that me and one of my old friends gave to him when we moved on to high school football. It meant a lot to me to see that somebody who was very inspirational in my life appreciated only a small token of my extreme gratitude.

Following the services for Aunt B., which Papa obviously couldn't attend due to his worsening health, his sister, Pat, called me out of the blue to ask me how he was doing.

"Let me give you his number," I told her. "You can call him and find out."

I was actually pretty pissed off about that. *Why couldn't she call her own brother, instead of his grandson, if she wanted to know how he was doing?* None of his siblings, except for Bill (who had been dead for several years by then) ever went to visit him since he moved to Newport in the mid-90's. Yet any time he came over this way, he would make every effort to visit them. "The road runs both ways," as he would say.

Papa was still plugging along by the end of March, though it was getting harder and harder for him to do so. While he was still in good enough shape, I went over there for the weekend on my own to spend two days with him without anyone else around. It was the only time that the two of us were together alone for that amount of time and I knew that it was likely going to be the last. I wasn't sad about it, I was happy, because he was still functioning on his own and I was able to spend some real quality time with him. None of his other grandchildren did that—only me.

He smiled on the outside, but I knew that he was struggling on the inside.

"I'm tryin' Ed, but I'm having a hard time. Everything I eat and drink tastes like shit. I only eat it 'cause I have to. Then I go to chemo—it puts me on my ass for three days. The first day I start feeling good again, I gotta go right back in there for another fuckin' round."

I gave him a hug before I left him for what I was sure was going to be the last time and I told him that I loved him, which was something that I never really did.

"I love you too, Ed. And I'm damn proud of you."

Papa died on July 14, 2010. It marked the second death in my family in less than a week. Four days earlier on July 10, Grandma Murrow died at the age of ninety-four. At first, neither passing really affected me. Papa died on the other side of the state and I wasn't there to see it. As for Grandma Murrow, how can you feel sad for someone who lives to be nearly a hundred years old? Although it wasn't, her funeral should have been more like a celebration of life.

That all changed a week or so later during a family gathering to spread Papa's ashes. In my lifetime there hasn't been tons, but still a fair amount of deaths in the family. Up to this point, it was Tuco's passing that hit me the hardest. I didn't cry at Aunt B.'s because I hadn't been that close to her for several years. Same with Grandma's death in 2008—I had just begun to see her again after ten years had gone by. Papa was different. I had spent much more time with him and was a hell of a lot closer to him than I was to the rest.

I tried to put on the "tough guy" look so nobody would see me get upset. Dad and I, and maybe even Jen, rode down on our motorcycles to Burlington to a boat launch along the Skagit River. I say "maybe Jen" because things started getting blurry for me on the ride down and I really don't remember. My mind was getting overrun with emotion as I started having flashbacks of the four wheeler rides, the bike trips, the hunting trips—everything. It was setting in that things like that weren't ever going to happen again. The temperature outside was probably in the mid-seventies, but it felt to me like it was in the hundreds. I was very hot and getting lightheaded.

Poor Dad, who has zero experience in public speaking, stammered through a speech as he dumped his father's ashes into the river. Dozens of family members stood just behind him throughout the ordeal, including Sharon and the girls. I stood twenty feet away from everyone else on my own. I was still trying to hold it all in and keep my feelings to myself the only way that I knew how—to keep it all locked inside so nobody feels sorry for me because I'm in pain. Once everyone else started crying, I couldn't stand it anymore and I left—before the service was even concluded. It just killed me inside to stand and watch it. At any second I was going to cry, puke, pass out, or all of the above and I just had to jump on my bike and get some air. I may have looked like a horse's ass by leaving early and I didn't mean anything by it, but I just wasn't strong enough to stay.

I bawled the whole ride home. The tears were flowing so much that the cars behind me had to turn on their windshield wipers. When I got home, I parked my bike, grabbed a bottle of Gatorade (seriously), and went and sat in the shade. I was shaking so bad but after downing all of those wonderful electrolytes, I started feeling better. Most people would reach for a bottle of something else, but not me—bad things happen if your mind starts thinking that alcohol is the only way to ease pain.

An hour or so later, I went up to Dad's for a barbeque along with everyone else. Nobody even brought it up about me leaving early. The crying time was over and now came the fun stories and such. The only somewhat emotional part came when Gladys gave me Papa's cowboy hat that I ran over with my dirt bike twenty years earlier. After looking at the hat, I couldn't help but burst out into—laughter—as the tire tracks were still on it!

After Papa's death, Gladys too was diagnosed with lung cancer. (Kids, whatever you do, don't smoke fucking cigarettes! They will kill you!) She has since moved back over to this side of the mountains and continues to battle it.

In June of 2010, I surpassed the ten year mark working at Dairy Valley and subsequently earned four weeks of vacation time per calendar year. Although I can't take them all at once, I split them up not far apart from each other. In fact, I did it to where I only had to work eleven out of a fifteen week span. I was going on vacation so much that every time I told my customers that I was going, their eyes would bulge and they would say, "Again?! Are you guys hiring?" I set my first week aside for a bike trip for the third-straight year, paying for it with the money that I made from announcing wrestling matches all season like I always did. For my second and third week, I was going to take those back-to-back for our family trip. For my fourth week, Sharon and I were going to Las Vegas together by ourselves to celebrate our fifth wedding anniversary.

Following the disappointing bike trip a year earlier, I opted to ride alone for this one. I had taken long rides on my own before, some for up to two nights, but not nearly for a full week. While it can be potentially dangerous if you were to break down or were to get into an accident alone in the middle of nowhere, it can actually be a very peaceful experience. Having done everything on the West Coast except for the coast itself, I set my sights on that. I packed and loaded my bike down on Thursday afternoon so I could leave directly from work on Friday when I was finished for the day. Before noon, I was southbound on I-5 and heading for the Mexican border, where I would then turn around and ride the coastline all of the way home. That was my tentative plan anyway.

After hitting some shitty traffic in Portland and again a few hours later in Eugene, I called my first audible and jumped off the freeway and headed east over Willamette Pass towards US-97. A few miles short of the summit, I found a perfect little turnout alongside a bridge where I could spend the night. Although I brought a tent, I declined to use it and just laid out under the stars. No city or house lights, no traffic—just me and the sound of the gently roaring creek spending a night of serenity.

I was up by daylight, sometime around 5:00, packed up, and moved out. Within a half-hour, I was on US-97 and heading south towards California. Short of the state line, I took a shortcut over to US-395 and ran that the rest of the day, through Reno, and back into California to a resort town east of Yosemite National Park called Mammoth Lakes. Right around dusk, I again found a perfect spot for me to spend the night just off of the main highway.

Following another night under the stars, I headed south through the misery that is the Mojave Desert and hit I-15 around San Bernardino. I spent the next two hours in miserable traffic, after which I turned and headed for the coast about a hundred miles north of the Mexican border. Aside from missing out on getting a picture at the border, of which I couldn't even cross because I was traveling with a gun, I was saving myself time in the long run by skipping San Diego and the surrounding vicinity. I wasn't going to be missing out on my coastal ride at all, as Highway 1 began at Dana Point, right from where my escape from I-15 dumped me out at.

I hit the Pacific Highway at Dana Point and began heading towards home. The beaches and surrounding towns were absolutely packed with people. First it was Laguna Beach, then Newport Beach, then Huntington Beach, and then Long Beach. Each town had more and more people and traffic.

I had lots of time to scope out the scene because I hit every single stoplight that I came up to. At first I sat through four or five light changes at a single intersection, but then I noticed other motorcyclists riding in between the two northbound lanes. Around home that is a good way to get door-jacked by a car, but it was 100% accepted down there. In fact, traffic will even move over a little bit to allow bikes to pass them. So I followed suit and rode along with a group of sport bikes for a while until I eventually decided that I had enough of the beach scene. I figured that I would have more fun in the mountains, so I called my third audible. I hit the freeways again in Anaheim and figured on riding until I was out of the Los Angeles area altogether. Unfortunately I ran out of daylight in Valencia, California, the home of Six Flags Magic Mountain. Believe it or not, I found a place to spend the night just over the hill from the park in an abandoned gravel pit.

The next morning, I jumped on I-5 and rode it for a few hours until the turnoff to San Francisco. After crossing both the Bay Bridge and the Golden Gate Bridge, I was back on the Pacific Highway. I spent that night in Garberville, about an hour south of Eureka, in a beautiful spot off of the road that had access to a creek. After four days of riding hard, I stripped naked and dove in to wash all of the road grime and sweat off of my body.

On Tuesday morning, I rode into Redwood National Park to ride alongside some of the tallest trees in the world on the Avenue of the Giants. I soon crossed into Oregon and rode the foggy coastline up the entire state, crossing scores of the coolest bridges that I have ever seen. Made of steel, cement, and even wood, all of the bridges were completely different from each other.

After my fifth consecutive night of sleeping for free under the stars like a drifter from a century ago, I headed for home on Wednesday morning. I finished with just short of 3,000 miles, none of which were ridden in the rain. It was peaceful, relaxing, and enjoyable (except for some of the traffic). I stopped when I wanted to and for as long as I wanted to, ate where, when, and if I wanted to, and I had nobody to answer to. It was a nice alternative to the trips that I had been on in the past. That being said, it is much funner going with others.

Two months later marked our rather unique family trip. For all of our previous trips, it has always been us cramming as much as we could possibly fit into a small period of time. Having done that for so many years, Sharon wanted one vacation where she could just sit around and do absolutely nothing the entire time. While that isn't my cup of tea, it was only fair that she get to choose once in a while. This time we were going to go to Puerto Vallarta, Jalisco, Mexico—and we wouldn't be going alone.

It had been since 1997's trip to Las Vegas since I had spent a vacation with Mom, or any extended period of time for that matter. Having traveled around with various different people, I knew that sometimes it could be a recipe for disaster. Sometimes Sharon and Mom didn't get along (usually when alcohol was involved) and let's face it, Mike and I didn't always see things from the same point of view (probably because I can't fit my head up my ass). Knowing what could potentially happen, I still gave in and agreed for the six of us to spend almost a week on the beach in Mexico. Because Mom and Mike had a time share, all we were out was the airfare. The all-inclusive stay at the resort came with their plan.

We took separate flights down there, saving us $200 per ticket. The downside was that we would spend an extra hour both in the air and in between flights on the way home. We traded planes in Phoenix, Arizona and got down to Puerto Vallarta a couple of hours ahead of them. Knowing zero about Mexican people and culture, we waited for them before leaving for the resort.

The roads and towns in Mexico are straight out of the old west. The bigger cities have department stores and buildings that you would find in the United States, but the outline areas have shacks and dirt roads with livestock walking up and down them. Barefooted kids were running along jagged rocks to jump into a mud hole that they used for a swimming pool. It made poverty look like living in a mansion on the hill.

Once through the gates of the resort, it was a new world. Mexican servants wait on your every need. They bring you anything that you want to eat or drink, save spots on the beach or at the pool for you, and even give you cart rides around the resort. Again it's not my deal to lay around on the beach all day, but the kids sure loved it.

There were other things to do in the resort as well besides cooking in the sun. Every night, they had a different themed event where they would serve a specific food to coincide with it. We ate barbeque on "Western Night," Mexican food on "Fiesta Night," and seafood on "Tropical Night." After dinner, they had games, contests, and dancing for the entire family.

I took part in every game or contest that they offered. I rode the mechanical bull, sang karaoke, played volleyball and water polo, and even won a beer drinking contest by slamming cervecas faster than anyone else in the room. While it isn't my style to drink that much alcohol that fast, it was a contest and I'm not going to lose at anything in front of my wife and kids.

I wish I had more to tell you about our five days down there, but I don't. To my surprise, everyone got along perfect. There was no fighting or arguing of any kind. Sharon got her wish of a lazy vacation and Mom and Mike got what they wanted by getting us to go with them on a trip. Elizabeth swam until she couldn't take it anymore and outside of splitting her head open, Katelynn had the time of her life. Me—I beat every other tourist in every contest, so I was happy too!

Five weeks later at the beginning of November, Sharon and I celebrated our fifth wedding anniversary with a five night stay in Las Vegas. We got a killer deal with two round trip tickets out of Bellingham and five nights in the Excalibur Hotel and Casino for just $600. This was our third trip down there since we had met, but it was the first without kids or friends. Finally, it was just going to be the two of us. We often joke about how we have been together for a higher number of years than the number of our actual dates. Although our dates usually involve something big like a concert, they are still few and far between. Since the two of us had seen George Thorogood at the Mount Baker Theater back in May, we hadn't spent so much as an evening alone.

We drove a mere forty minutes up to Bellingham on a Sunday afternoon, boarded a plane, and was in the air for our two hour flight in less time than it takes to watch the evening news. By 8:00 we were on the ground at McCarran International, where a shuttle bus loaded us up and took us the short little jaunt to the Excalibur. By 9:00 we were checked in, unpacked, and ready to hit the town.

As soon as we left the casino, we were instantly hit up by people pushing either tickets for free shows, or photo cards with telephone numbers for local hookers. Since Sharon wasn't into the hooker idea, we listened to the free show ticket peddlers instead. Just like when we were down in Vegas before, we got free tickets for several shows for listening to a two hour presentation on time shares the next morning. Although Monday was our anniversary, we figured that we would be done with the speech by 10:00 and have the rest of the week to do whatever we wanted—and with show tickets as well.

We had heard the whole bit before when we were down there for our wedding—about how Las Vegas was going to increase to astronomical amounts of people and everyone should buy as much deeded property as possible while they still could. But unlike last time, buying a time share actually made sense for us. After all, we make it a point to vacation every single year. Since our first trip to Disneyland in 2002, we have only missed a vacation one time. We had a good excuse, as that was in 2003 when we bought a house and Elizabeth was born within two months of each other. Although this was going to cost us ten grand, we would eventually save money in the long run. Let's put it this way—a one week stay in a five star resort anywhere in the world costs us a grand total of $200. It just made perfect sense to us, so we bought a time share right there on the spot.

Upon signing the paperwork, we got our free tickets that we were promised at the start as well as another pile of tickets and coupons that they threw in on top of that. Among them were two tickets to see hypnotist Marc Savard at Planet Hollywood that night. Even though it was our anniversary night, all we really had planned was to go out for a nice dinner. The show wasn't until ten p.m., so we would still be able to take our time and enjoy our meal.

Before we even walked into the theater, I told Sharon that I wanted to volunteer to be hypnotized so I could be a part of the show. I tried to get her to go up with me, but she didn't want to.

"I'm not going to make a fool out of myself," she said.

I didn't care—the dumber I was on stage, the more entertained the people in the audience would be.

I was always skeptical of the whole hypnosis thing to begin with. While I had seen it done on my graduation night a decade earlier, I still wasn't sold on the legitimacy of the deal. After listening to Savard's explanation of how everybody passes through hypnosis on their way to sleep each night, I could understand it.

What happens is that as your brain relaxes and prepares for sleep, you are still aware of what's going on around you. Sounds trigger certain things in your subconscious and you can literally wake up while still being asleep at the same time. It's kind of like if you have ever woken up and said something completely off the wall, or if you sleep walk—you remember doing it, but you don't know why you did it.

I didn't listen to everything he said during his introduction to the show because I was too anxious to be sure that I was going to get a spot on stage. He called up about thirty people, myself included, and he began attempting to hypnotize us collectively. As he went further along, we would remove people that weren't being affected in order to narrow it down to the eight or ten people that he would then use for the show.

As he talked, we listened to soothing music. He said that the key was to keep our eyes closed at all times, so I made sure that mine stayed shut. The whole process was said to have taken about ten minutes, most of which I don't remember. All I know is, I was still on the stage when he started picking up the pace and having us do some things with our eyes closed. Now I don't remember everything that I'm going to tell you that happened that night, but I do remember some of it. The rest of it I had to watch with my own eyes after Sharon bought the DVD of the night's show. The only way I can describe what I remembered doing is that while I knew it was happening, I couldn't stop myself from doing it.

After he weeded through some of the volunteers, he asked for us to play an imaginary instrument at a symphonic concert while our eyes remained closed. For no particular reason, I started pretending that I was playing a trombone. As he instructed, I started out slow and then picked it up as the music got faster. As the music shifted to an even faster song, he had us switch instruments. I chose a saxophone this time, even though they were playing heavy metal music, because I was still thinking that we were supposed to use big band instruments. I played faster and harder as the music got louder because I was supposed to be competing with the person next to me for a spot in a rock and roll band. Not to be outdone, I blew my face out like I was putting on a show down on Beale Street in Memphis. My eyes were still closed, so I just had to do the best I could in order to rock out better than the rest.

Then came the funny stuff. He asked us to play whatever instrument that we had backwards. The best I could think of was to start blowing through the opposite end of the horn. After a minute or so, he then asked us to play our same instruments with our asses. So I lifted my leg, pretended to shove the sax up my butt, and started to bear down on it like I was straining to fart or trying to shit out a bowel-clogging turd.

When the concert ended, we opened our eyes for the first time and were introduced to the audience. Upon shaking hands with our host, some of the people did things like rub their crotches, act all horny, or begin to cry. Thankfully, I wasn't amongst them. While I was aware that they were acting that way, I had no idea why until I watched the video later on. What happened was while I was sleeping in my chair on stage, he had instructed certain people to act that way upon the handshake.

Following introductions, he brought out a voodoo doll and poked its eyes, twisted its nipples, tickled its belly, and shoved his finger up its ass. We all reacted like we felt everything, and I swear to you I did. Although I don't remember this, Sharon said that he accidentally dropped the doll at one point and we all hit the deck.

He did some other stuff, like offer us pretend joints (which I still declined even in my hypnotic state), had us act like strippers, and have us feeling like we were on fire one minute and freezing the next. After that, he lined us all up and used magic to turn a belt into a rattlesnake. Of course it was still only a belt, but to me it hissed and rattled so I jumped off the stage and ran for my life. After Savard saw that, he found what he was looking for—a man who was scared to death of snakes. Once I was led back to the stage, he wrapped it around my neck as I trembled uncontrollably.

For the finale, he asked us all to select porn star names and told us that we were going to be auditioning for an upcoming adult film. I chose "Axl Steele," which I pulled from the Nintendo Wii's *Guitar Hero* game. Other guys were "Dick Biggly" and "Fill 'em Up Chuck." He then passed out blow—up dolls, one of which was a guy doll, and we all broke out into an orgy right there on stage. I wonder how the guy that humped a man on stage felt when he saw the video the next day? Needless to say, it became the most watched video around when we got home. I have yet to see anyone who has watched that DVD laugh harder as they did the first time they watched that show.

The next night, we went across the street to the Luxor to see Criss Angel perform his twisted illusions. I can't even begin to put into words what I saw him do. He hooked fish hooks in his cheeks and was raised up into the air. He stood in the center of the stage, clapped his hands, and was instantly up in the balcony. He sawed a girl in half with a saw, took each half of her across separate sides of the room, and she walked normally back across the stage. Sharon and I were speechless after the show.

Th rest of our days were spent down at the north end of town at the Sahara, where we played $1 blackjack for ten hours at a time. We didn't win much, but we didn't lose much either. We just had a great time playing cards and enjoying the other person's company. We were sad to see it all end when it was time to go home because we knew it would be a while until our next time out on the town with just the two of us.

In fact it was almost six months until we went out alone, this time to see Travis Tritt play a show in Tacoma. Not only was it a good show, but it crossed another name off my list of people that I want to see perform live. At the end of the show, he threw out towels and shirts and stuff from the stage. We were in about the fifth or sixth row center, but most of the merchandise went over my head. All except for one, as I jumped and fell backwards into a lady's lap to pull down a sweaty towel for my wife to take home as a souvenir.

At the beginning of 2011 and right out of thin air, Katelynn hit us with the news that she wanted to move in with her dad. She refuses to let us know the reason why she wants to "try it out," but I am certain that I know what it is—she doesn't like me. In her defense, it has got to be tough to go back and forth from home to home and to adhere to the different rules of each place, as perhaps one isn't as strict as the other. Around here, both Sharon and I make the rules. The problem is with Sharon's work schedule, usually I'm the one that has to enforce them. Fair or unfair, rules are rules and they have to be followed.

I can really trace it all back to 2007 when she started spending more time at her dad's. When she would come home after a weekend, she would constantly use the word "sucks." I know that there are worse words out there and that particular word is socially acceptable nowadays but to me, it is still short for "sucks dick" and I don't want to hear it out of a little girl's mouth. If she said it once or twice like any other word that slipped out of her mouth from time to time, I wouldn't care. But "this sucks," "that sucks," "they suck," and "I suck," was too much. After two or three warnings (which was more than fair), I made her write sentences. They weren't Mr. Prange sentences (that were more like paragraphs) they were basic, five-word sentences like "I will not say sucks." The first offense was ten times, then twenty, until I made her do a hundred, which took her from Libby, Montana until we got to Spokane to complete. It sounds brutal to say that I made her write through three states, but it was only a few hours in reality.

That was only the beginning. The fall of 2007 also marked the start of third grade for her. Now instead of coloring and light reading and math, things were starting to get a bit more challenging. In addition to doing cursive, multiplication, and book reports, she was also starting to receive actual letter grades, instead of just a star for completing an assignment whether it is done right or not. When she brought home a lower grade, I did what any good parent would do—go over it with her so she could understand it and then have her fix it.

After a few months of this, her grades got much better. The work that she brought home rarely had more than one or two answers wrong on them. But when her report card came home, her quarterly grade wasn't where I felt that it should be based on her work that I was seeing. After going up to the school to talk to her teacher, I found out that she was only bringing home the good papers. The bad papers would just get shoved into her desk.

That was three years ago, and she still does the same thing. She says that she does it so that she won't get punished for a bad grade. I don't know how many times I have told her that having her redo it in order to understand it isn't a punishment. It's when she hides her poor work for the whole quarter and gets a well-deserved poor grade on her report card that gets her the punishments. All of her subjects—math, spelling, social studies—they all can be better if she just practices. The thing about her is, she's lazy. She knows that it will require more work if she brings home things that I will likely have her correct. She would rather hide everything so she can immediately take part in family time. She knows damn well what will happen at the end of the quarter, but she does it anyway.

Another excuse for her having poor grades is that she "lost a few of her assignments." Looking at her backpack (that looks more like a trash can) and her desk (that looks more like a trash compactor), I can see why. At first I would ask her to clean it, explaining to her that if she stayed organized she would be less likely to lose things. When that only lasted for about a week,

I would dump her bag out on the floor and would even go to her school and dump her desk on the floor. Still, she would revert back and continue to have missing assignments.

In the past three years, I have explained myself countless times about organization and the importance of it as well as the importance of doing good work. When that didn't work, I threatened punishment. When that didn't work, I would punish her by taking away TV, video games, and desserts. When that didn't work, I put her in her room and only let her out to eat and to go to the bathroom. I even called it "jail" as a metaphor for what happens to repeat offenders in real life. What is wrong with that? It's not unfair. I'm not abusing her in any way, I'm just trying to get her to do the right thing. These things worked on me, they work on Elizabeth, why don't she get it?

I stew over this on a daily basis. I know that she is a girl and that the intimidation and slightly humiliating tactics that my parents, teachers, and coaches used on me to light a fire under my ass, don't work with her. That's okay, but she still needs to do what's right. If I give up and let her fail, which she will do if I don't keep on her, then I'm a loser. I have to stay on her so that she will not slip out of control but at the same time, I can't go to school and do the work for her. She must show responsibility and do it on her own, but she don't.

I have explained it to her in ways that she will understand and in a very calm tone. I tell her that I am holding out my hand for her to take so she doesn't fall into the mud, but she refuses to grab it. I tell her about how a well-lit path through the woods is easier to travel than the dark and scary path and that what I'm trying to do is be the one that lights her path. But it's no use, she just won't do it.

The only thing that I can possibly think, and I knew it was going to happen someday, is that I'm not her father. No shit! I've never claimed to be. I didn't deny her being my child. I didn't miss the first four years of her life. I don't just come around when it is convenient for me. I'm not the one who never once calls the house to see how school went. Instead, I'm just the asshole who potty trained her, taught her to ride a bike, coached her baseball team, and took her all over the country. God forbid I have to punish her when she makes mistakes, but I'm only human.

It doesn't help that she goes down there and whines to her coddling dad. He wouldn't dare say anything to my face because he knows that I will kick his yellow teeth so far down his throat that he would be able to chew on his own ass for his last supper. Instead he does the worst thing that anyone could do—he babies her. Never once does he say anything about her grades other than it must be the school's fault. He'll call Sharon and bitch at her because Katelynn is being punished too much for small problems. Are you fucking serious? Boy, is he going to be in for a rude awakening when he becomes a full-time parent for the first time in his pathetic life. I'm only sorry that Katelynn is the one who will be affected by it the most. I just hope that it won't be too late when the time comes that she realizes who was right in this whole thing, but I would be lying if I said that I didn't have my doubts.

In case that there was any doubt in your mind that I wasn't the problem, I'll clear that up with the coup de grace. The very next day after the four of us watched Papa's ashes drift down the Skagit River, she came to me after I told her to do twenty-five push-ups for telling a lie and told me that she "wishes that I was dead." If she was my own daughter I would have popped her in the mouth on the spot, but I can't do that with her. Instead, I just got up and walked away. She was eleven and just saw the pain and suffering that happens when you lose someone you love and admire—there was no way she didn't understand what she was saying.

So when she came to us and told us that she wanted to move, we agreed to let her do it right then and there. We don't really want her to go but if she isn't happy here, it isn't good for her or for the rest of us. I hate to say it, but the three of us get along better without her. Don't get me wrong, we miss her when she's gone, but we don't have near the household drama when she isn't around. Not that Elizabeth is perfect (she has her moments too), but she learns from her mistakes and won't continuously do things in spite of me. The only good thing about Katelynn's problems and shitty attitude is that Lizzy is learning how NOT to act.

I feel so sorry for Sharon, though. This marks her third child that is going away. Her only saving grace from a hell that I can't even imagine is the love that comes from Elizabeth and I. She, more so than us, will struggle with this the most and we've got to be here for her—and we will.

As for Katelynn, I hope that she is happy with her choice. If she ever comes back, she is welcome. If she never does, then that's okay too. I only hope that her other family keeps her on a tight leash because she needs it. My biggest fear is that she is only doing this because it is the easier road and she can get away with anything there. I can only hope that she is doing this because she missed so much time with her father in the past. We'll see.

Though there has been a lot of loss in one way or another as of late, there has been an abundance of good as well. Sharon is the acting store manager at Nine West while her boss is going on maternity leave for a few months. It is only a matter of time before she runs the whole show, proving what happens if you keep your chin up, accept what life dishes out to you no matter how bad, and never, ever quit.

Elizabeth is finishing up the second grade and is reading chapter books and doing multiplication. Watching her is like looking in the mirror, as her attitude, desire, charisma, and toughness is the exact same as mine.

Dad and Debbie still live up on Pinelli Road. They have found happiness in each other and who could ask for more? Over the years, Dad and I have repaired and strengthened our relationship compared to what it once was in the early part of the new millennium. In fact there is word about the two of us going on a bike trip together, which will totally contradict what I said about our Texas trip in 2001.

What can I say about Mom and Mike? Together, they lived with Grandpa at his house after Grandma died for almost two years before they moved back into their house. I don't throw praise lightly, but it takes a hell of a man to put up with that. Mom will do anything for anyone and ask for nothing in return. She doesn't work anymore but with her dad to look after, who has the time?

Jen graduated from Skagit Valley College and works at a school/daycare in Burlington. She is single, still looking for the future "Mr. Thramer."

Grandpa is still alive and kicking as is Grandma Chadwick, who now lives in Mount Vernon after Milt died a few years ago. If you would have told me that they would be my last two remaining grandparents, I would have laughed in your face. Funny how life turns out, huh?

I remember way back when I first put the pen to the paper telling you that I didn't know both how long this book was going to be or how it would end. While I knew for a fact that I would still be a married father, I didn't know that the eldest of my girls would be fixing to move away or that I would be living in the house of my dreams. While I knew that I would still be driving truck, I didn't know that I would be nearing my thirtieth birthday or that Papa and Aunt B. would die within a few months of each other.

It just goes to show you that life is short, as you hold my entire life right here in your hands. It also goes quick, as you clearly don't know when your time is up. I'm a natural competitor and will try to win at anything I do, whether it is a reading contest, a wrestling match, a farting contest, or a simple game of tic-tack-toe. The one opponent that I can't beat is the clock. I don't know who or what is out there that is in charge of pulling one's number but when its time for mine to come up, it's okay. My story has now been written for myself and for anyone else who cares or is ever going to care, so I'm ready when you call me—but give me just a little more time.
May 18, 2011

The End
(for now)

ACKNOWLEDGMENTS

T HESE ARE NOT in any way in order of importance, but rather in appearance. In addition to everyone that I have mentioned in this book, both positively and negatively, I would especially like to thank the following for making me into the person that I am today:

Dad—You are everything that I have ever wanted to be in my life. From the time I was born, I wanted to be just like you. Thank you for instilling into me the values that I live my life by everyday. Just like you, I will always put everything I have into my family, my work, and everything else that I set out to do.

Mom—You are the most giving person on the face of this Earth. Thank you for everything you do for me, my wife, and my kids. I can never repay you for your nurturing, your compassion, or your sacrifices.

Jen—You and I have had our moments, both good and bad. I have never wanted anything more for you than success and happiness. I just didn't realize that it meant being your own person instead of being just like me. Thank you for putting up with me.

Papa—Outside of my father, I have learned more from you about being a man than anyone else. Thank you for being such an inspiration. I miss you.

Grandpa—I will never, ever be able to express in words the gratitude that I have for you and what you have done for me and my family.

Uncle Robbie—I have had some of the greatest moments of my life alongside of you. Whatever I didn't get from Dad, I got from you.

Hulk Hogan—This may sound stupid to some people, but I don't care. Although I have never met you or your character in person, I have walked the line because of you. I will never let a drug into my body, never give up on anything, and will always believe in myself because of your advise that you said on TV so many years ago. If you ever intended to be a role model for anyone, you succeeded.

Joey—You are the only friend that I have who I would do anything for. In a world where everyone looks out for themselves, it's nice to know that I have a tag team partner if I need one.

Ron, Dale, and **Jay**—Gentlemen, it was an honor and a privilege to have been mentored by you. Thank you for the years of fun and excitement and a lifetime of mental toughness.

Tuco—It's been five years to the day since we said goodbye and not a day goes by that I don't think of you. Thank you so much for finding me on that Thursday afternoon in 1996. I couldn't have made it through those ten years without you to listen to my troubles. I miss you every day of my life.

Mike—I guess things in life happen for a reason. Thank you for being so good to my mom and thank you for the opportunity to live my dream.

Debbie—I'm truly sorry for how I treated you in the past. There are no excuses. Thank you for helping Dad find himself.

Sharon—You are the toughest person I know. Thank you for putting up with the person that I am. I am the luckiest guy in the world to have a wife like you.

Katelynn—You kept me on the ground when most people would be flying high. Thank you for teaching me the difference between a father and a dad.

Elizabeth—You are the single greatest accomplishment in my entire life. When I look at you, I see me. I get to relive my childhood again by watching you.

Everyone who is reading this—If you've reached this point, that means you have taken at least some interest in my story. Thank you for reading and I hope that you enjoyed it.